# Knowledge-Based Neurocomputing

edited by Ian Cloete and Jacek M. Zurada

## Knowledge-Based Neurocomputing

The MIT Press
Cambridge, Massachusetts
London, England

This book was printed and bound in the United States of America.

Library of Congress Cataloging-in-Publication Data

Cloete, Ian.
  Knowledge-based neurocomputing / Ian Cloete and J. M. Zurada.
  p.  cm.
  Includes bibliographical references and index.
  ISBN 0-262-03274-0 (hc. : alk. paper)
  1. Neural computers. 2. Expert systems (Computer science).
I. Zurada, Jacek M. II. Title.
QA76.87.C57   1999
006.3'2—dc21                                                    99-41770
                                                                    CIP

# Contents

# Preface

Knowledge-based neurocomputing concerns the utilization of problem-specific knowledge within the neurocomputing paradigm. The novelty of this book is that it illustrates the use of explicit comprehensible knowledge, a feature not always available within artificial neural networks. We believe that the issue of explicit knowledge manipulation within the neurocomputing paradigm has matured to such an extent, and is of such importance, that it warrants a volume dedicated to the review and exposition of approaches addressing this issue. This book is an outgrowth of that belief.

Uses of knowledge include prior knowledge about the problem domain, and the extraction, refinement and revision of knowledge about a specific problem domain contained within a neurocomputing system. The book also gives a thorough introduction to this field, describes the state-of-the-art methods, and points out the emergent directions for future research.

The book will be useful not only to those in the neurocomputing community, who wish to know more about the integration of knowledge-based principles and artificial neural networks, but also to the Artificial Intelligence community with its rich history of symbolic knowledge representation formalisms. The architectural issues addressed will aid developers aiming at connectionist-symbolic integration and the use of knowledge in hybrid intelligent systems.

The first part of the book (chapters 1 to 5) presents a taxonomy and reviews of methods for obtaining comprehensible neural network topologies by learning, as well as the encoding, extraction and refinement of symbolic knowledge within a neural network. The latter part presents wide ranging examples of applications of this technology, including rule extraction for chemical engineering systems, encoding and parameter estimation for differential equations describing known properties of a dynamical system, control systems development, time series analysis and prediction, and a neural expert system.

This book will therefore be valuable to researchers, graduate students and interested laymen in the areas of engineering, computer science, artificial intelligence, machine learning and neurocomputing, who require a comprehensive introduction to the subject, as well as keeping up with the latest research and the issues relevant to this exciting field.

# Acknowledgments

We would like to thank Reg Dodds for his expert assistance with the preparation of the manuscript.

# Contributors

**C Aldrich**
ca1@maties.sun.ac.za
Department of Chemical Engineering,
University of Stellenbosch,
7602 Stellenbosch, South Africa

**J Cervenka**
sima@uivt.cas.vz
Department of Theoretical Informatics,
Institute of Computer Science,
Academy of Sciences of the Czech
Republic,
Pod vodarenskou vezi 2, 182 07 Prague
8, Czech Republic

**I Cloete**
ian.cloete@i-u.de
International University in Germany,
D-76646 Bruchsal,
Germany

**RA Cozzio**
cozzio@comexar.com
COMEXAR Engineering Ltd.,
PO Box 441, Breitenstr. 15,
CH-8853 Lachen, Switzerland

**R Drossu**
rdrossu@eecs.wsu.edu
School of Electrical Engineering and
Computer Science,
Washington State University,
Pullman, Washington, 99164-2752

**J Fletcher**
jfletche@halcyon.com
School of Electrical Engineering and
Computer Science,
Washington State University,
Pullman, Washington, 99164-2752

**CL Giles**
giles@research.nj.nec.com
NEC Research Institute,
Princeton, NJ 08540, USA
and
UMIACS, U. of Maryland,
College Park, MD 20742, USA

**FS Gouws**
ca1@maties.sun.ac.za
Department of Chemical Engineering,
University of Stellenbosch,
7602 Stellenbosch, South Africa

**M Hilario**
Melanie.Hilario@cui.unige.ch
Computer Science Center,
University of Geneva, CH-1211
Geneva 4, Switzerland

**M Ishikawa**
ishikawa@ces.kyutech.ac.jp
Department of Control Engineering and
Science,
Kyushu Institute of Technology,
Iizuka, Fukuoka 820, Japan

**A Lozowski**

jmzura02@homer.louisville.edu
University of Louisville,
Louisville, Kentucky 40292, USA


**Z Obradovic**

zoran@eecs.wsu.edu
School of Electrical Engineering and
Computer Science,
Washington State University,
Pullman, Washington, 99164-2752


**CW Omlin**

omlin@cs.sun.ac.za
Department of Computer Science,
University of Stellenbosch,
7602 Stellenbosch, South Africa


**M Riedmiller**

riedml@ira.uka.de
Department of Computer Science,
University of Karlsruhe,
Karlsruhe, Germany


**P Romero**

promero@eecs.wsu.edu
School of Electrical Engineering and
Computer Science,
Washington State University,
Pullman, Washington, 99164-2752


**GPJ Schmitz**

ca1@maties.sun.ac.za
Department of Chemical Engineering,
University of Stellenbosch,
Stellenbosch 7602, South Africa


**J Sima**

sima@uivt.cas.cz
Department of Theoretical Informatics,
Institute of Computer Science,
Academy of Sciences of the Czech
Republic,
Pod vodarenskou vezi 2, 182 07 Prague
8, Czech Republic


**A Sperduti**

perso@di.unipi.it
Dipartimento di Informatica,
Università di Pisa,
Corso Italia 40,
I-56125 Pisa, Italy


**M Spott**

spott@ipd.info.uni-karlsruhe.de
Department of Computer Science,
University of Karlsruhe,
Karlsruhe, Germany


**J Weisbrod**

weisbrod@fzi.de
Forschungszentrum Informatik (FZI),
Karlsruhe, Germany


**JM Zurada**

jmzura02@homer.louisville.edu
University of Louisville,
Louisville, Kentucky 40292, USA

# 1     Knowledge-Based Neurocomputing: Past, Present, and Future

Ian Cloete

*Knowledge-Based Neurocomputing concerns the application of problem-specific knowledge within the neurocomputing paradigm. The old adage, "Knowledge is power," also applies to neurocomputing. This chapter addresses various methods of utilizing knowledge, and presents several dimensions for the classification of the various approaches. The chapter concludes with a view of the future prospects of knowledge-based neurocomputing.*

## 1.1    The Past

The paradigm of *neurocomputing*, as opposed to conventional procedural methods of computing, has evoked wide-spread interest since the first international conference on artificial neural networks in 1987. Neurocomputing methods are loosely based on an artificial model of the brain as a network of simple interconnected processing elements, corresponding to biological neurons. These methods derive their power by the collective processing of artificial neurons, the main advantage being that such systems can learn and adapt to a changing environment. Several other terms have been coined previously for this rapidly advancing area, such as *connectionist processing* (Shastri, 1995), *parallel distributed processing* (PDP) (Rumelhart and McClelland, 1986), *artificial neural networks* (ANN) (Hassoun, 1995; Rojas, 1996), and *artificial neural systems* (Zurada, 1992). This book assumes a basic familiarity with neurocomputing. However, those readers requiring more information should page to Chapter 13 where an introduction is given.

In *knowledge-based* neurocomputing the emphasis is on the use and representation of knowledge about an application within the neurocomputing paradigm. Despite the powerful processing capabilities of a neurocomputing system, explicit modeling of the *knowledge* represented by such a system remains a major research topic. The reason is simply that a human finds it very difficult to interpret the numeric representation of a neural network. It is therefore the aim of this book to address this issue from various perspectives, and to present the state-of-the-art in knowledge-based neurocomputing in an easily accessible form. The key assumption of knowledge-based neurocomputing is that knowledge is obtainable from, or can be represented by a neurocomputing system, in a humanly comprehensible form. By humanly comprehensible it is meant that the knowledge imbedded in the neuro-computing system is also representable in a symbolic or well-structured form, such as Boolean functions, automata, rules, or in similar well-understood ways. The focus of knowledge-based neurocomputing is therefore on methods to encode prior knowledge, and to extract, refine and revise knowledge within a neurocomputing system.

Why is knowledge-based neurocomputing important? Understanding the knowl-edge imbedded in the system would make neurocomputing systems more acceptable in a variety of application areas. Safety-critical or life-supporting medical applica-tions using a neurocomputing system, for instance, have to be verified to perform to specifications—this process will be much improved if the system's knowledge is comprehensible. There is also another advantage to a comprehensible knowl-edge representation scheme. It brings the research of symbolic Artificial Intelligence methods to bear on the knowledge-based neurocomputing paradigm.

Knowledge-based neurocomputing was inspired by two historically separate re-search areas, namely artificial intelligence (AI) and (artificial) neural networks. Artificial intelligence developed as a subarea of traditional computer science, with the goal to mimic human intelligence. Two viewpoints of what constitutes AI are cited below:

*Artificial intelligence is the study of the computations that make it possible to perceive, reason and act.* (Winston, 1992, p.5)

Russell and Norvig view AI from an "agent" perspective, leading to the following definition of an ideal rational agent:

*For each possible percept sequence, an ideal rational agent should do whatever action is expected to maximize its performance measure, on the basis of the evi-dence provided by the percept sequence and whatever built-in knowledge the agent has.* (Russel and Norvig, 1995, p.33)

Conventional AI is strongly based on symbol manipulation and formal languages in an attempt to mimic human intelligence. The representation and manipulation of symbolically structured knowledge has always played a central role. It is exactly this strong point which led to the development of so-called expert systems (ES), also named knowledge-based systems (KBS). These systems, if sufficient explicit "expert" knowledge about a narrow problem domain is available, provide capabil-ities to symbolically represent the knowledge and reason with it, for instance for diagnostic tasks (Gonzalez and Dankel, 1993). The advantages of these systems lie in their ability to represent comprehensible knowledge.

In the field of artificial neural networks, on the other hand, the analogy with human intelligence is based on a model of the human/animal brain, and an attempt to model explicit symbol manipulation is largely absent. Golden says the following:

*An artificial neural network (ANN) system is an abstract mathematical model inspired by brain structures, mechanisms and functions. An important hope of many researchers is that ANN systems may be used as a universal language by cognitive scientists, engineers, computer scientists, psychologists, biologists, neuroscientists, physicists, and mathematicians for specifying and testing theories of neural information processing.* (Golden, 1996, p.1)

Neurocomputing systems have demonstrated that they model some aspects of human intelligence very well, as recent advances in areas such as vision and speech illustrate (Arbib, 1995). A particularly appealing feature is their ability to acquire knowledge by learning from data. The problem is that this internal knowledge representation developed by the artificial neural network is largely incomprehensible to humans, and thus it cannot be manipulated easily.

We note that the issue of knowledge is common to both classical AI and neurocomputing. The boundaries between these computing paradigms are becoming less and less distinct, as is evidenced by the growing number of AI textbooks which now include material on neurocomputing (Winston, 1992; Russel and Norvig, 1995). he growing number of fuzzy-neural systems (Jang et al., 1997), which present yet another form of knowledge representation and processing, is further evidence of the importance of knowledge when modeling an application.

We believe that the issue of explicit knowledge manipulation within the neurocomputing paradigm has matured to such an extent, and is of such importance, that it warrants a volume dedicated to the review and exposition of approaches addressing this issue. This book is an outgrowth of that belief, and we therefore propose a broad categorization of knowledge-based neurocomputing as follows:

*Knowledge-based neurocomputing (KBN) concerns methods to address the explicit representation and processing of knowledge where a neurocomputing system is involved.*

This definition is of necessity fuzzy to accomodate the large variety of approaches. In this book we concentrate mainly on an engineering perspective to this field. I will return to this point in the next section.

Having discussed the motivation and sources of inspiration for KBN, the layout of the remainder of the chapter is as follows: The next section presents a review of approaches to KBN (which is also further exemplified in Chapter 2), followed by an overview of the book's chapters. The last section discusses the future of KBN, and lists several open questions within the field of KBN.

## 1.2   The Present

### 1.2.1   A Taxonomy

A taxonomy of approaches to KBN is useful since it facilitates understanding and allows the grouping together of related methods that share common characteristics. Three main dimensions are useful for this purpose:

- The motivating perspective of the approach followed,
- architectural considerations, and
- intrinsic characteristics of the methods.

#### *1.2.1.1   The Motivating Perspective*

Researchers' philosophical perspective has played an important role in determining the approach adopted to KBN. Many previous research efforts have concentrated on bringing other knowledge processing paradigms to bear on neurocomputing, with the underlying aim to improve the computational power and capabilities of these systems, or to model a particular aspect of the paradigm within a neurocomputing system, or to prove or disprove a certain theory. In one way or another, it introduces additonal knowledge to the modeling effort. Four broad motivating perspectives are outlined below, with varying degrees of overlap among them. The terms coined to describe the research from a particular perspective frequently provide a hint to its underlying motivation.

Neurobiological:
Research with a neurobiological perspective suggests biological/neural reality of the resulting neurocomputing system. The objective of Neuronal Symbol Processing (NSP), for instance, is to model the brain's high-level functions (Hilario, 1997) starting in a bottom-up fashion from the biological neuron. Edelman's neural Darwinism (Edelman, 1987, 1992), or neuronal group selection (TNGS), thus presents a theory which attempts a biological account of the full range of cognitive phenomena, ranging from sensorimotor responses to concept formation, language and higher-order consciousness (Hilario, 1997).
Examples of research areas impinging on the neurobiological perspective are neuroscience, biology, physiology, aspects of philosophy and psychology, etc.

Cognitive:
Research motivated from a cognitive perspective attempts to model aspects of the "mind," "intelligence" or behavior, though not necessarily requiring neurobiological reality. Cognitive science brings together computer models from AI and experimental techniques from psychology to try to construct testable theories of the workings of the human mind (Russel and Norvig, 1995). From this perspective, for instance, several approaches to language modeling and reasoning with knowledge have been proposed.

"Connectionism" is motivated from the belief that attention must be paid to the computational characteristics of the brain (Shastri, 1995), where the *structured connectionist* approach is distinguished from the *fully distributed* approach. The structured connectionist approach recognizes the importance of neurally motivated constraints, but also acknowledges that insights from disciplines such as psychology, linguistics, computer science, AI and learning theory will have to be incorporated to address complex problems in AI and cognitive science. Models following the structured connectionist approach frequently use a local representation (*localist*, see also Chapter 2) in which concepts are identified with individual nodes, and relationships among them are encoded by excitatory and inhibitory links; and where computation proceeds by spreading activation and lateral inhibition. These models, as well as neurally plausible systems, are limited in their representation of composite structures in a dynamic system, for instance, representing appropriate bindings between roles and fillers in semantic representations of language.

The fully distributed approach, on the other end of the representation spectrum, assumes that each item (concept or mental object) is represented as a pattern of activity over a common pool of units (Shastri, 1995).

The structured connectionist approach further emphasizes the importance of prior ANN structure to facilitate learning, i.e. prior knowledge. In contrast, the fully distributed approach assumes that all the necessary structure is developed by general purpose learning, starting from a *tabula rasa* view with a general purpose ANN architecture.

Examples of the structured connectionist approach include the following: The interactive activation model for letter perception (Rumelhart and McClelland, 1986) which has an interconnection pattern that allows bottom-up perceptual processing to be guided by top-down expectations; the connectionist semantic model (CSM) (Shastri, 1988) that represents memory as concepts organized in an Is-A hierarchy and that allows the attachment of property values to concepts; and the SHRUTI system (Shastri, 1995) which encodes large numbers of facts, general rules and Is-A relations between concepts, and which employ synchronous firing to correspond to dynamic facts.

In contrast to localist encoding of knowledge, some distributed representations employ *coarse coding*, a representation method that uses populations of broadly tuned units to encode a value collectively (Touretzky, 1995). Each unit responds to a range of values, and is active when the input to be encoded falls within its *receptive field*. The Distributed Connectionist Production System (DCPS) (Touretzky and Hinton, 1988), which is discussed below from the symbolic perspective, shows how coarse coding can be applied to symbolic representations.

Another method of distributed encoding of knowledge uses feature vectors. Smolensky, for instance, coined the term "sub-symbolic" to refer to certain types of microfeature representations which encode low-level features (Smolensky, 1988).

Other earlier work on knowledge representations used recurrent networks, such as Elman's simple recurrent networks which learned to process sentences a word at a time and to predict at every time step what the next word would be (Elman,

1995). A simple recurrent network saves hidden unit activations in another layer and then feeds them back to these hidden units on the next time step. Words were represented by a localist encoding in which a single bit was turned on. Analysis of the hidden unit activation vectors showed that the hidden unit space had been partitioned into broad regions corresponding to the grammatical category of the words.

In Chapters 3 and 4 further knowledge representations based on recurrent networks, which have more of a symbolic than a cognitive motivation, are presented and briefly discussed below as motivated from a symbolic perspective.

Further examples of research areas which contribute to a cognitive perspective of KBN are the social/behavioral sciences in general, psychiatry, linguistics, as well as other aspects of the medical, physical, and mathematical sciences that are pertinent to the study of cognition.

  Symbolic:

Research motivated from a symbolic perspective has a kind of AI flavor where symbol processing plays a role in the neurocomputing model. Early attempts in this direction started in the 1980's, of which Touretzky and Hinton's work on the implementation of a production system within the neurocomputing paradigm is a good example (Touretzky and Hinton, 1988). The connectionist expert system MACIE illustrates automated reasoning, a field for which classical AI is well-known (Gallant, 1993). BoltzCONS, for instance, is a connectionist model that dynamically creates and manipulates linked lists, showing how a neurocomputing system is capable of high-level symbol processing (Touretzky, 1995).

The CLARION (Connectionist Learning with Adaptive Rule Induction ONline) system (Sun and Peterson, 1996; Sun and Peterson, 1997), of which the CONSYDERR system (Sun, 1995) (CONnectionist SYstem with Dual-representation for Evidential Robust Reasoning) is a forerunner, has a two-level architecture that represents declarative (i.e. symbolic) knowledge in the form of rules at the top level, and procedural knowledge in the form of reactive routines at the bottom level. The central idea is that the different representations should be developed simultaneously along side each other. The bottom level learns procedural knowledge by reinforcement learning (Q-learning) (Sutton and Barto, 1998), while the top level learns by rule extraction, and generalization and specialization of the extracted rules. If some action decided upon by the reactive level is successful, then the top level extracts a rule corresponding to the reaction, since this provides the opportunity to obtain general knowledge about a particular action. The bottom level is implemented as a three layer network learning Q-values by backpropagation, with a fourth layer (a single unit) that performs stochastic decision making.

Chapters 3 and 4 discuss knowledge representations based on recurrent networks, e.g. various types of automata (deterministic finite-state automata (DFA), fuzzy automata (FFA), subclasses of DFA, such as definite memory machines, etc.), and, especially significant, labeled graphs which include many structured representations such as decision trees, frontier-to-root tree automata, neural trees, etc. Graph representations have played an important role in classical AI, and therefore methods to manipulate labeled graphs within the KBN paradigm will have far-reaching consequences.

Further examples of research areas which contribute to a symbolic perspective (other than AI) are many application areas of computer science and engineering, e.g. robotics, vision, learning, speech, etc.

Engineering:

Research motivated from an engineering perspective focuses on the task or function to be accomplished using whatever appropriate tools are available. Generally the underlying theory stems from mathematical, engineering or physical considerations. Many systems, classified below as *hybrid* combinations of symbolic and neurocomputing modules, attempt a synergistic integration of appropriate techniques to solve a particular problem. Chapter 9, for instance, presents a hybrid neural network and fuzzy system architecture called FYNESSE.

### *1.2.1.2   Architecture*

A second important dimension for classifying KBN systems is their architecture. We distinguish three main architectural approaches to neurosymbolic integration (see also Chapter 2 which provides further architectural perspectives). This classification dimension should be seen as a continuum where "unified" and "hybrid" approaches are the two endpoints.

- Unified architectures
- Translational architectures
- Hybrid architectures

In *unified* approaches symbol processing capabilities are modeled within the neurocomputing paradigm, i.e. no explicit symbolic functionality is programmed into the system in the classical AI sense. Knowledge is modeled using localist, distributed and combined localist/distributed connections between artificial neurons. Examples of this so-called connectionist symbol processing systems are Shastri's SHRUTI system and connectionist semantic model (CSN) (Shastri, 1988), and DCPS (Touretzky and Hinton, 1988), all mentioned above. Many of these types of systems are motivated from a cognitive or symbolic perspective.

The other types of unified architecture are those attempting to model neurobiological reality, such as Edelman's neural Darwinism mentioned in the previous section.

In *hybrid* systems separate neural network and symbolic modules are identifiable, i.e. as distinct components in a software system, where each is responsible for particular functions, and knowledge may be shared or transferred between them. Medsker, for instance, identifies five different integration strategies for expert systems and neural networks where the tightness of the coupling between the neural network and expert system increases from the first to the last model (Medsker, 1994): Stand-alone, transformational, loosely coupled, tightly coupled, and fully integrated models. Fu also identifies five integration strategies for neural networks and knowledge-based components, named as follows (Fu, 1995): Completely overlapped, partially overlapped, parallel, sequential, and embedded. Chapter 2 discusses the degree of integration between the neural network and symbolic modules, ranging from loose to tight coupling, and the method of integration (i.e. communication of data, knowledge and control information) among the modules. Four cooperation methods are identified: Chainprocessing, subprocessing, metaprocessing, and coprocessing.

Most systems classified as hybrids of symbolic and neurocomputational systems are motivated from an engineering perspective, focusing on accomplishment of the task at hand and choosing appropriate techniques from both (classical) AI and artificial neural networks. For example, Chapter 9 describes the hybrid neuro-fuzzy system FYNESSE for self-learning control of nonlinear dynamical systems. The INNS (Incremental Neuro-Symbolic) system of Osorio and Amy uses a coprocessing mode to integrate and transfer knowledge between a symbolic and ANN module(Osorio and Amy, 1998). The system learns incrementally by repeating the rule insertion, ANN learning, rule extraction and rule validation process, using the cascade-correlation learning method (Fahlman and Lebiere, 1990) which can grow the ANN to structure the topology and knowledge during the learning process. The symbolic module uses CLIPS (C Language Integrated Production System) (Giarratano, 1993) as inference engine.

*Translational* architectures typically have the following sequence of steps:

1. Obtain knowledge about the problem in a symbolic, i.e. structured, form.

2. Translate the knowledge to an equivalent ANN.

3. Train the ANN to revise and/or refine the knowledge imbedded in the ANN, using training techniques from neurocomputing.

4. Extract symbolic knowledge from the ANN.

5. Refine the symbolic knowledge.

Step 1 can be performed using machine learning algorithms, such as BEXA which produces propositional rules in $VL_1$ format (Theron and Cloete, 1996). Chapter 10 considers data mining techniques to obtain knowledge in a structured form. Chapters 5 to 8 provide examples of step 2. Some architectures start at step 3 to derive an ANN topology that is suited to symbolic knowledge extraction. This process assumes that suitable training data are available. Chapters 5, 9, 10 and 13 address step 3; and Chapters 5, 9, 11, 12 and 13 provide examples of step 4. Most current systems do not have step 5, however, we describe two such systems below. Steps 4 and 5 could also be seen as a knowledge verification and validation process typical of knowledge-based systems (Gonzalez and Dankel, 1993). This process can be performed by comparing the extracted knowledge with existing knowledge, by using an expert, or by using test data. For example, the hybrid INNS (Incremental Neuro-Symbolic) system of Osorio and Amy (described before) validates rules after each incremental rule acquisition phase to detect incorrect rules(Osorio and Amy,

1998). The cooperative symbolic and ANN learning framework (Viktor and Cloete, 1998), using various forms of team learning among agents, refines extracted symbolic knowledge before distributing it to other team members (Viktor et al., 1998).

### *1.2.1.3   Characteristics of Translational Methods*

Translational KBN architectures can be distinguished further based on intrinsic features of the methodology they follow to acquire comprehensible knowledge, that is, how they address some or all of steps 1 to 4 (Cloete, 1996a). This section elaborates further on this classification dimension and points the reader to relevant material in the book. KBN systems are influenced by the following issues:

- Type of representation of prior and final knowledge
The knowledge representation format influences the architecture of the ANN. For instance, symbolic knowledge in the form of propositional rules (Chapter 6) can be represented using a feed-forward ANN, while automata require a recurrent ANN (Chapter 3). Representing labeled graphs (Chapter 4) requires more powerful processing capabilities, such as recursive neurons (in contrast to "standard" units). Decision trees have been used both as prior knowledge (Ivanova and Kubat, 1995) for a KBN system, and as the extracted final symbolic knowledge representation (Chapter 11).

- Restrictions placed on the ANN architecture
General, i.e. unconstrained, ANN architectures are not necessarily able to facilitate the representation of symbolic knowledge within an ANN, and thus the ANN architecture is constrained to allow correspondence with a symbolic knowledge representation. Constraints include

  □ restricting the network architecture so that it maps to a desired structured representation,
  for instance, constructing the topology as a feed-forward ANN to follow IF-THEN type rules (see Chapter 6 or KBCNN (Fu, 1993)), or a specific topology suited to the representation of differential equations (see Chapter 8), or a recurrent structure to facilitate representation of automata (see Chapters 3 and 4), etc.

  □ restricting the number of layers of the network, e.g. to the level required to map rules to the ANN topology,

  □ restricting the types of activation functions, e.g. only sigmoid activation functions with a high gain are used (Towell and Shavlik, 1994), or certainty factor-based activation functions are used (Fu, 1994),

  □ constraints on weights, e.g. to the sets $\{-1, 0, 1\}$, $\{-H, +H\}$ (see Chapter 3), preferring equally valued weights incoming to a unit (Shavlik, 1996), or restricting weight values to the range [-1,1] for certainty factor-based activation functions (Fu, 1994),

  □ constraints on inputs, e.g. to the sets $\{0, 1\}$ or $\{-1, 1\}$ (Towell and Shavlik, 1994).

- **Characteristics of the training method**

Training methods are specially adapted to obtain comprehensible representations, such as

> □ Placing restrictions on parameters during training, e.g. allow weight or bias weight changes only, fix selected weights only (see Chapter 8), or fix the weight values of the hidden-output layer in a 3-layer feed-forward architecture,

> □ Making modifications to the topology, e.g. add/delete units: TOPGEN looks for units in the ANN with high error rates and then adds new units to these parts of the network (Opitz and Shavlik, 1995),

> □ Changing of the usual objective function,

> for instance, regularization terms are added to the error function. In this approach the "standard" error function is extended by adding additional penalty terms intended to prefer certain parameter values, e.g. desiring weight values in the set $\{-1, 0, 1\}$ (Denoeux and Lengellé, 1992). Structural Learning with Forgetting (SLF) (see Chapter 5) tailors the objective functions used at different stages of the training process to derive a required architecture. The training process consists of three steps: 1. Learning with forgetting, where the objective function includes a constant weight decay term to obtain a skeletal network. 2. Learning with hidden units clarification, where the objective function now forces hidden units to be fully active or inactive (i.e. get rid of the "distributed" representation of knowledge). 3. Learning with selective forgetting, where an objective function is used that makes only those weights decay whose absolute values are smaller than a certain threshold.

- **Method of knowledge extraction**

In addition to distinguishing the characteristics addressed above, here we note that knowledge extraction or acquisition methods usually rely on (1) specialized training requirements and a constrained ANN architecture, or (2) is targeted towards a "general" ANN without any of these restrictions. These two divisions represent a continuum where methods which require fewer restrictions are computationally more demanding because more search is required. Methods of type (1) derive an ANN architecture where the topology can be directly related to the structure of the symbolic knowledge which is extracted or acquired during the process. Methods of type (2) usually perform post processing on a trained ANN, using search mechanisms to extract symbolic descriptions from the "distributed" representation of the ANN. The trained ANN is treated as a black box and used to map inputs to outputs or to cluster some parameter values of the ANN, where this association is then re-represented in some symbolic knowledge structure.

In the special case where extracted knowledge is in the form of rules, these rule extraction techniques have been labeled as *decompositional*, *pedagogical* and *eclectic* (Andrews et al., 1995). The decompositional approach focuses on extracting rules at the level of the hidden and output associations. The decompositional approach is therefore applicable to a constrained ANN architecture which either originated from a set of rules, so-called rule-based connectionist networks (RBCN) (Fu, 1994), or where the topology of the ANN maps to a symbolic rule representation. The pedagogical approach corresponds to methods of type (2) at the other end of the continuum which treat the trained ANN as a black box and performs rule extraction from unconstrained architectures. The eclectic approach to rule extraction is a combination of the decompositional and pedagogical approaches.

This classification can readily be extended to the extraction of other types of symbolic knowledge representations, and to the continuum of "constrained" to "unconstrained" (general) architectures, as proposed above. The following redefinition is proposed: *Decompositional* knowledge extraction methods find a suitable mapping from the structure of a constrained ANN architecture to the desired symbolic knowledge representation scheme. *Pedagogical* knowledge extraction methods use the association between inputs and outputs developed by the ANN as the input to another procedure which creates a symbolic knowledge structure, independent of the original ANN architecture or training procedure. *Eclectic* knowledge extraction methods lie on the continuum from decompositional to pedagogical—the extent to which it belongs to one or the other is determined by the severity of the constraints and/or special training procedure requirements to extract knowledge.

The MOFN algorithm (Shavlik, 1996) is a decompositional method that extracts $m$–of–$n$ rules from trained knowledge-based neural networks. The INNS system (Osorio and Amy, 1998), using a decompositional knowledge extraction method, reduces the complexity of the rule extraction process by only analyzing the units newly added to the ANN due to cascade-correlation learning (Fahlman and Lebiere, 1990). The IMLP (Interpretable Multi-Layer Perceptron) of Bologna and Pellegrini decodes its internal representation to extract zero order conjunctive rules, even with continuous input attributes(Bologna and Pellegrini, 1998). Shavlik also demonstrated that the MOFN algorithm can be applied to ordinary ANNs by using a special training procedure, incorporating a variant of soft-weight sharing, which encourages weights to cluster during training. This version of the algorithm is classified as eclectic. SLF (Chapter 5) is an eclectic knowledge extraction method which derives a constrained ANN architecture through a special training regime. This procedure facilitates understanding of the neural network and the ability to extract comprehensible knowledge. Chapter 3 presents a clustering technique based on the pedagogical approach, while Chapter 11 presents an example of decision tree extraction, and Chapter 12 discusses a fuzzy rule extraction method.

This section concludes the review of current approaches to knowledge-based neurocomputing. The next section summarizes the chapter contributions to this volume, and the final section speculates about the future of knowledge-based neurocomputing.

### 1.2.2   Overview of the Book

The first and second chapters in the book provide an introduction and taxonomy of approaches followed to date in knowledge-based neurocomputing.

Chapters 3 to 5 concentrate on theory and methods for obtaining knowledge in a symbolic form. Knowledge representations used/acquired by both feedforward and recurrent artificial neural networks include Boolean functions, trees, general graphs and automata of various types (including fuzzy automata). Chapters 6 to 12 present methods for and applications of the encoding of prior knowledge, and the extraction, refinement and revision of knowledge within a neurocomputing system. Finally, Chapter 13 discusses knowledge-based neurocomputing in the context of expert and neural expert systems and presents the neural expert system EXPSYS.

The emphasis of the book is on an engineering approach to the design and use of knowledge within artificial neural networks. Thus the applications relate mainly to engineering problems, although the methods have also been applied to more symbolic AI and cognitive science oriented research, e.g. the methods of Chapters 3 and 4.

### 1.2.3   Overview by Chapters

#### 1.2.3.1   Chapter 2

Chapter 2 traces the origins of knowledge-based neurocomputing from the original ideas of *neurosymbolic integration* through to the state-of-the-art architectures of present day systems.

The goal of neurosymbolic integration is to build intelligent systems that exploit the synergy of symbolic and neural processing. Initially this term itself had a biologically inspired connotation where full symbol processing functionality is assumed to emerge from neural structures and processes, i.e. there is no need for symbolic structures and processes as such. This approach is termed "unified" since the capabilities of the systems stem only from a neurocomputing model. However, this unified approach to connectionist symbol processing now finds implementation in localist, distributed and localist/distributed architectures, of which a succinct overview is given. Thus the foundations of knowledge-based neurocomputing are examined, and a taxonomy is proposed mainly from an architectural viewpoint which examines the integration of neurosymbolic systems.

Subsequently, the design of neural networks is examined in the context of the extent to which prior knowledge is used to preprocess input data, to configure the neural network model (i.e. connections, topology, weights, etc.), and to train the neural network. The prior knowledge for a particular domain varies from one extreme where no domain knowledge is present, to the other extreme where perfect knowledge is available. Depending on the amount of prior knowledge, one can distinguish appropriate design techniques where almost perfect domain knowledge is available, knowledge-primed techniques for partial domain knowledge, and knowledge-free techniques where no prior knowledge is available.

The chapter concludes with a description of the SCANDAL system, whose main goal is to apply knowledge (both general knowledge about neural networks, and prior knowledge about a particular problem to be solved) to the design process of a neurocomputing model. The system is currently an experimental workbench consisting of two metalevels and a base level, of which all components are implemented as agents on a distributed system platform. At the highest level a superior agent is responsible for activating the appropriate configuration agents at the next metalevel, based on its background knowledge and the task description at hand. The configuration agents represent a range of topology design techniques covering the spectrum from knowledge-rich to no prior domain knowledge applications. These agents, in turn, are responsible for controlling simulation agents who actually use the suggested neural network architecture and input data to train a neural network model.

### 1.2.3.2   Chapter 3

We have previously stressed the importance of an interpretable and comprehensible knowledge representation, and the fact that there exist several knowledge representation schemes which are well known in the symbolic computation paradigm. Omlin and Giles demonstrate several methods for *symbolic knowledge representation* using *recurrent neural networks* in Chapter 3. Their underlying premise is that if a neural model cannot represent a certain knowledge structure, then it cannot learn it either. The chapter's most important contribution is the relationship established between theoretical models of computation and the corresponding implementation using a recurrent neural network. Issues which are addressed include the following:

- Temporal symbolic knowledge, encoded by finite-state automata, can be represented by recurrent neural networks.

This means that formal languages, their complexities and computational capabilities, as well as their corresponding implementations as deterministic finite-state automata (DFA), also serve as a framework to discuss the capability of various neural network architectures to represent spatio-temporal patterns. Subclasses of DFA, such as definite memory machines and finite memory machines, are shown to be representable by NNFIR (neural network finite impulse response) and NNIIR (neural network infinite impulse response) architectures respectively, while pushdown automata (a computationally more powerful DFA augmented with an infinite stack) can be learned by recurrent networks with an external stack. Although recurrent neural networks are computationally as powerful as Turing machines, this equivalence requires infinite precision in the network computation, and thus for all practical purposes Turing machines cannot be simulated by recurrent neural networks.

Chapter 3 further illustrates a method for encoding a DFA as a recurrent network, analyzes the stability and scalability of the encoding, and compares it to other methods for this purpose. The algorithm uses no more neurons than the best of all methods, and consistently uses fewer weights and smaller fan-out size than the others. This DFA encoding is then extended in two ways to yield a crisp representation of *fuzzy automata* (FFA), and a fuzzy FFA representation using a fuzzy representation of states.

- A method of *real-time on-line* training of recurrent neural networks.

▪ Extraction of rules from recurrent neural networks.

By means of cluster analysis of hidden neuron state space, several different consistent DFAs can be extracted. A heuristic algorithm is devised to make a choice among them.

▪ Insertion and refinement of prior knowledge in recurrent neural networks.

Chapter 3 illustrates how to insert prior knowledge about a DFA into dynamically-driven recurrent neural networks, using the known states and state transitions of the DFA. In addition, refinement and correction of the resulting DFA through subsequent training is illustrated, even in the presence of malicious hints, i.e. incorrect prior knowledge.

### 1.2.3.3   *Chapter 4*

Knowledge about a structured domain can frequently be represented using a graph structure, for instance labeled graphs which represent chemical compounds, or decision trees representing some classification task. In the early 1990's the first publications appeared on the processing of trees using a neural network approach. However, significant progress on the representation and learning of graphs with neural networks only occurred very recently. Sperduti has been a significant contributor to this development, and in Chapter 4, he reviews the state of the art for the classification of structures and presents his latest results in a tutorial style.

Processing of graph structures thus opens up a significant new area for the representation of knowledge in a structured form; an area which was previously developed only by the AI community. These methods are especially significant because they open the door for traditional knowledge representation formalisms of AI to be explored within the knowledge-based neurocomputing paradigm.

Chapter 4 therefore first discusses the basic concepts of graphs, graph transductions, tree grammars and frontier-to-root tree automata (FRA). Then a recursive neuron (as opposed to a standard or recurrent neuron) is introduced as a more powerful transfer function which enables neural graph transductions to be performed.

Backpropagation Through Structure (BPTS) has been proposed as a supervised learning method for these neural graph representations. Similar to backpropagation through time, which unfolds a recurrent network in time into an equivalent feedforward network, BPTS uses recursive neurons to encode and learn structures. The chapter illustrates how to extend Real-Time Recurrent Learning (RTRL), Recurrent Cascade Correlation and Neural Tree architectures to recursive neurons and the learning of neural graph transductions. For learning in the case of a cyclic graph extensions of backpropagation and RTRL are also proposed.

The chapter concludes by considering the computational power and complexity of several neural network architectures for the processing of structures since this characterizes the class of functions which can potentially be computed by these networks. It is shown that a simple recurrent network (Elman-style) can simulate any frontier-to-root tree automaton, while neither the Cascade-Correlation network for structures nor the Neural Tree for structures can simulate any FRA. The node complexity of the implementation of FRAs as recursive neural networks is addressed as well, and new upper bounds for three and four layer recursive networks are derived. As a special case, a new bound is derived by a constructive method for the implementation of finite-state automata (also discussed in Chapter 3), which may prove very useful for practical applications.

### *1.2.3.4   Chapter 5*

In Chapter 5 Masumi Ishikawa presents a comprehensive description of his novel method, with several variations, for training artificial neural networks, called Structural Learning with Forgetting (SLF). This training strategy finds a suitable network topology during training in such a way that the resulting network structure is comprehensible, i.e. the network structure has a well-defined symbolic interpretation. The training process consists of three successive steps: (1) Learning with forgetting. (2) Learning with hidden units clarification. (3) Learning with selective forgetting. Ishikawa also extends the process to apply to recurrent neural networks, and then presents a series of examples to illustrate the effectiveness of SLF versus other methods for various tasks. These tasks include:

- Discovery of Boolean functions: Functions with binary valued inputs and outputs.

- Classification of irises: Classification functions with continuous inputs and binary outputs.

- Discovery of recurrent networks: Jordan and buffer networks for time series are trained using SLF, or rather generalized SLF (GSLF) for recurrent networks.

- Adapting to a changing environment: When changes in input data indicate that the neural network structure needs to be changed in response, SLF is capable of on-line modification of the network topology.

- Discovery of propositional rules: Knowledge represented as rules can be discovered by SLF.

- Discovery of modular structured neural networks: SLF is capable of discovering useful subnetworks (modules) and both intra-module and inter-module connections. The advantages of modular components in a network are better understanding of the required knowledge organized into "knowledge" subcomponents, easier learning compared to a monolithic structure, and reduced computational cost during training.

### *1.2.3.5   Chapter 6*

Chapter 6 presents $VL_1ANN$, a method for transforming rules represented in Variable-valued Logic I format (Michalski, 1975) (and induced by the symbolic learning method BEXA (Theron and Cloete, 1996)) to a feedforward neural network. The $VL_1ANN$ algorithm is thus an example of a translational approach to obtain an equivalent ANN architecture. This allows further training of the neural network to refine the rules, and possibly to discover other decision regions not well-represented by the axis-parallel decision regions of the VL$_1$ rules.

### 1.2.3.6   Chapter 7

Partial or incomplete knowledge about a particular problem domain is frequently available from different sources and in different knowledge representation formalisms. For instance, a group of human experts may share knowledge of a problem, but each is more knowledgeable regarding a particular aspect of the problem. Previous chapters considered various approaches of introducing partial knowledge into a knowledge-based neurocomputing model, however, most approaches were based on transforming the prior knowledge into a neural network model before further processing could be performed. Chapter 7, on the other hand, addresses the problem of integrating heterogeneous sources of partial domain knowledge into a knowledge-based neurocomputing model. These knowledge sources include (symbolic) decision trees, rule-based expert systems and trained neural networks.

The chapter investigates several different methods for improving classification results by integrating prior knowledge and learning from data. First, domain and range transformations of the original problem are considered. These transformations are integrated with a neurocomputing model of a single source of prior knowledge, where the neural network can grow incrementally when needed. Alternatively a pre-existing expert system is imbedded directly into this constructive neural network learning model. Integration of multiple sources of prior knowledge is addressed next. Methods include the direct imbedding of multiple experts and a symbolic decision tree, while two neural network approaches are presented, namely a trainable combiner network, and the competitive integration of heterogeneous experts using a trainable gating network whose output units employ the differentiable softmax activation function.

Finally the methods presented in this chapter are evaluated in the context of two quite different benchmark problems: (1) Solving the classification of the well-known two spirals problem using several experts, and (2) a financial advising problem. The results illustrate how the expertise of each partial knowledge source influences the system's output by identifying regions of the input space where individual experts are good classifiers. The results also illustrate that the integration of techniques not performing well on their own may result in improved classification; and that the competitive neural network approach to integrate multiple experts is proved superior both to the other integration methods investigated and to each individual source of prior knowledge.

### 1.2.3.7   Chapter 8

Prior knowledge about a task at hand can take several forms, for instance production rules encoded to provide the initial neural network structure. Chapter 8 considers a novel method for encoding prior knowledge about a dynamical system in the form of differential equations. For many engineering problems and physical systems it is frequently the case that partial prior knowledge about the system dynamics is available as differential equations. Cozzio proposes a method of using this knowledge to construct both the architecture and initial weights of a neural network for modeling such a system. Training of such a network from observed data can then serve to refine the model and estimate unknown parameters of the system.

The chapter starts off with the necessary theoretical derivations by generalizing the Taylor series method for polynomial approximations to nonpolynomial approximation functions, from which suitable neural network approximators can be derived. A set of conditions depending on the properties of the derivatives of the neural network is identified to guarantee the solvability of the encoded differential equations. Any type of neural network, which adheres to these conditions, can serve as a suitable approximator. It is then proved that Radial Basis Function Networks and a new proposed architecture, Modified Logistic Networks, satisfy these conditions.

The resulting four-layer network architecture contains an input layer, a preprocessing layer for polynomial expressions of the inputs, a middle layer and an output layer. All weights are determined in advance; some of which are fixed, and include direct connections between inputs and outputs. Thus a Higher-Order Radial Basis Function Network or Higher-Order Modified Logistic Network is constructed. The chapter concludes with single-step and multi-step integration tests for forecasting time series generated by sampling the Lorenz system of chaotic differential equations. The proposed Modified Logistic Networks outperformed the Radial Basis Function Networks in all cases. The chapter thus illustrates how *prior* knowledge in the form of ordinary differential equations can be integrated with the learning from data approach, leading to advantages such as improved generalization and training efficiency, as well as less need for training data.

### *1.2.3.8   Chapter 9*

In practice, many neural network based solutions suffer from a lack of user acceptance due to their black-box nature, i.e. the system's knowledge is not explicit, but distributed, hidden within the neural network, and thus not interpretable by users. Chapter 9 proposes a hybrid neural network and fuzzy system architecture called FYNESSE, a self-learning controller of nonlinear dynamical systems. The main features of the controller are that it represents its control strategy as fuzzy relations which can be interpreted by end-users in terms of fuzzy rules, and which allow the integration of *prior* knowledge about the dynamical system in the form of fuzzy rules.

This chapter of the book introduces several novelties: First, it presents a *control system* with feedback, an application area that is only addressed in this chapter. This means that the temporal effects of nonlinear dynamical systems must be addressed by solving the difficult temporal credit assignment problem. Second, its knowledge representation scheme is fuzzy rules and fuzzy relations, instead of crisp rules in variants of propositional logic. Thus the desirable property of comprehensibility of prior and acquired knowledge is maintained. Third, a novel method is presented for learning the fuzzy control relation by modeling both the support (positive knowledge) and possibility (negative knowledge) of actions in a particular state. The method further includes the treatment of ignorance and inconsistent knowledge.

The chapter starts off by distinguishing five design requirements and points out that an architecture satisfying these requirements is a hybrid model with two strictly separate but interacting modules—a fuzzy module and a neural network. Various modes and levels of interaction establish degrees of freedom from which the user can choose according to the requirements of a particular control task. The system employs dynamic programming to implement reinforcement learning (Sutton and Barto, 1998), i.e. a learning situation where only a judgement about success or failure is available. In addition this judgement is delayed until the end of a trial, requiring that the temporal credit assignment problem be solved. Finally, the chapter illustrates a very successful benchmark test of the self-learning controller against a carefully designed analytical controller for which complete knowledge is available.

### 1.2.3.9   Chapter 10

Chapter 10 focuses on three important issues in knowledge-based neurocomputing: (1) The extraction of knowledge from data, (2) use of this knowledge to design appropriate neurcomputing architectures and (3) application of this knowledge to time series predictions. The chapter explains the problems of predicting non-stationary time series and then proceeds by proposing two categories of knowledge imbedding: direct and indirect.

For direct knowledge imbedding, techniques from information theory, nonlinear dynamical systems and stochastic analysis are used for exploratory data analysis of the time series to be predicted. Knowledge extracted in this way serves as prior knowledge to design an appropriate neural network architecture, set initial parameter values of the network before training commences, and suggests an adequate data sampling rate for the time series. These techniques are also applied to a real-life time series of compressed video traffic data, and to an artificial nonlinear chaotic time series, generated from the well-known Mackey-Glass differential equation.

Indirect knowledge imbedding concerns the use of *a priori* known properties of the target function to be approximated/predicted by the neural network, as well as general knowledge about non-stationary time series prediction which can be indirectly used "on-line" to improve predictions. Novel examples of the use of the last mentioned indirect knowledge imbedding, are various methods of detecting, during the prediction phase, that the characteristic parameters of the non-stationary time series have changed, and that the prediction method must therefore be modified accordingly.

### 1.2.3.10   Chapter 11

The importance of a comprehensible knowledge representation scheme has been stressed earlier. Decision trees have been used extensively in symbolic machine learning methods: Here choices are represented at the nodes of the tree, and the outcomes at the leaves. Chapter 11 proposes an algorithm, ANN-DT, to extract a binary decision tree from a trained neural network.

The basic idea of the algorithm is to sample the input space and use the trained neural network as a satisfactory model to compute the output associated with each input vector. In this way an artificial data set is created which serves as training data for a decision tree generator. The ANN-DT algorithm has several novel features to ensure that a faithful decision tree representation of the neural network model is generated:

- The generated artificial data must have the same distribution as the original data. Several similarity measures and sampling procedures are used to cater for both discrete and continuous variables.

- Two variants of the algorithm explore different methods to select the next attribute and its threshold when generating the tree. In particular, the chapter also proposes a new method to analyze attribute significance.

- Statistical tests, such as the Pearson's chi-square test and the F-test, are employed as stopping criteria when generating further decision tree splits. To prevent unnecessarily large (and thus incomprehensible) trees from being generated, a user defined maximum tree depth constraint, a lower branching limit constraint, and a constraint on the variance of the output of a node for continuous outputs are introduced.

In addition, note that the algorithm can be used for continuous outputs as well as discrete classifications, while the decision tree representation can also be converted to the customary propositional rules.

The algorithm is compared with other machine learning methods, such as CART, ID3 and C4.5 (Quinlan, 1993), on modeling problems involving both axis-parallel and nonlinear decision regions. In all case studies a faithful rule representation was extracted from the trained neural network, where the ANN-DT(e) variant of the algorithm performed better on classification problems, while the ANN-DT(s) variant showed more robust performance on continuous output data.

### 1.2.3.11   Chapter 12

Soft quantization of continuous inputs and outputs, and linguistic variables allow interpretable fuzzy rules to be constructed. Chapter 12 presents a pedagogical algorithm for fuzzy rule extraction from a neural network. The ANN is trained to approximate the classification problem at hand, and is then used as a black-box classifier which predicts the output given a sample from the input space. The input space is soft quantized by changing real-valued inputs into fuzzy numbers using appropriate fuzzy membership functions to produce values between 0 and 1. The input domain is systematically sampled, and the numerical coordinates of each example are mapped into corresponding linguistic variable values. The ANN approximator is then used to predict the output value for each numerical example. This procedure allows a fuzzy rule to be constructed which maps the input linguistic variable values to a decision indicated by the ANN. Since systematic sampling tends to produce a plethora of rules, the authors introduce an uncertainty margin to limit the number of extracted rules to represent the accuracy of approximation required.

The chapter illustrates the rule extraction method using the Exclusive-Or problem, and then applies it to the real-world problem of predicting the dosage of gentamycin necessary to treat kidney disease. The method is also applied to the well-known iris flower classification problem. These results allow comparison with many other machine learning algorithms which were tested on the same benchmark data.

### 1.2.3.12 Chapter 13

Expert systems captured the attention more than a decade ago as systems which contain specialized knowledge about a problem domain with a reasoning and explanation capability to address a user's query. The knowledge contained in these systems (typically in the form of production rules) is explicit and comprehensible to the experts, and can be inspected and modified when necessary.

Present day expert systems, also termed Knowledge-Based Systems (Gonzalez and Dankel, 1993), feature well-defined system architectures with several types of inferencing and appropriate knowledge representation formalisms available. The commonality between knowledge-based neurocomputing and these knowledge-based (expert) systems lies in the concept of comprehensible explicit knowledge. It is therefore natural to inquire if the KBN paradigm has similar capabilities to offer as those found in symbolic expert systems. In this regard, Chapter 13 presents an overview of hybrid expert systems which contain a neural processing component, and of expert systems wholly implemented within the KBN paradigm. Such systems, with reference to the preceding chapters, require that knowledge about the application domain either be encoded as prior knowledge and/or learned (refined) from examples, thus bringing all the techniques for using or refining prior knowledge to bear on the challenge of constructing a *neural expert system*.

The chapter starts off with a brief overview of the purpose and architecture of expert systems. Then the integration strategies of hybrid expert systems, i.e. expert systems that contain some form of knowledge-based neurocomputing model, are discussed. The last part of the chapter addresses neural expert systems. A review of the system MACIE (Gallant, 1993) is given, followed by a description of EXPSYS. The latter system has, among others, two noteworthy features: First, it uses interval neurons and encodes its input values appropriately. Second, it employs a modified form of the well-known backpropagation algorithm for training of these differentiable neuron activation functions, while MACIE uses the pocket algorithm for training. The chapter concludes by working through a complete example to illustrate all its salient features.

## 1.3   The Future

We believe that KBN has a bright future ahead, in both the short and longer term. Emergent directions in the near future indicate that the technology will be affected by three important issues: (1) New integration strategies, (2) developments in distributed processing and (3) the need to demonstrate practical applications.

New integration strategies allow models from different perspectives or disciplines to work together to solve a problem. KBN has its roots in two traditionally distinct research areas, namely artificial intelligence (AI) and (artificial) neural networks. Researchers from both main stream camps, as well as from numerous other disciplines, e.g. the behavioral and physiological sciences, and from other research areas which have an interest in modeling "intelligent" behavior, have realized the potential benefits of combining different approaches in a synergistic manner. The idea is simply that a hybrid approach can build on the strengths of the individual approaches, and so obtain better performance by utilizing complementary, but different, knowledge sources. Evidence of this phenomenon occurs in many places, for example, the creation of new subareas within AI which can incorporate a neural network component (such as data mining, intelligent diagnosis, etc.), modeling of financial data using a knowledge component based on neural networks, and so on. A further strong pointer to this expansion is the development of so-called "soft computing." Soft Computing consists of several computing paradigms, including neural networks, fuzzy set theory, approximate reasoning, and derivative-free optimization methods such as genetic algorithms and simulated annealing (Jang et al., 1997).

Developments in distributed processing will have a beneficial influence on knowledge-based neurocomputing. Examples are the development of distributed artificial intelligence and agent technology (Müller et al., 1997), and the CORBA (Common Object Resource Broker Architecture) specification of a standard object-oriented architecture for applications (Ryan, 1997). These technologies have to address the problems of communication, coordination, control and knowledge sharing between cooperating distributed processes on potentially heterogeneous computing platforms. These problems are shared by hybrid knowledge-based neurocomputing systems, i.e. systems with distinct neural network and symbolic components as discussed in Section 1.2.1.2. Although most current hybrid KBN systems are not distributed, progress on these problems will enable the wider implementation of KBN on distributed computing platforms and the imbedding of this technology in other software applications.

The rapid development of information technology in recent years demand practical applications which can use knowledge from diverse sources, cope with the impreciseness of the real world, and adapt to a changing environment. Knowledge-based neurocomputing is admirably suited to fulfill such a role. It has the ability for fusion of knowledge from complementary sources and different representations, and is tolerant of noise. KBN further provides both data driven and model driven learning. These capabilities will ensure its integration into conventional software applications in the future.

Despite the progress in knowledge-based neurocomputing, important open prob-

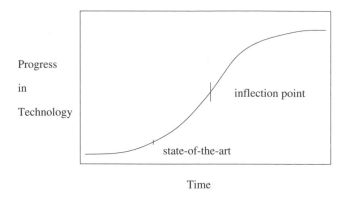

**Figure 1.1**   The expected technology S-curve for KBN

lems remain. KBN cannot yet harness the full power of predicate logic representations frequently used in AI. Although good progress has been made to represent symbolic structures in KBN (see Chapter 4), the dynamic variable binding problem remains to be solved (Park et al., 1995). Further questions to address include the development of new integration strategies and more diverse types of knowledge representations, e.g. procedural knowledge, methods to exchange knowledge, and reasoning capabilities.

So where is the knowledge-based neurocomputing technology at present? Company strategists often use the so-called *technology S-curve* to anticipate technological progress (Asthana, 1995). The technology S-curve tracks the progress of a base technology as a function of research and development (R&D) effort or, if R&D is constant, as a function of time. It most often assumes the approximate shape of an S (or for the ANN community, the shape of a sigmoid function): In the beginning technological progress is slow; as expertise builds up, progress is faster, and may even be exponential. When the technology matures, progress slows down. In the beginning of KBN technology (1980's, early 1990's), progress was slow; relatively few scientific papers on the subject appeared. Since then the interest has grown considerably, as is evidenced by several special sessions, workshops and tutorials on the topic organized at major international conferences. Examples include (Sun and Alexandre, 1997), (Fu, 1996), (Ghosh, 1997), (Cloete, 1996b), (Kozma, 1996), (Cloete et al., 1997) and (Alexandre and Cloete, 1998). There is no sign that the tempo of progress in KBN technology is slowing down, on the contrary, the growth rate is increasing. This leads me to believe that the state-of-the-art in KBN development is well below the inflection point of the S-curve depicted in Figure 1.1.

In conclusion, we expect that knowledge-based neurocomputing will continue to grow and stand to benefit from developments in conventional AI, machine learning, computational intelligence and soft computing, and from the many other disciplines whose intention it is to model comprehensible knowledge.

# References

Alexandre, F. and Cloete, I. 1998. Knowledge-based applications of artificial neural networks. In *Proceedings of the Fourth International Conference on Neural Networks and their Applications. (NEURAP'98) Special session.*, pp. 367–418, Marseille.

Andrews, R., Diederich, J., and Tickle, A. B. 1995. Survey and critique of techniques for extracting rules from trained artificial neural networks. *Knowledge-based Systems*, 8(6):373–389.

Arbib, M. A., ed. 1995. *The Handbook of Brain Theory and Neural Networks.* Cambridge, MA: MIT Press.

Asthana, P. 1995. Jumping the technology s-curve. *IEEE Spectrum*, pp. 49–54.

Bologna, G. and Pellegrini, C. 1998. Symbolic rule extraction from modular transparant boxes. In *Proceedings of the Fourth International Conference on Neural Networks and their Applications (NEURAP'98)*, pp. 393–398, Marseille, France.

Cloete, I. 1996a. Email invitation to contributors of this volume.

Cloete, I. 1996b. Knowledge-based neural networks. In *Proceedings of the IEEE International Concernece on Neural Networks. Special session S2.*, pp. 59–93, Washington D.C.

Cloete, I., Kozma, R., and Giles, C. L. 1997. Knowledge-based methods in neural networks. In *Proceedings of the IEEE International Conference on Neural Networks. Special sessions SS9 (A and B)*, pp. 2519–2559, Houston, USA.

Denoeux, T. and Lengellé, R. 1992. Production rules generation and refinement in back propagation networks. Tech. rep., Université de Technologie de Compiégne, France.

Edelman, G. M. 1987. *Neural Darwinism, the Theory of Neuronal Group Selection.* New York: Basic Books.

Edelman, G. M. 1992. *Bright Air, Brilliant Fire. On the Matter of the Mind.* New York: Basic Books.

Elman, J. L. 1995. Language processing. In Arbib (1995), pp. 508–513.

Fahlman, S. E. and Lebiere, C. 1990. The cascade-correlation learning architecture. Tech. Rep. CMU-CS-90-100, Carnegie Mellon University. Web address: http://www.cs.cmu.edu/Reports/index.html.

Fu, L. M. 1993. Knowledge-based connectionism for revising domain theories. *IEEE Transactions on Systems, Man and Cybernetics*, 23(1):173–182.

Fu, L. M. 1994. *Neural Networks in Computer Intelligence.* New York: McGraw-Hill.

Fu, L. M. 1995. Editorial. *Knowledge-based Systems*, 8(6):298.

Fu, L. M. 1996. Knowledge and neural heuristics: Tutorial lecture. In *IEEE*

*International Conference on Neural Networks*, Washington, D.C.

Gallant, S. I. 1993. *Neural Network Learning and Expert Systems*. Cambridge: MIT Press.

Ghosh, J. 1997. Network ensembles and hybrid systems. tutorial lecture. In *IEEE International Conference on Neural Networks*.

Giarratano, J. C. 1993. *CLIPS User Guide*. USA: NASA Software Technology Branch.

Golden, R. M. 1996. *Mathematical Methods for Neural Network Analysis and Design*. Cambridge, MA: MIT Press.

Gonzalez, A. J. and Dankel, D. D. 1993. *The Engineering of Knowledge-Based Systems*. Englewood Cliffs, NJ: Prentice-Hall International.

Hassoun, M. 1995. *Fundamentals of Artificial Neural Networks*. Cambridge: MIT Press.

Hilario, M. 1997. An overview of strategies for neurosymbolic integration. In *Connectionist-Symbolic Integration*, eds. R. Sun and F. Alexandre, pp. 13–35. Hillside, New Jersey: Lawrence Erlbaum Ass.

Ivanova, I. and Kubat, M. 1995. Initialization of neural networks by means of decision trees. *Knowledge-based Systems*, 8(6):333–344.

Jang, J. S., Sun, C.-T., and Mizutani, Z. 1997. *Neuro-Fuzzy and Soft Computing: A Computational Approach to Learning and Machine Intelligence*. Englewood Cliffs, NJ: Prentice-Hall International.

Kozma, R. 1996. Knowledge monitoring by neuro-fuzzy methods. In *Proceedings of the IEEE International Conference on Neural Networks. Spesial session S3*, pp. 94–123, Washington, D. C.

Medsker, L. 1994. Design and development of hybrid neural networks and expert systems. In *Proceedings of the IEEE International Conference on Neural Networks*, pp. 1470–1474, Orlando, Florida.

Michalski, R. S. 1975. Variable-valued logic and its applications to pattern recognition and machine learning. In *Computer Science and Multiple-valued logic: Theory and applications*, ed. D. C. Rine, pp. 506–534. North Holland.

Müller, J. P., Wooldridge, M. J., and Jennings, N. R. 1997. Intelligent agents III: Agent theories, architectures and languages. *Springer Verlag Lecture Notes in Artificial Intelligence*, 1193.

Opitz, D. W. and Shavlik, J. W. 1995. Dynamically adding symbolically meaningful nodes to knowledge-based neural networks. *Knowledge-based Systems*, 8(6):301–311.

Osorio, F. S. and Amy, B. 1998. INSS: A hybrid system for constructive machine learning. In *Proceedings of the Fourth International Conference on Neural Networks and their Apllications (NEURAP'98)*, pp. 369–376, Marseille, France.

Park, N. S., Robertson, D., and Stenning, K. 1995. Extension of the temporal synchrony approach to dynamic variable binding in a connectionist inference system. *Knowledge-based Systems*, 8(6):345–357.

Quinlan, J. R. 1993. *C4.5: Programs for Machine Learning*. San Mateo, California: Morgan Kaufman Publishers.

Rojas, R. 1996. *Neural Networks: A Systematic Introduction*. Berlin: Springer Verlag.

Rumelhart, D. E. and McClelland, J. L. 1986. *Parallel Distributed Processing: Volume 1, Foundations*. Cambridge, MA: MIT Press.

Russel, S. J. and Norvig, P. 1995. *Artificial Intelligence: A Modern Approach*. Englewood Cliffs, New Jersey: Prentice-Hall International.

Ryan, T. W. 1997. *Distributed Object Technology: Concepts and Applications*. Upper Saddle River, New Jersey: Prentice-Hall International.

Shastri, L. 1988. *Semantic Networks: An Evidential Formulation and its Connectionist Realization*. London: Pitman.

Shastri, L. 1995. Structured connectionist models. In Arbib (1995), pp. 949–952.

Shavlik, J. W. 1996. An overview of research at Wisconsin on knowledge-based neural networks. In *Proceedings of the IEEE International Conference on Neural Networks. Special session S2*, pp. 65–69, Washington, D.C.

Smolensky, P. 1988. On the proper treatment of connectionism. *Behav. Brain. Sci.*, 11:1–74.

Sun, R. 1995. A two-level hybrid architecture for structuring knowledge for commonsense reasoning. In *Computational Architectures Integrating Neural and Symbolic Processes*, eds. R. Sun and L. A. Bookman, pp. 247–281. Boston: Kluwer Academic Publishers.

Sun, R. and Alexandre, F. 1997. *Connectionist-Symbolic Integration*. Hillside, New Jersey: Lawrence Erlbaum Ass.

Sutton, R. S. and Barto, A. G. 1998. *Reinforcement Learning: An Introduction*. Cambridge: MIT Press.

Theron, H. and Cloete, I. 1996. BEXA: A covering algorithm for learning propositional concept descriptions. *Machine Learning*, 24:5–40.

Touretzky, D. S. 1995. Connectionist and symbolic representations. In Arbib (1995), pp. 243–247.

Touretzky, D. S. and Hinton, G. E. 1988. A distributed connectionist production system. *Cognitive Science*, 12(3):423–466.

Towell, G. G. and Shavlik, J. W. 1994. Knowledge-based artificial neural networks. *Artificial Intelligence*, 70:119–165.

Viktor, H. L. and Cloete, I. 1998. Inductive learning with a computational network. *Journal of Intelligent and Robotic Systems*, 21(2):131–141.

Viktor, H. L., Engelbrecht, A. P., and Cloete, I. 1998. Incorporating rule extraction from ANNs into a cooperative learning environment. In *Proceedings of the*

*Fourth International Conference on Neural Networks and their Applications (NEURAP'98)*, pp. 385–392, Marseille, France.

Winston, P. H. 1992. *Artificial Intelligence*. New York: Addison-Wesley.

Zurada, J. M. 1992. *Introduction to Artificial Neural Systems*. Boston: PWS.

# 2 Architectures and Techniques for Knowledge-Based Neurocomputing

Melanie Hilario

*In its early form, knowledge-based neurocomputing consisted mainly in mapping symbolic knowledge structures, e.g. rules, onto neural network nodes and links. It was shown that the resulting networks learned more quickly and attained higher accuracy than those developed without the help of prior knowledge. In the meantime, researchers have explored other ways of using domain knowledge in neural network development. This chapter proposes an extended definition of knowledge-based neurocomputing (KBN) which covers all efforts to incorporate knowledge into neural networks, without restriction to translational neurosymbolic models. It then surveys techniques for KBN as redefined and proposes a metalevel architecture for integrating these techniques into a system for knowledge-based neural network design and training. The chapter concludes with a discussion of challenging research issues and directions.*

## 2.1 The Knowledge-Data Trade-Off

The knowledge-data trade-off in machine learning reflects the fact that most learning takes place between two extremes. On the one hand, when a system's initial knowledge is complete and correct, the only relevant learning approach is analytical learning—a non-ampliative form of learning that merely reformulates (operationalizes) what is already known in order to increase efficiency in the performance of certain tasks. Analytical learning hardly requires data; in its pure form, explanation-based learning uses a single training instance (Mitchell et al., 1986). On the other hand, when prior knowledge is nil, the only recourse is data-driven learning; most theoretical guarantees about convergence and generalization apply mainly to this form of tabula rasa learning and assume asymptotic conditions where the amount of data tends toward infinity (Valiant, 1984; Baum and Haussler, 1989). However, learning in the real world typically starts out with some knowledge about a problem domain and a variable—but rarely infinite—amount of data for a given learning task. In this more realistic context, the knowledge-data trade-off in learning can be expressed as follows: the less knowledge you have, the more data you need; conversely, the less data you have, the more knowledge you need. In more general terms, learning can be viewed as the task of bringing *a priori* knowledge to bear on the available data in view of extracting *a posteriori* knowledge from these data.

There is a wide range of possibilities between pure knowledge-driven and pure data-driven learning. Depending on which end of the spectrum is closer, the problem of combining knowledge and data can be addressed from two different angles. First, one can use data to improve knowledge-driven learning; this approach has been embodied in many attempts to combine explanation-based learning with more empirical methods, thus allowing for graceful degradation in the presence of an incomplete or incorrect domain theory. Examples of this approach are UNIMEM (Lebowitz, 1986), IOE (Flann and Dietterich, 1989), GEMINI (Danyluk, 1994), DISCIPLE (Tecuci and Kodratoff, 1990), ML-SMART (Bergadano and Giordana, 1990) and others (Rajamoney and DeJong, 1987; Rajamoney et al., 1985; Segre, 1987). Alternatively, one can use prior knowledge to guide and reduce search during data-driven learning, as in FOCL (Pazzani and Kibler, 1992) and WHY (Saitta et al., 1993).

The above examples have been drawn from the symbolic paradigm to highlight the fact that the knowledge-data trade-off is as real a problem in symbolic learning as it is in neural network (NN) learning, which is the focus of this paper. Moreover, at the intersection of these two learning paradigms, the knowledge-data trade-off has been a major driving force behind *neurosymbolic integration*, a research area currently aimed at intelligent systems that exploit the synergy of symbolic and neural processing. Neural networks can be used to improve knowledge-driven learning; in EBNN, for instance, a set of neural networks combines analytical and inductive learning to refine imperfect, previously learned domain theories (Thrun and Mitchell, 1993; Mitchell and Thrun, 1994). NNs can also provide processing support to knowledge-based systems which have no learning capabilities. The SETHEO theorem prover relies on neural networks for diverse tasks: multilayer perceptrons are used to induce search control heuristics and limit combinatorics in theorem proving (Goller, 1994), whereas LRAAMs (Sperduti, 1994) are used in the classification of first-order logical terms (Goller and Kuechler, 1996). The complementary approach consists in using knowledge to improve connectionist learning. This has given rise to a host of neurosymbolic systems in which knowledge expressed in symbolic formalisms such as rules is used to configure and initialize neural networks. Some representatives of this approach are KBANN (Towell and Shavlik, 1994), TopGen (Opitz and Shavlik, 1993), RAPTURE (Mahoney and Mooney, 1993), KBCNN (Fu and Fu, 1990), and Lacher et al.'s work (Lacher et al., 1992). The neural networks created with this approach have been called knowledge-based neural networks and form the original core around which the field of *knowledge-based neurocomputing* (KBN) has developed.

Neurosymbolic integration is now a major research area at the confluence of classical AI and neurocomputing, and controlling the knowledge-data trade-off in machine learning remains one of its persistent concerns. Knowledge-based neuro-computing emerged as a specific subarea of neurosymbolic integration, but KBN has assumed a much broader scope than the simple mapping of symbolic structures into neural networks. To clarify this claim, Section 2.2 presents a taxonomy of architectures for neurosymbolic integration, which is then used as a framework to propose a redefinition of knowledge-based neurocomputing. Section 2.3 explores ways of building prior knowledge into neural networks and in the process unveils the extensive range of techniques available for knowledge-based neurocomputing. Many of these techniques have been integrated into a metalevel architecture for knowledge-based neural network development, described in Section 2.4. Finally, Section 2.5 concludes on a number of related issues and directions for future research.

## 2.2 Foundations for Knowledge-Based Neurocomputing

To grasp the intent and scope of knowledge-based neurocomputing, we examine the nurturing field in which it took root, that of neurosymbolic integration.

### 2.2.1 Architectures for Neurosymbolic Integration

As we have seen, neurosymbolic integration is the generic term that covers all efforts at combining symbolic and connectionist processing. These have given rise to three major architectural classes. *Unified* architectures attain neural and symbolic capabilities using neural networks alone. *Translational* architectures use symbolic structures as source formalisms: these are mapped onto neural networks, which subsequently take over the learning and performance tasks. *Hybrid* architectures combine neural networks and symbolic processors which can interact in a variety of ways (Fig. 2.1).

#### *2.2.1.1 Unified Architectures*

The unified approach is premised on the claim that there is no need for symbolic structures and processes as such: full symbol processing functionalities emerge from neural structures and processes. If we eliminate biologically inspired approaches which attempt to ground higher cognitive processing on the biological neuron, the unified approach consists mainly in *connectionist symbol processing* (CSP) (Hinton, 1991). Work in this area can be classified along two dimensions. From the point of view of the underlying representation scheme, CSP architectures can be localist, distributed, and combined localist/distributed. *Localist architectures* are based on a one-to-one mapping between network nodes and symbolic structures. Each node represents a feature, a value, a concept or a combination of concepts, e.g. a two-place predicate, a relation or a rule (Shastri, 1988; Ajjanagadde and Shastri, 1991; Sohn and Gaudiot, 1991; Lange, 1992; Feldman and Ballard, 1982). The principal disadvantage of localist architectures is that they quickly succumb to combinatorial

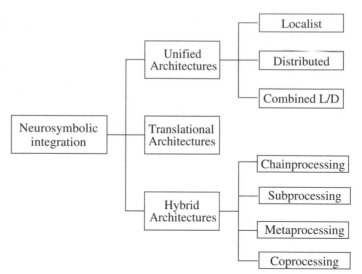

**Figure 2.1**   Classification of integrated neurosymbolic systems.

explosion as the number of individual concepts increases. This has motivated the development of *distributed architectures*, , where the most elementary concepts emerge from the interaction of several different nodes. Each knowledge item, e.g. concept, fact or rule, is represented using a combination of several units, and each unit can be used in the representation of several items. DCPS (Touretzky and Hinton, 1988), for example, is a distributed connectionist production system that uses coarse coding to store all entities manipulated by the rule interpreter. Its main advantage is that the working memory requires far fewer units than the number of facts that can potentially be stored. Coarse coding is also used in BoltzCONS (Touretzky, 1990b) to represent symbolic structures such as lists and stacks, whereas recursive distributed representations introduced in Pollack's RAAM (Pollack, 1990) have been used to implement tree-matching (Stolcke and Wu, 1992). Finally, *mixed local/distributed architectures* combine systems using these two representations in separate modules. The main strength of these systems is that they combine the efficiency of distributed representations with the power of localist representations. For instance, whereas DCPS is a highly constrained system that can represent only two triples in a rule's left-hand side, RUBICON (Samad, 1992), a connectionist rule-based system that uses a combined localist/distributed rule-based system, allows for a variable number of expressions in the left and right hand sides of each rule. It also supports chain inferencing as well as addition and deletion of working memory elements. Other systems that use combined localist/distributed representations are CONSYDERR (Sun, 1991) and its descendant CLARION (Sun et al., 1996).

From the point of view of system tasks, the unified approach has been actively investigated in a variety of task domains, particularly in automated reasoning and natural language understanding. The CHCL system (Hölldobler and Kurfess, 1991) is a connectionist inference mechanism which uses W. Bibel's connection method

(Bibel, 1987) to perform inferencing on Horn clauses using a matrix representation. An important subarea of work on logic and reasoning concerns variable binding (Ajjanagadde and Shastri, 1991; Touretzky and Hinton, 1988; Chen, 1992; Smolensky, 1990; Pinkas, 1994; Park and Robertson, 1995); a deeper insight into this problem will certainly help neural networks to attain the reasoning power of many symbolic systems, which perform first-order predicate logic tasks as a matter of routine. Techniques experimented in the field of automated reasoning via neural networks have been used in connectionist expert systems such as MACIE (Gallant, 1988, 1993), TheoNet (Bradshaw et al., 1989) and others (Saito and Nakano, 1988; Hayashi, 1991). Finally, natural language processing via connectionist symbol processing is a research field in itself; examples of work in this field can be found in (Bookman, 1987; Dyer, 1991; McClelland and Kawamoto, 1986; Gasser, 1988).

### 2.2.1.2 *Translational Architectures*

Translational architectures can be viewed as an intermediate class between unified and hybrid architectures. Like unified models, they rely only on neural networks as processors—but they can start from or end with symbolic structures. Most often, the symbolic structures used are propositional rules, whether categorical (Towell and Shavlik, 1994; Opitz and Shavlik, 1993; Fletcher and Obradovic, 1993) or probabilistic(Romachandran and Mooney, 1996), or rules with certainty factors (Mahoney and Mooney, 1993; Kuncicky et al., 1992; Fu and Fu, 1990; Taha and Ghosh, 1995). Neural networks have also been built from decision trees (Brent, 1991; Sethi and Otten, 1990; Ivanova and Kubat, 1995), ordinary differential equations (Cozzio, 1995), and deterministic finite-state automata (Maclin and Shavlik, 1993). However, symbolic structures are not processed as such in translational models; for instance, rules are not applied by an inference engine but only serve as source or target representations of network input or output data. They can thus be considered semi-hybrid systems in the sense that they use symbolic structures without the corresponding symbolic processors. Typically, translational models compile symbolic structures into neural networks before processing, or extract symbolic structures from neural networks after processing. Often, compilation into neural networks is followed by refinement of preexisting symbolic knowledge via connectionist learning, then by extraction of symbolic structures in view of communicating the knowledge thus refined to other systems (either humans or symbol-processing systems). Here again, the symbolic structures extracted from neural networks are typically rules (see (Andrews et al., 1995) for a survey of rule extraction methods), but attempts have also been made to extract schemata (Crucianu and Memmi, 1992). Translational architectures have also been called transformational models (Medsker, 1994).

Translational methods have been discussed extensively in Chapter 1 (this volume). Section 1.2.1.2 describes the major steps involved in building translational architectures while Section 1.2.1.3 discusses their distinctive features.

### 2.2.1.3   Hybrid Architectures

The hybrid approach rests on the assumption that only the synergistic combination of neural and symbolic models can attain the full range of cognitive and computational powers. In contrast to translational approaches, hybrid architectures incorporate *complete* symbolic and connectionist components: in addition to neural networks, they comprise both symbolic structures and their corresponding processors, e.g., rule interpreters, parsers, case-based reasoners and theorem provers.

Hybrid systems can be distinguished along different dimensions such as their target problem or task domain, the symbolic (e.g. rule-based reasoning, case-based reasoning) and neural (e.g. multilayer perceptrons, Kohonen networks) models used, or the role played by the neural (N) and symbolic (S) components in relation to each other and to the overall system. Though such dimensions allow for more or less clear distinctions between individual systems, they have little bearing on the central issues of neurosymbolic integration. We therefore propose a taxonomy of hybrid systems based on the mode and level of integration of the N and S components.

The **degree of integration** is a quantitative criterion: one can imagine a continuum going from the simple juxtaposition of symbolic and neural components under a common supervisor, to systems characterized by strong and repeated, if not constant, interaction between the two components. Though this spectrum can be graded numerically to represent progression from one extreme to another, we shall simplify by distinguishing two main degrees of integration—loose and tight coupling. Unfortunately, though the difference between them is intuitively clear, it is difficult to distinguish them more precisely without delving into implementation considerations. In *loosely coupled* systems, interaction between the two components is clearly localized in space and time: control and data can be transferred directly between N and S components, e.g. by function or procedure calls, or via some intermediate external structure, e.g. domain or control blackboards accessible to both components, or agent, e.g. a supervisor. However, interaction is always explicitly initiated by one of the components or by an external agent. In *tightly coupled* systems, knowledge and data are not only transferred, they can be shared by the N and S components via common internal structures (as opposed to structures such as blackboards which are shared by loosely coupled components but remain outside them). Thus a change which affects these common structures in one component has immediate repercussions on the other component *without need for explicit interaction initiatives*. For instance, in the SCRAPS/NN system (Hendler, 1989), a semantic marker-passing net and a distributed neural network have a set of common nodes, so that any activations in these nodes necessarily propagate in both the symbolic and the neural network. Within this category, too, coupling is not uniformly tight from one system to another: a slightly weaker example of tight coupling can be found in SYNHESYS (Giacometti, 1992), where the shared structures are simple links or pointers between the neural network and the symbolic component, in this case a rule-based system.

Along the qualitative dimension, the **integration mode** or scheme refers to the way in which the neural and symbolic components are configured in relation to each other and to the overall system. Four integration schemes have been identified: chainprocessing, subprocessing, metaprocessing and coprocessing. To define them, we suppose a system comprising one neural and one symbolic module, with the understanding that for more complex systems, there can be as many integration schemes as pairs of neural and symbolic components.

In *chainprocessing*, one of the (N or S) components is the main processor whereas the other takes charge of pre and/or postprocessing tasks. In (Hayes et al., 1992), for instance, a neural network preprocesses data from a respiratory monitor to determine qualitative states which are then fed as facts into a classical expert system. The same approach has been applied to market survey data to determine the effectiveness an advertising campaign (Ciesielski and Palstra, 1996); time series data concerning consumer attitudes and behavior are fed into neural networks which output symbolically meaningful classifications of the current trend, e.g. high rise, no change. These are then fed into a rule-based expert system which uses its knowledge of events and the market domain to complete the analysis. Conversely, a neural network can be assisted by a symbolic preprocessor; e.g. a decision tree generator selects significant features to be input into a backpropagation network, thus reducing learning and processing time (Piramuthu and Shaw, 1994). Another example is WATTS, a system which uses a Hopfield network to solve wastewater treatment optimization problems. A case-based reasoner retrieves the previously solved problem that most closely matches the current one and uses it to initialize the Hopfield net. It has been shown that this method leads to faster convergence than the usual random initialization of neural networks (Krovvidy and Wee, 1992).

In *subprocessing*, one of the two components is embedded in and subordinated to the other, which is the main problem solver. Typically, the S component is the main processor and the N component the subprocessor. It is an open question whether the reverse setup is at all possible. An example of neural subprocessing is INNATE/QUALMS: the main processor, a fault diagnosis expert system, calls on a set of multilayer perceptrons to generate a candidate fault, then either confirms their diagnosis or offers an alternative solution (Becraft et al., 1991). Others examples are SETHEO, a symbolic theorem prover which delegates to a neural net the task of learning search control heuristics (Goller, 1994), and SCRAPS/NN, in which a symbolic problem solver uses a neural network to extract perceptual similarities which can then be used in complex reasoning tasks like planning.

In *metaprocessing*, one component is the baselevel problem solver and the other plays a metalevel role (such as monitoring, control, or performance improvement). *Symbolic metaprocessing* is illustrated in ALVINN, a system for guiding autonomous vehicles (Pomerleau et al., 1991). Multiple networks are trained to become experts in specialized aspects of the autonomous vehicle control task, e.g. single-lane road driving, highway driving, collision avoidance. At the metalevel, a rule-based arbitrator examines the decisions of the driving neural nets and decides which network to follow and therefore how to steer. To take a decision, the arbitrator relies on an annotated map which stores geometric information such as the location of roads and landmarks, or the type of road the vehicle is in. A symbolic metaprocessor can also supervise both symbolic and neural components, as in the Robotic Skill Acquisition Architecture (RSA[2]) (Handelman et al., 1989, 1992). The system's goal is to develop robots which perform complex tasks using designer-supplied instructions and self-induced practice. At the baselevel, a rule-based system provides a declarative representation of human expert knowledge whereas neural networks embody reflexive procedural knowledge that comes with practice. A rule-based execution monitor supervises the training of the neural networks and controls the operation of the system during the learning process. At the outset, performance is ensured by a knowledge-based component, but as the networks develop robust patterns of learned behavior, task execution is increasingly shared between the symbolic and connectionist components under the control of the execution monitor.

In *coprocessing*, the N and S components are equal partners in the problem-solving process: each can interact directly with environment, each can transmit information to and receive information from the other. They can compete under the supervision of a metaprocessor, or they can cooperate in various ways, e.g. by performing different subtasks, or by doing the same task in different ways and/or under different conditions. Coprocessing by execution of specialized subtasks is illustrated in a system where a decision tree (timing classifier) and a neural network (morphology classifier) work together to detect arrythmia in heart patients (Jabri et al., 1992). In SYNHESYS (Giacometti, 1992), on the contrary, the same diagnostic task is executed by a rule-based system and a prototype-based neural network; if the neural component comes up with a diagnostic, this output is validated by the rulebase in backward chaining mode; otherwise, the rulebase is activated in forward chaining mode and its diagnostic is used to train the neural network.

### 2.2.2  Knowledge-Based Neurocomputing: A Redefinition

The following definition expresses the original, restrictive view of knowledge-based neurocomputing: *"Knowledge-based neural networks are neural networks whose topology and initial connection weights are determined by symbolic knowledge represented in particular formalisms, such as production rules and decision trees"* (Fu, 1995). Knowledge-based neural networks thus defined correspond exactly to what we call translational models (Section 2.2.1.2). However, as suggested in Section 2.1, knowledge-based neurocomputing can be characterized more generally by the use of prior domain knowledge to improve data-driven learning in neural networks. There is a vast range of techniques for integrating knowledge into NNs, and compilation of symbolic structures is just a subclass of these. As a matter of fact, the knowledge used in determining NN structure need not preexist in any symbolic formalism at all. We therefore propose the following enlarged definition: *Knowledge-based neural networks (KBNNs) are neural networks which have been designed and/or trained with the help of prior knowledge, that is, any information about the problem domain or the function to be learned.* This definition certainly has a broader scope because it abstracts away all considerations of implementation or formalism; in other words, it is a knowledge-level definition in the sense of Newell (Newell, 1982). An added advantage of this definition is that it remains valid despite the many new techniques that might yet be developed for inserting prior knowledge into neural nets.

With this generic definition, we can revisit our taxonomy of neurosymbolic integration systems and identify architectures, aside from translational models, which can be used for knowledge-based neurocomputing. Not surprisingly, unified architectures might have been designed for knowledge-based neurocomputing in the broad sense. Many unified architectures such as BoltzCONS (Touretzky, 1990b) and RAAM (Pollack, 1990) have been developed to show that neural networks can exhibit properties—such as compositionality (recursive combining into more complex structures)—which are essential for effective knowledge representation. As a result, all three subclasses of unified architectures can boast of examples of knowledge-based neural networks, though these are typically handcrafted by the system designers. To illustrate this, we take a system that uses both localist and distributed representation schemes. CLARION is composed of two levels: at the reactive level, a distributed network learns procedural skills through reinforcement learning; at the rule level, a localist network represents generic knowledge; rules are extracted from previous experiences of the reinforcement learner and wired up directly into the rule network (Sun et al., 1996). No symbolic-rule-to-network mapping takes place, yet there is no doubt that CLARION's rule network is a KBNN in the sense that it incrementally incorporates previously learned knowledge.

Whereas the original idea underlying unified architectures was to show that neural networks can be endowed with representational powers equal to those of symbolic systems, hybrid architectures address the representation problem from another angle. If symbolic systems have the representation capabilities that are missing in neural networks, why not couple both to overcome this limitation of neural networks? *A priori*, then, there is no need for knowledge-based neural networks in hybrid architectures, since domain knowledge can be stored in the symbolic components. This would be true if knowledge representation were the only motivation for KBNNs; however, it turns out that an even more important reason for using background knowledge in the design of neural networks is to accelerate learning and improve network performance (Bishop, 1995). Thus, even in hybrid architectures, the incorporation of prior knowledge into the neural component remains an added value. In addition, the symbolic component can play an important role in performing this knowledge integration task. For instance, a symbolic preprocessor can be used to analyze the training data and extract knowledge, e.g. about domain-dependent class probability densities, which can then be used in the design of the neural network. Or a symbolic metaprocessor might have prior knowledge of specific properties of the function to be learned; it can then generate training examples illustrating these properties to ensure that this prior knowledge is incorporated into the network structure through the training process. In short, the symbolic components of hybrid architectures can become powerful tools for automating the design of knowledge-based neural networks. This will be substantiated in the remainder of this chapter.

### 2.2.3   KBN and the Bias-Variance Trade-Off

In the context of NN learning, prior knowledge designates any information concerning the task domain or the target function. This knowledge may come from different sources: it can be provided by human experts or accumulated by the system from previous experience, e.g. from previous training episodes in the case of incremental neural network learners. Alternatively, it can be acquired by transfer of knowledge from other neural networks (Pratt, 1994; Thrun and Mitchell, 1993). Finally, it can even be knowledge derived from the current training data prior to NN development, usually by exploratory data analysis methods.

Whatever its source, prior knowledge can be used during any of the two main stages of neural network development—configuration (or design) and training. NN *configuration* consists in defining the network topology, e.g. the number of hidden layers, the number of input, hidden, and output units and their interconnection patterns. NN *training* consists in using the data to iteratively adjust the connection weights until a predefined error threshold is reached. These two processes may be effected sequentially (the topology is defined before training starts) or simultaneously (network topology evolves during training).

The use of prior knowledge in NN configuration or training is a promising way of addressing the bias-variance trade-off in neural network learning. The generalization error in neural networks (as in other estimators) can be decomposed into two parts: bias (squared) plus variance (Geman et al., 1992). Bias captures the notion of systematic error for all training sets of a given size; it is that part of the error that depends only on the learning model (in the case of neural networks, the architecture—or more precisely, the number of free parameters). An incorrect or inflexible model leads to high bias: in the limit, such a biased model will take no heed of the training data. Its contribution to the error can be diminished only by adjusting model complexity. Variance, on the other hand, depends on the training sample; a model that is too complex or too flexible in relation to the training data leads to large variance; in the limit, it will not generalize but simply (over)fit the data points.

The trade-off between bias and variance is such that reducing bias often increases variance and vice versa. To reduce bias, we add structure to the model, e.g. by adding hidden units; but increasing model complexity may lead to high variance. The problem, then, is to find a compromise between the conflicting requirements of bias and variance in order to minimize the total generalization error. Various techniques such as regularization and cross-validation have been proposed to balance bias and variance, but these are computationally expensive tools. Prior knowledge or hints can be used as an alternative or as a complement to such techniques.

The role of prior knowledge in mitigating the bias-variance dilemma can be formulated as follows. In knowledge-based configuration, background knowledge is used to introduce the right level of complexity into the initial model, thus obviating bias (Sections 2.3.1 and 2.3.2.1). On the other hand, the goal of knowledge-based training is to control variance by expanding the training set, either by increasing the

| Domain knowledge | NN Design Techniques |
|---|---|
| Almost perfect domain knowledge | **Knowledge-intensive or translational techniques**<br>e.g. Rule compilation |
| Partial domain knowledge | **Knowledge-primed or hint-based techniques**<br>e.g. Weight sharing, Virtual examples |
| No domain knowledge | **Knowledge-free or search-based techniques**<br>e.g. Constructive algorithms |

**Figure 2.2** Prior domain knowledge and NN development techniques.

number of training instances or by adding training knowledge other than simple target values to each instance (Section 2.3.2.2). In both phases, the use of prior knowledge ensures consistency with the unknown target function, so that it becomes possible to reduce both bias and variance at the same time.

## 2.3 Techniques for Building Prior Knowledge into Neural Networks

Many techniques have been proposed for neural network development, and the choice of technique depends primarily on the amount of prior knowledge available in the application domain. Existing methods can be situated along an axis representing the amount of domain knowledge available—going from one endpoint where no knowledge is available to the other extreme where domain knowledge forms an approximate, i.e. almost complete and correct, theory. Between these two extremes are a number of intermediate points representing the availability of specific and partial domain knowledge (see Fig. 2.2).

In this section, we investigate a number of NN development techniques in the three main subregions of the (domain) knowledge spectrum. Knowledge-intensive, knowledge-primed, and knowledge-free techniques are discussed successively.

### 2.3.1 Knowledge-Intensive or Translational Techniques

Translational approaches, as described in Sections 1.2.1 and 2.2.1.2, consist in mapping symbolically expressed knowledge such as rules onto neural network structures. Pioneers of this approach stress the need for an approximately complete and correct domain theory as a prerequisite for successful training (Towell and Shavlik, 1994). For this reason, translational techniques can be characterized succinctly as techniques for knowledge-intensive neural network configuration.

The problem with translational techniques is that they have a limited area of applicability due to the drastic constraints they impose on the amount and quality of prior knowledge. Approximately perfect domain theories are relatively rare in real-world problems; furthermore, even when a domain theory is available, it is difficult to assess its completeness or correctness. Although Towell and Shavlik's requirement of an approximate domain theory may have been due to system-specific limitations of KBANN, which was incapable of learning new rules, it has not been shown that very partial or noisy theories can yield good results when translated into neural networks that can grow or shrink dynamically during training. Thus, in the absence of an approximate theory, so-called hint-based techniques might prove more useful.

### 2.3.2    Knowledge-Primed or Hint-Based Techniques

The most common situation in neural network development is one in which some domain knowledge is available without, however, qualifying as an approximate domain theory. Such partial, often piecemeal, knowledge (aka hints) can be used to prime neural network design and training. Hints come in many flavors. One type of hint involves the structure of the application task. Another type of hint concerns the application domain: for instance, in stock market trend prediction, it is known that extraneous events such as domestic or international political crises can have a major impact on market behavior. Yet another type of partial prior knowledge formulates global constraints on the function to be learned, or partial information about its implementation. In pattern recognition tasks, for instance, it is often known *a priori* that the target function is invariant under certain transformations such as shift, rotation or scaling. Other function characteristics which might prove useful in other domains are symmetry, monotonicity, or parity.

Knowledge-primed or hint-based techniques are those which make use of partial task domain knowledge in building neural networks. In the following subsections, we examine ways in which hints are incorporated during the two main stages of NN development as well as during preliminary data preprocessing. We thus distinguish three broad classes of hint-based techniques: hint-based configuration, hint-based training and hint-based preprocessing.

#### 2.3.2.1    *Hint-Based Configuration*

In hint-based configuration , any information about the problem domain can be used to determine the initial structure of the neural system. First of all, when a task is too complex to be solved by a single network, knowledge of the task decomposition can be used to *generate a neural macrostructure*: the task is broken down into subtasks which can be solved sequentially or in parallel by a set of neural networks. This gives rise to modular neural networks, which have been the focus of intense research but which lie beyond the scope of this chapter (Ballard, 1987; Jacobs and Jordan, 1991; Jacobs et al., 1990; Bottou and Gallinari, 1991; Hrycej, 1992; de Francesco, 1994). At the level of the individual network, the configuration task involves the following subtasks: choose the input and output units (and their encoding), determine the number of hidden layers and units, the connectivity pattern and initial connection weights. Hints can be used to support any of these subtasks.

Neural network inputs and outputs are generally selected during preliminary task analysis, but prior knowledge can be used to add input or output variables which are not intrinsic to the original task specification. For instance, prior knowledge can be injected as *extra outputs of a neural network*. Practically, this means constraining the network to learn both the original task and a second task that is known to be related to the first. Once training is completed, the extra outputs can be removed and performance is restricted to the original task. The size of the training set itself is not increased, but the original training patterns need to be modified to incorporate the additional target values. To borrow a simple example from (Yu and Simmons, 1990), the N-bit parity problem gets increasingly harder as N gets larger, due to local minima. To train a neural network more easily on this task, one can train the network on a related task like counting the number of 1's in the input. This means augmenting the original binary output with a set of units which act as a counter. The key result is that multitask learning improves a network's generalization performance on each of the individual tasks to be learned. Experiments reported in (Caruana, 1993) show that this improvement is not due to a simple regularization effect such as that produced by adding random noise; rather, it comes from the fact that training for each individual task benefits from the extra knowledge provided by the training values for the other related tasks.

Multitask learning via extra outputs not only improves generalization, it also decreases learning time. For instance, it has been observed that non monotonic functions like the fuzzy predicate *medium height* are more difficult to learn than monotonic functions such as *tallness*. A 1–4–1 neural network trained using backpropagation took 2913 epochs to learn the concept of medium height; when an output unit representing the concept of tallness was added, the resulting 1–4–2 network took only 1433 epochs to learn both concepts (Suddarth and Kergosien, 1990). This method has been tested on a more complex application task, the control of a simulated planetary lander. The goal is to land the craft at low velocity; the network's task is to determine the thrust value required to land the craft on the basis of three inputs—altitude, actual velocity and fuel. Training data were drawn from actions of a human during a simulation landing. Prior knowledge about a related task—determining the desired velocity—was used to generate extra outputs for the available training instances. The 'hinted' network (3–8–2) converged in 17% of the training time required for the same network without the hint (3–8–1) (Suddarth and Holden, 1991).

Another hint-based configuration technique is the *addition of 'heuristic' input units*, i.e. units which, contrary to typical input variables, play only a heuristic role in the mapping to be learned. In financial forecasting, for example, it is common knowledge that major political or other non-economic events can have as direct an influence on stock market trends as classical economic indicators. This heuristic was integrated into the network in the form of an extra input unit whose default value is 0.5 (no significant event); newspaper headlines were examined daily, and this input node was set to 1 in the case of positive event knowledge, e.g. cold war ends, or to -1 in the case of negative event knowledge, e.g. House of Representatives to dissolve. Tests showed that use of this hint increased prediction accuracy, though nothing is said about the statistical significance of this increase (Kohara and Ishikawa, 1994).

Moreover, prior knowledge can be used to improve generalization by *modifying input or output encoding*. For example, (Lendaris and Harb, 1990) compared two feedforward neural network architectures for character recognition which differed only with respect to the encoding of the output units. The networks had 256 inputs (training examples were 16x16-pixel images) and 2 hidden layers. The first network had 26 outputs, one for each of the 26 capital letters of the alphabet. In the second network, output encoding was based on observations that humans adopt a higher-level representation of these letters in terms of component parts and their relations. For instance, the letter A is thought of as two long lines touching each other at one end and connected by a shorter line somewhere in the middle. In addition to cognitive plausibility, this representation has the advantage of being invariant to such transformations as rotations and translations. Thus the second network's output layer was a concept-relation vector consisting of 21 binary-valued elements. The first network's accuracy was between 66% and 83%; with the new output layer, the second network's accuracy jumped to the 93%-96% interval. Complementary tests aimed at explaining the improvement ruled out alternative hypotheses and confirmed that the change was in fact due to the change in output representation.

Determining inter-unit connections and their weights is an essential part of network configuration, since the long-term knowledge of the network is stored in these weights. Prior knowledge can be used in several ways to configure a network's connections. First of all, domain-specific hints can directly *determine the connectivity pattern*. For instance, a neural net that forecasts the trend of the Tokyo stock market index should somehow express the fact that the influence of economic indicators on market trends persists for some time after a given instant $t$. One way of translating this persistence into neural network structure is by means of feedback connections: in one such forecasting system, hidden units are self-connected, with the effect that the hidden layer at time $t$ becomes the context layer at time $t + 1$ (Kohara and Ishikawa, 1994).

Prior knowledge can be formulated as *permanent constraints on connections and weights*. In pattern recognition, for instance, one can encode invariance knowledge by structuring the network in such a way that transformed versions of the same input produce the same output. The best-known technique for doing this is *weight sharing*, i.e. constraining different connections to have equal weights (LeCun et al., 1990; Rumelhart et al., 1986). Weight sharing has also been used in time-delay neural networks for speech recognition (Waibel et al., 1989) as well as in higher-order recurrent networks (Giles and Maxwell, 1987; Perantonis and Lisboa, 1992). LeCun has generalized weight sharing into a technique called weight space transformation (LeCun, 1989).

Hints can also be used to *determine initial connection weights* in a more task-specific fashion than the usual random method. Frasconi et al.(Frasconi et al., 1995) use first-order recurrent networks for sequence learning, e.g. isolated word recognition, but complement pure learning from examples with prior knowledge in the form of automaton rules. Automaton states are encoded as neuron activations; transition rules are used not only to determine constraints on connection weights but also to initialize these weights by using a technique based on linear programming. In a speaker-independent test on 284 words, recognition rate attained 92.3%, but more importantly, the proposed model seems to scale up well with the lexicon's dimension.

Giles et al. use a similar technique to incorporate grammatical rules into second-order recurrent neural networks for regular language recognition. These rules are expressed as state transitions in the corresponding deterministic finite-state automata (DFAs). Known transitions are used to program some of the initial weights to $\pm H$, where $H$ is a large rational number representing the strength of the hint. All other connection weights are set to small random values. Any number of known rules can be injected into the network in this way; the only condition is that the number of network units be larger than the number of DFA states. Tests have shown that when correct rules are inserted, training time decreases with the hint strength $H$; in one trial where the entire ruleset was inserted, training time went down to zero (no training was needed) for $H \geq 7$. This method allows for the integration of a variable amount of prior knowledge, from single rules reflecting very partial knowledge to rule sets corresponding to entirely known DFAs (Giles and Omlin, 1993; Omlin and Giles, 1992). Even in the latter case, however, this technique remains hint-based rather than translational, since prior knowledge is used to determine only a particular subtask of the network design process.

The above examples show that prior knowledge can be injected into practically any component of a network's initial structure. However, the diversity of hint-based configuration techniques discussed above is equalled only by their task-specific, often ad hoc nature. Most of the techniques described in this section depend heavily on handcrafting, and it is difficult to imagine, at least in the short term, how they can be transferred to other application domains. The techniques themselves seem quite generic and capable of representing different types of prior knowledge, but for the moment, they have met with a certain degree of success mainly in image and speech recognition tasks. This task-dependency is clearly an artefact of the state of the art: a lot of work remains to be done before an extensive mapping of hint types onto network structural constraints is obtained across different application tasks and domains.

### 2.3.2.2   Hint-Based Training

Rather than being wired directly into the network structure, prior knowledge can be incorporated indirectly via the training process. The first and most common way of doing this is to expand the training set by *generating a sufficiently large number of examples that illustrate the hint.* Abu-Mostafa (Abu-Mostafa, 1990, 1995b) has identified a variety of hints concerning the function to be learned and proposed two ways of integrating them into the training set. The simplest way is by means of duplicate examples: for some hints, we can take available examples of the target function, duplicate them, and modify the copies to express the hint. For instance, given the prior knowledge that the target function is even, i.e. $y(x) = y(-x)$, and given a training example $y(2) = 4$, we can generate a second example $y(-2) = 4$. An alternative way is the use of virtual examples. For the evenness hint, a virtual example would have the form $y(x) = y(-x)$ for a particular input $x$. One can generate as many examples as needed by picking different values of $x$. There is no need to know the target value to generate the example; however the use of virtual examples involves a modification of the objective function to be used during the training process. For regular training instances, the objective function is some measure of the discrepancy between the target value and the actual value; since virtual examples do not contain target values, the error measure is dependent on the hint; e.g. for the evenness hint, it should measure the distance between $y(x)$ and $y(-x)$. If several hints are involved in a given task, they can all be integrated following a fixed or dynamic scheduling scheme. This form of hint-based training has been applied to foreign exchange rate forecasting, where data is both noisy and non stationary (Abu-Mostafa, 1995a).

A similar approach was adopted by Röscheisen et al. (Röscheisen et al., 1992) to preset the rolling force in a steel rollmill. Previously, the rolling force was determined using a parameterized analytical model that gave only approximate predictions which had to be adjusted on-line, resulting in a lot of steel band waste. When a neural network solution was implemented, the imperfect knowledge contained in the imperfect model was used to artificially generate training data; these were then combined with data derived from on-line measurements to train a neural network using backpropagation.

Prem et al. also use prior knowledge to generate additional training data (Prem et al., 1993); however, their jmethod differs in that the hint-generated data are used only in a pretraining phase. In a medical application aimed at diagnosing coronary heart disease, heuristic rules from a medical expert are used to create pretraining data. A randomly initialized network is trained on these examples, and the weights thus obtained define the initial state from which the second phase, regular example-based training, is conducted. Another form of knowledge injection, called concept support, consists in introducing concepts which are deemed relevant using the same pretraining technique. For instance, to incorporate the hint that the patient's sex is relevant to heart disease, a network with two output units representing the male-female distinction is trained; in the second phase, the two output units are replaced by a single unit representing the presence or absence of coronary heart disease, and the network is trained on the original task. Experiments have shown that the method consistently improves generalization with respect to levels achieved through knowledge-free training.

The second main approach to hint-based training is *direct incorporation of hints into the training data*. Since the number of training instances is not increased, convergence is not slowed down due to artificial expansion of the dataset. This hint-based training technique is illustrated by TangentProp (Simard et al., 1992). In handwritten character recognition, for example, a useful hint concerns invariance of the target function to minor transformations of the input such as rotation or translation. The preceding section described examples in which invariance knowledge is built into the neural net structure. Alternatively, this knowledge can be expressed by adding training derivatives of the usual training values. For instance, rotational invariance is expressed by assigning a value of zero to the derivative of the target function with respect to a rotation parameter. To exploit this hint, however, the learning algorithm needs to be modified; in particular, the error function needs to take account of the difference not only between the training value and the actual value, but also between the training derivative and the actual derivative. TangentProp is a modification of standard backpropagation which obliges the networks to have zero derivatives in some directions. For particular transformations, the standard error function is augmented with a regularization term which penalizes discrepancies between the training and the actual derivatives. If several transformations are specified, the algorithm ensures that local invariance to each results in invariance to the composed transformation. Experiments showed that TangentProp achieves significantly higher classification accuracy and converges more quickly than standard backpropagation with no prior knowledge.

To summarize, hint-based training reduces variance by expanding the training set, either by generating new examples that express the hint or by incorporating the hint into each original example. In principle, reducing variance in this way does not lead to increased bias, since the information content added by prior knowledge ensures consistency with the unknown target function.

### 2.3.2.3  *Hint-Based Preprocessing*

Invariance in object recognition is probably the most popular form of partial knowledge used in neural network development. As in NN configuration and training, this type of knowledge has also been used for hint-based preprocessing. For instance, (Bishop, 1995) shows that extraction of central moments from input data yields translation-invariant features, and that normalizing these moments makes them invariant to scale. He also points out the disadvantages of using moments as input features, in particular the computational cost of extracting them from each new input image. An alternative approach is feature transformation: input data are transformed so that the features themselves exhibit invariance properties (Barnard and Casasent, 1991). This is done in two steps: first, determine an appropriate set of constraints; second, transform all measurements to satisfy these constraints. Tested in a vehicle identification task under limited image resolution, this approach led to accuracy in the range of 93–97% for neural networks as well as nonneural classifiers.

In hint-based preprocessing, the hints are known beforehand and the input data are transformed to express these hints. Data preprocessing can serve another related purpose; when prior knowledge is lacking, data can be explored in order to extract hints that might prove useful in network configuration and training, indeed even in other data preprocessing tasks. Thus a closely related issue is that of *hint extraction via data preprocessing.* For certain applications, one might know which type of hint is needed and how it will be used, without however knowing the exact content or value of that hint. Consider a network whose task is to associate an input pattern $x$ to an output pattern $y$ while simultaneously correcting all errors that lie within a distance less than $d/2$, where $d$ is the minimum Hamming distance between the input patterns. Here the hint is the minimum Hamming distance, which is used in the training phase by a modified backpropagation algorithm. When this hint is not known *a priori*, it can be extracted from the training examples themselves during the preprocessing stage (Al-Mashouq and Reed, 1991). Similarly, the TangentProp algorithm (see Section 2.3.2.2) uses invariance hints in the form of training derivatives, which need to be introduced manually by the user. EBNN (Thrun and Mitchell, 1993; Thrun, 1996) relieves the user of this burden; prior to neural network training, an analytical learner uses a domain theory to explain a given training example, then uses the explanation to compute the required derivative.

In many applications, however, one has no precise domain-specific information to look for in the data; the idea is simply to explore the data with the hope of finding clues that may lead to more effective neural network design and training. For instance, human designers routinely analyse application data and the insights gained are put to use in subsequent NN development tasks such as task decomposition, variable selection and missing value imputation. Hint extraction via preprocessing is an attempt to automate this process. In (Rida et al., 1999), for instance, the input data is assumed to be a mixture of Gaussians; during the preprocessing stage, an improved Kohonen network (DeSieno, 1988) is used to cluster the input data into overlapping subspaces. Local experts, e.g. a multilayer perceptron, are assigned to these subspaces and their outputs combined either by weighted averaging or by stacked generalization (Wolpert, 1992). Experiments showed that stacking with subsamples based on preliminary distribution analysis led to significantly higher accuracy than stacking with randomly generated subsamples. Combinations of experts have been shown to lead to more accurate learning than single experts in general (see for instance (Sharkey, 1995)); in the case of these two combination schemes, however, the difference in performance was due precisely to the knowledge acquired prior to learning about the probability distribution of the input space.

### 2.3.3   Knowledge-Free or Search-Based Techniques

At the other extreme, where domain knowledge is scarce or unusable, NN design techniques rely mainly on guided search. These knowledge-free methods can be subdivided into dynamic and static methods. In static configuration the network topology is chosen *before* the training process, whereas in dynamic configuration it is dynamically modified *during* training.

An example of static configuration is Vysniauskas et al.'s method, which estimates the number of hidden units $h$ needed by a single-hidden-layer network to approximate a function to a desired accuracy. The approximation error $\epsilon$ of a network is expressed as a function of $h$ and the number of training instances $N$. Two models of this error function are available, and the parameters of a model can be determined by experimentation on the training set. The resulting parameterized model of the approximation error can then be used to determine the number of hidden units $h$, given a training set and a user-selected error threshold (Vysniauskas et al., 1993). For classification tasks, Bose and Garga propose a design algorithm based on the construction of Voronoi diagrams over the set of data points in the training set. These diagrams are then analysed to determine which design options to take on the basis of observed characteristics, e.g. linear separability, convexity. Contrary to the preceding technique, which estimates only the number of hidden units, this is a complete configuration procedure that determines the number of hidden layers and hidden units per layer, as well as the connections and corresponding weights of the network before training (Bose and Garga, 1993).

Dynamic configuration methods can be divided into constructive (or growing) and destructive (or pruning) algorithms. Constructive methods start out with a minimal network structure, e.g. the input and output layers, and progressively add hidden layers and/or units until a stopping criterion is met. Some algorithms, like Neural Trees (Sirat and Nadal, 1990) and Cascade-Correlation (Fahlman and Lebiere, 1990), approximate the discriminant function by piecewise linear separation of the input space. Others, like GAL (Alpaydin, 1991), use a technique similar to the nearest neighbour decision rule in order to define regions of influence where patterns of a given class are most likely to appear. Though most constructive methods are aimed at classification tasks, Cascade2 (Fahlman and Boyan, 1996) and IRO (Lengellé and Denoeux, 1996) can also perform regression, i.e. tasks with continuous-valued outputs. Destructive methods adopt the reverse approach: they start from an initially complex model and prune units and/or links until the desired out-of-sample accuracy is attained. The pruning process can take place during training, as in weight decay (Krogh and Hertz, 1992) and weight elimination (Weigend et al., 1991), or after training, as in Optimal Brain Damage (LeCun et al., 1990) and Optimal Brain Surgeon (Hassibi and Stork, 1993).

This quick review of knowledge-free methods has been included for the sake of completeness, though they clearly do not produce knowledge-based neural networks. However, it should be noted that knowledge-free methods incorporate an enormous amount of implicit metaknowledge concerning neural networks in order to reduce the space of search for a reasonable network architecture. It could be worthwhile to extract this embedded metaknowledge in view of representing and using it explicitly in neural network design and training.

## 2.4 A Metalevel Architecture for Knowledge-Based Neurocomputing

SCANDAL (Symbolic-Connectionist Architecture for Neural Network Design and Learning) is an experimental workbench for exploring the use of prior knowledge— both domain and metalevel—in the design of neural networks. This section describes its architecture and the strategies for building prior knowledge into neural networks.

### 2.4.1   Overview of SCANDAL

The architecture consists of a connectionist baselevel and a symbolic metalevel (Fig. 2.3), each implemented as a set of agents interacting via a distributed platform (Gonzalez et al., 1997). The baselevel consists of agents which execute decisions taken by metalevel design agents concerning NN configuration and training as well as data preprocessing. At the metalevel, a supervisor receives the application task definition and, on the basis of its knowledge of the domain and of neural networks in general, selects one or several design agents. Each design agent embodies a class of techniques for accomplishing one or several design subtasks. A data preprocessor analyses available data and calls on the competent base level agents as needed: data cleaners fill in missing values or discretize continuous attributes on request, knowledge extractors are symbolic learners such as C4.5 which induce rules for use in subsequent phases of NN design, and artificial data generators are routines which generate training examples from hints expressed as rules or as functional constraints. Several configuration agents are available. A rule compilation agent translates a domain theory expressed as rules into a feedforward network. In the current version, this agent can handle categorical as well as certainty-factor rules. A hint-based configuration agent uses knowledge of related tasks to add extra output units to a network.

Partial knowledge can also be used to improve the training process. For instance, when data deficiency is a problem, the pretraining agent uses knowledge-based artificial examples produced by the data generators to pretrain the network before training on real examples. In knowledge-lean domains, the supervisor has two alternatives: either attempt to exploit domain hints induced from data by the knowledge extractors, or have the search-based agents, e.g. constructive configuration agents, resort to iterative experimentation.

Metalevel design agents are implemented in an object-oriented representation which blends a global ontology with agent-specific rules and methods. The system's ontology provides a unifying framework for domain as well as metalevel knowledge; it is by inspecting this ontology that design agents can access domain knowledge and use it to determine NN structure and development. In addition, base level entities such as network links and weights, nodes and activations, which typically remain invisible in standard simulators, have associated meta-objects which are periodically updated to reflect their current state. Via this dual representation scheme, the internal state of the network remains accessible for explicit reasoning and decision making by the supervisor, the design agents, and the user.

### 2.4.2   Strategies for Knowledge Utilization

SCANDAL's basic bias is towards the maximum use of domain knowledge in the different stages of NN development. Knowledge-based configuration (KBC) consists in

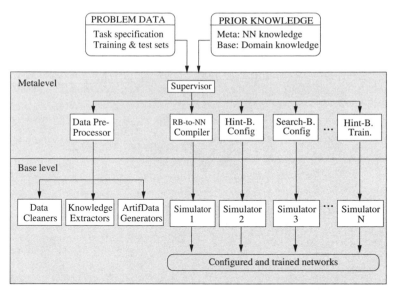

**Figure 2.3**   The SCANDAL architecture.

using domain knowledge to determine the network's architecture, while knowledge-based training (KBT) integrates domain knowledge into the training process. When background knowledge is insufficient or inaccessible, the system attempts knowledge extraction from data (KEX) to gather hints that might guide the design process. For instance, any rule induction algorithm may be called to generate domain rules for use in subsequent phases. These elementary processes—knowledge extraction from data, knowledge-based configuration, and knowledge-based training—may be combined in four different ways, depending on the adequacy of the knowledge and data available. The four variants of the knowledge-based approach to NN design are summarized in Table 2.1.

As discussed in Section 2.3, SCANDAL integrates different techniques for exploiting knowledge during the three phases of NN development. However, in the remainder of this chapter, we shall focus on rule-based methods to illustrate knowledge-based NN design: rule induction by C4.5 for KEX, rule mapping onto neural nets for KBC, and rule-based generation of artificial training data for KBT.

### 2.4.3   Experiments

This section reports on experiments conducted on these four strategies for incorporating knowledge into NN learning. To compare the knowledge-based approach with a state-of-the-art search-based method, the SCANDAL implementation of the Orthogonal Incremental Learning (OIL) algorithm (Vysniauskas et al., 1995) was used. OIL is an incremental approach to NN design which adds one hidden unit at a time while the rest of the network remains fixed. A feature of OIL is that it minimizes the parameters to be tuned with each hidden node addition, thus leading to extremely fast training. Both search- and knowledge-based approaches were evalu-

**Table 2.1**   Four strategies for knowledge-based neural network design. KBC stands for knowledge-based configuration, KBT for knowledge-based training, and KEX for knowledge extraction from data.

Adequate prior knowledge (K) and data (D) → KBC
  1. KBC: Compile K into a neural network
  2. Train NN on D
Deficient prior knowledge and adequate data → KEX-KBC
  1. KEX: Extract K' from D
  2. KBC: Compile (K+K') into an NN
  3. Train NN on D
Adequate prior knowledge and deficient data → KBC-KBT
  1. KBC: Compile K into a neural network
  2. KBT: Generate artificial data D' from K
      Pretrain NN on D'
      Train pretrained NN on D
Deficient prior knowledge and data → KEX-KBC-KBT
  (in preference to search-based design)
  1. KEX: Extract K' from D
  2. KBC: Compile (K+K') into NN
  3. KBT: Generate D' from (K+K')
      Pretrain NN on D'
      Train pretrained NN on D alone

ated on several benchmarks from the UCI Machine Learning Repository (Murphy and Aha, 1991). All experiments used 10 network initializations, each tested on 10 different permutations of a given dataset. Each experiment thus consisted of 100 training/test runs, each using ten-fold stratified cross-validation. The following subsections present evaluation results for these four strategies in turn.

### 2.4.3.1   Adequate Knowledge and Data

When both knowledge and data are adequate (in particular when there is an approximate domain theory), the knowledge-based approach is reduced to mapping domain rules onto a neural network, followed by standard training from data. We shall illustrate the effectiveness of this simple approach on two benchmarks. The student loan benchmark contained a relational dataset and rulebase, both of which were rewritten in propositional form. The domain task is to decide, on the basis of 7 features, whether a student is exempted from reimbursing a loan; the 18-rule theory was mapped onto a four-layer 21–6–2–1 neural network. The dataset contains 1000 instances. In the tic-tac-toe endgame benchmark, the task is to determine in which cases player X will win, assuming she played first. The benchmark does not include a domain theory, but it was quite straightforward to define winning endgame configurations in 8 simple rules. However, of the 8 rules which would have defined a complete domain theory, two were purposely eliminated to test the neural network's ability to recover from the lesioned initial theory.

**Table 2.2** Results on benchmarks with adequate prior knowledge and data. In this and the following tables, I is the number of inputs, N the dataset size. Performance measures are classification accuracy on the test set (mean percentage of cases classified correctly $\pm$ the standard deviation) and the number of training epochs. The default accuracy rate is that attained by simply selecting the most frequent class. For the incremental algorithm OIL, training time is represented by the number of training cycles for all candidate hidden units (in brackets), followed by the number of the training cycles for the tenured hidden units alone.

| **Loans** (I=21  N=1000) | Accuracy (Def=64.3%) | Training cycles | |
|---|---|---|---|
| OIL | 94.88 ± 0.09 | [940] | 98 |
| KBC | 94.89 ± 0.11 | | 12 |
| **Tic-tac-toe** (I=27  N=958) | Accuracy (Def=64.7%) | Training cycles | |
| OIL | 98.50 ± 3.10 | [1194] | 122 |
| KBC | 99.00 ± 1.80 | | 53 |

Since prior knowledge is meant to add information value when a dataset is deficient, in this particular case prior knowledge is not expected to improve generalization. This is confirmed by the results shown in Table 2.2; the knowledge-based and search-based methods attain equivalent mean off-sample accuracy rates. However, the decisive difference lies in the complexity value added by prior knowledge; counting only the number of cycles spent on training the tenured hidden units, KBC is twice as fast as OIL on the second benchmark and 8 times faster on the first. If we take into account the training cycles spent on discarded candidate units, KBC is 22 times faster than OIL on the tic-tac-toe benchmark and 78 times faster on the student loan dataset.

### 2.4.3.2 Deficient Knowledge and Adequate Data

To illustrate the utility of knowledge extraction when there is sufficent data, C4.5 (Quinlan, 1993) was used to generate rules for two benchmarks which came with no domain theory. In the first, the task is to predict contact lenses prescription (soft, hard, or none) from four features such as age and tear production; in the second, party affiliation is predicted on the basis of a congressman's vote on 17 crucial issues. Rules generated by C4.5 were compiled into a 9–2–3 network for the lenses domain and a 48–2–2 network for the votes domain. Training results are shown in Table 2.3. The 80.0% accuracy obtained by KEX-KBC on the lenses problem is significantly higher than known previous results which range from 65% accuracy for ID3 and 76.7% for backpropagation to 80.5% for FLARE using prior knowledge and 83.3% for CN2. In the votes domain, KEX-KBC scores 95.6%, as compared with past results: 93.8% for CN2, 95.4% for ID3, 96% for backpropagation, and 94.5% for FLARE using prior knowledge (all past results reported on these two benchmarks are based on (Giraud-Carrier, 1995)). It was also interesting to find out if the inductive

**Table 2.3**   Results on benchmarks with deficient knowledge and adequate data.

| Lenses(I=9  N−24) | Accuracy (Def=62.5%) | Training cycles | |
|---|---|---|---|
| OIL | 47.03 ± 8.65 | [11918] | 1101 |
| KEX-KBC | 89.93 ± 2.00 | | 3 |
| **Votes** (I=48  N=435) | Accuracy (Def=61%) | Training cycles | |
| OIL | 95.03 ± 0.69 | [1725] | 277 |
| KEX-KBC | 95.60 ± 0.50 | | 12 |

**Table 2.4**   Results on a benchmark with adequate prior knowledge and deficient data. For KBC-KBT, the number of training cycles includes those for pretraining on artificial data (in brackets), followed by training on the original data.

| **Credit** (I=25  N=125) | Accuracy (Def=68%) | Training cycles | |
|---|---|---|---|
| OIL | 75.52 ± 2.45 | [16692] | 2392 |
| KBC | 77.05 ± 2.34 | | 36 |
| KBC-KBT | 82.42 ± 2.09 | [42] | 14 |

method used for knowledge extraction would not have solved these tasks directly; a 10-fold cross-validation run on C4.5 yielded a mean accuracy of 83.3% for lenses and 94% for votes—in both cases lower than the KEX-KBC results.

### 2.4.3.3   *Adequate Knowledge and Deficient Data*

When prior domain knowledge is available to remedy data deficiency, the combination of knowledge-based configuration and knowledge-based training seems to be the most effective strategy. A network is compiled from domain rules as before; in addition, the same rules are recycled to fulfill another function, the generation of artificial data. These are used to pretrain the network before actual training on the original dataset. This strategy proved appropriate for the Japanese credit screening benchmark, which has a dataset of only 125 instances but includes a domain theory developed in cooperation with domain experts from a Japanese credit company. The original first-order rules were rewritten in propositional form and mapped onto a 25–7–2–1–2 network.

The results in Table 2.4 show the improvement added by knowledge-based training to knowledge-based configuration: on average, KBC alone achieves an accuracy of 77% after 36 training epochs whereas KBC-KBT reaches an accuracy of 82.4% in 14 epochs. Of course, the overhead consists of the 42 cycles used to pretrain the network on the knowledge-based examples. This pretraining, which can be seen as a refinement of the weight initializations effected by knowledge-based configuration, seems to improve both generalization and convergence speed during the actual training on the original data. A one-tailed two-sample test on

**Table 2.5**   Results on two problems with deficient knowledge and deficient data.

| **Hepatitis** (I=59  N=155) | Accuracy (Def=79.4%) | Training cycles | |
|---|---|---|---|
| OIL | 83.4 ± 1.8 | [5179] | 1427 |
| KEX-KBC | 85.1 ± 1.3 | | 11 |
| KEX-KBC-KBT | 86.1 ± 1.2 | [52] | 11 |
| **Toxic Coma** (I=30  N=505) | Accuracy (Def=52.5%) | Training cycles | |
| OIL | 55.2 ± 4.4 | [10636] | 1615 |
| KEX-KBC | 60.3 ± 1.4 | | 10 |
| KEX-KBC-KBT | 62.3 ± 1.8 | [46] | 18 |

these two variants showed that the improvement in accuracy for this problem is statistically significant at the 0.01 level.

### 2.4.3.4   Deficient Knowledge and Data

When both knowledge and data are deficient, the SCANDAL strategy is to try the knowledge-based approach anyway, since it is not yet clear under which conditions search-based methods can prove more appropriate. For instance, in the hepatitis benchmark and in a medical application concerning the diagnosis of comas induced by tricyclic antidepressants, both KEX-KBC and KEX-KBC-KBT still attain higher accuracies than OIL, as shown in Table 2.4.3.4.

The hepatitis problem has no available domain knowledge whereas in the coma problem expert rules are incomplete—they detect the present of antidepressants in isolated form, but not in combination with other toxins. Interestingly, rules extracted by C4.5 proved to be a perfect complement to the expert's rules: induced rules concluded on the absence of antidepressants or their combination with other toxins, but not on their presence in isolation. Both problems are reputedly difficult; for the toxic coma problem, alternative approaches such as maximum entropy probabilistic methods (Amy et al., 1997) barely bypassed the baseline accuracy, while the best past result for the hepatitis benchmark is 83% accuracy (Murphy and Aha, 1991). However, it must be said that the improvement brought by adding KBT to KBC is generally less significant when knowledge is extracted from data than in cases where adequate knowledge from domain experts effectively complete or correct deficient data.

### 2.4.4   Summary of Findings

The particularity of the approach presented in this section lies in the combination of techniques for knowledge-based configuration and knowledge-based training, whereas previous approaches (cf. Section 2.3) have focused on a specific technique for a single design subtask. Experiments reported in the preceding section show that these different techniques can be combined synergistically to improve neural network performance. These are borne out by the following findings:

- Generalization power (as measured by off-sample accuracy) generally increases and training time (as measured by the number of training cycles) generally decreases with the amount of knowledge built into a neural network.

- As the size of the dataset increases, the impact of background knowledge on final accuracy diminishes in the sense that a knowledge-free technique will eventually attain accuracy levels comparable to that of a knowledge-based neural network. However, it will do so in a considerably larger number of training epochs (by several orders of magnitude, counting time spent on training pools of candidate hidden units).

- When training data are deficient, the same knowledge that was compiled to configure and initialize a neural net can be recycled to generate artificial examples and obtain higher accuracy levels. More extensive studies will be needed to determine the minimum amount of artificial data needed to obtain significant improvement levels.

- Finally, when both knowledge and data are deficient, knowledge can be extracted from the original data and used both to configure the network and to generate additional training examples. In our experiments, this combination of knowledge extraction with knowledge-based configuration and training led to both higher accuracy and faster learning than search-intensive methods. In particular, rule compilation appears to achieve these effects even when the available rules are far from being approximately complete and correct. Although these findings have to be confirmed by further experimentation, they raise hopes that time-consuming iterative search can be avoided even in knowledge-lean domains.

## 2.5   Open Research Issues

As a recent research field, knowledge-based neurocomputing still has a number of shortcomings to remedy and open frontiers to explore. The major drawback of most knowledge incorporation techniques is their task-specific, often ad hoc nature. Many hint-based techniques, in particular, depend heavily on handcrafting, and it is difficult to imagine, at least in the short term, how they can be transferred across application domains. Some techniques such as weight sharing seem quite generic and capable of representing different types of prior knowledge; but for the moment, they have been successful mainly in image and speech recognition tasks. This task-dependency is clearly an artefact of the state of the art: a lot of work remains to be done before an extensive mapping of hint types onto network structural constraints is obtained across different application tasks and domains. A priority task on the research agenda is therefore the need to abstract from successful application-dependent implementations a set of generic techniques that are valid for broader classes of problems.

Another research challenge consists in widening the range of knowledge types that can be incorporated into NN, as well as the repertoire of techniques for incorporating them. This implies tackling a number of *representational issues*, the foremost of which is the restricted representational power of state-of-the-art neural networks. The overwhelming majority of these are limited to propositional representations and thus cannot convey relational knowledge which is essential in many real-world domains. Despite vigorous research on the variable-binding problem in neural networks, the main hurdle is that of scaling up the proposed architectures to solve real-world problems. A related issue is representing structured knowledge in neural networks. Symbolic artificial intelligence (AI) boasts of a plethora of structured representations, e.g. trees, frames, objects, semantic networks and belief networks, to convey the rich internal structure of knowledge. Information in neural networks is typically encoded in vector or matrix form; the problem is how to fit highly complex knowledge structures into this representational straitjacket.

Progress in knowledge-based neurocomputing also depends on resolving certain open *learning issues*. One of these is coping with complex multistep tasks: many NN learning tasks are cast as elementary tasks which can be categorized under either classification or regression. However, real-world applications are typically composite, and the first step is to reformulate the original problem as a combination of these elementary tasks. This issue is being investigated independently in the connectionist community by specialists in modular NNs (see Section 2.3.2.1) and in symbolic machine learning under the label of structured induction (Langley and Simon, 1995). A convergence of these two research streams might have interesting repercussions on knowledge-based neural networks. Another issue is building architectures for neurosymbolic learning. The knowledge-data tradeoff has spawned a variety of multistrategy learning systems in symbolic AI, but multistrategy symbolic-connectionist learning has not really taken off: the most common approach in hybrid systems is to combine neural network learning with non-learning symbolic models. Hybrid architectures for knowledge-based NN design would certainly gain in power and versatility if the symbolic component, whose task is to improve NN learning, were itself endowed with learning capabilities.

## Acknowledgments

Thanks to Ahmed Rida who performed the experiments on the OIL algorithm.

## References

Abu-Mostafa, Y. S. 1990. Learning from hints in neural networks. *Journal of Complexity*, 6:192–198.

Abu-Mostafa, Y. S. 1995a. Financial market applications of learning from hints.

In Refenes, A. P., editor, *Neural Networks in the Capital Markets*, chapter 15, pages 221–232. Wiley.

Abu-Mostafa, Y. S. 1995b. Hints. *Neural Computation*, 7:639–671.

Ajjanagadde, V. and Shastri, L. 1991. Rules and variables in neural nets. *Neural Computation*, (3):121–134.

Al-Mashouq, K. A. and Reed, I. S. 1991. Including hints in training neural networks. *Neural Computation*, 3:418–427.

Alpaydin, E. 1991. GAL : Networks that grow when they learn and shrink when they forget. Technical Report TR-91-032, International Computer Science Institute, Berkeley.

Amy, B., Danel, V., Ertel, W., Gonzalez, J., Hilario, M., Malek, M., Nerot, O., Osorio, F., Rialle, V., Rida, A., Schultz, S., Velasco, J., and Velasco, L. 1997. Medical application (final report). Esprit Project MIX Deliverable D16.

Andrews, R., Diederich, J., and Tickle, A. 1995. A survey and critique of techniques for extracting rules from neural networks. Technical report, Neurocomputing Research Centre, Queensland.

Ballard, D. H. 1987. Modular learning in neural networks. In *Proceedings of the National Conference in Artificial Intelligence (AAAI-87)*.

Barnard, E. and Casasent, D. 1991. Invariance and neural nets. *IEEE Transactions on Neural Networks*, 2:498–508.

Baum, E. B. and Haussler, D. 1989. What size net gives valid generalization? *Neural Computation*, 1:151–160.

Becraft, W. R., Lee, P. L., and Newell, R. B. 1991. Integration of neural networks and expert systems. In *Proc. of the 12th International Joint Conference on Artificial Intelligence*, pages 832–837, Sydney, Australia. Morgan Kaufmann.

Bergadano, F. and Giordana, A. 1990. Using induction with domain theories. In Kodratoff and Michalski (1990), chapter 17, pages 474–492.

Bibel, W. 1987. *Automated Theorem Proving*. Vieweg Verlag, Braunschweig, Germany.

Bishop, C. M. 1995. *Neural Networks for Pattern Recognition*. Oxford University Press.

Bookman, L. 1987. A microfeature based scheme for modelling semantics. In Proc. IJCAI-87 (1987).

Bose, N. K. and Garga, A. K. 1993. Neural network design using Voronoi diagrams. *IEEE Transactions on Neural Networks*, 4(5):778–787.

Bottou, L. and Gallinari, P. 1991. A framework for the cooperation of learning algorithms. In Lippman et al. (1991), pages 781–788.

Bradshaw, G., Fozzard, R., and Ceci, L. 1989. A connectionist expert system that actually works. In Touretzky, D. S., editor, *Advances in Neural Information Processing, 1*, pages 248–255. Morgan Kaufmann, San Mateo, CA.

Brent, R. P. 1991. Fast training algorithms for multilayer neural nets. *IEEE Transactions on Neural Networks*, 2(3):346–353.

Caruana, R. A. 1993. Multitask learning: A knolwedge-based source of inductive bias. In Utgoff, P., editor, *Proc. of the 10th International Conference on Machine Learning*, pages 41–48, Amherst, MA. Morgan Kaufmann.

Chen, J. R. 1992. A connectionist composition of formula, variable binding and learning. In Sun et al. (1992).

Ciesielski, V. and Palstra, G. 1996. Using a hybrid neural/expert system for data base mining in market survey data. In Sismoudis, E., Han, K., and Fayyad, U., editors, *Proc. Second International Conference on Knowledge Discovery and Data Mining*, pages 38–43, Portland, OR. AAAI Press.

Cozzio, R. 1995. *The Design of Neural Networks Using A Priori Knowledge*. PhD thesis, ETHZ, Zurich.

Crucianu, M. and Memmi, D. 1992. Extracting structure from an connectionist network. In *Artificial Intelligence and Simulation of Behaviour, Special Issue on Hybrid Models - part II*, pages 31–35.

Danyluk, A. 1994. Gemini: An integration of analytical and empirical learning. In Michalski, R. S. and Tecuci, G., editors, *Machine Learning. A Multistrategy Approach*, chapter 7, pages 189–216. Morgan Kaufmann.

de Francesco, M. 1994. *Functional Networks. A New Computational Framework for the Specification, Simulation and Algebraic Manipulation of Modular Neural Systems*. PhD thesis, CUI, University of Geneva.

DeSieno, D. 1988. Adding conscience to competitive learning. In *Proc. International Conference on Neural Networks*, volume I, pages 117–124, NY. IEEE Press.

Dyer, M. 1991. Symbolic neuroengineering for natural language processing: A multilevel research approach. In Barnden, J. A. and Pollack, J. B., editors, *Advances in Connectionist and Neural Computation Theory. Vol.1: High-Level Connectionist Models*, pages 32–86. Ablex Publishing.

Fahlman, S. E. and Boyan, . A. 1996. The Cascade 2 learning architecture. Technical Report CMU-CS-96-184, Carnegie-Mellon.

Fahlman, S. E. and Lebiere, C. 1990. The Cascade-Correlation learning architecture. Technical Report CMU-CS-90-100, Carnegie Mellon University.

Feldman, J. and Ballard, D. 1982. Connectionist models and their properties. *Cognitive Science*, 6:205–254.

Flann, N. S. and Dietterich, T. G. 1989. A study of explanation-based methods for inductive learning. *Machine Learning*, 4(2):187–226.

Fletcher, J. and Obradovic, Z. 1993. Combining prior symbolic knowledge and constructive neural network learning. *Connection Science*, 5(3 & 4):365–375.

Frasconi, P., Gori, M., Maggini, M., and Soda, G. 1995. Unified integration of explicit knowledge and learning by example in recurrent networks. *IEEE*

*Transactions on Knowledge and Data Engineering*, 7(2):340–346.

Fu, L. M., editor 1994. *International Symposium on Integrating Knowledge and Neural Heuristics*, Pensacola, FL.

Fu, L. M. 1995.   Special issue: Knowledge-based neural networks (editorial). *Knowledge-Based Systems*, 8(6):298.

Fu, L. M. and Fu, L. C. 1990. Mapping rule-based systems into neural architecture. *Knowledge-Based Systems*, 3(1):48–56.

Gallant, S. I. 1988. Connectionist expert systems. *Communications of the ACM*, 31(2):152–169.

Gallant, S. I. 1993. *Neural Network Learning and Expert Systems*. Bradford/MIT, Cambridge, MA.

Gasser, M. E. 1988.   A connectionist model of sentence generation in a first and second language. Technical Report Report UCLA-AI-88-13, University of California, Los Angeles, CA.

Geman, S., Bienenstock, E., and Doursat, R. 1992.   Neural networks and the bias/variance dilemma. *Neural Computation*, 4:1–58.

Giacometti, A. 1992. *Modèles hybrides de l'expertise*. PhD thesis, ENST, Paris.

Giles, C. L. and Maxwell, T. 1987. Learning, invariance and generalization in high-order neural networks. *Applied Optics*, 26(23):4972–4978.

Giles, C. L. and Omlin, C. W. 1993.   Extraction, insertion and refinement of symbolic rules in dynamicallly driven recurrent neural networks. *Connection Science*, 5(3–4):307–337.

Giraud-Carrier, C. 1995.   An integrated framework for learning and reasoning. *Journal of Artificial Intelligence Research*, 3:147–185.

Goller, C. 1994.   A connectionist control component for the theorem prover SETHEO. In Hilario, M., editor, *ECAI'94 Workshop on Combining Symbolic and Connectionist Processing*, pages 88–93, Amsterdam.

Goller, C. and Kuechler, A. 1996. Learning task-dependent distributed representations by backpropagation through structure. In Proc. ICNN-96 (1996), pages 347–352.

Gonzalez, J. C., Velasco, J. R., and Iglesias, C. A. 1997. A distributed platform for symbolic-connectionist integration. In Sun, R. and Alexandre, F., editors, *Connectionist-Symbolic Integration: From Unified to Hybrid Approaches*, chapter 10. L. Erlbaum.

Handelman, D. A., Lane, S. H., and Gelfand, J. J. 1989. Integrating knowledge-based system and neural network techniques for robotic skill acquisition. In *Proc. of the 11th International Joint Conference on Artificial Intelligence*, pages 193–198, Detroit, MI. Morgan Kaufmann.

Handelman, D. A., Lane, S. H., and J. J, G. 1992. Robotic skill acquisition based on biological principles. In Kandel and Langholz (1992), chapter 14, pages 301–327.

Hassibi, B. and Stork, D. 1993. Second-order derivatives for network pruning: Optimal brain surgeon. In Hanson, S., Cowan, J. D., and Giles, C. L., editors, *Advances in Neural Information Processing, 5.* Morgan-Kaufmann, San Mateo, CA.

Hayashi, Y. 1991. A neural expert system with automated extraction of fuzzy if-then rules and its application to medical diagnosis. In Lippman et al. (1991), pages 578–584.

Hayes, S., Ciesielski, V. B., and Kelly, W. 1992. A comparison of an expert system and a neural network for respiratory system monitoring. Technical Report TR #92/1, Royal Melbourne Institute of Technology.

Hendler, J. A. 1989. Problem solving and reasoning: A connectionist perspective. In Pfeifer et al. (1989), pages 229–243.

Hinton, G., editor 1991. *Connectionist Symbol Processing.* MIT-Elsevier.

Hölldobler, S. and Kurfess, F. 1991. CHCL—A connectionist inference system. In Fronhoefer, B. and Wrightson, G., editors, *Parallelization in Inference Systems.* Springer-Verlag, New York.

Hrycej, T. 1992. *Modular Learning in Neural Networks.* John Wiley & Sons.

Ivanova, I. and Kubat, M. 1995. Initialization of neural networks by means of decision trees. *Knowledge-Based Systems*, 8(6):333–343.

Jabri, M., Pickard, S., Leong, P., Chi, Z., Flower, B., and Xie, Y. 1992. Ann based classification for heart difibrillators. In Moody et al. (1992), pages 637–644.

Jacobs, R. A. and Jordan, M. I. 1991. A competitive modular architecture. In Lippman et al. (1991), pages 767–773.

Jacobs, R. A., Jordan, M. I., and Barto, A. G. 1990. Task decomposition through competition in a modular connectionist architecture: the what and where vision tasks. Technical Report 90-27, DCIS, University of Massachusetts, Amherst, MA.

Kandel, A. and Langholz, G., editors 1992. *Hybrid Architectures for Intelligent Systems.* CRC Press, Boca Raton, FL.

Kodratoff, Y. and Michalski, R. S., editors 1990. *Machine Learning. An Artificial Intelligence Approach, Vol. 3.* Morgan Kaufmann.

Kohara, K. and Ishikawa, T. 1994. Multivariate prediction using prior knowledge and neural heuristics. In Fu (1994), pages 179–188.

Krogh, A. and Hertz, J. A. 1992. A simple weight decay can improve generalization. In Moody et al. (1992), pages 950–057.

Krovvidy, S. and Wee, W. G. 1992. An intelligent hybrid system for wastewater treatment. In Kandel and Langholz (1992), chapter 17, pages 358–377.

Kuncicky, D. C., Hruska, S. I., and Lacher, R. C. 1992. Hybrid systems: The equivalence of rule-based expert system and artificial neural network inference. *International Journal of Expert Systems*, 4(3):281–297.

Lacher, R. C., Hruska, S. I., and Kuncicky, D. C. 1992. Backpropagatin learning in expert networks. *IEEE Transactions on Neural Networks*, 3:63–72.

Lange, T. E. 1992. Issues in controlling activation and inferencing for natural language understanding in structured connectionist networks. In Sun et al. (1992), pages 31–38.

Langley, P. and Simon, H. A. 1995. Applications of machine learning and rule induction. *Communications of the ACM*, 38(11):54–64.

Lebowitz, M. 1986. Integrated learning: controlling explanation. *Cognitive Science*, 10:219–240.

LeCun, Y. 1989. Generalization and network design strategies. In Pfeifer et al. (1989), pages 143–155.

LeCun, Y., Boser, B., Denker, J. S., et al. 1990. Handwritten digit recognition with a back-propagation network. In Touretzky (1990a), pages 396–404.

LeCun, Y., Denker, J. S., and Solla, S. A. 1990. Optimal brain damage. In Touretzky (1990a), pages 598–605.

Lendaris, G. C. and Harb, I. A. 1990. Improved generalization in ANN's via use of conceptual graphs: a character recognition task as as example case. In Proc. IJCNN–90 (1990), pages I 551–555.

Lengellé, R. and Denoeux, T. 1996. Training MLPs layer by layer using an objective function for internal representations. *IEEE Transactions on Neural Networks*, 9(1):83–97.

Lippman, R. P., Moody, J. E., and Touretzky, D. S., editors 1991. *Advances in Neural Information Processing, 3*. Morgan-Kaufmann, San Mateo, CA.

Maclin, R. and Shavlik, J. W. 1993. Using knowledge-based neural networks to improve algorithms: refining the Chou-Fasman algorithm for protein folding. In Michalski (1993), pages 195–215.

Mahoney, J. J. and Mooney, R. J. 1993. Combining connectionist and symbolic learning to refine certainty factor rule bases. *Connection Science*, 5(3 & 4):339–393.

McClelland, J. L. and Kawamoto, A. H. 1986. Parallel distributed processing. explorations in the microstructure of cognition. In McClelland, J. L., Rumelhart, D. E., and the PDP Research Group, editors, *Parallel Distributed Processing. Explorations in the Microstructure of Cognition*, volume 2, chapter 19, pages 272–325. MIT Press, Cambridge, MA.

Medsker, L. R. 1994. *Hybrid Neural Network and Expert Systems*. Kluwer Academic Publishers, Boston.

Michalski, R., editor 1993. *Machine Learning, Special Issue on Multistrategy Learning*, volume 11. Kluwer.

Mitchell, T. M., Keller, R., and Kedar-Cabelli, S. 1986. Explanation-based generalization: a unifying view. *Machine Learning*, 1:47–80.

Mitchell, T. M. and Thrun, S. B. 1994. Explanation based learning: A comparison of symbolic and neural network approaches. In Cohen, W. W. and Hirsh, H., editors, *Proc. of the 11th International Conference on Machine Learning*, pages 197–204, Rutgers, NJ. Morgan Kaufmann.

Moody, J. E., Hanson, S., and Lippman, R. P., editors 1992. *Advances in Neural Information Processing, 4*. Morgan-Kaufmann, San Mateo, CA.

Murphy, P. M. and Aha, D. 1991. UCI machine learning repository. http://www.ics.uci.edu/ mlearn/MLRepository.html. Irvine, CA: University of California, Dept. of Information and Computer Science.

Newell, A. 1982. The knowledge level. *Artificial Intelligence*, 18:87–127.

Omlin, C. W. and Giles, C. L. 1992. Training second-order recurrent neural networks using hints. In Sleeman, D. and Edwards, P., editors, *Proc. of the 9th International Workshop on Machine Learning*, pages 361–366. Morgan Kaufmann.

Opitz, D. W. and Shavlik, J. W. 1993. Heuristically expanding knowledge-based neural networks. In Proc. IJCAI–93 (1993), pages 1360–1365.

Park, N. S. and Robertson, D. 1995. A localist network architecture for logical inference based on temporal asynchrony approach to dynamic variable binding. In Sun, R. and Alexandre, F., editors, *IJCAI–95 Workshop on Connectionist-Symbolic Integration: From Unified to Hybrid Approaches*, pages 63–68, Montreal, CN.

Pazzani, M. and Kibler, D. 1992. The utility of knowledge in inductive learning. *Machine Learning*, 9(1):57–93.

Perantonis, S. J. and Lisboa, P. J. G. 1992. Translation, rotation and scale-invariant pattern recognition by high-order neural networks and moment classifiers. *IEEE Transactions on Neural Networks*, 3(2):241–251.

Pfeifer, R., Schreter, Z., and Fogelman-Soulié, F., editors 1989. *Connectionism in Perspective*. Elsevier.

Pinkas, G. 1994. Propositional logic, nonmonotonic reasoning and symmetric networks—On bridging the gap between symbolic and connectionist knowledge representation. In Levine, D. S. and IV, M. A., editors, *Neural Networks for Knowledge Representation and Inference*, chapter 7, pages 175–203. Lawrence Erlbaum Associates Inc., Hillsdale, NJ.

Piramuthu, S. and Shaw, M. I. 1994. On using decision tree as feature selector for feed-forward neural networks. In Fu (1994), pages 67–74.

Pollack, J. B. 1990. Recursive distributed representations. *Artificial Intelligence*, 46:77–105.

Pomerleau, D. A., Gowdy, J., and Thorpe, C. E. 1991. Combining artificial neural networks and symbolic processing for autonomous robot guidance. *Engineering Applications of Artificial Intelligence*, 4(4):279–285.

Pratt, L. Y. 1994. Experiments on the transfer of knowledge between neural networks. In Hanson, S. J., Drastal, G. A., and Rivest, R. L., editors, *Computational Learning Theory and Natural Learning Systems*, volume I, chapter 19, pages 523–

560. MIT Press.

Prem, E., Mackinger, M., Dorffner, G., Porenta, G., and Sochor, H. 1993. Concept support as a method for programming neural networks with symbolic knowledge. In *GAI-92: Advances in Artificial Intelligence.* Springer.

Proc. ICNN–96 1996. *Proc. IEEE International Conference on Neural Networks,* Washington, DC.

Proc. IJCAI–87 1987. *Proc. of the 10th International Joint Conference on Artificial Intelligence,* Milan, Italy. Morgan Kaufmann.

Proc. IJCAI–93 1993. *Proc. of the 13th International Joint Conference on Artificial Intelligence,* Chambéry, France. Morgan Kaufmann.

Proc. IJCNN–90 1990. *International Joint Conference on Neural Networks,* San Diego, CA.

Quinlan, J. R. 1993. *C4.5: Programs for Machine Learning.* Morgan Kaufmann, San Mateo, CA.

Rajamoney, S. and DeJong, G. 1987. The classification, detection and handling of imperfect theory problems. In Proc. IJCAI–87 (1987), pages 205–207.

Rajamoney, S., DeJong, G., and Faltings, B. 1985. Toward a model of conceptual knowledge acquisition through directed experimentation. In *Proc. of the 9th International Joint Conference on Artificial Intelligence,* pages 688–690, Los Angeles, CA. Morgan Kaufmann.

Rida, A., Labbi, A., and Pellegrini, C. 1999. Local experts combination through density decomposition. In *Uncertainty–99,* Ft. Lauerdale, Florida.

Romachandran, S. and Mooney, R. 1996. Revising Bayesian network parameters using backpropagation. In Proc. ICNN-96 (1996), pages 82–87.

Röscheisen, M., Hofmann, R., and Tresp, V. 1992. Neural control for rolling mills: incorporating domain theories to overcome data deficiency. In Moody et al. (1992), pages 659–666.

Rumelhart, D. E., Hinton, G. E., and Williams, R. J. 1986. Learning internal representations by error propagation. In Rumelhart, D. E., McClelland, J. L., and the PDP Research Group, editors, *Parallel Distributed Processing. Explorations in the Microstructure of Cognition,* volume 1, chapter 8, pages 318–362. MIT Press.

Saito, K. and Nakano, R. 1988. Medical diagnostic expert system based on pdp model. In *Proc. IEEE International Conference on Neural Networks,* pages 255–262, San Diego, CA.

Saitta, L., Botta, M., and Neri, F. 1993. Multistrategy learning and theory revision. In Michalski (1993), pages 45–172.

Samad, T. 1992. Hybrid distributed/local connectionist architectures. In Kandel and Langholz (1992), chapter 10, pages 200–219.

Segre, A. 1987. On the operationality/generality tradeoff in explanation-based learning. In Proc. IJCAI–87 (1987), pages 242–248.

Sethi, I. K. and Otten, M. 1990. Comparison between entropy net and decision tree classifiers. In *International Joint Conference on Neural Networks*, volume III, pages 63–68, San Diego, California.

Sharkey, A. J. C. 1995. Special issue: Combining artifical neural nets: Ensemble approaches. *Connection Science*, 8.

Shastri, L. 1988. A connectionist approach to knowledge representation and limited inference. *Cognitive Science*, 12:331–392.

Simard, P., Victorri, B., LeCun, Y., and Denker, J. 1992. TangentProp—a formalism for specifying selected invariances in an adaptive network. In Moody et al. (1992), pages 895–903.

Sirat, J. A. and Nadal, J. P. 1990. Neural trees: a new tool for classification. *Network*, 1:423–438.

Smolensky, P. 1990. Tensor product variable binding and the representation of symbolic structures in connectionist systems. *Artificial Intelligence*, (46):159–216.

Sohn, A. and Gaudiot, J. 1991. Connectionist production systems in local and hierarchical representation. In Bourbakis, N., editor, *Applications of Learning and Planning Methods*, pages 165–180. World Scientific Publishing, Singapore.

Sperduti, A. 1994. Labelling recursive auto-associative memory. *Connection Science*, 6:429–460.

Stolcke, A. and Wu, D. 1992. Tree matching with recursive distributed representations. In Sun et al. (1992).

Suddarth, S. C. and Holden, A. D. C. 1991. Symbolic-neural systems and the use of hints for developing complex systems. *International Journal of Man-Machine Studies*, 35(291–311).

Suddarth, S. C. and Kergosien, Y. L. 1990. Rule-injection hints as a means of improving network performance and learning time. In Almeida, L. and Wellekens, C., editors, *Neural Networks: Proc. EURASIP Workshop*, volume 412 of *Lecture Notes in Computer Science*, Berlin. Springer.

Sun, R. 1991. *Integrating Rules and Connectionism for Robust Reasoning. A Connectionist Architecture with Dual Representation*. PhD thesis, Brandeis University, Waltham, MA 02254. Technical Report CS-91-160.

Sun, R., Bookman, L., and Shekar, S., editors 1992. *AAAI 92 Workshop on Integrating Neural and Symbolic Processes: The Cognitive Dimension*.

Sun, R., Peterson, T., and Merrill, E. 1996. Bottom-up skill learning in reactive sequential decision tasks. In *Proc. Cognitive Science Conference*.

Taha, I. and Ghosh, J. 1995. A hybrid intelligent architecture for refining input characterization and domain knowledge. In *Proc. World Congress on Neural Networks*, pages II: 284–87, Washington, DC.

Tecuci, G. and Kodratoff, Y. 1990. Apprenticeship learning in imperfect domain theories. In Kodratoff and Michalski (1990), chapter 19, pages 514–551.

Thrun, S. B. 1996. *Explanation-Based Neural Network Learning: A Lifelong Approach.* Kluwer.

Thrun, S. B. and Mitchell, T. M. 1993. Integrating inductive neural network learning and explanation-based learning. In Proc. IJCAI–93 (1993), pages 930–936.

Touretzky, D., editor 1990a. *Advances in Neural Information Processing, 2.* Morgan-Kaufmann, San Mateo, CA.

Touretzky, D. S. 1990b. Boltzcons : Dynamic symbol structures in a connectionist network. *Artificial Intelligence*, 46(1–2).

Touretzky, D. S. and Hinton, G. E. 1988. A distributed connectionist production system. *Cognitive Science*, 12:423–466.

Towell, G. G. and Shavlik, J. W. 1994. Knowledge-based artificial neural networks. *Artificial Intelligence*, 70:119–165.

Valiant, L. G. 1984. A theory of the learnable. *Communications of the ACM*, 27:1134–1142.

Vysniauskas, V., Groen, F. C. A., and Kröse, B. 1993. The optimal number of learning samples and hidden units in function approximation with a feedforward network. Technical Report CS-93-15, CSD, University of Amsterdam.

Vysniauskas, V., Groen, F. C. A., and Kröse, B. J. A. 1995. Orthogonal incremental learning of a feedforward network. In *International Conference on Artificial Neural Networks*, Paris.

Waibel, A., Hanazawa, T., Hinton, G., Shikano, K., and Lang, K. 1989. Phoneme recognition using time-delay neural networks. *IEEE Transactions on Acoustics, Speech and Signal Processing*, 37:328–339.

Weigend, A. S., Rumelhart, D. E., and Huberman, B. A. 1991. Generalization by weight elimination with application to forecasting. In Lippman et al. (1991), pages 875–882.

Wolpert, D. H. 1992. Stacked generalization. *Neural Networks*, 5.

Yu, Y. H. and Simmons, R. F. 1990. Extra output biased learning. In Proc. IJCNN–90 (1990), pages III 161–166.

**3** Symbolic Knowledge Representation in Recurrent Neural Networks: Insights from Theoretical Models of Computation

Christian W. Omlin and C. Lee Giles

*This chapter gives an overview of some of the fundamental issues found in the realm of recurrent neural networks. Theoretical models of computation are used to characterize the representational, computational, and learning capabilities of recurrent network models. We discuss how results derived for deterministic models can be generalized to fuzzy models and then address how these theoretical models can be utilized within the knowledge-based neurocomputing paradigm for training recurrent networks, for extracting symbolic knowledge from trained networks, and for improving network training and generalization performance by making effective use of prior knowledge about a problem domain.*

## 3.1 Introduction

This chapter addresses some fundamental issues in regard to recurrent neural network architectures and learning algorithms, their computational power, their suitability for different classes of applications, and their ability to acquire symbolic knowledge through learning. We have found it convenient to investigate some of those issues in the paradigm of theoretical models of computation, formal languages, and dynamical systems theory. We briefly outline some of the issues we discuss in this chapter.

### 3.1.1 Why Neural Networks?

Neural networks were for a long time considered to belong outside the realm of mainstream artificial intelligence. The development of powerful new architectures and learning algorithms and the success of neural networks at solving real-world problems in a wide variety of fields has established a presence for neural networks as part of the toolbox for building intelligent systems. The reasons why neural networks enjoy tremendous popularity include their ability to learn from examples and to generalize to new data, and their superior performance compared to more traditional approaches for solving some real-world problems. Furthermore, they are universal computational devices; virtually identical network architectures and training algorithms can be applied to very different types of applications. Successful applications of neural networks include optical character recognition, robotics, speaker recognition and identification, credit rating and credit card fraud detection, and timeseries prediction.

### 3.1.2    Theoretical Aspects of Neural Networks

Despite that neural networks have had a significant impact, their theoretical foundations generally lag behind their tremendous popularity. For instance, feedforward neural networks with hidden layers were in use long before it was shown that a single hidden layer of sigmoidal neurons is sufficient for approximating continuous functions with arbitrary precision (Cybenko, 1989). Furthermore, determining the size of the hidden layer for a particular application remains an open question; in the absence of definitive theoretical results, heuristics for on-line growing and pruning of network architectures have been proposed (Fahlman, 1990, 1991; Cun et al., 1990; Mozer and Smolensky, 1989; Giles and Omlin, 1994). Similarly, recent theoretical results relate network size and size of training sets to a network's generalization performance (Baum and Haussler, 1989), but there exist no results which guarantee that a network can be trained to reach that generalization performance or more importantly, that training even converges to a solution. Developers side-step that problem by measuring generalization performance using test sets or crossvalidation.

Even though negative theoretical results demonstrate that training neural networks is a computationally difficult problem (Judd, 1987), neural networks have and will continue to enjoy tremendous popularity. In addition, methods and heuristics have been developed which ease, but do not eliminate the computational challenges; they include use of parallel learning algorithms (Deprit, 1989), use of partial prior system information (Omlin and Giles, 1992; Towell and Shavlik, 1994), and training data selection and presentation heuristics. Thus, it appears that theoretical results generally have little bearing on how neural networks are used, particularly when the results do not give hands-on recipes. This is also the case for some of the theoretical results regarding the computational power of recurrent neural networks which we will discuss here while others have the potential to have a direct impact on applications.

### 3.1.3    What Kind of Architecture Is Appropriate?

Selecting the size of the hidden layer of a feedforward neural network is only one example of how to choose a network architecture for a particular application. A more fundamental choice is dictated by the nature of the application: Is the application limited to dealing with spatial patterns (in the general sense) which are invariant over time or are they time-varying or so-called spatio-temporal patterns? Speech and stock markets are good examples of time-varying patterns.

The computational capabilities of feedforward networks are sufficient for learning input-output mapping between fixed, spatial patterns. If an application deals with time-varying patterns, we may still be able to use feedforward neural networks. Tapped delay neural networks (TDNNs) are a class of feedforward neural networks proposed for speech recognition, more precisely phoneme recognition (Lang et al., 1990). The success of TDNNs is based on the very limited context of the sampled speech signals that is required for phoneme identification. Similarly, feedforward networks may be sufficient for control applications where all system states are observable, i.e. there are no hidden states, even though we are dealing with time-varying patterns which require long-term context. What do we gain by using recurrent neural networks with hidden states, and how does it affect training? We maintain the position that recurrent network architectures significantly expand the range of problems that neural networks can be applied to.

### 3.1.4 Recurrent Networks and Models of Computation

Recurrent neural networks are appropriate tools for modeling time-varying systems, e.g. financial markets, physical dynamical systems, speech recognition, etc. Networks can be used to recognize pattern sequences, e.g. speech recognition, or they can be used for forecasting future patterns, e.g. financial markets. These applications are generally not well-suited for addressing fundamental issues of recurrent neural networks such as training algorithms and knowledge representation because they come with a host of application-specific characteristics which muddle the fundamental issues, e.g. financial data is generally non-stationary, or feature extraction may be necessary for speaker identification.

We will discuss the capabilities of recurrent neural networks and related issues in the framework of theoretical models of computation (Hopcroft and Ullman, 1979). Models such as finite-state automata and their corresponding language can be viewed as a general paradigm of temporal, symbolic knowledge. No feature extraction is necessary to learn these languages from examples, and there exist correspondences between levels of complexity of formal languages, their accepting automata, and neural network models. Furthermore, the dynamics induced into recurrent neural networks through learning has a nice correspondence with the dynamics of finite-state automata. Similar approaches have been used for characterizing physical systems (Crutchfield and Young, 1991) Even though formal languages and automata models may lack the semantics and complexities of natural languages and some dynamical processes, they have great expressive power, and results from these investigations are likely to have an impact on natural language learning (Lawrence et al., 1996) and nonlinear system identification and control.

### 3.1.5    Knowledge Representation and Acquisition

We can view *representation* of automata as a prerequisite for *learning* their corresponding languages, i.e. if an architecture cannot represent an automaton, then it cannot learn it either. These questions have been answered for some automata and some network models (Giles et al., 1995; Kremer, 1995). In some cases, results not only show that network models can represent certain automata, but also how the actual mapping "automata → recurrent network" can be accomplished (Alquezar and Sanfeliu, 1995; Frasconi et al., 1996; Omlin and Giles, 1996a).

### 3.1.6    Are Neural Networks Black Boxes?

One of the reasons why expert sytems have found acceptance more easily than neural networks is their capability to explain how they arrive at a solution for a given problem. The explanation component is a by-product of the automated reasoning process using the knowledge base and a set of rules describing a domain. Neural networks, on the other hand, do not provide an explanation as part of their information processing. The knowledge that neural networks have gained through training is stored in their weights. Until recently, it was a widely accepted myth that neural networks were black boxes, i.e. the knowledge stored in their weights after training was not accessible to inspection, analysis, and verification. Since then, research on that topic has resulted in a number of algorithms for extracting knowledge in symbolic form from trained neural networks.

   For feedforward networks, that knowledge has typically been in the form of Boolean and fuzzy if-then clauses (Fu, 1994; Hayashi and Imura, 1990; Towell and Shavlik, 1993); excellent overviews of the current state-of-the-art can be found in several chapters of this book and in (Andrews and Diederich, 1996; Andrews et al., 1995). For recurrent networks, finite-state automata have been the main paradigm of temporal symbolic knowledge extraction (Cleeremans et al., 1989; Frasconi et al., 1991; Giles et al., 1992a; Omlin and Giles, 1996b; Watrous and Kuhn, 1992a; Zeng et al., 1993). Clearly, neural networks are no longer black boxes. Some applications (e.g. application of neural networks to credit rating and lending policy and critical applications such as aircraft control) may require that neural networks undergo validation prior to being deployed. Knowledge extraction could be an important stage in that process.

### 3.1.7    Overcoming the Bias/Variance Dilemma

It has been accepted for a long time that neural networks cannot be expected to learn anything useful without some significant prior structure (Minsky and Papert, 1969). Recent theoretical results support that point of view (Geman et al., 1992). Therefore, learning with prior knowledge (also known as learning with hints) has attracted increasing attention. The philosophy of learning with hints is that since training neural networks is an inherently difficult problem, advantage should be taken of any and all prior knowledge that is available. One approach is to prestructure or initialize a network with knowledge prior to training (Omlin and Giles, 1992; Towell and Shavlik, 1994). The goal is to reduce training time and possibly improve network generalization performance. Thus, the role of neural networks then becomes that of *knowledge refinement* or even *knowledge revision* in the case where the prior knowledge is incorrect (Omlin and Giles, 1996c).

## 3.2   Representation of Symbolic Knowledge in Neural Networks

We give a brief general discussion of the significance of knowledge extraction and initialization of neural networks with prior knowledge. We then discuss how these two processes can be combined for knowledge refinement and revision.

### 3.2.1   Importance of Knowledge Extraction

The goal of knowledge extraction is to generate a concise symbolic description of the knowledge stored in a network's weights. Summaries of some existing knowledge extraction methods can be found in several chapters of this book and in (Andrews and Diedcrich, 1996; Andrews et al., 1995). Of particular concern—and an open issue—is *fidelity* of the extraction process, i.e. how accurately the extracted knowledge corresponds to the knowledge stored in the network. Fidelity can be measured by comparing, for a given test set, the performance of a trained network with the performance of extracted rules. Unfortunately, rule extraction is a computationally very hard problem. For feedforward networks, it has been shown that there do not exist polynomial-time algorithms for concise knowledge extraction (Golea, 1996). Although no corresponding results exist in the literature for recurrent networks, it is likely that a similar result applies. Thus, heuristics have been developed for overcoming the combinatorial complexity of the problem.

The merits of rule extraction include discovery of unknown salient features and nonlinear relationships in data sets, explanation capability leading to increased user acceptance, improved generalization performance, and possibly transfer of knowledge to new, yet similar learning problems. As we will see later, improved generalization performance applies particularly to recurrent networks whose nonlinear dynamical characteristics can easily lead to deteriorating generalization performance.

Extraction algorithms can broadly be divided into three classes (Andrews et al., 1995): Decompositional methods infer rules from the internal network structure (individual nodes and weights). Pedagogical methods view neural networks as black boxes, and use some machine learning algorithm for deriving rules which explain the network input/output behavior. Algorithms which do not clearly fit into either class are referred to as "eclectic," i.e. they may have aspects of decompositional and pedagogical methods.

### 3.2.2   Significance of Prior Knowledge

Partial prior knowledge has shown to be useful for network training and generalization. The prior knowledge may be in the form of explicit rules which can be encoded into networks by programming some of the weights (Towell et al., 1990a), or an initial analysis of the data may provide hints about a suitable architecture (Tresp et al., 1993). Fidelity of the mapping of the prior knowledge into a network is also important since a network may not be able to take full advantage of poorly encoded prior knowledge or, if the encoding alters the essence of the prior knowledge, the prior knowledge may actually hinder the learning process.

### 3.2.3   Neural Networks for Knowledge Refinement

Rule insertion and extraction can be combined to perform knowledge refinement or revision with neural networks (Shavlik, 1994). The goal is to use neural network learning and rule extraction techniques to produce a better or refined set of symbolic rules that apply to a problem domain. Initial domain knowledge, which may also contain information that is inconsistent with the available training data, is encoded into a neural network; this encoding typically consists of programming some of a network's weights. Rather than starting with a network whose weights are initialized to small random values, these programmed weights presumably provide a better starting point for finding a solution in weight space. A network is then trained on the available data set; training typically requires several passes through the training set, depending on how close the initial symbolic knowledge is to the final solution. Refined, or revised rules in the case of wrong prior knowledge, can then be extracted from the trained network. The impact of using prior knowledge in training feedforward neural networks on the generalization capability and the required sample size for valid generalization has been theoretically investigated in (Abu-Mostafa, 1990; Fu, 1996).

## 3.3   Computational Models as Symbolic Knowledge

### 3.3.1   A Hierarchy of Automata and Languages

This section introduces theoretical models of computation and formal languages as a convenient framework in which to study the computational capabilities of various network models. Even though these synthetic languages may lack some of the characteristics of natural languages, they capture some of those characteristics and, more importantly, they allow a classification of various levels of language complexities.

We will discuss various network architectures and relate them to formal automata in terms of their capability to represent spatio-temporal patterns. This discussion will build a hierarchy from simple to more powerful network architectures and

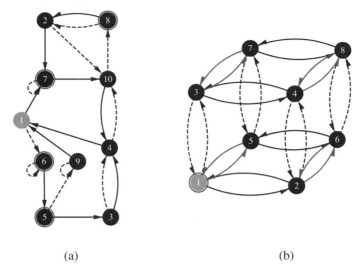

$$(a) \qquad\qquad\qquad (b)$$

**Figure 3.1**   Examples of DFAs: Shown are two unique, minimal DFAs. **(a)** Randomly generated DFA with 10 states and two input symbols. State 1 is the DFAs start state. Accepting states are shown with double circles. **(b)** DFA for triple parity which accepts all strings over the alphabet $\Sigma = \{0, 1, 2\}$ which contains a multiple of 3 zeroes.

(© IEEE Press, used with permission, see Copyright Acknowledgments)

models of computations. We will not discuss the details of training algorithms or proofs of equivalence here. Instead, we will summarize results reported in the literature. This will also provide a context for the more detailed discussions to follow later on.

### 3.3.2   Finite-State Automata

A large class of discrete processes can be modeled by deterministic finite-state automata (DFAs). They also form the basic building blocks of theoretical models of computation. More powerful models of computation can be obtained by adding new elements to DFAs; restrictions to the topology of DFAs yield special subclasses of DFAs with characteristic properties.

We will use the following definition of DFAs in the remainder of this chapter:

**Definition 3.1**
A DFA $M$ is a 5-tuple $M - \langle \Sigma, Q, R, \Gamma, \delta \rangle$ where $\Sigma = \{a_1, \dots, a_k\}$ is the alphabet of the language $L$, $Q = \{s_1, \dots, s_{N_s}\}$ is a set of states, $R \in Q$ is the start state, $F \subseteq Q$ is a set of accepting states and $\delta : Q \times \Sigma \to Q$ defines state transitions in $M$.

Two examples of DFAs are shown in Figure 3.1. A string $x$ is accepted by the DFA $M$ and hence is a member of the regular language $L(M)$ if an accepting state is reached after the entire string $x$ has been read by $M$. Alternatively, a DFA $M$

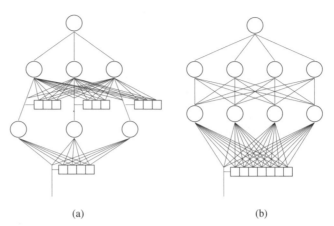

**Figure 3.2** Network architectures for definite memory machines: **(a)** Neural Network Finite Impulse Response (NNFIR) **(b)** Input Delayed Neural Networks (IDNNs)

(© IEEE Press, used with permission, see Copyright Acknowledgments)

can be interpreted as a grammar which generates the regular language $L(M)$. A sequential finite-state machine (Kohavi, 1978) is the actual implementation in some logical form consisting of logic (or neurons) and delay elements that will recognize $L$ when the strings are encoded as temporal sequences. It is this type of representation that the recurrent neural network will learn.

Since we will focus our discussion on learning regular languages, we give a brief description of regular grammars; see (Hopcroft and Ullman, 1979) for more details. Regular languages represent the smallest and simplest class of formal languages in the Chomsky hierarchy and are generated by regular grammars. A regular grammar $G$ is a quadruple $G = \langle S, V, T, P \rangle$ where S is the start symbol, V and T are respectively non-terminal and terminal symbols and $P$ are productions of the form $A \rightarrow a$ or $A \rightarrow aB$ where $A, B \in V$ and $a \in T$. The regular language generated by $G$ is denoted $L(G)$. A deterministic finite-state automaton (DFA) $M$ is the recognizer of each regular language $L$: $L(G) = L(M)$.

The process of learning grammars from example strings is also known as *grammatical inference* (Fu, 1982; Angluin and Smith, 1983; Miclet, 1990). The inference of regular grammars from positive and negative example strings has been shown to be an NP-complete problem in the worst case (Golden, 1978). However, good heuristic methods have recently been developed for randomly generated DFAs (Lang, 1992).

We will show in later sections how DFAs can be mapped into fully recurrent network architectures such that the DFA and the recurrent network are equivalent, i.e. accept the same language.

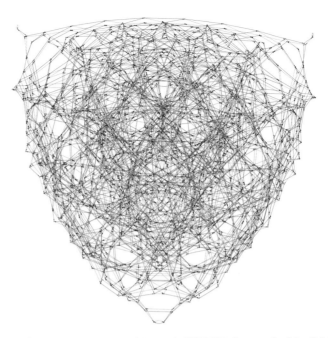

**Figure 3.3** Definite memory machine: A NNFIR learned this DMM with 2048 states

(© IEEE Press, used with permission, see Copyright Acknowledgments)

### 3.3.3 Subclasses of Finite-State Automata

We can identify two network architecture which are capable of representing subclasses of DFAs.

The first architecture—called Neural Network Finite Impulse Response (NNFIR)—is a feedforward network implemented with tapped delay lines, see Figure 3.2. In general, each neuron has a tapped delay line which stores the outputs of the previous $d$ time steps. The output of that node and the stored values are inputs to nodes in the next layer. The length of the tapped delay line determines the range of input history to which the network is sensitive. It has been shown that NNFIR networks are equivalent with IDNNs (Input-Delayed Neural Networks) which only have delay lines for the network input layer (Clouse et al., 1997). It is obvious that NNFIR can only represent DFAs whose state depends on a limited input history.

In order to understand the representational capabilities of NNFIRs, an intuitive argument based on network topology has been made that DFAs can be mapped into sequential machines (Kohavi, 1978) using combinational logic and memory elements. The machines whose current state can always be determined uniquely from the knowledge of the last $d$ inputs are called *definite memory machines* (DMMs). It is obvious that combinational logic can be implemented by a feedforward neural network with tapped input delay lines.

The transition diagrams of DFAs that can be mapped into DMMs are essentially shift registers, i.e. only a small amount of 'logic' is necessary to compute the next state from the current state and previous inputs. Contrary to what one's intuition about feedforward network architectures may suggest, these DFAs *can* have loops and thus can accept strings of arbitrary length. IDNN architectures can learn DMMs with a large number of states (in the order of 1000 states) if the 'logic' is sufficiently simple. Such a large DMM is shown in Figure 3.3.

The representational capability of NNFIR can be increased by augmenting the network architecture with output tapped delay lines that are fed back into the network as inputs; this network architecture is also referred to as Neural Network Infinite Impulse Response (NNIIR) because of its similarity to infinite response filters. This topology of NNIIR is the same as that of Finite Memory Machines (FMMs) which can be implemented as sequential machines using combinatorial logic, e.g. memory and combinational logic.

FMMs are a subclass of DFAs for which the present state can always be determined uniquely from the knowledge of the last $n$ inputs and last $m$ outputs for all possible sequences of length $max(n, m)$—also referred to as FMMs of input-order $n$ and output-order $m$. Given an arbitrary finite-state machine, there exist efficient algorithms for determining if the machine has finite memory and its corresponding order (Kohavi, 1978). As in the case of DMMs , large FMMs (i.e., machines with on the order of 100 states) can be learned if the corresponding logic is relatively simple. It is fairly obvious that the class of finite memory machines includes the class of definite memory machines: DMMs are FFMs with output order 0.

### 3.3.4   Push-Down Automata

The computational power of DFAs can be increased by adding an infinite stack. In addition to reading input symbols and performing state transitions, input symbols may also be pushed and popped onto and from the stack, respectively. This enriched model is called the pushdown automaton (PDA). The language $L(P)$ is called context-free; a string $x$ is a member of the language $L(P)$ if the pushdown automaton arrives at an accepting state after $x$ has been read. Similarly to the regular languages, there exists a context-free grammar $G$ which generates exactly the strings accepted by $P$: $L(G) = L(P)$.

In order to gain an intuitive understanding why PDAs are computationally more powerful than DFAs, consider the language $L = \{a^n b^n | n \geq 0\}$. Examples are $ab, aabb, aaabbb, \ldots$ . In order for a machine to determine whether or not a string $x$ is a member of the language, it needs to count the number of $a$'s it has seen and check the number of $b$'s that follow the $a$'s. This can be achieved by pushing the $a$'s onto the stack and popping the $a$'s from the stack as soon as the first $b$ is encountered. This task cannot be performed by a DFA *if* the length of the strings is *arbitrary*. From this discussion, it is obvious that PDAs can also recognize regular languages (we simply ignore the stack), but DFAs cannot recognize context-free languages.

PDAs can be learned by recurrent networks with an external stack (Das et al.,

1992). More recently, methods for training recurrent networks without the use of an external stack have been investigated (Wiles and Bollard, 1996). While recurrent networks have in principle the computational power of PDAs they cannot simulate arbitrary context-free languages. PDAs require infinite stack depth; this demands infinite precision in the computation of the recurrent network which is not possible. Nevertheless, research into the representation of 'context-free' languages in recurrent networks seems promising since some interesting questions regarding the dynamics of networks trained to recognize context-free languages can be addressed.

### 3.3.5 Turing Machines

The stack of PDAs determines the order in which symbols can be read from or written to a memory. We can relax that requirement by replacing the stack with an infinite input tape (or two stacks). This model is referred to as a Turing machine. In addition to performing state transitions, a Turing machine may read and write information from and to the tape, respectively. This model is the most powerful model of computation: It is capable of computing essentially all computable functions (computability of a function is often expressed in terms of Turing computability). Given the restrictions on how stored data can be accessed in PDAs, it is intuitively obvious that Turing machines are computationally more powerful than PDAs. It has been shown that recurrent neural networks are computationally as powerful as Turing machines (Siegelmann and Sontag, 1995). However, this equivalence requires infinite precision in the network computation. For all practical purposes, Turing machines cannot be simulated by recurrent neural networks.

### 3.3.6 Summary

We have developed a hierarchy of the computational power of recurrent network architectures by identifying the class of computation each of the neural network architectures discussed here can perform. Even though recurrent networks have in principle the power of Turing machines, they can in practice perform only DFA computation due to the finite precision with which neural networks can be simulated. Thus, we will limit our discussion to DFA computation in the remainder of this chapter.

---

## 3.4 Mapping Automata into Recurrent Neural Networks

### 3.4.1 Preliminaries

Recently, much work has focused on the representational capabilities of recurrent networks as opposed to their ability to learn certain tasks. The underlying premise is that if a network model cannot *represent* a certain structure, then it certainly cannot *learn* it either. A positive answer to the question of whether or not a given recurrent

network architecture can represent a certain structure can be of three types: (1) The network architecture is *in principle* computationally rich enough for representating a certain structure, but an equivalence with a theoretical model of computation would require infinite resources such as infinite precision (Siegelmann and Sontag, 1995) or infinitely many neurons (Sun et al., 1991). These answers establish the computational power of recurrent networks. (2) Networks can represent a certain structure with the given resources (Kremer, 1995, 1996; Sperduti, 1997). These results can guide the selection of a recurrent network architecture for a given application. However, no constructive algorithm is given which guarantees the existence of a solution for a chosen architecture, e.g. network size. (3) We can give an algorithm which maps the structure into a recurrent network architecture such that the structure and network perform the same computation on identical inputs for an arbitrary number of computation steps (Alon et al., 1991; Frasconi et al., 1996; Minsky and Papert, 1969; Omlin and Giles, 1996a). These results guarantee the existence of a solution, but do not guarantee that it can be learned. In the remainder of this section, we will primarily answer questions of the third type for DFAs.

### 3.4.2    DFA Encoding Algorithm

In showing how DFAs can be mapped into recurrent networks, we must address three issues: First, we must establish a mapping from DFA states to an internal representation in the network. Then, we must program the network weights such that the network dynamics mimic the DFA dynamics. Finally, we must prove that the DFA and the derived network perform the same computation for an arbitary number of time steps. This is not obvious: DFAs have a discrete state space whereas recurrent networks with sigmoidal discriminants can exhibit complicated nonlinear dynamics (Tino et al., 1995).

For ease of representation, we choose networks with second-order weights $W_{ijk}$ shown in Figure 3.4. The continuous network dynamics are described by the following equations:

$$S_i^{t+1} = g(a_i(t)) = \frac{1}{1 + e^{-a_i(t)}}, a_i(t) = b_i + \sum_{j,k} W_{ijk} S_j^t I_k^t,$$

where $b_i$ is the bias associated with hidden recurrent state neurons $S_i$; $I_k$ denotes input neurons; $g$ is the nonlinearity; and $a_i$ is the activation of the $i$th neuron.

An aspect of the second order recurrent neural network is that the product $S_j^t I_k^t$ in the recurrent network directly corresponds with the state transition $\delta(q_j, a_k) = q_i$ in the DFA. After a string has been processed, the output of a designated neuron $S_0$ decides whether the network accepts or rejects a string. The network accepts a given string if the value of the output neuron $S_0^t$ at the end of the string is greater than some preset value such as 0.5; otherwise, the network rejects the string. For the remainder of this chapter, we assume a one-hot encoding for input symbols $a_k$,

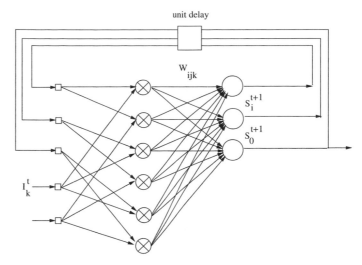

**Figure 3.4**  Second-order recurrent neural network.
(© ACM, used with permission, see Copyright Acknowledgments)

i.e. $I_k^t \in \{0, 1\}$.

Our DFA encoding algorithm follows directly from the similarity of state transitions in a DFA and the dynamics of a recurrent neural network: Consider a state transition $\delta(s_j, a_k) = s_i$. We arbitrarily identify DFA states $s_j$ and $s_i$ with state neurons $S_j$ and $S_i$, respectively. One method of representing this transition is to have state neuron $S_i$ have a high output $\approx 1$ and state neuron $S_j$ have a low output $\approx 0$ after the input symbol $a_k$ has entered the network via input neuron $I_k$. One implementation is to adjust the weights $W_{jjk}$ and $W_{ijk}$ accordingly: setting $W_{ijk}$ to a large positive value will ensure that $S_i^{t+1}$ will be high and setting $W_{jjk}$ to a large negative value will guarantee that the output $S_j^{t+1}$ will be low. All other weights are set to small random values. In addition to the encoding of the known DFA states, we also need to program the response neuron, indicating whether or not a DFA state is an accepting state. We program the weight $W_{0jk}$ as follows: If state $s_i$ is an accepting state, then we set the weight $W_{0jk}$ to a large positive value; otherwise, we will initialize the weight $W_{0jk}$ to a large negative value. We define the values for the programmed weights as a rational number $H$, and let large *programmed* weight values be $+H$ and small values $-H$. We will refer to $H$ as the *strength* of a rule. We set the value of the biases $b_i$ of state neurons that have been assigned to known DFA states to $-H/2$. This ensures that all state neurons which do not correspond to the the previous or the current DFA state have a low output. Thus, the rule insertion algorithm defines a nearly *orthonormal internal representation* of all known DFA states. We assume that the DFA generated the example strings starting in its initial state. Therefore, we can arbitrarily select the output of one of the state neurons to be 1 and set the output of all other state neurons initially to zero.

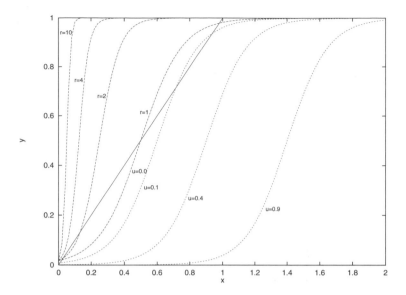

**Figure 3.5** Fixed points of the sigmoidal discriminant function: Shown are the graphs of the function $f(x, r) = \frac{1}{1+e^{H(1-2rx)/2}}$ (dashed graphs) for $H = 8$ and $r = \{1, 2, 4, 10\}$ and the function $p(x, u) = \frac{1}{1+e^{H(1-2(x-u))/2}}$ (dotted graphs) for $H = 8$ and $u = \{0.0, 0.1, 0.4, 0.9\}$. Their intersection with the function $y = x$ shows the existence and location of fixed points. In this example, $f(x, r)$ has three fixed points for $r = \{1, 2\}$, but only one fixed point for $r = \{4, 10\}$ and $p(x, u)$ has three fixed points for $u = \{0.0, 0.1\}$, but only one fixed point for $u = \{0.6, 0.9\}$.
(© ACM, used with permission, see Copyright Acknowledgments)

### 3.4.3   Stability of the DFA Representation

The encoding algorithm leads to the following special form of the equation governing the network dynamics:

$$S_i^{(t+1)} = h(x, H) = \frac{1}{1 + e^{H(1-2x)/2}}$$

where $x$ is the input to neuron $S_i$, and $H$ is the weight strength. The proof of stability of the internal DFA representation makes use of (1) the existence of three fixed points $\phi^-, \phi^0$ and $\phi^+$ of the sigmoidal discriminant, (2) $0 < \phi^- < \phi^0 < \phi^+ < 1$, (3) the stability of $\phi^-$ and $\phi^+$ (notice that the fixed point $\phi^0$ is unstable), and (4) two auxiliary sigmoidal functions $f$ and $g$ whose fixed points $\phi_f^-$ and $\phi_g^+$ provide upper and lower bounds on the low and high signals, respectively, in a constructed network. The graphs in Figure 3.5 illustrate the fixed points of the sigmoidal discriminant function.

As can be seen, the discriminant function may not have two stable fixed points for some choices of the parameters. However, the existence of two stable fixed points can be guaranteed by establishing a lower bound on the weight strength $H$

for given values of $n$. This is illustrated in Figure 3.5 (see figure caption for an explanation). Convergence to the fixed points $\phi^-$ and $\phi^+$ can be shown using a Lyapunov argument: An appropriate energy function can be defined and it can be shown that that function only reaches a minimum for either one of the two fixed points. The following result can be derived from the above analysis:

**Theorem 3.1**

For any given DFA $M$ with $r$ states and $m$ input symbols, a sparse recurrent neural network with $r+1$ sigmoidal state neurons and $m$ input neurons can be constructed from $M$ such that the internal state representation remains stable if the following three conditions are satisfied:

$$(1)\ \phi_f^-(r,H) < \frac{1}{r}\left(\frac{1}{2} + \frac{\phi_f^0(r,H)}{H}\right)$$

$$(2)\ \phi_g^+(r,H) > \frac{1}{2} + \phi_f^-(r,H) + \frac{\phi_g^0(r,H)}{H}$$

$$(3)\ H > max(H_0^-(r), H_0^+(r))$$

Furthermore, the constructed network has at most $3mr$ second-order weights with alphabet $\Sigma_w = \{-H, 0, +H\}$, $r+1$ biases with alphabet $\Sigma_b = \{-H/2\}$, and maximum fan-out $3m$.

The function $H_0(r)$ is shown in Figure 3.6 (see caption for an explanation). For any choice $H > H_0^-(r)$ and $H > H_0^+(r)$ for low and high signals, respectively, the sigmoidal discriminant function is guaranteed to have two stable fixed points. Stable encoding of DFA states is a necessary condition for a neural network to implement a given DFA. The network must also correctly classify all strings. The conditions for correct string classification are expressed in the following corollary:

**Corollary 3.1**

Let $L(M_{DFA})$ denote the regular language accepted by a DFA $M$ with $r$ states and let $L(M_{RNN})$ be the language accepted by the recurrent network constructed from $M$. Then, we have $L(M_{RNN}) = L(M_{DFA})$ if

$$(1)\quad \phi_g^+(r,H) > \frac{1}{2}\left(1 + \frac{1}{r} + \frac{2\,\phi_g^0(r,H)}{H}\right)$$

$$(2)\quad H > max(H_0^-(r), H_0^+(r))$$

### 3.4.4   Simulations

In order to empirically validate our analysis, we constructed networks from randomly generated DFAs with 10, 100 and 1,000 states. For each of the three DFAs, we randomly generated different test sets each consisting of 1,000 strings of length 10, 100, and 1,000, respectively. The networks' generalization performance on these test sets for rule strength $H = \{0.0, 0.1, 0.2, \ldots, 7.0\}$ are shown in Figures 3.7–

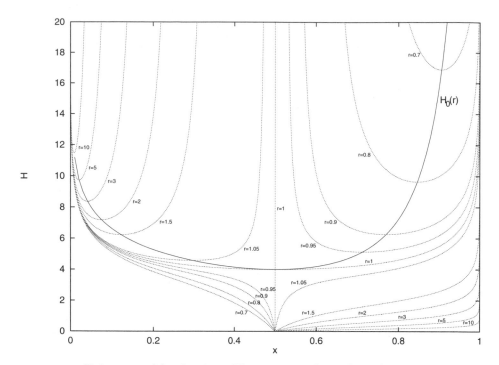

**Figure 3.6** Existence of fixed points: The contour plots of the function $h(x, r) = x$ (dotted graphs) show the relationship between $H$ and $x$ for various values of $r$. If $H$ is chosen such that $H > H_0(r)$ (solid graph), then a line parallel to the x-axis intersects the surface satisfying $h(x, r) = x$ in three points which are the fixed points of $h(x, r)$.

(© ACM, used with permission, see Copyright Acknowledgments)

3.9. A misclassification of these long strings for arbitrary large values of $H$ would indicate a network's failure to maintain the stable finite-state dynamics that was encoded. However, we observe that the networks can implement stable DFAs as indicated by the perfect generalization performance for some choice of the rule strength $H$ and a chosen test set. Thus, we have empirical evidence which supports our analysis.

All three networks achieve perfect generalization for all three test sets for approximately the same value of $H$. Apparently, the network size plays an insignificant role in determining for which value of $H$ stability of the internal DFA representation is reached, at least across the considered 3 orders of magnitude of network sizes.

In our simulations, no neurons ever exceeded or fell below the fixed points $\phi_f^-$ and $\phi_g^+$, respectively. Furthermore, the network has a built-in reset mechanism which allows low and high signals to be strengthened. Low signals $S_j^t$ are strengthened to $h(0, H)$ when there exists no state transition $\delta(\cdot, a_k) = q_j$. In that case, the neuron $S_j^t$ receives no inputs from any of the other neurons; its output becomes less than $\phi_f^-$ since $h(0, H) < \phi_f^-$. Similarly, high signals $S_i^t$ get strengthened if either low

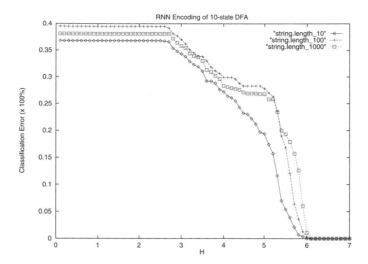

**Figure 3.7**  Performance of 10-state DFA: The network classification performance on three randomly-generated data sets consisting of 1,000 strings of length 10 ($\diamond$), 100 (+), and 1,000 ($\square$), respectively, as a function of the rule strength $H$ (in 0.1 increments) is shown. The network achieves perfect classification on the strings of length 1,000 for $H > 6.0$.

(© MIT Press, used with permission, see Copyright Acknowledgments)

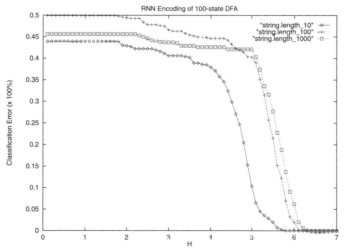

**Figure 3.8**  Performance of 100-state DFA: The network classification performance on three randomly-generated data sets consisting of 1,000 strings of length 10 ($\diamond$), 100 (+), and 1,000 ($\square$), respectively, as a function of the rule strength $H$ (in 0.1 increments) is shown. The network achieves perfect classification on the strings of length 1,000 for $H > 6.2$.

(© MIT Press, used with permission, see Copyright Acknowledgments)

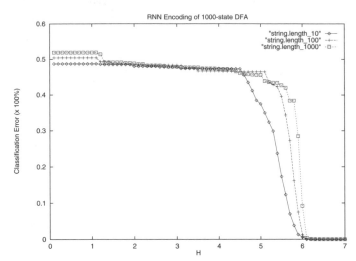

**Figure 3.9**   Performance of 1000-state DFA: The network classification performances on three randomly-generated data sets consisting of 1,000 strings of length 10 ($\diamond$), 100 (+), and 1,000 ($\square$), respectively, as a function of the rule strength $H$ (in 0.1 increments). The network achieves perfect classification on the strings of length 1,000 for $H > 6.1$.

(© MIT Press, used with permission, see Copyright Acknowledgments)

signals feeding into neuron $S_i$ on a current state transition $\delta(\{q_j\}, a_k) = q_i$ have been strengthened during the previous time step or when the number of positive residual inputs to neuron $S_i$ compensates for a weak high signal from neurons $\{q_j\}$. Since constructed networks are able to regenerate their internal signals and since typical DFAs do not have the worst case properties assumed in this analysis, the conditions guaranteeing stable low and high signals are generally much too strong for some given DFA.

### 3.4.5   Scaling Issues

The worst case analysis supports the following predictions about the implementation of arbitrary DFAs:

(1)   neural DFAs can be constructed that are stable for arbitrary string length for finite value of the weight strength $H$,

(2)   for most neural DFA implementations, network stability is achieved for values of $H$ that are smaller than the values required by the conditions in Theorem 3.1,

(3)   the value of $H$ scales with the DFA size, i.e. the larger the DFA and thus the network, the larger $H$ will be for guaranteed stability.

Predictions (1) and (2) are supported by our experiments. However, when we compare the values $H$ in the above experiments for DFAs of different sizes, we find that $H \approx 6$ for all three DFAs. This observation seems inconsistent with the theory. The reason for this inconsistency lies in the assumption of a *worst case* for the analysis, whereas the DFAs we implemented represent *average cases*. For the construction of the randomly generated 100-state DFA we found correct classification of strings of length 1,000 for $H = 6.3$. This value corresponds to a DFA whose states have 'average' indegree $n = 1.5$. [The magic value 6 also seems to occur for networks which are trained. Consider a neuron $S_i$; then, the weight which causes transitions between dynamical attractors often has a value $\approx 6$ (Tino, 1994).] However, there exist DFAs which exhibit the scaling behavior that is predicted by the theory. We will briefly discuss such DFAs. That discussion will be followed by an analysis of the condition for stable DFA encodings for asymptotically large DFAs.

### 3.4.6 DFA States with Large Indegree

We can approximate the worst case analysis by considering an extreme case of a DFA:

(1) Select an arbitrary DFA state $q_\rho$;

(2) select a fraction $\rho$ of states $q_j$ and set $\delta(q_j, a_k) = q_\rho$.

(3) For low values of $\rho$, a constructed network behaves similarly to a randomly generated DFA.

(4) As the number of states $q_j$ for which $\delta(q_j, a_k) = q_\rho$ increases, the behavior gradually moves toward the worst case analysis where one neuron receives a large number of residual inputs for a designated input symbol $a_k$.

We constructed a network from a randomly generated DFA $M_0$ with 100 states and two input symbols. We derived DFAs $M_{\rho_1}, M_{\rho_2}, \ldots, M_{\rho_R}$ where the fraction of DFA states $q_j$ from $M_{\rho_i}$ to $M_{\rho_{i+1}}$ with $\delta(q_j, a_k) = q_\rho$ increased by $\Delta\rho$; for our experiments, we chose $\Delta\rho = 0.05$. Obviously, the languages $L(M_{\rho_i})$ change for different values of $\rho_i$. The graph in Figure 3.10 shows for 10 randomly generated DFAs with 100 states the minimum weight strength $H$ necessary to correctly classify 100 strings of length 100—a new data set was randomly generated for each DFA— as a function of $\rho$ in 5% increments. We observe that $H$ generally increases with increasing values of $\rho$; in all cases, the hint strength $H$ sharply declines for some percentage value $\rho$. As the number of connections $+H$ to a single state neuron $S_i$ increases, the number of residual inputs which can cause unstable internal DFA representation and incorrect classification decreases.

We observed that there are two runs where outliers occur, i.e. $H_{\rho_i} > H_{\rho_{i+1}}$ even though we have $\rho_i < \rho_{i+1}$. Since the value $H_\rho$ depends on the randomly generated DFA, the choice for $q_\rho$ and the test set, we can expect such an uncharacteristic behavior to occur in some cases.

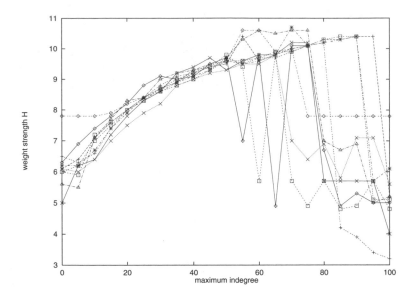

**Figure 3.10**  Scaling weight strength: An accepting state $q_\rho$ in 10 randomly generated 100-state DFAs was selected. The number of states $q_j$ for which $\delta(q_j, 0) = q_\rho$ was gradually increased in increments of 5% of all DFA states. The graph shows the minimum values of $H$ for the correct classification of 100 strings of length 100. $H$ increases up to $\rho = 75\%$; for $\rho > 75\%$, the DFA becomes degenerate causing $H$ to decrease again. (© MIT Press, used with permission, see Copyright Acknowledgments)

### 3.4.7  Comparison with Other Methods

Different methods (Alon et al., 1991; Frasconi et al., 1993, 1995; Horne and Hush, 1994; Minsky, 1967) for encoding DFAs with $n$ states and $m$ input symbols in recurrent networks are summarized in Table 3.1. The methods differ in the choice of the discriminant function (hard-limiting, sigmoidal, radial basis function), the size of the constructed network and the restrictions that are imposed on the weight alphabet, the neuron fan-in and fan-out. The results in (Horne and Hush, 1994) improve the upper and lower bounds reported in (Alon et al., 1991) for DFAs with only two input symbols. Those bounds can be generalized to DFAs with $m$ input symbols (Horne, 1994). Among the methods which use continuous discriminant functions, our algorithm uses no more neurons than the best of all methods, and consistently uses fewer weights and smaller fan-out size than all methods.

**Table 3.1** Comparison of different DFA encoding methods: The different methods use different amounts and types of resources to implement a given DFA with $n$ states and $m$ input symbols.

| Author(s) | Nonlinearity | Order | # Neurons | # Weights |
|---|---|---|---|---|
| Minsky (1967) | hard | first | $O(mn)$ | $O(mn)$ |
| Alon (1991) | hard | first | $O(n^{3/4})$ | — |
| Frasconi (1993) | sigmoid | first | $O(mn)$ | $O(n^2)$ |
| Horne (1994) | hard | first | $O(\sqrt{mn}\log n)$ | $O(mn\log n)$ |
| Frasconi (1996) | radial/sigmoid | first | $O(n)$ | $O(n^2)$ |
| Omlin (1996) | sigmoid | second | $O(n)$ | $O(mn)$ |

## 3.5 Extension to Fuzzy Domains

### 3.5.1 Preliminaries

There has been an increased interest in hybrid systems as more applications using hybrid models emerge. One example of hybrid systems is in combining artificial neural networks and fuzzy systems (Bezdek, 1992). Fuzzy logic (Zadeh, 1965) provides a mathematical foundation for approximate reasoning and has proven very successful in a variety of applications. Fuzzy finite-state automata (FFAs) have a long history (Dubois and Prade, 1980) and can be used as design tools for modeling a variety of systems (Cellier and Pan, 1995; Kosmatopoulos and Christodoulou, 1995). Such systems have two major characteristics: (1) the current state of the system depends on past states and current inputs, and (2) the knowledge about the system's current state is vague or uncertain.

A variety of implementations of FFAs have been proposed (Grantner and Patyra, 1994; Khan and Unal, 1995; Unal and Khan, 1994), some in digital systems. However, this is the first proof that such implementations in sigmoid activation RNNs are stable, i.e. guaranteed convergence to the correct prespecified membership (Omlin et al., 1998). Furthermore, this proof can be for different FFA representations, with and without fuzzy state representation: It is based on stably mapping deterministic finite-state automata (DFAs) into recurrent neural networks discussed above.

In contrast to DFAs, a *set* of FFA states can be occupied to *varying degrees* at any point in time; this fuzzification of states generally reduces the size of the model, and the dynamics of the system being modeled is often more accessible to a direct interpretation.

The proofs of representational properties of AI and machine learning structures are important for a number of reasons. Many users of a model want guarantees about what it can theoretically do, i.e. its performance and capabilities; others need this for use justification and acceptance. The capability of *representing* FFAs can be viewed as a foundation for the problem of *learning* FFAs from examples (if a network

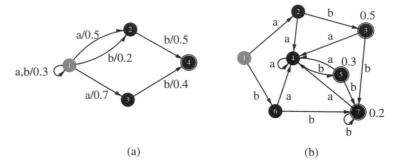

(a)                    (b)

**Figure 3.11**  Transformation of an FFA into its corresponding DFA: **(a)** A fuzzy finite-state automaton with weighted state transitions. State 1 is the automaton's start state; accepting states are drawn with double circles. Only paths that can lead to an accepting state are shown (transitions to garbage states are not shown explicitly). A transition from state $q_j$ to $q_i$ on input symbol $a_k$ with weight $\theta$ is represented as a directed arc from $q_j$ to $q_i$ labeled $a_k/\theta$. **(b)** corresponding deterministic finite-state automaton which computes the membership function strings. The accepting states are labeled with the degree of membership. Notice that all transitions in the DFA have weight 1.
(© IEEE Press, used with permission, see Copyright Acknowledgments)

cannot represent FFAs, then it certainly will have difficulty in learning them). A stable encoding of knowledge means that the model will give the correct answer (membership in this case) independent of when the system is used or how long it is used. This can lead to robustness that is noise independent. Finally, with the extraction of knowledge from trained neural networks, the methods presented here could potentially be applied to incorporating and refining *a priori* fuzzy knowledge in recurrent neural networks (Maclin and Shavlik, 1993).

### 3.5.2    Crisp Representation of Fuzzy Automata

The following result allows us to immediately apply the DFA encoding algorithm and stability analysis discussed above in order to map FFA states and state transitions into recurrent networks (Thomason and Marinos, 1974):

***Theorem 3.2***
Given a regular fuzzy automaton $M$, there exists a deterministic finite-state automaton $M'$ with output alphabet $Z \subseteq \{\theta : \theta \text{ is a production weight}\} \cup \{0\}$ which computes the membership function $\mu : \Sigma^* \to [0, 1]$ of the language $L(M')$.

An example of such a transformation is shown in Figure 3.11. In order to complete the mapping, we just need to compute the fuzzy membership function of strings.

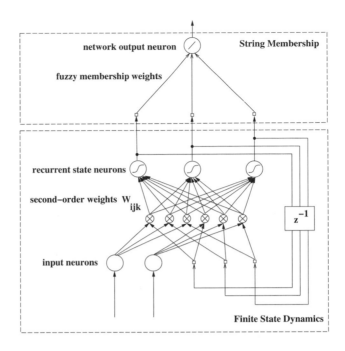

**Figure 3.12** Recurrent network architecture for crisp representation of fuzzy finite-state automata: The architecture consists of two parts: Recurrent state neurons encode the state transitions of the deterministic acceptor. These recurrent state neurons are connected to a linear output neuron which computes string membership.
(© IEEE Press, used with permission, see Copyright Acknowledgments)

The following lemma is useful:

**Lemma 3.1**
For the fixed points $\phi^-$ and $\phi^+$ of the sigmoidal discriminant, we have

$$\lim_{H \to \infty} \phi^- = 0 \ \ and \ \ \lim_{H \to \infty} \phi^+ = 1$$

Since exactly one neuron corresponding to the current automaton state has a high output at any given time and all other neurons have an output close to 0, we can simply multiply the outputs of all neurons by the fuzzy acceptance label of the corresponding automaton state and add up all values. Thus, we have the following result:

**Theorem 3.3**
Any fuzzy finite-state automaton $M$ can be represented in a second-order recurrent neural network with linear output layer which computes the fuzzy membership function of input strings with arbitrary accuracy.

An architecture for this mapping is shown in Figure 3.12. In order to empirically test our encoding methodology, we examine how well strings from randomly generated FFAs are classified by a recurrent neural network in which the FFA is encoded. We randomly generated deterministic acceptors for fuzzy regular languages over the alphabet $\{a, b\}$ with 100 states as follows: For each DFA state, we randomly generated a transition for each of the two input symbols to another state. Each accepting DFA state $q_i$ was assigned a membership $0 < \mu_i \leq 1$; for all non-accepting states $q_j$, we set $\mu_j = 0$. We encoded these acceptors into recurrent networks with 100 recurrent state neurons, two input neurons (one for each of the two input symbols 0 and 1), and one linear output neuron.

We measured their performance on 100 randomly generated strings of fixed length 100 whose membership was determined from their deterministic acceptors. The graphs in Figure 3.13 show the average absolute error of the network output as a function of the weight strength $H$ used to encode the finite-state dynamics for DFAs where 1%, 5%, 20%, 30%, 50% and 100% of all states had labels $0 < \mu_i \leq 1$. We observe that the error decreases exponentially with increasing hint strength $H$, i.e. the average output error can be made arbitrarily small. The DFA size has no significant impact on the network performance. The network performance depends on the stability of the internal representation of the finite-state dynamics; the value of $H$ for which the dynamics of all DFAs used in these experiments remains stable for strings of arbitrary length is approximately $H \simeq 9.8$. When the representation becomes unstable because the weight strength $H$ has been chosen too small, then that instability occurs for very short strings—typically less than five iterations.

We have also shown that network architectures such as shown in Figure 3.12 learn an internal representation of a deterministic acceptor when trained on fuzzy strings. A deterministic acceptor can then be extracted from a trained network using any of the known DFA extraction heuristics. Whether or not a *fuzzy* representation of an FFA can be extracted remains an open question.

### 3.5.3 Fuzzy FFA Representation

In this section, we present a method for encoding FFAs using a *fuzzy* representation of states. The method generalizes the algorithm for encoding finite-state transitions of DFAs. The objectives of the FFA encoding algorithm are (1) ease of encoding FFAs into recurrent networks, and (2) the direct representation of "fuzziness," i.e. the uncertainties $\theta$ of individual transitions in FFAs are also parameters in the recurrent networks. The stability analysis of recurrent networks representing DFAs generalizes to the stability of the fuzzy network representation of FFAs.

We extend the functionality of recurrent state neurons in order to represent fuzzy states as illustrated in Figure 3.14.

The main difference between the neuron discriminant function for DFAs and FFAs is that the neuron now receives as inputs the weight strength $H$, the signal $x$ which represents the collective input from all other neurons, and the transition weight $\theta_{ijk}$, where $\delta(a_k, q_j, \theta_{ijk}) = q_i$; we will denote this triple with $(x, H, \theta_{ijk})$.

The value of $\theta_{ijk}$ is different for each of the states that collectively make up the current fuzzy network state. This is consistent with the definition of FFAs.

The following generalized form of the sigmoidal discriminant function $g(\cdot)$ will be useful for representing FFA states:

$$S_i^{(t+1)} = \tilde{g}(x, H, \theta_{ijk}) = \frac{\theta_{ijk}}{1 + e^{H(\theta_{ijk} - 2x)/2\theta_{ijk}}}$$

Compared to the discriminant function $g(\cdot)$ for the encoding of DFAs, the weight $H$ which programs the network state transitions is strengthened by a factor $1/\theta_{ijk}$ ($0 < \theta_{ijk} \leq 1$); the range of the function $\tilde{g}(\cdot)$ is squashed to the interval $[0, \theta_{ijk}]$, and it has been shifted towards the origin. Setting $\theta_{ijk} = 1$ reduces the function to the sigmoidal discriminant function used for DFA encoding. More formally, the function $\tilde{g}(x, H, \theta)$ has the following important invariant property which will later simplify the analysis:

**Lemma 3.2**
$\tilde{g}(\theta x, H, \theta) = \theta \, \tilde{g}(x, H, 1)$.

Thus, $\tilde{g}(\theta x, H, \theta)$ can be obtained by scaling $\tilde{g}(x, H, 1)$ uniformly in the $x-$ and $y-$directions by a factor $\theta$.

The above property of $\tilde{g}$ allows a stability analysis of the internal FFA state representation similar to the analysis of the stability of the internal DFA state representation to be carried out.

We map FFAs into recurrent networks as follows: Consider state $q_j$ of FFA $M$ and the fuzzy state transition $\delta(a_k, q_j, \{\theta_{ijk}\}) = \{q_{i_1} \ldots q_{i_r}\}$. We assign recurrent state neuron $S_j$ to FFA state $q_j$ and neurons $S_{i_1} \ldots S_{i_r}$ to FFA states $q_{i_1} \ldots q_{i_r}$. The basic idea is as follows: The activation of recurrent state neuron $S_i$ represents the certainty $\theta_{ijk}$ with which some state transition $\delta(a_k, q_j, \theta_{ijk}) = q_i$ is carried out, i.e. $S_i^{t+1} \simeq \theta_{ijk}$. If $q_i$ is not reached at time $t+1$, then we have $S_i^{t+1} \simeq 0$.

We program the second-order weights $W_{ijk}$ as we did for DFAs with the exception that any neuron with a high output can drive the output of several other neurons to a high value. This encoding algorithm leaves open the possibility for ambiguities when an FFA is encoded in a recurrent network as follows: Consider two FFA states $q_j$ and $q_l$ with transitions $\delta(q_j, a_k, \theta_{ijk}) = \delta(q_l, a_k, \theta_{ilk}) = q_i$ where $q_i$ is one of all successor states reached from $q_j$ and $q_l$, respectively, on input symbol $a_k$. Further assume that $q_j$ and $q_l$ are members of the set of current FFA states, i.e. these states are occupied with some certainty. Then, the state transition $\delta(q_j, a_k, \theta_{ijk}) = q_i$ requires that recurrent state neuron $S_i$ have dynamic range $[0, \theta_{ijk}]$ while state transition $\delta(q_l, a_k, \theta_{ilk}) = q_i$ requires that state neuron $S_i$ asymptotically approach $\theta_{ilk}$. For $\theta_{ijk} \neq \theta_{ilk}$, we have ambiguity for the output range of neuron $S_i$:

**Definition 3.2**
We say an *ambiguity* occurs at state $q_i$ if there exist two states $q_j$ and $q_l$ with $\delta(q_j, a_k, \theta_{ijk}) = \delta(q_l, a_k, \theta_{ilk}) = q_i$ and $\theta_{ijk} \neq \theta_{ilk}$. An FFA $M$ is called *ambiguous* if an ambiguity occurs for any state $q_i \in M$.

However, there exists a simple algorithm which resolves these ambiguities by splitting each state for which an ambiguity exists into two or more new unambiguous states (Giles et al., 1999):

**Theorem 3.4**

Any FFA $M$ can be transformed into an equivalent, unambiguous FFA $M'$.

In order to prove the stability of a proposed fuzzy FFA encoding, we need to investigate under what conditions the existence of three fixed points of the fuzzy sigmoidal discriminant $g(\cdot)$ is guaranteed. See Equation (3) in Theorem 3.1. Fortunately, the following corollaries establish some useful invariant properties of the function $H_0(n, \theta)$:

**Corollary 3.2**

The value of the minimal $H(x, n, \theta)$ only depends on the value of $n$ and is independent of the particular values of $\theta$.

**Corollary 3.3**

For any value $\theta$ with $0 < \theta \leq 1$, the fixed points $[\phi]_\theta$ of the fuzzy discriminant function $g(x, H, \theta)$ have the following invariant relationship:

$$[\phi]_\theta = \theta \, [\phi]_1$$

Their significance is that (1) the fixed points of $\tilde{g}(\cdot)$ can be derived directly from the fixed points of a standard sigmoidal discriminant, and (2) we can use the same condition of Theorem 3.1 to guarantee the existence of three stable fixed points of the fuzzy sigmoidal discriminant function.

Applying the analysis technique from (Omlin and Giles, 1996a) to prove stability of the fuzzy internal representation of FFAs in recurrent neural networks yields the following result:

**Theorem 3.5**

For some given unambiguous FFA $M$ with $r$ states and $m$ input symbols, let $\theta_{min}$ and $\theta_{max}$ denote the minimum and maximum, respectively, of all transition weights $\theta_{ijk}$ in $M$. Then, a sparse recurrent neural network with $r$ states and $m$ input neurons can be constructed from $M$ such that the internal state representation remains stable if

$$(1) \quad [\phi_f^-]_1 < \frac{1}{r\,\theta_{max}} \left( \frac{1}{2} + \theta_{min} \frac{[\phi_f^0]_1}{H} \right)$$

$$(2) \quad [\phi_h^+]_1 > \frac{1}{\theta_{min}} \left( \frac{1}{2} + \theta_{max}[\phi_f^-]_1 + \frac{[\phi_f^0]_1}{H} \right)$$

$$(3) \quad H > max(H_0^-(r), H_0^+(r)) \, .$$

Furthermore, the constructed network has at most $3mr$ second-order weights with alphabet $\Sigma_w = \{-H, 0, +H\}$, $r + 1$ biases with alphabet $\Sigma_b = \{-H/2\}$, and

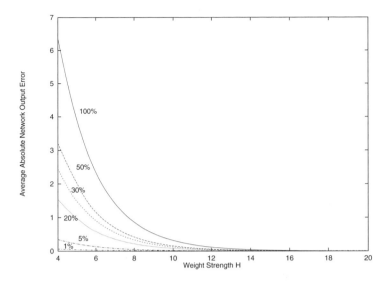

**Figure 3.13** Network performance: The graphs show average absolute error of the network output when tested on (a) 100 randomly generated strings of fixed length 100 and (b) on 100 randomly generated strings of length up to 100 as a function of the weight strength $H$ used to encode the finite-state dynamics of randomly generated DFAs with 100 states. The percentages of DFA states with $\mu_i > 0$ were 1%, 5%, 20%, 30%, 50% and 100% respectively, of all DFA states.
(© IEEE Press, used with permission, see Copyright Acknowledgments)

maximum fan-out $3m$.

For $\theta_{min} = \theta_{max} = 1$, conditions (1)-(3) of the above theorem reduce to those found for stable DFA encodings. This is consistent with a crisp representation of DFA states.

In order to validate our theory, we constructed a fuzzy encoding of a randomly generated FFA with 100 states (after the execution of the FFA transformation algorithm) over the input alphabet $\{a, b\}$. We randomly assigned weights in the range $[0, 1]$ to all transitions in increments of 0.1. We then tested the stability of the fuzzy internal state representation on 100 randomly generated strings of length 100 by comparing, at each time step, the output signal of each recurrent state neuron with its ideal output signal. Since each recurrent state neuron $S_i$ corresponds to a FFA state $q_i$, we know the degree to which $q_i$ is occupied after input symbol $a_k$ has been read: either 0 or $\theta_{ijk}$. A histogram of the differences between the ideal and the observed signal of state neurons for selected values of the weight strength $H$ over all state neurons and all tested strings is shown in Figure 3.15. As expected, the error decreases for increasing values of $H$. We observe that the number of discrepancies between the desired and the actual neuron output decreases 'smoothly' for the shown values of $H$—almost no change can be observed for values up to $H = 6$. The most significant change can be observed by comparing the histograms for $H = 9.7$

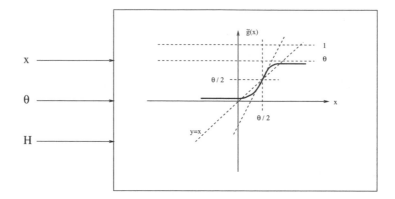

**Figure 3.14**  Fuzzy discriminant function for state representation: A neuron receives as input the collective signal $x$ from all other neurons, the weight strength $H$, and the transition certainty $\theta$ to compute the function $\tilde{g}(x, H, \theta) = \frac{\theta}{1+e^{H(\theta-2x)/2\theta}}$. Thus, the sigmoidal discriminant function used to represent FFA states has variable output range.

(© IEEE Press, used with permission, see Copyright Acknowledgments)

and $H = 9.75$: The existence of significant neuron output errors for $H = 9.7$ suggests that the internal FFA representation is unstable. For $H \geq 9.75$, the internal FFA state representation becomes stable. This discontinuous change can be explained by observing that there exists a critical value $H_0(r)$ such that the number of stable fixed points also changes discontinuously from one to two for $H < H_0(r)$ and $H > H_0(r)$, respectively.

The 'smooth' transition from large output errors to very small errors for most recurrent state neurons, Figures 3.15(a)-(e), can be explained by observing that not all recurrent state neurons receive the same number of inputs; some neurons may not receive any input for some given input symbol $a_k$ at time step $t$; in that case, the low signals of those neurons are strengthened to $\tilde{g}(0, H, \theta_{i.k}) \simeq 0$.

## 3.6  Learning Temporal Patterns with Recurrent Neural Networks

### 3.6.1  Motivation

It has become popular to use formal languages as testbeds for investigating fundamental issues, in particular computational capabilities and efficient learning algorithms. The advantages of using formal languages are (1) they represent temporal dependencies, (2) no feature extraction is necessary for learning, (3) they have a solid theoretical foundation and representation in the form of models of computation, and (4) they can serve as benchmark tests for new learning algorithms.

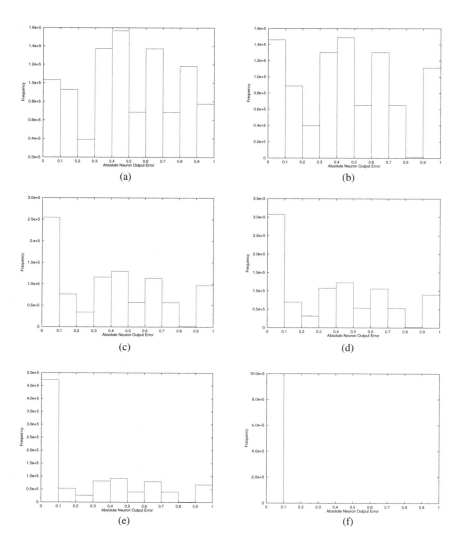

**Figure 3.15**   Stability of FFA state encoding: The histogram shows the absolute neuron output error of a network with 100 neurons that implements a randomly generated FFA, and reads 100 randomly generated strings of length 100 for different values of the weight strength $H$. The distribution of neuron output signal errors in increments of 0.1 are for weight strengths **(a)** $H = 6.0$, **(b)** $H = 9.0$, **(c)** $H = 9.60$, **(d)** $H = 9.65$, and **(e)** $H = 9.70$, and **(f)** $H = 9.75$.
(ⓒ IEEE Press, used with permission, see Copyright Acknowledgments)

### 3.6.2   Learning Algorithms

The two most popular learning algorithms for recurrent networks are real-time recurrent learning (RTRL) (Williams and Zipser, 1989) and backpropagation-through-time (BPTT) (Rumelhart et al., 1986). They are both gradient-descent learning algorithms and differ only in the manner in which the gradients are computed. The former computes the gradients in real-time as inputs are fed into a recurrent network whereas the latter unfolds the recurrent network in time and applies the backpropagation algorithm to this unfolded feedforward network. More recently, a new recurrent learning algorithm has been proposed which was designed to overcome some of the shortcomings of both RTRL and BPTT (Hochreiter and Schmidhuber, 1997). Although early results are very encouraging, it is too soon to say whether or not this new algorithm will fulfill its promise.

We will discuss the training algorithm for second-order recurrent networks introduced aboved. For a discussion of the training algorithms of other recurrent neural network models to recognize finite state languages, see for example (Cleeremans et al., 1989; Elman, 1990; Giles et al., 1992a; Horne et al., 1992; Mozer and Bachrach, 1990; Noda and Nagao, 1992; Pollack, 1991; Watrous and Kuhn, 1992b; Williams and Zipser, 1989). For a discussion of the training of neural networks to recognize context-free grammars and beyond, see for example (Allen, 1990; Das et al., 1992; Giles et al., 1990; Lucas and Damper, 1990; Pollack, 1990; Williams and Zipser, 1989).

### 3.6.3   Input Dynamics

We will discuss learning for second-order networks. Algorithms for first-order networks are analogous. Each input string is encoded into the input neurons one character per discrete time step $t$. Each hidden neuron $S_i$ in the above equation is updated to compute the next state vector **S** of the same hidden neurons at the next time step $t + 1$. This is why we call the recurrent network "dynamically-driven." Using a unary or one-hot encoding (Kohavi, 1978), there is one input neuron for each character in the string alphabet. After this the recurrent network is trained on strings generated by a regular grammar, it can be considered as a neural network finite state recognizer or DFA.

### 3.6.4   Real-Time On-Line Training Algorithm

For training, the error function and error update must be defined. In addition, the presentation of the training samples must be considered. The error function $E_0$ is defined by selecting a special "output" neuron $S_0$ of the hidden state neurons which is either on: $S_0 > 1 - \epsilon$, if an input string is accepted, or off: $S_0 < \epsilon$, if rejected, where $\epsilon$ is the tolerance of the response neuron. Two error cases result from this definition: (1) the network fails to reject a negative string, i.e. $S_0 > \epsilon$; (2) the network fails to accept a positive string, i.e., $S_0 < 1 - \epsilon$.

The error function is defined as:

$$E_0 = \tfrac{1}{2}(\tau_0 - S_0^{(f)})^2$$

where $\tau_0$ is the desired or *target* response value for the response neuron $S_0$. The target response is defined as $\tau_0 = 0.8$ for positive examples and $\tau_0 = 0.2$ for negative examples. The notation $S_0^{(f)}$ indicates the *final* value of $S_0$ after the final input symbol.

A popular training method is an on-line real-time algorithm that updates the weights at the end of each sample string presentation with a gradient-descent weight update rule:

$$\Delta W_{lmn} = -\alpha \, \tfrac{\partial E_0}{\partial W_{lmn}} = \alpha(\tau_0 - S_0^{(f)}) \cdot \tfrac{\partial S_0^{(f)}}{\partial W_{lmn}}$$

where $\alpha$ is the learning rate. We also add a momentum term $\eta$ as an additive update to $\Delta W_{lmn}$. To determine $\Delta W_{lmn}$, the $\partial S_i^{(f)}/\partial W_{lmn}$ must be evaluated. This training algorithm updates the weights at the *end* of the input string and should be contrasted to methods that train by predicting the next string (Cleeremans et al., 1989). From the recursive network state equation, we see that

$$\tfrac{\partial S_i^{(f)}}{\partial W_{lmn}} = g'(\Xi_i) \cdot \left[ \delta_{il} S_m^{(f-1)} I_n^{(f-1)} + \sum_{j,k} W_{ijk} I_k^{(f-1)} \tfrac{\partial S_j^{(f-1)}}{\partial W_{lmn}} \right]$$

where $g'$ is the derivative of the discriminant function. For the last time step $f$, replace $t$ and $t-1$ by $f$ and $f-1$. Note that this is a second-order form of the RTRL training method of Williams and Zipser (Williams and Zipser, 1989). Since these partial derivative terms are calculated one iteration per input symbol, the training rule can be implemented *on-line* and in *real-time*. The initial values are $\partial S_i^{(0)}/\partial W_{lmn}$ set to zero. Thus the error term is forward-propagated and accumulated at each time step t. Note that for this training algorithm each update of $\partial S_i^{(t)}/\partial W_{lmn}$ is computationally expensive and requires $O(N^4 \times K^2)$ terms. For $N >> K$, this update is $O(N^4)$ which is the same as a forward-propagated linear network. For scaling, it would be most useful to use a training algorithm that was not so computationally expensive such as gradient-descent back-propagation through time.

It is common to reinitialize the network state to a configuration at the beginning of each string which remains fixed throughout training. However, it is also possible to *learn* a network's initial state (Forcada and Carrasco, 1995).

### 3.6.5 Training Procedure

All strings used in training were accepted by the DFA in Figure 3.19(a) and Figure 3.1. This randomly generated automaton is minimal in size and has 4 accepting states with the initial state also a rejecting state. The training set consisted of the first 500 positive and 500 negative example strings. The presentation of strings was in alphabetical order, alternating between positive and negative examples (Elman,

1991; Giles et al., 1990; Porat and Feldman, 1991). The weights, unless initially programmed, were initialized to small random values in the interval $[-0.1, 0.1]$.

### 3.6.6    Deterioration of Generalization Performance

We observed that the generalization performance of recurrent networks tends to deteriorate for unseen strings of increasing lengths. This is due to the nonlinear dynamics of recurrent networks: Training a network on strings induces dynamical attractors such as fixed points and periodic orbits and trajectories between those attractors (these attractors and orbits correspond to DFA states and loops, respectively). These trajectories may deteriorate for strings that were not part of the training set. The deterioration becomes worse with increasing string length. Thus, the network dynamics may follow trajectories other than those induced through training. This can cause a network to output a wrong classification for some strings.

The problem of deterioration of generalization performance can be somewhat alleviated by continuously pruning and retraining a network that has found an initial solution (Giles and Omlin, 1994). We have found that pruning outperforms weight decay heuristics.

### 3.6.7    Learning Long-Term Dependencies

Even though recurrent neural networks have the computational capability to represent arbitrary nonlinear dynamical systems, gradient descent algorithms can have difficulties learning even simple dynamical behavior. This difficulty can be attributed to the problem of *long-term dependencies* (Bengio et al., 1994). This problem arises when the desired network output of a system at time $T$ depends on inputs presented at time $t << T$. In particular, it has been argued that if a system is to store information robustly, then the error information that the gradient contributes for inputs $n$ time steps in the past approaches zero as $n$ becomes large. Thus, the network will not remember inputs it has seen in the distant past that are crucial to computing the weight update.

Even though there exist no methods for completely eliminating the problem of vanishing gradient information, heuristics have been proposed which aim at alleviating the problem. These heuristics either address training data presentation and/or selection, or suggest ways in which to alter the basic network architecture.

For applications where input sequences of varying length are available in the training set (as was the case for learning regular languages), a data selection strategy which favors short strings in the early stages of training induces a good approximation of the desired long-term dynamical behavior of the recurrent network. Longer strings can then be used to refine that dynamical behavior. Similarly, partial prior knowledge about the desired dynamics (see Section 3.8) can facilitate the formation of the network behavior for longer strings (Giles and Omlin, 1993). In the absence of short training data or prior knowledge, other heuristics can be employed. Compression of the input history that makes global features more prominent is one way to lessen the problem of vanishing gradient information (Schmidhuber, 1992). The heuristic works well if input sequences contain local regularities that make them partially predictable. It fails, however,when such regularitiies are absent and when short-term dependencies are also important.

The above heuristics have all involved changing the presentation of the training data. One promising method which alters the network architecture in order to improve learning of long-term dependencies is the use of *embedded memory*; previous network states are stored and participate in the network's computation at pre-defined time-delay intervals. A comparison study has shown that the use of embedded memory (1) is universal in the sense that embedded memory can be added to any recurrent network architecture, and (2) the heuristic significantly enhances a network's ability to learn long-term dependencies (Lin et al., 1996a). An intuitive explanation can be given by observing that embedded memories provide a shorter path for propagation of gradient information since the stored states do not need to propagate through nonlinearities; thus, we eliminate the degradation of the error information. A special case of a network with embedded memory is the so called NARX architecture (Lin et al., 1996b). It uses a tapped delay line of previous network inputs and outputs. A different architectural modification proposes the use of high-order gates (Hochreiter and Schmidhuber, 1995). In benchmark tests, the method has been shown to be capable of bridging time intervals in excess of 1000 even in noisy learning environments. This is achieved by modifying the network architecture which enforces constant error flow of error information through special units. The heuristic, however, seems to have problems learning XOR type sequences, i.e. sequences where the presence (or absence) of a single input symbol changes the desired network output (Hochreiter, 1996).

## 3.7 Extraction of Rules from Recurrent Neural Networks

### 3.7.1 Cluster Hypothesis

Once the network is trained (or even during training), we want to extract meaningful internal representations of the network, such as rules. For related work on rule extraction from recurrent neural networks see (Cleeremans et al., 1989; Frasconi et al., 1991; Giles et al., 1992a; Watrous and Kuhn, 1992a; Zeng et al., 1993). The conclusion of (Cleeremans et al., 1989) was that the hidden unit activations represented past histories and that clusters of these activations can represent the states of the generating automaton. (Giles et al., 1992a) showed that a *complete deterministic finite-state automata and their equivalence classes* can be extracted from recurrent networks both *during and after training*. This was extended in (Giles et al., 1992b) to include a method for extracting bounded "unknown" grammars from a trained recurrent network. An alternative approach to state machine extraction was implemented by (Watrous and Kuhn, 1992b).

Since our interest is in "simple" production rules, we describe a heuristic for extracting rules from recurrent networks in the form of DFAs. Different extraction methods are described in (Cleeremans et al., 1989; Watrous and Kuhn, 1992b; Zeng et al., 1993). The algorithm we use is based on the observation that the outputs of the recurrent state neurons of a trained network tend to cluster in the neuron activation space, see Figure 3.16. The figure shows the outputs of two-dimensional projections of hidden neuron activations in the $(S_i, S_j)$-plane for all possible pairs $(S_i, S_j)$ (6 projections) for a well-trained 4-neuron recurrent network. This network was trained on strings from a 4-state DFA and tested on a small test set. If the recurrent network has learned a good representation of the DFA of the training set, then the same colors should cluster. For a hard-threshold logic neuron or gate, the clusters would represent points in the $N$ dimensional neuron space (Zeng et al., 1993). DFA extraction becomes identifying clusters in the output space $[0, 1]^N$ of all state neurons. We use a dynamical state space exploration which identifies the DFA states and at the same time avoids the computationally infeasible exploration of the entire space.

### 3.7.2   Extraction Algorithm

The extraction algorithm  divides the output of each of the $N$ state neurons into $q$ intervals or *quantization levels* of equal size, producing $q^N$ partitions in the space of the hidden state neurons. Starting in a defined initial network state, a string of inputs will cause the trained weights of the network to follow a discrete state trajectory connecting continuous state neuron values. The algorithm presents all strings up to a certain length in alphabetical order starting with length 1. This procedure generates a search tree with the initial state as its root and the number of successors of each node equal to the number of symbols in the input alphabet. Links between nodes correspond to transitions between DFA states. The search is performed in breadth-first order. Paths are made from one partition to another depending on the following: (1) When a previously visited partition is reached, then only the new transition is defined between the previous and the current partition, i.e. no new DFA state is created and the search tree is pruned at that node. (2) When an input causes a transition immediately to the same partition, then a loop is created and the search tree is pruned at that node. The algorithm terminates when no new DFA states are created from the string set initially chosen and all possible transitions from all DFA states have been extracted.

   Obviously, the extracted DFA depends on the quantization level $q$ chosen, i.e., in general, different DFAs will be extracted for different values of $q$. Furthermore, different DFAs may be extracted depending on the order of strings presented which leads to different successors of a node visited by the search tree. Usually these distinctions are not significant because the minimization algorithm (Hopcroft and Ullman, 1979) guarantees a unique, minimal representation for any extracted DFA. Thus, many different DFAs extracted for different initial conditions, different numbers of neurons, etc. collapse into *equivalence classes* (Giles et al., 1992a). Finally we must distinguish between accepting and nonaccepting states. If at the

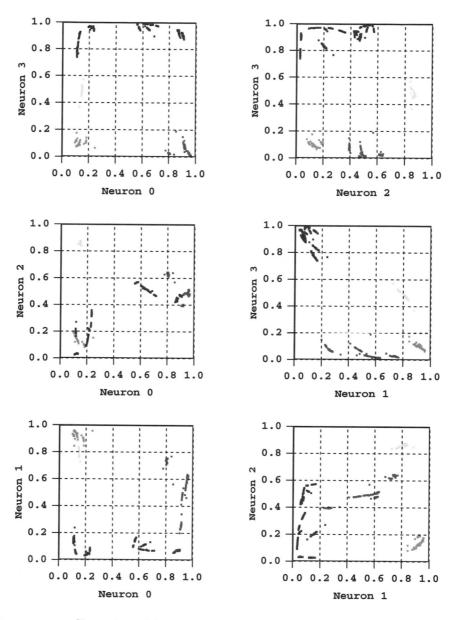

**Figure 3.10** Clustering of the states of a known DFA in hidden neuron state space. The network builds an internal representation of the learned DFA in the space of its hidden neurons. Two-dimensional projections of the hidden neuron state space $[0, 1]^4$ into the $(S_i, S_j)$-plane for all possible pairs $(S_i, S_j)$ are shown as the first 1024 strings are fed into the trained network. These clusters are the trained network's internal representation of the DFA's states. Transitions between clusters correspond to state transitions in the DFA.

(© Elsevier Science, used with permission, see Copyright Acknowledgments)

end of a string the output of the response neuron $S_0$ is larger than 0.5, the DFA state is accepting; otherwise, rejecting.

We believe that the extraction of DFAs from recurrent networks does not fit the decompositional class of extraction algorithms because the extraction relies on clustering of the state space of an *ensemble* of recurrent state neurons. The knowledge of the weights or activations of individual neurons is insufficient for extracting DFA states. The global (or input/output) behavior of the network is only used to label DFA states accept/reject but no learning is involved. Thus, our algorithm falls into the class of eclectic extraction methods within the taxonomy of (Andrews et al., 1995) which was extended in Chapters 1 and 2.

### 3.7.3  Example of DFA Extraction

An example of the extraction algorithm is illustrated in Figure 3.17. Assume a recurrent network with 2 state and 2 input neurons is trained on a data set. The range of possible values of $S_0$ and $S_1$ can be represented as a unit square in the $(S_0, S_1)$-plane. For illustration, choose a quantization level $q = 3$, i.e. the activation of each of the two state neurons is divided into 3 equal length intervals, defining $3^2 = 9$ discrete partitions. Each of these partitions corresponds to a hypothetical state in an unknown DFA. Assign labels *1, 2, 3, ...* to the partitions in the order in which they are visited for the first time.

The start state of the to-be-extracted DFA is the initial network state vector used in training—partition *1* in Figure 3.17(a) which is also an accepting state (denoted by a shaded circle) since the output of the response neuron ($S_0$) is larger than 0.5. On input '0' and '1', the network makes a transition into partitions *1* and *2*, respectively. This causes the creation of a transition to a new accepting DFA state 2 and a transition from state 1 to itself. In the next step, transitions occur from partition *2* into partitions *3* and *4* on input '0' and '1', respectively. The resulting partial DFA is shown in Figure 3.17(b). The DFA in Figure 3.17(c) shows the current knowledge about the DFA after all state transitions from states 3 and 4 have been extracted from the network. In the last step, only one more new state is created. See Figure 3.17(d). When the final string of this string set is seen, the extraction algorithm terminates. Notice that not all partitions have been assigned to DFA states. The algorithm usually only visits a subset of all available partitions for the DFA extraction. Many more partitions are reached when large test sets are used, especially when they contain many long strings, e.g. when measuring the generalization performance on a large test set. The extracted DFA can be transformed into a unique, minimized representation.

### 3.7.4  Selection of DFA Models

If several DFAs are extracted with different quantization levels $q_i$, then one or more of the extracted DFAs $M_{q_i}$ may be consistent with the given training set, i.e correctly classify the training set. To make a choice between different consistent

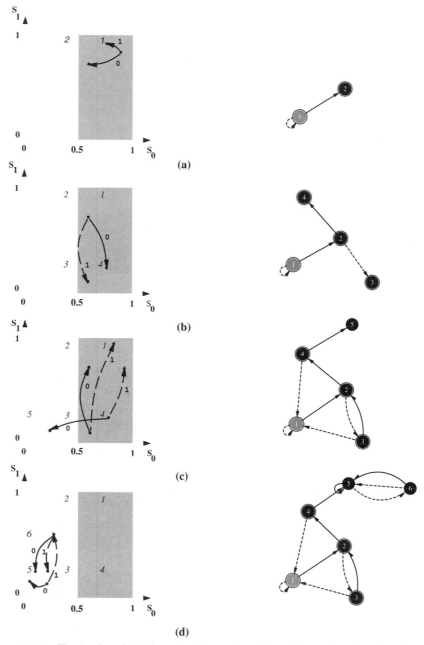

**Figure 3.17**   Example of DFA extraction algorithm. Example of extraction of a DFA from a recurrent network with 2 state neurons. The state space is represented as a unit square in the $(S_0, S_1)$-plane. The output range of each state neuron has been divided into 3 intervals of equal length resulting in 9 partitions in the networks state space. Shaded states are accepting states. The figures show the transitions performed between partitions and the (partial) extracted DFA at different stages of the extraction algorithm: **(a)** the initial state 1 and all possible transitions, **(b)** all transitions from state 2, **(c)** all transitions from states 3 and 4, and **(d)** all possible transitions from states 5 and 6.

DFAs, we devise a heuristic algorithm (Omlin et al., 1992).

Let $M$ denote the unknown DFA and $L(M)$ the language accepted by $M$. By choosing a particular quantization level $q_i$, we extract a minimized finite-state automaton, the *hypothesis* $M_{q_i}$ for the grammar to be inferred. A DFA $M$ is defined as *consistent* if it correctly classifies all strings of the training set; otherwise, it is an *inconsistent* model of the unknown source grammar. Given a set of consistent hypotheses $M_{q_1}, M_{q_2}, \ldots, M_{q_Q}$ we need a criterion for model selection that permits the choice of a hypothesis that best represents the unknown language $L(M)$. A possible heuristic for model selection would be to split a given data set into two disjoint sets (training and testing set), to train the network on the training set and to test the network's generalization performance on the test set. However, by disregarding a subset of the original data set for training, we may be eliminating valuable data from the training set which would improve the network's generalization performance if the entire data set were used for training. However, we wish to make a model selection based solely on simple properties of the extracted DFAs and not resort to a test set. (Keep in mind that all DFAs discussed here will accept strings of arbitrary length.) The model selection algorithm will be motivated by the simulation results and discussed next.

An example of model selection and performance is shown in Figure 3.18. Minimized DFAs are extracted from a trained network for quantization levels $q = 3$, $q = 6$ and $q = 8$. All three DFAs are consistent with the training set, i.e. they correctly classified all strings in the training set. But which DFA best models the unknown source $M$?

Simulations demonstrated that a policy for selecting a "good" model of the unknown source grammar can be formulated. We choose the DFA $M_s$ which is the smallest consistent DFA. $M_s$ can be found by extracting DFAs $M_2, \ldots, M_{s-1}, M_s$ in that order and the best model is the first consistent DFA $M_s$. We rely on the hypothesis that there always exists an $s$ such that $M_s$ is the smallest consistent DFA. This is an example of *Occam's Razor*—complex models should not be preferred over simple models that explain the phenomena equally well.

The quality of the extracted rules can be improved through continous network pruning and retraining (Giles and Omlin, 1994).

### 3.7.5 Controversy and Theoretical Foundations

As seen above, our DFA extraction algorithm depends on the discretization of the continuous state space into a finite number of regions. It has been argued (Kolen, 1994), that this approach to understanding the computation performed by recurrent neural networks is problematic for the following reasons: (1) Recurrent neural networks are nonlinear dynamical systems which are sensitive to initial conditions capable of producing nondeterministic machines: Their trajectories are determined by both the initial state of the network and the dynamics of the state transitions. Extraction methods which use single transitions between regions are insufficient because initially nearby states will become separated across several state

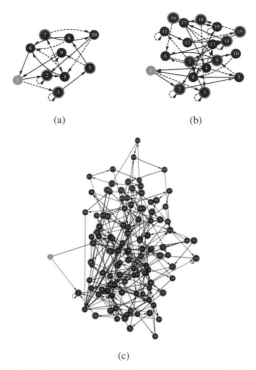

(a)                                    (b)

(c)

**Figure 3.18**  Examples of extracted DFAs. Minimized DFAs extracted from a trained network with quantization levels **(a)** q=3 **(b)** q=6 and **(c)** q=8. All three DFAs are consistent with the training set, i.e. they correctly classify each string in the set. Which DFA best models the unknown regular grammar? We contend DFA (a) because it has the least number of states.

(ⓒ Elsevier Science, used with permission, see Copyright Acknowledgments)

regions over time. Thus, no matter how fine a discrete quantization of the continuous state space we use, we eventually encounter the situation where an extracted state splits into multiple trajectories independent of the future input sequence; this is characteristic of a nondeterministic state transition. It is, at the very least, very difficult to distinguish between a nondeterministic automaton with few states and a deterministic automaton with a large number of states. (2) It is the observer's bias which determines that a dynamical system is equivalent to a finite-state automaton, i.e. trivial changes in observation strategies may result in a behavioral description from a range of complexity classes for a single system.

It has subsequently been shown analytically that objection (1) can be resolved by noting that sensitivity to initial conditions itself does not pose any problem for DFA extraction: If the reachable points in a partition state are mapped to more than one other partition state and the recurrent network robustly models some DFA, then the target partition states must be equivalent. Thus, the following result establishes the theoretical foundation for DFA extraction from recurrent networks:

**Theorem 3.6**

For recurrent neural networks that robustly model a given DFA, for sufficiently large quantization level $q$, it is sufficient to consider only partitions created by dividing each neuron's range into $q$ equal partitions to always succeed in extracting the DFA that is being modeled.

This follows from the observation that a recurrent neural network that robustly models some DFA must have mutually disjoint, closed sets that correspond to DFA states. An immediate consequence of the above result is the following corollary:

**Corollary 3.4**

A finite dimensional recurrent neural network can robustly only perform finite-state machine computations.

The above result follows from the observation that a network's phase space can only contain a finite number of disjoint sets due to its compactness. It is relevant in the context of on-going research on learning and extracting context-free languages from trained recurrent neural networks (Wiles and Bollard, 1996).

Objection (2) can be resolved by noting that we use models of sufficient complexity that adequately explain the given data. Even in cases where the dynamics underlying an unknown system are more complex than that of finite-state automata, this simple model may in some sense approximate the real dynamics and extraction of this model may offer important insights not available otherwise.

---

## 3.8   Recurrent Neural Networks for Knowledge Refinement

### 3.8.1   Introduction

The importance of using prior knowledge in a learning problem has been noted by many. (Minsky and Papert, 1969) state that *"... significant learning at significant success rate presupposes some significant prior structure. Simple learning schemes based on adjusting coefficients can indeed be practical and valuable when the partial functions are reasonably matched on the task ..."*. More recently, (Geman et al., 1992) have investigated the strengths and weaknesses of neural learning from a statistical viewpoint. In formulating the bias/variance dilemma, they conclude that *"... important properties must be built-in or hard-wired, perhaps to be tuned later by experience, but not learned in any statistical meaningful way"*. Recently, the use of prior knowledge about a learning task to be solved with a neural network has been studied by several authors.

Inserting *a priori* knowledge has been shown useful in training feed-forward neural networks, e.g. see Chapters 1, 2, 6 and (Abu-Mostafa, 1990; Berenji, 1991; Giles and Maxwell, 1987; Pratt, 1992; Suddarth and Holden, 1991; Towell et al., 1990b). The resulting networks usually performed better than networks that were trained without *a priori* knowledge. In the context of training feed-forward networks, it has been pointed out by (Abu-Mostafa, 1990) that using partial information about the implementation of a function $f$ which uses input-output examples may be valuable to the learning process in two ways: (1) It may reduce the number of functions that are candidates for $f$ and (2) it may reduce the number of steps needed to find the implementation. In related work, (Al-Mashouq and Reed, 1991) have trained feed-forward networks using hints, thus improving the learning time and the generalization performance; while Chapter 6 and (Towell et al., 1990a) show how approximate rules about a domain are translated into a feed-forward network.

Our focus has been on methods for inserting prior knowledge into dynamically-driven *recurrent* neural networks (Das et al., 1992; Frasconi et al., 1991, 1994; Giles and Omlin, 1992; Maclin and Shavlik, 1992; Omlin and Giles, 1992; Sanfeliu and Alquezar, 1992).The work by (Frasconi et al., 1991) inserts rules into first-order recurrent networks by solving a linear programming problem for the weights. The theoretical foundation for this approach is discussed in (Frasconi et al., 1994). However, (Goudreau et al., 1994) have shown that there exist simple deterministic finite-state automata which cannot be represented with a first-order, single-layer fully recurrent network architecture unless additional layers of weights (or an end symbol) are added. Giving the recurrent network helpful hints about the strings, such as too long, etc., has also been shown to help learning (Das et al., 1992). It is also useful to put rules directly into the sample strings themselves (Maclin and Shavlik, 1992).

We encode prior knowledge about the DFA using the algorithm presented in Section 3.4.2. The only difference is that we may not map entire DFAs into recurrent networks, but only *known* states and state transitions. These hints are encoded as rules which are then inserted *directly* before training into the *recurrence* of the neural network. We demonstrate the approach by training recurrent neural networks with *inserted rules* to learn to recognize regular languages from grammatical string examples. Our simulations show that training recurrent networks with different amounts of partial knowledge to recognize simple grammars usually improves the training time by orders of magnitude, even when only a small fraction of all transitions are inserted as rules. In addition there appears to be no loss in generalization performance.

When all known rule transitions have been inserted into the network by encoding the weights according to the above scheme, the network is trained. Notice that all weights including the ones that have been programmed are *still adaptable* - they are not fixed.

### 3.8.2   Variety of Inserted Rules

Rules (or DFAs) to be inserted prior to training are shown in Figures 3.19 and 3.20. They represent various amounts of prior information and also some incorrect prior knowledge.

For a baseline comparison, Figure 3.19(a) represents the entire rule set. Rules shown in Figures 3.19(b) and 3.19(c)-(f) represent respectively no knowledge of self-

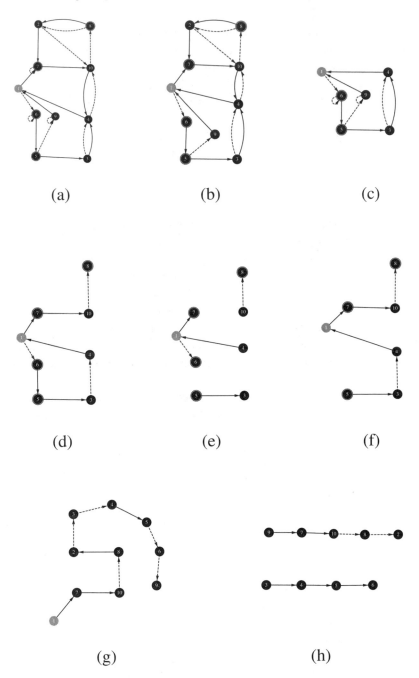

**Figure 3.19** Partial rules inserted into networks. Shown are the rules inserted into the recurrent neural network before training. State 1 is the start state. State transitions on input symbols '0' and '1' are shown respectively as solid and dashed arcs. The figures show: **(a)** all rules (entire DFA), **(b)** all rules except self-loops, **(c)** partial DFA, **(d)** rules for string '(10010)*001', **(e)** rules for disjointed transitions, **(f)** rules that do not start with a start state, **(g)** rules for string '001011011' without programming loop, **(h)** rules for separate strings '000' and '0011'

(© Carfax Publishing Ltd. used with permission, see Copyright Acknowledgments) loops and partial knowledge of complete segments of the DFA. Figures 3.19(g)-(h) represent strings that the DFA accepts but without knowledge of start or accepting states. In this sense these rules can be considered "incorrect." Figures 3.20(i)-(m) are very incorrect rules which we term "malicious."

We made the following significant observations: (1) The improvement in training times was roughly 'proportional' to the amount of correct, prior knowledge for a suitable choice of the weight strength $H$. (2) The generalization performances of networks trained with and without prior knowledge were comparable. (3) The inserted knowledge could also be extracted after network training. (4) The choice of the weight strength value $H$ had a significant impact on the training times. When small values were chosen for $H$, then the learning bias was not sufficiently strong for a significant speed-up. When $H$ was chosen too large, then the network had difficulties converging to a solution because the bias stifled the networks' variance necessary to converge to a solution. We investigated different methods for choosing a 'good' value for $H$. (1) Choosing the minimum value $H$ such that the encoded knowledge could also be extracted from the network prior to training, and (2) choosing $H$ such that the function $\frac{\partial E}{\partial H}$ had a maximum seemed to work well, i.e. the methods determined initial values for $H$ which compared favorably with the optimal value found through exhaustive search (Omlin, 1994).

The problem of changing incorrect rules has been addressed for rule-based systems (Ginsberg, 1988; Pazzani, 1989; Oursten and Mooney, 1990). We demonstrated that recurrent networks can be used successfully for rule verification and revision, i.e. inserted rules can be verified and also corrected. Rule verification consists of four stages: (1) Encode knowledge into the weights of a network. (2) Train the network on the data set. (3) Check the inserted rules by extracting rules in the form of DFAs from the trained network. (4) Compare the rules in the extracted DFA with the initial prior knowledge.

## 3.9  Summary and Future Research Directions

It has been argued that learning formal languages is not a well-suited application for neural networks, particularly since the languages learnt to date are generally simpler, e.g. in terms of the complexity of the corresponding grammar. We agree that, with current learning algorithms, neural networks cannot compete with algorithms that are tailored to the problem of grammatical inference. However, using theoretical models of computation as a testbed has led to the successful investigation of many fundamental issues. They include computational capabilities of different recurrent network architectures, knowledge representation, extraction of symbolic knowledge from trained networks, and use of prior knowledge for improved learning and generalization performance. Even though not all real-world applications can be cast into a symbolic domain, the lessons learned may be useful for nonsymbolic applications. Furthermore, some applications which at first glance seem incompatible with a symbolic interpretation, e.g. financial forecasting, may

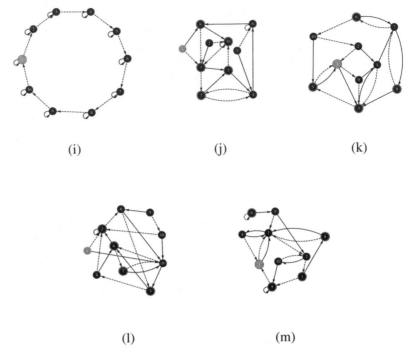

(i)                    (j)                    (k)

(l)                              (m)

**Figure 3.20  Malicious hints**: Rule **(i)**: DFA accepting all strings where the number of 1's is a multiple of 10. Rules **(j)**–**(m)**: Randomly generated DFAs with 10 states.
(© Carfax Publishing Ltd., used with permission, see Copyright Acknowledgments)

turn out to be amendable to a symbolic analysis after all, e.g. (Lawrence et al., 1997).

There are few real-world applications small enough such that neural networks alone could solve the problem. It is much more likely that neural networks will be successful as components of larger intelligent systems. The challenge for the near future lies in the design of such hybrid systems which requires that components such as neural networks interface with other technologies.

---

# Copyright Acknowledgments

Figure 3.1 reprinted from *IEEE Transactions on Neural Networks*, Vol 5, No 5, Giles, C.L. and Omlin, C.W., Pruning recurrent neural networks for improved generalization performance, 848–851, © (1994), with permission from the Institute of Electrical and Electronics Engineers.

Figures 3.2 and 3.3 reprinted from *IEEE Transactions on Neural Networks*, Vol 8, No 5, Clouse, D.S., Giles, C.L., Horne, B.G., and Cottrell, G.W., Time-delay neural networks: representation and induction of finite state machines, 1065–1070, © (1997), with permission from the Institue of Electrical and Electronics Engineers.

Figures 3.4-3.6 and some text of Sections 3.4.1-3.4.4 and Section 3.4.7 reprinted from *Journal of the ACM*, Vol 43, No 6, Omlin, C.W. and Giles, C.L., Constructing deterministic finite-state automata in recurrent neural networks. 937–972, © (1996), with permission from Association for Computing Machinery.

Figures 3.7-3.10 and some text of Sections 3.4.5-3.4.6 reprinted from Omlin, C.W. and Giles, C.L., *Neural Computation*, Vol 8, No 7, Stable encoding of large finite-state automata in recurrent neural networks with sigmoid discriminants, 675–696, © (1996), with permission from Massachusetts Institute of Technology.

Figures 3.11-3.13 and some text of Sections 3.5.1-3.5.2 reprinted from Omlin, C.W. Thornber, K.K., and Giles, C.L., *IEEE Transactions on Fuzzy Systems*, Vol 6, No 1, Fuzzy finite-state automata can be deterministically encoded into recurrent neural networks, 76–89, © (1996), with permission from Electrical and Electronics Engineers.

Figures 3.14-3.15 and some text of Section 3.5.3 reprinted from Omlin, C.W. Thornber, K.K., and Giles, C.L., *Proceedings of the IEEE, Special Issue on Computational Intelligence*, D. Fogel, (Ed), Equivalence in knowledge representation: automata, recurrent neural networks, and dynamical fuzzy systems, accepted for publication, © (1998), with permission from Electrical and Electronics Engineers.

Figures 3.16-3.18 and some text of Section 3.7 reprinted from Omlin, C.W. and Giles, C.L., *Neural Networks*, Vol 9, No 1, Extraction of rules from discrete-time recurrent neural networks, 41–52, © (1996), with permission from Pergamon Press.

Figures 3.19-3.20 and some text of Section 3.8 reprinted from Giles, C.L. and Omlin, C.W., *Connection Science*, Vol 5, No 3/4, Extraction, insertion and refinement of symbolic rules in dynamically driven recurrent neural networks, 307–337, © (1993), with permission from Carfax Publishing, 11 New Fetter Lane, London EC4P 4EE, United Kingdom.

# References

Abu-Mostafa, Y. S. 1990. Learning from hints in neural networks. *Journal of Complexity*, 6:192.

Al-Mashouq, K. A. and Reed, I. S. 1991. Including hints in training neural nets. *Neural Computation*, 3(4):418.

Allen, R. B. 1990. Connectionist language users. *Connection Science*, 2(4):279.

Alon, N., Dewdney, A. K., and Ott, T. J. 1991. Efficient simulation of finite automata by neural nets. *Journal of the Association for Computing Machinery*, 38(2):495–514.

Alquezar, R. and Sanfeliu, A. 1995. An algebraic framework to represent finite state machines in single-layer recurrent neural networks. *Neural Computation*, 7(5):931.

Andrews, R. and Diederich, J., eds. 1996. *Proceedings of the NIPS'96 Rule Extrac-*

*tion from Trained Artificial Neural Network Workshop*, Snowmass, Colorado.

Andrews, R., Diederich, J., and Tickle, A. B. 1995. Survey and critique of techniques for extracting rules from trained artificial neural networks. *Knowledge-based Systems*, 8(6):373–389.

Angluin, D. and Smith, C. H. 1983. Inductive inference: Theory and methods. *ACM Computing Surveys*, 15(3):237–269.

Baum, E. B. and Haussler, D. 1989. What size net gives valid generalization? *Neural Computation*, 1(1):151.

Bengio, Y., Simard, P., and Frasconi, P. 1994. Learning long-term dependencies with gradient descent is difficult. *IEEE Transactions on Neural Networks*, 5:157–166. Special Issue on Recurrent Neural Networks.

Berenji, H. R. 1991. Refinement of approximate reasoning-based controllers by reinforcement learning. In *Machine Learning, Proceedings of the Eighth International International Workshop*, eds. L. A. Birnbaum and G. C. Collins, pp. 475–479, San Mateo, CA. Morgan Kaufmann Publishers.

Bezdek, J., ed. 1992. *IEEE Transactions on Neural Networks—Special Issue on Fuzzy Logic and Neural Networks*, vol. 3. IEEE Neural Networks Council.

Cellier, F. E. and Pan, Y. D. 1995. Fuzzy adaptive recurrent counterpropagation neural networks: A tool for efficient implementation of qualitative models of dynamic processes. *J. Systems Engineering*, 5(4):207–222.

Cleeremans, A., Servan-Schreiber, D., and McClelland, J. 1989. Finite state automata and simple recurrent recurrent networks. *Neural Computation*, 1(3):372–381.

Clouse, D. S., Giles, C. L., Horne, B. G., and Cottrell, G. W. 1997. Time-delay neural networks: Representation and induction of finite state machines. *IEEE Transactions on Neural Networks*, 8(5):1065–1070.

Crutchfield, J. P. and Young, K. 1991. Computation at the onset of chaos. In *Proceedings of the 1988 Workshop on Complexity, Entropy and the Physics of Information*, ed. W. H. Zurek, pp. 223–269, Redwood City, CA. Addison-Wesley.

Cun, Y. L., Denker, J. S., and Solla, S. 1990. Optimal brain damage. In *Advances in Neural Information Processing Systems 2*, ed. D. S. Touretzky, San Mateo, CA. Morgan Kaufmann Publishers.

Cybenko, G. 1989. Approximation by superpositions of a sigmoidal function. *Mathematics of Control, Signals, and Systems*, 2:303–314.

Das, S., Giles, C. L., and Sun, G. Z. 1992. Learning context-free grammars: Limitations of a recurrent neural network with an external stack memory. In *Proceedings of The Fourteenth Annual Conference of the Cognitive Science Society*, pp. 791–795, San Mateo, CA. Morgan Kaufmann Publishers.

Deprit, E. 1989. Implementing recurrent back-propagation on the connection machine. *Neural Networks*, 2(4):295–314.

Dubois, D. and Prade, H. 1980. *Fuzzy sets and systems: theory and applications*, vol. 144 of *Mathematics in Science and Engineering*, pp. 220–226. Academic Press.

Elman, J. L. 1990. Finding structure in time. *Cognitive Science*, 14:179–211.

Elman, J. L. 1991. Incremental learning, or the importance of starting small. Tech. Rep. CRL Tech Report 9101, Center for Research in Language, University of California at San Diego, La Jolla, CA.

Fahlman, S. E. 1990. The cascade-correlation learning architecture. In *Advances in Neural Information Processing Systems 2*, ed. D. S. Touretzky, pp. 524–532, San Mateo, CA. Morgan Kaufmann Publishers.

Fahlman, S. E. 1991. The recurrent cascade-correlation architecture. In *Advances in Neural Information Processing Systems 3*, eds. R. P. Lippmann, J. E. Moody, and D. S. Touretzky, pp. 190–196, San Mateo, CA. Morgan Kaufmann Publishers.

Forcada, M. L. and Carrasco, R. C. 1995. Learning the initial state of a second-order recurrent neural network during regular-language inference. *Neural Computation*, 7(5):923–930.

Frasconi, P., Gori, M., Maggini, M., and Soda, G. 1991. A unified approach for integrating explicit knowledge and learning by example in recurrent networks. In *Proceedings of the International Joint Conference on Neural Networks*, vol. 1, p. 811. IEEE 91CH3049-4.

Frasconi, P., Gori, M., Maggini, M., and Soda, G. 1995. Representation of finite state automata in recurrent radial basis function networks. *Machine Learning*. In press.

Frasconi, P., Gori, M., Maggini, M., and Soda, G. 1996. Representation of finite state automata in recurrent radial basis function networks. *Machine Learning*, 23(1):5–32.

Frasconi, P., Gori, M., and Soda, G. 1993. Injecting nondeterministic finite state automata into recurrent networks. Tech. rep., Dipartimento di Sistemi e Informatica, Università di Firenze, Italy, Florence, Italy.

Frasconi, P., Gori, M., and Soda, G. 1994. Recurrent neural networks and prior knowledge for sequence processing: A constrained nondeterministic approach. *Knowledge-Based Systems*. Submitted.

Fu, K. S. 1982. *Syntactic Pattern Recognition and Applications*. Englewood Cliffs, N. J: Prentice-Hall.

Fu, L. M. 1994. Rule generation from neural networks. *IEEE Transactions on Systems, Man, and Cybernetics*, 24(8):1114–1124.

Fu, L. M. 1996. Learning capacity and sample complexity on expert networks. *IEEE Transactions on Neural Networks*, 7(6):1517–1520.

Geman, S., Bienenstock, E., and Dourstat, R. 1992. Neural networks and the bias/variance dilemma. *Neural Computation*, 4(1):1–58.

Giles, C. L., Chen, D., Sun, G. Z., Chen, H. H., Lee, Y. C., and Goudreau, M. W. 1995. Constructive learning of recurrent neural networks: limitations of recurrent cascade correlation and a simple solution. *IEEE Transactions on Neural Networks*. To be published.

Giles, C. L. and Maxwell, T. 1987. Learning, invariance, and generalization in high-order neural networks. *Applied Optics*, 26(23):4972.

Giles, C. L., Miller, C. B., Chen, D., Chen, H. H., Sun, G. Z., and Lee, Y. C. 1992a. Learning and extracting finite state automata with second-order recurrent neural networks. *Neural Computation*, 4(3):380.

Giles, C. L., Miller, C. B., Chen, D., Sun, G. Z., Chen, H. H., and Lee, Y. C. 1992b. Extracting and learning an unknown grammar with recurrent neural networks. In *Advances in Neural Information Processing Systems 4*, eds. J. E. Moody, S. J. Hanson, and R. P. Lippmann, pp. 317–324, San Mateo, CA. Morgan Kaufmann Publishers.

Giles, C. L. and Omlin, C. W. 1992. Inserting rules into recurrent neural networks. In *Neural Networks for Signal Processing II, Proceedings of The 1992 IEEE Workshop*, eds. S. Y. Kung, F. Fallside, J. A. Sorenson, and C. A. Kamm, pp. 13–22. IEEE Press.

Giles, C. L. and Omlin, C. W. 1993. Extraction, insertion and refinement of symbolic rules in dynamically driven recurrent neural networks. *Connection Science*, 5(3 & 4):307–337.

Giles, C. L. and Omlin, C. W. 1994. Pruning recurrent neural networks for improved generalization performance. *IEEE Transactions on Neural Networks*, 5(5):848–851.

Giles, C. L., Omlin, C. W., and Thornber, K. K. 1999. Equivalence in knowledge representation: Automata, recurrent neural networks and dynamical fuzzy systems. In *Proceedings of the IEEE (Special Issue on Computational Intelligence)*, eds. D. B. Fogel, T. Fukada, and L. Guan.

Giles, C. L., Sun, G. Z., Chen, H. H., Lee, Y. C., and Chen, D. 1990. Higher order recurrent networks & grammatical inference. In *Advances in Neural Information Processing Systems 2*, ed. D. S. Touretzky, pp. 380–387, San Mateo, CA. Morgan Kaufmann Publishers.

Ginsberg, A. 1988. Theory revision via prior operationalization. In *Proceedings of the Sixth National Conference on Artificial Intelligence*, p. 590.

Golden, E. M. 1978. Complexity of automaton identification from given data. *Information and Control*, 37:302–320.

Golea, M. 1996. On the complexity of rule-extraction from neural networks and network-querying. Tech. rep., Department of Systems Engineering, Australian National University, Canberra, Australia.

Goudreau, M. W., Giles, C. L., Chakradhar, S., and Chen, D. 1994. First-order vs. second-order single-layer recurrent neural networks. *IEEE Transactions on*

*Neural Networks*, 5(3):511–513.

Grantner, J. and Patyra, M. J. 1994. Synthesis and analysis of fuzzy logic finite state machine models. In *Proceedings of the Third IEEE Conference on Fuzzy Systems*, vol. I, pp. 205–210.

Hayashi, Y. and Imura, A. 1990. Fuzzy neural expert system with automated extraction of fuzzy if-then rules from a trained neural network. In *Proceedings of the First IEEE Conference on Fuzzy Systems*, pp. 489–494.

Hochreiter, S. 1996. Private communication.

Hochreiter, S. and Schmidhuber, J. 1995. Long short term memory. Tech. Rep. FKI-207-95, Fakultaet fuer Informatik, Technische Universitaet Muenchen.

Hochreiter, S. and Schmidhuber, J. 1997. Long short term memory. *Neural Computation*, 9(8):123–141.

Hopcroft, J. E. and Ullman, J. D. 1979. *Introduction to Automata Theory, Languages, and Computation*. Reading, MA: Addison-Wesley Publishing Company, Inc.

Horne, B. G. 1994. Personal Communication.

Horne, B. G. and Hush, D. 1994. Bounds on the complexity of recurrent neural network implementations of finite state machines. In *Advances in Neural Information Processing Systems 6*, pp. 359–366. Morgan Kaufmann.

Horne, B. G., Hush, D. R., and Abdallah, C. 1992. The state space recurrent neural network with application to regular grammatical inference. Tech. Rep. UNM Technical Report No. EECE 92-002, Department of Electrical and Computer Engineering, University of New Mexico, Albuquerque, NM, 87131.

Judd, S. 1987. Learning in networks is hard. In *Proccedings of the First IEEE Annual Conference on Neural Networks*.

Khan, E. and Unal, F. 1995. Recurrent fuzzy logic using neural networks. In *Advances in fuzzy logic, neural networks, and genetic algorithms*, ed. T. Furuhashi, Lecture Notes in Artificial Intelligence. Berlin: Springer Verlag.

Kohavi, Z. 1978. *Switching and Finite Automata Theory*. New York, NY: McGraw-Hill, Inc., 2nd edn.

Kolen, J. F. 1994. Fool's gold: Extracting finite state automata from recurrent network dynamics. In *Advanves in Neural Information Processing Systems 6*, eds. J. D. Cowan, G. Tesauro, and J. Alspector, pp. 501–508, San Francisco, CA. Morgan Kaufmann.

Kosmatopoulos, E. B. and Christodoulou, M. A. 1995. Neural networks for identification of fuzzy dynamical systems: Approximation, convergence, and stability and an application to identification of vehicle highway systems. Tech. rep., Department of Electronic and Computer Engineering, Technical University of Crete.

Kremer, S. C. 1995. On the computational power of Elman-style recurrent networks. *IEEE Transactions on Neural Networks*, 6(4):1000–1004.

Kremer, S. C. 1996. Comments on "constructive learning of recurrent neural networks": Cascading the proof describing limitations of recurrent cascade correlation. *IEEE Transactions on Neural Networks*.

Lang, K. J. 1992. Random DFAs can be approximately learned from sparse uniform examples. In *Proceedings of the Fifth ACM Workshop on Computational Learning Theory*, Pittsburgh, PA.

Lang, K. J., Waibel, A. H., and Hinton, G. E. 1990. A time-delay neural network architecture for isolated word recognition. *Neural Networks*, 3(1):23–43.

Lawrence, S., Fong, S., and Giles, C. L. 1996. Natural language grammatical inference: A comparison of recurrent neural networks and machine learning methods. In *Symbolic, Connectionist, and Statistical Approaches to Learning for Natural Language Processing*, eds. S. Wermter, E. Riloff, and G. Scheler, Lecture notes in AI, pp. 33–47. Berlin: Springer-Verlag.

Lawrence, S., Giles, C. L., and Tsoi, A. C. 1997. Symbolic conversion, grammatical inference and rule extraction for foreign exchange rate prediction. In *Proceedings of the Fourth International Conference on Neural Networks in the Capital Markets*, eds. A. S. W. Y. Abu-Mostafa and A.-P. N. Refenes. Singapore: World Scientific.

Lin, T., Horne, B. G., and Giles, C. L. 1996a. How embedded memory in recurrent neural network architectures helps learning long-term temporal dependencies. Tech. Rep. UMIACS-TR-96-28 and CS-TR-3626, Institute for Advanced Computer Studies, University of Maryland, College Park, MD.

Lin, T., Horne, B. G., Tino, P., and Giles, C. L. 1996b. Learning long-term dependencies in NARX recurrent neural networks. *IEEE Transactions on Neural Networks*, 7(6):1329–1338.

Lucas, S. and Damper, R. 1990. Syntactic neural networks. *Connection Science*, 2:199–225.

Maclin, R. and Shavlik, J. W. 1992. Refining algorithms with knowledge-based neural networks: Improving the Chou-Fasman algorithm for protein folding. In *Computational Learning Theory and Natural Learning Systems*, eds. S. Hanson, G. Drastal, and R. Rivest. MIT Press.

Maclin, R. and Shavlik, J. W. 1993. Using knowledge-based neural networks to improve algorithms: Refining the Chou-Fasman algorithm for protein folding. *Machine Learning*, 11:195–215.

Miclet, L. 1990. Grammatical inference. In *Syntactic and Structural Pattern Recognition; Theory and Applications*, eds. H. Bunke and A. Sanfeliu, chap. 9. Singapore: World Scientific.

Minsky, M. 1967. *Computation: Finite and Infinite Machines*, chap. 3, pp. 32–66. Englewood Cliffs, NJ: Prentice-Hall, Inc.

Minsky, M. L. and Papert, S. A. 1969. *Perceptrons*. Cambridge, MA: MIT Press.

Mozer, M. C. and Bachrach, J. 1990. Discovering the structure of a reactive environment by exploration. *Neural Computation*, 2(4):447.

Mozer, M. C. and Smolensky, P. 1989. Skeletonization: A technique for trimming the fat from a network via relevance assessment. In *Advances in Neural Information Processing Systems 1*, ed. D. S. Touretzky, pp. 107–115, San Mateo, CA. Morgan Kaufmann Publishers.

Noda, I. and Nagao, M. 1992. A learning method for recurrent networks based on minimization of finite automata. In *Proceedings International Joint Conference on Neural Networks 1992*, vol. I, pp. 27–32.

Omlin, C. W. 1994. *Symbolic Information in Recurrent Neural Networks: Issues of Learning and Representation*. Ph.D. thesis, Rensselaer Polytechnic Institute, Troy, NY.

Omlin, C. W. and Giles, C. L. 1992. Training second-order recurrent neural networks using hints. In *Proceedings of the Ninth International Conference on Machine Learning*, eds. D. Sleeman and P. Edwards, pp. 363–368, San Mateo, CA. Morgan Kaufmann Publishers.

Omlin, C. W. and Giles, C. L. 1996a. Constructing deterministic finite-state automata in recurrent neural networks. *Journal of the ACM*, 43(6):937–972.

Omlin, C. W. and Giles, C. L. 1996b. Extraction of rules from discrete-time recurrent neural networks. *Neural Networks*, 9(1):41–52.

Omlin, C. W. and Giles, C. L. 1996c. Rule revision with recurrent neural networks. *IEEE Transactions on Knowledge and Data Engineering*, 8(1):183–188.

Omlin, C. W., Giles, C. L., and Miller, C. B. 1992. Heuristics for the extraction of rules from discrete-time recurrent neural networks. In *Proceedings International Joint Conference on Neural Networks 1992*, vol. I, pp. 33–38.

Omlin, C. W., Thornber, K. K., and Giles, C. L. 1998. Fuzzy finite-state automata can be deterministically encoded into recurrent neural networks. *IEEE Transactions on Fuzzy Systems*, 6(1):76–89.

Oursten, D. and Mooney, R. J. 1990. Changing rules: A comprehensive approach to theory refinement. In *Proceedings of the Eighth National Conference on Artificial Intelligence*, p. 815.

Pazzani, M. J. 1989. Detecting and correcting errors of omission after explanation-based learning. In *Proceedings of the Eleventh International Joint Conference on Artificial Intelligence*, p. 713.

Pollack, J. B. 1990. Recursive distributed representations. *Journal of Artificial Intelligence*, 46:77.

Pollack, J. B. 1991. The induction of dynamical recognizers. *Machine Learning*, 7:227–252.

Porat, S. and Feldman, J. A. 1991. Learning automata from ordered examples. *Machine Learning*, 7(2-3):109.

Pratt, L. Y. 1992. Non-literal transfer of information among inductive learners. In

*Neural Networks: Theory and Applications II*, eds. R. J. Mammone and Y. Y. Zeevi. Academic Press.

Rumelhart, D. E., Hinton, G. E., and Williams, R. J. 1986. Learning internal representations by error propagation. In *Parallel Distributed Processing*, chap. 8. Cambridge, MA: MIT Press.

Sanfeliu, A. and Alquezar, R. 1992. Understanding neural networks for grammatical inference and recognition. In *Advances in Structural and Syntactic Pattern Recognition*, ed. H. Bunke. World Scientific.

Schmidhuber, J. 1992. Learning complex, extended sequences using the principle of history compression. *Neural Computation*, 4(2):234–242.

Shavlik, J. W. 1994. Combining symbolic and neural learning. *Machine Learning*, 14(3):321–331.

Siegelmann, H. T. and Sontag, E. D. 1995. On the computational power of neural nets. *Journal of Computer and System Sciences*, 50(1):132–150.

Sperduti, A. 1997. On the computational power of recurrent neural networks for structures. *Neural Networks*, 10(3).

Suddarth, S. and Holden, A. 1991. Symbolic neural systems and the use of hints for developing complex systems. *International Journal of Man-Machine Studies*, 34:291.

Sun, G. Z., Chen, H. H., Lee, Y. C., and Giles, C. L. 1991. Turing equivalence of neural networks with second order connection weights. In *1991 IEEE INNS International Joint Conference on Neural Networks—Seattle*, vol. II, pp. 357–362, Piscataway, NJ. IEEE Press.

Thomason, M. G. and Marinos, P. N. 1974. Deterministic acceptors of regular fuzzy languages. *IEEE Transactions on Systems, Man, and Cybernetics*, (3):228–230.

Tino, P. 1994. Personal communication.

Tino, P., Horne, B. G., and L.Giles, C. 1995. Finite state machines and recurrent neural networks – automata and dynamical systems approaches. Tech. Rep. UMIACS-TR–95–1, Institute for Advance Computer Studies, University of Maryland, College Park, MD 20742.

Towell, G. G., Craven, M. W., and Shavlik, J. W. 1990a. Constructive induction using knowledge-based neural networks. In *Eighth International Machine Learning Workshop*, eds. L. A. Birnbaum and G. C. Collins, p. 213, San Mateo, CA. Morgan Kaufmann Publishers.

Towell, G. G. and Shavlik, J. W. 1993. The extraction of refined rules from knowledge-based neural networks. *Machine Learning*, 13(1):71–101.

Towell, G. G. and Shavlik, J. W. 1994. Knowledge-based artificial neural networks. *Artificial Intelligence*, 70. To appear.

Towell, G. G., Shavlik, J. W., and Noordewier, M. O. 1990b. Refinement of approximately correct domain theories by knowledge-based neural networks. In

*Proceedings of the Eighth National Conference on Artificial Intelligence*, p. 861, San Mateo, CA. Morgan Kaufmann Publishers.

Tresp, V., Hollatz, J., and Ahmad, S. 1993. Network structuring and training using rule-based knowledge. In *Advances in Neural Information Processing Systems 4*, eds. C. L. Giles, S. J. Hanson, and J. D. Cowan, San Mateo, CA. Morgan Kaufmann Publishers.

Unal, F. A. and Khan, E. 1994. A fuzzy finite state machine implementation based on a neural fuzzy system. In *Proceedings of the Third International Conference on Fuzzy Systems*, vol. 3, pp. 1749–1754.

Watrous, R. L. and Kuhn, G. M. 1992a. Induction of finite-state languages using second-order recurrent networks. *Neural Computation*, 4(3):406.

Watrous, R. L. and Kuhn, G. M. 1992b. Induction of finite state languages using second-order recurrent networks. In *Advances in Neural Information Processing Systems 4*, eds. J. E. Moody, S. J. Hanson, and R. P. Lippmann, pp. 309–316, San Mateo, CA. Morgan Kaufmann Publishers.

Wiles, J. and Bollard, S. 1996. Beyond finite state machines: Steps towards representing and extracting context-free languages from recurrent neural networks. In *NIPS'96 Rule Extraction from Trained Artificial Neural Networks Workshop*, eds. R. Andrews and J. Diederich, p. 70.

Williams, R. J. and Zipser, D. 1989. A learning algorithm for continually running fully recurrent neural networks. *Neural Computation*, 1:270–280.

Zadeh, L. 1965. Fuzzy sets. *Information and Control*, 8:338–353.

Zeng, Z., Goodman, R. M., and Smyth, P. 1993. Learning finite state machines with self-clustering recurrent networks. *Neural Computation*, 5(6):976–990.

# 4 A Tutorial on Neurocomputing of Structures

Alessandro Sperduti

*In this chapter we present a tutorial on neural networks for the processing of structured information. Fundamental concepts on structured domains are first introduced. Then earlier work on representing data structures within traditional neural networks is briefly reviewed. This review introduces some basic concepts which are exploited to realize graph transductions. We discuss neural realizations of a specific class of graph transductions for the classification of labeled acyclic graphs. We show how the standard definition of neuron and neural learning algorithms can be extended to deal with structured domains. A section is then devoted to the case of cyclic graphs. In the second part of the chapter, computational and complexity results concerning this class of neural networks are reviewed. Almost all these results exploit Tree Automata Theory as a medium to assess the computational capabilities and functional complexity of this kind of neural network.*

## 4.1 Introduction

Structured representations are ubiquitous in different fields such as knowledge representation, language modeling and pattern recognition. Examples of application domains where structures are extensively used are medical and technical diagnoses, molecular biology, chemistry, automated reasoning, and so on.

While algorithms that manipulate symbolic information are capable of dealing with highly structured data, adaptive neural networks are usually regarded as learning models for domains in which instances are organized into *static* data structures, like records or fixed size arrays. Recurrent neural networks, that generalize feedforward networks to sequences (a particular case of dynamically structured data) are perhaps the best known exception.

Interest in developing connectionist architectures capable of dealing with these rich representations, as opposed to "flat" or vector-based representations, can be traced back to the end of the 80's (Touretzky, 1990; Pollack, 1990; Hinton, 1990; Plate, 1995; Smolensky, 1990). However, only during the last few years a general framework for the development of neural networks for the representation and processing of structures has been developed (Sperduti and Starita, 1997; Frasconi et al., 1998). In particular, these neural networks are a generalization of recurrent networks for processing sequences, i.e. linear chains from a graphical point of view, to the case of (mainly) directed acyclic graphs.

There are several reasons for being interested in processing of structures by neural networks. First of all, neural networks are universal approximators. Moreover, they are good classifiers and they are robust to the presence of noise. These capabilities are important when considering real-world applications in structured domains. In order to exemplify, let us consider the classification of labeled graphs which represent chemical compounds. The standard approach consists of encoding each graph $X$ as a fixed-size vector which is then given as input to a feedforward neural network for classification. This approach is motivated by the fact that neural networks only have a fixed number of input units while graphs are variable in size. The encoding process is usually defined *a priori* and does not depend on the classification task, e.g. in molecular biology and chemistry, the encoding process is performed through the definition of *topological indexes* (Hall and Kier, 1991), which are designed by a very expensive trial and error approach.

The *a priori* definition of the encoding process faces the *specificity-generality dilemma*, i.e. if the encoding is too specific, new features must be devised (by suitable experts) for each new computational problem; on the other hand, if the encoding is too general, the representing features are weakly relevant with respect to the specific target and so they turn out to be difficult to classify. To overcome the dilemma, the encoding process should be adapted automatically to the specific classification task at hand. This can be done by implementing the encoding process through an additional neural network which is trained, alongside the neural network performing the classification, to learn the best way to encode the graphs for the given classification task.

Of course, neither standard neurons nor recurrent neurons are powerful enough to be used in such a network. This is because the former were devised for processing unstructured patterns, while the latter can only naturally process sequences. However, by extending the concept of recurrent neuron it is possible to formalize several supervised models for the classification of structures which stem very naturally from well known models, such as Backpropagation Through Time networks, Real-Time Recurrent networks, Simple Recurrent networks, Recurrent Cascade-Correlation networks, and Neural Trees.

When developing a new computational model, it is important to understand its computational power and complexity. This evaluation is typically done by resorting to known results in related models. For example, it is well known that recurrent neural networks can simulate any finite-state automata (Alon et al., 1991; Omlin and Giles, 1996) as well as any multi-stack Turing machine in real time (Siegelmann and Sontag, 1995). When constraining the network architecture, however, this computational power may no longer hold. For example, Elman-style Recurrent Networks can simulate any finite-state automata (Goudreau et al., 1994;

Kremer, 1995), while Recurrent Cascade-Correlation networks cannot (Giles et al., 1995; Kremer, 1996). Here we discuss the computational capabilities of Elman-style Recurrent Networks, Recurrent Cascade Correlation networks, and Neural Trees with respect to the classification of structures. We will relate them to Frontier-to-Root Tree Automata (FRA) (Thatcher, 1973; Gonzalez and Thomason, 1978) and show that Elman-style Recurrent Networks can simulate any FRA, while neither Cascade-Correlation networks, nor Neural Trees can. Moreover, we briefly report a known result which states that, if the set of possible labels (alphabet) is finite, then any mapping from trees to the set of reals can be implemented by a neural network for structures having a sufficient number of parameters.

Computational complexity of the model is important as well. Here we give both upper and lower bounds on the number of neurons (or connections) needed to implement an arbitrary frontier-to-root Tree Automaton into the most powerful model. Some results on the complexity of learning are sketched as well.

## 4.2   Basic Concepts

Here we consider structured domains which are sets of annotated directed ordered graphs (DOGs). A DOG is a directed graph $Y$ with vertex set vert$(Y)$ and edge set $edg(Y)$, where for each vertex $v \in$ vert$(Y)$ a total order on the edges leaving from $v$ is defined. Moreover, vertices are annotated by labels which are tuples of variables. The void DOG will be denoted by the special symbol $\xi$.

For example, in the case of graphs representing logical terms with variables, denoted by capital letters, the order on outgoing edges is immediately induced by the order of the arguments to a function; e.g. the logical term `f(X,g(X,c))` can be represented as

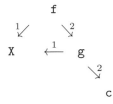

Note that, since the variable X is shared, a single node is used to represent it.

In problems of structure classification, we shall require the DOG either to be empty or to possess a supersource, i.e. a vertex $s \in$ vert$(Y)$ such that every vertex in vert$(Y)$ can be reached by a directed path starting from $s$. Note that if a DOG does not possess a supersource, it is still possible to define a convention for adding an extra vertex $s$ (with a minimal number of outgoing edges), such that $s$ is a supersource for the expanded DOG (Sperduti and Starita, 1997). When considering a DOAG, i.e. an acyclic DOG, the function $source(Y)$ returns the unique supersource of $Y$. We also assume that a convention is defined in such a way that, given a cyclic DOG, the function *source*($\boldsymbol{Y}$) returns a predetermined supersource within the set of supersources[1].

Given a DOAG $\boldsymbol{Y}$ and $v \in \text{vert}(\boldsymbol{Y})$, we denote by pa[$v$] the set of parents of $v$, by ch[$v$] the set of children of $v$, by de[$v$] the set of descendants of $v$, and by an[$v$] the set of ancestors of $v$. We will use the notation $\text{ch}_j[v]$ to refer to the $j$-th child of $v$. The *indegree* of $v$ is the cardinality of the set pa[$v$] the *outdegree* of $v$ is the cardinality of the set ch[$v$]. In the following, we shall denote by $\#^{(i,o)}$ the class of DOAGs with maximum indegree $i$ and maximum outdegree $o$. In our logical terms example, the maximum outdegree corresponds to the maximum arity of the functions being considered, e.g. the maximum outdegree of f(X,g(X,c)) is 2. A generic class of DOAGs with bounded (but unspecified) indegree and outdegree, will simply be denoted by $\#$.

Subscript notation will be used when referencing the labels attached to vertices in a data structure. Hence $\boldsymbol{Y}_v$ denotes the set of variables labeling vertex $v \in \text{vert}(\boldsymbol{Y})$.

Given a data structure $\boldsymbol{Y}$, the DOG obtained by ignoring all node labels will be referred to as the *skeleton* of $\boldsymbol{Y}$, denoted skel($\boldsymbol{Y}$). Clearly, any two data structures can be distinguished because they have different skeletons, or, if they have the same skeleton, because they have different node labels. The class of all data structures defined over the label universe domain $\mathcal{Y}$ and skeleton in $\#^{(i,o)}$ will be denoted as $\mathcal{Y}^{\#^{(i,o)}}$.

We define a *structured domain* $\mathcal{D}$, over the set of labels $\Sigma$, as any (possibly infinite) set of graphs over $\Sigma$. The *valence of a domain* $\mathcal{D}$ is defined as the maximum among the out-degrees of the graphs belonging to $\mathcal{D}$.

Since we deal with learning, we need to define the target function we want to learn. In approximation tasks, a *target function* $d(\cdot)$ over $\mathcal{D}^{\#}$ is defined as any function $d : \mathcal{D}^{\#} \to \mathbb{R}^k$, where $k$ is the output dimension, while in (binary) classification tasks we have $d : \mathcal{D}^{\#} \to \{0,1\}^k$, i.e. $d : \mathcal{D}^{\#} \to \{-1,1\}^k$. A training set $T$ on a domain $\mathcal{D}^{\#}$ is defined as a set of couples $(\boldsymbol{X}, d(\boldsymbol{X}))$, where $\boldsymbol{X} \in \mathcal{U}^{\#} \subseteq \mathcal{D}^{\#}$ and $d(\cdot)$ is a target function defined on $\mathcal{D}^{\#}$.

Finally, for the sake of completeness, here we recall the basic definitions of standard and recurrent neurons. The output $o^{(s)}$ of a standard neuron is given by

$$o^{(s)} = f(\sum_i w_i I_i), \tag{4.1}$$

where $f(\cdot)$ is some non-linear squashing function applied to the weighted sum[2] of inputs $I$. A recurrent neuron with a single self-recurrent connection, on the other

---

1. A cyclic graph may have several supersources.
2. The threshold of the neuron is included in the weight vector by always expanding the input vector with a component equal to 1.

hand, computes its output $o^{(r)}(t)$ as follows

$$o^{(r)}(t) = f(\sum_i w_i I_i(t) + w_s o^{(r)}(t-1)), \tag{4.2}$$

where $f(\cdot)$ is applied to the weighted sum of inputs $I$ plus the self-weight, $w_s$, times the previous output. The above formula can be extended by considering both several interconnected recurrent neurons and delayed versions of the outputs (Haykin, 1994).

## 4.3 Representing Structures in Neural Networks

Structures may be represented in a neural network by using either a *localist representation* or a *distributed representation*. In the localist representation each neuron represents a component of the structure, while each connection represents a relation between components. This way of representing structures is trivial and not efficient, since different structures need to be represented by different networks. For this reason, several researchers have developed neural systems using different types of distributed representation, such as in DCPS (Touretzky and Hinton, 1988), Boltz-CONS (Touretzky, 1990), Tensor Products (Smolensky, 1990), RAAM (Pollack, 1990) and LRAAM (Sperduti, 1994a,b), Convolution-based models (CHARM (Metcalfe, 1991), TODAM2 (Murdock, 1993)) and Holographic Reduced Representations (Plate, 1995). In the following we discuss the RAAM family of models, since they can be considered the precursors of the models presented in this chapter.

### 4.3.1 The RAAM Family

The task of a network in the RAAM family (Sperduti and Starita, 1996) consists of devising a reduced descriptor for each structure (and substructure) in a given set of structures, i.e. the training set. Hinton first introduced the concept of the reduced descriptor (Hinton, 1990). The basic idea is to represent complex conceptual structures in distributed representations. These representations, however, should satisfy four desiderata:

1. **Representational adequacy:** It should be possible to reconstruct the full representation of the structure from the reduced descriptor;

2. **Reduction:** The reduced descriptor should require the allocation of fewer units than the full explicit representation of the structure;

3. **Systematicity**: The reduced descriptor should be related in a systematic way to the full representation;

4. **informativeness**: The reduced descriptor should tell us something about the concept that it refers to, without it being necessary to reconstruct the full representation.

All these desiderata are satisfied by the networks in the RAAM family; see Figure 4.1. Depending on the nature of the structures at hand and on how they are represented, different networks of the RAAM family can be used. A standard RAAM network is able to generate reduced descriptors for trees with information stored in the leaves; an SRAAM network is, instead, suited for lists and an LRAAM network (which is a generalization of the SRAAM network) can deal with labeled directed graphs.

The general form of a neural network of the RAAM family is defined by a $N_I - N_H - N_O$ feedforward encoder network, where both the input and output layers are partitioned in one label field and $n$ reduced descriptor (pointer) fields, i.e. $N_I = N_O = N_l + nN_H$, where $N_l \geq 0$ is the size of the label field; moreover, the reduced descriptor fields and the hidden layer have the same size. In this formulation, the network for a RAAM network is obtained by setting $N_l = 0$ and the network for an SRAAM by setting $n = 1$. The set of equations describing the network are as follows:

$$\boldsymbol{F}_E(\vec{i}) = \boldsymbol{F}(E\vec{i} + \vec{\theta}_H) \equiv \vec{h}, \qquad (4.3)$$

$$\boldsymbol{F}_D(\vec{h}) = \boldsymbol{F}(D\vec{h} + \vec{\theta}_O) \equiv \vec{o}, \qquad (4.4)$$

where $\vec{h}, \vec{\theta}_H \in \mathbb{R}^{N_H}$, $\vec{o}, \vec{i}, \vec{\theta}_O \in \mathbb{R}^{N_l+nN_H}$, $\boldsymbol{F}(\vec{i})_j = f(\vec{i}_j)$, and $f(\cdot)$ is a sigmoid-shaped function. The vectors $\vec{\theta}_H$ and $\vec{\theta}_O$ are the bias vectors for the hidden and output layers, respectively, $\vec{i}$ is the input pattern to the network, $\vec{h}$ is the hidden activation, and $\vec{o}$ is the output of the network. The matrix $E \in \mathbb{R}^{N_H \times N_I}$ is the Encoding matrix, i.e. the weight matrix between the input layer ($N_I = N_l + nN_H$ units) and the hidden layer ($N_H$ units); and $D \in \mathbb{R}^{N_O \times N_H}$ is the Decoding matrix, i.e. the weight matrix between the hidden layer and the output layer ($N_O = N_I$). In the following, the index $t$ will vary on the output units, $s$ on the hidden units, and $q$ on the input units.

A pattern[3] in the training set of a general RAAM network assumes the form $\vec{p} = [\vec{c}_1, \ldots, \vec{c}_m]$, where $\vec{c}_j \in \mathbb{R}^{N_H}$ can be either a reduced descriptor or a label. When considering an SRAAM network the typical form of a pattern becomes $\vec{p} = [\vec{l}, \vec{rd}]$, where $\vec{l} \in \mathbb{R}^{N_l}$ is a label and $\vec{rd} \in \mathbb{R}^{N_H}$ is a reduced descriptor. An LRAAM network generalizes this form, allowing multiple reduced descriptors: $\vec{p} = [\vec{l}, \vec{rd}_1, \ldots, \vec{rd}_k]$.

The learning algorithm for RAAM and SRAAM networks was originally developed by J. B. Pollack and it essentially remains the same for the LRAAM (Pollack, 1990). The algorithm combines a standard gradient descent with a dynamical adaptation of the training set. Specifically, the goal of the gradient descent consists of

---

3. For the sake of notation, in the following, we omit the transpose operator: the notation $\vec{p} = [\vec{y}_1, \ldots, \vec{y}_k]$ must be read as $\vec{p}^{\,t} = [\vec{y}_1^{\,t}, \ldots, \vec{y}_k^{\,t}]$.

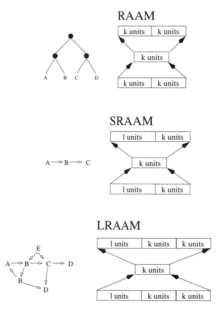

**Figure 4.1** The models belonging to the RAAM family: The RAAM is able to encode trees with labels on the leaves, the SRAAM encodes sequences, while the LRAAM is able to encode labeled directed graphs.

minimizing the following cost function:

$$C_0 = \frac{1}{2} \sum_k^P \|\vec{p}^{\,(k)} - \boldsymbol{F}_D(\boldsymbol{F}_E(\vec{p}^{\,(k)}))\|^2, \tag{4.5}$$

where $P$ is the number of patterns (substructures) in the training set.

If the learning is able to reach zero error, then the network implements a perfect compressor-reconstructor couple for the training set. Furthermore, if each reduced descriptor $\vec{rd}^{\,(k)}$ in the training set is equal to $\vec{h}^{(k)} = \boldsymbol{F}_E(\vec{p}^{\,(k)})$, then the network is also a member of the RAAM family, in the sense that each reduced descriptor retains all the information contained in the pattern $\vec{p}^{\,(k)}$. In fact, this information can be reconstructed by decoding $\vec{rd}^{\,(k)}$, i.e. $\vec{p}^{\,(k)} = \boldsymbol{F}_D(\vec{rd}^{\,(k)})$. Pollack's algorithm fulfills this constraint by modifying the training set during learning: at each epoch of learning every reduced descriptor $\vec{rd}^{\,(k)}$ is replaced by the corresponding hidden layer activity $\vec{h}^{(k)}$. Note that, this technique guarantees the consistency of the model only at global minima of $C_0$. Practically, however, even a point in the weights space which is in the proximity of a global minimum works well.

For LRAAM networks, this author introduced an additional learning rule for dealing with void descriptors (Sperduti, 1994b). This rule is necessary because in LRAAM networks there is no commitment to a particular representation for the void descriptor, i.e. the void descriptor can get multiple representations. These representations are distinguished from non-void descriptors thanks to a void condition bit allocated in the label for each reduced descriptor field of the network. The learning rule for void descriptors consists of copying the output representations for the void descriptor into the training set at each epoch of learning.

The main theoretical concern about Pollack's algorithm (and its LRAAM generalization) is whether it is possible to give it a better mathematical characterization, since an improved understanding of the underpinning mathematics should eventually either help in improving the efficiency of the algorithm or in disclosing the limitations of the RAAM family.

## 4.4   From Graph Representation to Graph Transductions

In the previous section, we discussed a specific way of representing labeled graphs within a RAAM neural network. The basic idea is to implement a mechanism for encoding the graph into a vectorial representation, preserving all the information needed for subsequent decoding of the vectorial representation in order to reconstruct the original graph. In this section, we discuss how the encoding function can be fruitfully combined with a transformation to obtain a specific type of graph transduction[4].

A functional graph transduction $\mathcal{T} : \mathcal{I} \to \mathcal{O}$ is defined as a mapping from an input structured domain $\mathcal{I}$ (over $\Sigma_{\mathcal{I}}$) to an output structured domain $\mathcal{O}$ (over $\Sigma_{\mathcal{O}}$). A special case of transduction that we will consider is the one where $\mathcal{O}$ is the trivial set of structures compounded by a single labeled node. In fact, it is not difficult to recognize that when this is the case, with $\Sigma_{\mathcal{O}} = \{0, 1\}$, the transduction can be interpreted as a classification function of the structures in $\mathcal{I}$.

In general, however, graph transductions can assume several forms. For the purpose of this chapter we mainly focus on the class of transductions, defined on domains of DOAGS with supersources, which can be represented in the following form

$$\mathcal{T} = g \circ \hat{\tau} \tag{4.6}$$

where $g$ is the *output* function and $\hat{\tau}$ is the *encoding* (or *state transition*) function. Specifically, $\hat{\tau}$ is defined recursively as

$$\hat{\tau}(\boldsymbol{Y}) = \begin{cases} nil & \text{if } \boldsymbol{Y} = \xi \\ \tau(s, \boldsymbol{Y}_s, \hat{\tau}(\boldsymbol{Y}^{(1)}), \ldots, \hat{\tau}(\boldsymbol{Y}^{(o)})) & \text{otherwise} \end{cases} \tag{4.7}$$

where $\tau : vert(\mathcal{I}^{\#}) \times \mathcal{I} \times \mathcal{X}^o \to \mathcal{X}$ is the *c-model* function, $s = source(\boldsymbol{Y})$, $nil \in \mathcal{X}$ is used to represent the void graph, and $\boldsymbol{Y}^{(1)}, \ldots, \boldsymbol{Y}^{(o)}$ are the subgraphs pointed

---

4. Some experimental results obtained on combining an LRAAM network with a perceptron are reported in (Sperduti et al., 1995).

to by $s$, i.e. $source(\boldsymbol{Y}^{(i)}) = ch_i[s]$. The function $\tau$ is called a c-model function since it defines a computational model for the encoding function.

Note that, because of Equation 4.7, $\mathcal{T}$ is *causal* since $\tau$ only depends on the current node and nodes descending from it. Moreover, when $\tau$ does not depend on any specific vertex, i.e. $\tau(\boldsymbol{Y}_s, \hat{\tau}(\boldsymbol{Y}^{(1)}), \ldots, \hat{\tau}(\boldsymbol{Y}^{(o)}))$, then $\mathcal{T}$ is also *stationary transduction*. We will mainly focus on stationary transductions.

Of course, for general DOGs, the above definition of $\hat{\tau}(\cdot)$ is not adequate. In Section 4.8 we will also discuss how to deal with cyclic DOGs.

**Example 4.1**
Given a stationary encoding function $\hat{\tau}$, the encoding of the labeled structure

$$
\begin{array}{c}
\phantom{xxxx} b \\
\phantom{xxx} {\scriptstyle 1}\nearrow \\
a \\
\phantom{xxx} {\scriptstyle 2}\searrow \\
\phantom{xxxxxx} c \xrightarrow{1} a
\end{array}
$$

is defined by the following set of equations

$$
\hat{\tau}\left(
\begin{array}{c}
b \\
{\scriptstyle 1}\nearrow \\
a \\
{\scriptstyle 2}\searrow \\
c \xrightarrow{1} a
\end{array}
\right) = \tau(a, \hat{\tau}(\mathbf{b}), \hat{\tau}(c \xrightarrow{1} a)),
$$

$$
\hat{\tau}(\mathbf{b}) = \tau(b, nil, nil),
$$

$$
\hat{\tau}(c \xrightarrow{1} a) = \tau(c, \hat{\tau}(\mathbf{a}), nil),
$$

$$
\hat{\tau}(\mathbf{a}) = \tau(a, nil, nil),
$$

where $\mathbf{b}$ and $\mathbf{a}$ denote the graphs with a single node labeled b, and a, respectively. By proper substitutions, the encoding can finally be written as

$$
\hat{\tau}\left(
\begin{array}{c}
b \\
{\scriptstyle 1}\nearrow \\
a \\
{\scriptstyle 2}\searrow \\
c \xrightarrow{1} a
\end{array}
\right) =
$$

$$= \tau(\text{a}, \tau(\text{b}, nil, nil), \tau(\text{c}, \tau(\text{a}, nil, nil), nil))$$

It should be noted that causal stationary transductions cannot compute any function of the input DOAG. For example, consider the following two DOAGs

Any given transduction described by Equations 4.6-4.7 will necessarily map these two graphs into the same output, regardless of the form of functions $g(\cdot)$ and $\tau(\cdot)$. This is because the graph's processing is bottom-up, so it is not possible to recognize that in the right-hand side graph $pa[\text{a}]$ is constituted by two nodes, i.e. the ones labeled h and q.

This computational limitation, however, allows one to improve the efficiency of the computation. In fact, when considering DOAGs, the training set can be optimized by allowing only one occurrence of the same subgraph: if there are graphs $\boldsymbol{X}^{(1)}, \ldots, \boldsymbol{X}^{(q)}$ which share a common subgraph $\hat{\boldsymbol{X}}$, then $\hat{\boldsymbol{X}}$ can be represented only once. This is obtained by merging all the graphs in a single minimal DOAG. After that, a topological sort on the vertices of the minimal DOAG is performed to determine the updating order on the vertices for the recursive network. The advantage of having this topological order is that all the reduced representations and also their derivatives with respect to the weights can be computed by a single ordered scan of the training set.

Both the merging[5] and sorting operations can be done efficiently (almost linearly) with respect to the size of all DOAGs and the size of the minimal DOAG, respectively. Moreover, the use of the minimal DOAG leads to a considerable reduction in space complexity. In some cases, such reduction can even be exponential.

## 4.5   Neural Graph Transductions

The implementation of graph transductions through standard and recurrent neural networks can only be realized by resorting to complex and very unnatural encoding protocols which map structures onto fixed-size unstructured patterns or sequences. A more natural approach, instead, can be obtained by proper instantiation of the input and output domains for $g$, $\hat{\tau}$, and $\tau$.

Specifically, let $\mathcal{I}^{\#}$ be the input structured domain with real valued vectors as labels $\mathcal{I} = \mathbb{R}^n$, and $\mathcal{O} = \mathbb{R}^k$. The encoding function $\hat{\tau}$ is completely defined by

---

5. The merging operation can be performed by using either hash tables or AVL trees.

choosing a representation for the void graph and by defining the c-model function $\tau$. By choosing $\mathcal{X} = I\!\!R^m$, any real valued vector would be fine for representing the void graph, however, for computational reasons which will be clear in the following, we choose the null vector for representing the void graph, i.e. $nil = \mathbf{0} \in I\!\!R^m$. Consequently the c-model function $\tau$ will be defined as

$$\tau : I\!\!R^n \times \underbrace{I\!\!R^m \times \cdots \times I\!\!R^m}_{\text{o times}} \to I\!\!R^m \tag{4.8}$$

where the first domain of the cartesian product denotes the label space, while the remaining domains represent the encoded subgraph spaces up to the maximum outdegree of the input domain $\mathcal{I}^{\#}$. Finally, we can define the output function $g$ as

$$g : I\!\!R^m \to I\!\!R^k. \tag{4.9}$$

Note that Equations 4.8 and 4.9 only describe the general form for $\tau$ and $g$. Different realizations can be given which satisfy the above equations. For example, both $\tau$ and $g$ can be implemented by feedforward neural networks. Before reaching such a level of complexity, however, it is worth exploring simpler realizations. Specifically, in the following section we study recursive neurons.

## 4.6   Recursive Neurons

First consider the case in which $m = 1$. The simplest non-linear neural realization for $\tau(\cdot)$ is given by

$$\tau(l, x_1, \ldots, x_o) = f(\sum_{i=1}^{n} w_i l_i + \sum_{j=1}^{o} \hat{w}_j x_j + \theta), \tag{4.10}$$

where $f$ is a sigmoidal function, $w_i$ are the weights associated with the label space, $\hat{w}_j$ are the weights associated with the subgraphs spaces, $\theta$ is the bias, $l$ is the current input label, and $x_1, \ldots, x_o$ are the encoded representations of subgraphs.

***Example 4.2 Logical term f(a,g(b),c).***
Let us define a coding function

$$\phi : \{\mathsf{a}, \mathsf{b}, \mathsf{c}, \mathsf{f}, \mathsf{g}\} \to \{0, 1\}^5$$

which encodes the symbolic labels into binary vectors, i.e. $\phi(\mathsf{a}) = [1, 0, 0, 0, 0]$, $\phi(\mathsf{b}) = [0, 1, 0, 0, 0]$, $\phi(\mathsf{c}) = [0, 0, 1, 0, 0]$, $\phi(\mathsf{f}) = [0, 0, 0, 1, 0]$, $\phi(\mathsf{g}) = [0, 0, 0, 0, 1]$, and $nil = 0$. Thus, $\tau(\cdot)$ will be defined by five parameters for the label, i.e. $w_1, \ldots, w_5$, three parameters for the subgraphs (maximum outdegree), i.e. $\hat{w}_1$, $\hat{w}_2$, and $\hat{w}_3$, and the bias $\theta$.

Then,

$$\hat{\tau}\left(\begin{array}{ccc} & \text{f} & \\ {}^{1}\swarrow & {}^{2}\downarrow & \searrow^{3} \\ \text{a} & \text{g} & \text{c} \\ & {}^{1}\downarrow & \\ & \text{b} & \end{array}\right) =$$

$$= f(\sum_{i=1}^{5} w_i \phi_i(\text{f})) + \hat{w}_1 \overbrace{f(\sum_{i=1}^{5} w_i \phi_i(\text{a}) + \theta)}^{\hat{\tau}(\mathbf{a})} +$$

$$\overbrace{\hat{w}_2 f(\sum_{i=1}^{5} w_i \phi_i(\text{g}) + \hat{w}_1 \underbrace{f(\sum_{i=1}^{5} w_i \phi_i(\text{b}) + \theta)}_{\hat{\tau}(\mathbf{b})} + \theta)}^{\hat{\tau}(\mathbf{g}\xrightarrow{1}\mathbf{b})}$$

$$+ \hat{w}_3 \underbrace{f(\sum_{i=1}^{5} w_i \phi_i(\text{c}) + \theta)}_{\hat{\tau}(\mathbf{c})} + \theta).$$

A graphical representation of the above equation is given in Figure 4.2.

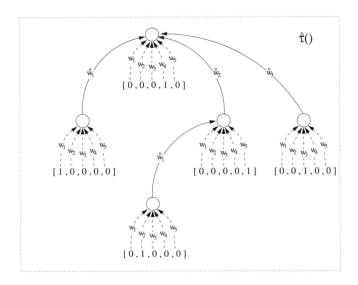

**Figure 4.2**  Graphical representation for the encoding function of Example 4.2.

When $m > 1$, $\tau(\cdot) \in \mathbb{R}^m$ can be written as

$$\tau(\boldsymbol{l}, \boldsymbol{x}^{(1)}, \dots, \boldsymbol{x}^{(o)}) = \boldsymbol{F}(\boldsymbol{W}\boldsymbol{l} + \sum_{j=1}^{o} \widehat{\boldsymbol{W}}_j \boldsymbol{x}^{(j)} + \boldsymbol{\theta}), \qquad (4.11)$$

where $\boldsymbol{F}_i(\boldsymbol{v}) = f(v_i)$, $\boldsymbol{l} \in \mathbb{R}^n$, $\boldsymbol{\theta} \in \mathbb{R}^m$, $\boldsymbol{W} \in \mathbb{R}^{m \times n}$, $\boldsymbol{x}^{(j)} \in \mathbb{R}^m$, $\widehat{\boldsymbol{W}}_j \in \mathbb{R}^{m \times m}$.

Concerning the output function $g(\cdot)$, it can be defined as a standard neuron taking its input as the encoded representation of the graph, i.e.

$$g(\boldsymbol{x}) = \boldsymbol{F}(\boldsymbol{M}\boldsymbol{x} + \beta), \qquad (4.12)$$

where $\boldsymbol{M} \in \mathbb{R}^{k \times m}$ and $\beta \in \mathbb{R}^k$ are the weight matrix and bias terms defining $g(\cdot)$, respectively.

As a special case, $g(\cdot)$ can be defined as a function which selects a subset of the state vector in $\mathbb{R}^m$. For example,

$$g(\boldsymbol{x}) = \boldsymbol{M}\boldsymbol{x}, \qquad (4.13)$$

where $\boldsymbol{M} \in \mathbb{R}^{k \times m}$ is a 0-1 matrix with a single 1 for each row and at most a single 1 for each column. This corresponds with letting the selected components of the state vector contribute to both the output and the coding of the state.

The relationship between recurrent and recursive neurons is clarified by the following example.

**Example 4.3**

A recurrent neuron can be considered as a special case of a recursive neuron applied to lists, i.e. labeled graphs with $o=1$; in that case, the position of a vertex within the list corresponds to the time of processing; e.g. given the list

$$\boldsymbol{L} \equiv \boldsymbol{l}^{(k)} \rightarrow \boldsymbol{l}^{(k-1)} \rightarrow \dots \rightarrow \boldsymbol{l}^{(1)}$$

the set of equations derived by the recursive application of Equation 4.10 is

$$x_1 = \tau(\boldsymbol{l}^{(1)}, nil) = f(\sum_{j=1}^{n} w_j l_j^{(1)})$$

$$x_i = \tau(\boldsymbol{l}^{(i)}, x_{i-1}) = f(\sum_{j=1}^{n} w_j l_j^{(i)} + \hat{w}_1 x_{i-1}) \quad i = 2, \dots, k$$

where $\hat{w}_1$ is the weight on the recursive connection; by making the time $t$ of processing explicit, the above equations can be rewritten as the output $o(\cdot)$ of a recurrent neuron as follows

$$o(t = 1) = f(\sum_{j=1}^{n} w_j l_j^{(1)})$$

$$o(t) = f(\sum_{j=1}^{n} w_j l_j^{(t)} + \hat{w}_1 o(t-1)) \quad t = 2, \dots, k.$$

## 4.7 Learning Algorithms

In this section, we discuss how several standard supervised algorithms for neural networks can be extended to structures.

### 4.7.1 Backpropagation through Structure

The task addressed by backpropagation through time networks (Rumelhart and McClelland, 1986) is to produce particular output sequences in response to specific input sequences. These networks are, generally, fully recurrent, in which any unit may be connected to any other. Consequently, they cannot be trained by using plain backpropagation. A trick, however, can be used to turn an arbitrary recurrent network into an equivalent feedforward network when the input sequences have a maximum length $T$. In this case, all the units of the network can be duplicated $T$ times (*unfolding of time*), so that the state of a unit in the recurrent network at time $t$ is held by the $t$-th copy of the same unit in the feedforward network. By preserving the same weight values through the layers of the feedforward network, it is not difficult to see that the two networks will behave identically for $T$ time steps. The feedforward network can be trained by backpropagation, taking care to preserve the identity constraint between weights of different layers. This can be guaranteed by adding together the individual gradient contributions of corresponding copies of the same weight and then changing all copies by the total amount.

Backpropagation through Time can easily be extended to structures. The basic idea is to use recursive neurons to encode the structures, i.e. $\hat{\tau}(\cdot)$; the representations obtained are then classified or used to approximate an unknown function by a standard feedforward network, i.e. $g(\cdot)$.

Following our framework, given an input graph $\boldsymbol{X}$, the network output $\mathcal{T}(\boldsymbol{X})$ can be expressed as the composition of the encoding function $\hat{\tau}(\cdot)$ and the classification (or approximation) function $g(\cdot)$:

$$\mathcal{T}(\boldsymbol{X}) = g(\hat{\tau}(\boldsymbol{X})). \tag{4.14}$$

Learning the set of weights $\boldsymbol{W}_g$ can be implemented by plain backpropagation on the feedforward network realizing $g(\cdot)$

$$\Delta \boldsymbol{W}_g = -\eta \frac{\partial Error(g(\boldsymbol{y}))}{\partial \boldsymbol{W}_g}, \tag{4.15}$$

where $\boldsymbol{y} = \hat{\tau}(\boldsymbol{X})$, i.e. the input to the feedforward network, while learning the set of weights, $\boldsymbol{W}_{\hat{\tau}}$, realizing $\hat{\tau}(\cdot)$ can be implemented by

$$\Delta \boldsymbol{W}_{\hat{\tau}} = -\eta \frac{\partial Error(g(\boldsymbol{y}))}{\partial \boldsymbol{y}} \frac{\partial \boldsymbol{y}}{\partial \boldsymbol{W}_{\hat{\tau}}}, \tag{4.16}$$

where the first term represents the error coming from the feedforward network and the second one represents the error due to the encoding function $\hat{\tau}(\cdot)$. Note that $\boldsymbol{W}_{\hat{\tau}}$ actually refers to the weights associated with the c-model function $\tau(\cdot)$. Thus, in order to clarify this point we will denote this weight matrix as $\boldsymbol{W}_{\tau}$

Goller and Küchler (Goller and Küchler, 1996) devised a learning algorithm, namely *Backpropagation Through Structure*, on the basis of the above equations. The basic idea it to observe that $\frac{\partial \boldsymbol{y}}{\partial \boldsymbol{W}_{\tau}}$ can be computed by backpropagating the error from the feedforward network implementing $g(\cdot)$ through the network implementing the encoding function $\hat{\tau}(\boldsymbol{X})$. As in backpropagation through time, the gradient contributions of corresponding copies of the same weight are collected for each structure. The total amount is then used to change all the copies of the same weight. If learning is performed by *structure*, then the weights are updated after the presentation of each individual structure, otherwise, the gradient contributions are collected through the whole training set and the weights changed after all the structures in the training set have been presented to the network. Recalling that the encoding network of a graph $\boldsymbol{X}$ is defined as the composition of the network implementing $\hat{\tau}(\boldsymbol{X})$ with the network implementing $g(\cdot)$, the learning algorithm for an optimized training set of $L$ structures can be summarized in the following way:

**Backpropagation through Structure**

**Repeat**

**for** $l = 1$ **to** L

Compute $\mathcal{T}(\boldsymbol{X})$;

Compute the gradient using the Backpropagation Algorithm over the encoding network of $\boldsymbol{X}$;

Collect (add) the gradient for the different instances of weights in $\boldsymbol{W}_{\tau}$;

Update $\boldsymbol{W}_{\tau}$ and $\boldsymbol{W}_{g}$;

**Until** Convergence

### 4.7.2 Extension of Real-Time Recurrent Learning

The extension of Real-Time Recurrent Learning (Williams and Zipser, 1989) to recursive neurons does not present particular problems. Here we consider a neural model where $g(\cdot)$ is implemented as in Equation 4.13, while the encoding is performed by $m$ recursive neurons, i.e. (by including the bias into the label weight matrix)

$$\hat{\tau}(\boldsymbol{X}) = \tau(\boldsymbol{l}, \boldsymbol{x}^{(1)}, \ldots, \boldsymbol{x}^{(o)}) = \boldsymbol{F}(\boldsymbol{W}\boldsymbol{l} + \sum_{j=1}^{o} \widehat{\boldsymbol{W}}_j \boldsymbol{x}^{(j)}), \qquad (4.17)$$

where $\boldsymbol{x}^{(j)} = \hat{\tau}(\boldsymbol{X}^{(j)})$ with $source(\boldsymbol{X}^{(j)}) = ch_j[source(\boldsymbol{X})]$, and

$$\boldsymbol{W}_\tau = [\boldsymbol{W}, \widehat{\boldsymbol{W}}_1, \ldots, \widehat{\boldsymbol{W}}_o]. \qquad (4.18)$$

Here we show how to compute the derivatives of $\hat{\tau}(\boldsymbol{X})$ leaving to the reader the derivation of the final learning rule according to the chosen error function.

The derivatives of $\hat{\tau}(\boldsymbol{X})$ with respect to $\boldsymbol{W}$ and $\widehat{\boldsymbol{W}}_i$ ($i \in [1, \ldots, o]$) can be computed as follows:

$$\frac{\partial \hat{\tau}_p(\boldsymbol{X})}{\partial W_{tk}} = \tau_p'(l_k \delta_{pt} + \sum_{j=1}^{o} (\widehat{\boldsymbol{W}}_j)_p \frac{\partial \boldsymbol{x}^{(j)}}{\partial W_{tk}}), \qquad (4.19)$$

where $\tau_p'$ is the first derivative of the $p$-th component of $\tau(\cdot)$ computed on the supersource of $\boldsymbol{X}$, $\delta_{mt}$ is the Kronecker delta, $p = 1, \ldots, m$, $t = 1, \ldots, m$, $k = 0, \ldots, n$ and $(\widehat{\boldsymbol{W}}_j)_p$ is the $p$th row of $\widehat{\boldsymbol{W}}_j$;

$$\frac{\partial \hat{\tau}_p(\boldsymbol{X})}{\partial (\widehat{\boldsymbol{W}}_i)_{tq}} = \tau_p'(\boldsymbol{x}_p^{(j)} \delta_{pt} + \sum_{j=1}^{o} (\widehat{\boldsymbol{W}}_j)_t \frac{\partial \boldsymbol{x}^{(j)}}{\partial (\widehat{\boldsymbol{W}}_i)_{tq}}), \qquad (4.20)$$

where $t = 1, \ldots, m$, and $q = 1, \ldots, m$.

These equations are recursive on the structure $\boldsymbol{X}$, and can be computed by noting that if $\boldsymbol{V}$ is a graph composed of a single vertex, then

$$\frac{\partial \hat{\tau}_p(\boldsymbol{V})}{\partial W_{tk}} = \tau_p'(l_{source(\boldsymbol{V})})_k \delta_{pt}, \text{ and } \frac{\partial \hat{\tau}_t(\boldsymbol{V})}{\partial (\widehat{\boldsymbol{W}}_i)_{tq}} = 0. \qquad (4.21)$$

This allows the computation of the derivatives in real time alongside the computation of the neural representations for the graphs.

### 4.7.3   Recursive Cascade Correlation

In this section we discuss how a neural graph transduction $\mathcal{T}$ can be learned using an extension of the Cascade-Correlation algorithm. The standard Cascade-Correlation algorithm (Fahlman and Lebiere, 1990) creates a neural network using an incremental approach for the classification or regression of unstructured patterns. The starting network $\mathcal{N}_0$ is a network without hidden nodes trained by a Least Mean Square algorithm. If network $\mathcal{N}_0$ is not able to solve the problem, a hidden unit $u_1$ is added such that the *correlation* between the output of the unit and the residual error of network $\mathcal{N}_0$ is maximized[6]. The weights of $u_1$ are frozen and the remaining weights are retrained. If the obtained network $\mathcal{N}_1$ cannot solve the problem, new hidden units are added which are connected, with frozen weights, with all the inputs and previously installed hidden units. The resulting network is a *cascade* of nodes. Fahlman extended the algorithm to the classification of sequences, obtaining good results (Fahlman, 1991).

In the following, we show that Cascade Correlation can be further extended to structures by using our computational scheme (Sperduti et al., 1996). In fact, the shape of the c-model function can be expressed component-wise by the following set of equations:

$$\tau_1 = h_1(\boldsymbol{l}, \hat{\tau}_1(\boldsymbol{Y}^{(1)}), \dots, \hat{\tau}_1(\boldsymbol{Y}^{(o)})) \tag{4.22}$$

$$\tau_2 = h_2(\boldsymbol{l}, \hat{\tau}_1(\boldsymbol{Y}^{(1)}), \dots, \hat{\tau}_1(\boldsymbol{Y}^{(o)}), \tag{4.23}$$
$$\hat{\tau}_2(\boldsymbol{Y}^{(1)}), \dots, \hat{\tau}_2(\boldsymbol{Y}^{(o)}), \hat{\tau}_1(\boldsymbol{Y}))$$

$$\vdots$$

$$\tau_m = h_m(\boldsymbol{l}, \hat{\tau}_1(\boldsymbol{Y}^{(1)}), \dots, \hat{\tau}_1(\boldsymbol{Y}^{(o)}), \tag{4.24}$$
$$\hat{\tau}_2(\boldsymbol{Y}^{(1)}), \dots, \hat{\tau}_2(\boldsymbol{Y}^{(o)}), \dots$$
$$\dots, \hat{\tau}_m(\boldsymbol{Y}^{(1)}), \dots, \hat{\tau}_m(\boldsymbol{Y}^{(o)}), \tag{4.25}$$
$$\hat{\tau}_1(\boldsymbol{Y}), \dots, \hat{\tau}_{m-1}(\boldsymbol{Y}))$$

where the $h_i$ are suitable nonlinear functions of the arguments.

Specifically, the output of the $k$-th hidden unit, in our framework, can be computed as

$$\tau_k(\boldsymbol{l}, \boldsymbol{x}^{(1)}, \dots, \boldsymbol{x}^{(o)}) = f(\sum_{i=0}^{n} w_i^{(k)} l_i + \sum_{v=1}^{k} \sum_{j=1}^{o} \hat{w}_{(v,j)}^{(k)} \boldsymbol{x}_v^{(j)} +$$
$$+ \sum_{q=1}^{k-1} \bar{w}_q^{(k)} \tau_q(\boldsymbol{l}, \boldsymbol{x}^{(1)}, \dots, \boldsymbol{x}^{(o)})), \tag{4.26}$$

where $w_{(v,j)}^{(k)}$ is the weight of the $k$-th hidden unit associated with the output of the $v$-th hidden unit computed on the $j$-th subgraph code $\boldsymbol{x}^{(j)}$, and $\bar{w}_q^{(k)}$ is the weight of the connection from the $q$-th (frozen) hidden unit, $q < k$, and the $k$-th hidden unit. The output of the network (with $k$ inserted hidden units) is then computed according to Equation 4.12.

Learning is performed as in standard Cascade Correlation by interleaving the minimization of the total error function (LMS) and the maximization of the correlation of the new inserted hidden unit with the residual error. The main difference with respect to standard Cascade Correlation is in the calculation of

---

6. Since the maximization of the correlation is obtained using a gradient ascent technique on a surface with several maxima, a pool of hidden units is trained and the best one selected.

the derivatives. According to Equation 4.26, the derivatives of $\tau_k(\boldsymbol{l}, \boldsymbol{x}^{(1)}, \ldots, \boldsymbol{x}^{(o)})$ with respect to the weights are computed as

$$\frac{\partial \tau_k(\boldsymbol{l}, \boldsymbol{x}^{(1)}, \ldots, \boldsymbol{x}^{(o)})}{\partial w_i^{(k)}} = f'(l_i + \sum_{j=1}^{o} \hat{w}_{(k,j)}^{(k)} \frac{\partial \boldsymbol{x}_k^{(j)}}{\partial w_i^{(k)}}) \tag{4.27}$$

$$\frac{\partial \tau_k(\boldsymbol{l}, \boldsymbol{x}^{(1)}, \ldots, \boldsymbol{x}^{(o)})}{\partial \bar{w}_q^{(k)}} = f'(\tau_q(\boldsymbol{l}, \boldsymbol{x}^{(1)}, \ldots, \boldsymbol{x}^{(o)}) + \tag{4.28}$$

$$+ \sum_{j=1}^{o} \hat{w}_{(k,j)}^{(k)} \frac{\partial \boldsymbol{x}_k^{(j)}}{\partial \bar{w}_q^{(k)}})$$

$$\frac{\partial \tau_k(\boldsymbol{l}, \boldsymbol{x}^{(1)}, \ldots, \boldsymbol{x}^{(o)})}{\partial \hat{w}_{(v,t)}^{(k)}} = f'(\boldsymbol{x}_v^{(t)} + \sum_{j=1}^{o} \hat{w}_{(k,j)}^{(k)} \frac{\partial \boldsymbol{x}_k^{(j)}}{\partial \hat{w}_{(v,t)}^{(k)}}) \tag{4.29}$$

where $i = 0, \ldots, n$; $q = 1, \ldots, (k-1)$; $v = 1, \ldots, k$; $t = 1, \ldots, o$ and $f'$ is the derivative of $f(\cdot)$. The above equations are recurrent on the structures and can be computed by observing that for graphs composed by a single vertex Equation 4.27 reduces to $\frac{\partial \boldsymbol{x}_k}{\partial w_i^{(k)}} = l_i f'$, $\frac{\partial \boldsymbol{x}_k}{\partial \bar{w}_q^{(k)}} = \boldsymbol{x}_q f'$ (for $q < k$), and all the remaining derivatives are null. Consequently, we only need to store the output values of the unit and its derivatives for each component of a structure.

Learning of the output weights proceeds as for standard Cascade Correlation.

### 4.7.4    Extension of Neural Trees

Neural Trees (NT) have recently been proposed as a fast learning method in classification tasks. They are decision trees (Breiman et al., 1984) where the splitting of the data for each vertex, i.e. the classification of a pattern according to some features, is performed by a perceptron (Sirat and Nadal, 1990) or a more complex neural network (Sankar and Mammone, 1991). After learning, each vertex at every level of the tree corresponds to an exclusive subset of the training data and the leaf nodes of the tree completely partition the training set. In the operative mode, the internal nodes route the input pattern to the appropriate leaf node which represents its class.

One advantage of the neural tree approach is that the tree structure is constructed dynamically during learning and not linked to a static structure like a standard feedforward network. Moreover, it allows incremental learning, since subtrees can be added as well as deleted to recognize new classes of patterns or to improve generalization. Both supervised (Sirat and Nadal, 1990; Sethi, 1990; Atlas et al., 1992; Sankar and Mammone, 1991) and unsupervised (Perrone and Intrator, 1992; Li et al., 1992; Perrone, 1992) splitting of the data have been proposed.

The learning and classification algorithms for binary and general trees can be found in (Sankar and Mammone, 1991). The extension of these algorithms to structures is straightforward: the standard discriminator (or network) associated with each node of the tree is replaced by a recursive discriminator (or network) which can be trained with any of the learning algorithms we have presented so far.

## 4.8   Cyclic Graphs

Up to now we have considered DOAGs. In fact, the processing of graphs with cycles poses at least two main problems: *(i)* How to modify the definition of $\hat{\tau}(\cdot)$ in such a way to attain an unambiguous neural representation of the graph? *(ii)* How to modify the learning algorithm? Of course, the answer to question *(ii)* depends on the answer to question *(i)*. Here we propose a solution to both problems, which, however, must be considered partial since it is not guaranteed to be valid under all conditions. The nature of this limitation will be clear in the following.

Given a cyclic DOG $Y$, with $h$ vertices, define the associated set of equations

$$\mathcal{S}(Y) \;=\; \begin{cases} \mathbf{x}_{v_1} = \tau(v_1, Y_{v_1}, \mathbf{x}_{ch_1[v_1]}, \dots, \mathbf{x}_{ch_o[v_1]}) \\ \mathbf{x}_{v_2} = \tau(v_2, Y_{v_2}, \mathbf{x}_{ch_1[v_2]}, \dots, \mathbf{x}_{ch_o[v_2]}) \\ \vdots \\ \mathbf{x}_{v_h} = \tau(v_h, Y_{v_h}, \mathbf{x}_{ch_1[v_h]}, \dots, \mathbf{x}_{ch_o[v_h]}) \end{cases} \tag{4.30}$$

where there is one equation for each vertex $v_j \in vert(Y)$, and if $ch_i[v_j]$ is void, then $\mathbf{x}_{ch_i[v_j]} = nil$. Then, if $\mathcal{S}(Y)$ admits a (unique) solution, we define

$$\hat{\tau}(Y) = \mathbf{x}_{source(Y)}, \tag{4.31}$$

where we exploit the fact that, by definition, $source(Y)$ returns a predefined supersource of $Y$ among all possible ones. Note that if $Y$ is acyclic, then the system $\mathcal{S}(Y)$ has a unique solution given by Equation 4.7. So, Equation 4.31 is more general than Equation 4.7. The system $\mathcal{S}(Y)$, however, in general may not allow a solution, or if it does, it may admit multiple solutions. Consequently, according to the way $\tau(\cdot)$ is actually implemented, sufficient conditions should be derived to guarantee the existence of a (unique) solution, thus solving problem *(i)*. Such conditions should then also be extended to cope with the perturbations introduced by the learning algorithm over the parametric implementation of $\tau(\cdot)$.

The neural implementation of Equation 4.31 can still be obtained by resorting to Equations 4.10-4.12. In this case the encoding function $\hat{\tau}(Y)$ is computed by a recurrent neural network $\mathcal{N}(Y)$ defined according to $\mathcal{S}(Y)$: $\mathcal{N}(Y)$ will contain a pool of recursive neurons[7] for each distinct equation in $\mathcal{S}(Y)$ and the connections between pools of neurons is defined according to the functional dependencies expressed by each single equation in the system.

---

7. The number of recursive units in the pool is given by $m$.

**Example 4.4**

Let us consider the following graph

$$\boldsymbol{Y} \;=\; \boldsymbol{l}^{(6)} \;\xrightarrow{1}\; \boldsymbol{l}^{(5)} \;\xleftarrow{1}\; \boldsymbol{l}^{(4)}$$

$$1\downarrow \qquad\qquad 1\uparrow$$

$$\boldsymbol{l}^{(3)} \;\xrightarrow{2}\; \boldsymbol{l}^{(2)} \;\xrightarrow{2}\; \boldsymbol{l}^{(1)}$$

$$1\downarrow$$

$$\boldsymbol{l}^{(0)}$$

where $\boldsymbol{l}^{(0)} = [1,0,0,0,0]$, $\boldsymbol{l}^{(1)} = [0,1,0,0,0]$, $\boldsymbol{l}^{(2)} = [1,1,0,0,0]$, $\boldsymbol{l}^{(3)} = [0,0,1,0,0]$, $\boldsymbol{l}^{(4)} = [1,0,1,0,0]$, $\boldsymbol{l}^{(5)} = [0,0,0,1,0]$ and $\boldsymbol{l}^{(6)} = [0,0,1,0,1]$. Consider a single recursive neuron ($m = 1$). In this case, $\tau(\cdot)$ is defined by five parameters for the label, i.e. $w_1, \ldots, w_5$, two parameters for the pointers, i.e. $\hat{w}_1$, and $\hat{w}_2$, and the bias $\theta$. The corresponding system $\mathcal{S}(\boldsymbol{Y})$ is

$$\mathcal{S}(\boldsymbol{Y}) \;=\; \begin{cases} x_{v_0} &=\; f(\sum_{j=1}^{5} w_j l_j^{(0)} + \theta) \\[4pt] x_{v_1} &=\; f(\sum_{j=1}^{5} w_j l_j^{(1)} + \theta) \\[4pt] x_{v_2} &=\; f(\sum_{j=1}^{5} w_j l_j^{(2)} + \hat{w}_1 x_{v_4} + \\ &\qquad + \hat{w}_2 x_{v_1} + \theta) \\[4pt] x_{v_3} &=\; f(\sum_{j=1}^{5} w_j l_j^{(3)} + \hat{w}_1 x_{v_0} + \\ &\qquad + \hat{w}_2 x_{v_2} + \theta) \\[4pt] x_{v_4} &=\; f(\sum_{j=1}^{5} w_j l_j^{(4)} + \hat{w}_1 x_{v_5} + \theta) \\[4pt] x_{v_5} &=\; f(\sum_{j=1}^{5} w_j l_j^{(5)} + \hat{w}_1 x_{v_3} + \theta) \\[4pt] x_{v_6} &=\; f(\sum_{j=1}^{5} w_j l_j^{(6)} + \hat{w}_1 x_{v_5} + \theta) \end{cases} \qquad (4.32)$$

The resulting network $\mathcal{N}(\boldsymbol{Y})$ is shown in Figure 4.3.

Satisfactory sufficient conditions to guarantee the existence of a unique solution to system $\mathcal{S}(\boldsymbol{Y})$ when using recursive neurons are still missing. In fact, it is well known that if the weight matrix of a recurrent network, such as the network $\mathcal{N}(\boldsymbol{Y})$, is symmetric, an additive network with first order connections possesses a Lyapunov function and is convergent (Hopfield, 1984; Cohen and Grossberg, 1983). Moreover, Almeida proved a more general symmetry condition than the symmetry of the weight matrix, i.e. a system satisfying *detailed balance* is guaranteed to possess a Lyapunov function as well (Almeida, 1987). Finally, if the norm of the weight matrix (not necessarily symmetric) is sufficiently small, the network's dynamics can be shown to go to a unique equilibrium for a given input (Atiya, 1988). The above results, however, may impose too many constraints on the class of functions which can be computed and they also do not solve the stability problem for learning, i.e. the weights of the network $\mathcal{N}(\boldsymbol{Y})$ change with learning and there is no guarantee that learning will preserve the stability of the network.

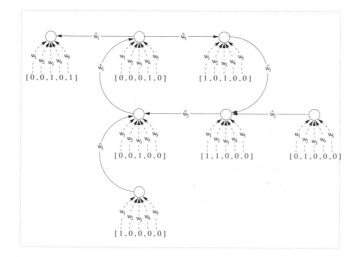

**Figure 4.3**   Graphical representation for the encoding function of the cyclic graph.

## 4.9   Learning with Cycles

In this section we formulate a proposal on how learning in the case of cyclic graphs can be performed. Extensions of both Backpropagation and Real-Time learning are discussed.

### 4.9.1   Backpropagation

Let consider the framework introduced in Section 4.7.1. Since the network implementing $\hat{\tau}(\cdot)$ is recurrent, $\frac{\partial \boldsymbol{y}}{\partial \boldsymbol{W}_\tau}$ can only be computed by resorting to *recurrent backpropagation* (Pineda, 1988), which has been defined to cope with neural networks containing cycles.

In the standard formulation, a recurrent backpropagation network $\mathcal{N}$ with $p$ units is defined as

$$\boldsymbol{o}^{(rbp)}(t+1) = \boldsymbol{F}(\boldsymbol{W}^{(rbp)}\boldsymbol{o}^{(rbp)}(t) + \boldsymbol{I}^{(rbp)}), \tag{4.33}$$

where $\boldsymbol{I}^{(rbp)} \in \mathbb{R}^p$ is the input vector for the network, and $\boldsymbol{W}^{(rbp)} \in \mathbb{R}^p \times \mathbb{R}^p$ the weight matrix. The learning rule for a weight of the network is given by

$$\Delta w_{rs}^{(rbp)} = \eta o_s^{(rbp)} o_r'^{(rbp)} \sum_k e_k (\boldsymbol{L}^{-1})_{kr} \tag{4.34}$$

where all the quantities are taken at a fixed point of the recurrent network, $e_k$ is the error between the current output of unit $k$ and the desired one, $L_{ji} = \delta_{ji} - o_j'^{(rbp)} w_{ji}$

($\delta_{ji}$ is a Kronecker delta), and the quantity

$$y_j^{(rbp)} = \sum_k e_k (\boldsymbol{L}^{-1})_{kj} = \sum_i o'^{(rbp)}_i w_{ij} y_i^{(rbp)} + e_i \qquad (4.35)$$

can be computed by relaxing the *adjoint* network $\mathcal{N}'$, i.e. a network obtained from $\mathcal{N}$ by reversing the direction of the connections[8]. The weight $w_{ji}$ from neuron $i$ to neuron $j$ in $\mathcal{N}$ is replaced by $o_i^{(rbp)} w_{ij}$ from neuron $j$ to neuron $i$ in $\mathcal{N}'$. The activation functions of $\mathcal{N}'$ are linear and the output units in $\mathcal{N}$ become input units in $\mathcal{N}'$ with $e_i$ as input.

Given a cyclic graph $\boldsymbol{Y}$, let $h = \#vert(\boldsymbol{Y})$, $m$ be the number of recursive neurons and $\boldsymbol{o}_i(t)$ be the output at time $t$ of these recursive neurons for $v_i \in vert(\boldsymbol{Y})$. We define the global state vector of $\mathcal{N}(\boldsymbol{Y})$ at time $t$ as

$$\boldsymbol{o}(t) = \begin{bmatrix} \boldsymbol{o}_1(t) \\ \boldsymbol{o}_2(t) \\ \vdots \\ \boldsymbol{o}_h(t) \end{bmatrix} \qquad (4.36)$$

where, for convention, $\boldsymbol{o}_1(t)$ is the output of the neurons representing $source(\boldsymbol{Y})$.

To account for the labels, we have to modify Equation 4.33 slightly

$$\boldsymbol{o}(t+1) = \boldsymbol{F}(\widehat{\boldsymbol{W}}_\tau \boldsymbol{o}(t) + \boldsymbol{W}_\tau \boldsymbol{I}), \qquad (4.37)$$

where

$$\boldsymbol{I} = \begin{bmatrix} l_1 \\ \vdots \\ l_h \end{bmatrix} \qquad (4.38)$$

is the vector collecting all the labels of $\boldsymbol{Y}$, and

$$\boldsymbol{W}_\tau = \underbrace{\begin{bmatrix} \boldsymbol{W} & & \boldsymbol{0} \\ & \ddots & \\ \boldsymbol{0} & & \boldsymbol{W} \end{bmatrix}}_{h \ repetitions \ of \ \boldsymbol{W}} \qquad (4.39)$$

and $\widehat{\boldsymbol{W}}_\tau \in \Re^{hm \times hm}$ is defined according to the topology of $\boldsymbol{Y}$.

The input of the adjoint network is $e_k = (\frac{\partial Error(g(\boldsymbol{y}))}{\partial \boldsymbol{y}})_k$, and the learning rules become:

---

8. Note that, in this case, the directions of the connections agree with the directions of the corresponding edges in the input graph.

$$\Delta \hat{w}_{rs} = \eta o_s o'_r \sum_k e_k (\boldsymbol{L}^{-1})_{kr}, \qquad (4.40)$$

$$\Delta w_{rs} = \eta I_s o'_r \sum_k e_k (\boldsymbol{L}^{-1})_{kr}. \qquad (4.41)$$

Of course, as in Backpropagation Through Structure, all the changes referring to the same weight are added and then all copies of the same weight are changed by the total amount. It must be noted that each graph gives rise to a new adjoint network and independently contributes to the variations of the weights. Moreover, the above formulation is more general than Backpropagation Through Structure: when used for DOAGs the adjoint network becomes a feedforward network representing the backpropagation of errors.

As for standard recurrent networks, in this case it may also be necessary to force the creation of new fixed points in the dynamics of the network by using *teacher forcing*, a variation of recurrent Backpropagation proposed by Pineda (Pineda, 1988). However, while the effects of this technique are quite well understood in standard recurrent networks, it is not clear to us how it can influence the dynamics of the networks associated with the input graphs. In fact, given a set of graphs $\{\boldsymbol{Y}^{(1)}, \ldots, \boldsymbol{Y}^{(p)}\}$, the associated networks $\mathcal{N}(\boldsymbol{Y}^{(1)}), \ldots, \mathcal{N}(\boldsymbol{Y}^{(p)})$ are interdependent since they share the same set of weights. A more accurate study on how this sharing of resources affects the dynamics of the system when using teacher forcing is needed.

### 4.9.2   Real-Time

Before proceeding with definitions and equations, we need to clarify a basic assumption inherent to the application of real-time learning to cyclic graphs. In fact, the original real-time algorithm was defined for sequences, where the order of presentation of the input data is trivially defined. This order can naturally be extended when dealing with DOAGs: A node is presented only if all its offspring have been presented. Of course, the application of this convention does not work for cyclic graphs since the presence of a cycle traversing all the vertices of the graph will render the application of a real-time algorithm impractical: The encoding of the graph can be computed only at the time all the vertices of the graph are presented and the corresponding network is relaxed. Thus, in this case, it is more efficient to use the extension of Backpropagation presented in the previous section. Consequently, in the following we only consider graphs with local cycles, i.e. cycles involving few vertices. In this case, it is useful to resort to two strictly related concepts, the strongly connected components of a graph and the related definition of a component graph.

### Definition 1 *Strongly Connected Component*
A strongly connected component of a directed graph $\boldsymbol{G}$ is a maximal set of vertices $U \subseteq \text{vert}(\boldsymbol{G})$ such that for each pair of vertices $u$ and $v$ in $U$, there exists a path from $u$ to $v$ and vice-versa, i.e. $u$ and $v$ are reachable from each other.

### Definition 2  Component Graph

The (acyclic) component graph of $\boldsymbol{G}$ is defined as the graph $\boldsymbol{G}^{SCC}$, where $vert(\boldsymbol{G}^{SCC})$ contains one vertex for each strongly connected component of $\boldsymbol{G}$, and $edg(\boldsymbol{G}^{SCC})$ contains the edge $(u, v)$ if there is a directed edge from a vertex in the strongly connected component of $\boldsymbol{G}$ corresponding to $u$ to a vertex in the strongly connected component of $\boldsymbol{G}$ corresponding to $v$.

The computation of the strongly connected components of a graph $\boldsymbol{G}$ and its component graph $\boldsymbol{G}^{SCC}$ can be performed by combining two depth-first searches in $\Theta(\#vert(\boldsymbol{G}) + \#edg(\boldsymbol{G}))$ time (Cormen et al., 1990).

The basic assumption is that vertices of input graphs are presented to the recursive network according to the preorder defined by the corresponding component graphs. Once the vertices belonging to a strongly connected component are presented, the partial encoding of the corresponding subgraph can be computed alongside with the relevant derivatives. It is in this sense that we perform real-time processing.

Thus, the computation of the derivatives in real time for a graph $\boldsymbol{Y}$ can be done by observing that

1. Equations 4.19 and 4.20 are still valid;

2. each strongly connected component of $\boldsymbol{Y}$ corresponds to a set of interdependent equations of this kind;

3. $\boldsymbol{Y}^{SCC}$ defines the dependences between sets of equations.

### Example 4.5

Consider a single recursive neuron $(m = 1)$ and the graph shown in Example 4.4. The component graph $\boldsymbol{Y}^{SCC}$ is given by

$$u_3 \quad \rightarrow \quad u_2 \quad \rightarrow \quad u_1$$
$$\downarrow$$
$$u_0$$

where

$$
\begin{array}{lll}
u_0 \overset{\text{def}}{=} \boldsymbol{l}^{(0)} & & \boldsymbol{l}^{(5)} \leftarrow \boldsymbol{l}^{(4)} \\
u_1 \overset{\text{def}}{=} \boldsymbol{l}^{(1)} & u_2 \overset{\text{def}}{=} \quad \downarrow \qquad \uparrow \\
u_3 \overset{\text{def}}{=} \boldsymbol{l}^{(6)} & & \boldsymbol{l}^{(3)} \rightarrow \boldsymbol{l}^{(2)}
\end{array}
$$

Let us consider the derivatives $x'_{v_j} = \frac{\partial x_{v_j}}{\partial \hat{w}_1}$ with $v_j \in vert(\boldsymbol{Y})$. They are the solutions of the set of equations (derived by Equation 4.20)

$$
\begin{cases}
\text{component } u_0 \\
x'_{v_0} = 0 \\
\text{component } u_1 \\
x'_{v_1} = 0 \\
\text{component } u_2 \\
x'_{v_2} = f'(x_{v_4} + \hat{w}_1 x'_{v_4} + \hat{w}_2 x'_{v_1}) \\
x'_{v_3} = f'(x_{v_0} + \hat{w}_1 x'_{v_0} + \hat{w}_2 x'_{v_2}) \\
x'_{v_4} = f'(x_{v_5} + \hat{w}_1 x'_{v_5}) \\
x'_{v_5} = f'(x_{v_3} + \hat{w}_1 x'_{v_3}) \\
\text{component } u_3 \\
x'_{v_6} = f'(x_{v_5} + \hat{w}_1 x'_{v_5})
\end{cases}
$$

which can be decomposed according to the component graph. By substituting the solution for $x'_{v_1}$ into the equation for $x'_{v_2}$, and the solution for $x'_{v_0}$ into the equation for $x'_{v_3}$, the subset of equations corresponding to the strongly connected component $u_2$ can be solved through a relaxation process. Finally, once the solution value for $x'_{v_5}$ is known, the last equation corresponding to component $u_3$ can be solved by direct substitution. In general, by taking into account the dependencies established by the component graph, both the output of the recursive neuron and its derivatives can be computed in real-time with respect to the component graph.

## 4.10  Computational Power

It is well known that recurrent neural networks can simulate any finite-state automata (Alon et al., 1991; Omlin and Giles, 1996) as well as any multi-stack Turing machine in real time (Siegelmann and Sontag, 1995). When constraining the network architecture, however, this computational power may no longer hold. For example, Elman-style Recurrent Networks can simulate any finite-state automata (Goudreau et al., 1994; Kremer, 1995), while Recurrent Cascade-Correlation Networks cannot (Giles et al., 1995; Kremer, 1996). For this reason, it is of paramount importance to assess the computational power of a given network architecture, since this characterizes the class of functions which, in principle, can be computed by such network. Given an application domain, and based on the observation that the difficulty of training a network is directly proportional to the computational power exhibited by the network, computational results can be used to select the least complex architecture able to deal with the application.

To assess the computational capability of recursive neural networks, it is useful to resort to Tree Automata theory. In the next section we give a brief introduction to Tree Grammars and to a specific class of Tree Automata, i.e. Frontier-to-Root Tree Automata.

### 4.10.1   Tree Grammars and Tree Automata

A *tree grammar* is defined as a four-tuple $G_t = (V, r, P, S)$ where $V = N \cup \Sigma$ is the grammar alphabet (nonterminals and terminals); $(V, r)$ a ranked alphabet; productions in $P$ are of the form $T_i \to T_j$, where $T_i$ and $T_j$ are trees; and $S$ in $T_V$ is a finite set of "starting trees," where $T_V$ denotes the set of trees with nodes labeled by elements in $V$.

A tree grammar is in *expansive form* if all its productions are of the form

A (deterministic) *frontier-to-root tree automaton* (FRA) is a system $\mathcal{A}_t = (Q, F, \{f_a | a \text{ in } \Sigma\})$ where $\Sigma$ is a ranked alphabet; $Q$ is a finite set of states; $F, F \subseteq Q$, is a set of final states; $\{f_a | a \text{ in } \Sigma\}$ is a set of transition functions $f_a : Q^m \to Q$ such that $m$ is a rank of the symbol $a \in \Sigma$. The recognition process computed by the automaton can be described intuitively by the following computational stages: first of all, the frontier of the state tree is labeled $q_0$ (the status associated to nodes with $m = 0$, i.e. the leaves); then, for any node in the input labeled $l$ with rank $m$, the corresponding node of the state tree is labeled $f_l(q_1, \ldots, q_m)$, where $q_1, \ldots, q_m$ are the states labeling the offspring of that state tree node. Finally, an input tree is accepted by $\mathcal{A}_t$ if the automaton can enter a final state upon encountering the root.

According to the above definition, the *language recognized* by $\mathcal{A}_t$ is the set $T(\mathcal{A}_t) = \{T | T \text{ in } T_\Sigma, \ \mathcal{A}_t \text{ can halt in a state in } F \text{ when the root of } T \text{ is reached}\}$.

It is not difficult to realize that, given an expansive tree grammar $G_t(V, r, S, P)$ generating the set $L(G_t)$ of trees with nodes labeled with elements in $\Sigma$, it is always possible to construct a FRA $\mathcal{A}_t$ that recognizes $L(G_t)$. In fact, let $Q = N$ with $F = \{S\}$ and, for each symbol $a$ in $\Sigma$, define a transition function $f_a$ such that $f_a(X_1, \ldots, X_n) = X$ *iff* there is in $G_t$ a production

### 4.10.2   Computational Results

All the results reported in this section are based on the observation that a sigmoid function can approximate a step function to an arbitrary degree of precision by augmenting the modulus of the associated weight vector. Thus, if it is demonstrated that a recursive network with step functions can implement any FRA, the result holds for recursive networks with sigmoids as well.

Elman-style networks, i.e. recursive networks with fully interconnected hidden units, turn out to be powerful enough to simulate any FRA (Sperduti, 1997):

### Theorem 4.10.1
An Elman-style network can simulate any FRA.

The proof is based on a constructive procedure using step function units: there will be a hidden unit for each transition function of the FRA, and a state is represented by the set of units associated to transition functions which introduce the same state in the computation.

Unfortunately, not all the neural networks for the processing of structures are as powerful as Elman-style networks. In fact, the following theorems state that both Cascade-Correlation networks and Neural Trees cannot simulate any FRA (Sperduti, 1997).

### Theorem 4.10.2
A Cascade-Correlation network for structures cannot simulate any FRA.

The proof for this theorem is obtained by observing that a Cascade-Correlation network for structures is a generalization of a Recurrent Cascade-Correlation network which has been proved unable to simulate any finite-state machine (Giles et al., 1995; Kremer, 1996). Since a finite-state machine is equivalent to an FRA with relations having rank 1, it follows that a Cascade-Correlation network for structures, which in the finite-state machine case reduces to a Recurrent Cascade-Correlation network, cannot simulate any FRA.

The same kind of limitation is proved for Neural Trees.

### Theorem 4.10.3
A Neural Tree for structures cannot simulate any FRA.

This is demonstrated by showing the following result (Sperduti, 1997):

### Theorem 4.10.4
Any Neural Tree for structures can be implemented by a Cascade-Correlation network for structures.

The above theorem holds since it is observed that a Neural Tree can be cast in the form of a three-layer feedforward network. The trick is to retain all the units associated with internal nodes of the Neural Tree as units of the first layer. The second layer of units is then used to represent all the possible paths from the root to one leaf. Finally, the output layer will implement the **or** of the paths associated to leaves of the corresponding class. The proof is then concluded by observing that the feedforward network belongs to the class of architectures implemented by Cascade-Correlation for structures.

Note that from the previous two theorems, and from the fact that Cascade-Correlation networks and Neural Trees for structures are generalizations of Recurrent Cascade-Correlation networks and Neural Trees for sequences, respectively, we have

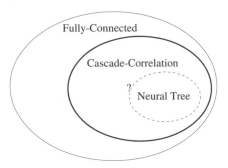

**Figure 4.4**  Graphical representation of the computational relationships between different recursive neural network architectures.

### Corollary 1
A Neural Tree for sequences cannot simulate any Finite-State Machine.

and

### Corollary 2
Any Neural Tree for sequences can be simulated by a Recurrent Cascade-Correlation network.

A summary of the computational results is given in graphical form in Figure 4.4.

### 4.10.3   Function Approximation

Theoretical results on the capacity of recursive neural networks to approximate an arbitrary mapping from a set of labeled trees to the reals have been developed in (Hammer and Sperschneider, 1997). Specifically, given

- a set $\mathcal{S}$ of trees with labels in a finite set;
- a function $\bar{f} : \mathcal{S} \to \mathbb{R}^q$;
- set of functions $\mathcal{F}$ implementable by a recursive neural network defined as in (Goller and Küchler, 1996);

the following result holds

### Theorem 4.10.5
For any $\epsilon > 0$ there exists a function $f^\epsilon \in \mathcal{F}$ such that $\forall s \in \mathcal{S}, \; P(|f^\epsilon(s) - \bar{f}(s)| > \epsilon) < \epsilon$

This result is quite interesting, since it states that if the set of possible labels is finite, then any mapping from trees to the set of reals can be implemented by a recursive neural network having a sufficient number of parameters. No universal mapping result for arbitrary real valued vectors as labels, however, has been established up to now.

---

## 4.11 Complexity Issues

A usual problem in neural networks is the evaluation of how many resources a network needs to implement a desired function. In this section, we explore this problem from a node-complexity perspective when considering the implementation of *Frontier-to-Root Tree Automata with Output* (FRAO) into recursive neural networks.

Here we report upper bounds on the number of units needed to implement a given FRAO in four-, three-, and two-layer recursive networks. While the bound for four-layer networks constitutes a generalization of the bound discussed in (Horne and Hush, 1996) for the implementation of Finite-State Machines (FSM) in recurrent networks, the bound for three-layer networks produces, as a special case, a new bound to the implementation of Finite-State Automata (FSA) in three-layer networks. Moreover, the bound for three-layer networks is constructive. Thus, it may become useful for practical applications where *a priori* knowledge available in the form of formal languages or inferred by symbolic machine learning approaches can be injected into the neural network. For the case of recurrent neural networks see Chapter 3 and (Omlin and Giles, 1996; Frasconi et al., 1995). Its constructive proof is based on the encoding of each possible input configuration of the FRA by a different integer in a predefined interval. This integer is then processed by the repeated application of the *telescopic* technique (Siu et al., 1995), which is so called because it consists of the progressive activation of a set of units according to the magnitude of the processed integer. On the basis of this progressive encoding, it is possible to implement both the transition and output function of the desired FRAO.

Finally, a lower bound based on a counting argument is reported, which demonstrates the optimality of the upper bound obtained for four-layer recursive networks.

### 4.11.1 Representing FRAO as Boolean Functions

In (Horne and Hush, 1996) the $m$ states of a FSA are encoded through $\log m$ bits. Hence, the state and output transition functions can be implemented by a boolean function

$$\{0,1\}^{\log m + \log l} \to \{0,1\}^{\log m + \log l} \tag{4.42}$$

where $\log m$ bits in the input are used to encode the current status, while the remaining $\log l$ bits are used to encode the current input label. Similarly, $\log m$ bits in the output are used to encode the new status and one bit to encode the output bit.

In a similar way an FRAO can be implemented by a boolean function

$$\{0,1\}^{\log l + N \log m} \to \{0,1\}^{\log l + \log m} \tag{4.43}$$

where $\log l$ is the number of bits encoding the input-output symbols, and $N$ is the maximum rank for the symbols.

### 4.11.2   Upper Bounds

Even in this case, the fact that a sigmoid function can approximate a step function to an arbitrary degree of precision by augmenting the modulus of the associated weight vector, implies that any complexity bound based on threshold gates is also valid for sigmoidal networks.

It is known that Finite-State Automata with $m$ states and binary alphabet can be inserted in four-layer recurrent neural networks with $O(\sqrt{m})$ units (Horne and Hush, 1996). This result was obtained by exploiting the following lemma by Lupanov (Lupanov, 1972):

***Lemma 4.1***
Arbitrary boolean logic functions of the form $f : \{0,1\}^x \to \{0,1\}^y$ can be implemented in a four-layer network of perceptrons with a node complexity of $O(\sqrt{\frac{y2^x}{x - \log y}})$.

Using the same lemma the following theorem can be proved:

***Theorem 4.11.1   Four-Layer Insertion***
Any FRAO with $m$ states, $l$ input-output labels, and maximum rank $N$, can be implemented by a four-layer recursive neural network with a node complexity of $O(\sqrt{\frac{(\log l + \log m) l m^N}{\log l + N \log m}})$.

If $l < m$ the node complexity can be simplified to $O(\sqrt{\frac{l m^N}{N}})$.

If the network is constrained to have three layers, then by using the telescopic technique (Siu et al., 1995) it can be proven that:

***Theorem 4.11.2   Three-Layer Insertion***
Any FRAO with $m$ states, $l$ input-output labels, and maximum rank $N$, can be implemented by a three-layer recursive neural network with a node complexity of $O((\log l + \log m)\sqrt{l m^N})$ and with $O((\log l + \log m) l m^N)$ connections.

Note that the result stated in the theorem gives a direct upper bound to the insertion of FSA in three-layer recurrent networks as well:

***Corollary 3***
A three-layer recurrent neural network can implement FSMs having $m$ states, and $l$ input-output labels, with a node complexity of $O((\log l + \log m)\sqrt{l m})$ and with $O((\log l + \log m) l m)$ connections.

Finally, when considering two-layer networks, the application of the telescopic technique allows the establishment of the following theorem

### Theorem 4.11.3  Two-Layer Implementation
Any FRAO with $m$ states, $l$ input-output labels, and maximum rank $N$, can be implemented by a two-layer recursive neural network with a node complexity of $O(lm^N)$ and with $O((\log l + N \log m)lm^N)$ connections.

### 4.11.3   A Lower Bound on the Node Complexity

When considering the minimum number of neurons that are required to implement arbitrary FRAO into recursive networks, a first naive consideration would lead to $\Omega(\log l + \log m)$ since $l$ different input symbols and $m$ states can effectively be encoded by $\log l + \log m$ units.

However, by using counting arguments similar in nature to the ones used by Alon et al. and Horn and Hush (lower bounds on the node complexity for recurrent network implementations of FSA (Alon et al., 1991; Horne and Hush, 1996)), it is possible to derive an improved lower bound:

### Theorem 4.11.4  Lower Bound, Node Complexity
The node complexity required to implement an arbitrary FRAO with $m$ states, $l$ input-output labels and maximum rank $N$ in a recursive neural network is $\Omega(\sqrt{\frac{(\log l + \log m)lm^N}{\log l + N \log m}})$.

This result clearly states the optimality of the upper bound for the four-layer networks.

### 4.11.4   Bounds on Learning

It is well known that any neural network learning algorithm may be seriously plagued by the presence of local minima in the associated error function. This is also true for the class of algorithms we have introduced here. Recently, however, the efficiency of learning the membership of DOAGs in terms of local minima of the error surface, by relying on the principle that their absence is a guarantee of efficient learning, has been analyzed (Frasconi et al., 1997). The authors give a sufficient condition under which the error surface is free of local minima. In particular, they define a topological index associated with a collection of DOAGs that make it possible to design the architecture so as to avoid local minima. The condition they give holds for any training set composed of graphs with symbolic nodes and a neural network capable of learning the assigned data.

Finally, it is worth mentioning that some preliminary results on the VC-dimension of a specific type of recursive neural network are given in (Hammer, 1997).

## 4.12    Conclusions

The possibility of representing and processing structures in a neural network greatly increases the potential of integration between neural networks and symbol systems in a knowledge-based neurocomputing system. In fact, structures generated by a symbolic module can be evaluated by this type of network and their evaluation can be used to modify the behavior of the symbolic module. An instance of this integration scheme is given, for example, by learning heuristics for automated deduction systems. Goller reported very successful results in using a Backpropagation Through Structure network within the SETHEO theorem prover (Goller, 1997). On the other hand, it is not difficult to figure out, in analogy with finite-state automata extraction from recurrent networks, how to extract tree automata from a neural network for structures. This would allow the above scheme to work the other way around, with a neural module which is driven by a symbolic subsystem.

Another application domain where neurocomputing of structures has already shown promising results is in chemistry (Bianucci et al., 1999). In this domain, compounds are naturally represented as labeled graphs. However, the main computational target typically consists of assigning numerical ratings to chemical compounds in order to establish their usefulness in specific applications. Neural networks for structures are particularly good at performing this kind of task.

From the above examples it should be clear that neural networks for structures have the potential of building a very natural bridge between two totally different ways of representing concepts. This constitutes a contribution towards the development of a homogeneous and systematic methodology for the integration of components of different types in a knowledge-based system.

## References

Almeida, L. B. 1987. A learning rule for asynchronous perceptrons with feedback in a combinatorial environment. In *Proceedings of the IEEE First Annual International Conference on Neural Networks*, eds. M. Caudil and C. Butler, pp. 609–618, San Diego, CA. IEEE.

Alon, N., Dewdney, A. K., and Ott, T. J. 1991. Efficient Simulation of Finite Automata by Neural Nets. *Journal of the ACM*, 38(2):495–514.

Atiya, A. 1988. Learning on a general network. In *Neural Information Processing Systems*, ed. D. Z. Anderson, pp. 22–30. New York: AIP.

Atlas, L. E., Cole, R., Muthusamy, Y., Lippman, A., Connor, J. T., Park, D., El-Sharkawi, M., and Marks, R. J. 1992. A performance comparison of trained multilayer perceptrons and trained classification trees. *Proceedings of the IEEE*, 78:1614–1619.

Bianucci, A. M., Micheli, A., Sperduti, A., and Starita, A. 1999. Application of cascade-correlation networks for structures to chemistry. *Applied Intelligence*. To appear.

Breiman, L., Friedman, J., Olshen, R., and Stone, C. 1984. *Classification and Regression Trees*. Wadsworth International Group.

Cohen, M. A. and Grossberg, S. 1983. Absolute stability of global pattern formation and parallel memory storage by competitive neural networks. *IEEE Trans. on Systems, Man, and Cybernetics*, 13:815–826.

Cormen, T. H., Leiserson, C. E., and Rivest, R. L. 1990. *Introduction to Algorithms*. MIT Press.

Fahlman, S. E. 1991. The recurrent cascade-correlation architecture. In *Advances in Neural Information Processing Systems 3*, eds. R. P. Lippmann, J. E. Moody, and D. S. Touretzky, pp. 190–196, San Mateo, CA. Morgan Kaufmann Publishers.

Fahlman, S. E. and Lebiere, C. 1990. The cascade-correlation learning architecture. In *Advances in Neural Information Processing Systems 2*, ed. D. S. Touretzky, pp. 524–532. San Mateo, CA: Morgan Kaufmann.

Frasconi, P., Gori, M., and Soda, G. 1995. Recurrent Neural Networks and Prior Knowledge for Sequence Processing: A Constrained Nondeterministic Approach. *Knowledge-Based Systems*, 8(6):313–332.

Frasconi, P., Gori, M., and Sperduti, A. 1997. On the efficient classification of data structures by neural networks. In *Proceedings of the International Joint Conference on Artificial Intelligence*, pp. 1066–1071.

Frasconi, P., Gori, M., and Sperduti, A. 1998. A framework for adaptive data structures processing. *IEEE Transactions on Neural Networks*, 9(5):768–786.

Giles, C. L., Chen, D., Sun, G. Z., Chen, H. H., Lee, Y. C., and Goudreau, M. W. 1995. Constructive learning of recurrent neural networks: Limitations of recurrent casade correlation and a simple solution. *IEEE Transactions on Neural Networks*, 6(4):829–836.

Goller, C. 1997. *A Connectionist Approach for Learning Search-Control Heuristics for Automated Deduction Systems*. PhD thesis, Technical University Munich, Faculty of Computer Science.

Goller, C. and Küchler, A. 1996. Learning task-dependent distributed structure-representations by backpropagation through structure. In *IEEE International Conference on Neural Networks*, pp. 347–352.

Gonzalez, R. C. and Thomason, M. G. 1978. *Syntactical Pattern Recognition*. Addison-Wesley.

Goudreau, M. W., Giles, C. L., Chakradhar, S. T., and Chen, D. 1994. First-order vs. second-order single-layer recurrent neural networks. *IEEE Transactions on Neural Networks*, 5(3):511–513.

Hall, L. H. and Kier, L. B. 1991. Chapter 9. The molecular connectivity Chi indexes and Kappa shape indexes in structure-property modeling. In *Reviews in Computational Chemistry*, eds. K. B. Lipkowitz and D. B. Boyd, pp. 367–422.

VCH Publishers, Inc.: New York.

Hammer, B. 1997. Learning recursive data is intractable. Osnabrücker Schriften zur Mathematik Reihe P, Heft 194, Fachbereich Mathematik/Informatik, Universität Osnabrück, 49069 Osnabrück.

Hammer, B. and Sperschneider, V. 1997. Neural networks can approximate mappings on structured objects. In *ICCIN '97, 2nd International Conference on Computational Intelligence and Neuroscience*.

Haykin, S. 1994. *Neural Networks: A Comprehensive Foundation*. Piscataway, NJ: IEEE Press.

Hinton, G. E. 1990. Mapping part-whole hierarchies into connectionist networks. *Artificial Intelligence*, 46:47–75.

Hopfield, J. J. 1984. Neurons with graded response have collective computational properties like those of two-state neurons. In *Proc. Natl. Acad. Sci.*, pp. 3088–3092.

Horne, B. G. and Hush, D. R. 1996. Bounds on the complexity of recurrent neural network implementations of finite state machines. *Neural Networks*, 9(2):243–252.

Kremer, S. C. 1995. On the computational power of Elman-style recurrent networks. *IEEE Transactions on Neural Networks*, 6(4):1000–1004.

Kremer, S. C. 1996. Finite state automata that recurrent cascade-correlation cannot represent. In *Advances in Neural Information Processing Systems 7*, eds. D. Touretzky, M. Mozer, and M. Hasselmo. MIT Press. 612–618.

Li, T., Fang, L., and Jennings, A. 1992. Structurally adaptive self-organizing neural trees. In *International Joint Conference on Neural Networks*, pp. 329–334.

Lupanov, O. 1972. Circuits using Threshold elements. *Soviet Physics—Doklady*, 17(2):91–93.

Metcalfe, E. J. 1991. Recognition failure and charm. *Psychological Review*, 98(4):529–553.

Murdock, B. B. 1993. TODAM2: A model for the storage and retrieval of item, associative, and serial-order information. *Psychological Review*, 100(2):183–203.

Omlin, C. W. and Giles, C. L. 1996. Constructing Deterministic Finite-State Automata in Recurrent Neural Networks. *Journal of the ACM*, 43(2):937–972.

Perrone, M. P. 1992. A soft-competitive splitting rule for adaptive tree-structured neural networks. In *International Joint Conference on Neural Networks*, pp. 689–693.

Perrone, M. P. and Intrator, N. 1992. Unsupervised splitting rules for neural tree classifiers. In *International Joint Conference on Neural Networks*, pp. 820–825.

Pineda, F. J. 1988. Dynamics and architecture for neural computation. *Journal of Complexity*, 4:216–245.

Plate, T. A. 1995. Holographic reduced representations. *IEEE Transactions on Neural Networks*, 6(3):623–641.

Pollack, J. B. 1990. Recursive distributed representations. *Artificial Intelligence*, 46(1-2):77–106.

Rumelhart, D. E. and McClelland, J. L. 1986. *Parallel Distributed Processing: Explorations in the Microstructure of Cognition*. MIT Press.

Sankar, A. and Mammone, R. 1991. Neural tree networks. In *Neural Networks: Theory and Applications*, eds. R. Mammone and Y. Zeevi, pp. 281–302. Academic Press.

Sethi, I. K. 1990. Entropy nets: From decision trees to neural networks. *Proceedings of the IEEE*, 78:1605–1613.

Siegelmann, H. T. and Sontag, E. D. 1995. On the computational power of neural nets. *Journal of Computer and System Sciences*, 50(1):132–150.

Sirat, J. A. and Nadal, J.-P. 1990. Neural trees: A new tool for classification. *Network*, 1:423–438.

Siu, K.-Y., Roychowdhury, V., and Kailath, T. 1995. *Discrete Neural Computation*. Englewood Cliffs, New Jersey: Prentice Hall.

Smolensky, P. 1990. Tensor product variable binding and the representation of symbolic structures in connectionist systems. *Artificial Intelligence*, 46:159–216.

Sperduti, A. 1994a. Encoding of Labeled Graphs by Labeling RAAM. In *Advances in Neural Information Processing Systems 6*, eds. J. D. Cowan, G. Tesauro, and J. Alspector, pp. 1125–1132. San Mateo, CA: Morgan Kaufmann.

Sperduti, A. 1994b. Labeling RAAM. *Connection Science*, 6(4):429–459.

Sperduti, A. 1997. On the computational power of recurrent neural networks for structures. *Neural Networks*, 10(3).

Sperduti, A., Majidi, D., and Starita, A. 1996. Extended cascade-correlation for syntactic and structural pattern recognition. In *Advances in Structural and Syntactical Pattern Recognition*, eds. P. Perner, P. Wang, and A. Rosenfeld, Lecture notes in Computer Science, pp. 90–99. Berlin: Springer-Verlag.

Sperduti, A. and Starita, A. 1996. A general learning framework for the RAAM family. In *Neural Nets WIRN Vietri–95*, eds. M. Marinaro and R. Tagliaferri, pp. 136–141. Singapore: World Scientific.

Sperduti, A. and Starita, A. 1997. Supervised neural networks for the classification of structures. *IEEE Transactions on Neural Networks*, 8(3):714–735.

Sperduti, A., Starita, A., and Goller, C. 1995. Learning distributed representations for the classification of terms. In *Proceedings of the International Joint Conference on Artificial Intelligence*, pp. 509–515.

Thatcher, J. W. 1973. Tree automata: An informal survey. In *Currents in the Theory of Computing*, ed. A. V. Aho. Englewood Cliffs, NJ: Prentice-Hall.

Touretzky, D. S. 1990. BoltzCONS: Dynamic symbol structures in a connectionist network. *Artificial Intellicence*, 46:5–46.

Touretzky, D. S. and Hinton, G. E. 1988. A distributed connectionist production system. *Cognitive science*, 12(3):423–466.

Williams, R. J. and Zipser, D. 1989. A learning algorithm for continually running fully recurrent neural networks. *Neural Computation*, 1:270–280.

# 5     Structural Learning and Rule Discovery

Masumi Ishikawa

*An overview of structural learning is presented. This is followed by a detailed description of structural learning with forgetting. In contrast to backpropagation learning, it adopts local representation to facilitate the interpretation of hidden units. Various applications such as classification, discovery of recurrent network structure, time series prediction and so forth are presented. Adaptive characteristics are also evaluated. Various methods of rule extraction or rule discovery using neural networks are summarized. Comparative studies among various methods using neural networks and artificial intelligence are shown, emphasizing the importance of structural learning. Learning of modular structured networks and its applications are presented. Integration of symbols and patterns is discussed.*

## 5.1   Introduction

Neural networks have been used extensively in various application domains since their resurgence in the middle of the 1980s. Notwithstanding the similarity of neural networks and brains, many users feel strongly that neural networks are difficult to handle because of their black-box character; the resulting networks are often hard to understand.

It is widely known that, despite its popularity, backpropagation (BP) learning suffers from serious difficulties. The first difficulty is the necessity of prior specification of a network structure. Needless to say, the selection of a network structure is important; if the size of a network is too large, it generalizes poorly, and if it is too small, learning of training samples becomes insufficient. Since prior structural information is hardly available in most cases, learning with trial and error becomes inevitable. The second difficulty is the interpretation of hidden units. It is attributed to excess degrees of freedom of a network and to distributed representation on hidden layers. The third difficulty is a scaling problem: computational cost grows rapidly as the network size increases. The fourth difficulty is a local minima problem, which becomes more and more serious as the network size increases.

There have been various studies aiming at the solution of the first two difficulties. I call these methods *structural learning*. Most structural learning methods have focused on the decrease in computational cost and the number of units or connections in a network. Still more important, I believe, is to obtain a network with a white-box character. This facilitates the discovery of regularities or rules from data. There have been many structural learning algorithms, but, as far as I know, there are only a few algorithms which face this difficulty squarely. I have proposed a novel structural learning method called a structural learning with forgetting (hereafter referred to as SLF), which aims at obtaining neural networks with a white-box character (Ishikawa, 1989, 1994b,c, 1996d).

The following section provides an overview of structural learning. It is followed by a detailed description of SLF. To evaluate its effectiveness, it is applied to several examples: the discovery of Boolean functions, classification of irises, discovery of recurrent network structure and prediction of time series. The adaptive character of SLF is also evaluated. Rule extraction or rule discovery is becoming popular in an attempt to automate knowledge acquisition. An overview of rule extraction or rule discovery using neural networks is described. SLF is particularly suitable for rule discovery. Its applications to various databases are also presented. SLF is also effective in the learning of modular structured networks and is considered to be a promising solution to the third and the fourth difficulties of BP learning. Last, integration of symbols and patterns is discussed.

## 5.2   Structural Learning Methods

Structural learning methods aim at ameliorating the first and the second difficulties of BP learning mentioned in the Introduction: prior specification of network structure and the interpretation of hidden units. They are roughly classified into four categories: various pruning algorithms by adding a penalty term to the conventional quadratic criterion of the mean square error (MSE) (Reed, 1993), the deletion of hidden units with little contribution to the MSE, the deletion of connections with little contribution to the MSE, and the incremental increase in the number of hidden units until the MSE becomes sufficiently small.

The above first three categories are called *destructive* learning and the last one is called *constructive* learning. Since the former starts with a large-size network and the latter starts with a small-size one, the computational cost for the former is larger than that for the latter. On the other hand, the former is expected to have larger generalization ability than the latter, because the former optimizes the connection weights simultaneously, whereas the latter optimizes a part of them sequentially.

### 5.2.1    Addition of a Penalty Term

The simplest additional term is the sum of squares of the connection weights (Nowlan and Hinton, 1986).

$$J_q = J + \frac{\lambda}{2} \sum_{i,j} w_{ij}^2 = \sum_k (o_k - t_k)^2 + \frac{\lambda}{2} \sum_{i,j} w_{ij}^2 \tag{5.1}$$

where $J$ is the quadratic criterion in BP learning, $\lambda$ is the relative importance of the additional penalty term, $w_{ij}$ is the connection weight from unit $j$ to unit $i$, $o_k$ is the output of output unit $k$, and $t_k$ is its target.

The penalty term in Equation 5.1 causes exponential decay to connection weights, i.e. the amount of decay is proportional to the corresponding connection weight. This characteristic causes two difficulties. First, a small amount of decay for weak connections makes the decay speed extremely slow. Thus it takes a long time for weak connections to fade out completely. Second, a large amount of decay for strong connections causes severe degradation of the learning performance in terms of the MSE.

Rumelhart proposed the following penalty term, $C$, representing the complexity of a network(Rumelhart, 1988).

$$J_c = \lambda J + (1 - \lambda)C \tag{5.2}$$

$$C = \sum_{i,j} \frac{w_{ij}^2}{1 + w_{ij}^2} + \sum_{i,j} \frac{w_{ij}^2}{1 + \sum_k w_{ik}^2} \tag{5.3}$$

where $\lambda$ and $(1 - \lambda)$ indicate the relative importance of the quadratic criterion and that of the penalty term, respectively. However, it has a deficiency similar to the exponential weight decay for weak connections, because each term on the right of Equation 5.3 is approximated as $w_{ij}^2$ for weak connections.

Structural learning with forgetting (SLF) (Ishikawa, 1989, 1996d) will be described in detail in the following section.

Minimum entropy learning (Ishikawa and Uchida, 1992) adopts an entropy function, $H$, as a penalty term.

$$J_e = J + \lambda H = J - \lambda \sum_{i,j} P_{ij} \log_2 P_{ij} \tag{5.4}$$

$$P_{ij} = \frac{|w_{ij}|}{\sum_{m,n} |w_{mn}|} \tag{5.5}$$

where $\lambda$ indicates the relative importance of the penalty term and $P_{ij}$ represents a relative connection weight. Its advantage is that the penalty term has a clear meaning based on information theory.

Lateral inhibition learning uses the following equation for weight change (Yasui, 1992).

$$\Delta w_{ij} = \Delta w'_{ij} - \varepsilon sgn(w_{ij}) \sum_{k=1, \neq j}^{n} |w_{ik}| \qquad (5.6)$$

where $\Delta w'_{ij}$ is the weight change due to backpropagation learning, and $sgn(x)$ is the sign function., i.e. 1 when $x$ is positive and $-1$ otherwise. It was originally proposed as the above form, but can also be formulated as an additional term.

Bayesian learning (Buntine and Weigend, 1991; MacKay, 1995; Ishikawa, 1996a) may also be regarded as belonging to this category, and provides a procedure for finding the optimal relative weight of a penalty or a regularization term.

### 5.2.2   Deletion of Unnecessary Units

Structural learning methods in this category try to optimize the number of hidden units.

Mozer and Smolensky proposed a skeletonization method: estimate the increase in MSE due to the removal of a hidden unit and delete the one with the smallest increase (Mozer and Smolensky, 1989). This approach has the following difficulties. First, the estimation is difficult and can only be an approximation. Second, it is assumed implicitly that the optimal structure can be obtained by adjusting the number of hidden units. However, this assumption does not necessarily hold; the optimal structure might be sparse as is seen in subsequent examples.

### 5.2.3   Deletion of Unnecessary Connections

Structural learning methods in this category include Optimal Brain Damage (OBD) (Cun et al., 1990) and Optimal Brain Surgeon (OBS)(Hassibi et al., 1994).

OBD deletes connections which have little contribution to the MSE and train the network again. This process is repeated until the deletion of any connection causes a large increase in the MSE. The following second derivative of the quadratic criterion, $s_{ij}$, estimates the increase in the quadratic criterion, when the connection $w_{ij}$ is removed from a network.

$$s_{ij} = \frac{1}{2} w_{ij}^{o2} \frac{\partial^2 J}{\partial w_{ij}^2}|_{w_{ij}=w_{ij}^o} \qquad (5.7)$$

where $w_{ij}^o$ is the connection weight which minimizes the quadratic criterion.

To be noted is that the estimate in Equation 5.7 is the product of the squared connection weight and the second derivative of the quadratic criterion. It clearly indicates that it is not appropriate to remove connections simply because their weights are small; weak connections with large second derivatives can be significant.

In the above estimation, the Hessian matrix is approximated with a diagonal matrix. OBS uses the full Hessian matrix for the estimation.

### 5.2.4  Constructive Learning

In constructive learning, the number of hidden units is incrementally increased until the MSE becomes sufficiently small. Gallant proposes a Tower construction algorithm for binary inputs and outputs (Gallant, 1986). Ash proposes simple incremental learning (Ash, 1989). Fahlman et al. propose a cascade-correlation learning architecture (Fahlman and Lebiere, 1990).

## 5.3  Structural Learning with Forgetting

SLF is composed of three successive algorithms: learning with forgetting, learning with hidden units clarification and learning with selective forgetting. SLF can be extended to recurrent networks. The interpretation of forgetting and its determination are also discussed.

### 5.3.1  Learning with Forgetting

The criterion function in the learning with forgetting is,

$$J_f = J + \varepsilon' \sum_{i,j} |w_{ij}| = \sum_k (o_k - t_k)^2 + \varepsilon' \sum_{i,j} |w_{ij}| \tag{5.8}$$

where the first term on the right side, $J$, is the quadratic criterion in BP learning, the second term is a penalty term, $\varepsilon'$ is its relative weight, and $J_f$ is a total criterion.

The weight change, $\Delta w_{ij}$, is obtained by differentiating Equation 5.8 with respect to the connection weight, $w_{ij}$,

$$\Delta w_{ij} = -\eta \frac{\partial J_f}{\partial w_{ij}} = \Delta w'_{ij} - \varepsilon\, sgn(w_{ij}) \tag{5.9}$$

where $\Delta w'_{ij} (= -\eta \frac{\partial J}{\partial w_{ij}})$ is the weight change due to BP learning, $\eta$ is a learning rate, $\varepsilon\, (= \eta\varepsilon')$ is the amount of decay at each weight change, and $sgn(w_{ij})$ is the sign function.

As shown in Equation 5.9, a key idea of SLF is constant decay of connection weights in contrast to exponential decay(Nowlan and Hinton, 1986). The difference may seem trivial, but results are quite different. The learning with forgetting or constant decay has twofold advantages. First, unnecessary connections fade away and a skeletal network emerges. Because of this, prior specification of the network structure is no longer required. The resulting skeletal networks enable the discovery of regularity or rules from data. Second, the MSE is much smaller than that from learning with exponential decay.

Learning with forgetting, however, causes two difficulties. The first is the emergence of distributed representation on hidden layers, which hinders the discovery of regularity or rules. Learning with *hidden units clarification*, which succeeds learning with forgetting, solves this difficulty. The second difficulty is that the MSE of learning with forgetting is still larger than that of BP learning. Learning with *selective* forgetting solves this deficiency.

### 5.3.2   Learning with Hidden Units Clarification

Distributed representation prevents hidden units from being fully active (1) or inactive (0). Learning with hidden units clarification using the following criterion dissipates distributed representation by forcing each hidden unit to be fully active or inactive.

$$J_h = J_f + c \sum_i min\{1 - h_i, h_i\} \tag{5.10}$$

where $h_i$ is the output of hidden unit $i$ satisfying $h_i \in [0, 1]$, and $c$ is a relative weight of the penalty term.

The minimization of the penalty term can easily be carried out by taking the derivative of $1 - h$, $h > 0.5$, or $h$, $h < 0.5$, with respect to the connection weight $w_{ij}$. In the present paper, however, a simple three-layer network which approximates a nonlinear mapping from $h_i$ to $min\{1 - h_i, h_i\}$ is used instead.

### 5.3.3   Learning with Selective Forgetting

The MSE of learning with forgetting is larger than that of BP learning, because the former minimizes the total criterion, $J_f$, instead of the quadratic criterion, $J$. The following criterion makes only those connection weights decay whose absolute values are smaller than a threshold, $\theta$.

$$J_s = J + \varepsilon' \sum_{|w_{ij}| < \theta} |w_{ij}| \tag{5.11}$$

This penalty term makes the MSE much smaller than that of learning with forgetting, because the summation is restricted only to weak connections. It also prevents the revival of deleted connections.

### 5.3.4   Procedure of SLF

SLF is composed of the following three steps.

1. Train a neural network by learning with forgetting to obtain a rough skeletal structure.

2. Train it by both learning with forgetting and with hidden units clarification in order to dissipate distributed representation. This is skipped when target outputs are not binary.

3. Train it by both learning with selective forgetting and that with hidden units clarification to get better learning performance in terms of the MSE.

There are two ways of dealing with deleted connections. One method is to keep the deleted connections alive, i.e. continue computation even for zero-weight connections. In this case computational cost does not decrease, even if the number of zero-weight connections increases. However, it makes adaptive learning possible; once deleted connections can revive due to the change in the environment. The alternative is to discard deleted connections from the computation. This reduces computational cost, but can no longer learn adaptively.

### 5.3.5   Extension to Recurrent Networks

Backpropagation through time (BPTT) (Williams and Zipser, 1995) trains a recurrent network based on given sequences of external inputs and target outputs. A basic idea of BPTT is the conversion of a recurrent network into a multi-layer feedforward network whose number of layers equals the number of time steps. BPTT, however, has a similar drawback to BP; the resulting network tends to use up all the connections provided, preventing the extraction of structural information such as the location of feedback loops in a network. Generalized SLF (GSLF), a combination of SLF and BPTT, can solve this difficulty.

In BTPP, the following criterion function $J(t_0, t_1)$ is adopted,

$$J(t_0, t_1) = \sum_t J(t) = \sum_{t=t_0}^{t_1} \sum_j e_j(t)^2 \tag{5.12}$$

where $e_j(t)$ is the output error of output unit $j$ at time $t$. The weight change of connection weight $w_{ij}$ in GSLF is given by,

$$\Delta w_{ij}(t) = -\eta \frac{\partial J(t_0, t_1)}{\partial w_{ij}} - \varepsilon\, sgn(w_{ij})$$
$$= \eta \sum_t \delta_i(t) y_j(t-1) - \varepsilon\, sgn(w_{ij}) \tag{5.13}$$

### 5.3.6   Interpretation of Forgetting

The connection weight, $w_{ij}$, fades away due to forgetting, provided the total criterion $J_f$ becomes the minimum at $w_{ij} = 0$. From Equation 5.8, this condition can be written as,

$$\frac{\partial J_f}{\partial w_{ij}}|_{w_{ij}=0+} = \frac{\partial J}{\partial w_{ij}}|_{w_{ij}=0} + \varepsilon' > 0$$
$$\frac{\partial J_f}{\partial w_{ij}}|_{w_{ij}=0-} = \frac{\partial J}{\partial w_{ij}}|_{w_{ij}=0} - \varepsilon' < 0 \tag{5.14}$$

Equation 5.14 is equivalent to,

$$-\varepsilon' < \frac{\partial J}{\partial w_{ij}}|_{w_{ij}=0} < \varepsilon' \tag{5.15}$$

Equation 5.15 is the condition under which the connection weight, $w_{ij}$, fades away due to forgetting.

Consider now the similarity and the difference between SLF and OBD (Cun et al., 1990). Let $w_{ij}^o$ be the connection weight which minimizes the quadratic criterion. The middle term in Equation 5.15 can be approximated as follows by expansion around $w_{ij}^o$, provided $w_{ij}$ is small.

$$\frac{\partial J}{\partial w_{ij}}|_{w_{ij}=0} \approx \frac{\partial J}{\partial w_{ij}}|_{w_{ij}=w_{ij}^o} - w_{ij}^o \frac{\partial^2 J}{\partial w_{ij}^2}|_{w_{ij}=w_{ij}^o}$$

$$= -w_{ij}^o \frac{\partial^2 J}{\partial w_{ij}^2}|_{w_{ij}=w_{ij}^o} \tag{5.16}$$

where $\frac{\partial J}{\partial w_{ij}}|_{w_{ij}=w_{ij}^o}$ equals zero by definition. Therefore, Equation 5.15 is rewritten as the following using Equation 5.16.

$$-\varepsilon' < w_{ij}^o \frac{\partial^2 J}{\partial w_{ij}^2}|_{w_{ij}=w_{ij}^o} < \varepsilon' \tag{5.17}$$

OBD uses $\frac{1}{2} w_{ij}^{o2} \frac{\partial^2 J}{\partial w_{ij}^2}|_{w_{ij}=w_{ij}^o}$ as an estimate of the increase in the MSE when the connection $w_{ij}$ is removed. Connections with small estimates are removed from a network. Simply removing a connection with a small weight is not appropriate, because it causes severe degradation in the MSE when the corresponding second derivative is large. This estimate is close to the one in Equation 5.17, representing the estimate of the derivative of the quadratic criterion. It indicates close similarity between SLF and OBD.

They differ in the manner that estimates are obtained and used. In OBD, the estimate must be explicitly calculated, and the connections with estimates smaller than a threshold are deleted by a model builder. In SLF, on the contrary, there is no need to explicitly calculate the estimate in Equation 5.17, and unnecessary connections fade away automatically. This simplicity is a big advantage of SLF over OBD.

From a Bayesian point of view (MacKay, 1995), a penalty term represents a prior distribution of connection weights. In the case of quadratic weights (Nowlan and Hinton, 1986), the prior distribution of each connection weight is Gaussian. In the case of the penalty criterion in Equation 5.8, the prior distribution is exponential. The difference between the Gaussian and exponential distributions is that the latter has a much broader tail than the former.

### 5.3.7   Determination of the Amount of Decay

Needless to say, the determination of the amount of decay in Equation 5.9, $\varepsilon$, or a regularization parameter in Equation 5.8, $\varepsilon'$, is important. If $\varepsilon$ is too large, even the necessary connections fade away, causing severe degradation in the MSE. On the other hand, if $\varepsilon$ is too small, unnecessary connections do not fade away, resulting in a network far from skeletal.

There are three methods of determining $\varepsilon$. First, the MSE for test data $(\text{MSE}_p)$, is used. Its disadvantage is the requirement of test data in addition to training data. It is intuitively understandable, but when the number of samples is small, it is difficult to apply due to the shortage of data.

Second, an information criterion, AIC, evaluates the goodness of fit of given models based on MSE for training data and the number of estimated parameters (Akaike, 1974; Fogel, 1991; Kurita, 1990).

$$AIC = -2\log(\text{maximum likelihood}) + 2K \qquad (5.18)$$

where $K$ is the number of independently estimated parameters. If output errors are statistically independent of each other and follow normal distribution with zero mean and a constant variance, Equation 5.18 can be approximated as,

$$AIC = Nk\log(\hat{\sigma}^2) + 2K \qquad (5.19)$$

where $N$ is the number of training data, $k$ is the number of output units and $\hat{\sigma}^2$ is the maximum likelihood estimate of the MSE. In the presence of a regularizer, the Network Information Criterion (NIC) (Murata et al., 1994) is more appropriate to use than AIC, because NIC is formulated for a criterion with a regularizer.

In the above two methods, models are trained with various $\varepsilon$'s. Among them, the one with the smallest measure is selected as optimal. This is equivalent to the determination of the amount of decay.

Third, a Bayesian approach is used for determining regularization parameters (Buntine and Weigend, 1991; MacKay, 1995; Ishikawa, 1996a), which is also equivalent to the determination of the amount of decay. Its advantage is that, in contrast to other methods, training of only one model is sufficient. This is because regularization parameters are iteratively adjusted during training.

### 5.3.8 Model Selection

Although AIC or $\text{MSE}_p$ is useful in evaluating the goodness of fit of a given model, it is difficult to find the model with the largest goodness of fit from among all the possible models due to the huge search space. Consider a network with $n$ connections. Its submodels are obtained by removing a part of its connections. Since the number of submodels is $2^n - 1$, the search space is too large to examine all of them, unless $n$ is very small. In most cases, therefore, only a small part of it is actually examined to make the search feasible.

The difficulty is caused by the fact that AIC or $\text{MSE}_p$ does not provide prior information on which models should be examined. In the case of a three-layer network with $N_H$ hidden units, only the fully connected three-layer subnetworks with $h$ hidden units $(1 \le h \le N_H)$ are usually examined. However, the true model is not necessarily fully connected.

Recently, similar indicators such as FIS (Final Information Statistic) (Fogel, 1991), GPE (Generalized Prediction Error) (Moody, 1992) and NIC (Network

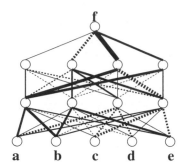

**Figure 5.1**  The resulting network in the discovery of the Boolean function, $f = (a \cup b) \cap (c \cup e)$, by BP learning. Solid lines and dashed lines represent positive and negative connection weights, respectively. The thickness of each connection is approximately proportional to the absolute value of its weight. The learning parameters are: learning rate $\eta = 0.1$ and a momentum $\alpha = 0.2$.

Information Criterion) (Murata et al., 1994) have been proposed. They share similar characteristics with AIC.

AIC or $\mathrm{MSE}_p$ provides useful information on the goodness of fit of given models, but does not provide prior information on which connections should be deleted. On the other hand, SLF provides the latter, but not the former. In other words, SLF deletes unnecessary connections with small derivatives, but does not tell us when to stop the deletion. These complementary characteristics necessitate the use of both SLF and AIC or $\mathrm{MSE}_p$.

## 5.4   Discovery of a Boolean Function

The discovery of a Boolean function is chosen as an example of binary inputs and outputs. The Boolean function to be discovered is,

$$f = (a \cup b) \cap (c \cup e) \qquad (5.20)$$

where the output, $f$, is the Boolean function with the inputs, $a$, $b$, $c$ and $e$, and $\cup$ and $\cap$ denote disjunction and conjunction, respectively.

The network structure adopted here is a 4-layer network: an input layer with five units, the first hidden layer with four units, the second hidden layer with four units, and an output layer with one unit. Although $f$ has four inputs, the irrelevant input, $d$, is included to evaluate the ability to detect irrelevances. Equation 5.20 suggests that a 3-layer network with 2 hidden units is sufficient for its representation, but a 4-layer network with sufficient hidden units is used to evaluate the ability of structure discovery.

There are $32(=2^5)$ pairs of input and output data, of which 26 pairs are used for training. Figure 5.1 illustrates the resulting network by BP learning. Its distributed

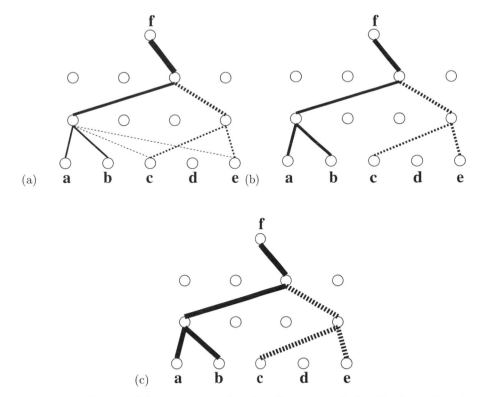

**Figure 5.2**   The resulting networks in the discovery of the Boolean function, $f = (a \cup b) \cap (c \cup e)$, by **(a)** learning with forgetting, **(b)** the combined use of learning with forgetting and learning with hidden units clarification, and **(c)** the combined use of learning with selective forgetting and learning with hidden units clarification. In (a) and (b), connections with weights smaller than 0.005 are not drawn for simplicity. (a) and (b) have 9 and 7 undrawn weak connections, respectively. (c) does not have such weak connections; all the connections are either strong or zero. The learning parameters are: $\eta = 0.1$, $\alpha = 0.2$, the amount of decay $\varepsilon = 10^{-4}$, and the threshold in selective forgetting $\theta = 0.1$.

representation prevents the discovery of the Boolean function. Also note that there are outgoing connections from the irrelevant input, $d$.

Learning with forgetting generates the network in Figure 5.2(a). It shows that on the first hidden layer only the first and the fourth units are used, the first representing $(a \cup b)$ and the fourth representing $(c \cup e)$. Closer observation reveals that the first unit also represents $(c \cup e)$, a minor term in the distributed representation on this layer. On the second hidden layer only the third unit is used, representing $(a \cup b) \cap (c \cup e)$. Learning with hidden units clarification dissipates distributed representation as in Figure 5.2(b). To improve the learning performance in terms of the MSE, both learning with selective forgetting and that with hidden units clarification are carried out, resulting in the network in Figure 5.2(c). It clearly indicates

**Table 5.1**  Performance comparison of SLF in the discovery of the Boolean function, $f = (a \cup b) \cap (c \cup e)$. $MSE_f$ is the MSE by learning with forgetting. The MSE and the $MSE_p$ correspond to the combined use of learning with selective forgetting and that with hidden units clarification. $K$ is the number of connections and biases.

| $\varepsilon$ $\times 10^{-4}$ | $MSE_f$ $\times 10^{-2}$ | $MSE$ $\times 10^{-2}$ | $MSE_p$ $\times 10^{-2}$ | $K$ | AIC |
|---|---|---|---|---|---|
| 0.0 | 0.0062 | 0.0062 | 0.0086 | 49 | $-153.90$ |
| 0.1 | 0.049 | 0.0058 | 0.0056 | 11 | $-231.63$ |
| 0.2 | 0.104 | 0.0060 | 0.0058 | 11 | $-230.75$ |
| 0.5 | 0.244 | 0.0064 | 0.0060 | 11 | $-229.07$ |
| 1.0 | 0.595 | 0.0052 | 0.0050 | 11 | $-234.47$ |
| 2.0 | 1.245 | 0.0060 | 0.0056 | 11 | $-230.75$ |
| 5.0 | 5.19 | 0.0054 | 0.0052 | 11 | $-233.49$ |
| 6.0 | 8.76 | 0.0056 | 0.0052 | 11 | $-232.54$ |
| 7.0 | 25.24 | 25.0 | 25.0 | 0 | $-36.04$ |

that only one hidden layer with two hidden units is enough.

Three cases are tried starting from different initial connection weights. All the resulting networks share the same network structure. Table 5.1 compares the performance of SLF for various amounts of decay. It indicates that as the amount of decay increases, the MSE of learning with forgetting becomes larger. However, the MSE resulting from the combined use of learning with selective forgetting and learning with hidden units clarification remains almost the same for networks with the amount of decay between $10^{-5}$ and $6 \times 10^{-4}$. These networks share the same network structure as in Figure 5.2(c). Their AICs are also approximately the same. They show the robustness of the resulting network due to the change of the amount of decay in this example. The amount of decay of 0.0 corresponds to BP learning. When $\varepsilon$ is larger than $6 \times 10^{-4}$, all the connections and biases fade away due to excess decay.

Table 5.2 compares the performance of various structural learning methods. The task is the discovery of the Boolean function, $f = (a \cup c) \cap (b \cup d)$ using a 3-layer network: an input layer with four units, a hidden layer with four units, and an output layer with one unit. In this case all 16 data pairs are used for training. "Bayesian" here means that a penalty term is the sum of quadratic weights and its relative weight is estimated by a cheap Bayesian algorithm (MacKay, 1995). The resulting network is far from skeletal; the absolute values of all the connections are larger than 0.6. Although the Bayesian method is effective in adjusting the relative weight, it becomes powerless in cases where the penalty term is not appropriate such as in this case.

Table 5.2 indicates that SLF, entropy minimum learning, lateral inhibition learning and OBD generate skeletal networks. Furthermore, SLF, entropy minimum learning and OBD have small values of AIC. SLF is also computationally inexpen-

**Table 5.2**  Performance comparison of various structural learning methods in the discovery of the Boolean function, $f = (a \cup c) \cap (b \cup d)$. CPU time is normalized.

| learning method | MSE $\times 10^{-2}$ | $K$ | AIC | CPU time |
|---|---|---|---|---|
| BP | 0.0048 | 25 | −109.11 | 1.00 |
| complexity | 0.0536 | 13 | −94.50 | 47 |
| SLF | 0.0050 | 9 | −140.46 | 3.17 |
| entropy | 0.0054 | 9 | −139.22 | 45 |
| lateral inhibition | 0.324 | 9 | −73.71 | 11.3 |
| OBD | 0.0050 | 10 | −138.46 | 11.3 |
| Bayesian | 6.00 | 25 | 4.972 | 5.52 |

**Table 5.3**  Generalization ability in the classification of irises. $\#e$ stands for the number of classification errors for test data and is the average over five trials starting from different initial connection weights.

| no. of data | | $\#e$ | |
|---|---|---|---|
| training | test | SLF | BP |
| 9 | 141 | 19.2 | 18.6 |
| 15 | 135 | 10.2 | 16.6 |
| 21 | 129 | 6.8 | 16.2 |
| 30 | 120 | 5.0 | 6.4 |
| 60 | 90 | 5.2 | 4.8 |
| 90 | 60 | 5.0 | 5.0 |

sive in addition to the above two advantages.

---

## 5.5  Classification of Irises

The classification of irises (Fisher, 1936) is chosen as an example of continuous valued inputs and binary outputs. Irises are classified into three categories: setosa, versicolor and virginica. Each category has 50 samples. Each sample possesses four attributes: sepal length, sepal width, petal length and petal width. The network structure used here is a 3-layer network: an input layer with four units corresponding to four attributes, a hidden layer with four units and an output layer with three units representing three categories. A subset of data is randomly chosen for training, and the generalization ability of the resulting network is evaluated by AIC or $\text{MSE}_p$.

BP learning tends to use up all the units and connections provided. Table 5.3 indicates the generalization ability of BP learning and SLF. When the number of training data is 15, 21 or 30, SLF generalizes better than BP learning. This suggests

**Table 5.4**   Performance comparison of various structural learning methods in the classification of irises. $\#e$ is the number of classification errors.

| learning method | MSE $\times 10^{-2}$ | MSE$_p$ $\times 10^{-2}$ | $K$ | AIC | $\#e$ | CPU time |
|---|---|---|---|---|---|---|
| BP | 0.0076 | 5.52 | 35 | −527.54 | 12 | 1.00 |
| complexity | 0.1044 | 3.42 | 27 | −378.48 | 7 | 70 |
| SLF | 0.0064 | 4.09 | 13 | −582.37 | 9 | 5.9 |
| entropy | 0.0526 | 3.59 | 13 | −449.66 | 8 | 37 |
| lateral inh. | 0.3340 | 3.11 | 12 | −335.21 | 8 | 25 |
| OBD | 0.0056 | 4.36 | 28 | −560.78 | 13 | 3.9 |
| Bayesian | 4.351 | 7.70 | 35 | −127.49 | 18 | 1.35 |

the robustness of SLF for small samples. When the number of training data is 9, both methods have insufficient generalization ability. When it is 60 or 90, both methods have sufficiently large generalization ability.

Table 5.4 compares various structural learning methods. BP learning, SLF and OBD perform well in terms of the MSE. Resulting networks by SLF, entropy minimum learning and lateral inhibition learning are skeletal. The resulting network by OBD is far from skeletal; one more deletion of a connection makes the MSE much larger, i.e. from 0.0056 to 0.0290. SLF and OBD have small values of AIC. Learning with a complexity term, SLF, entropy minimum learning and lateral inhibition learning have less classification errors. BP learning, SLF, OBD and Bayesian learning need less CPU time. From these SLF is the best choice among them in this example.

## 5.6   Discovery of Recurrent Networks

The discovery of a recurrent network structure is chosen as an example of continuous valued inputs   and outputs. The example used here is the discovery of the simple Jordan network in Figure 5.3(a), which has one external input and one visible unit, i.e. a unit with a target output. A fully recurrent network with five sigmoidal units is used as an initial network structure, i.e. the number of initial connections is 25. The initial determination of the number of units does not matter much as long as the network is large enough for realizing the mapping from input to output.

Starting from different random connection weights, three networks are generated by a generalized SLF (GSLF). Figure 5.3(b) indicates the resulting network in case 1. The structure is the same as the original one in Figure 5.3(a). Two excess units vanish in the sense that all the incoming connections into and outgoing connections from them fade away. Only 4 out of 25 connections remain after learning. The resulting network in case 2 in Figure 5.3(c) is different from the original one, but it can be interpreted that the role of the state unit 3 in Figure 5.3(a) is split into

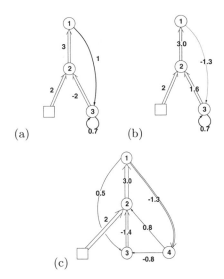

**Figure 5.3**  Discovery of recurrent networks. **(a)** Original network structure. **(b)** The resulting network structure in case 1. **(c)** The resulting network structure in case 2. A square indicates an external input. A number within a circle indicates the unit number. The external input sequence is given to unit 2 and the target output sequence is given to unit 1 . A number along a connection represents the value of its weight. The lengths of the input and target output sequences are 20. The parameters during learning are: $\eta = 0.1$, $\alpha = 0.2$, $\varepsilon = 10^{-4}$ and $\theta = 0.1$.

**Table 5.5**  Performance comparison of three learning methods in the discovery of recurrent networks. The learning parameters are: $\eta = 0.1$ and $\alpha = 0.2$, $\varepsilon = 10^{-4}$ and $\theta = 0.1$.

| learning method | MSE $\times 10^{-2}$ | MSE$_p$ $\times 10^{-2}$ | $K$ | AIC |
|---|---|---|---|---|
| BPTT | 0.0036 | 0.0752 | 25 | −155 |
| GSLF | 0.0004 | 0.0948 | 4 | −241 |
| Bayesian | 1.886 | 2.270 | 4 | −71 |

units 3 and 4 in Figure 5.3(c). The network structure in case 3 is the same as in Figure 5.3(a).

BPTT learning, on the other hand, uses up all the connections. Most of the connection weights are not close enough to 0. Twenty out of 25 connections have weights whose absolute values are larger than 0.1. The cheap Bayesian learning generates a skeletal network, but the resulting structure is quite different from the original one. Table 5.5 summarizes the comparison of these methods. BPTT and GSLF give good performance in the MSE both for training data and test data. GSLF and Bayesian learning generate skeletal networks. They indicate the superiority of GSLF.

## 5.7   Prediction of Time Series

### 5.7.1   Recurrent Networks for Time Series

Neural networks for time series are categorized roughly into two: simple recurrent networks and recurrent networks. The former includes Jordan networks, Elman networks and buffer networks (Jordan, 1986; Elman, 1990; Weigend and Gershenfeld, 1994). They are primarily feedforward networks with additional feedback loops or self loops for implementing dynamics. They usually employ approximate learning methods such as BP learning.

The latter, on the other hand, uses fully recurrent networks and employs learning methods such as backpropagation through time (BPTT) (Williams and Zipser, 1995). BP learning is an approximation in the sense that errors at some time back propagate only one time step ahead. In BPTT, on the other hand, errors at some time back propagate all the way through the initial time.

In this section, Jordan networks and buffer networks with sigmoidal units are employed (Ishikawa and Moriyama, 1996). The Jordan network in Figure 5.4 retains the following history of outputs in the context layer.

$$\boldsymbol{y}_{t-1} + (1-d)\boldsymbol{y}_{t-2} + (1-d)^2\boldsymbol{y}_{t-3} + (1-d)^3\boldsymbol{y}_{t-4} + \cdots \tag{5.21}$$

where $\boldsymbol{y}_{t-i}$ is the output $i$ steps before and $d$ is a decay rate of outputs. History of outputs in the context layer decays exponentially. Therefore, the determination of the decay rate, which determines the effective length of history, is crucial.

As mentioned earlier, it is difficult to acquire prior information on the structure of a network. In case of BP learning, therefore, the determination of the number of hidden units necessitates trial and error based on some criterion such as $\mathrm{MSE}_p$. The determination of the decay rate, $d$, also requires trial and error.

The buffer network in Figure 5.5 stores $(m+1)$ most recent inputs and $n$ most recent outputs in the input and output buffers, respectively. The buffer network retains complete history of inputs and outputs for a specified time interval, while entirely disregarding inputs and outputs outside of this interval. Therefore, the

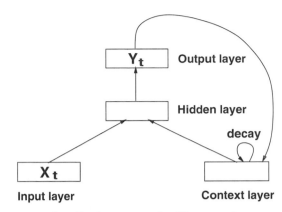

**Figure 5.4** Structure of a Jordan network. History of outputs is stored in the context layer.
(© Elsevier Science, used with permission, see Copyright Acknowledgments)

determination of the length of buffers is crucial for the learning of time series.

In case of BP learning, a buffer network requires much more structural parameters than a Jordan network. Structural parameters of the former are composed of the number of hidden units, the length of a buffer and its content, i.e. the specification of a subset of $\{x_t, x_{t-1}, ..., x_{t-m}\}$ and $\{\mathbf{y}_{t-1}, \mathbf{y}_{t-2}, ..., \mathbf{y}_{t-n}\}$. Especially the last one necessitates a huge number of trials to find the best buffer network structure by BP learning.

Consider the selection of the number of hidden units and the length of a buffer. Suppose the maximum number of hidden units is $N_H$ and the maximum length of a buffer is $N_B$. The number of trials is at most $N_H N_B$. In contrast to this, the determination of the content of a buffer is far more laborious. Consider a network with a buffer of length $N$. Suppose its submodel has a smaller buffer with length less than or equal to $N$. There can be $2^N - 1$ submodels. However, at most $N$ submodels are usually examined as in the case of this paper, assuming that a buffer is composed of the most recent successive inputs and outputs. This clearly indicates that the number of trials for determining the content of a buffer is far larger than that for determining the number of hidden units and the length of a buffer.

Data measured every hour at some building (Kreider and Haberl, 1993) are used for the prediction of time series. These data originally had three output variables, but we use only one of them in this paper. Figure 5.6 shows the inputs and the output of these data: temperature, humidity ratio, solar flux, wind speed, and an indicator showing weekday(0)/holiday(1) as the inputs, and the consumption of electricity as the output. These data are recorded from Sep. 1, 1989, through Dec. 31, 1989. We use the data for the two weeks: from Sep. 8 through Sep. 21. These data are normalized from 0 to 1 based on the data of the entire period. Data for the first week are used for training and those for the succeeding week are used for test. During the test period, only an input sequence is given; one week prediction

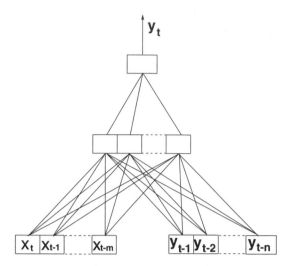

**Figure 5.5**   Structure of a buffer network. $\{x_t, x_{t-1}, ..., x_{t-m}\}$ constitute the input buffer and $\{\mathbf{y}_{t-1}, \mathbf{y}_{t-2}, ..., \mathbf{y}_{t-n}\}$ constitute the output buffer.
(© Elsevier Science, used with permission, see Copyright Acknowledgments)

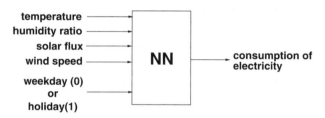

**Figure 5.6**   Five input variables and one output variable of time series data
(© Elsevier Science, used with permission, see Copyright Acknowledgments)

is adopted here instead of a series of one hour predictions.

### 5.7.2   Prediction Using Jordan Networks

First, training of Jordan networks is carried out by BP learning. Table 5.6 shows the learning and prediction performance of Jordan networks with various decay rates. $\text{MSE}_p$ reaches a minimum of 0.01625 at the decay rate of 0.1. The decay rate of 0.1 means that information of 24 hours ago decreases to $8\%(\approx 0.9^{24})$ of its original value. However, the model which minimizes $\text{MSE}_p$ does not minimize AIC. This mismatch sometimes occurs and its reason will be discussed later.

Table 5.7 indicates that the learning and prediction performance of Jordan networks with various numbers of hidden units using the optimal decay rate of 0.1. $\text{MSE}_p$ becomes a minimum of 0.00749 for the network with 2 hidden units. In other words the model with 2 hidden units and the decay rate of 0.1 has the

**Table 5.6**  Learning and prediction performance of Jordan networks by BP learning. The number of hidden units is 5. $K$ is the number of connections and biases. The learning parameters are: $\eta = 0.01$ and $\alpha = 0.2$. Both MSE and AIC are the average of three trials starting from different initial connection weights.

| decay rate, $d$ | MSE training | MSE test | $K$ | AIC |
|---|---|---|---|---|
| 0.05 | 0.00275 | 0.04060 | 41 | −908 |
| 0.1 | 0.00315 | 0.01625 | 41 | −899 |
| 0.2 | 0.00237 | 0.03360 | 41 | −923 |
| 0.3 | 0.00233 | 0.02134 | 41 | −935 |
| 0.4 | 0.00246 | 0.02082 | 41 | −925 |

**Table 5.7**  Learning and prediction performance of Jordan networks by BP learning. $N_h$ is the number of hidden units and the decay rate is 0.1. The learning parameters are the same as those in Table 5.6. Both MSE and AIC are the average of three trials.

| $N_h$ | MSE training | MSE test | $K$ | AIC |
|---|---|---|---|---|
| 1 | 0.00545 | 0.00960 | 9 | −856 |
| 2 | 0.00387 | 0.00749 | 17 | −898 |
| 3 | 0.00371 | 0.01163 | 25 | −887 |
| 4 | 0.00312 | 0.01433 | 33 | −903 |
| 5 | 0.00315 | 0.01625 | 41 | −899 |

smallest $\mathrm{MSE}_p$, i.e. the best generalization ability, among the examined models. The value of AIC of this model is −898, but the model with 4 hidden units has a slightly smaller value of AIC.

In the next stage, SLF is applied to Jordan networks with 5 hidden units and the decay rate of 0.1 for various values of $\varepsilon$'s. The initial determination of the number of hidden units does not matter much as long as it is large enough, because excessive hidden units lose all the incoming and outgoing connections during learning. Table 5.8 indicates that $\mathrm{MSE}_p$ becomes the minimum at the amount of decay of $\varepsilon = 9 \times 10^{-4}$. The numbers of hidden units actually used in this case are 1, 2 and 2 for 3 trials. It clearly demonstrates that the initial determination of the number of hidden units does not affect the resulting models much.

Table 5.9 summarizes the performance comparison of Jordan networks by BP learning and SLF. Case A clearly indicates the deterioration of $\mathrm{MSE}_p$ for a large-size network. Case B substantially improves $\mathrm{MSE}_p$ by decreasing the number of hidden units. In case C, although the MSE for training data is the largest, the MSE for test data is the smallest among 3 cases. This shows the superiority of the

**Table 5.8**    Learning and prediction performance of Jordan networks by SLF. The number of hidden units is 5 and the decay rate is 0.1. The learning parameters are: $\eta = 0.01$, $\alpha = 0.2$, and $\theta = 0.1$. Both MSE and AIC are the average of three trials.

| amount of | MSE | | $K$ | AIC |
|---|---|---|---|---|
| decay, $\varepsilon$ | training | test | | |
| $1 \times 10^{-4}$ | 0.00376 | 0.01415 | 22.3 | −893 |
| $5 \times 10^{-4}$ | 0.00610 | 0.00882 | 11.0 | −833 |
| $9 \times 10^{-4}$ | 0.00657 | 0.00674 | 7.7 | −827 |

**Table 5.9**    Performance comparison of learning and prediction of Jordan networks by BP learning and SLF. $N_h$ is the number of hidden units. In case A the same network structure is used as the initial structure in case C. Case B corresponds to the best network in Table 5.7, i.e. $N_h = 2$. Case C corresponds to the best network in Table 5.8, i.e. $\varepsilon = 9 \times 10^{-4}$. The decay rate is 0.1. The learning parameters are: $\eta = 0.01$, $\alpha = 0.2$, $\varepsilon = 9 \times 10^{-4}$ and $\theta = 0.1$.

| case | learning | $N_h$ | MSE | | $K$ | AIC |
|---|---|---|---|---|---|---|
| | method | | training | test | | |
| A | BP | 5 | 0.00315 | 0.01642 | 41 | −882 |
| B | BP | 2 | 0.00387 | 0.00749 | 17 | −898 |
| C | SLF | 5 | 0.00657 | 0.00674 | 7.7 | −827 |

network model obtained by SLF in terms of $\text{MSE}_p$. However, AIC selects a different model. This mismatch will be discussed later.

Figures 5.7 and 5.8 illustrate the output sequence and the target output sequence of cases B and C in Table 5.9. The actual output, i.e. the consumption of electricity, is used as the target output here. The training period is from Sep. 8 through 14 and the test period is from Sep. 15 through 21. Sep. 9, 10, 16 and 17 are holidays as can be seen from the low consumption rate of electricity.

### 5.7.3   Prediction Using Buffer Networks

First, training of buffer networks is carried out by BP learning. The input buffer here is composed of the 5 most recent inputs and the output buffer is composed of the $n$ most recent outputs. Table 5.10 indicates that $\text{MSE}_p$ becomes the minimum of 0.01002 for the output buffer of length 5. The value of AIC of this model is −978, but some other models have slightly smaller values of AICs.

In the next stage, SLF is applied. Table 5.11 shows the learning and prediction performance of buffer networks by SLF for various values of decay. The network has 8 hidden units and the output buffer of length 10. As before, the initial determination of the number of hidden units and the buffer length does not matter

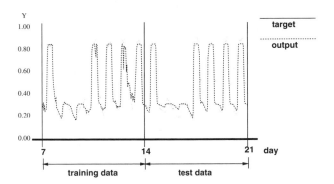

**Figure 5.7** Output and target output sequences of the Jordan network by BP learning (case B in Table 5.9). The number of hidden units is 2 and the decay rate is 0.1. The learning parameters are: $\eta = 0.01$ and $\alpha = 0.2$.
(© Elsevier Science, used with permission, see Copyright Acknowledgments)

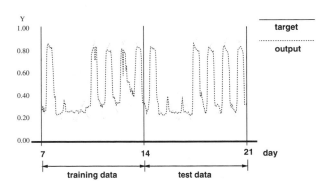

**Figure 5.8** Output and target output sequences of the Jordan network by SLF (case C in Table 5.9). The number of hidden units is 5 and the decay rate is 0.1. The learning parameters are: $\eta = 0.01$, $\alpha = 0.2$, $\varepsilon = 9 \times 10^{-4}$, and $\theta = 0.1$
(© Elsevier Science, used with permission, see Copyright Acknowledgments)

**Table 5.10**  Learning and prediction of buffer networks by BP learning. The number of hidden units is 6. The learning parameters are: $\eta = 0.01$ and $\alpha = 0.2$.

| buffer length | MSE training | MSE test | $K$ | AIC |
|:---:|:---:|:---:|:---:|:---:|
| 3 | 0.00174 | 0.04829 | 61 | −946 |
| 4 | 0.00171 | 0.01287 | 67 | −937 |
| 5 | 0.00125 | 0.01002 | 73 | −978 |
| 6 | 0.00112 | 0.01171 | 79 | −983 |
| 10 | 0.00085 | 0.06208 | 103 | −981 |

**Table 5.11**  Learning and prediction of buffer networks by SLF. The number of hidden units is 8 and the length of the output buffer is 10. The learning parameters are: $\eta = 0.01$, $\alpha = 0.2$ and $\theta = 0.1$.

| amount of decay, $\varepsilon$ forgetting | MSE training | MSE test | $K$ | AIC |
|:---:|:---:|:---:|:---:|:---:|
| $1 \times 10^{-4}$ | 0.00134 | 0.01135 | 26 | −1059 |
| $2 \times 10^{-4}$ | 0.00196 | 0.00469 | 21 | −1005 |
| $3 \times 10^{-4}$ | 0.00239 | 0.00576 | 17 | −980 |
| $5 \times 10^{-4}$ | 0.00539 | 0.00959 | 10 | −858 |

much as long as they are large enough. Table 5.11 indicates that the model with the amount of decay $\varepsilon = 2 \times 10^{-4}$ has the smallest $\mathrm{MSE}_p$, i.e. the best generalization ability. Figure 5.9 illustrates the corresponding buffer network. The output buffer contains outputs of 1, 3, 5, 6, 7 and 10 hours before. In the hidden layer, only 3 out of 8 units are actually used. This intermittent output buffer and parsimonious usage of hidden units make the number of connections much smaller than that by BP learning. This greatly contributes to the improvement of the generalization ability of the resulting model.

Table 5.12 summarizes the results by BP learning and SLF. The generalization ability in terms of $\mathrm{MSE}_p$ is maximized in case F. In SLF the number of hidden units, the length of a buffer and its content are determined concurrently with the learning of connection weights. It is to be noted that much trial and error is required in obtaining the result of case E. In Table 5.12, AIC chooses the model with the smallest $\mathrm{MSE}_p$. Figures 5.10 and 5.11 illustrate the output sequences and the target output sequences in cases B and C in Table 5.12, respectively, for both the training period and the test period.

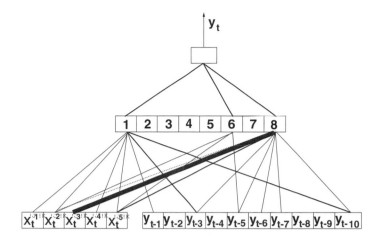

**Figure 5.9**  The resulting buffer network by SLF. $\{x_t^{(1)}, x_t^{(2)}, ..., x_t^{(5)}\}$ is the current input and $\{\mathbf{y}_{t-1}, \mathbf{y}_{t-2}, ..., \mathbf{y}_{t-10}\}$ constitute the output buffer. The learning parameters are: $\eta = 0.01$, $\alpha = 0.2$, $\varepsilon = 2 \times 10^{-4}$ and $\theta = 0.1$.

(© Elsevier Science, used with permission, see Copyright Acknowledgments)

**Table 5.12**  Performance comparison of the learning and prediction of buffer networks by BP learning and SLF. $N_h$ is the number of hidden units and $N_b$ is the length of a buffer. In case D the same network structure is used as the initial structure in case F. Case E corresponds to the best network in Table 5.10, i.e. $N_b = 5$. Case F corresponds to the best network in Table 5.11, i.e. $\varepsilon = 2 \times 10^{-4}$. The learning parameters are the same as those in Figure 5.9.

| case | learning method | $N_h$ | $N_b$ | MSE | | $K$ | AIC |
|------|--------|-------|-------|----------|---------|-----|-----|
|      |        |       |       | training | test    |     |     |
| D    | BP     | 8     | 10    | 0.00060  | 0.02160 | 137 | −971 |
| E    | BP     | 6     | 5     | 0.00118  | 0.01273 | 73  | −985 |
| F    | SLF    | 8     | 10    | 0.00204  | 0.00685 | 21  | −996 |

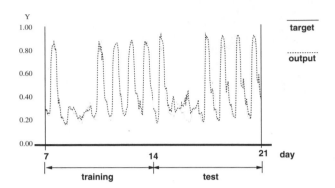

**Figure 5.10** Output and target output sequences of the buffer network by BP learning (case E in Table 5.12). The number of hidden units is 6, the length of the output buffer is 5. The learning parameters are: $\eta = 0.01$ and $\alpha = 0.2$.

(© Elsevier Science, used with permission, see Copyright Acknowledgments)

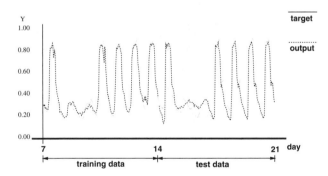

**Figure 5.11** Output and target output sequences of the buffer network by SLF (case F in Table 5.12). The number of hidden units is 8 and the length of the output buffer is 10. The learning parameters are the same as those in Figure 5.9.

(© Elsevier Science, used with permission, see Copyright Acknowledgments)

**Table 5.13** Autocorrelation function of output errors. $r_J(t)$ is the autocorrelation function of output errors by the Jordan network of case C in Table 5.9. $r_b(t)$ is the one by the buffer network of Case F in Table 5.12.

| t | $r_J(t)$ | $r_b(t)$ |
|---|---|---|
| 0 | 1.000 | 1.000 |
| 1 | 0.686 | 0.676 |
| 2 | 0.328 | 0.318 |
| 3 | 0.131 | 0.123 |
| 4 | 0.045 | 0.071 |
| 5 | 0.004 | 0.055 |

### 5.7.4 Discussion

In the learning of neural networks, various structural parameters should be specified in advance: the number of hidden units in Jordan networks, and the number of hidden units, the length of a buffer and its content in buffer networks. Extensive trial and error is needed to determine these parameters. Since exhaustive search is, in most cases, impossible, only a small portion of search space is usually examined.

SLF solves this difficulty by simultaneously carrying out the determination of these structural parameters and the learning of connection weights. Simulation results demonstrate that SLF has better generalization ability than BP learning both in Jordan networks and buffer networks in this example.

The mismatch between $\text{MSE}_p$ and AIC is considered to occur due to the following reasons. First, both $\text{MSE}_p$ and AIC are subject to statistical variation. Second, the independence assumption of output errors underlying Equation 5.19 does not necessarily hold in actual cases. The autocorrelation function of output errors in Table 5.13 clearly indicates that they have temporal correlation. Third, due to slow learning speed, the MSE for training data decreases very slowly. Therefore it might be larger than it should be due to immature learning. In this paper, $\text{MSE}_p$ is considered to be more reliable than AIC due mainly to the second reason. The clarification of these is left for further study.

## 5.8 Adaptive Learning

In this section the adaptive !indexlearning!adaptive ability of a network in a changing environment is evaluated. SLF has the advantage of generating the simplest possible network structure given data from the environment. This advantage, in contrast to BP learning, facilitates the adaptability of a network in a changing environment.

To evaluate this ability, the following Boolean function and its subsets are used to realize the changing environment.

$$g = (a \cup b) \cap (c \cup d) \cap (e \cup f) \tag{5.22}$$

There are in total $64(=2^6)$ samples. Various subsets of samples are given for training.

First, SLF is used to train a 3-layer network with 5 hidden units. In the first stage, 36 samples for which $(c \cup d) \cap (e \cup f)$ is always true are given for training. Figure 5.12(a) illustrates the resulting network structure representing $(a \cup b)$, which is the simplest rule explaining the given data. In the second stage, 48 samples for which $(e \cup f)$ is always true are given for training. The network structure adaptively changes and Figure 5.12(b) is generated. $(a \cup b) \cap (c \cup d)$ is the simplest rule. In the third stage, all 64 samples are given for training and Figure 5.12(c) is obtained. The Boolean function in Equation 5.22 is the simplest rule. So far, sprouting of connections occurs.

In the fourth stage, 48 samples for which $(a \cup b)$ is always true are given for training. Adaptive learning produces Figure 5.12(d), eliminating unnecessary connections. $(c \cup d) \cap (e \cup f)$ is the simplest rule. In the final stage, 36 samples for which $(a \cup b) \cap (c \cup d)$ is always true are given for training. Adaptive learning generates Figure 5.12(e), representing $(e \cup f)$. These five figures well demonstrate the adaptive learning capability of SLF.

Second, BP learning is used for training. In the first stage, all 64 samples are given for training. Figure 5.13(a) is generated, but is hard to understand due to distributed representation. In the second stage, 36 samples for which $(a \cup b) \cap (c \cup d)$ is always true are used for training. However, since MSE is small even right after the change of the environment, modification of connection weights do not occur. Therefore, the resulting network structure in Figure 5.13(b) remains almost the same as Figure 5.13(a). In other words, BP learning has no adaptive ability in the changing environment.

## 5.9   Methods of Rule Extraction/Discovery

Knowledge acquisition is, needless to say, important, because it is a key to the solution to one of the bottlenecks in artificial intelligence (AI). In addition to numerous studies on knowledge acquisition in machine learning such as ID3 and C4.5 (Quinlan, 1993), the neural-network approach has attracted wide attention recently because of its computational simplicity and ability to generalize. Rule extraction or rule discovery using neural networks, however, is not easy due mainly to distributed representation in a network. Most of the existing methods suffer from this difficulty, hence the crucial issue has been how to extract rules from trained neural networks.

This section surveys various methods for obtaining rules from data using neural networks. They are roughly classified into two categories: those with prior theories

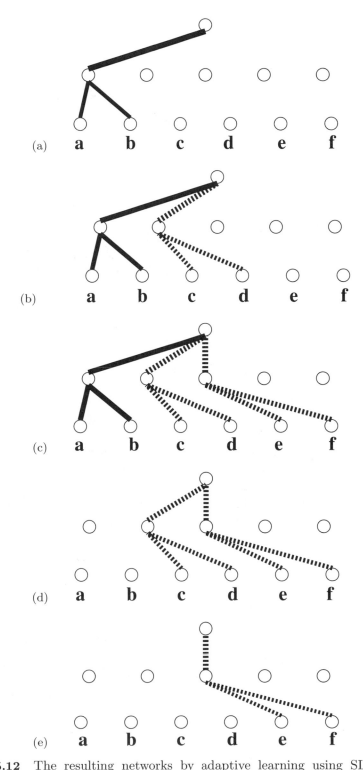

**Figure 5.12** The resulting networks by adaptive learning using SLF. **(a)** 36 training samples satisfying $(c \cup d) \cap (e \cup f)$. (Stage 1). **(b)** 48 training samples satisfying $(e \cup f)$. (Stage 2). **(c)** All 64 samples are used for training. (Stage 3). **(d)** 48 training samples satisfying $(a \cup b)$. (Stage 4). **(e)** 36 training samples satisfying $(a \cup b) \cap (c \cup d)$. (Stage 5).

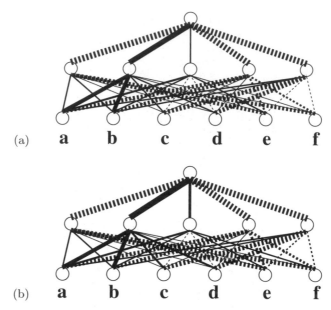

(a)          **a     b     c     d     e     f**

(b)          **a     b     c     d     e     f**

**Figure 5.13**   The resulting networks by BP learning. **(a)** All 64 samples are used for training. (Stage 1). **(b)** 36 training samples satisfying $(a \cup b) \cap (c \cup d)$. (Stage 2).

and those without them. The former assumes prior theories, and modifies, adds and deletes them by learning based on data. The latter, on the other hand, assumes no theory and depends solely on learning based on data. Because of this difference, I would like to use different terminologies in this chapter; *rule extraction* for the former and *rule discovery* for the latter.

Andrews et al. have made an extensive survey of various methods of rule extraction or discovery using neural networks, and clarified comparative performance using the MONK's problems and mushroom database (Andrews et al., 1995, 1996). Thrun et al. have also made an extensive comparative study on various methods ranging from machine learning to neural networks using the MONK's problems (Thrun et al., 1991). Methods using neural networks include BP, BP with weight decay, and cascade-correlation learning. However, the purpose of this comparative study is not to evaluate the performance of rule extraction or discovery, but to evaluate mapping performance. Therefore, this is not our present concern.

Kowalczyk et al. proposed a rule discovery method using higher order neural networks (Ferrá and Gardiner, 1991). It is applied to the classification of mushrooms. Its good performance, however, is due mainly to the pre-selection of a small number of useful attributes by a statistical method.

Sestito and Dillon proposed the Building Representations for AI using Neural NEtworks (BRAINNE) method (Sestito and Dillon, 1994). In BRAINNE an expanded 3-layer network architecture with additional inputs representing target outputs is adopted. In the selection of the defining attributes for a conjunctive rule, a measure of relevance between input and output is proposed. However, a cut-off point may not be determined clearly when data are corrupted by noise. A disjunctive rule can also be obtained by an extension of the original BRAINNE. This is in contrast to SLF, in which a universal procedure generates either conjunctive or disjunctive rules depending on given data. BRAINNE can also be extended to continuous valued inputs. Again in contrast to SLF, generated rules are restricted in the sense that only one attribute is allowed for each term of a rule, i.e. each attribute has lower and/or upper bounds. In its application to the classification of mushrooms and irises, BRAINNE generates more rules than SLF; 46 rules in the former and 11 rules in the latter.

McMillan, Mozer and Smolensky proposed RuleNet (McMillan et al., 1992). It is a combination of learning of a simple mapping and local expert architecture by Jacobs, Jordan, Nowlan and Hinton (Jacobs and Nowlan, 1991). It deals with only symbolic inputs and outputs. Local expert architecture generates context. Therefore, it is a good architecture for cognitive models, but its ability to discover rules from real world data is not clear, because no benchmark data are presented.

Towell and Shavlik propose the following framework: insert knowledge into a neural network using KBANN (Knowledge-Based Neural Network), train the network using a set of data and extract rules from the trained network (Towell and Shavlik, 1993). The last extraction phase is the most difficult part. They propose a Subset algorithm and an MofN algorithm for the extraction phase. The Subset algorithm generates a set of rules by selecting a subset of input units which guarantee full activation of the corresponding non-input unit using a branch and bound algorithm. The MofN algorithm generates a simpler set of rules by clustering, averaging, eliminating, optimizing, extracting and simplifying incoming connection weights of each non-input unit. The proposed method is applied to the classification of DNA sequences and the MONK's problems. Detailed analyses of the rule extraction performance is also presented (Towell and Shavlik, 1994).

Fu (Fu, 1993) proposes aKnowledge-Based Conceptual Neural Network (KBCNN),, which is similar to the framework by Towell and Shavlik (Towell and Shavlik, 1993). During the learning phase, it uses heuristic procedures such as ignoring weak connections. During the rule extraction phase, the KT algorithm which is similar to the Subset algorithm is adopted. The whole procedure is somewhat more complex than the one by Towell and Shavlik. This method is applied to the classification of DNA sequences. Since all the data are used for training, the generalization ability is not reported.

Fu proposes another method which does not require prior information on problem domains. During the extraction phase it uses the KT method (Fu, 1994). A heuristic search using three kinds of thresholds is carried out, which influences the resulting rules. The proposed method is applied to three kinds of examples, i.e. the classification of irises, hepatitis prognosis prediction and hypothyroid diagnosis. The first one has continuous valued inputs, and the last two have both continuous and discrete valued inputs. It, however, extracts only the simplest rules similar to C4.5, i.e. each term of a rule contains only one attribute.

Most of the existing methods focus on how to extract rules from trained neural networks, because this is the most difficult part. I would say that this is the result of using unsophisticated learning algorithms such as BP learning.

As mentioned in the Introduction, it is widely known that BP learning suffers from such difficulties as prior specification of network structure and the interpretation of hidden units. To overcome these difficulties, various structural learning methods have been proposed as shown in Section 5.2. However, these two fields, i.e. rule extraction or discovery and structural learning, have developed almost independently. Furthermore, most of the structural learning methods put emphasis on the decrease in computational cost and in the number of connections, and put less emphasis on the interpretation of the resulting networks. I claim that learning methods which are capable of generating skeletal structure with easy interpretation should be applied to rule extraction or rule discovery.

## 5.10   Rule Discovery by SLF

SLF is effective in obtaining skeletal network structure with easy interpretation of hidden units (Ishikawa, 1989, 1996d). SLF is also efficacious in rule discovery from data with discrete valued inputs (Ishikawa, 1995b, 1996b,c), because the resulting network structure is skeletal and hidden units are binary owing to the learning with hidden units clarification. These characteristics make ad hoc procedures such as ignoring weak connections unnecessary.

An input or an output unit with a discrete value can be converted to a set of binary units. Therefore, without loss of generality, we can assume that all the input and output units are binary. The discovery of rules is carried out in the following steps.

1. Train a neural network by the learning with forgetting to obtain a rough skeletal network structure.

2. Train it by both the learning with forgetting and that with hidden units clarification to dissipate distributed representation.

3. Train it by both learning with selective forgetting and that with hidden units clarification to get a smaller MSE. At this step, all the hidden units become binary.

4. Represent each hidden unit by a Boolean function of input units.

5. Represent each output unit by a Boolean function of hidden units.

6. By combining the above two Boolean functions, each output unit can be represented by a Boolean function of input units. These are the rules we seek for.

Another advantage of SLF is that it can be extended to the discovery of rules from data with continuous valued inputs (Ishikawa, 1997). A direct application of SLF, however, is not powerful enough because of the inherent difficulty of continuous valued inputs. To overcome this difficulty, neural networks of various degrees of complexity are trained. The degree of complexity, here, is defined by the maximum

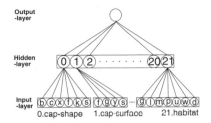

**Figure 5.14**  The network structure for the classification of mushroom data. Each hidden unit represents an attribute and is connected to the corresponding attribute values in the input layer.

number of incoming connections to each hidden unit. From among these, the one with the smallest AIC (Akaike, 1974) is selected as optimal. Since outputs of hidden units are binary owing to the learning with hidden units clarification, incoming connection weights to each hidden unit determine the corresponding discriminating hyperplane. A logical combination of these hyperplanes provides rules.

## 5.11  Classification of Mushrooms

The mushroom database contains 8124 samples (Murphy and Aha, 1992). Each sample has 22 attributes and each attribute has from 2 to 12 nominal attribute values. The total number of attribute values is 126. Each sample is also given a categorical value, e.g. edible or poisonous. Figure 5.14 illustrates the network structure adopted here. Out of 8124 samples, 812 samples are randomly chosen for training. Learning is carried out by two methods: BP learning and SLF.

SLF can select appropriate attributes without pre-selection. In this case, 2, 4 or 6 significant attributes is chosen depending on the amount of decay, $\varepsilon$. In a 2-attribute case, two attributes, *odor* and *spore_print_color,* are selected. The former attribute has {*almond, anise, creosote, fishy, foul, musty, none, pungent, spicy*} as its attribute values. The latter has attribute values of {*black, brown, buff, chocolate, green, orange, purple, white, yellow*}. The discovered rule for edible mushrooms in the 2-attribute case is,

$$(odor = almond \cup anise \cup none) \cap (spore\_print\_color = \neg green) \qquad (5.23)$$

where $\neg$ stands for negation. Figure 5.15 illustrates the corresponding network structure (Ishikawa, 1998). Out of 22 attributes, only the relevant 2 attributes are shown here. The discovered rule for edible mushrooms in the 4-attribute case is,

$$(odor = almond \cup anise \cup none)$$
$$\cap(spore\_print\_color = \neg green)$$
$$\cap\{(stalk\_surface\_below\_ring = \neg scaly)$$
$$\cup(population = \neg several \cap \neg clustered)\} \tag{5.24}$$

ID3, a popular inductive learning algorithm in AI, is selected for comparison. The information expected from the entire data, $E$, is represented as,

$$M(E) = -p(e) \log_2 p(e) - p(p) \log_2 p(p) \tag{5.25}$$

where $p(e)$ and $p(p)$ are the probabilities that a sample belongs to the class $e$ and class $p$, respectively.

The information expected when the attribute $A$ is selected is,

$$B(A) = \sum_i p(A_i) M(C_i) \tag{5.26}$$

where the attribute $A$ has attribute values $A_i (i = 1, ..., n)$, $C_i$ is a set of samples with attribute values $A_i$, $p(A_i)$ is the probability that the attribute $A$ has attribute value $A_i$. $M(C_i)$ is the expected information when the attribute value is $A_i$ and can be obtained in a similar way as $M(E)$. The attribute which maximizes $M(E) - B(A)$ is selected as the most significant one, because it acquires the largest amount of information. This procedure continues recursively.

Table 5.14 indicates the results by BP learning, SLF and ID3. It is to be noted that BP learning, in contrast to SLF and ID3, cannot discover any explicit rules. Since the number of attributes is 22 in case of BP learning, it requires data on all attributes during the test phase. This is a serious disadvantage of BP learning. Table 5.14 also shows that SLF is superior to BP and ID3 in terms of the number of classification errors. By adding 8 erroneous samples in the 4-attribute case to 812 training data, it becomes possible to obtain a classification rule with 6 attributes which correctly classifies all mushrooms.

## 5.12  MONK's Problems

The MONK's problems are composed of three classification tasks. One of them is the MONK's problem I. Table 5.15 shows a list of attributes and the corresponding attribute values. There are 6 attributes and 17 nominal attribute values. Table 5.16 indicates 4 correct classification rules. Figure 5.16 illustrates the network architecture used in the MONK's problem I. Each unit in the Hidden1 layer represents one of the attributes. The total number of samples is 432 ($= 3 \times 3 \times 2 \times 3 \times 4 \times 2$) as can be calculated from Table 5.15.

The number of training samples is 85, 70 or 50. These training samples are

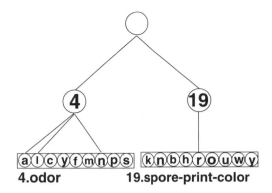

4.odor       19.spore-print-color

**Figure 5.15** The resulting network by SLF in the classification of mushrooms. The learning parameters are: $\eta = 0.05$, $\alpha = 0.9$, $\varepsilon = 7 \times 10^{-5}$ and $\theta = 0.1$. (© Springer-Verlag, used with permission, see Copyright Acknowledgments)

**Table 5.14** Performance comparison of the classification of mushrooms. The numbers of training data and the total data are 812 and 8124, respectively. #A stands for the number of attributes. MSE and $\text{MSE}_T$ are MSEs for training data and the total data, respectively. $\#e_1$ and $\#e_2$ stand for the numbers of classification errors for training data and the total data, respectively. The parameters of learning are: $\eta = 0.05$, $\alpha = 0.9$ and $\theta = 0.1$.

| method | $\varepsilon \times 10^{-5}$ | #A | MSE | $\text{MSE}_T$ | $\#e_1$ | $\#e_2$ |
|--------|------|----|-----|------|------|------|
| BP | – | 22 | 0.00006 | 0.00606 | 0 | 56 |
| SLF | 7 | 2 | 0.00676 | 0.00639 | 5 | 48 |
|     | 1 | 4 | 0.00014 | 0.00109 | 0 | 8 |
| ID3 | – | 2 | – | – | 5 | 48 |
|     | – | 3 | – | – | 2 | 24 |
|     | – | 4 | – | – | 2 | 24 |

**Table 5.15** Attributes and the corresponding attribute values in the MONK's problems.

| attribute | attribute values |
|-----------|------------------|
| head-shape | round, square, octagon |
| body-shape | round, square, octagon |
| smiling | yes, no |
| holding | sword, balloon, flag |
| jacket-color | red, yellow, green, blue |
| has-tie | yes, no |

**Table 5.16**   Correct classification rules for the MONK's problem I.

| No. | rule |
|-----|------|
| 1 | (head-shape=round) ∩ (body-shape=round) |
| 2 | (head-shape=square) ∩ (body-shape=square) |
| 3 | (head-shape=octagon) ∩ (body-shape=octagon) |
| 4 | jacket-color=red |

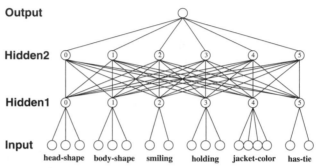

**Figure 5.16**   The network architecture for the MONK's problem I.
(© Springer-Verlag, used with permission, see Copyright Acknowledgments)

randomly chosen. Four cases, corresponding to different subsets of training samples, are tried as shown in Table 5.17. An example of the resulting network by BP learning in Figure 5.17 indicates that it is far from skeletal. Another example of the resulting network by SLF in Figure 5.18 clearly indicates its skeletal character. Table 5.17 summarizes the performance comparison of BP learning, SLF and ID3. It shows that SLF is superior to BP, and BP is superior to ID3 in terms of the number of classification errors. SLF succeeds in discovering the correct set of rules in 11 out of 12 trials for 85 training samples and in 10 out of 12 trials for 70 training samples. Although the experiments by Subset and MofN are carried out somewhat differently (Towell and Shavlik, 1993), the results suggest that they are inferior to SLF.

## 5.13   Modular Structured Networks

As mentioned in the Introduction, neural networks suffer from the local minima problem and the rapid increase in computational cost when the size of a network becomes large (Minsky and Papert, 1988). Modular structured networks are expected to solve these difficulties, because the size of each module is modest. In modular structured networks, mixtures of experts architecture is popular (Jacobs and Nowlan, 1991). SLF is also applicable to this architecture (Ishikawa and Yoshino,

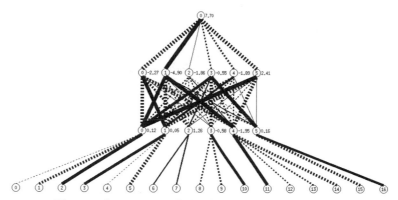

**Figure 5.17**   The resulting network by BP learning in the MONK's problem I. The learning parameters are: $\eta = 0.05$ and $\alpha = 0.9$.

(© Springer-Verlag, used with permission, see Copyright Acknowledgments)

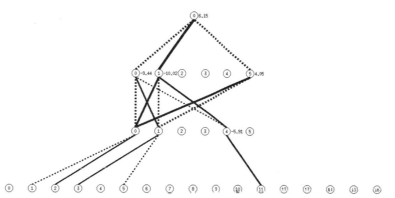

**Figure 5.18**   The resulting network by SLF in the MONK's problem I. The learning parameters are: $\eta = 0.05$, $\alpha = 0.9$, $\varepsilon = 3.4 \times 10^{-4}$, and $\theta = 0.1$.

(© Springer-Verlag, used with permission, see Copyright Acknowledgments)

**Table 5.17**  Performance comparison of BP learning, SLF and ID3 in the MONK's problem I. In each case, 3 initial connection weights are tried. The learning parameters are the same as those in Figures 5.17 and 5.18.

| no. of samples | case | no. of errors | | |
|---|---|---|---|---|
| | | BP | SLF | ID3 |
| 85 | 1 | 0 | 0 | 56 |
| | 2 | 0 | 0 | 48 |
| | 3 | 52.7 | 0 | 66 |
| | 4 | 28.7 | 4.0 | 60 |
| | mean | 20.4 | 1.0 | 57.5 |
| 70 | 1 | 41.3 | 0 | 12 |
| | 2 | 27.0 | 28.0 | 50 |
| | 3 | 26.0 | 0 | 36 |
| | 4 | 25.3 | 0 | 92 |
| | mean | 29.9 | 7.0 | 47.5 |
| 50 | 1 | 92.3 | 36.0 | 68 |
| | 2 | 85.7 | 57.3 | 92 |
| | 3 | 95.0 | 52.0 | 60 |
| | 4 | 55.0 | 54.0 | 110 |
| | mean | 82.0 | 49.8 | 82.5 |

1993). In this section, another approach is pursued (Ishikawa, 1995a); both intra-module and inter-module connections are trained by SLF to realize understandable modular structured networks.

### 5.13.1   Module Formation and Learning of Modular Networks

The learning of modular structured networks is carried out here in two stages: the first stage being the learning of connection weights in each module and the second stage being that of inter-module connection weights. The advantages of using modular networks are the following: First, because each module is small, computational cost and the local minima problem in the first stage are not serious.

Second, computational cost in the second stage is not as serious as that of a homogeneous structured network, because the component modules have already been learned.

Third, a resulting modular network is easy to understand, because understanding how component modules are connected to each other is far simpler than understanding how separate units are connected to each other. Whether or not this advantage holds depends on a learning method. As shown previously, SLF generates networks with a small number of connections. This characteristic greatly helps understand the resulting modular networks. BP learning, on the other hand, does not share this characteristic.

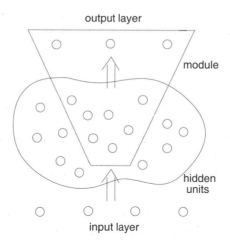

**Figure 5.19** Formation of a module. (© Elsevier Science, used with permission, see Copyright Acknowledgments)

Last, as will be shown later, learning becomes more efficient as it proceeds, because many previously learned modules become available. This advantage is not only useful from a practical point of view, but also interesting from a cognitive science perspective because of its similarity to the learning of humans.

Figure 5.19 illustrates how a module is formed. A task is given to a group of units (called output units) from the outside world as pairs of input and target outputs. Suppose the input layer contains all the necessary information to do the given task. The network is composed of a group of hidden units in addition to those input and output units, and can freely use these hidden units. SLF generates a subnetwork with a small number of input and hidden units due to the elimination of connections. The resulting subnetwork in Figure 5.19 can be interpreted as a module composed of output units and relevant hidden units. In contrast to this, BP learning tends to use up all the input and hidden units. Therefore the resulting network cannot be interpreted as a module.

It is not a realistic assumption that the learning of a module is based solely on information from the input layer. The more complex a task becomes, the larger the size of a resulting module becomes. This increases the impact of the computational cost and the local minima problem for the learning of a new module.

A more realistic assumption is that a module, during learning, may acquire information either from the input layer or from previously learned modules. Figure 5.20 illustrates a simple example of a 2-module network. Suppose module A is to learn a task, and module B has already learned its subtask. Suppose further that the input layer contains all the necessary information on these tasks. Module A, during learning, acquires information on the subtask from module B, not from the input layer. The reason is the following. Information in module B is more condensed than that in the input layer. Therefore, a module acquiring information

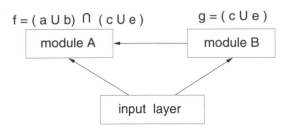

**Figure 5.20** An example of a network composed of two modules and the input layer.
(© Elsevier Science, used with permission, see Copyright Acknowledgments)

from module B is simpler than the one acquiring information solely from the input layer. The parsimonious characteristic of SLF enables the acquisition of information from module B.

Generally speaking, if a module uses outputs of previously learned modules, its learning becomes more efficient and a resulting network is constructed by assembling the previously learned modules. The penalty term in Equation 5.8 helps the generation of this simplified network.

As learning proceeds, the number of available modules increases. The essential problem is this: from where does a module acquire information for its learning? This problem becomes serious as the number of available modules increases. As will be shown later, appropriate modules can be selected without any supervision, provided SLF is adopted.

### 5.13.2    Boolean Functions

The purpose of learning a Boolean function is not merely to realize the mapping from input to output, but to discover a Boolean function explicitly based on input and output data.

#### 5.13.2.1   Sequential Learning of a 2-Module Network

The problem considered here is sequential learning, i.e. module B has finished learning and module A learns making use of the output of module B. In other words, the information flow between two modules is uni-directional.

Suppose module A in Figure 5.20 is to learn the Boolean function, $f = (a \cup b) \cap (c \cup e)$. Suppose further that module B has already learned its subtask, $g = (c \cup e)$, to some degree. If module B were not present, module A acquires information solely from the input layer. The existence of module B is expected to accelerate the learning of module A.

Figure 5.21 illustrates output patterns of module B for various degrees of learning performance in terms of the MSE: complete learning, 500-iteration learning, 200-iteration learning, 100-iteration learning and 50-iteration learning. The output pattern in the complete learning case is the same as the target output pattern. The 50-iteration learning case is quite immature, and can barely differentiate between 0 and 1.

In the complete learning case, it is highly expected that module A makes use of the output of module B during learning. An interesting question arising next is whether or not module A acquires information on $(c \cup e)$ from the incompletely learned module B instead of from the input layer.

Figure 5.22 displays the percentages of the connection weight from module B to module A. It indicates that in all cases except the 50-learning case the connection weights from the input units, $c$ and $e$, to module A diminishes to zero, and the connection weight from module B to module A increases during learning. In the 50-learning case the learning performance of module B is too poor to be used by module A. In the 100-learning case, although only partly shown in Figure 5.22, the connection weight from module B to module A becomes completely dominant after 50,000 iterations. It also illustrates that the better the learning performance of module B is, the faster the connections from module B to module A becomes dominant.

Figure 5.23 shows that the higher the learning performance of module B is, the faster the learning of module A becomes. This is in accordance with the difference of the speed at which the connection from module B to module A becomes dominant as shown in Figure 5.22.

Reorganization of modular structured networks is also noteworthy. Figure 5.24 illustrates the result of learning; modules A and B independently learn their tasks using SLF based on information from the input layer. Starting from this modular network, SLF generates Figure 5.25. These two figures indicate that the initial connections from the input units, $c$ and $e$, to module A are completely replaced by the connection from module B to module A. This can be regarded as a simple example of the process in which pieces of knowledge are reorganized into more coherent and amalgamated knowledge.

### 5.13.2.2  Sequential Learning of a Multiple-Module Network

Suppose a new module may acquire information from either previously learned modules or the input layer. From where does the new module acquire information for its learning?

Module A is to learn the Boolean function, $f = (a \cup b) \cap (c \cup e)$. Five modules, $B_1, B_2, B_3, B_4$ and $B_5$, are to learn the Boolean function, $(c \cup e)$, which correspond with complete-learning, 500-iteration learning, 200-iteration learning, 100-iteration learning and 50-iteration learning, respectively. Figure 5.26 displays how the information source on $(c \cup e)$ changes as learning proceeds. It shows that in the initial stage information both from the modules, $B_i$, and from the inputs, $c$ and $e$, are used, but as learning proceeds information from the best learned module, $B_1$, to module A becomes dominant.

In other words, in cases where multiple modules are available, the best module

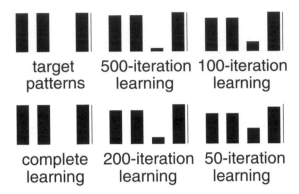

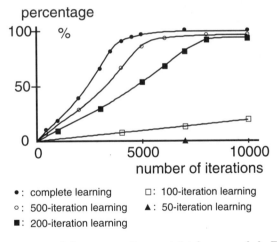

**Figure 5.21**   Output and target output patterns of module B for various degrees of learning performance in terms of the MSE. The height of each bar indicates the output value. Four bars in a row illustrate the output values corresponding to the 4 training inputs: $(c, e) = (1, 0), (0, 1), (0, 0)$ and $(1, 1)$. The length of the solid line on the right signifies the value of 1.

(© Elsevier Science, used with permission, see Copyright Acknowledgments)

**Figure 5.22**   Percentages of the connection weight from module B to module A, i.e. $100 \times |W_{AB}| / (|W_{AB}| + |W_{A,input}|)$, where $|W_{AB}|$ is the absolute value of the connection weight from module B to module A, and $|W_{A,input}|$ is the sum of the absolute values of the connection weights from the input units, $c$ and $e$, to module A. The vertical axis indicates the percentage. The horizontal axis represents the number of iterations during learning. Since the initial connection weight from module B to module A is set to zero, the initial value of the percentage is also zero. The percentage of connections from the input units, $c$ and $e$, to module A is calculated by subtracting the above percentage from 100. The learning parameters are: $\eta = 0.1$, $\alpha = 0.2$ and $\varepsilon = 10^{-4}$.

(© Elsevier Science, used with permission, see Copyright Acknowledgments)

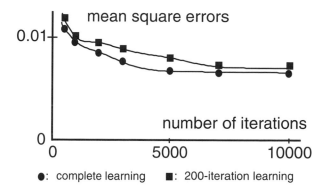

**Figure 5.23**  Learning speed of module A for various degrees of learning performance of module B. The parameters of learning are the same as those in Figure 5.22.

(© Elsevier Science, used with permission, see Copyright Acknowledgments)

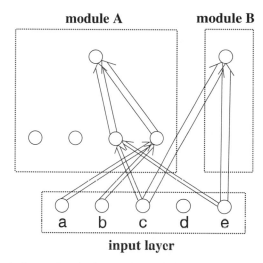

**Figure 5.24**  The independently learned modular structured network. Module A learns $f = (a \cup b) \cap (c \cup e)$, and module B learns $g = (c \cup e)$. The parameters of learning are the same as those in Figure 5.22.

(© Elsevier Science, used with permission, see Copyright Acknowledgments)

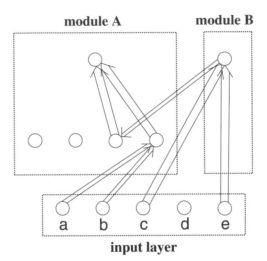

**Figure 5.25** The modular structured network after reorganization. Module B learns $g = (c \cup e)$, and module A learns $f = (a \cup b) \cap (c \cup e)$ making use of the output of module B. The learning parameters are the same as those in Figure 5.22. (© Elsevier Science, used with permission, see Copyright Acknowledgments)

for learning of the new module is automatically selected, provided SLF is used. This characteristic of the appropriate selection without any supervision is valuable for the learning of modular structured networks.

In the case of BP learning, on the other hand, the information on $(c \cup e)$ comes from all the modules and the input layer as shown in Figure 5.27. Generally speaking, in BP learning a new module acquires information from modules whose outputs have correlation with the current target output. For this reason, BP learning is not suited for the learning of modular structured networks.

### 5.13.2.3   Concurrent Learning of a 2-Module Network

Suppose two modules learn concurrently, i.e. each module can make use of the output of the other. Module A is to learn the Boolean function, $f = (a \cup b) \cap (c \cup e)$, and module B is to learn $g = (c \cup e)$. These two modules start learning at the same time. Qualitatively speaking, the learning of module B precedes that of module A due to its simplicity.

In the beginning stage of learning, both modules acquire information on $(c \cup e)$ from the input layer. Since the learning of module B becomes almost complete in about 2,000 iterations, module A begins to acquire information on $(c \cup e)$ from module B instead of the input layer. Figure 5.28 illustrates that the percentage of the connection weight from module B to module A increases and that from module A to module B diminishes to zero as learning proceeds. The percentage of connection weights from the input layer to module A is calculated by subtracting

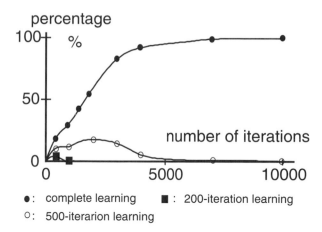

**Figure 5.26**   The percentage of the connection weight concerning $(c \cup e)$ from each module, $B_i$, to module A. The cases where the percentage is almost zero throughout learning are not shown here. The initial connection weight from each module, $B_i$, to module A is set to zero. The percentage of connection weights from the inputs, $c$ and $e$, to module A is calculated by subtracting the sum of the above percentages from 100. The learning parameters are the same as those in Figure 5.22.

(© Elsevier Science, used with permission, see Copyright Acknowledgments)

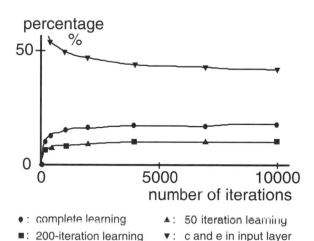

**Figure 5.27**   The percentage of the connection weight concerning $(c \cup e)$ from each module, $B_i$, to module A. Not all the cases are shown here for visibility. The parameters of learning are: $\eta = 0.1$ and $\alpha = 0.2$.

(© Elsevier Science, used with permission, see Copyright Acknowledgments)

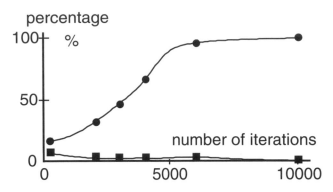

percentage

**Figure 5.28**   The percentage of the connection weight concerning $(c \cup e)$ from one module to the other. The learning parameters are the same as those in Figure 5.22. (© Elsevier Science, used with permission, see Copyright Acknowledgments)

the above percentage from 100.

This result demonstrates well that even if multiple modules learn concurrently, a simple modular structured network emerges, provided there exist part-whole relations among tasks to be learned.

### 5.13.3   Parity Problems

A parity problem is to judge whether the number of 1's in a binary input vector is odd or even; when it is odd, the output is 1 and when it is even, the output is 0. A parity problem with $n$ inputs is called a parity problem of order $n$.

As the order of a parity problem increases, its learning becomes more and more difficult due to the local minima problem. When a parity problem of some order has already been solved, it helps solve parity problems of higher orders because of the similarity among parity problems of various orders.

In this section, a trial is performed to solve a higher order parity problem under the assumption that lower order parity problems have already been solved and their outputs are available for its learning.

Let the parity problems of orders 2, 3 and 4 be $P_2$, $P_3$ and $P_4$, respectively, and their inputs be $(x_1, x_2)$, $(x_1, x_2, x_3)$ and $(x_1, x_2, x_3, x_4)$, respectively. Suppose, in the learning of the parity problem of order 5, $P_5$, not only the inputs, $(x_1, x_2, x_3, x_4, x_5)$, but also the outputs of lower order parity problems, $P_2, P_3$ and $P_4$ are available as shown in Figure 5.29. SLF using all $32(= 2^5)$ training samples generates the modular network constructed as the *exclusive or* of two information sources: $P_4$, which has the largest similarity to $P_5$ among modules and the additional input unit, $x_5$. It clearly reveals the structure of the parity problem $P_5$. It is to be noted that the inputs, $(x_1, x_2, x_3, x_4)$, and lower order parity problems, $P_2$ and $P_3$, are not used in

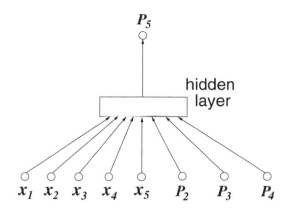

**Figure 5.29** Learning of the parity problem of order 5 using the modular structured network. The learning parameters are: $\eta = 0.1$, $\alpha = 0.2$ and $\varepsilon = 10^{-4}$.
(© Elsevier Science, used with permission, see Copyright Acknowledgments)

solving the parity problem, $P_5$.

This result can be extended to parity problems of higher orders. The parity problem of order $n$, $P_n$, can be represented by a modular network of the *exclusive or* of $P_{n-1}$ and the additional input unit, $x_n$.

### 5.13.4 Geometrical Transformation of Figures

The characteristic that only appropriate modules among previously learned ones are made use of and all the connections from other modules diminish without any supervision is valuable in the learning of modular structured networks. Up to now all the previously learned modules are located at the same level as the input layer. In other words, only, as it were, flat modular networks have been considered.

In this section, the learning of a sequence of modules is considered by dynamically concatenating previously learned modules. As an example, geometric transformation of simple figures is adopted here. Table 5.18 shows a list of elementary geometric transformations. Each of these geometric transformations corresponds to a module.

Here, a simple geometric transformation realized by concatenating two modules is considered. Figure 5.30 illustrates an example of a multi-layer modular structured network. Both the first and the second module layers have 8 modules in Table 5.18. Each module can easily be realized by a 2-layer neural subnetwork and is kept frozen during the learning of a modular network. At first glance Figure 5.30 seems to be a 6-layer network, but since the input layer and the lower layer of the first module layer is one and the same layer, it actually is a 5-layer network. In Figure 5.30 all the layers except the output layer use linear units instead of sigmoidal units.

The problem considered here is to discover a sequence of geometric transformation modules based on 4 pairs of input and output figures in Figure 5.31. The supposed solution to this problem is the rotation of $90^o$ clockwise followed by the upward

**Table 5.18**   Modules for elementary geometric transformations.

| module | geometric transformation |
|--------|-------------------------|
| $M_1$ | no transformation |
| $M_2$ | rotation of $90^o$ clockwise |
| $M_3$ | rotation of $180^o$ clockwise |
| $M_4$ | rotation of $270^o$ clockwise |
| $M_5$ | rightward translation by 1 block |
| $M_6$ | leftward translation by 1 block |
| $M_7$ | upward translation by 1 block |
| $M_8$ | downward translation by 1 block |

translation by 1 block.

If BP learning is used for this problem, the realization of the mapping from an input figure to an output figure is straightforward, but the resulting inter-module connections cannot be interpreted as a sequence of geometric transformations. Instead, they correspond to a complex combination of all the transformations and are impossible to implement or understand. On the other hand, SLF plays an essential role in discovering a sequence of geometric transformation modules.

Given 4 pairs of input figures and target output figures, inter-module connections are trained. SLF generates a single path or at most a few parallel paths from input to output, explicitly providing a sequence of geometric transformation modules.

Ten different initial connection weights are tried. The solution of leftward translation by 1 block followed by rotation of $90^o$ clockwise is obtained 5 times. In this case, only the connections from $M_6$ in the first module layer to $M_2$ in the second module layer and the connections from this $M_2$ to the output layer remain, and all other connections fade out. In 3 out of 10 cases, the supposed solution of the rotation of $90^o$ clockwise followed by the upward translation by 1 block is obtained. In 2 out of 10 cases, both solutions appear simultaneously.

Generally speaking, it is impossible to know *a priori* how many layers of modules are necessary. Preparing an excess number of module layers solves this problem; if the number of module layers is too large, no transformation, $M_1$, in Table 5.18 can be used for necessary number of times.

In cases where a given task does not depend on a *sequence* of modules, the problem is reduced to the discovery of a subset of modules instead of a sequence of modules. In other words, only one module layer is sufficient to solve this kind of problems.

### 5.13.5   Discussion

In the section, I have demonstrated that SLF can efficiently construct modular networks in various examples: Boolean functions, parity problems, and the transformation of geometric figures. The characteristic that appropriate modules can

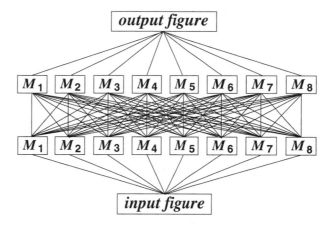

**Figure 5.30**   The 2-layer modular structured network. Each module layer is composed of 8 modules. Each module is realized by a 2-layer subnetwork.
(© Elsevier Science, used with permission, see Copyright Acknowledgments)

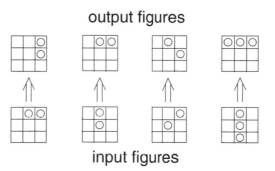

**Figure 5.31**   Input figures and target output figures. The former is the figure before transformation and the latter is the one after transformation.
(© Elsevier Science, used with permission, see Copyright Acknowledgments)

automatically be selected without any supervision is especially important in the learning of modular networks.

The use of previously learned modules helps shorten the required learning time. It also simplifies the resulting modular networks, because previously learned modules can be utilized as building blocks. This could be seen as a model of progressive learning based on the previously learned results and is similar to the *layers of society* in the society of mind (Minsky, 1985).

## 5.14   Toward Hybrid Intelligence

Information processing is categorized roughly into connectionism and symbolism. Let us review these two types of information processing. Connectionism is good at learning and self-organization. Associative memory and recall, which is readily available, is similar to human memory. Because its basic mechanism is similarity-based inference, its information processing is flexible and robust to noise and distortion. Since it can represent physical signals, it is compatible with the physical world rather than symbolism.

On the other hand, symbolism is good at structural knowledge representation. Variables and recursive processing are also possible.

These complementary characteristics have motivated studies on the integration of connectionism and symbolism to achieve flexible and effective information processing (Sun and Alexandre, 1995). From the viewpoint of cognitive science, the integration sounds reasonable, because humans seem to use both types of information processing.

However, *ad hoc* integration will not lead to literally flexible and effective information processing. For example, symbolic information processing using neural networks which lacks the advantages of connectionism is almost meaningless. Therefore, preserving the advantages of both types of information processing is indispensable.

There have been various studies towards this integration: introduction of flexibility into symbolic systems (Touretzky, 1990), injection of symbolic ingredients into neural systems (Ishikawa, 1996d), introduction of modularity into network structure (Ishikawa, 1995a), building of schemas to bridge the gap (Leow and Miikkulainen, 1994; Miikkulainen and Leow, 1995), the subsymbol hypothesis (Smolensky et al., 1992), emergence of symbols or rules out of pattern information (Ishikawa, 1994b, 1996c), modeling of the interaction between them (Ishikawa, 1994a; Ishikawa and Kawashima, 1997; Sun, 1994), and so forth (Hinton, 1991).

One of the various studies, which I believe is promising, is the injection of symbolic ingredients into neural systems. This will be made possible by structural learning methods which facilitate generating skeletal networks and modular networks. This is because symbols will emerge out of a uniform structured network and the meaning of its component units will be clarified.

Another approach, which I believe is also promising, is the modeling of the interaction between symbols and patterns. This is an example of hierarchical integration. Toward this end, I have developed an integrated model of pattern and symbolic information for the recognition of an object in various contexts (Ishikawa, 1994a). This is composed of a pattern module and a symbol module, interacting with each other to realize flexible information processing. Another model which I have developed is an integrated neural network model for the recognition of complex figures (Ishikawa and Kawashima, 1997). It realizes both locally shift invariant and globally location dependent recognition.

Development of an information processing system in which the integration plays an essential role in the real world is a challenging task to be pursued.

## 5.15  Conclusion

This chapter proposes a simple and effective learning method called structural learning with forgetting (SLF). Various applications demonstrate that it has the following significant advantages.

1. SLF can discover regularities in or discover rules from data without initial theories and preprocessing.

2. Learning with trial and error for finding appropriate network structure is no longer necessary, because a skeletal network emerges.

3. SLF has good generalization ability due to the simplicity of the resulting network structure.

4. SLF has a simple criterion function and learning rule. Therefore it needs only little extra computational cost.

5. In cooperation with AIC or MSE for test data, SLF can determine a relative weight of a penalty term.

6. SLF can easily be extended to the learning of recurrent network structure.

7. SLF has adaptive learning capability.

8. SLF is effective in discovering rules from data.

9. SLF is effective in the learning of modular structured networks.

10. SLF is expected to play an important role in the integration of connectionism and symbolism.

As mentioned in the Introduction, the first advantage is the most essential. It enables the acquisition of white box models instead of black-box models.

## Acknowledgments

I would like to thank Hirotsugu Yamamoto and Jyunji Shimizu, former students in my laboratory, for their contributions to this research. The work was partially supported by Grant-in-Aid for Scientific Research (c)07680404 and (c)09680371 by the Ministry of Education, Science, Sports and Culture, Japan.

## Copyright Acknowledgments

## References

Akaike, H. 1974. A new look at the statistical model identification. *IEEE Trans. on AC*, AC-19(6):716–723.

Andrews, R. et al. 1996. An evaluation and comparison of techniques for extracting and refining rules from artificial neural networks. Tech. rep., QUT NRC Technical Report.

Andrews, R., Diederich, J., and Tickle, A. B. 1995. Survey and critique of techniques for extracting rules from trained artificial neural networks. *Knowledge-Based Systems*, 8(6):373–389.

Ash, T. 1989. Dynamic node creation in backpropagation networks. *Connection Science*, 1(4):365–375.

Buntine, W. and Weigend, A. S. 1991. Bayesian backpropagation. *Complex Systems*, 5:603–643.

Cun, Y. L., Denker, J. S., and Solla, S. 1990. Optimal brain damage. In *Advances in Neural Information Processing Systems 2*, ed. D. S. Touretzky, San Mateo, CA. Morgan Kaufmann Publishers.

Elman, J. L. 1990. Finding structure in time. *Cognitive Science*, 14:179–211.

Fahlman, S. E. and Lebiere, C. 1990. The cascade-correlation learning architecture.

In *Advances in Neural Information Processing Systems*, ed. D. S. Touretzky, vol. 2, pp. 642–649, San Mateo, CA. Morgan Kaufmann.

Ferrá, A. K. H. L. and Gardiner, K. 1991. Discovering production rules with higher order neural networks: a case study. In *Proceedings of Machine Learning*, pp. 158–162.

Fisher, R. A. 1936. The use of multiple measurements in taxonomic problem. *Annals of Eugenics*, 7:179–188. Part 2.

Fogel, D. B. 1991. An information criterion for optimal neural network selection. *IEEE Trans. on Neural Networks*, 2(5):490–497.

Fu, L. M. 1993. Knowledge-based connectionism for revising domain theories. *IEEE Trans. on SMC*, 23(1):173–182.

Fu, L. M. 1994. Rule generation from neural networks. *IEEE Trans. on SMC*, 24(8):1114–1124.

Gallant, S. I. 1986. Three constructive algorithms for network learning. In *Proceedings of the Cognitive Science Society*, pp. 652–660, Amherst, MA.

Hassibi, B., Stork, D. G., Wolf, G., and Watanabe, T. 1994. Optimal brain surgeon: Extensions and performance comparisons. In *Advances in Neural Information Processing Systems*, eds. J. D. Cowan, G. Tesauro, and J. Alspector, vol. 6, pp. 263–270. Morgan Kaufmann.

Hinton, G., ed. 1991. *Connectionist Symbol Processing*. MIT Press.

Ishikawa, M. 1989. A structural learning algorithm with forgetting of link weights. In *IJCNN*, Washington DC.

Ishikawa, M. 1994a. An integrated model of pattern and symbolic information for the recognition of an object in context. In *ICNN*, pp. 1810–1814, Orlando FL.

Ishikawa, M. 1994b. Structural learning and its applications to rule extraction. In *Proceedings of ICNN'94*, pp. 354–359, Orlando FL.

Ishikawa, M. 1994c. Structural learning in neural networks. In *Proceedings of 3rd International Conference on Fuzzy Logic, Neural Nets and Soft Computing (IIZUKA'94)*, pp. 37–44, Iizuka, Japan.

Ishikawa, M. 1995a. Learning of modular structured networks. *Artificial Intelligence*, 75:51 62.

Ishikawa, M. 1995b. Neural networks approach to rule extraction. In *ANNES'95*, pp. 6–9.

Ishikawa, M. 1996a. Bayesian estimation in structural learning of neural networks. In *ICONIP'96*, pp. 1377–1380, Hong Kong.

Ishikawa, M. 1996b. Rule extraction by successive regularization. In *IEEE ICNN'96*, pp. 1139–1143, Washington D.C.

Ishikawa, M. 1996c. Structural learning and knowledge acquisition. In *IEEE ICNN'96*, pp. 100–105, Washington D.C.

Ishikawa, M. 1996d. Structural learning with forgetting. *Neural Networks*, 9(3):509–

521.

Ishikawa, M. 1997. Structural learning approach to rule discovery from data with continuous valued inputs. In *ICONIP'97*.

Ishikawa, M. 1998. Structural learning and rule discovery from data. In *Brain-Like Computing and Intelligent Information Systems*, eds. S. Amari and N. Kasabov. Springer.

Ishikawa, M. and Kawashima, S. 1997. An integrated neural network model for the recognition of complex figures—combination of shift invariance and location dependence. In *1997 Real World Computing Symposium (RWC'97)*, pp. 312–317, Tokyo.

Ishikawa, M. and Moriyama, T. 1996. Prediction of time series by a structural learning of neural networks. *Fuzzy Sets and Systems*, 82:167–176.

Ishikawa, M. and Uchida, H. 1992. A structural learning of neural networks based on an entropy criterion. In *IJCNN'92*, pp. II375–380, Beijing.

Ishikawa, M. and Yoshino, K. 1993. Automatic task decomposition in modular networks by structural learning with forgetting. In *Proceedings of 1993 International Joint Conference on Neural Networks*, pp. 1345–1348.

Jacobs, R. A. and Nowlan, S. J. 1991. Adaptive mixtures of local experts. *Neural Computation*, 3(1):79–87.

Jordan, M. I. 1986. Serial order—a parallel distributed processing approach. Tech. rep., ICS Report, UC San Diego.

Kreider, J. and Haberl, J. 1993. The great energy prediction shootout concept and summary of the first building data analysis and prediction competition. Unpublished.

Kurita, T. 1990. A method to determine the number of hidden units of three layered neural networks by information criteria. *Trans. of the Institute of Electronics Information and Communication Engineers*, J73-D-II(11):1872–1878.

Leow, W. K. and Miikkulainen, R. 1994. Visor: Schema-based scene analysis with structured neural networks. *Neural Processing Letters*, 1.1(2):18–23.

MacKay, D. J. C. 1995. Probable networks and plausible predictions—a review of practical bayesian methods for supervised neural networks. *Network: Computation in Neural Systems*, 6:469–505.

McMillan, C., Mozer, M. C., and Smolensky, P. 1992. Rule induction through integrated symbolic and subsymbolic processing. In *Advances in Neural Information Processing Systems*, vol. 4, pp. 969–976. Morgan Kaufmann Publishers.

Miikkulainen, R. and Leow, W. K. 1995. Visual schemas in object recognition and scene analysis. In *The Handbook of Brain Theory and Neural Networks*, ed. in M. A. Arbib, pp. 1029–1031, Cambridge MA. MIT Press.

Minsky, M. 1985. *The Society of Mind*. Simon and Schuster.

Minsky, M. and Papert, S. 1988. *Perceptrons*. MIT Press.

Moody, J. E. 1992. *The effective number of parameters: an analysis of generalization and regularization in nonlinear learning systems*, vol. 4, pp. 847–854. San Mateo CA: Morgan Kaufmann.

Mozer, M. C. and Smolensky, P. 1989. Using relevance to reduce network size automatically. *Connection Science*, 1(1):3–16.

Murata, N., Yoshizawa, S., and Amari, S. 1994. Network information criterion—determining the number of hidden units for an artificial neural network model. *IEEE Trans. on Neural Networks*, 5(6):865–872.

Murphy, P. M. and Aha, D. W. 1992. UCI repository of machine learning databases. Department of Information and Computer Science, University of California, Irvine, CA.

Nowlan, D. C. P. S. J. and Hinton, G. E. 1986. Experiments on learning by back propagation. Tech. Rep. CMU-CS-86-126, Carnegie-Mellon Univ.

Quinlan, J. R. 1993. *C4 5: Programs for Machine Learning*. Morgan Kaufmann.

Reed, R. 1993. Pruning algorithms—a survey. *IEEE Trans. on Neural Networks*, 4(5):740–747.

Rumelhart, D. E. 1988. Parallel distributed processing. Plenary session.

Sestito, S. and Dillon, T. S. 1994. *Automated Knowledge Acquisition*. Prentice Hall.

Smolensky, P., Legendre, G., and Miyata, Y. 1992. Principles for an integrated connectionist/symbolic theory of higher cognition. Tech. Rep. CU-CS-600-92, University of of Colorado.

Sun, R. 1994. *Integrating rules and connectionism for robust commonsense reasoning*. New York: John Wiley & Sons.

Sun, R. and Alexandre, F., eds. 1995. *The Working Notes of the IJCAI Workshop on Connectionist-symbolic Integration*.

Thrun, S. B., Bala, J., Bloedorn, E., Bratko, I., Cestnik, B., Cheng, J., Jong, K. D., Dzeroski, S., Fahlman, S. E., Fisher, D., Hamann, R., Kaufman, K., Keller, S., Kononenko, I., Kreuziger, J., Michalski, R. S., Mitchell, T., Pachowicz, P., Vafaie, Y. R. H., de Welde, W. V., Wenzel, W., Wnek, J., and Zhang, J. 1991. The MONK's problems—A performance comparison of different learning algorithms. Tech. Rep. CMU-CS-91-197, Carnegie Mellon University Technical Report.

Touretzky, D. S. 1990. BoltzCONS: Dynamic symbol structures in a connectionist network. *Artificial Intelligence*, 40:5–46.

Towell, G. G. and Shavlik, J. W. 1993 Extracting refined rules from knowledge-based neural networks. *Machine Learning*, 13:71–101.

Towell, G. G. and Shavlik, J. W. 1994. Knowledge-based artificial neural networks. *Artificial Intelligence*, 70:119–165.

Weigend, A. S. and Gershenfeld, N. A. 1994. *Time Series Prediction: Forecasting the future and understanding the past*. Addison-Wesley.

Williams, R. J. and Zipser, D. 1995. Gradient-based learning algorithm for recurrent networks. In *Back-propagation: theory architectures and applications*, eds. in Y. Chauvin and D. E. Rumelhart, Hillsdale NJ. Erlbaum.

Yasui, S. 1992. A new method to remove redundant connections in backpropagation neural networks: Introduction of parametric lateral inhibition fields. In *IJCNN'92*, pp. II360–367, Beijing.

# 6     VL₁ANN: Transformation of Rules to Artificial Neural Networks

Ian Cloete

*An algorithm for the translation of symbolic classification rules into feedforward artificial neural networks is presented. The syntax of the rules for which the algorithm caters is followed closely by a wide variety of machine learning algorithms, thus allowing domain theories acquired by these programs to be incorporated into a neural network. Several methods are also proposed to tune fuzziness in the network's decision.*

## 6.1   Introduction

Symbolic knowledge about a problem domain is frequently available in the form of classification or production rules. This chapter presents a translational neurocomputing architecture that transforms symbolic rules into an equivalent feedforward Artificial Neural Network (ANN).

In machine learning the area of *empirical learning* is concerned with the problem of deriving application-specific information from a set of examples. Many empirical machine learning algorithms for deriving classification information, such as BEXA (Theron and Cloete, 1996), CN2 (Clark and Boswell, 1991) and C4.5 (Quinlan, 1993), represent their domain theories in the form of symbolic rules. These rules represent hyperrectangular decision regions formed in the input variable space, and cannot represent more complex decisions such as arithmetic combinations of input variables (Quinlan, 1993).

An artificial neural network, on the other hand, has the ability to encode complex decision regions by linear and non-linear transformations of its inputs (Zurada, 1992). Its knowledge about an application is encoded in terms of numeric values, the so-called weights of the network. The challenge is to integrate the symbolic domain theory derived by symbolic learning methods into the ANN. Incorporation of symbolic rules into the ANN then allows prior knowledge about an application to be used by the ANN, while the numerical learning techniques of the ANN can be applied to refine the domain theory and to augment it with more complex decision regions of which it is capable. This integration of symbolic and connectionist knowledge representations holds the promise of combining the best features of each approach to construct computationally intelligent systems.

This chapter thus addresses the issue of converting symbolic rules to an ANN to represent the same domain theory. The algorithm that is proposed, $VL_1$ANN, incorporates tunable fuzziness in the decision by adjusting the rule representation together with the representation of the input data (Cloete, 1996).

The chapter is organized as follows. Section 6.2 discusses the rule syntax and description of input data. Section 6.3 is devoted to the algorithm for rule translation and the representation of input data, and Section 6.4 contains an example. In Section 6.5 the algorithm is also briefly compared to related approaches to encode rules into a neural network. The method is summarized in Section 6.6 and suggestions for future research are given.

## 6.2  Data Representation and Rule Syntax

The variables (attributes) of a data set accepted by $VL_1$ANN are of two basic types: continuous numeric values and nominal values. The continuous numeric values are real or integer valued (linearly ordered) variables, while the nominal attributes (e.g. a variable taking a string value such as *green*) include linearly ordered nominals (e.g. an attribute *weight* taking the string values *light*, *medium* and *heavy*) binary nominals (e.g. the boolean values *false* and *true* or any two-valued nominal attribute) and unordered nominal values.

Syntax of the symbolic classification rules adhere to the conventions of $VL_1$ (Theron and Cloete, 1996), Michalski's multiple-valued extension to propositional logic (Michalski, 1975). The description below follows Haussler (1988) and describes the relevant subset of $VL_1$ using standard logic terminology (Haussler, 1988; Theron and Cloete, 1996). Let $A_i$ denote an attribute with domain $D_i$ and let $a_i$ denote any value in $D_i$. Attributes are related to values via *atoms*. *Elementary* atoms take the form $[A_i = a_i]$ for nominal attributes, e.g. `[weight = light]`. For linearly ordered attributes elementary atoms take the form $[A_i \ \# \ a_i]$   with $\# \in \{=, <, \leq, >, \geq\}$ or $[a_i \ \# \ A_i \ \# \ b_i]$ with $\# \in \{<, \leq\}$, e.g. `[age < 10]` and `[20 < weight ≤ 100]`.

$VL_1$ *expressions* are defined as follows. (1) An atom is an expression. (2) A *conjunctive* expression is the conjunction of one or more atoms. Adjacent atoms have an implicit $\land$ (and) between them. (3) A *disjunctive* expression is the disjunction of one or more conjunctions. (4) An expression that implies a concept is called a *rule*. A set of disjunctive rules can always be written as an equivalent set of *production rules* and vice versa. Therefore all disjunctive rules are given to $VL_1$ANN in the form of production rules such as: `IF conjunction THEN concept description`. The *concept description* following THEN in the production rule assigns one of its values to a nominal attribute $A_i$, where $A_i$ was designated as an output variable, e.g. `IF [autumn = no][temp < 25] THEN PlayOutside = +`.

## 6.3   The VL$_1$ANN Algorithm for Rule Representation

The VL$_1$ANN algorithm for rule representation assumes that the neural network architecture into which the rules are mapped is a feedforward network, i.e. without recurrent connections, with differentiable activation functions. This network representation allows training by neural network learning methods, such as backpropagation (Zurada, 1992), at a later stage to refine the network's decisions. The network typically has four layers (not counting the inputs at layer 0) and sigmoid activation functions for all units at layers 1 to 4, the output layer. Unit $i$ at layer $l$ takes its inputs from the $n$ units connected to it from layer $l-1$ with outputs $x_j$ and weights $w_{ji}$. The sigmoid function $f(x)$ maps any real-valued input to a non-negative output in the range $(0,1)$, where $f(x_i) = 1/(1 + e^{-s_i x_i})$, and the net input $x_i$ to unit $i$ is $x_i = \sum_{j=1}^{n} w_{ji}x_j + \theta_i$. The parameter $s_i$ controls the slope of the sigmoid function. By setting it to an appropriately high value, say $s_i > 5$, the activation function approaches a threshold logic unit with outputs near 0 or 1. The parameter $\theta_i$ serves as the bias for a unit. If the net input exceeds 0 the unit outputs a value closer to 1, otherwise a value closer to 0, since $f$ is a monotonic increasing function with $f(0) = 0.5$.

Since an ANN accepts only real valued inputs, all input data must be converted to real values. The basic idea underpinning VL$_1$ANN is that a neural network unit which approximates a threshold logic unit can divide an input variable's values into two sets: those for which the unit outputs a value closer to 1 and those for which the unit outputs a value closer to 0. The response of the unit can be graded by adjusting the activation function's slope, while the bias value selects the input value projected onto the midpoint of the activation function's output values. In this way one or more units can be programmed to implement any of the relational conditions (atoms) listed in Section 6.2. These conditions are implemented at layer 1, i.e. the first hidden layer, of the ANN constructed by VL$_1$ANN and will be referred to as "relational" units at the "relational" layer or level of the ANN. These relational tests create special surfaces in the input space, namely hyperplanes that are orthogonal to the axis of a tested attribute and parallel to all other axes. Thus this layer removes the restriction that inputs be represented as propositions.

The condition parts of production rules are interpreted conjunctively; so all atoms of the same production rule are connected to a unit approximating a threshold logic AND function (Kohavi, 1978) at layer 2 of the ANN. This conjunctive interpretation of connected inputs creates decision regions that are all hyperrectangles.

At layer 3 all AND units implementing production rules with identical conclusions are connected to a unit approximating a threshold logic OR function (Kohavi, 1978). The construction of layer 4 is discussed after each of these successive steps have been explained in more detail below.

THE VL$_1$ANN ALGORITHM:

1. Encode input variables to real (numeric) values.

2. FOR each rule DO:

2.1 FOR each atom of the rule DO:

2.1.1 Encode the atom as new relational units at layer 1 connected to the input in layer 0.

2.2 Connect all the relational units of the rule to a new AND unit in layer 2.

3. Connect all the AND units representing rules with the same conclusion to a new OR unit in layer 3.

4. FOR each output variable *Attr* not orthogonally encoded DO:

4.1 Map all the OR units for *Attr* in layer 3 to a single new output unit in layer 4.

In Step 1 continuous inputs are scaled to a specified range at the discretion of the user, while each nominal value is encoded as a real value. For input nominal attributes, the real values representing each nominal value are placed around 0, equally spaced unless the user specifies the mapping, and maintain the original order in the case of totally ordered nominal values, in such a way that no nominal input value is mapped to 0. This ensures that when the network is trained using backpropagation, the weight corresponding to each nominal value will be adjusted. For output nominal attributes, the nominal values are mapped similarly to real values within the output range of the activation functions in the output layer of the ANN. Mapping a nominal value to 0.5 is not allowed, since this value is used to indicate an unknown decision for the sigmoid activation function.

Step 2.1.1: Rule representation is intertwined with the representation of the input data. Spacing of the real values and the strength of the response by each relational unit mutually influence one another. Consider the representation of the atom [X ≤ 4], X a continuous-valued attribute. Assume that the next larger observed value for X in the data set was 6 and that the user wants the relational unit for this rule to output at least 0.9 when the condition is satisfied. $VL_1ANN$ then computes a *cut-point* in the interval between these observed values to separate them. The bias of the unit determines this cut-point, which is set by default to the midpoint of the interval. The slope of the sigmoid function is computed (using its inverse function) to output the desired value when $X = 4$. All weights of relational units are set to either a positive or a negative constant $C$. For $C = 1$ this unit has a weight value of $-1$, slope value of 2.198 and bias value of 5. For the observed value 6 this unit will output approximately 0.1. The default placing of the cut-point, i.e. at the midpoint or closer to the value specified in an atom, and the desired output of a unit are user-specified parameters. In this way a relational unit can produce a graded response, which can be further tuned by adjusting the scaling of a variable's values to a specified range. For instance, scaling the range of the variable $X$ to produce a larger sized interval between observed values, leads to a smaller slope value for the relational unit while still implementing the same atom. (A flatter slope for an activation function benefits subsequent backpropagation training.)

For each of the relational operators $(<, \leq, >, \geq)$ one relational unit is added to the ANN. The operator $>$ requires a cut-point to the "right" of the value specified in an atom, but the unit's weight is the positive constant $C$ in order to output values close to 1 for all inputs greater than the cut-point. The operators $\geq$ and $<$ are currently treated similarly to the operators discussed above by placing a cut-point to the "left" of the value specified in an atom. For the operator $=$ two relational units are constructed which implement cut-points on both sides of the value. Atoms of the form $[a_i \ \# \ A_i \ \# \ b_i]$, with $\# \in \{<, \leq\}$, are treated as the two atoms $[a_i \ \# \ A_i]$ and $[A_i \ \# \ b_i]$, conjunctively interpreted and connected to the same AND unit.

Nominal attributes are treated like the continuous attributes, except that a simplification is possible in two cases. For an atom $[X = a]$, where $a$ is mapped to the smallest real value representing the attribute's values, only a single relational unit is needed. The same applies when $a$ is mapped to the largest real value. Ordered nominal attributes are treated like continuous attributes.

This type of representation chosen for inputs allows linear combinations of variables to be discovered and the cut-points between input values to be adjusted by subsequent learning procedures. It also avoids the prior discretization of inputs typically required by other approaches, and incorporates trainable/adjustable fuzziness into the representation.

In Step 2.2 an AND unit is constructed by setting the bias of a unit with $n$ inputs (each approximating 0 or 1) to a value between $-n*w$ and $-(n-1)*w$, with $w$ the positive weight value on each of the incoming connections (Kohavi, 1978). Again the response of the unit can be graded by adjusting the slope of the activation function, by changing the magnitude of $w$, or by setting the bias to a value $-n*w*k$ with $0 < k < 1$. The last adjustment may allow the AND unit to fire when less than $n$ units are activated or some inputs are not as highly activated as others.

In Step 3 an OR unit computes the disjunction of all production rules with the same conclusion, again constructed in the usual way (Kohavi, 1978). The comments for softening an AND unit's decision also applies. Such an OR unit represents an "orthogonal" encoding of an output attributes' values, i.e. one output unit representing the presence (output approximately 1) or absence (output approximately 0) of each of the nominal attributes' values. Recall that a conclusion is specified as `Attribute = value`. Step 4.1 of VL₁ ANN is not used for this type of encoding of nominal outputs. However, in the case that a single unit at layer 4 must output any of the real values corresponding to a nominal value of the variable, Step 4.1 constructs a unit to compute such a mapping.

Step 4.1: The unit's bias is set to 0 and its slope to the default value of 0.5. This more gradual slope allows a larger input range to project onto a small range of output values, thus allowing for variations in the inputs while still projecting the inputs close to the desired output value. All the units in layer 3 that assign a value to this same output attribute are connected as inputs. Exactly one of these inputs takes a value close to 1, the rest a value close to 0. Then the real value to be computed for each nominal value is mapped to a corresponding weight value using the inverse activation function. For example, an OR unit at layer 3 which fires for the concept description `Color = blue`, blue mapped to 0.8, is connected to the output unit with a weight of 2.773.

Lastly, what happens when none of the production rules fire? In this situation each orthogonally encoded output unit outputs a value approximating 0, while each continuously encoded unit outputs a value approximating 0.5 (unknown classification). For this reason also, no nominal output value is represented by 0.5. $VL_1ANN$ also has a post-processor which maps the network's output values to the original symbolic data representation.

In certain cases not all four layers of the network need to be constructed. It may occur, for instance, that for a particular decision only one production rule exists, thus obviating the need to construct a disjunctive (OR) unit for this decision. Similarly, an AND unit (conjunction) can be ommitted when a decision requires exactly one atom. The next section illustrates $VL_1ANN$ with an example.

## 6.4  Example

Consider the following three illustrative rules suggested by BEXA when learning classification rules for the well-known data set:

1. IF [petal-width ≤ 6] THEN iris-type = setosa
2. IF [petal-length ≤ 49] AND [6 < petal-width ≤ 16] THEN iris-type = versicolor
3. IF [petal-length > 49] AND [petal-width > 16] THEN iris-type = virginica

The aim of the iris data set is to determine to which of three types an iris belongs based on its petal length and width, and sepal length and width. The data set contains four integer valued input attributes measured in milimeters (*sepal-length, sepal-width, petal-length, petal-width*) and the class attribute *iris-type* with possible values *setosa, virginica* and *versicolor*. The unpruned rules above use only two of the input attributes. *petal-length* varies from 10 to 69mm, while *petal-width* takes values from 1 to 25 with no values observed in the data between 6 and 10.

The network constructed by $VL_1ANN$ to encode the three rules above is shown in Figure 6.1.

Firstly, the relational layer encodes each of the 6 tests in the rules above (the number of an atom corresponds to the number of the unit in the figure):

1. petal-width ≤ 6
2. petal-width ≤ 16
3. petal-width > 6
4. petal-length ≤ 49
5. petal-length > 49
6. petal-width > 16

The value of the parameter $s_i$ is given next to each unit, weight values are next to each link and the bias values are given on the links not connected to any lower layer unit. Only connetions dictated by the production rules above are included in the figure. Note that conditions 1 and 3 specify a bias value of 8 and $s_i = 1.099$. Because the values between 6 and 10 for *petal-width* has not been observed in the

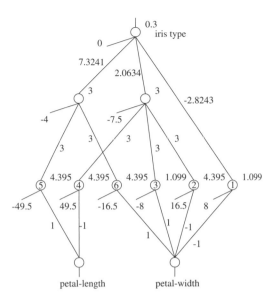

**Figure 6.1**   Network constructed for three iris rules

data set, VL$_1$ANN chooses the cut-point as the middle of the interval inbetween (by default) and adjusts the slope of the sigmoid transfer function accordingly. Similarly, the bias values of the other units and their $s_i$ parameters are set to the midpoint between the observed integer values. Unit 1 is connected directly to the output unit because a single atom is adequate for the decision that the iris type is *setosa*.

At the next layer the AND units form the conjunction of the input conditions. In this case an OR unit is not required as explained before, so these units are connected directly to the output unit.

The nominal output values corresponding to the possible values *setosa*, *virginica* and *versicolor* have been chosen as 0.3, 0.9 and 0.65, respectively. The output unit has a bias value of 0. Its $s_i$ value of 0.3 produces a 'flatter' sigmoid transfer function which reduces the effect of slightly activated inputs other than the actual decision to be output.

## 6.5   Related Work

The translational approach to constructing a knowledge-based neurocomputing system has been termed *rule-based connectionist modeling* (Fu, 1996) which produces rule-based connectionist networks (RBCN). Each rule has an antecedent (premise) consisting of one or more conditions and a consequent. In this approach the rules are first transformed into a set of equivalent rules with conjunctive conditions (propositional variables) only and a single consequent, while the rules are interpreted disjunctively. In the neural network configuration all the conjunctive conditions of a rule are linked to a conjunction unit and all rules (i.e. conjunction units) for the same concept are linked to a disjunction unit, where the firing of each such unit represents that concept. That is why the disjunction unit has also been called a concept unit, which can be an intermediate conclusion or an output unit. This leads to a two layer network, not counting the input layer.

This approach is followed by both KBCNN (Knowledge-Based Conceptual Neural Network) (Fu, 1993) and the KBANN (Knowledge-Based Artificial Neural Network) algorithm (Towell and Shavlik, 1994). KBANN uses sigmoid activation functions where weights from a positive attribute and from a negative attribute are set to $w$ and $-w$ respectively. KBCNN also caters for certainty factor based activation functions with weight values bounded between $-1$ and 1. These systems accept rules in the form of propositional Horn clauses, while nominal inputs are translated to orthogonal input variables (i.e. one input unit for each nominal value of the variable) taking values in $\{0, 1\}$ or $\{-1, 1\}$ to yield a false/true interpretation.

Although KBANN accepts rules in the form of propositions (variable free Horn clauses), it also caters for linearly ordered inputs (Towell and Shavlik, 1994). Nominal inputs are always translated to orthogonal variables, while linear inputs are translated to user-defined subranges. Each subrange is represented by a normalized input value with the midpoint of the subrange having the highest value. Ordered nominals are also orthogonally translated, except that each input unit is assigned a value which is scaled according to its distance from the given input value. These last two encodings of inputs enforce the use of several input units to represent a single input attribute, while the linear transformation also requires the *a priori* selection of subranges to which a variable should be mapped.

The $VL_1ANN$ algorithm follows the same general correspondence and rule-based semantics as these systems: Data attributes and input variables are mapped to input units, target concepts are mapped to output units, intermediate concepts are mapped to hidden units, and the domain rules determine how the attributes and concepts link. However, the $VL_1ANN$ algorithm caters for relational expressions as inputs instead of propositions only, thus inserting an extra pre-processing layer to create orthogonal decision boundaries in the input space. Nominal inputs may be mapped to numeric values in a specified range and "relational units" are used to define subranges, thus avoiding a restriction to an orthogonal encoding of inputs. Each relational unit (hidden unit in the first hidden layer) is connected to exactly one input unit, in the case that a relational unit is used.

$VL_1ANN$ also extends the representation of outputs by catering for output variables which require a specific numeric value to be output instead of a false/true encoding only, i.e. output units are not restricted to an orthogonal representation.

The most significant differences are thus that $VL_1ANN$ accepts relational conditions in a very natural syntax used by many machine learning programs, and that the translation of rules allow decisions to be made less crisp while also catering for outputs which are not orthogonally encoded as propositions. This representation allows linear combinations of variables to be discovered and the cut-points between input values to be adjusted by subsequent learning procedures, while avoiding prior discretization of inputs.

## 6.6   Summary

This chapter presents an algorithm for the translation of symbolic classification rules into artificial neural networks. The syntax of the rules for which the algorithm caters is used by a wide variety of machine learning algorithms, thus allowing domain theories acquired by these programs to be incorporated into an ANN. This approach overcomes an important limitation that input values be restricted to binary values as is typical for the representation of propositions; instead any real value is acceptable. In addition four ways of representing tunable fuzziness in a decision was proposed: (1) Adjust the bias value of relational units to set the threshold between adjacent observed input values in the data set. (2) Adjust the slope of the sigmoid activation function of a relational unit and the scaling of its input values to cause a graded response by the unit. (3) Adjust the bias value of AND units so that a unit may fire with fewer inputs than given in the original rule. (4) Adjust the bias value of OR units so that a unit may fire at a lower threshold, i.e. an input may be close to 1 to cause the OR unit to fire, or more than one input being close to 1 can be viewed as additional evidence that the OR unit should fire.

## Acknowledgments

The UCI Repository of Machine Learning Databases and Domain theories (ml-repository@ics.uci.edu) kindly supplied the iris data.

## References

Clark, P. and Boswell, R. 1991. Rule induction with CN2: some recent improvements. In *Machine Learning—European Working Session on Learning*, ed. Y. Kodratoff, pp. 151–163. Berlin: Springer-Verlag.

Cloete, I. 1996. $VL_1$ANN: An algorithm for fusion of rules and artificial neural networks. In *Proceedings of the Workshop on Foundations of Information/Decision Fusion with Applications to Engineering Problems*, pp. 40–45, Washington, D. C.

Fu, L. M. 1993. Knowledge-based connectionism for revising domain theories. *IEEE Transactions on Systems, Man and Cybernetics*, 23(1):173–182.

Fu, L. M. 1996. Knowledge and neural heuristics: Tutorial lecture. In *IEEE International Conference on Neural Networks*, Washington, D.C.

Haussler, D. 1988. Quantifying inductive bias: AI learning algorithms and Valiant's learning framework. *Artificial Intelligence*, 36:177–221.

Kohavi, Z. 1978. *Switching and Finite Automata Theory*. New York: McGraw Hill Book Company.

Michalski, R. S. 1975. Variable-valued logic and its applications to pattern recognition and machine learning. In *Computer Science and Multiple-valued logic: Theory and applications*, ed. D. C. Rine, pp. 506–534. North Holland.

Quinlan, J. R. 1993. *C4.5: Programs for Machine Learning*. San Mateo, California: Morgan Kaufman Publishers.

Theron, H. and Cloete, I. 1996. Bexa: A covering algorithm for learning propositional concept descriptions. *Machine Learning*, 24:5–40.

Towell, G. G. and Shavlik, J. W. 1994. Knowledge-based artificial neural networks. *Artificial Intelligence*, 70:119–165.

Zurada, J. M. 1992. *Introduction to Artificial Neural Systems*. Boston: PWS.

# 7    Integration of Heterogeneous Sources of Partial Domain Knowledge

Pedro Romero, Zoran Obradović and Justin Fletcher

*This chapter explores the possibility of achieving better classification results using systems that integrate prior knowledge and learning from examples. This integration is first discussed as a transformation of either the original problem's domain or its range. A domain transforming neural network model that starts from a single source of prior knowledge and grows incrementally as needed is introduced next. In this model two integration techniques are explored: (1) converting the expert system rule base into a corresponding neural network and then extending this network by constructive learning; and (2) embedding the pre-existing expert system directly into a constructive neural network learning system. Domain transforming and range transforming methods for integrating multiple prior-knowledge sources simultaneously are also considered. Various experiments carried out on the two-spirals and a financial advising classification problem showed that prior knowledge can indeed help improve the results obtainable by learning from examples alone. When integrating multiple sources of prior knowledge, a competitive neural network based integration technique significantly outperformed the individual classifiers, a symbolic based method and a cooperative neural network based technique.*

## 7.1   Introduction

Automatically classifying data into categories is an important problem in many real life domains. When data is two-dimensional, classification tasks can be simple for humans but still quite difficult for automatic systems (e.g. determining whether a point is inside or outside of nested spirals is a well known benchmark problem for classification systems (Fahlman and Lebiere, 1990)). Higher-dimensional data classification is typically challenging for humans too, and sometimes more accurate results are achievable by automatic classifiers (e.g. determining protein disorder from amino acid sequence (Romero et al., 1997)).

There are two traditional ways for a computer system to acquire knowledge required to perform classification tasks. The *knowledge based* approach translates information obtained from human domain experts into a form that is interpretable by a computer system (Hayes-Roth et al., 1983). This knowledge base is the core of an *expert system*, which emulates human decision-making skills. The alternative approach, called *machine learning*, is an attempt to extract knowledge directly from data (Dietterich and Michalski, 1983).

Each of these two approaches has its advantages and disadvantages. An expert system represents knowledge in symbolic form allowing relatively easy manipulation and incorporation of newly obtained knowledge. In addition, its classification engine may be readily interpreted by humans. A machine learning system is less dependent on human understanding of the phenomena and can, in principle, be applied to any domain with sufficient amount of available data. However, both approaches are based on strong modeling assumptions. Expert systems assume human understanding of the phenomena and availability of an expert capable of explaining domain knowledge to a computer programmer. The knowledge used to build an expert system is typically acquired from the expertise of many individuals and thus, it can be inconsistent and incomplete. Similarly, a data set used to build a machine learning system can be noisy, conflicting and sparse. Even if these problems are not present in a given data set, extrtacting complex nonlinear relationships directly from data through machine learning can still be a difficult nonlinear optimization task.

*Hybrid intelligent systems* (Michalski and G. Tecuci, 1994) that integrate knowledge extraction from data and the use of existing alternative sources of domain specific knowledge have had considerable practical success (Drossu and Obradović, 1996; Fletcher and Obradović, 1993; Towell et al., 1990). Typical systems of this type use trading rules, stochastic analysis, nonlinear dynamics, genetic algorithms, fuzzy logic or other approaches to complement limited training data information and create more accurate prediction systems.

An inspection of recent literature indicates that the most popular approaches for integrating multiple learning components are: (1) combining expert modules through various averaging scenarios; and (2) selecting the most competent local expert for any given example. The combining approach can potentially be used to reduce the variance of an unstable predictor without increasing its bias (Breiman, 1996). This is very attractive when applying neural network modeling in complex domains where these models are very likely to be unstable (Chan et al., 1996; Chenoweth and Obradović, 1996; Shimshoni and Intrator, 1996). In the selection approach each expert module tends to learn only a subset of the training data, thus devoting itself to a sub-region of the input space (Jacobs et al., 1991). This showed quite promising results when forecasting a non-stationary time series (Weigend et al., 1995).

In particular, current research has been directed towards systems in which neural network machine learning techniques are combined with expert systems in order to complement and enhance their capabilities (Kandel and G. Langholz, 1992; Medsker and Bailey, 1992). This combination has been carried out in several directions including:

**Transformational models.** Here, one type of system is transformed into another, i.e. either an expert system is transformed into a neural network or vice versa (Gallant, 1988; Samad, 1988). Neural nets are transformed into expert systems whenever knowledge documentation and justification facilities are needed. Conversely, an expert system can be transformed into a neural network when speed, adaptability and robustness are a priority.

**Fully-integrated models.** Here several systems share data structures and knowledge representation. The most common variation of this model is the connectionist expert system, in which symbolic nodes are connected by weighted links (Gallant, 1988). These systems are robust and have improved problem solving characteristics, but the complexity of the system makes it difficult to develop and maintain.

**Loosely-coupled models.** This is an integrational model in which neural network and knowledge-based systems interact through shared data files. Examples include one system serving as a preprocessor, post-processor, co-processor or interface for the other (Benachenhou et al., 1990). These systems are easier to develop than more integrated models, allowing for the use of commercial software for both expert systems and neural networks, but at the cost of slower operation, redundancy in computational capabilities, overlap in data input requirements and high communication cost.

**Tightly-coupled models.** As in loosely-coupled models, this type of architecture uses independent neural net and expert systems. The difference is that here the interaction is by means of memory resident data structures, so communication and operation velocities are vastly improved. System development is not much more difficult than that for loosely-coupled systems, but redundancy is also an issue here (Gutknecht et al., 1991; Hanson and Brekke, 1988; Hendler and Dickens, 1991).

The approaches just explained are used in this chapter to integrate neural network learning from examples with sources of partial domain knowledge obtained from human symbolic reasoning (henceforth called *experts*). This integration has been carried out in two ways:

**Embedding transformed experts.** This is a transformational approach in which the expert is converted into a neural network that serves as a starting point for learning from examples.

**Embedding experts directly.** In this approach the experts are embedded without modifications in the hybrid classification system, which means that no knowledge of their internal mechanisms is required. Thus, in this case, the definition of an expert can be expanded to include any system used to encapsulate pre-existing knowledge: traditional expert systems, statistical prediction systems, nearest neighbor algorithms, inductive algorithms, computer programs, fuzzy logic, genetic algorithms, neural networks and the like.

In addition, the hybrid systems discussed in this study are organized into:

**Single expert expansion systems.** In this approach, all expert knowledge comes from a single source, which is further expanded through neural network learning.

**Multiple experts integration systems.** Here multiple, possibly heterogeneous, experts are integrated into a hybrid classification system.

The integration of partial domain knowledge sources can be viewed as a transformation of either the problem domain or its range, as illustrated in Section 7.2. Section 7.3 describes three single expert expansion systems, two being transformational, and one fully-integrated model that embeds an expert directly. Three multiple experts integration techniques that embed prior knowledge sources directly are presented in Section 7.4. Finally, Section 7.5 contains experimental comparisons of these models for two classification problems.

## 7.2   Experts Integration: Domain or Range Transformation   Dilemma

A classification problem can be viewed as identification of an appropriate mapping from a given *domain* to a *range* of categories. For example, a classification problem that takes a pattern composed of $n$ real numbers as input and tries to classify it as belonging to one of two classes, defined as "0" or "1," can be seen as a mapping:

$$\Re^n \to \{0, 1\}$$

where $\Re^n$ is the domain of the mapping and $\{0,1\}$ represents its range.

When integrating prior knowledge sources, the classification problem is hopefully simplified by transforming its corresponding mapping. This can be achieved by modifying either the problem domain or its range as discussed in this section.

### 7.2.1   Domain Transformation

When using the outputs of several experts as inputs to a new classifier (called a *combiner*), the original input space is transformed to an entirely new one, its dimensionality being defined by the number of experts used and their output representation.

For example, suppose $K$ experts are to be combined to solve an $n$-input, $m$-class classification problem. Assuming that each expert uses $m$ outputs, the combining classifier will have $mK$ inputs, thus transforming the problem domain from $n$ dimensions onto $mK$ dimensions. Figure 7.1 shows schematically how this process works.

When transforming the problem domain as explained, the hope is that it will be easier to identify an appropriate mapping using the new problem domain. This can be the result of one or more of the following reasons:

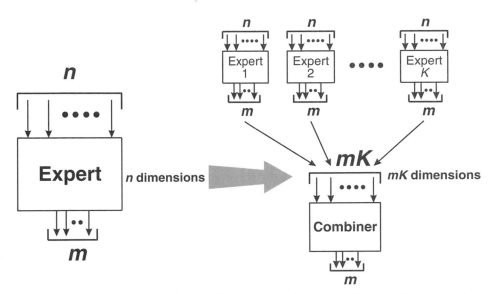

**Figure 7.1**   Integrating $m$ experts: domain transformation from $n$-dimensional to $mK$-dimensional.

**Reduced domain dimensionality.** This results in models with less parameters, which, due to the curse of dimensionality, can be a significant advantage when designing a model from a limited data set (Bishop, 1995).

**Input preprocessing.** The domain transformation can be regarded as a feature extraction process (Fukunaga, 1990). This can help eliminate the effect of irrelevant or noisy input variables.

**Simpler decision regions.** Even if the original dimensionality is not significantly reduced through a transformation, classes in the new domain may be easier to separate due to more favorable clustering of the patterns.

It is important to observe that information can be lost when transforming the domain, resulting in a poor classifier. This is especially true for experts with low resolution output representations, e.g. one bit representation for each output dimension. This is illustrated in Figure 7.2, where two experts, whose outputs are one-bit numbers, are to be combined. In that figure, class 0 and class 1 patterns are represented as circles and crosses respectively. The domain is partitioned into regions according to the experts' outputs, shown as pairs $(a, b)$ for each region. Notice that each pair $(a, b)$ represents an input vector for the combiner. In this example, the transformed domain is not faithful in any of the regions, meaning that for each region there are examples that belong to different classes and that are mapped to the same input vector for the combiner. This information loss makes it impossible for a combiner to resolve the problem completely.

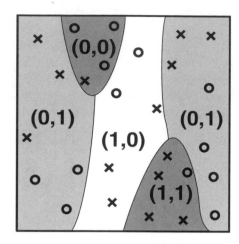

**Figure 7.2**    Decision regions for two experts with binary outputs.

## 7.2.2   Range Transformation

In this case, a classifier is trained to integrate the various experts by partitioning the domain and assigning disjoint regions to individual experts. Here, the original problem domain does not change, but the integrating classifier has a different class range defined by the number of experts.

Suppose that $K$ experts are to be integrated in this manner. The problem is reduced to assigning each expert exclusively to its "region of expertise," that is, a sub-domain where a given expert's classification performance is superior to that of the other experts. So, the original $m$-class problem is transformed into a new problem with $f(K)$ classes.

For $K = 2$, the classifier could be trained to recognize the following possibilities:

Class 0    None of the local experts classifies this example correctly;

Class 1    Expert 1 alone classifies the example correctly;

Class 2    Expert 2 alone classifies the example correctly;

Class 3    Both local experts classify the example correctly.

Figure 7.3(a) shows a schematic view of the input space of a 2-class problem and a possible range transformation into a 4-class problem according to the method just explained for $K = 2$ experts. Notice that in this case the number of classes is *increased*, but this is done anticipating that the new decision regions are simpler in the transformed problem than in the original one. Whether or not this will be the case depends on the characteristics of the problem and the quality of the experts used.

This transformation leads to $f(K) = 2^K$, so the number of classes grows exponentially with the number of experts used. A better alternative for this example would be to use only 2 classes:

**2 classes**  **4 classes**

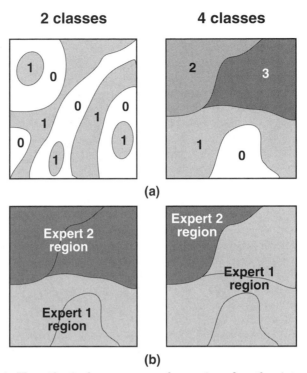

**(a)**

**(b)**

**Figure 7.3** (a) Hypothetical range transformation for the integration of two experts in a 2-class problem. (b) Two of the possible distributions of the input space between the two experts.

Class 1    Use expert 1 to classify the example;

Class 2    Use expert 2.

However, the new problem here is that of assigning the patterns for which both experts are correct (or incorrect). Figure 7.3(b) depicts two of the possible ways to distribute the input space between the two experts. Notice that any decision boundary lying within the region where both experts are correct (class 3 on the right hand side of Figure 7.3(a)) is acceptable for this distribution: Figure 7.3(b) just shows the extreme cases, that is, assigning the whole "class 3" region to either expert. Similarly, the "class 0" region could have been assigned to expert 2 or even distributed randomly between both experts. In any event, the decision regions thus created would have been a lot more complex. In a problem with more dimensions or experts, this assignment task gets even more complicated.

Hybrid systems relying on range transformation can provide various advantages over original classifiers, specifically the following:

**Simpler decision regions.** As in the domain transformation case, it is anticipated that the transformed problem will have simpler decision regions than the original one, thus being easier to solve and requiring a less complex classifier to do

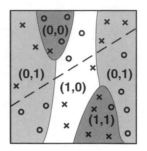

**Figure 7.4**   Range transformation for the problem of Figure 7.2.

the job.

**Restricted domain for local training.** Assigning a portion of the domain to a specific classifier allows local training of machine learning based experts on the remaining region or regions. Examples of this approach are studied in Sections 7.3 and 7.4.

**Insensibility to output representation.** Range transformation works in the same way regardless of the experts' output representation. Indeed, the technique can even work with experts whose output representations differ from one another. Figure 7.4 shows the same hypothetical problem shown in Figure 7.2, but this time the range transformation produces two distinct and easily separable regions corresponding to the "areas of expertise" of each expert. Remember that this problem was impossible to solve appropriately when transforming the domain.

## 7.3   Incremental Single Expert Expansion

In (Towell et al., 1990), Towel, Shavlik and Noordwier propose a knowledge-based artificial neural network approach called *KBANN*, that generates neural networks from hierarchically-structured rules. In these neural networks units correspond to rules, while connection weights and thresholds correspond to rule dependencies. Each layer is then fully connected with the weights of the new links set to small random values. This type of transformational approach is also addressed and extended in Chapter 6, and is demonstrated using a financial advising example in the results section of this chapter. Finally, the initial knowledge is refined by neural network training from examples using the backpropagation algorithm (Werbos, 1995).

The hyperplane determination from examples algorithm (HDE) proposed by Fletcher and Obradovic (Fletcher and Obradović, 1995) belongs to the class of *constructive algorithms*. These algorithms, in addition to optimizing the model's parameter values, also search for an appropriate neural network topology by growing hidden units in a greedy optimization manner. In contrast to the well known cascade-correlation technique (Fahlman and Lebiere, 1990), which grows neurons in depth, HDE is used to construct a 2-layer neural network starting from a single hidden unit and adding new hidden units as necessary.

This algorithm can be used to build a hybrid classification system by using an expert to build the initial neural network and then applying HDE to add new hidden units to improve classification performance. Similar to the KBANN technique, the expert can be converted into a rule base and then transformed into a neural network (Fletcher and Obradović, 1993). Alternatively, the source of prior knowledge can be used in a "black box" fashion by treating it as a single hidden unit (called an *expert unit*). A more detailed explanation of this domain transforming hybrid model is provided in the following subsections.

### 7.3.1 The HDE Algorithm

An interesting iterative construction of hidden units in a feed-forward neural network with a single hidden layer was proposed by Baum (Baum, 1991; Baum and Lang, 1991). His algorithm constructs a two layer neural network given examples and the ability to query an oracle for the classification of specific points within the problem domain. The algorithm is very efficient, but in practice the required oracle may either be too expensive or not available.

Inspired by Baum's work on learning from queries, our HDE algorithm constructs the hidden units in a feedforward neural network from examples alone (Fletcher and Obradović, 1995). Construction of the HDE neural network is performed in three phases:

1. Determination of points on the decision boundary;

2. Generation of a pool of candidate hyperplanes from the obtained points; and

3. Selection of the final separating hyperplanes from the candidate pool and creation of hidden units from selected hyperplanes.

These phases will be described using as an example the construction of a neural network approximating the ideal decision boundary shown in Figure 7.5(a). For simplicity of explanation, we will assume that the examples from the training set $T$ shown in the figure belong to two classes $T_1$ and $T_2$.

For all pairs of training examples belonging to different classes, a search for corresponding points on the boundary separating those examples is performed. Approximations to points on the decision boundary are determined by repeatedly interpolating between example points of the classes $T_1$ and $T_2$. The interpolation begins by selecting two examples $m \in T_1$, $n \in T_2$. The *unknown region* between $m$ and $n$ is defined as the circle centered at the midpoint of $m$ and $n$ with a diameter of the distance between $m$ and $n$, as shown in Figure 7.5(b). The unknown region between $m$ and $n$ is then searched for the training example nearest to the midpoint of $m$ and $n$. If such an example $q$ is found and $q \in T_1$ ($T_2$) the search is then repeated in the smaller unknown region between $q$ and $n$ ($m$). The next unknown

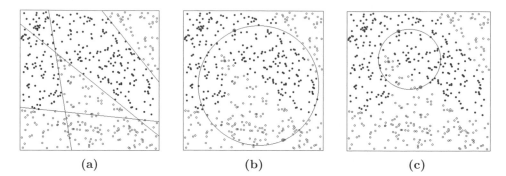

(a)                              (b)                              (c)

**Figure 7.5**   HDE algorithm example: **(a)** ideal decision region; **(b)** initial unknown region; **(c)** next unknown region.

(**(b)** and **(c)** © Dynamic Publishers, Inc., used with permission, see Copyright Acknowledgments)

region is shown in Figure 7.5(c).

If no point from $T$ is found in the current unknown region (Figure 7.6(a)), its midpoint is the closest approximation to a point on the decision boundary (Figure 7.6(b)). If the radius of this known region is within a specified tolerance, the boundary point is stored provided it has not been previously determined. Boundary points continue to be generated until a pre-determined number have been found or a number of data points have been examined without finding a new point on a decision boundary. The resultant boundary points are shown in Figure 7.6(c).

Once the points on the decision boundary have been found, their $k$-1 nearest boundary points are determined. As previously, $k$ is the domain dimensionality. A pool of hyperplanes is then determined through solution of the equation system defined by each set of the $k$ boundary points. Figure 7.7(a) shows such a candidate pool with their associated boundary points.

The first hidden unit is created from the candidate hyperplane which best classifies the training data. This hyperplane is then removed from the candidate list. Each remaining hidden unit is created by evaluation of the remaining candidate hyperplanes in conjunction with the previously created hidden units. This is accomplished by creating a hidden unit and iteratively setting the input layer connection weights to the corresponding equation of each of the candidate hyperplanes. The output layer weights for a candidate for the next intermediate network are then determined by learning from the training examples using the ratcheted pocket algorithm (Gallant, 1990). This procedure continues until no candidate hyperplane results in a significant improvement in classification on the training set.

A final selection of hidden layer hyperplanes is shown in Figure 7.7(b) with the resultant decision boundary depicted in Figure 7.7(c).

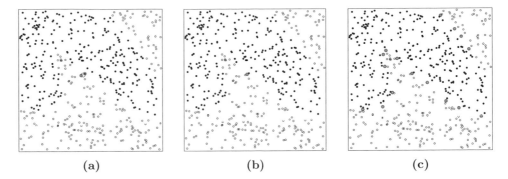

(a)                                   (b)                                   (c)

**Figure 7.6**  HDE algorithm example: **(a)** last unknown region; **(b)** a point on the decision boundary; **(c)** more points on the decision boundary.

((**c**) © Dynamic Publishers, Inc., used with permission, see Copyright Acknowledgments)

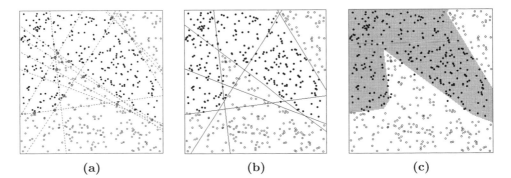

(a)                                   (b)                                   (c)

**Figure 7.7**  HDE algorithm example: **(a)** candidate hyperplanes; **(b)** selected hyperplanes; **(c)** resultant decision boundary.

(© Dynamic Publishers, Inc., used with permission, see Copyright Acknowledgments)

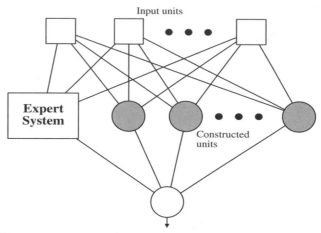

**Figure 7.8**   Direct integration of an expert into HDE construction.

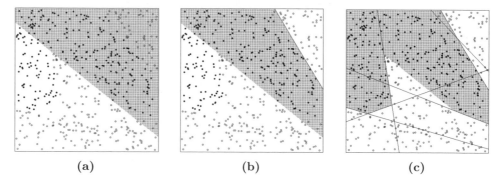

**Figure 7.9**   Direct expert integration example: **(a)** first modification of the decision boundary; **(b)** next decision boundary; **(c)** final decision boundary.

### 7.3.2   Embedding of Transformed Prior Knowledge

Here, a symbolic expert is transformed into a neural network as in the KBANN method. However, in a neural network obtained from the original rule base, the KBANN stage in which the layers are fully connected is omitted. Instead, the HDE algorithm is used to add neurons to the last layer of the initial neural network. The output weights of the starting network are modified after each new hidden unit is added through HDE construction.

The obtained hybrid system is a transformational model in which a symbolic rule base is required to build the original neural network using the KBANN technique. This means that in this case it is not possible to use an arbitrary type of expert since the source of prior knowledge has to be a known AND/OR structured rule base.

### 7.3.3 Direct Integration of Prior Knowledge

In this approach, no transformation of the expert system is required. Instead, a hybrid architecture is constructed with the expert system directly embedded into the neural network as shown in Figure 7.8.

The three-phase process of the HDE algorithm is followed with certain small exceptions. An initial network consisting of the input layer, a single hidden unit and an output unit is created. The hidden unit is designated as an *expert unit*, which, instead of computing the usual activation function, calls the expert system to determine the unit's output. The expert unit, then, acts as the initial hidden unit, contributing with its decision boundary, such as the simple one shown in Figure 7.9(a).

As before, a set of candidate hyperplanes is built, and they are tested as new hidden units in conjunction with the original one (the expert unit) in order to create an intermediate network. The first hyperplane added in this example is shown in Figure 7.9(b).

Any remaining hidden units are then created by evaluating each of the remaining candidate hyperplanes with the intermediate hybrid network. This process continues until either the candidate pool is exhausted or no significant improvement is gained by integrating any candidate hyperplane. The final output layer weights are again determined through the use of the pocket algorithm. A final decision boundary is shown in Figure 7.9(c).

In contrast to this simple example, an expert can contribute with a more complex decision boundary that helps reduce the number of hidden units needed in the integrated system as compared to that of a simple neural network constructed similarly. This process has the same effect as an input space reduction through range transformation as explained in Section 7.2.2, that is, the generation of new hidden units is carried out only in the regions of the input space where classification based on prior knowledge is unsatisfactory, effectively reducing the input space to be solved. On the other hand, the hidden units act as experts, producing a domain-transformed problem for the output layer to solve.

This classifier is an example of a fully integrated hybrid system with direct expert embedding. Since the expert is not modified in any way, any kind of classifier can be used as an expert neuron.

## 7.4 Multiple Experts Integration

Three techniques designed to integrate several sources of prior knowledge are discussed in this section.

### 7.4.1   Cooperative Combination of Heterogeneous Experts

The domain transformation through cooperative combination of multiple experts has been successfully applied to a number of real-life classification problems, e.g. protein structure prediction (Zhang et al., 1992).

In this chapter, a feedforward neural network is used as a combiner for $K$ *local experts* as shown in Figure 7.10. Here, each example for the combiner training process is constructed from an input vector $\mathbf{x}$ and a desired response vector $\mathbf{y}^*$. First, a vector $\mathbf{z} = [\mathbf{y}_1\mathbf{y}_2 \ldots \mathbf{y}_K]$ is assembled using the output vectors $\mathbf{y}_1, \mathbf{y}_2, \ldots,$ $\mathbf{y}_K$ obtained from the $K$ experts when presented with the input vector $\mathbf{x}$. Second, vector $\mathbf{z}$ is fed to the combining neural network, which finally produces the output vector $\mathbf{y}$.

The combining module is trained by means of the backpropagation learning algorithm (Werbos, 1995), using the $\mathbf{z}$ vectors as inputs, and the desired response vectors ($\mathbf{y}^*$) as targets. Once the combiner is trained, the whole system can be used, as shown in Figure 7.10, to classify new patterns.

### 7.4.2   Symbolic Integration Using Decision Trees

This technique, considered in (Romero and Obradović, 1995), trains a decision tree to select among the $K$ local experts to be integrated. Because there is no simple way to decide how to assign the patterns for which none, all or several experts make a correct classification, the decision tree has to learn a $2^K$-class problem. This corresponds to a range transformation, as explained in Section 7.2.

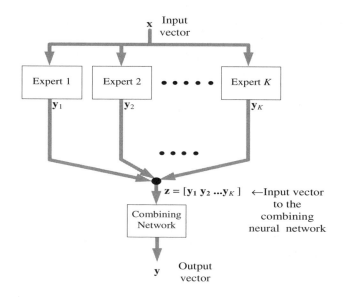

**Figure 7.10**   Neural network based cooperative combination.

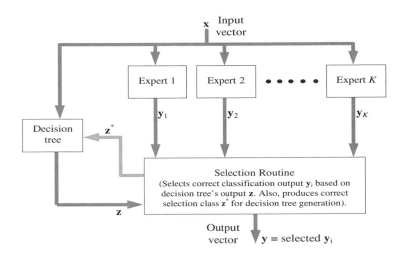

**Figure 7.11**   Decision tree symbolic integration.

**Table 7.1**   Range transformation through decision tree integration.

| Classifier | input vector | output (class) vector |
|---|---|---|
| Expert | $\mathbf{x}$ | $\mathbf{y}$ |
| Decision tree | $\mathbf{x}$ | $\mathbf{z}$ |

Figure 7.11 shows an implementation of the proposed system. Again, each training pattern consists of an input vector $\mathbf{x}$ and a desired response vector $\mathbf{y}^*$. Each local expert outputs a response $\mathbf{y}_i$ which is fed to a selection routine. This class information is used for the decision tree generation.

The selection routine compares the local experts' outputs ($\mathbf{y}_i$) to the desired response $\mathbf{y}^*$. Then, it assigns the input $\mathbf{x}$ to a desired class $\mathbf{z}^*$. Thus, the decision tree is generated from modified patterns, as illustrated in Table 7.1.

After the tree is generated, the system works as follows: The input vector $\mathbf{x}$ is fed to the decision tree and to all local experts. The decision tree produces a response $z$ and each expert $i$ outputs a response $y_i$. All these responses are given to the selection routine, which, based on the value of $z$, selects one of the $y_i$'s. The selected value is then output as the system's response.

When all experts are wrong, the system's output can be generated randomly or inferred from the data. For example, when solving a binary classification (2-class) problem using 2 experts that are both incorrect on a given example, the system has to output the opposite class from that selected by both experts.

The construction of the decision tree can be carried out using various decision tree generation  methods. In this study, GID3* (Fayyad, 1994) was used. This technique

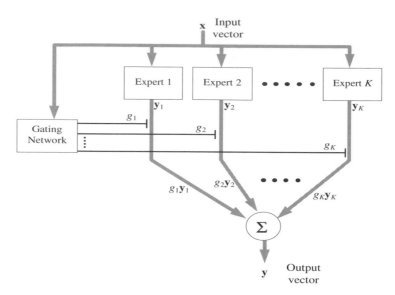

**Figure 7.12**   Competitive neural network based integration.

groups together irrelevant attribute values before generating the tree using the ID3 algorithm (Quinlan, 1986). The classification problem addressed in this paper has real valued attributes which have to be discretized before using GID3*. This is achieved by using a multiple-interval discretization technique proposed in (Fayyad and Irani, 1993). The common approach is to discretize the attributes at each node of the decision tree. For the problem studied here, we found that a single discretization step performed on each input variable before tree generation always achieved better generalization, and so the results reported here were obtained using the latter technique.

### 7.4.3   Competitive Integration of Heterogeneous Experts

The competitive integration of heterogeneous experts, proposed in (Romero and Obradović, 1995), is an extension of Jacobs, Jordan, Nowlan and Hinton's mixture of local experts architecture (Jacobs et al., 1991) which uses a *gating network* to integrate the responses of all local experts, selecting the most competent local expert for any given example (see Figure 7.12).

In the original architecture from (Jacobs et al., 1991) all $K$ local experts are backpropagation neural networks. A supervised learning process is carried out using a set of training examples, each consisting of an input vector $\mathbf{x}$ and a desired response vector $\mathbf{y}^*$. In the basic model, the input vector $\mathbf{x}$ is applied to both the local expert networks and the gating network. The gating network used in this study is a one-layer feedforward neural network whose output units use a *softmax* activation function

$$g_i = \frac{e^{s_i}}{\sum_{j=1}^{K} e^{s_j}}$$

where $s_i$ is the weighted input sum of the $i$th output unit. This activation function ensures that the system's output $\mathbf{y} = \sum_{i=1}^{K} g_i \mathbf{y}_i$ corresponds to a weighted average of the individual expert's outputs $\mathbf{y}_1, \ldots, \mathbf{y}_K$. It is interesting to notice that the softmax function is a continuous (differentiable) version of the "winner take all" selection criteria, suitable for use in a gradient descent technique such as backpropagation.

All experts use a special error function

$$E = -\ln L = -\ln \sum_{i=1}^{K} l_i = -\ln \sum_{i=1}^{K} g_i e^{-\frac{1}{2\sigma_i^2} \|\mathbf{y}^* - \mathbf{y}_i\|^2}$$

where $\ln L$ represents the log likelihood of generating a response vector $\mathbf{y}^*$, and $\sigma_i^2$ is a scaling term. The summation term is called $l_i$ for clarity purposes. The system is trained to minimize $-\ln L$ (maximize the log likelihood), which allows a competitive learning process by training only the most competent local expert(s) on a given example. This is best understood when examining the last hidden layer weight update term for the $i$th expert network:

$$(\Delta w_{jk})_i = \eta \delta_{ji}(g_i) o_k$$

where $w_{jk}$ is the weight of the connection between hidden layer unit $k$ and output unit $j$, $\eta$ is the learning rate, $o_k$ is the output of hidden unit $k$, and $\delta_{ji}(g_i)$ represents the back-propagated error for output unit $j$ of expert $I$ ($\delta_{ji}$), which is a function of $g_i$. It can be seen that the $i$th expert network weight change is dependent on $g_i$, so only the networks selected for a given example (those with $g_i$ greater than 0) will have their weights updated, i.e. will "learn" that example.

The weights' update for the gating network is given by

$$\Delta \mathbf{u}_i = \eta (g_i - h_i) \mathbf{x}$$

where $\mathbf{u}_i$ represents the weight vector associated to output unit $I$, and $h_i = \frac{l_i}{L}$. In a statistical sense, the $g_i$'s can be regarded as *prior* probabilities of selecting the $i$th expert, while the $h_i$'s represent *posterior* probabilities of expert $i$ generating the desired output vector. Thus, as the gating network learns, the prior probabilities of selecting an expert move towards the posterior probability of that expert generating the desired response.

In an extended model, the gating network can receive an additional input $\mathbf{x}'$ either in conjunction with, or instead of the expert networks' input $\mathbf{x}$. Using an additional input for the gating network could be useful as a "hint" on the correct distribution of experts. For example, the gating network might work better if provided with the sex of the speaker in a vowel recognition problem (Nowlan and Hinton, 1991).

In the competitive integration system used in this chapter we assume that the local experts need not only be neural networks, but can also be various sources of prior knowledge (Romero and Obradović, 1995). We will also assume that only the gating network and any neural network components do the learning as explained above, while the other expert components are fixed and can only be used to respond to the input patterns.

## 7.5   Results

The systems discussed in previous sections are evaluated in the context of two quite different benchmark problems. The first problem has a 2-dimensional domain, but it requires generation of an extremely complex decision region, whereas the second one is six-dimensional, but it can be solved by using a classifier with a simpler decision region. Classification results of various hybrid systems applied to these two problems are summarized in this section.

Some common parameters have been defined in order to standardize comparisons. For the HDE-based approaches' default configuration, the maximum number of points on the decision boundary is set to ten times the dimensionality of the input space, or stopped if one thousand example pairs are examined without determining a new boundary point. Gallant's parameter recommendations for the pocket algorithm, used for determination of the final output layer weights, are followed (ten thousand initial iterations, increased by fifty percent if the pocket is updated in the final eighty percent of the iterations). The learning rate for the pocket algorithm is standardized at 30%, and no additional hyperplanes are selected if the overall classification improvement is less than 0.5%. The gating neural networks used on the competitive integration experiments are all single layer networks, i.e. with no hidden units. Gating networks can in principle be multi-layered, but the principal idea was to show how problem transformation can simplify a classification mapping so that a basic classifier is able to achieve good integration.

### 7.5.1   The Two-Spirals Problem

The two-spirals problem was proposed by A. Wieland of MITRE Corporation as a task constructed to test the ability of neural networks to deal with complex decision regions. This well known benchmark (Fahlman and Lebiere, 1990) differs from many others by testing only the memorization ability, rather than the ability to generalize over the problem domain. The input space consists of two dimensional data points arranged into two spirals on the x-y plane. This is a 2-class problem: all points on a given spiral are of one class, while the points on the other spiral belong to the opposite class, as shown in Figure 7.13.

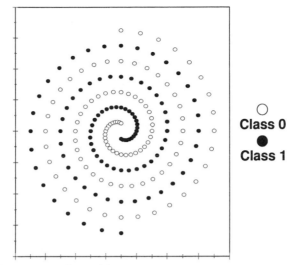

**Figure 7.13**   The two-spirals problem.

**Table 7.2**   Distance metrics for the two-spirals experts used in this work.

| Experts | Distance metric | Success rate |
|---------|-----------------|--------------|
| Expert 0 | $dist = \sqrt{x^2 + y^2}$ | 50.00% |
| Expert 1 | $dist = \sqrt{(x + 0.5)^2 + (y + 0.5)^2}$ | 52.99% |
| Expert 2 | $dist = \sqrt{x^2 + y^2} + 0.5$ | 53.61% |
| Expert 3 | $dist = \sqrt{x^2 + y^2} + 1.0$ | 53.09% |

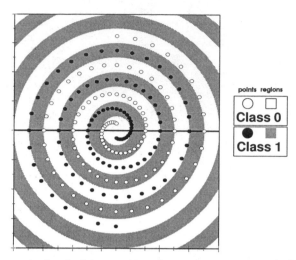

**Figure 7.14**    Two-spirals: decision regions for expert system "0" from Table 7.2.

### 7.5.1.1   Sources of Partial Domain Knowledge

Both the incremental construction and the competitive integration approaches were applied to this problem in order to illustrate the effects of using sources of partial domain knowledge to construct improved classifiers. To simulate partial domain knowledge, it is assumed that a human expert is under the impression that the class of a given point depends on its polar radius, that is, on its distance to the origin. Using this assumption, several experts were developed. Based on a distance metric, the experts classify a given data point as follows:

$$Class = \begin{cases} 0 & \text{if } dist \bmod 2 < 1 \\ 1 & \text{otherwise} \end{cases}$$

Each of the various experts used in this chapter employs a different distance metric *dist*, as defined in Table 7.2, where $x$ and $y$ refer to the pattern's coordinates in the 2-dimensional input space. As an example, Figure 7.14 shows the decision regions for Expert 0 from Table 7.2. Although the global classification rate for this expert is only 50%, it actually contains information. In fact, this expert correctly classifies points lying above the $x$ axis (horizontal line in Figure 7.14). Similarly, for experts 1, 2 and 3 it is also possible to identify regions of the input space where they are reasonably good classifiers.

### 7.5.1.2   Incremental Model Construction

The results summarized in Table 7.3 and the corresponding decision boundary shown in Figure 7.15(a) were obtained by the HDE algorithm using the default learning parameters. This may be viewed as rather dismal results especially if compared to cascade-correlation, which reports 100% classification using between 12 and 19 units (Fahlman and Lebiere, 1990). However, these results may be somewhat improved if three additional steps are taken. First, the number of decision boundary points is not limited to ten times the problem dimensionality but instead continue to be generated until one thousand pairs are examined without generating a new boundary point. This results in a significantly larger candidate hyperplane pool (Figure 7.15(b)). Second, the hyperplane selection phase is eliminated as a hidden unit is constructed for each candidate hyperplane. Finally, the initial number of iterations of the pocket algorithm  during final output layer weight training is increased from ten thousand to twenty-five thousand. Table 7.4 shows the new results with a representative decision boundary shown in Figure 7.15(c).

While this results in near-perfect classification (one of the ten experiments resulted in 98.45% accuracy), the algorithm generated a very large network architecture, which is not likely to generalize well on new data. A preferred approach would be to integrate an existing knowledge base in order to reduce the complexity of the classifier.

As shown in Table 7.2, Expert 0 has a success rate of 50%. If we embed this expert, hyperplanes are selected in such a fashion as to take advantage of the areas where the expert successfully classifies the input space (the region above the horizontal line on Figure 14). Table 7.5 shows an improvement in classification ability of over ten percent when integrating Expert 0 as compared to the original HDE algorithm (Table 7.3). The default learning parameters were used in both cases.

A number of items are made apparent by this benchmark. The basic approaches to determining decision boundary points and constructing the candidate hyperplane pool appear to be appropriate, but the proper number of decision boundary points will vary with the problem. It is also apparent that process parameters may need to be adjusted for each individual problem. However, an important point made by this benchmark is that the integration of two techniques which do not perform well

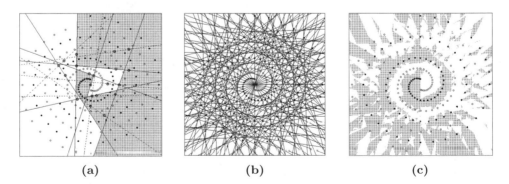

|  (a)  |  (b)  |  (c)  |

**Figure 7.15**   HDE algorithm application on the two-spirals problem: **(a)** decision boundary using default learning parameters; **(b)** candidate pool of decision boundaries; **(c)** final decision boundary.

**Table 7.3**   Two-spirals: default HDE network construction.

|  | Average | Min. | Max. |
|---|---|---|---|
| Boundary Points | 20 | 20 | 20 |
| Candidate Hyperplanes | 15.7 | 18 | 18 |
| Hidden Units | 4.3 | 1 | 7 |
| Accuracy | 61.49 | 56.19 | 65.98 |

**Table 7.4**   Two-spirals: modified HDE network construction.

|  | Average | Min. | Max. |
|---|---|---|---|
| Boundary Points | 159.6 | 157 | 163 |
| Candidate Hyperplanes | 152.1 | 150 | 156 |
| Hidden Units | 152 | 152 | 152 |
| Accuracy | 99.84 | 98.45 | 100.0 |

**Table 7.5**   Two-spirals: Expert 0 + default HDE hybrid network construction.

|  | Average | Min. | Max. |
|---|---|---|---|
| Boundary Points | 20 | 20 | 20 |
| Candidate Hyperplanes | 15.7 | 13 | 18 |
| Hidden Units | 3.5 | 3 | 6 |
| Accuracy | 74.43 | 68.56 | 76.29 |

independently may result in improved classification when combined into a hybrid system.

### 7.5.1.3   Multiple Experts Integration

The experts shown in Table 7.2 can be combined in order to obtain a better classifier. Due to the fact that these experts have single one-bit outputs, this example is not suitable for domain transformation approaches as explained in Section 7.2. (Figure 7.2). Indeed, the very nature of the decision regions generated by these experts (see Figure 7.14) guarantees that different patterns from each of the classes will get transformed into identical input vectors for the combiner.

On the other hand, range transformation approaches can work very well on this problem. Figure 7.16, corresponding to the integration of Expert 0 and Expert 2, shows graphically how the use of local experts can simplify the decision regions in the input space. As explained in Section 7.2, the integration of two local experts can result in the input space being partitioned in up to four different decision regions, shown in the left picture of Figure 7.16. These regions correspond to the

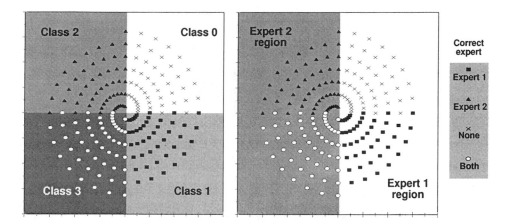

**Figure 7.16** Integration of experts 0 and 2 for the two-spirals problem: (left) 4-class decision region; (right) one of the possible experts' assignment.

**Table 7.6** Two-spirals problem: Success rates for local experts and their combinations.

| Local experts | Success rate on training data | |
| --- | --- | --- |
| | Upper bound | Integrated system |
| 0+1 | 66.49% | 66.49% |
| 0+2 | 76.80% | 76.80% |
| 0+3 | 100.00% | 100.00% |

ones shown in Figure 7.3(a), that is: (0) data points misclassified by both experts; (1) data points correctly classified only by the first expert; (2) data points correctly classified only by the second expert; and (3) data points correctly classified by both experts. The right hand side of Figure 7.16 shows one possible domain partitioning between the two experts in the manner illustrated in Figure 7.3(b).

The competitive integration technique for multiple experts integration was tested on this problem. The experiments summarized in Table 7.6 were performed by integrating Expert 0 with one of the other experts shown in Table 7.14. The upper bounds for the success rate are measured as the maximum accuracy obtainable by combining experts perfectly, that is, always selecting the best expert for the job. The difference from 100% corresponds to the examples that neither expert classified correctly. As can be seen in the table, the competitive integration system always achieved the maximum possible success rate, which means that the system always performed an optimal integration. Figure 7.17 depicts the decision region found by the gating network for the integration of experts 0+2, which can be compared to that shown on the right hand side of Figure 7.16. Notice that both solutions

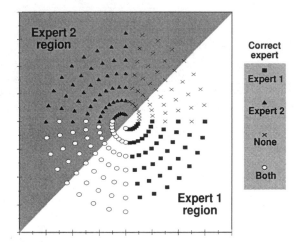

**Figure 7.17**   Gating network experts' assignment for the integration of experts 0 and 2 shown in Figure 7.16.

are equally effective for integrating these experts, since they keep the areas where only one of the experts is correct on opposite sides of the decision boundary, while distributing the regions where both experts perform identically.

### 7.5.2   A Financial Advising Problem

This problem is a modified version of the simple financial advisor from (Luger and Stubblefield, 1989). The task is to advise whether an individual should invest capital in additional savings or in the stock market. Although the rule based model shown in Table 7.7 is extremely simplified, it illustrates issues involved in realistic financial advising.

The system's input consists of six real variables, shown in italics in Table 7.7: annual income, if the income source is steady, current assets, current savings, annual debt payments and the number of dependents. The output variable, **invest_stocks**, can have two possible values, corresponding to advising "yes" or "no." The AND/OR graph corresponding to the rule base from Table 7.7 is shown in Figure 7.18.

#### 7.5.2.1   *Sources of Partial Domain Knowledge*

Pruned versions (i.e. with one or more rules missing) of the rule-base were used to create imperfect local expert systems with diverse performances, which were used as models of real-life, rule-based financial advising systems developed using incomplete knowledge. The experts used to test the constructive integration approach are shown in Table 7.8. This table identifies each expert by its pruning point. As an example, the elimination of the *savings_ok* rule and its antecedents

**Table 7.7**   Financial advisor rule base.

| Label | Rule | |
|-------|------|---|
| (1) | if (savings_ok and income_ok) then | **invest_stocks** |
| (2) | if dependent_savings_ok then | savings_ok |
| (3) | if assets_high then | savings_ok |
| (4) | if (dependent_income_ok and *earnings_steady*) then | income_ok |
| (5) | if debt_low then | income_ok |
| (6) | if ($savings \geq dependents \times 5000$) then | dependent_savings_ok |
| (7) | if ($income \geq 25000 + 4000 \times dependents$ ) then | dependent_income_ok |
| (8) | if ($assets \geq income \times 10$) then | assets_high |
| (9) | if ($annual\_debt < income \times 0.30$) then | debt_low |

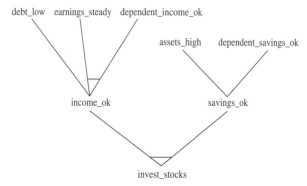

**Figure 7.18**   Financial advisor AND/OR graph.

*dependent_savings_ok* and *assets_high* is indicated by a prior knowledge pruning point of *savings_ok*. The expert system rule base of Table 7.7 is used to generate example data.

The expert systems shown in Table 7.9 were used to test the multiple experts integration approaches. The pruned rules for each expert are designated with rule numbers corresponding to those used in Table 7.7. A fixed, previously trained neural network, named "NN" was also used as a local expert. The output representations for both symbolic and neural experts were treated as real numbers in the range $[0, 1]$. Notice that these experts can be separated into three classes: pessimistic, optimistic and mixed. A pessimistic expert's errors are always false negative predictions, that is, errors in which the output is 0 (recommending to stay out of stocks) when it should be 1 (recommending to invest). On the other hand, an optimistic expert's errors are all false positive predictions (it outputs 1 when it should say 0). A mixed expert makes both kinds of errors.

### 7.5.2.2   *Incremental Model Construction*

As already explained, the expert system rule base of Table 7.7 is used to generate example data. Five hundred training examples and five thousand test examples were randomly generated consistent with the full rule base.

For these experiments, pruned versions of the AND/OR graph from Figure 7.18 were transformed into neural networks as in the KBANN technique, but without fully connecting the network. Then, the HDE algorithm was used to add units to the last hidden layer. As an example, Figure 7.19 illustrates the initial neural network obtained by transforming the original AND/OR graph from Figure 7.18 with no pruning.

Average results of five experiments are shown in Table 7.8. Observe that the hybrid system's performance was always equal or superior to those of the rule based experts and learning from examples alone. Also, note that when learning without the *debt_low* rooted subtree of the rule base, the constructive algorithm showed an impressive increase in prediction quality. Predictive quality of 61.76% from rules

**Table 7.8**   Individual experts vs. hybrid systems classification accuracy.

| Prior knowledge pruning point | Size (hidden units) | Generalization | |
|---|---|---|---|
| | | rules alone | rules + examples |
| no pruning | 0 | 100% | 100% |
| no prior knowledge | 4.1 | n/a | 81.06% |
| dependent_savings_ok | 3.4 | 74.95% | 86.19% |
| assets_high | 0 | 93.36% | 93.36% |
| dependent_income_ok | 0 | 95.2% | 95.2% |
| earnings_steady | 0 | 95.6% | 95.6% |
| debt_low | 5.7 | 61.76% | 82.22% |
| savings_ok | 0.4 | 90.18% | 91.17% |
| income_ok | 4.7 | 67.54% | 85.02% |

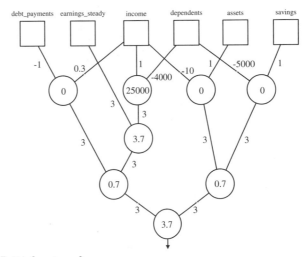

**Figure 7.19**   Initial network.

alone increased to 82.22% for rules and examples. In comparison, the knowledge refinement technique of the extended KBANN rule-based network using additional connections and backpropagation as in (Towell et al., 1990) provided an increase to only 64.64%. It is also important to observe that when the expert was able to classify the sample data well no hidden units were constructed.

### 7.5.2.3   Multiple Experts Integration

In the experiments carried out with the neural network combiners the training and testing sets were generated independently, with 1,000 examples in the training set and 10,000 in the test set. For the decision tree approach different training sets were

**Table 7.9**   Local experts used in multiple experts integration approaches.

| System | Success Rate | False prediction negative | positive | Pruned rules | Expert type |
|--------|--------------|---------------------------|----------|--------------|-------------|
| Expert 1 | 65% | 100% | 0% | (2),(6) | pessimistic |
| Expert 2 | 69% | 100% | 0% | (5),(9) | pessimistic |
| Expert 3 | 82% | 100% | 0% | (3),(4),(7),(8) | pessimistic |
| Expert 4 | 73% | 0% | 100% | (7),(4) | optimistic |
| NN | 87% | 57% | 43% | not applicable | mixed |

**Table 7.10**   Financial advising: Integration of two experts.

| Expert systems | Generalization Upper bound | Decision tree | Cooperative network | Competitive network |
|----------------|-------------|---------------|---------------------|---------------------|
| Experts 1 + 2 | 86.05% | 67.75% | 86.05% | 85.78% |
| Experts 1 + 3 | 90.37% | 68.60% | 90.37% | 90.02% |
| Experts 2 + 3 | 95.56% | 70.00% | 95.56% | 94.53% |
| Experts 1 + 4 | 100.00% | 68.60% | 58.62% | 90.60% |

used, ranging from 120 to 500 examples, and the test set was the same one used for the neural network based integration techniques. Experiments were performed by applying the three integration techniques discussed in Section 7.4 to different combinations of expert systems and/or neural networks. For comparison purposes, an upper bound on the success rate of each combination was computed for the given test data set. As in the two-spirals problem (Table 7.6), this upper bound represents the maximum possible success rate achievable by always following the correct advice, i.e. selecting the expert that best classifies the given example. Also, a bound below 100% means that there are cases where all local experts classification responses are wrong, and so it is impossible to output a correct answer either by selecting one of them, or by combining their outputs. Notice that this upper bound is by no means tight. For example, a pair of "dumb" experts, in which one of the modules always outputs 0 and the other always outputs 1, has an upper bound of 100% (they are never both wrong), but the information they provide is nil. Thus, the cooperative combiner network can only achieve a very limited performance, while the gating network used in the competitive approach is left with the task of learning to classify the patterns by itself. Actually, the gating network has the advantage of being fed the original input in addition to the outputs of the "dumb" experts, and so it can learn to some extent how to classify the patterns. For the financial advising problem, a gating network combining two "dumb" experts achieved a test set success rate close to 72%.

The results of integrating several pairs of expert systems are shown in Table 7.10.

The table presents the computed upper bound on the accuracy of each combination and the generalization (testing data) success rates obtained by implementing the decision tree, cooperative and competitive network, respectively. The results shown for the decision tree approach are averaged over twelve training sets of different sizes (120, 200, 300 and 500 examples). It is interesting to note here that the monostrategy decision tree approach, i.e. using a decision tree to solve the original classification problem, gave a better result (74.75%) than all the decision tree integrated systems tested here. Notice that, when combining pairs of pessimistic experts, both neural network-based methods produce excellent results. This is so because it is very easy to combine either two or more pessimistic or two or more optimistic experts by feeding their outputs to an AND gate (if the experts are optimistic) or an OR gate (if the experts are pessimistic). Obviously, both problems can be learned by a single neuron.

In contrast, the combination of pairs of experts of different types (1+4) proves to be much more difficult for the cooperative combiner approach. In this case, the competitive network achieves around 90% accuracy, and the decision tree does a better job than the cooperative combiner. This is another example of the domain transformation's shortcomings  when dealing with low resolution outputs, as explained in Section 7.2.

The results of combining two of the expert systems with a neural network are summarized in Table 7.11. The upper bound for the success rate is measured using the symbolic expert and the fixed neural network. The table shows two different implementations of the competitive network. In the fixed neural network case, the neural network shown in Table 7.9 was used as an expert system, i.e. it only responded to the inputs, with no further training. In the dynamic learning method, the neural network local expert was trained at the same time as the gating network.

Notice that, in this case, the cooperative combiner's performance when combining "mixed" experts improves significantly over that in Table 7.10. This is caused by the fact that the output from one of the experts (NN) is now a real number, instead of a one-bit value. This increase in resolution facilitates the generation of a more adequate decision region on the transformed domain. The gating network, on the other hand does a very good job on integrating these systems, especially

**Table 7.11**   Financial advising: Integration of one expert and a neural network.

| Expert systems | Generalization | | | | |
| --- | --- | --- | --- | --- | --- |
| | Upper bound | Decision tree | Cooperative network | Competitive network | |
| | | | | Fixed NN | Dynamic NN |
| Expert 1 + NN | 96.24% | 71.40% | 91.79% | 96.32% | |
| Expert 2 + NN | 97.27% | 71.40% | 93.92% | 95.22% | |
| Expert 3 + NN | 94.11% | 74.05% | 72.10% | 89.00% | 93.24% |
| Expert 4 + NN | 96.62% | 66.10% | 78.21% | 91.45% | 95.33% |
| Expert 5 + NN | 96.62% | 79.40% | 88.89% | 93.79% | |

when the local expert neural network is allowed to learn simultaneously with the gating network. The decision tree approach managed to outperform the cooperative combiner in one of the cases, but its results continued to be very poor.

## 7.6   Conclusions

Several approaches to the development of hybrid classification systems integrating existing classifiers and learning from examples are discussed and compared on two domains. It was demonstrated that incremental single expert expansion can provide generalization improvement over both the expert and learning from examples alone. Also, it was evident that some of the multiple experts integration techniques can take advantage of multiple heterogeneous sources of partial domain knowledge. In particular, the competitive neural network approach was found to be superior to the other multiple experts integration methods studied, and to each of the sources of prior knowledge.

It is important to observe that single expert expansion and multiple experts integration are not mutually exclusive approaches. Once heterogeneous experts are efficiently integrated, the obtained system can be used as prior knowledge for single expert expansion. Conversely, in multiple experts integration systems, a single expert extended through incremental learning can be treated as one of several sources of partial domain knowledge. Further research is needed to characterize which approach is more appropriate for specific problem classes.

## Copyright Acknowledgments

## References

Baum, E. B. 1991.  Neural net algorithms that learn in polynomial time from examples and queries. *IEEE Transactions on Neural Networks*, 2(1):5–19.

Baum, E. B. and Lang, K. J. 1991.  Constructing hidden units using examples and queries. In *Advances in Neural Information Processing Systems*, eds. R. P. Lippmann, J. E. Moody, and D. S. Touretzky, vol. 3, pp. 904–910, Denver 1990. Morgan Kaufmann, San Mateo.

Benachenhou, D., Cader, M., Szu, H., Medsker, L., Wittwer, C., and Garling, D. 1990.  Neural networks for computing invariant clustering of a large open set of DNA-PCR primers generated by a feature-knowledge based system. In *Proc. International Joint Conference on Neural Networks*, vol. 2, pp. 83–89, San Diego,

CA.

Bishop, C. M. 1995. *Neural Networks for Pattern Recognition.* Oxford: Clarendon Press.

Breiman, L. 1996. Bagging predictors. *Machine Learning,* 24(2):123–140.

Chan, P., Stolfo, S., and Wolpert, D. 1996. *Working Notes of The 1996 AAAI Workshop on Integrating Multiple Learned Models for Improving and Scaling Machine Learning Algorithms, held in conjunction with National Conference on Artificial Intelligence AAAI. WWW location http://cs.fit.edu/~imlm/.* Portland, OR.

Chenoweth, T. and Obradović, Z. 1996. A multi-component nonlinear prediction system for the S&P 500 index. *Neurocomputing,* 10(3):275–290.

Dietterich, T. G. and Michalski, R. S. 1983. A comparative review of selected methods for learning from examples. In *Machine Learning,* eds. R. S. Michalski, J. G. Carbonell, and T. M. Mitchell, pp. 41–82. San Mateo: Morgan Kaufmann.

Drossu, R. and Obradović, Z. 1996. Rapid design of neural networks for time series prediction. *IEEE Computational Science and Engineering,* 3(2):78–89.

Fahlman, S. E. and Lebiere, C. 1990. The cascade-correlation learning architecture. In *Advances in Neural Information Processing Systems,* ed. D. S. Touretzky, vol. 2, pp. 524–532, Denver 1989. Morgan Kaufmann, San Mateo.

Fayyad, U. M. 1994. Branching on attribute values for decision tree generation. In *Proc. of the 12th National Conference on Artificial Intelligence,* pp. 601–606.

Fayyad, U. M. and Irani, K. B. 1993. Multi-interval discretization of continuous-valued attributes for classification learning. In *Proc. of the International Joint Conference on Artificial Intelligence, IJCAI-93,* pp. 1022–1027.

Fletcher, J. and Obradović, Z. 1993. Combining prior symbolic knowledge and constructive neural network learning. *Connection Science,* 5(3,4):365–375.

Fletcher, J. and Obradović, Z. 1995. A discrete approach to constructive neural network learning. *Neural, Parallel and Scientific Computations,* 3(3):307–320.

Fukunaga, K. 1990. *Introduction to statistical pattern recognition.* San Diego: Academic Press.

Gallant, S. I. 1988. Connectionist expert systems. *Communications of the ACM,* 31(2):152–169.

Gallant, S. I. 1990. Perceptron-based learning algorithms. *IEEE Transactions on Neural Networks,* 1(2):179–191.

Gutknecht, M., Pfeifer, R., and Stolze, M. 1991. Cooperative hybrid systems. Tech. rep., Universitat Zurich.

Hanson, M. A. and Brekke, R. L. 1988. Workload management expert system—combining neural networks and rule-based programming in an operational application. In *Proc. Instrument Society of America,* vol. 24, pp. 1721–1726.

Hayes-Roth, F., Waterman, D. A., and Lenat, D. B., eds. 1983. *Building Expert*

*Systems*. Reading, MA: Addison-Wesley.

Hendler, J. and Dickens, L. 1991. Integrating neural network and expert reasoning: An example. In *Proc. AISB Conf. on Developments of Biological Standardization*.

Jacobs, R. A., Jordan, M. I., Nowlan, S. J., and Hinton, G. E. 1991. Adaptive mixtures of local experts. *Neural Computation*, 3:79–87.

Kandel, A. and G. Langholz, e. 1992. *Hybrid Architectures for Intelligent Systems*. Boca Raton: CRC Press, Inc.

Luger, G. F. and Stubblefield, W. A. 1989. *Artificial Intelligence and the Design of Expert Systems*. Redwood City, CA: Benjamin/Cummings.

Medsker, L. and Bailey, D. 1992. Models and guidelines for integrating expert systems and neural networks. In *Hybrid Architectures for Intelligent Systems*, eds. A. Kandel and G. Langholz. Boca Raton: CRC Press, Inc.

Michalski, R. S. and G. Tecuci, e. 1994. *Machine Learning. A Multistrategy approach*, vol. 4. Morgan Kaufmann.

Nowlan, S. J. and Hinton, G. E. 1991. Evaluation of adaptive mixtures of competing experts. In *Advances in Neural Information Processing Systems*, eds. R. P. Lippmann, J. E. Moody, and D. J. Touretzky, vol. 3, pp. 774–780. San Mateo, CA: Morgan Kaufmann.

Quinlan, J. 1986. Induction of decision trees. *Machine Learning*, 1:81–106.

Romero, P. R. and Obradović, Z. 1995. Comparison of symbolic and connectionist approaches to local experts integration. In *IEEE Technical Applications Conference at Northcon/95*, pp. 105–110, Portland, OR.

Romero, P. R., Obradović, Z., Kissinger, C., Villafranca, J. E., and Dunker, A. K. 1997. Identifying disordered regions in proteins from amino acid sequence. In *Proc. IEEE International Conference on Neural Networks*, vol. 1, pp. 90–95, Houston, TX.

Samad, T. 1988. Towards connectionist rule-based systems. In *Proceedings of the IEEE International Conference on Neural Networks*, vol. 2, pp. 525–532, San Diego.

Shimshoni, Y. and Intrator, N. 1996. On the integration of ensembles of neural networks: Application to seismic signal classification. In *Working Notes of the 1996 AAAI Workshop on Integrating Multiple Learned Models for Improving and Scaling Machine Learning Algorithms, held in conjunction with National Conference on Artificial Intelligence AAAI, WWW location http://cs.fit.edu/~imlm/*, eds. P. Chan, S. Stolfo, and D. Wolpert, Portland, OR.

Towell, G. G., Shavlik, J. W., and Noordwier, M. O. 1990. Refinement of approximate domain theories by knowledge-based neural networks. In *Proceedings of the Eighth National Conference on Artificial Intelligence*, pp. 861–866, Boston, MA.

Weigend, A. S., Mangeas, M., and Srivastava, A. N. 1995. Nonlinear gated experts for time series: Discovering regimes and avoiding overfitting. *Int. J. of Neural Systems*, 6:373–399.

Werbos, P. 1995. *Beyond regression: New tools for predicting and analysis in the behavioral sciences. Harvard University, Ph.D. Thesis, 1974.* Wiley and Sons (Reprinted).

Zhang, X., Mesirov, J. P., and Waltz, D. L. 1992. Hybrid system for protein secondary structure prediction. *Journal of Molecular Biology*, 225:1049–1063.

# 8     Approximation of Differential Equations Using Neural Networks

Rico A. Cozzio

*Knowledge-based neurocomputing tries to exploit problem-specific knowledge within the neurocomputing paradigm. Differential equations are an important type of a priori knowledge available in engineering problems and physical systems. We consider a novel method for using this knowledge to generate a neural network that implements an initial model of the system dynamics described by differential equations. A design algorithm is developed that determines the structure as well as the weights of the network. This algorithm can be used for all neural network architectures that satisfy the necessary mathematical restrictions. Specifically, Radial Basis Function networks and a new architecture, Modified Logistic Networks, satisfy these conditions. After initial design of the neural network using this algorithm, additional training can then serve to refine the model and estimate unknown parameters of the system. We use the proposed algorithm to construct single-step and multi-step integrators for forecasting time series generated by sampling the Lorenz system of chaotic differential equations. In our tests, the Modified Logistic Networks outperformed the Radial Basis Function Networks. The advantages of our translational approach are integration of prior knowledge in the form of differential equations with learning from data, therefore leading to improved generalization and training efficiency, as well as the need for less training data.*

## 8.1   Motivation

Differential equations are very important mathematical tools used in engineering. They are the dominant technique for modeling dynamic systems, because the causal relations between physical variables present in engineering problems can be described well by differential equations.

However, if the dynamics of a physical system are unknown, we face the problem of identifying the process driving the system. This nonlinear modeling problem can be approached using a general model, whose parameters are estimated from observations of the system. These *system identification* and *parameter estimation* tasks can be attacked with neural networks, where the network corresponds to the model and the network weights are the free parameters. A learning algorithm searches for the optimal network weights that fit the network output to the actual system observations. Nevertheless, finding optimal weights for large neural networks is difficult. An overview of the usage of neural networks for system identification and parameter estimation tasks typically found in control applications is given in (Narendra and Parthasarathy, 1990) and (White and Sofge, 1992).

Many engineering problems share some characteristics of both problem specifications: It is common that partial knowledge about the dynamics of a system is available as differential equations, but they are insufficient for modeling purposes. Assume for example, only the structure of the differential equations describing a system is known, but some physical constants are missing. The standard approach of applying neural networks to such problems uses only system observations for modeling and the available differential equations are ignored. However, an optimal usage of information tries to integrate both the observation data and the structured knowledge into the neural networks. If we manage to combine both aspects of modeling in the networks, the accuracy, stability and efficiency of neural modeling can be improved, and the networks generalize better from observed data.

In this chapter, a method to exploit ordinary differential equations for the design of neural networks is presented. Both the architecture and the weights of the networks are determined from the differential equations. Single-step and multi-step numerical integration procedures for the approximation of the differential equations are derived using the resulting neural networks as basic building blocks. After initial design, the neural networks can be trained from observation data in order to account for the modeling deficiencies of the differential equations. The approximation quality of constructed networks is demonstrated by forecasting the Lorenz system of chaotic differential equations.

## 8.2   Local Approximation by Taylor Series

Assume we have a first order ordinary differential equation of the form (8.1) with initial condition (8.2).

$$x'(t) = f(t, x(t)) \qquad (8.1)$$

$$x(t_0) = x_0 \qquad (8.2)$$

If $x(t)$ and the functional $f$ are analytic in the neighborhood of the initial value $t_0$, we can successively differentiate the differential equation to obtain Equations 8.3.

$$x^{(k)}(t_0) = f(t, x(t))^{(k-1)}\Big|_{t=t_0}, k = 1 \ldots K \qquad (8.3)$$

Since the solution $x(t)$ is assumed to be analytic at $t_0$, it can be approximated near $t_0$ by a power series (8.4), whose derivatives are given in (8.5).

$$x(t) \approx \sum_{k=0}^{\infty} a_k \cdot (t - t_0)^k \tag{8.4}$$

$$x^{(k)}(t_0) = a_k \cdot k! \tag{8.5}$$

Solving Equation 8.5 for the coefficients $a_k$ gives the solution (8.6), which turns (8.4) into the well known Taylor series (8.7) with convergence radius $\rho$.

$$a_k = \frac{x^{(k)}(t_0)}{k!} = \frac{1}{k!} \cdot f(t, x(t))^{(k-1)} \Big|_{t=t_0} \tag{8.6}$$

$$x(t) = \sum_{k=0}^{\infty} \frac{x^{(k)}(t_0)}{k!} \cdot (t - t_0)^k, t \in [t_0 - \rho, t_0 + \rho] \tag{8.7}$$

A local approximation (8.8) near $t_0$ is obtained by truncating the Taylor series after $K$ terms.

$$x(t_0 + \Delta t) \approx \sum_{k=0}^{K} a_k \cdot \Delta t^k, \text{ where } a_k = \frac{x^{(k)}(t_0)}{k!} \tag{8.8}$$

This straightforward method to compute polynomial approximations (8.8) of differential equations is very old. Isaac Newton already used infinite power series for the approximation of differential equations (Hairer et al., 1991, p. 4). The result of the Taylor series method is a local approximation (8.8) of the differential equation (8.1), given as a polynomial of the step size $\Delta t$. The coefficients $a_k$ are functions of the initial conditions (8.2), and they are determined by the solution of Equation 8.5. Provided that the step size $\Delta t$ is smaller than the convergence radius of the series and enough terms of the truncated series are used, the local approximation (8.8) of the solution of the differential equation allows the construction of a single-step integrator, which is sufficiently accurate to compute good approximations over a large interval. Taylor coefficients can be computed recursively and methods to choose a good step size do exist (Henrici, 1956; Campbel et al., 1961; Leavitt, 1966; Barton et al., 1971; Fairén et al., 1988), or for a short summary (Hairer et al., 1991, p. 47). Hence, many computer programs for the automatic approximation of differential equations based on long truncated power series have been implemented (see (Chang, 1974), (Norman, 1976), (Corliss and Lowery, 1977), (Barton, 1980), (Corliss and Chang, 1982)).

## 8.3   Generalization of the Taylor Series Method

In this section, we keep the basic idea of the Taylor series method, but we extend the power series approximation to more general approximation functions. The power series (8.4) is replaced by a parametrized local approximation function (8.9), with finitely many parameters $a_k$.

$$x(t) \approx \Phi_k(t; t_0; a_0, a_1, \ldots, a_k), t \in [t_0 - \rho, t_0 + \rho] \tag{8.9}$$

The method of successive differentiation can be generalized to approximation function $\Phi_K$, if $\Phi_K$ satisfies the following conditions:

*Solvability:* After substituting the approximation $\Phi_K$ for $x(t)$, the equations generated by the successive differentiation method (8.3) must be solvable for the parameters $a_k$. The following requirements enforce solvability:

*Triangulation condition:*

$$\left. \Phi_K(t; t_0; a_0, a_1, \ldots, a_K)^{(k)} \right|_{t=t_0} = \Theta_k^\Phi(a_0 \ldots a_k), \text{ where } k \leq K \tag{8.10}$$

The k-th derivative $\Theta_k^\Phi$ of the approximation function $\Phi_K$ at initial value $t_0$ must depend only on the parameters $a_0 \ldots a_k$.

*Invertibility:*

$$\begin{aligned}
y &= \Theta_k^\Phi(a_0 \ldots a_k) \\
a_k &= \Theta_k^{\Phi^{-1}}(y; a_0 \ldots a_{k-1}) \\
&= \Theta_k^{\Phi^{-1}}(\Theta_k^\Phi(a_0 \ldots a_k); a_0 \ldots a_{k-1})
\end{aligned} \tag{8.11}$$

The k-th derivative $\Theta_k^\Phi$ of the approximation function $\Phi_K$ at initial value $t_0$ must be invertible for the parameter $a_k$.

*Convergence:*

$$\lim_{K \to \infty} |x(t) - \Phi_k(t; t_0; a_0, \ldots, a_k)| = 0, t \in [t_0 - \rho, t_0 + \rho] \tag{8.12}$$
$$\text{for some norm } |\ldots|$$

With increasing number of parameters $a_k$, the sequence of truncated approximation functions $\Phi_K$ must converge to the solution $x(t)$ of the differential equation in a region near the initial value $t_0$.

If the approximation function $\Phi_K$ and the functional $f$ are analytic at initial value $t_0$, and if $\Phi_K$ obeys the condition (8.10), the successive differentiation method (8.3) generates the following Equations 8.13:

$$\begin{aligned}
\Theta_0^\Phi(a_0) &= x_0 \\
\Theta_k^\Phi(a_0 \ldots a_k) &= \left. f(t, \Phi_k(t; t_0; a_0, \ldots, a_k))^{(k-1)} \right|_{t=t_0} \\
&= g_{k-1}(t_0; \Theta_0^\Phi(a_0), \ldots, \Theta_{k-1}^\Phi(a_0 \ldots a_{k-1})), k = 1 \ldots K
\end{aligned} \tag{8.13}$$

The solution of (8.13) for parameter $a_k$ is given in Equation 8.14:

$$a_k = \Theta_k^{\Phi^{-1}}(g_{k-1}(t_0; \Theta_0^{\Phi}(a_0), \dots, \Theta_{k-1}^{\Phi}(a_0 \dots a_{k-1})); a_0 \dots a_{k-1}) \qquad (8.14)$$

After having solved the first $k$ Equations of (8.13) for the parameters $a_0 \dots a_k$, the $k+1$-th equation contains only the unknown parameter $a_k$. Consequently, Equations 8.13 can be solved iteratively, generating one parameter $a_k$ after the other. If both the derivatives $g_k$ of $f$ and $\Theta_k^{\Phi}$ are linear, (8.13) turns into a linear equation system, whose matrix is triangular [1] because of condition (8.10). For complex functions $\Theta_k^{\Phi}$, more sophisticated methods may be needed (see (Wu, 1984)). The following theorem demonstrates that the method of successive differentiation suffices to guarantee the convergence of the sequence of approximations $\Phi_K$ to $x(t)$. The proof is based on the fact that Taylor series with identical coefficients converge to the same function (for the proof see (Cozzio, 1995)):

### Theorem 8.1
Let $x(t)$ be an analytic function defined by the differential equation (8.15), and let $\Phi_K$ be an analytic local approximation function of the form (8.16) with $K$ parameters $a_k$.

$$x'(t) = f(t, x(t)) \qquad (8.15)$$
$$x(t_0) = x_0$$

$$x(t) \approx \Phi_k(t; t_0; a_0, \dots, a_k), t \in [t_0 - \rho, t_0 + \rho] \qquad (8.16)$$

$$\Phi_k(t; t_0; a_0, \dots, a_k) = x_0 \qquad (8.17)$$
$$\Phi_k(t; t_0; a_0, \dots, a_k)\Big|_{t=t_0} = f(t, \Phi_k(t; t_0; a_0, \dots, a_k))^{(k-1)}\Big|_{t=t_0}, k = 1 \dots K$$

If the parameters $a_k$ satisfy Equations 8.17, then for any $t$ within a radius $\rho$ of $t_0$, the approximation $\Phi_K$ converges to $x(t)$ with increasing $K$, where $\rho$ equals the radius of the Taylor series expansion of $x(t)$:

$$\lim_{K \to \infty} |x(t) - \Phi_k(t; t_0; a_0, \dots, a_k)| = 0, t \in [t_0 - \rho, t_0 + \rho] \qquad (8.18)$$

The result of Theorem 8.1 is independent of the specific form of approximation function $\Phi_K$ that is used. Consequently, if we select a specific function $\Phi_K$, only conditions (8.10), (8.11) and (8.17) have to be checked and the convergence (8.12) of $\Phi_K$ to $x(t)$ is implied.

---

1. Since condition (8.10) generates triangular matrices for linear systems, it is called the *triangulation condition*.

## 8.4   Choice of Suitable Neural Network Approximators

In Section 8.3, the Taylor series method for generating polynomial approximations has been generalized to non-polynomial functions $\Phi_K$. This method allows the construction of neural networks for the approximation of differential equations, if neural network architectures can be found for $\Phi_K$ that satisfy conditions (8.10) and (8.11).

Although many standard neural network models have been proven to be universal function approximators (e.g., see (Cybenko, 1989), (Funahashi, 1989), (Stinchcombe and White, 1989), (Girosi and Poggio, 1990), (Hartman et al., 1990), (Hornik et al., 1990), (Park and Sandberg, 1991), (Ito, 1992), (Cotter and Conwell, 1993), (Park and Sandberg, 1993)), most of them do not satisfy property (8.10), which requires that the network parameters $a_{i>k}$ vanish when the $k$-th derivative is taken at the initial value $t_0$. This strong requirement is necessary for solving Equations (8.13) iteratively, but it is satisfied trivially only by polynomials.

This attractive property of power series suggests that we should look for neural network architectures which can be rewritten as variants of power series. The derivation of power series of some basis function can take advantage of the fact that the concatenation of two functions turns into multiplication of their derivatives. Thus, if the derivatives of the underlying power series vanish, the derivatives of the modified series also vanish.

There exist classes of neural networks that satisfy additive and multiplicative closure, which means that power series of network functions can again be implemented by a neural network of the same class. The classes of neural networks satisfying the Stone-Weierstrass theorem share this property:

***Theorem 8.2 Stone-Weierstrass, see (Cotter and Conwell, 1990)***
Let domain $D$ be a compact space of $N$ dimensions, and let $F$ be a set of continuous real-valued functions on $D$, satisfying the following criteria:

*Identity function:* The constant function $f(x) = 1$ is in $F$.

*Separability:* For any two points $x_1 \neq x_2 \in D$, there is an $f \in F$ such that $f(x_1) \neq f(x_2)$.

*Algebraic closure:* If $f$ and $g$ are any two functions in $F$, $f \cdot g$ and $a \cdot f + b \cdot g$ are in $F$ for any two real numbers $a$ and $b$.

Then $F$ is dense in $C(D)$, the set of continuous real-valued functions on $D$. In other words, for any $\epsilon > 0$ and any function $g \in C(D)$, there is a function $f \in F$ such that $|g(x) - f(x)| < \epsilon$ for all $x \in D$.

Consequently, classes of neural networks satisfying the Stone-Weierstrass theorem are guaranteed to be universal function approximators for continuous real-valued functions. In the following Sections 8.4.1 and 8.4.2, two such neural network architectures are investigated: the *Modified Logistic Network* and the *Radial Basis Function Network* with Gaussian units.

### 8.4.1 Modified Logistic Networks

The application of neural networks to systems of differential equations requires only networks with a single output unit, because every variable of a differential equation system can be approximated by a different network. A traditional three-layered neural network model with sigmoidal units in the hidden layer and a linear output unit is represented by function (8.19).

$$y(\overline{x}; \overline{z}_1 \ldots \overline{z}_k, \theta_1 \ldots \theta_k, w_1 \ldots w_k) = \sum_{k=1}^{K} w_k \cdot \text{sigmoid}(\overline{z}_k \cdot \overline{x} - \theta_k) \tag{8.19}$$

$$\text{where e.g., sigmoid}(x) = tanh(x)$$

Unfortunately, networks (8.19) using sigmoidal functions like *tanh* do not satisfy algebraic closure. Consequently, they can only approximate polynomials of their own activation function, but they cannot implement them exactly.

In (Cotter and Conwell, 1990), Cotter proposes a variant of this network, the *Modified Logistic Network* (8.20), which satisfies the Stone-Weierstrass theorem and which compensates for this defect.

$$y(\overline{x}; \overline{z}_{1,1} \ldots \overline{z}_{I,K}, w_1 \ldots w_K) = \sum_{k=1}^{K} w_k \cdot \frac{1}{1 + \sum_{i=1}^{I} e^{-\overline{z}_{i,k} \cdot \overline{x}}} \tag{8.20}$$

Note that the traditional networks (8.19) using the function tanh are a subset of the class of Modified Logistic Networks, because tanh satisfies the identity (8.21). Polynoms of tanh functions, however, do not belong to the class of tanh networks any more.

$$\tanh(x) = \frac{e^x - e^{-x}}{e^x + e^{-x}} = \frac{e^{2x} - 1}{e^{2x} + 1} = 1 - \frac{2}{1 + e^{2x}} \tag{8.21}$$

We now propose the neural network (8.22) for approximation function $\Phi_K$. $\Phi_K^{MLG}$ is a polynomial of networks (8.19), which can be represented as a Modified Logistic Network (8.20) after transforming tanh according to identity (8.21) and after expanding all multiplications.

$$\Phi_K^{MLG}(t; t_0; a_0, \ldots, a_K) =$$
$$a_0 + \sum_{k-1}^{K} \left[ \tanh(t - t_0)^{k-1} \cdot \sum_{i=0}^{\lfloor \frac{K}{2} \rfloor} \frac{\tanh(a_k(t-t_0))^{2i+1}}{2i+1} \right] \tag{8.22}$$

The derivatives of the approximation function $\Phi_K^{MLG}$ at the initial value $t_0$ are given in (8.23). Its coefficients $c_{k,i}$ are shown in Table 8.1, where empty entries denote 0.

$$\Phi_K^{MLG}(t; t_0; a_0, \ldots, a_K)^{(k \leq K)} \Big|_{t=t_0} = \Theta_k^{MLG}(a_0 \ldots a_k) = \sum_{i=0}^{k} c_{k,i} \cdot a_i \tag{8.23}$$

**Table 8.1**    Coefficients $c_{k,i}$.

| $k$ | $c_{k,0}$ | $c_{k,1}$ | $c_{k,2}$ | $c_{k,3}$ | $c_{k,4}$ | $c_{k,5}$ | $\dots$ |
|-----|-----------|-----------|-----------|-----------|-----------|-----------|---------|
| 0 | 1 | | | | | | |
| 1 | | 1 | | | | | |
| 2 | | | 2 | | | | |
| 3 | | | | 6 | | | |
| 4 | | | $-8$ | | 24 | | |
| 5 | | | | $-80$ | | 120 | |
| $\dots$ | $\dots$ | $\dots$ | $\dots$ | $\dots$ | $\dots$ | $\dots$ | $\dots$ |

### Theorem 8.3

(For the proof see (Cozzio, 1995)) A Modified Logistic Network of the form (8.22) allows the application of the method of successive differentiation (8.13) for the local approximation of differential equations. The equations generated by (8.13) can be recursively solved for parameters $a_k$ with Equation 8.14.

Since the derivatives of the approximation function $\Phi_K^{MLG}$ are linear expressions of the parameters $a_k$, the equation system (8.13) is not significantly more complex to solve than for polynomial approximation functions. This makes the Modified Logistic Network $\Phi_K^{MLG}$ a good choice for the local approximations of differential equations.

### 8.4.2   Radial Basis Function Networks

Radial basis functions are well known in approximation theory. Some of their properties relevant to multidimensional approximation are documented in (Powell, 1987) and (Poggio, 1990).

For our purposes, we use three-layered neural networks with one input layer, one hidden layer with Gaussian radial basis function units and one output layer with a single linear unit. Since every variable of the system of differential equations is approximated by a different neural network, we need only one output unit, which computes the function (8.24).

$$y(\overline{x}; \overline{z}_1 \dots \overline{z}_K, w_1 \dots w_K) = \sum_{k=1}^{K} w_k \cdot e^{-\left(\frac{\overline{x} - \overline{z}_k}{\sigma_k}\right)^2}, \text{ where } \sigma_k > 0 \qquad (8.24)$$

### Theorem 8.4

Let the class $RBF$ of functions of the form (8.24) be called *Radial Basis Function Networks*. Then, all functions $f \in RBF$ satisfy the Stone-Weierstrass Theorem 8.2.

### Proof

*Identity function:* The constant function $f(x) = 1$ is in $RBF$ if we allow $\sigma \to \infty$:

$$f(x) = \lim_{\sigma \to \infty} e^{-\left(\frac{x}{\sigma}\right)^2} = 1 \tag{8.25}$$

*Separability:* For any two points $x_1 \neq x_2 \in D$, there is an $f \in RBF$ such that $f(x_1) \neq f(x_2)$ :

$$f(x) = e^{-(x-x_1)^2} \tag{8.26}$$

*Algebraic closure:* If $f$ and $g$ are any two functions in $RBF$, $f \cdot g$ and $a \cdot f + b \cdot g$ are in $RBF$ for any two real numbers $a$ and $b$:

Since the output layer is linear, the sum of two networks can be trivially implemented by one network. The product of two networks is transformed into a sum of products of the hidden layer activation functions, which again can be represented by Gaussian units. This transformation is justified by the identity (8.27).

$$w_1 \cdot e^{-\left(\frac{\bar{x}-\bar{z}_1}{\sigma_1}\right)^2} \cdot w_2 \cdot e^{-\left(\frac{\bar{x}-\bar{z}_2}{\sigma_2}\right)^2} = w_3 \cdot e^{-\left(\frac{\bar{x}-\bar{z}_3}{\sigma_3}\right)^2} \tag{8.27}$$

$$\bar{z}_3 = \frac{\sigma_1^2 \cdot \bar{z}_2 + \sigma_2^2 \cdot \bar{z}_1}{\sigma_1^2 + \sigma_2^2}, \sigma_3^2 = \frac{\sigma_1^2 \cdot \sigma_2^2}{\sigma_1^2 + \sigma_2^2}, w_3 = w_1 \cdot w_2 \cdot e^{\frac{-(\bar{z}_1 - \bar{z}_2)^2}{\sigma_1^2 + \sigma_2^2}}$$

The generalization of Equation 8.27 to multiple products is given in (8.28).

$$\prod_{k=1}^{N} w_k \cdot e^{-\left(\frac{\bar{x}-\bar{z}_k}{\sigma_k}\right)^2} = w \cdot e^{-\left(\frac{\bar{x}-\bar{z}}{\sigma}\right)^2}$$

$$\bar{z} = \frac{\sum_{k=1}^{N} \bar{z}_k \cdot \prod_{i=1,i\neq k}^{N} \sigma_i^2}{\tilde{\sigma}}, \quad \sigma^2 = \frac{\prod_{i=1}^{N} \sigma_i^2}{\tilde{\sigma}}, \quad \tilde{\sigma} = \sum_{k=1}^{N} \left( \prod_{i=1,i\neq k}^{N} \sigma_i^2 \right) \tag{8.28}$$

$$w = \exp\left(\frac{-1}{\tilde{\sigma}} \sum_{k=1}^{N} \bar{z}_k \cdot \left[ \bar{z}_k \cdot \sum_{i=1,i\neq k}^{N} \left( \prod_{j=1,j\neq k,j\neq i}^{N} \sigma_j^2 \right) - \sum_{i=1,i\neq k}^{N} \bar{z}_i \cdot \prod_{j=1,j\neq k,j\neq i}^{N} \sigma_j^2 \right] \right) \cdot$$
$$\prod_{k=1}^{N} w_k$$

Therefore, Radial Basis Function Networks (8.24) satisfy algebraic closure. ∎

We now present the neural network (8.29) for the approximation function $\Phi_K$, which can be converted into a Radial Basis Function Network of the form (8.24) for constant $\Delta t = t - t_0$.

$$\Phi_K^{RBF}(t; t_0; a_0, \ldots, a_K) =$$

$$a_0 + \sum_{k=1}^{K} \left[ \left( \frac{1}{e} - e^{-((t-t_0)-1)^2} \right)^{k-1} \cdot \sum_{i=1}^{K} \frac{b_i \cdot e^{i-1}}{2^i \cdot i!} \cdot \left( \frac{1}{e} - e^{-(a_k \cdot (t-t_0)-1)^2} \right)^i \right] \tag{8.29}$$

**Table 8.2**   Coefficients $b_i$.

| |
|---|
| $b_1 = 1$ |
| $b_2 = 1$ |
| $b_3 = 5$ |
| $b_4 = 25$ |
| $b_5 = 209$ |
| $b_6 = 1961$ |
| $b_7 = 23589$ |
| $\dots$ |

The transformation (8.30) translates the arguments of the Gaussian units in Equation 8.29 into their equivalent in (8.24), where the parameters $a_k$ correspond to the inputs into the Gaussian layer.

$$x_k = a_k, \sigma_k = \frac{1}{t - t_0} = \frac{1}{\Delta t}, z_k = \sigma_k \tag{8.30}$$

After expanding all multiplications in Equation 8.29, the approximation function $\Phi_K^{RBF}$ can be rewritten as a polynomial of Gaussian functions. Identity (8.28) for multiple products transforms $\Phi_K^{RBF}$ into a Radial Basis Function Network (8.24). The coefficients $b_i$ of the neural network (8.29) are given in Table 8.2. They are calculated by solving condition (8.10).

Although we have not found an explicit mathematical formula for the coefficients $b_i$, they can be computed easily by using the recursive equation (8.32), which is derived from the simplified approximation function (8.31).

$$\tilde{\Phi}_K^{RBF}(t; t_0; a_0, a_1) = a_0 + \sum_{i=1}^{K} \frac{b_i \cdot e^{i-1}}{2^i \cdot i!} \cdot \left( \frac{1}{e} - e^{-(a_1 \cdot (t-t_0)-1)^2} \right)^i \tag{8.31}$$

$$b_1 = 1, b_k = \frac{e \cdot (-1)^{k-1}}{a_1{}^k} \cdot \tilde{\Phi}_{k-1}^{RBF}(t; t_0; a_0, a_1)^{(k)} \bigg|_{t=t_0} \tag{8.32}$$

The derivatives of the approximation function $\Phi_K^{RBF}$ at the initial value $t_0$ are given in Equation 8.33. Their coefficients $c_{k,i}$ are shown in Table 8.3, where empty entries denote 0.

$$\Phi_K^{RBF}(t; t_0; a_0, \dots, a_K)^{(k \le K)} \bigg|_{t=t_0} = \Theta_k^{RBF}(a_0 \dots a_k) = \sum_{i=0}^{k} \frac{c_{k,i}}{e^i} \cdot a_i \tag{8.33}$$

**Theorem 8.5**

(For the proof see (Cozzio, 1995)) A Radial Basis Function Network of the form (8.29) allows the application of the method of successive differentiation (8.13) for the local approximation of differential equations. The equations generated

**Table 8.3**   Coefficients $c_{k,i}$.

| $k$ | $c_{k,0}$ | $c_{k,1}$ | $c_{k,2}$ | $c_{k,3}$ | $c_{k,4}$ | $c_{k,5}$ | $\cdots$ |
|-----|-----------|-----------|-----------|-----------|-----------|-----------|----------|
| 0 | 1 | | | | | | |
| 1 | | $-1$ | | | | | |
| 2 | | | 4 | | | | |
| 3 | | | 6 | $-24$ | | | |
| 4 | | | $-16$ | $-96$ | 192 | | |
| 5 | | | $-100$ | 200 | 1440 | $-1920$ | |
| $\cdots$ | $\cdots$ | $\cdots$ | $\cdots$ | $\cdots$ | $\cdots$ | $\cdots$ | $\cdots$ |

by (8.13) can be recursively solved for parameters $a_k$ with Equation 8.14.

According to Theorem 8.5, the approximation function (8.29) describes a Radial Basis Function Network which allows the application of the method of successive differentiation (8.13) for the local approximation of differential equations. Since the derivatives of the approximation function $\Phi_K^{RBF}$ are linear expressions of the parameters $a_k$, the equation system (8.13) is only slightly more complex to solve than for polynomial approximation functions. This makes the Radial Basis Function Network $\Phi_K^{RBF}$ another good choice as an approximation function.

## 8.5    Transformation of Differential Equations into Approximable Form

In Sections 8.4.1 and 8.4.2, the Modified Logistic Network (8.22) and the Radial Basis Function Network (8.29) have been proposed for approximation function $\Phi_K$. They both satisfy the convergence and solvability conditions described in Section 8.3. Fortunately, their derivatives $\Theta_k$ are linear expressions of the unknown parameters $a_k$, which generates particularly simple solutions to Equations 8.13. Consequently, the parameters $a_k$ depend only on the functional $f$, respectively on its derivatives $g_k$.

The architecture of the resulting neural networks looks as follows: The functional dependency of the parameters $a_k$ on the initial conditions (8.2) of the differential equation determines the structure of a preprocessing layer. It is followed by a middle and an output layer, whose network weights are independent of the differential equation (see Figure 8.1).

In case the functional $f$ is linear and independent of time $t$, Equations 8.13 are also linear and can be solved by backsubstitution. In this case, the parameters $a_k$ depend linearly on the initial conditions of the differential equation and both types of neural networks do not need an intermediate preprocessing layer.

If the functional $f$ is nonlinear, however, a nonlinear preprocessing layer between the input and the middle layer is needed, which is not regarded as a standard neural network architecture any more.

Since we want to keep standard architectures if possible, we try to solve this

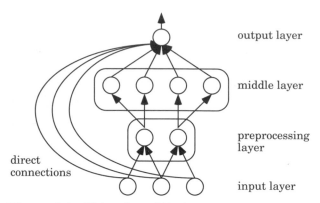

**Figure 8.1**    Network architecture.

problem by a suitable transformation of the differential equation, turning nonlinear functionals $f$ into polynomials. In (Kerner, 1981) and (Fairén et al., 1988), a set of transformation rules is offered, which cover a very general class of functionals $f$. Actually, Kerner demonstrates that polynomial systems can be even further simplified to quadratic systems, which are called *Riccati-systems* (Kerner, 1981). Consequently, the quadratic representation can be regarded as a *normal form* for differential equations, and a very general class of differential equations can be reduced to this form. The neural networks that result from such quadratic or polynomial functionals $f$ use polynomial preprocessing layers. In the literature, these networks are known as *higher-order neural networks* (see (Sejnowski, 1986), (Lee et al., 1986) or (Pineda, 1987)).

The transformation method is simple: Complex expressions are replaced by new variables, which are then defined by additional differential equations and their corresponding initial conditions. Since most "interesting" functions are themselves generated by rational differential equations, this transformation allows the reduction of these functions to their associated rational derivatives. After repeated application of the transformation rules, polynomial differential equations are obtained. This method covers rational, irrational and most transcendental functions usually encountered in physical modeling. Basically, all functions controlled by differential equations of finite order can be treated this way (a counterexample is the gamma function, which does not obey a differential equation of finite order).

In Table 8.4, some transformation rules are listed which serve to eliminate nonlinear functions. Note that the first transformation rule in Table 8.4 formally erases the distinction between autonomous and nonautonomous  differential equations by the near-trivial introduction of a variable.

### *Theorem 8.6*

Let differential equations of polynomial form be called being of *approximable form*. Then, if a differential equation of the form (8.1) can be transformed into a system of differential equations of approximable form by repeated transformation of the functional $f$, the differential equations can be locally approximated within the convergence radius to any desired accuracy by higher-order neural networks of

**Table 8.4**  Example of transformation rules.

| Replaced Functions | Added Differential Equations | Added Initial conditions |
|:---:|:---:|:---:|
| $c \cdot t \to a(t)$ | $a'(t) = c$ | $a(t_0) = c \cdot t_0$ |
| $\frac{1}{x(t)} \to a(t)$ | $a'(t) = -a(t)^2 \cdot x'(t)$ | $a(t_0) = \frac{1}{x(t_0)}$ |
| $\sin(x(t)) \to a(t)$ | $a'(t) = b(t) \cdot x'(t)$ | $a(t_0) = \sin(x(t_0))$ |
| $\cos(x(t)) \to b(t)$ | $b'(t) = -a(t) \cdot x'(t)$ | $b(t_0) = \cos(x(t_0))$ |
| $\ln(x(t)) \to a(t)$ | $a'(t) = \frac{x'(t)}{x(t)}$ | $a(t_0) = \ln(x(t_0))$ |
| $e^{x(t)} \to a(t)$ | $a'(t) = a(t) \cdot x'(t)$ | $a(t_0) = e^{x(t_0)}$ |
| $\tanh(x(t)) \to a(t)$ | $a'(t) = (1 - a(t)^2) \cdot x'(t)$ | $a(t_0) = \tanh(x(t_0))$ |

type (8.22) or (8.29) with polynomial preprocessing layers.

***Proof***   If the functional $f$ can be transformed into polynomial form by introducing new variables, each variable can be approximated by a neural network. The parameters of the networks (8.22) or (8.29) are the solutions of Equations 8.14, which result in polynomial expressions of the initial conditions of the differential equations. Therefore, the preprocessing layer of the network consists of polynomials determined by the differential equations, whereas the weights of the middle and the output layer are independent of the differential equations and remain fixed. The accuracy of the approximation is controlled by the number of parameters $a_k$ that are included, which also determines the size of the neural networks. According to Theorems 8.3 and 8.5, the differential equations can be approximated to any desired accuracy within the convergence radius $\rho$.  ∎

The following example illustrates the transformation process (individual transformation steps are marked by arrows that are labeled by the transformation rule used):

1. Using the transformation rules of Table 8.4, the rational differential Equation 8.34 with initial condition (8.35) is first transformed into Equations 8.36 and 8.37, which introduces the new variable $a(t)$. Differential Equations 8.36 are now in polynomial form.

$$x'(t) = \frac{1}{x(t)^2} \tag{8.34}$$

$$x(t_0) = x_0 \tag{8.35}$$

$$\Big\downarrow \quad \frac{1}{x(t)^2} \to a(t)$$

$$x'(t) = a(t)$$

$$a'(t) = -a(t)^2 \cdot 2x(t) \cdot x'(t) \tag{8.36}$$
$$= -2a(t)^3 \cdot x(t)$$

$$x(t_0) = x_0$$

$$a(t_0) = \frac{1}{x_0{}^2} \tag{8.37}$$

2. Then, Equations 8.36 are transformed successively into quadratic form, resulting

in Equations 8.44 and 8.45, which introduce the new variables $b(t) \ldots f(t)$.

$$x'(t) = a(t)$$
$$a'(t) = -2a(t)^3 \cdot x(t) \tag{8.38}$$

$$\Big\downarrow \quad a(t)^3 \rightarrow b(t)$$

$$a'(t) = -2b(t) \cdot x(t)$$
$$b'(t) = -6a(t)^2 \cdot b(t) \cdot x(t) \tag{8.39}$$

$$\Big\downarrow \quad a(t)^2 \rightarrow c(t)$$

$$b'(t) = -6b(t) \cdot c(t) \cdot x(t)$$
$$c'(t) = -4a(t) \cdot b(t) \cdot x(t) \tag{8.40}$$

$$\Big\downarrow \quad x(t) \cdot b(t) \rightarrow d(t)$$

$$b'(t) = -6c(t) \cdot d(t)$$
$$c'(t) = -4a(t) \cdot d(t) \tag{8.41}$$
$$d'(t) = a(t) \cdot b(t) - 6c(t) \cdot d(t) \cdot x(t)$$

$$\Big\downarrow \quad x(t) \cdot c(t) \rightarrow e(t)$$

$$d'(t) = a(t) \cdot b(t) - 6d(t) \cdot e(t)$$
$$e'(t) = a(t) \cdot c(t) - 4a(t) \cdot d(t) \cdot x(t) \tag{8.42}$$

$$\Big\downarrow \quad x(t) \cdot a(t) \rightarrow f(t)$$

$$e'(t) = a(t) \cdot c(t) - 4d(t) \cdot f(t)$$
$$f'(t) = c(t) - 2d(t) \cdot x(t) \tag{8.43}$$

$$\Big\downarrow$$

$$x'(t) = a(t)$$
$$a'(t) = -2d(t)$$
$$b'(t) = -6c(t) \cdot d(t)(t)$$
$$c'(t) = -4a(t) \cdot d(t) \tag{8.44}$$
$$d'(t) = a(t) \cdot b(t) - 6d(t) \cdot e(t)$$
$$e'(t) = a(t) \cdot c(t) - 4d(t) \cdot f(t)$$
$$f'(t) = c(t) - 2d(t) \cdot x(t)$$

$$x(t_0) = x_0$$
$$a(t_0) = \frac{1}{x_0{}^2}, b(t_0) = \frac{1}{x_0{}^6}$$
$$c(t_0) = \frac{1}{x_0{}^4}, d(t_0) = \frac{1}{x_0{}^5} \tag{8.45}$$
$$e(t_0) = \frac{1}{x_0{}^3}, f(t_0) = \frac{1}{x_0}$$

The substitution of compound expressions by new variables has a serious drawback, however: Since for each new variable another differential equation is introduced, the size of the system of differential equations may be increased substantially. The worst case occurs if full transformation to Riccati-form is desired, which our example (8.44) demonstrates (see (Kerner, 1981) for an estimation of the increase in size). We also encounter a difference in numerical precision between the approximations of the original and the transformed differential equations: After transforming the differential equation by differentiating away the nonlinear functions, we actually reverse this transformation by numerical integration. In most cases this gives worse results. Thus, approximating the transformed differential equations in general requires smaller integration steps than approximating the original equations.

On the other hand, if we transform a system of differential equations into quadratic form, and if we apply the method of successive differentiation and solve the generated equations, we still get polynomial solutions, not quadratic ones. This is already the case for very simple differential equations. Equations 8.47 generated by successive differentiation of example (8.46) demonstrate this phenomenon.

$$x'(t) = x(t)^2 \tag{8.46}$$
$$x(t_0) = x_0$$

$$
\begin{aligned}
x'(t_0) &= x(t_0)^2 \\
x''(t_0) &= \left(x(t)^2\right)'\Big|_{t=t_0} = 2x(t) \cdot x'(t)\Big|_{t=t_0} = 2x(t_0)^3 \\
x'''(t_0) &= \left(2x(t)^3\right)'\Big|_{t=t_0} = 6x(t)^2 \cdot x'(t)\Big|_{t=t_0} = 6x(t_0)^4 \\
&\cdots
\end{aligned}
\tag{8.47}
$$

Since quadratic differential equations still generate preprocessing layers with polynomials of unrestricted degree, the transformation from polynomial to quadratic form is not worth the effort. It only increases the complexity of the resulting neural networks. We therefore recommend to transform the differential equations only into polynomial form, not into (quadratic) normal form.

## 8.6 Single-Step and Multi-Step Integration Procedures

So far, we have discussed the construction of neural networks for the local approximation of differential equations in the neighborhood of $t_0$. Using the approximation function $\Phi_K$, we can construct a single-step numerical integration method (8.48).

$$x(t_0 + \Delta t) \approx \Phi_K(t_0 + \Delta t; t_0; a_0, \dots, a_K), \quad \text{where } \Delta t < \rho \tag{8.48}$$

If the function $\Phi_K(t_0 + \Delta t; t_0; a_0, \dots, a_K)$ is independent [2] of $t_0$ and if the parameters $a_k$ are resolved using the method of successive differentiation from Section 8.3, the single-step method corresponds to an iterated map (8.49).

$$x(t_0) = x_0$$
$$x_{k+1} = \varphi_\Phi(\Delta t; x_k) \tag{8.49}$$

If the step size $\Delta t$ is chosen smaller than the convergence radius $\rho$, the successive values $x_k$ at the points $t_k = t_0 + k \cdot \Delta t$ provide good approximations of the solution of the differential equation. This is a standard method used in numerical algorithms, where truncated Taylor series approximations $\Phi_K$ are reduced to linear functions $\varphi_\Phi$, e.g. see (Hairer et al., 1991).

Up to now, we exclusively treated first order differential equations. In order to handle higher-order differential equations, there are two approaches:

1. We can transform every higher order differential equation into a system of first order differential equations, which can be treated as usual. This approach is useful only if we know the derivatives at the initial value $t_0$, which is the case in example (8.50).

$$x''(t) = -x(t)$$
$$x(t_0) = x_0 \tag{8.50}$$
$$x'(t_0) = x_0'$$
$$\Big\downarrow \quad x'(t) \to a(t)$$
$$x'(t) = a(t)$$
$$a'(t) = -x(t) \tag{8.51}$$
$$x(t_0) = x_0$$
$$a(t_0) = x'(t_0) = x_0'$$

2. In example 8.52, however, there are two boundary conditions given for $x(t)$ instead of the initial conditions for $x(t)$ and $x'(t)$. Therefore, the first approach is not applicable to this case.

$$x''(t) = -x(t)$$
$$x(t_0) = x_0 \tag{8.52}$$
$$x(t_1) = x_1$$

There is a basic problem with systems like (8.52). This is revealed when we look at

---

2. Note that general differential equations can be transformed into autonomous systems using the first transformation rule of Table 8.4 shown in Section 8.5.

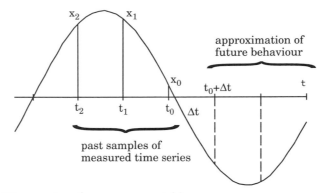

**Figure 8.2**  Time series of a process variable.

Equations 8.53 generated by successive differentiation:

$$x(t_0) = x_0$$
$$x(t_1) = x_1$$
$$x''(t) = -x(t) \quad\quad\quad\quad\quad\quad\quad\quad\quad (8.53)$$
$$x'''(t) = -x'(t)$$
$$x^{(k)}(t) = \begin{cases} (-1)^{\frac{k}{2}} \cdot x(t) & \text{for even } k \\ (-1)^{\frac{k-1}{2}} \cdot x'(t) & \text{for odd } k \end{cases}$$

For first order systems, the derivatives of the approximation function $\Phi_K$ satisfy the differential equation exactly up to order $K$ at initial value $t_0$. This is possible because the equations generated by successive differentiation specify precise conditions for all derivatives of $\Phi_K$ up to order $K$. For the second order differential equation (8.53), however, there is no condition for the first derivative $\Phi_K'$, because it is replaced by a boundary condition in the differential equation. Therefore, any approximation error of the derivative $x'(t)$ will be duplicated in all higher derivatives of odd order.

Since the exact derivative is not available, it is very important that a good approximation be used instead.

The following solution provides good estimates of the derivative: If the variable described by the differential equation is sampled periodically, the time series of the past evolution of the process is available as in Figure 8.2.

A natural way to approximate the derivative numerically is to take the derivative of a Lagrange interpolation (8.54) of the past samples $x_0 \ldots x_M$.

$$x(t) \approx \Psi(t; t_0 \ldots t_M; x_0 \ldots x_m) = \sum_{i=0}^{M} x_i \cdot \prod_{j=0, j \neq i}^{M} \frac{t-t_j}{t_i-t_j}, \quad\quad (8.54)$$

where $M - 1 \geq$ order $m$ of the differential equation

The derivatives $\Psi^{(k)}$ at initial value $t_0$ of the Lagrange interpolation (8.54) are linear in the samples $x_0 \ldots x_M$. They are substituted for the unknown derivatives of $\Phi_K$, which finally results in a multi-step numerical integration procedure using several past values for the next integration step. In case the points $x_k$ are distributed on the grid $t_k = t_0 + k \cdot \Delta t, \Delta t < \rho$, an integration step is performed by executing one iteration of the map (8.55). Note that the step size $\Delta t$ must be smaller than the convergence radius $\rho$.

$$x(t_0 - k \cdot \Delta t) = x_{-k}, k = 0 \ldots M$$
$$x_{k+1} = \varphi_\Psi(\Delta t; x_{k-M} \ldots x_k) \tag{8.55}$$

In the next two sections, we substitute the neural networks $\Phi_K^{MLG}$ and $\Phi_K^{RBF}$ for the local approximation function $\Phi_K$, and we discuss the resulting neural network architectures.

### 8.6.1  Modified Logistic Networks

It is not quite clear which parts of a Modified Logistic Network should actually be called a *unit* or *neuron*. We differ from (Cotter and Conwell, 1990), who decompose a Modified Logistic Network into a network of specialized units, and we call a unit with activation function (8.57) a *Modified Logistic Unit*. This terminology is consistent with the generalization of the logistic function (8.56) to function (8.57).

$$y(\overline{x}; \overline{z}) = \frac{1}{1 + e^{-\overline{z} \cdot \overline{x}}} \tag{8.56}$$

$$y(\overline{x}; \overline{z}_1 \ldots \overline{z}_I) = \frac{1}{1 + \sum_{i=1}^{I} e^{-\overline{z}_i \cdot \overline{x}}} \tag{8.57}$$

It has been shown in Section 8.5 that the transformation of differential equations into normal form may generate equations with polynomial solutions for the parameters $a_k$ of a Modified Logistic Network. Therefore, the most general architecture for a Modified Logistic Network of the form (8.22) needs a polynomial preprocessing layer. It feeds its outputs into a layer of Modified Logistic Units, whose outputs are summed up in a linear output unit. See Figure 8.3.

Additionally, there are direct connections from the input to the output layer. All weights in the network are determined by the differential equation to be approximated, and they are computed by the method described in Section 8.3. If we approximate a system of several differential equations, there is one such neural network for each variable, and the past values of all variables are used as inputs to the networks.

### Theorem 8.7
According to the definition of a Modified Logistic Unit (8.57), a network (8.22) with $K$ parameters $a_k$ and constant $\Delta t = t - t_0$, needs $K \cdot \left(\left\lfloor \frac{K}{2} \right\rfloor + 1\right) \cdot \left(2 \cdot \left\lfloor \frac{K}{2} \right\rfloor + 1\right)$ units in the middle layer, which increases with $O(K^3)$ relative to the number of parameters $a_k$.

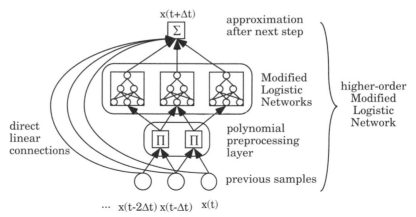

**Figure 8.3**   Architecture of modified logistic network.

***Proof***   The function tanh can be represented by one Modified Logistic Unit because of identity $\tanh(x) = 1 - \frac{2}{1+e^{2x}}$. Since the product of two Modified Logistic Units is again a Modified Logistic Unit, the power $\tanh(x)^i$ can be represented by $\sum_{j=1}^{i} j = \frac{i \cdot (i+1)}{2}$ units. The sum of powers of $\tanh(x)^{2i+1}$ in (8.22) needs only as many units as the highest power of tanh, because the lower powers are contained therein and their units can be merged. Consequently, the total number of needed Modified Logistic Units is $K \cdot \left( \left\lfloor \frac{K}{2} \right\rfloor + 1 \right) \cdot \left( 2 \cdot \left\lfloor \frac{K}{2} \right\rfloor + 1 \right)$.   ∎

### 8.6.2   Radial Basis Function Networks

If we use the Radial Basis Function Network (8.29) presented in Section 8.4.2 for the local approximation function $\Phi_K$, the resulting architecture in Figure 8.4 looks similar to the higher-order Modified Logistic Network, except for the layer of Modified Logistic Units, which is replaced by a layer of Gaussian units of the form (8.24).

***Theorem 8.8***

A Radial Basis Function Network (8.29) with $K$ parameters $a_k$ and constant $\Delta t = t - t_0$ needs $K \cdot \frac{K \cdot (K+1)}{2} = \frac{K^3 + K^2}{2}$ Gaussian units in the middle layer. Therefore, the network size increases with $O(K^3)$ relative to the number of parameters $a_k$.

***Proof***   Since the product of two Gaussian units is again a Gaussian unit, the power $\left( \frac{1}{e} - e^{-(a_k \cdot (t - t_0) - 1)^2} \right)^i$ can be represented by $\sum_{j=1}^{i} j = \frac{i \cdot (i+1)}{2}$ units. The sum of such powers in (8.29) needs only as many units as the highest power in (8.29), because the lower powers are contained therein and their units can be merged. Consequently, the total number of needed Gaussian units is $K \cdot \frac{K \cdot (K+1)}{2}$.   ∎

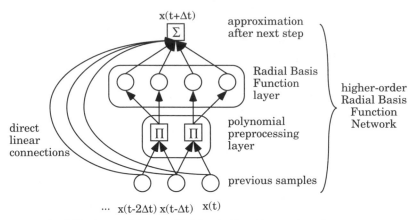

**Figure 8.4** Architecture of the radial basis function network.

### 8.6.3 Example: Second Order Differential Equation

The following example shows how to construct a *multi-step numerical integration procedure* for the *second order differential equation* (8.58):

$$x''(t) = -x(t)$$
$$x(t_0) = x_0 \tag{8.58}$$
$$x(t_1) = x_1$$

1. The differential equation is already in polynomial form, therefore, no transformation is necessary.

2. We have to choose an approximation function of type (8.22) for the second order differential equation (8.58). We select a Modified Logistic Network (8.59) with four parameters $a_0..a_3$ for that purpose, see Section 8.4.1.

$$\Phi_K^{MLG}(t; t_0; a_0, \dots, a_3) =$$
$$a_0 + \sum_{k=1}^{3} \left[ \tanh(t - t_0)^{k-1} \cdot \sum_{i=0}^{1} \frac{\tanh(a_k(t-t_0))^{2i+1}}{2i+1} \right] \tag{8.59}$$

3. The Equations 8.60 generated by successive differentiation of (8.58) require the first derivative of $x(t)$. It is approximated by the derivative of the Lagrange interpolation function (8.61), using the samples $x_0$ and $x_1$.

$$x''(t_0) = -x(t_0)$$
$$x'''(t_0) = -x'(t_0) \tag{8.60}$$
$$x(t_0) = x_0$$
$$x(t_1) = x_1$$

$$\Psi(t; t_0, t_1; x_0, x_1) = x_0 \cdot \frac{t - t_1}{t_0 - t_1} + x_1 \cdot \frac{t - t_0}{t_1 - t_0} \tag{8.61}$$

If we substitute the approximation function $\Phi_3^{MLG}$ for $x(t)$ in the Equations 8.60, and if we replace $t_1 = t_0 - \Delta t$ and $x'(t_0) = \Psi'(t; t_0, t_1; x_0, x_1)\big|_{t=t_0}$, we get the full equation system (8.62) for the parameters $a_k$.

$$\begin{aligned} a_0 &= x_0 \\ a_1 &= \frac{x_0 - x_1}{\Delta t} \\ 2a_2 &= -a_0 \\ 6a_3 &= -a_1 \end{aligned} \tag{8.62}$$

4. Equations 8.62 are solved for the parameters $a_k$, resulting in the values given by (8.63).

$$\begin{aligned} a_0 &= x_0 \\ a_1 &= \frac{x_0 - x_1}{\Delta t} \\ a_2 &= -\frac{1}{2} \cdot x_0 \\ a_3 &= -\frac{1}{6} \cdot \frac{x_0 - x_1}{\Delta t} \end{aligned} \tag{8.63}$$

5. The multi-step integration procedure (8.64) is completed by inserting the resolved parameters $a_k$ into $\Phi_3^{MLG}$.

$$x(t_0 + \Delta t) \approx \Phi_3^{MLG}(t_0 + \Delta t; a_0, \dots, a_3), \quad \text{where } \Delta t < \rho \tag{8.64}$$

6. Figure 8.5 compares the results computed by the multi-step procedure with the exact solution $x(t) = \sin(t)$, where the parameters $t_0 = 0, x_0 = 0, t_1 = -0.1, x_1 = \sin(-0.1), \Delta t = 0.1$ are used. Obviously, the approximated solution diverges quickly from the exact solution.

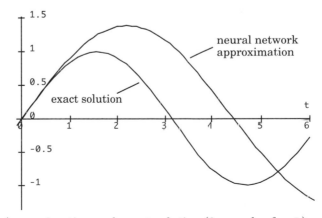

**Figure 8.5** Approximation and exact solution (2 samples for $\Psi$)

After increasing the number of past samples used for the Lagrange interpolation function $\Psi$ from 2 to 4, the approximation of the first derivative of $x(t)$ is improved considerably. Now, the results in Figures 8.6 and 8.7 show only small differences between the neural network output and the exact solution.

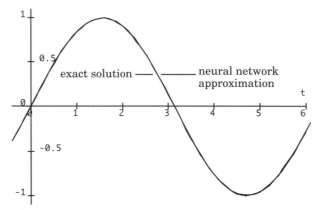

**Figure 8.6**   Approximation and exact solution (4 samples for $\Psi$)

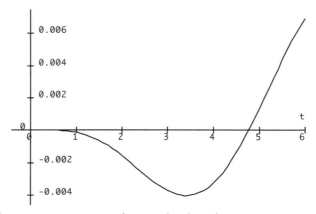

**Figure 8.7**   Approximation error (4 samples for $\Psi$)

## 8.7  Training Designed Neural Networks with Observation Data

The approximation quality of a neural network designed with our method depends on several factors. If the given differential equations and their physical parameters describe a dynamic system correctly, approximation errors are only introduced during the construction of the neural network. The size of the chosen network (the number of included parameters $a_k$) and the step size $\Delta t$ determine the achievable accuracy.

On the other hand, for modeling a dynamic system with differential equations, it is often necessary to rely on simplifying assumptions. Usually, not all influencing factors are known and approximation errors are introduced additionally by mis-specified differential equations.

If enough observation data of the dynamic system is available, we can train the neural network to reduce its approximation errors. In this way the knowledge embedded in the neural network can be refined or revised. First, an error function $E$ is constructed that measures the deviation of network approximations from observations. The mean-squared error (8.65) is typically used for that purpose:

$$E = \frac{1}{2} \sum_{i=1}^{N} \|\overline{x}_i - NN_i\|_2{}^2 \tag{8.65}$$

$\overline{x}_i = \overline{x}(t_0 + i \cdot \Delta t) = $ time series of observations

$\Delta t = $ time increment between observations

$N = $ length of time series

$NN_i = $ neural network output for observation $i$

Then, neural network training tries to minimize error $E$ by adapting the weights in the network. Recall the Modified Logistic Network (8.22) introduced in Section 8.4.1 and remember the network architecture described in Section 8.6.1. Note that the weights in the network described by Equation 8.22 are hardwired: The weights of the preprocessing layer (represented by the parameters $a_k$) are derived from the differential equation, whereas the weights of the middle and output layer are fixed. In order to train the network, we have to replace some of the fixed weights by flexible weights that can be adapted during training. There are several possibilities to do that:

1. The neural network represented by $\Phi_K^{MLG}(t; t_0; a_0, \dots, a_K)$ can be replaced by a composite network $\tilde{\Phi} = \Phi_K^{MLG}(t; t_0; a_0, \dots, a_K) + NN(t; t_0; \overline{w})$, where only the weights $\overline{w}$ of the second network $NN$ are trained. This network learns to compensate for the approximation errors of the initial network $\Phi_K^{MLG}$. There are no restrictions on the size or on the architecture of the neural network $NN$, but of course the total network will be larger than the initial network $\Phi_K^{MLG}$.

2. If we do not want to increase the size of the neural network, we can simply turn some of the fixed network weights into flexible weights. A good place to do that

are the middle and the output layer, because the number of weights is substantially smaller than in the preprocessing layer. If the backpropagation training algorithm is used, computing the gradient of the error function is also much easier for these weights than for those in the preprocessing layer. Basically, the arguments of the tanh functions in (8.22) are changed according to (8.66):

$$\tanh(a \cdot (t - t_0)) = tanh(a \cdot w - \theta) \tag{8.66}$$
$$w^0 = t - t_0 = \Delta t, \ \theta^0 = 0$$

After introducing the flexible network weights $v_k$, $w_{k,i}$ and the thresholds $\theta_{k,i}$, the network (8.22) turns into network (8.67). If the weights are initialized according to Equation 8.68, the function computed by the two networks is still identical, but network training will adapt the weights of (8.67) in order to minimize the network's approximation error.

$$\Phi_K^{MLG}(\overline{a}; \overline{v}, (w_{k,i}), (\theta_{k,i})) =$$
$$a_0 + \sum_{k=1}^{K} \left[ v_k \cdot \sum_{i=0}^{\lfloor \frac{K}{2} \rfloor} \frac{\tanh(a_k \cdot w_{k,i} - \theta_{k,i})^{2i+1}}{2i+1} \right] \tag{8.67}$$

$$v_k^0 = \tanh(t - t_0)^{k-1}, \ w_{k,i}^0 = t - t_0 = \Delta t, \ \theta_{k,i}^0 = 0 \tag{8.68}$$

The same strategy can be applied to the Radial Basis Function Network (8.29) of Section 8.4.2. Introducing the weights $v_k$, $z_{k,i}$ and $\sigma_{k,i}$ turns the network (8.29) into network (8.69). Again, initializing the weights according to (8.70) generates the same network output as (8.29).

$$\Phi_K^{RBF}(\overline{a}; \overline{v}, (z_{k,i}), (\sigma_{k,i})) =$$
$$a_0 + \sum_{k=1}^{K} \left[ v_k \cdot \sum_{i=1}^{K} \frac{b_i \cdot e^{i-1}}{2^i \cdot i!} \cdot \left[ \frac{1}{e} - e^{-\left(\frac{a_k - z_{k,i}}{\sigma_{k,i}}\right)^2} \right]^i \right] \tag{8.69}$$

$$v_k^0 = \left( \frac{1}{e} - e^{-((t-t_0)-1)^2} \right)^{k-1}, \ z_{k,i}^0 = \sigma_{k,i}^0 = \frac{1}{t - t_0} = \frac{1}{\Delta t} \tag{8.70}$$

After replacing some of the network's fixed weights by flexible weights, most neural network training algorithms can be applied to reduce the approximation error $E$. Gradient-based algorithms like the backpropagation algorithm described in (Rumelhart and McClelland, 1986) are well suited for these problems.

---

## 8.8    Application to Forecasting of Chaotic Time Series

A traditional application of neural networks is *time series forecasting* (see (Kimoto et al., 1990), (Weigend et al., 1990), (Dorronsoro and López, 1991), (Wong, 1991) or (Hoptroff, 1993)). A time series is a series of observations of a dynamic system which are taken at regular time intervals. If the future behavior of the dynamic system should be determined, we speak of *forecasting* or *predicting* the time series. Neural networks can be used as a black-box model of the unknown process generating the time series, and the network can be trained to forecast the future behavior, given the past observations of the series. Sometimes, the time series results from observing a deterministic physical process whose dynamic behavior is described by differential equations. For such applications, forecasting the future evolution of the series is equivalent to approximating the solution of the differential equation, given the current state as initial condition.

In this context, our neural network design algorithm can be used to construct neural networks for forecasting the future behavior of time series. In case the knowledge of the generating process is complete, the network will be fully specified by the design algorithm. If the knowledge is incomplete however, the network will contain free parameters, which can be determined by using common neural network learning algorithms. In this way, any knowledge in the form of differential equations can be incorporated into the neural network and the discrepancies with respect to the real process can be reduced or even removed by additional learning.

In this section, neural networks will be constructed for forecasting time series generated by chaotic differential equations. In science, *chaos* is used as a synonym for *irregular behavior*, whose long-term development is essentially *unpredictable*, see (Schuster, 1988). Chaotic differential equations exhibit not only irregular behavior, but they are also unstable with respect to small perturbations of their initial conditions. Consequently, it is difficult to forecast the future of time series based on chaotic differential equations, and they should be a good benchmark for a neural network design algorithm. In this section, we test the performance of the resulting neural networks for the Lorenz system of differential equations.

### 8.8.1  Lorenz System

The Lorenz system (8.71) of differential equations is an idealization of a hydrodynamic system, which serves as a simplified model for studying turbulence in fluids (see (Lorenz, 1963)):

$$
\begin{aligned}
x'(t) &= \sigma \cdot y(t) - \sigma \cdot x(t) \\
y'(t) &= -x(t) \cdot z(t) + r \cdot x(t) - y(t) \\
z'(t) &= x(t) \cdot y(t) - b \cdot z(t) \\
x(t_0) &= x_0 \\
y(t_0) &= y_0 \\
z(t_0) &= z_0
\end{aligned}
\tag{8.71}
$$

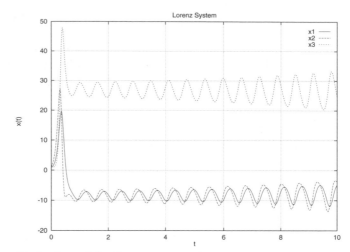

**Figure 8.8**   Evolution of the Lorenz system.

We use the notation introduced in Equations 8.72, which embeds the Lorenz system into our framework:

$$x_1'(t) = A \cdot (x_2(t) - x_1(t))$$
$$x_2'(t) = -x_1(t) \cdot x_3(t) + B \cdot x_1(t) - x_2(t)$$
$$x_3'(t) = x_1(t) \cdot x_2(t) - C \cdot x_3(t) \tag{8.72}$$
$$x_1(t_0) = x_{1,0}$$
$$x_2(t_0) = x_{2,0}$$
$$x_3(t_0) = x_{3,0}$$

Lorenz has shown that the behavior of system (8.72) becomes nonperiodic for some parameter sets. Moreover, it is unstable with respect to small modifications of the initial conditions, which is characteristic for chaotic systems.

The following Figures 8.8 and 8.9 illustrate the evolution of the Lorenz system for the critical parameters $A = 10, B = 28, C = 8/3$. Note that for this chapter, all reference models are generated with the numerical integration procedure *D02PCF* of the NAG-library [3] (see (NAG Library., 1994)). It is based on an adaptive Runge-Kutta method.

Figure 8.8 shows the evolution of the Lorenz system with initial conditions $t_0 = 0$, $x_{1,0} = x_{2,0} = x_{3,0} = 1$. First, periodic stationary behavior seems to establish, but Figure 8.9 reveals that after some time, nonperiodic chaotic behavior emerges.

We now develop a neural network for the approximation of the Lorenz system:

---

3. NAG is a registered trademark of The Numerical Algorithms Group Limited, Wilkinson House, Jordan Hill Road, Oxford, OX2 8DR, United Kingdom.

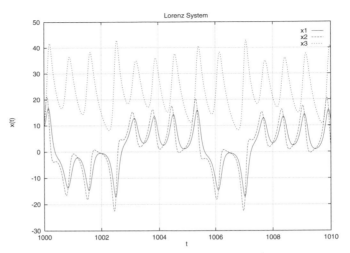

**Figure 8.9** Evolution of the Lorenz system after $t = 10^3$.

1. Since the differential equations are already in polynomial form, no transformation is necessary.

2. For each variable $x_1(t) \ldots x_3(t)$, we have to choose an approximation function $\Phi_K^i$. We select the Radial Basis Function Networks (8.73) with five parameters $a_{i,0} \ldots a_{i,4}$.

$$x_i(t) \approx \Phi_4^{RBF_i}(t; t_0; a_{i,0}, \ldots, a_{i,4}), \text{ for } i = 1 \ldots 3 \tag{8.73}$$

3. We substitute approximation functions $\Phi_4^{RBF_i}$ for $x_i(t)$ in the equations generated by successive differentiation, and we get an equation system for the parameters $a_{i,k}$ (omitted).

4. The equation system is solved for the parameters $a_{i,k}$, resulting in the values (8.74) to (8.85). The values of $a_{1,4}, a_{2,4}$ and $a_{3,4}$ are omitted, see (Cozzio, 1995) for all results.

$$a_{1,0} = x_{1,0} \tag{8.74}$$

$$a_{1,1} = (x_{1,0} - x_{2,0}) \cdot A \cdot e \tag{8.75}$$

$$a_{1,2} = \frac{A \cdot e^2}{4} (x_{1,0} \cdot (A + B) - x_{2,0} \cdot (A + 1) - x_{1,0} \cdot x_{3,0}) \tag{8.76}$$

$$a_{1,3} = \frac{A \cdot e^3}{48} \begin{pmatrix} x_{1,0} \cdot (3A + 5B + 4A \cdot B + 2A^2) - \\ x_{2,0} \cdot (5 + 5A + 2A \cdot B + 2A^2) - \\ x_{1,0} \cdot x_{3,0} \cdot (5 + 4A + 2C) + \\ x_{2,0} \cdot x_{3,0} \cdot 2A + x_{1,0}^2 \cdot x_{2,0} \cdot 2 \end{pmatrix} \tag{8.77}$$

$$a_{2,0} = x_{2,0} \tag{8.78}$$

$$a_{2,1} = -(x_{1,0} \cdot B - x_{2,0} - x_{1,0} \cdot x_{3,0}) \cdot e \tag{8.79}$$

$$a_{2,2} = \frac{-e^2}{4} \left( \begin{array}{l} x_{1,0} \cdot (B + A \cdot B) - x_{2,0} \cdot (A \cdot B + 1) - \\ x_{1,0} \cdot x_{3,0} \cdot (A + C + 1) + \\ x_{2,0} \cdot x_{3,0} \cdot A + x_{1,0}^2 \cdot x_{2,0} \end{array} \right) \tag{8.80}$$

$$a_{2,3} = \frac{-e^3}{48} \left( \begin{array}{l} x_{1,0} \cdot (A \cdot (5B + 2A \cdot B + 2B^2) + 5B) - \\ x_{2,0} \cdot (5 + 7A \cdot B + 2A^2 \cdot B) - \\ x_{1,0} \cdot x_{3,0} \cdot (5 + A \cdot (5 + 4B + 4C + 2A) + 5C + 2C^2) + \\ x_{2,0} \cdot x_{3,0} \cdot A \cdot (7 + 2A + 4C) + \\ x_{1,0}^2 \cdot x_{2,0} \cdot (7 + 6A + 2C) - x_{1,0} \cdot x_{2,0}^2 \cdot 6A + \\ x_{1,0} \cdot x_{3,0}^2 \cdot 2A - x_{1,0}^3 \cdot 2B + x_{1,0}^3 \cdot x_{3,0} \cdot 2 \end{array} \right) \tag{8.81}$$

$$a_{3,0} = x_{3,0} \tag{8.82}$$

$$a_{3,1} = (x_{3,0} \cdot C - x_{1,0} \cdot x_{2,0}) \cdot e \tag{8.83}$$

$$a_{3,2} = \frac{-e^2}{4} \left( \begin{array}{l} -x_{3,0} \cdot C^2 + x_{1,0} \cdot x_{2,0} \cdot (A + C + 1) - \\ x_{1,0}^2 \cdot B - x_{2,0}^2 \cdot A + x_{1,0}^2 \cdot x_{3,0} \end{array} \right) \tag{8.84}$$

$$a_{3,3} = \frac{-e^3}{48} \left( \begin{array}{l} -x_{3,0} \cdot (3C^2 + 2C^3) + \\ x_{1,0} \cdot x_{2,0} \cdot (5 + A \cdot (7 + 2A + 8B + 2C) + 5C + 2C^2) - \\ x_{1,0} \cdot x_{2,0} \cdot x_{3,0} \cdot 8A + x_{1,0}^2 \cdot B \cdot (2C - 6A - 5) - \\ x_{2,0}^2 \cdot A \cdot (9 + 2C + 2A) + \\ x_{1,0}^2 \cdot x_{3,0} \cdot (5 + 6A + 4C) - x_{1,0}^3 \cdot x_{2,0} \cdot 2 \end{array} \right) \tag{8.85}$$

5. The single-step integration procedure (8.86) is completed by inserting the re-solved parameters $a_{i,k}$ into $\Phi_4^{RBF_i}$.

$$\begin{aligned} x_i(t_0 + \Delta t) &\approx \Phi_4^{RBF_i}(t_0 + \Delta t; t_0; a_{i,0}, \dots, a_{i,4}) \\ &= \hat{\Phi}_4^{RBF_i}(\Delta t; x_{1,0}, x_{2,0}, x_{3,0}; A, B, C) \end{aligned} \tag{8.86}$$

## 8.8.2  One-Step-Ahead Forecasts

For our first experiment, we use the single-step integration procedure (8.86) for generating one-step-ahead forecasts of the Lorenz system. During each integration

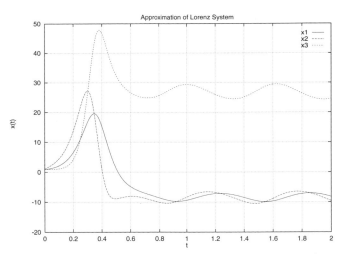

**Figure 8.10**   One-step-ahead forecasts and the reference model ($t_0 = 0$).

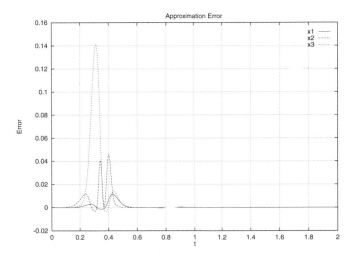

**Figure 8.11**   Approximation error of one-step-ahead forecasts ($t_0 = 0$).

step, the last state observation of the system is entered into the neural network to predict the new state after the next time step. Figure 8.10 illustrates the approximation quality that can be achieved with this method, showing only small approximation errors in Figure 8.11 ($A = 10, B = 28, C = 8/3, t_0 = 0, x_{1,0} = x_{2,0} = x_{3,0} = 1, \Delta t = 0.001$).

Figure 8.12 shows the one-step-ahead forecasts for the parameters $A = 10, B = 28, C = 8/3, t_0 = 10^3, x_{1,0} = x_{2,0} = x_{3,0} = 10, \Delta t = 0.001$. The approximation errors are displayed in Figure 8.13.

In general, the approximation errors of the one-step-ahead forecasts are quite small, but they are maximal wherever the trajectory of the Lorenz system changes

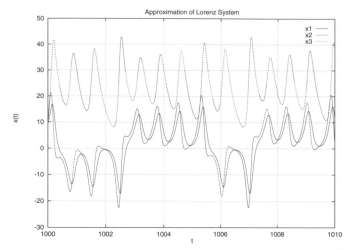

**Figure 8.12**  One-step-ahead forecasts and reference model ($t_0 = 10^3$).

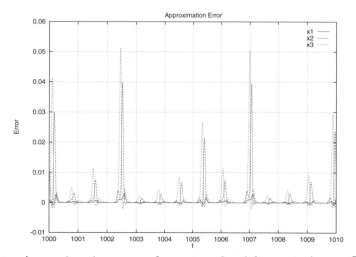

**Figure 8.13**  Approximation error of one-step-ahead forecasts ($t_0 = 10^3$).

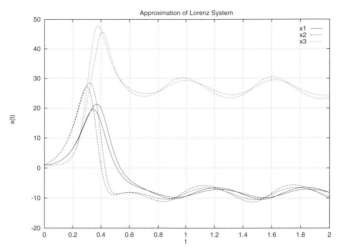

**Figure 8.14**   Repeated forecasts and reference model ($t_0 = 0$).

direction.

### 8.8.3   Repeated Forecasts

If forecasts for time horizons longer than one time step should be obtained, the standard approach of iterating a one-step-ahead forecasting procedure can be used. This is equivalent to iterating the single-step integration procedure for the approximation of differential equations, where intermediate approximation errors accumulate. Therefore, only the initial state is taken from the observations and all subsequent forecasts are generated by feeding back the previous forecasts as input into the network. Figure 8.14 compares the repeated forecasts of the neural network with the reference model. Again, we use the parameters $A = 10, B = 28, C = 8/3, t_0 = 0, x_{1,0} = x_{2,0} = x_{3,0} = 1$ with a step size of $\Delta t = 0.001$. The approximation errors are shown in Figure 8.15. The repeated forecasts diverge soon from the reference model, but the approximation error remains bounded.

The first neural network for the approximation of the Lorenz system is based on Radial Basis Function Networks. Of course, Modified Logistic Networks discussed in Section 8.4.1 can be chosen as well. The next experiment shown in Figure 8.16 demonstrates that a Modified Logistic Network provides better repeated forecasts of the Lorenz system with step size $\Delta t = 0.001$ than a Radial Basis Function Network. The approximation errors for the Modified Logistic Network are shown in Figure 8.17.

We repeat both experiments for the parameters $t_0 = 10^3, x_{1,0} = x_{2,0} = x_{3,0} = 10$. Figure 8.18 shows the repeated forecasts of the Radial Basis Function Network. Its approximation errors are displayed in Figure 8.19.

Figure 8.20 displays the forecasts of the Modified Logistic Network for $t_0 = 10^3$, where the corresponding approximation errors are illustrated in Figure 8.21.

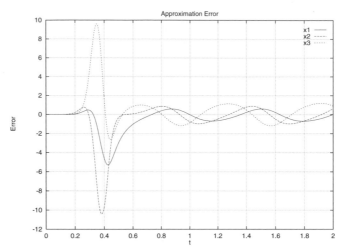

**Figure 8.15**   Approximation error of repeated forecasts ($t_0 = 0$).

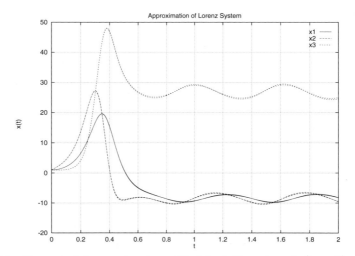

**Figure 8.16**   Repeated forecasts of modified logistic network ($t_0 = 0$).

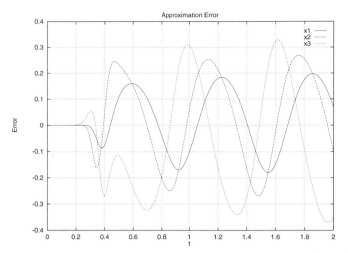

**Figure 8.17**   Approximation error of modified logistic network ($t_0 = 0$).

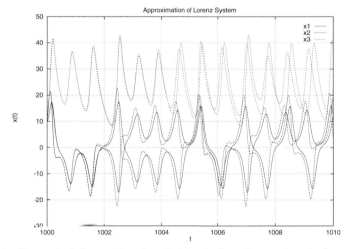

**Figure 8.18**   Repeated forecasts of radial basis function network ($t_0 = 10^3$).

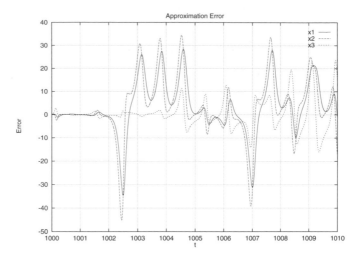

**Figure 8.19**   Approximation error of radial basis function network ($t_0 = 10^3$).

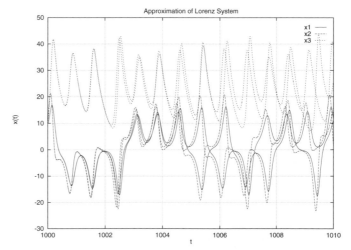

**Figure 8.20**   Repeated forecasts of modified logistic network ($t_0 = 10^3$).

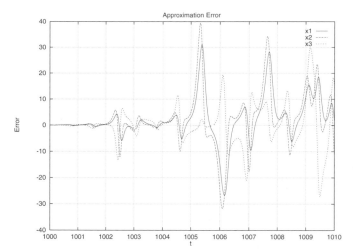

**Figure 8.21**   Approximation error of modified logistic network ($t_0 = 10^3$).

The repeated forecasts of the Modified Logistic Network exhibit superior long-term behavior, because they reach the error level of the Radial Basis Function Network much later.

## 8.9   Conclusions

In this chapter, we have explored a method for the design of neural networks that uses application specific knowledge. Although it is common in the field of neural networks to replace application specific knowledge and algorithms by data and learning, neglecting available knowledge is an inefficient usage of information. For complex problems, where neural networks reveal their own specific difficulties like inefficient learning or bad generalization, the usage of apriori knowledge can decide on success or failure. We therefore support the approach that all available information should be used, regardless of whether it is available as data or in the form of structured knowledge.

The main advantages of using apriori knowledge for the design of neural networks are smaller needs for learning data, improved training efficiency and better generalization. The potential for such improvements varies from application to application, but literature studies show consistent benefits for a wide range of different applications.

In this chapter, we have concentrated on the usage of differential equations for the design of neural networks, because they are an important type of *a priori* knowledge which has not been covered before. We have developed a method for constructing neural networks for the approximation of differential equations. The algorithm determines the structure as well as the weights of a network. It generates a set of equations for the network weights by the method of successive differentiation of the differential equations. This is a variant of the Taylor series method generalized to non-polynomial approximation functions.

We have identified a set of conditions to guarantee the solvability of these equations, which depends on the properties of the derivatives of a neural network. Consequently, our algorithm is not restricted to one specific neural network architecture. All classes of neural networks that satisfy the conditions can be used. Both the Radial Basis Function Networks and the Modified Logistic Networks have been shown to meet these requirements. They belong to special classes of neural networks that are able to implement polynomials of their members exactly. This property has made it much easier to derive networks that are suitable for our algorithm.

We have shown that most ordinary differential equations that are relevant for modeling physical processes can be transformed into polynomial first order systems. Consequently, the solutions of the network equations are polynomial expressions of the network inputs, which requires the introduction of a preprocessing layer in the network. If we restrict ourselves to linear differential equations, we do not need this preprocessing layer. In this case, we can keep the standard network architecture. Therefore, the general network architecture created by the design algorithm consists of four layers: An input layer, a preprocessing layer, a middle layer and an output layer. All weights of the network are specified: The weights from the middle layer to the output layer are fixed, and the weights from the polynomial preprocessing layer to the middle layer are derived from the differential equation. Also the direct connections from the input layer to the output layer are fixed. The final architecture is called *Higher-Order Radial Basis Function Network* or *Higher-Order Modified Logistic Network* respectively.

In principle, we can approximate virtually all differential equations of practical interest with neural networks designed by our algorithm. Nevertheless, the complexity of the resulting networks and the induced numerical problems pose practical limits. For example, the transformation of a system of differential equations into polynomial form can expand its size substantially. Moreover, the size of the generated network is of cubic order relative to the number of derivatives that should match the differential equation. This means that the complexity of the preprocessing layer increases quickly. Obviously, standard numerical integration procedures achieve the same results more efficiently. However, many applications are characterized by incomplete differential equations, where observation data is available. For such applications the learning capabilities of the neural networks outweigh the disadvantages. These are the applications we are aiming for.

The neural networks obtained by our design algorithm have been used to construct single-step and multi-step numerical integration procedures. Multi-step procedures for higher order differential equations can be constructed by approximating the lower order derivatives with finite differences. This introduces additional approximation errors, however it is useful for applications, where only the main variables can be measured, but not their derivatives.

We have tested the approximation quality of the networks by forecasting time series generated by sampling the Lorenz system of chaotic differential equations.

In all tests, the Modified Logistic Networks proved to be superior to the Radial Basis Function Networks. After initial design, these networks can still learn from observation data. This allows an optimal integration of both *a priori* knowledge and of learning data into neural networks.

# References

Barton, D. 1980. On Taylor series and stiff equations. *ACM Transactions on Mathematical Software*, 6(3):280–294.

Barton, D., Willers, I. M., and Zahar, R. V. M. 1971. The automatic solution of systems of ordinary differential equations by the method of Taylor series. *The Computer Journal*, 14(3):243–248.

Campbel, E. S., Buehler, R., Hirschfelder, J. O., and Hughes, D. 1961. Numerical construction of Taylor series approximations for a set of simultaneous first order differential equations. *Journal of the ACM*, 8:374–383.

Chang, Y. F. 1974. Automatic solution of differential equations. In *Constructive and Computational Methods for Differential and Integral Equations, Lecture Notes in Math. 430*. Springer-Verlag.

Corliss, G. and Chang, Y. F. 1982. Solving ordinary differential equations using Taylor series. *ACM Transactions on Mathematical Software*, 8(2):114–144.

Corliss, G. and Lowery, D. 1977. Choosing a step size for Taylor series methods for solving ODEs. *Journal of Computational and Applied Mathematics*, 3(4):251–256.

Cotter, N. E. and Conwell, P. R. 1990. The Stone-Weierstrass theorem and its application to neural networks. *IEEE Transactions on Neural Networks*, 1(4).

Cotter, N. E. and Conwell, P. R. 1993. Universal approximation by phase series and fixed-weight networks. *Neural Computation*, 5:359–362.

Cozzio, R. A. 1995. *The Design of Neural Networks using a priori Knowledge, Diss. ETH No. 10991*. Ph.D. thesis, Swiss Federal Institute of Technology, Zurich, Switzerland.

Cybenko, G. 1989. Approximation by superpositions of a sigmoidal function. *Math. Control Signals Systems*, 2:303–314.

Dorronsoro, J. R. and López, V. 1991. Neural network learning of polynomial formats for coupled time series. In *Artificial Neural Networks*, eds. T. Kohonen, K. Makisara, O. Simula, and J. Kangas, pp. 201–206. North-Holland.

Fairén, V., López, V., and Conde, L. 1988. Power series approximation to solutions of nonlinear systems of differential equations. *Am. J. Phys.*, 56(1).

Funahashi, K.-I. 1989. On the approximate realization of continuous mappings by neural networks. *Neural Networks*, 2:183–192.

Girosi, F. and Poggio, T. 1990. Networks and the best approximation property.

*Biological Cybernetics*, 63:169–176.

Hairer, E., Nørsett, S. P., and Wanner, G. 1991. *Solving Ordinary Differential Equations I: Nonstiff Problems*, vol. 8 of *Springer Series in Computational Mathematics*. Springer-Verlag, 2nd edn.

Hartman, E. J., Keeler, J. D., and Kowalski, J. M. 1990. Layered neural networks with Gaussian hidden units as universal approximations. *Neural Computation*, 2:210–215.

Henrici, P. 1956. Automatic computations with power series. *Journal of the ACM*, 3(1):15.

Hoptroff, R. G. 1993. The principles and practice of time series forecasting and business modelling using neural nets. *Neural Computing & Applications*, 1:59–66.

Hornik, K., Stinchcombe, M., and White, H. 1990. Universal approximation of an unknown mapping and its derivatives using multilayer feedforward networks. *Neural Networks*, 3:551–560.

Ito, Y. 1992. Approximations of continuous functions on rd by linear combinations of shifted rotations of a sigmoid function with and withoud scaling. *Neural Networks*, 5:105–115.

Kerner, E. H. 1981. Universal formats for nonlinear ordinary differential systems. *J. Math. Phys.*, 22(7):1366–1371.

Kimoto, T., Asakawa, K., Yoda, M., and Takeoka, M. 1990. Stock market prediction system with modular neural networks. In *Proceedings of the International Joint Conference on Neural Networks*, vol. 2, pp. 1–6.

Leavitt, J. A. 1966. Methods and applications of power series. *Mathematics of Computation*, 20:46–52.

Lee, Y. C., Doolen, G., Chen, H. H., Sun, G. Z., Maxwell, T., Lee, H. Y., and Giles, C. L. 1986. Machine learning using a higher order correlation network. *Physica D*, 22:276–306.

Lorenz, E. N. 1963. Deterministic nonperiodic flow. *Journal of the Atmospheric Sciences*, 20:130–141.

NAG Library. 1994. *The NAG Fortran Library Manual, Mark 16*, vol. 2. The Numerical Algorithms Group Limited.

Narendra, K. S. and Parthasarathy, K. 1990. Identification and control of dynamical systems using neural networks. *IEEE Transactions on Neural Networks*, 1(1):4–27.

Norman, A. C. 1976. Expanding the solutions of implicit sets of ordinary differential equations in power series. *The Computer Journal*, 19(1):63–68.

Park, J. and Sandberg, I. W. 1991. Universal approximation using radial-basis-function networks. *Neural Computation*, 3:246–257.

Park, J. and Sandberg, I. W. 1993. Approximation and radial-basis-function networks. *Neural Computation*, 5:305–316.

Pineda, F. J. 1987. Generalization of backpropagation to recurrent and higher order neural networks. In *Proceedings of the IEEE Conference on Neural Information Processing Systems (NIPS)*, pp. 602–611. IEEE.

Poggio, T. 1990. Networks for approximation and learning. *Proceedings of the IEEE*, 78(9):1481–1497.

Powell, M. J. D. 1987. Radial basis functions for multivariable interpolation: A review. In *Algorithms for Approximation*, eds. J. C. Mason and M. G. Cox. Clarendon Press, Oxford.

Rumelhart, D. E. and McClelland, J. L. 1986. *Parallel Distributed Processing: Explorations in the Microstructure of Cognition*, vol. I & II. MIT Press.

Schuster, H. G. 1988. *Deterministic Chaos*. VCH Verlagsgesellschaft mbH, 2nd edn.

Sejnowski, T. J. 1986. Higher-order Boltzmann machines. *Proceedings of American Institute of Physics*, 151:398–403.

Stinchcombe, M. and White, H. 1989. Universal approximation using feedforward networks with non-sigmod hidden layer activation functions. In *Proceedings of the International Joint Conference on Neural Networks*, vol. I, pp. 613–617. IEEE.

Weigend, A. S., Hubermann, B., and Rumelhart, D. E. 1990. Predicting the future: A connectionnist approach. *International Journal of Neural Systems*, 1(3):193–209.

White, D. A. and Sofge, D. A. 1992. *Handbook of Intelligent Control: Neural, Fuzzy, and Adaptive Approaches*. Multiscience Press, Inc.

Wong, F. S. 1991. Time series forecasting using backpropagation neural networks. In *Neurocomputing*, vol. 2, pp. 147–159.

Wu, W.-T. 1984. Basic principles of mechanical theorem proving in geometries. *Journal of Sys. Sci. and Math. Sci.*, 3(4):207–235.

# 9     Fynesse: A Hybrid Architecture for Self-Learning Control

Martin Riedmiller, Martin Spott and Joachim Weisbrod

*This chapter presents a novel controller design method that exploits principles of knowledge-based neurocomputing to realize a hybrid controller architecture that is able to learn to control a priori unknown nonlinear dynamical systems autonomously. It allows the user to interpret, examine and correct the acquired control strategy in every stage of learning. Based on five requirements that are essential for a widely applicable learning controller, the hybrid control architecture* FYNESSE *is derived: The control strategy is represented by a fuzzy relation that can be interpreted and contains* a priori *knowledge, whereas the more complex part of learning is solved by a neural network that is trained by* dynamic programming *methods. The advantages of both paradigms, learning capability of neural networks and interpretability of fuzzy systems, are preserved since the two modules are strictly separated. The application of the* FYNESSE *controller to a chemical plant demonstrates the high quality of autonomously learned control. Furthermore it shows the benefits of the integration of* a priori *knowledge and the interpretation of the controller in terms of fuzzy rules.*

## 9.1   Introduction

Self learning of appropriate control behavior assuming only a minimum of external knowledge about the system to be controlled is a field of growing research interest. The use of self-learning methods instead of costly analytical modeling promises the ability to control arbitrary systems without worrying about their probably very complex internal structure. The obvious advantage of an autonomously learning controller therefore lies in the fact that the effort to design an appropriate control law is removed from the human expert and executed instead by a machine. Another aspect which is perhaps less obvious but nevertheless of crucial importance is the modeling aspect: Analytical approaches are typically based on a mathematical model of the system to be controlled. Very often, linear models are used to approximate the system behavior, because they allow exploitation of a wide theory of linear controller design methods. But even if more complex models are used, it is unlikely that all effects that occur in a real system can be described exactly. Therefore, a model is always an approximation to reality, and analytical controller design can at most be as good as the validity of the model. Also, analytical statements about closed loop behavior, for example stability issues, are given with respect to the model rather than with respect to the real system itself.

A self-learning controller that is able to learn an appropriate control behavior by *directly* interacting with the real system and drawing the right conclusions, would not suffer from the above problem of an approximate mathematical model. Also, if reality may be sufficiently well described by a model, but the model is too complicated to be handled analytically, a learning controller might be more appropriate. However, some benefits of analytical controller design, for example the analytical proof of stability, will be sacrificed if no analytical model is assumed. Due to the importance of stability issues, other ways of guaranteeing the correct functioning of the controller, e.g. numerical methods or less rigorous checks for plausibility, have to be applied.

Although the concept of autonomously learning control is very appealing, several aspects known from classical control theory must be considered in order to find an approach that is a real alternative to classical methods. Unfortunately, as criticized in (Geva and Sitte, 1993), many learning approaches are tailored to a special application which make them difficult to compare and to apply in a more general framework.

Therefore, the design of the proposed FYNESSE[1] architecture was driven by five requirements that are fundamental for a reasonable and widely applicable learning controller. They include the demand for learning when only the control target is given and no other *a priori* knowledge can be assumed, the need for the correct treatment of temporal or dynamic effects and the possibility to integrate and extract control knowledge.

What we derive from our basic requirements turns out to be a hybrid system. It contains both a neural network and a fuzzy module. Recently, neuro-fuzzy systems have become a very active field of research. There are many attempts to combine learning capabilities with the possibility of interpreting and understanding knowledge. From this point of view, the combination of neural networks (learning capabilities) and fuzzy systems (natural language representation) seems very promising. Most of these systems realize a fuzzy controller by a neural network, e.g. (Berenji and Khedkar, 1992; Nauck et al., 1993; Sulzberger et al., 1993; Jang, 1992; Bersini et al., 1993; Glorennec, 1993; Wang, 1994; Eppler, 1993) by translating the concepts of fuzzy control to neural networks and by exploiting learning algorithms like backpropagation. The fusion of neuro and fuzzy systems are based on some compromises. On the one hand, special neural networks are used that tend to lose the basic property of distributed representations. In most neuro-fuzzy sys-

---

1. FYNESSE stands for (**F**uzz**y**-**Ne**uro control **s**yst**e**m)

tems, each neuron plays a distinct role with a fixed interpretation. There is no real room for self-organization; this leads to reduced learning capabilities. The embedded fuzzy systems, on the other hand, are simplified to parametrized models with restricted approximation capabilities. In many applications these compromises have been shown to work satisfactorily—for example in the case of supervised learning for function approximation.

Here we focus on another class of problems, namely the autonomous learning of control tasks. As we will see, to solve such problems, we will need important properties of each paradigm individually to appropriately address different aspects of the overall job. Hence within the FYNESSE architecture presented in this chapter, the fuzzy and the neural network paradigms are strictly separated and realized in two interacting (coprocessing) modules.

The contents of this chapter are organized as follows. In Section 9.2 five *essential requirements* for the control architecture are put forward that form the basis of our *design decisions* in Section 9.3. This leads to the introduction of the *main concepts* and *degrees of freedom* of the FYNESSE control architecture in Section 9.4. Section 9.5 explains the different parts and mechanisms of FYNESSE in detail, the procedure of self-learning to control a plant is demonstrated on the example of a chemical plant in Section 9.6. *Conclusions* close the chapter.

## 9.2 Essential Requirements

The design of the FYNESSE architecture has been guided by five fundamental requirements that are presented below. From our point of view, these requirements specify essential aspects that a system capable of learning to control should definitely address.

### 9.2.1 Dynamical Systems

In many real world control applications, the management of temporal effects plays a central role. This is due to the dynamic nature of physical systems, which means that a certain event may not only influence the immediate response, but may also have a considerabe influence on the behavior of the system for a long time in the future. As a consequence, if we want to influence a system to behave in a 'controlled' manner, we have to ensure that each control decision takes its future consequences into account. Every controller design method, whether analytical or not, has to address this important aspect. In classical control theory dynamical effects are handled within the framework of differential equations. In the context of learning systems, which is the focus of this chapter, the correct treatment of dynamic effects inevitably leads to the hard-to-solve situation which is known as the *temporal credit assignment* problem.

### Requirement 1
If we want to manage interesting real world systems, we have to take care of dynamic properties.

## 9.2.2   Autonomous Learning

In situations where we have an expert who already knows how to control a certain system, supervised learning methods may be applied simply to imitate the strategy of the expert. Reasons for this type of learning may be to substitute the expert in order to have a faster or cheaper control system. Additionally, one often aims at exploiting the generalization abilities of the learning mechanism, i.e. to find sensible answers in situations that have never been presented before. Nevertheless, in order to conduct learning from examples we need a teacher who already knows the correct answers for at least a sufficiently large number of situations.

Very often we are faced with the control of systems where no expert control knowledge is available. This is the scenario of *autonomous learning* which is the focus of this chapter. The idea behind this approach is that a learning system should be able to learn a given task, when it is told only if its current behavior is either good or bad. The situation gets even more complicated if this judgement is not given after each decision, but only after the result of a complete *sequence* of decisions is observed. Clearly, this corresponds perfectly with the properties already mentioned about dynamical systems: current events or decisions can influence the complete future behavior of a system. Consequently, only the final outcome can determine the appropriateness of each control decision taken so far.

### Requirement 2
In order to manage complex processes where no or hardly any *a priori* knowledge is available, the learning procedure should be able to learn from as little information as possible.

## 9.2.3   Quality of Control

Given a concrete controller task, in general there are different competitive optimization goals. If, for instance, the controller is to control the temperature of a class room, such goals could be:

- Reach the desired temperature as fast as possible.
- Reach the desired temperature without overshooting.
- Control the temperature as economically as possible.

When trying to develop control laws that lead to high quality control behavior, it is obviously important to be able to specify the actual optimization goal(s) at hand.

### Requirement 3
The learning mechanism should be able to cope with explicit optimization goals.

### 9.2.4 Integration of *a priori* Knowledge

To learn a complete control policy from scratch is not always feasible, especially in the situation where there is no computer simulation of the process at hand, and consequently the adaptation has to take place on the real process. In such a situation it is obvious that the initial controller cannot act in an arbitrary way: the system and/or the controller may get damaged and people may be endangered.

Therefore, for some tasks it is a fundamental requirement to be able to incorporate *a priori* control knowledge. In many situations, a coarse and basic controller strategy represents a prerequisite for adaptation without simulation.

If adaptation starts from such an initially sensitive controller, both convergence speed and chances for success may improve dramatically as well.

#### *Requirement 4*
If there is some *a priori* knowledge in the controller's strategy, we should be able to integrate this knowledge into the initial controller.

### 9.2.5 Interpretation

It is often important to understand a controller's strategy. There are several reasons for being interested in an interpretation of the control knowledge:

- First of all, this understanding may give insight into the process to be controlled.
- Especially in safety critical applications we need to understand why the controller is acting the way it does.
- Many people do not trust a black box. They need some plausible explanations to be convinced of the controller's performance.

Nevertheless, the most important task of a controller is to do its job as well as possible. Interpretation is less important. Therefore the ability to get an understanding of the controller strategy must not constrain the controller's adaptation facilities and performance.

#### *Requirement 5*
Whenever the controller makes a decision, we are interested in an explanation of this decision. Therefore we need ways to interpret and understand the controller's strategy, but interpretation facilities must not impose any constraints on controller performance.

## 9.3 Fundamental Design Decisions

In the following, we take a closer look at the above requirements and present methods that are able to address the different demands faced by an autonomously learning controller. As will be seen, the requirements are split roughly into two parts.

Requirements 1 to 3, control of dynamical systems, autonomous learning, and controller quality, mainly address the learning process. All three of them are concerned with the properties and characteristics that the learning mechanism can promise to hold for the emerging controller. On the other hand, Requirements 4 and 5, integration of *a priori* knowledge and interpretation, basically refer to the resulting controller itself, no matter how its control strategy has been developed. Requirements 1 to 3 influence the specification of the learning procedure (Section 9.3.1), whereas Requirements 4 and 5 apply to the representation of the controller knowledge (Section 9.3.2).

### 9.3.1  Autonomously Learning to Control

The desire for learning based on the simple information of success or failure requires finding a framework in which only the knowledge of the control target (and respectively avoidable situations) is sufficient for finding an appropriate solution. This means that the learning system should be able to evaluate previous trials accordingly, in order to finally find a suitable policy to reach the goal. Moreover, by Requirement 3 we want to be able to further specify the range of admissible solutions, such that the resulting policy fulfills certain aspects of quality. Finally, the desire to control dynamical systems requires the possibility of appropriately handling temporal effects. As we shall see in more detail in Section 9.5.1, all three aspects can be fulfilled within the framework of *Dynamic Programming*. Dynamic Programming methods aim at solving a certain class of optimization problems, where temporal effects play a central role. It will be shown later that the control tasks considered here fall into this class, and that the underlying learning problem can be formulated as a dynamic optimization problem.

However, there are two aspects of the considered problem situation that make the direct application of standard Dynamic Programming methods impossible:

- the dynamics of the process are unknown and
- the state space of the system is continuous.

These two aspects imply the need for a method that can learn and improve iteratively while interacting with the real process. A modified variant of Dynamic Programming therefore suggests that the optimization procedure is applied only to those situations that are actually visited during a control trial. This approach is called *Real-Time Dynamic Programming* (Barto et al., 1995) and will be discussed in further detail in Section 9.5.1. The idea is to execute control trials from different starting situations repeatedly, thereby improving the knowledge about the consequences of the current policy. This knowledge is represented in terms of estimated costs for each possible state and can be effectively used to optimize the policy.

The application of the above procedure to a system with a continuous state space immediately leads to the question of how to store the estimated costs for each state, since there are infinitely many possible states. This problem may be approached in various ways. One possibility is to partition the state space into a finite number of distinct boxes. The problem with this approach is that the granularity of the discretization must be determined in advance. Even worse, the number of boxes grows exponentially with the number of dimensions. For these reasons, we decided to use a feedforward neural network here. The costs are not explicitly stored for each state, but are computed by the neural network function. The neural mapping of states to their costs is determined by the parameters (weights) of the neural network, which are adapted during the learning phase. The advantage of the use of a neural network to represent the costs hence lies in the fact that a finite number of parameters is sufficient to represent an arbitrary mapping between continuous state information and the associated costs.

To summarize, we propose solving Requirements 1 to 3 using a neural network learning method based on Dynamic Programming. As we will see in Section 9.5.1, this offers the possibility of learning optimal control behavior when only minimal training information is available. However, the remaining Requirements 4 and 5 have not been considered up to now. To do so, we somehow have to represent the policy explicitly. This is explained in the following section.

### 9.3.2   Representation of Controller Knowledge

In order to be able to reason about controller strategies, we first of all need some explicit and intuitive representation of the controller knowledge. If, for instance, the controller is realized by a neural network, such an explicit and intuitive representation is missing. Therefore we are looking for a representation scheme that is both as general and as flexible as possible.

The job of a controller is to map inputs to outputs, i.e. sensory information to control actions. Ideally a controller is a mapping $c : I \to O$ from some input space $I$ into some output space $O$. Nevertheless, the following properties are not supported by such a simple mapping:

- In some situations there may be only one reasonable action, whereas in other states many control actions may be applicable.

- Some controller actions may be well established and resolute, whereas others are less determined. In the second case several control actions may be chosen as well.

- Especially when learning is complicated, it should be possible to represent stochastic information in order to explore the space of possible actions.

From this we conclude that representing the controller knowledge with a mapping is too restricted. By generalizing the notion of a mapping $c : I \to O$ we naturally derive the notion of a relation $C : I \times O \to \{0, 1\}$; then any sensory information may be mapped to more than one control action. Further generalizing the notion of a (crisp) relation into a fuzzy relation $\tilde{C} : I \times O \to [0, 1]$, we are finally able to differentiate the degree of applicability of several control actions.

The concept of a fuzzy control relation means: given some input state $i \in I$, for each $o \in O$ the value $\mu_C(i, o)$ represents the controller's knowledge concerning the "degree of applicability" of the control action $o$ in state $i$. Of course, there are several types of semantics on this "degree of applicability," see Section 9.4.2.2. There are numerous ways of deriving crisp answers from fuzzy relations, both deterministic and stochastic ones. And last but not least the crisp mapping $c$ from above is simply a special case of a fuzzy relation $\tilde{C}$.

With respect to Requirements 4 and 5, integration of *a priori* knowledge and interpretation, a fuzzy relation is a very reasonable choice. Relevant types of available *a priori* knowledge (Requirement 4) are fuzzy rule-based systems, statistical information (observation of human operators) and control mappings derived from classical control theory. All types can be represented by a fuzzy relation.

When it comes to the interpretation of a fuzzy relation (Requirement 5), we have to develop techniques to invert the above. In the first case of fuzzy rule-based systems, for instance, this means finding a set of rules with a relational representation matching the fuzzy relation at hand. If another form of intuitive knowledge representation is required, we have to develop corresponding approximation schemes. Since an exact approximation is not expected, these algorithms will be based on optimization procedures. Following Requirement 5 the main optimization goals are the comprehensibility of interpretation and, less important, the precision of approximation.

In conclusion, we observe that a fuzzy relation offers both the generality and the flexibility needed: Generality, since the notion of a fuzzy relation covers relevant types of control knowledge, and flexibility, since both the semantics of the membership degrees and the method of deriving control actions from fuzzy information are not restricted at all in contrast with other approaches (see Section 9.1).

## 9.4 The FYNESSE Architecture

The considerations above imply a combined approach, where learning and control facilities are divided into two separate modules with different properties. The two modules cooperate in order to solve the task as a whole (coprocessing). The first module, a neural feed-forward network that is used to implement an approximate Dynamic Programming method effectively and efficiently, takes care of satisfying Requirements 1 to 3. The second module, a fuzzy relation appropriate for integrating and extracting different types of information, is derived from Requirements 4 and 5.

At first glance it is not yet clear how to specify and where to put the interface between these two modules. Trying to answer these questions we found that there are actually two different learning tasks as well. The first task is to learn something about the future consequences when a certain action is applied in a current situation and what it means with respect to the desired global optimization goal. The second task is the local decision on whose action should be applied in a concrete situation. This division of the learning task into a critic and a controller module is already known in the literature in several variations and with different objectives; see e.g. (Barto et al., 1983), (Sutton, 1990), (Berenji and Khedkar, 1992). Since this approach perfectly matches the modularization into a neural network and a fuzzy relation derived from our requirements above, we decided to adapt the critic/controller paradigm to fit our needs.

In the following section, we explain how this concept is realized here and present the resulting FYNESSE architecture. In Section 9.4.2, we will discuss the remaining degrees of freedom and their impacts.

### 9.4.1   Main Concepts

From the above considerations that were derived from the requirements for a self-learning control architecture as stated in Section 9.1, we now formulate the concepts of the FYNESSE architecture. As we will see, besides some fundamental and fixed properties, the framework offers several degrees of freedom that can be parametrized according to the concrete requirements of the respective application.

The fundamental features of the FYNESSE control architecture are:

- use of two separate modules to learn to control and to explicitly represent the policy,

- learning is based on a neural implementation of Dynamic Programming methods and

- explicit representation of the controller by means of fuzzy relations

Both neural and fuzzy approaches are used within the FYNESSE architecture. Note, however, that crucially different from many neuro-fuzzy systems, within our framework no mixing of the two paradigms occurs. Instead, we allow the two separate modules to interact or communicate—the neural network based critic establishes the basis for changing the strategy represented by a fuzzy relation, and vice-versa, the explicit policy representation should help the critic to learn in a faster and more robust way. Originating from this concept of communication, various levels and modes of interaction can be derived. They establish various degrees of freedom which can be chosen according to the requirements of the respective control task. This is the focus of the following section.

### 9.4.2   Degrees of Freedom

#### *9.4.2.1   Types of a priori Knowledge*

As mentioned above, knowledge about the control strategy can be given in different ways:

- crisp control laws,
- fuzzy rules and

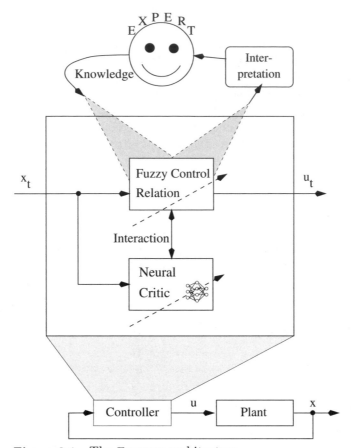

**Figure 9.1**    The FYNESSE architecture

■ statistical information.

Classical control theory leads to crisp control laws via an analytical model of the process. If that is not available or too difficult or expensive to develop an expert may formulate a controller in terms of fuzzy rules. Furthermore, by observing an existing controller (e.g. human operator) histograms may be obtained. All these types of a priori knowledge can be represented by a fuzzy relation.

### 9.4.2.2    Types of Fuzzy Control Relations

A single fuzzy control relation reflects the knowledge about the control strategy at a certain stage of learning. The uncertainty of the strategy may be measured by the *fuzziness* of the relation, but it is not possible to detect the stage of learning, i.e. locating situations that we have not yet learnt to handle. In (Weisbrod, 1996; Spott and Weisbrod, 1996) a concept was introduced that allows an explicit representation of ignorance and inconsistent knowledge. The idea is the use of two fuzzy relations, each attached to its own   semantics: one for positive and another for negative knowledge. In the case of complete ignorance, nothing can be supported (positive knowledge) and everything is possible (negative knowledge). Learning control then means that the support of good control actions will rise and bad ones will be forbidden. Since the neural critic itself changes during the learning phase, its evaluations of the controller's performance will be inconsistent over time. This case is reflected by the two relations: a control action may be supported and forbidden simultaneously. As it cannot be decided which evaluation is correct, inconsistent knowledge will be transformed into ignorance. The formal definition of consistent knowledge is that the level of possibility of a fact must be greater than or equal to the level of its support. In the case of an inconsistency, e.g. the support is greater than the possibility, we adapt the levels of support and possibility to enforce consistency. A simple method, for example, is to swap the values. In this way the level of inconsistency ($|possibility - support|$) becomes the level of ignorance.

Furthermore, the knowledge about regions of ignorance can be used for active control of the learning procedure: learn especially in those situations in which the controller is ignorant. In this way a good exploration of the system's state space can be guaranteed. All in all we have two basic possibilities to represent the fuzzy controller:

- one fuzzy control relation and
- two fuzzy control relations (positive/negative knowledge).

### 9.4.2.3 Application of the Fuzzy Control Relation

The fuzzy control relation maps a given (crisp or fuzzy) input onto a fuzzy output. As only crisp values can be applied to the plant the fuzzy output of the controller must be retransformed into a crisp value (*defuzzified*). Several methods are described in the literature of fuzzy systems, the choice of an appropriate one depends on the application:

- center of gravity,
- mean of maxima,
- stochastic defuzzification (in the learning phase) and
- others.

Since the control information in the fuzzy relation is induced by Dynamic Programming the method *mean of maxima* plays an important role in the context of FYNESSE (see Section 9.5.2.2).

### 9.4.2.4 Interpretation of the Controller's Strategy

Two main goals characterize the interpretation of the self-learned controller:

1. Comprehensibility of interpretation and
2. Quality of approximation.

The interpretation is intended as a mechanism that translates the numerical information in the fuzzy control relation into a form that can easily be understood by human experts. An intuitive form is given by fuzzy rules, e.g. "IF $x$ is $\tilde{A}$ THEN $u$ is $\tilde{B}$," where $x$ and $u$ are the input and output of the controller, $\tilde{A}$ and $\tilde{B}$ are fuzzy sets defined on the universes of input and output. The variables can be labeled with linguistic terms, i.e. we obtain linguistic rules like "IF *temperature* is high THEN open *valve* widely." Each rule represents partial knowledge about the control strategy. The aggregation of all rules covers and approximates the complete control relation. There are several degrees of freedom in the extraction of control rules:

- number of rules,
- shape of fuzzy sets $(\tilde{A}, \tilde{B})$,
- location of fuzzy sets and
- semantics of rules.

Since each expert applies his own standard to the interpretation, he should be able to restrict the degrees of freedom for his purpose. For example, he may want to restrict the number of rules or demand convex fuzzy sets. He must also lay down the semantics of "IF ... THEN ... " in the fuzzy rules: The most important interpretations are given by

- fuzzy logic (logical implication or logical conjunction) and a
- functional view (map $\tilde{A}$ onto $\tilde{B}$).

Especially the distribution of premises $\tilde{A}$ or conclusions $\tilde{B}$ may be too difficult for the expert, i.e. what part of the input/output space is covered by which rule. So, depending on the expert's requirements and his skills we can

- distribute premises or conclusions by hand or
- distribute premises or conclusions automatically.

The automation of rule extraction is one of our current research topics.

Clearly the main goals of interpretation are contradictory: The more exact the approximation of the control relation the more difficult the interpretation becomes for the expert. The reason for this is that the number of rules will increase and the shape and location of fuzzy sets will become incomprehensible with growing precision of approximation. Besides that, the control relation contains some noise that can be filtered out by a rougher approximation. On the whole the comprehensibility of interpretation is more important than its precision.

### 9.4.2.5  *Interaction between Critic and controller*

The main learning scheme in FYNESSE consists of three steps:

1. Incorporation of *a priori* knowledge,

2. Self-learning control and

3. Interpretation.

In the learning step the fuzzy relation and the neural network exchange information about the control strategy (see Figure 9.1). In the following both directions of information flow will be explained briefly. This leads to different possible types of interaction in the learning phase.

The neural network learns a cost function that represents an implicit controller. In Section 9.5.2.2 it is shown how an explicit controller can be obtained from this in a *transformation* step. The result is the fuzzy control relation. In this case control knowledge is passed from the neural network to the fuzzy relation. On the other hand, if we integrate *a priori* knowledge about the control strategy into the fuzzy relation, first of all the information must flow in the reverse direction. The neural cost function is trained to correspond with the control strategy.

There are some possible types of interaction between the neural network and the fuzzy relation. They can be characterized by the mechanism of knowledge transfer from the neural network to the fuzzy control relation:

- transformation

- adaptation.

The first is simply the *transformation* described above. The neural network is trained and the fuzzy relation exactly reflects the control knowledge embedded in the neural cost function. In this case learning is restricted to the neural network.

In the second approach the neural network and the fuzzy controller really interact, they learn from each other in contrast to the static transformation above. The idea is that the implicit control knowledge in the neural network is only used as a trend, i.e. some kind of critical signal. The fuzzy relation is then *adapted* according to this criticism instead of completely passing the current control knowledge from neural cost function into the fuzzy relation. The advantage is that the learning process will be smoothed, temporary bad local states in the net will not harm the controller. This is especially important in the early stages of learning.

## 9.5 Stepping into FYNESSE

### 9.5.1 The Learning Critic

#### *9.5.1.1 The Learning Scenario*

As pointed out, the task of the learning module is to solve the temporal credit assignment problem that inevitably occurs when dynamic effects have to be appropriately addressed. Here we assume additionally that no external training information is given. Only the control target and situations that are likely to be invalid are specified—this is the basis to decide about success or failure of the current behavior.

This situation is closely related to biological learning, where a successful trial yields a reward (e.g. food) and thus the corresponding behavioral patterns are strengthened or reinforced. Thus, learning situations where only a judgement about success or failure is provided are commonly termed *Reinforcement Learning (RL)*. Here we focus on a special class of reinforcement problems where the judgement over a decision comes with some delay, namely at the end of a trial. Recently, interest has been growing in the application of methods based upon the theory of Dynamic Programming (Bellman, 1957) to solve learning problems of the above kind (Watkins, 1989; Werbos, 1990; Barto et al., 1995; Bertsekas and Tsitsiklis, 1996; Riedmiller, 1996a,c). Dynamic Programming methods offer a solid mathematical foundation with the goal of finding optimal solutions for temporal optimization problems and therefor constitute an ideally suited framework for the class of learning problems that we want to solve by the FYNESSE control architecture. The ideas of dynamic programming are described in the following section.

### 9.5.1.2  Dynamic Programming

Dynamic programming was first introduced by Bellman to solve a special type of optimization task, where temporal relations play a central role (Bellman, 1957). Consider a dynamical system$^2$ described by the following system of equations

$$x_{t+1} = f(x_t, u_t), \quad y_t = g(x_t)$$

where $x_t$ denotes the current state of the system, $u_t$ is the action or control signal applied to the plant, and $f$ describes the system's transfer function. The output $y_t$ of the system is computed depending on state $x_t$ by the output function $g$. The control signal $u_t$ that is applied to the plant is determined by the control policy $\pi$

$$\pi : \mathcal{X} \to \mathcal{U}, \quad u_t := \pi(x_t),$$

which selects one control signal out of a finite set of available actions $\mathcal{U} = \{u_1, \ldots, u_n\}$. The goal of optimization is to find an optimal control strategy $\pi^*$ that minimizes the accumulated costs over a complete control trajectory when the the plant starts in state $x_0$:

$$J^*(x_0) = \min_{\pi \in \Pi} \sum_{t=0}^{\infty} r(x_t, \pi(x_t)).$$

Here, the function $r : (\mathcal{X}, \mathcal{U}) \to \mathbb{R}$ denotes the immediate costs that arise when action $u$ is applied in state $x$. Thus by choosing $r$, the quality of the control strategy can be specified. To solve the optimization problem, the *whole* trajectory of accumulated costs has to be considered: actions with low immediate costs $r(x, u)$

---

2. To simplify the notation, we refer to a deterministic system here. The approach can be extended easily to the treatment of stochastic systems.

may have advantages initially, but may have unfortunate consequences in the future.

The theory of dynamic programming provides several methods to solve problems of the above kind. One such method is the *value iteration* technique. The idea is to approximate the optimal accumulated cost function $J^*$ by improving estimates for the optimal costs for the states iteratively:

$$J_{k+1}(x) := \min_u \{r(x, u) + J_k(f(x, u))\}. \tag{9.1}$$

Under certain assumptions, which will be discussed in Section 9.5.1.3, the sequence $J_k$ converges $J^*$. Once $J^*$ has been determined, the optimal control strategy is also known:

$$\pi^*(x) := \arg\min_u \{r(x, u) + J^*(f(x, u))\}. \tag{9.2}$$

The optimal action minimizes the sum of *immediate* costs $r(x, u)$ and accumulated future costs $J^*$ that occur when this action is applied.

### *9.5.1.3   Conditions of Convergence*

There are several possible sets of assumptions, which guarantee the convergence of the *value iteration* method. One popular framework is the *shortest path* scenario, where an absorbing terminal state is assumed. Unfortunately, closed loop control of dynamic systems is an ongoing process, and typically no such terminal state does exist. Instead, we formulate other conditions under which convergence can be proven (for an exact specification of the assumptions and the proof the reader is referred to (Riedmiller, 1996b)):

1. There exists a set of states $\mathcal{X}^+$ with zero immediate costs:

$$\forall x \in \mathcal{X}^+ \, \forall u : r(x, u) = 0,$$

2. For all other states immediate costs are positive:

$$\forall x \notin \mathcal{X}^+ \, \forall u : r(x, u) > 0, \text{ and}$$

3. With the available control signals it is possible to
   (a) control the system from an arbitrary start state to a cost-free state and
   (b) keep the system within the cost-free states.

Then, the following can be shown:

- The *value iteration* method converges towards the optimal costs:

$$\lim_{k \to \infty} J_k = J^*,$$

- The optimal control policy $\pi^*$

▫ Controls the system to a cost-free state $x^+ \in \mathcal{X}^+$

▫ Then, the system is permanently kept within a (sub)set $\mathcal{X}^* \subseteq \mathcal{X}^+$ of cost-free states

$$x \in \mathcal{X}^* \Rightarrow f(x, \pi^*(x)) \in \mathcal{X}^*.$$

This theoretical framework has an important practical impact for the control problems that we try to solve by learning.

Consider a typical control task, where the output of the plant should be controlled to equal a given target value $y^{target}$. The controller has a finite set of different control signals $\mathcal{U}$ that may be applied to the plant. Now we are looking for an appropriate policy $\pi^* : \mathcal{X} \to \mathcal{U}$ that solves the task. The value iteration method is applied to approximate the optimal cost function and thus to solve the control task. To do so, the above assumptions must be fulfilled. We define

$$r(x, u) := 0 \Leftrightarrow |g(x) - y^{target}| < \delta,$$

where $\delta$ denotes the maximum allowed tolerance. If the output is not within that region, than we select $r(x, u) > 0$ (Assumptions 1 and 2). To fulfill Assumption 3a and 3b, it must then be *possible* to control the plant within the target region $\mathcal{X}^+$. To guarantee this, the set of available actions $\mathcal{U}$ has to be chosen accordingly. The proposal now states that the *value iteration* method will converge. Secondly it will automatically find a policy that controls the plant within the cost-free region. Due to our special choice of $r(x, u)$ this means that the output then equals the target value ($\pm\delta$). Thus, the resulting optimal control strategy solves the original control task.

### 9.5.1.4　Value Iteration and Learning

As pointed out, learning within this approach means to approximate the optimal value function. In the original *value iteration* method this is done by stepping through the set of all states, updating the values of the value function according to the equations in Section 9.1. This assumes that the state space is finite. If we do not want to assume a finite number of states—for example because the current state information is a vector of continuous sensor values—we have to apply another technique. The *Real-Time Dynamic Programming* approach proposed in (Barto et al., 1993) suggests to update only those states that occur during a control trial. The idea is to start the plant in one of a finite set of random starting situations, which will be denoted by $\mathcal{X}^0$. The plant is then controlled by choosing the action which is best according to the current knowledge, represented by the current approximation of the cost function, $J_k$:

$$u_t = \arg\min_{u \in \mathcal{U}}\{r(x_t, u) + J_k(f(x_t, u))\}. \tag{9.3}$$

Then, the selected control signal is applied to the plant which changes its state to $x_{t+1}$. This information can be used to update the approximation of the cost function:

$$J(x_t) := r(x_t, u_t) + J(x_{t+1}) \tag{9.4}$$

These three steps—action selection, Equation 9.3, application to the plant and update of the value function, Equation 9.4—then exactly implement the *value iteration* step in Equation 9.1 for state $x_t$.

#### 9.5.1.5 *Neural Value Iteration*

As already pointed out, due to the continuous nature of the state space, a neural network—more exactly a multilayer perceptron—is used to compute the values of the estimated value function. The input of this network is the current state information $x_t$ and the output represents the estimated cost value $J(x_t)$. When using a neural network, the assignment made by Equation 9.4 cannot be made directly. Instead, the assignment is expressed in terms of a minimization between actual output and new target value

$$e_{td} := (J(x_t) - (r(x_t, u_t) + J(x_{t+1})))^2.$$

To minimize the difference between the actual output of the network and its desired target value, the weights in the network have to be updated accordingly. This can be done by using standard gradient descent techniques based on the application of the backpropagation algorithm. What makes this update formula special is that the target value is not given externally, but is computed as the cost value of the successor state by the neural network itself. This special type of learning is therefore called *Temporal Difference (TD)* learning (Sutton, 1988).

#### 9.5.1.6 *Model Based and Model Free Approaches*

Finally, a word should be said concerning the use of an internal model. The pure value iteration idea as presented above assumes the evaluation of the states. This implies the need for a model $f$ of the process in order to choose the appropriate action (Equation 9.3). However, typically a model of the plant may not be available. A tricky solution to this problem is to represent the value of the costs for *state/actions* pairs $x, u$ directly. This is the idea of the *Q-Learning* approach presented in (Watkins, 1989). The relationship between the function $J$ which evaluates the states and $Q$ which evaluates state/action pairs is given by

$$J(x) = \min_u \{Q(x, u)\}.$$

The procedure of action selection then reduces simply to stepping through the $Q$ values of the available actions:

$$u_t = \arg \min_{u \in \mathcal{U}} \{Q(x_t, u)\}. \tag{9.5}$$

This alternative representation thus allows a complete renunciation of a plant model inside the control architecture.

### 9.5.2   The Explicit Controller

#### 9.5.2.1   *Introduction*

The neural network learned to control the plant, but we neither know its strategy nor the uncertainty of its strategy. Below we show that the implicit information about the strategy in the neural network is indeed uncertain, i.e. *fuzzy*. The idea is to transform this information into a fuzzy relation, i.e. explicit control knowledge. As pointed out in Section 9.4.2.5, this can be done by a static transformation in one step or by an adaptation of the fuzzy relation. In this chapter we focus on the case that the neural network is trained using *Q-Learning* (see Section 9.5.1.6).

The fuzzy control relation can be interpreted in terms of fuzzy rules, e.g. "If $x$ is negative small then $u$ is positive small" with input $x$ and output $u$ of the controller. These rules can easily be understood, verified and changed by humans. It is explained how the extraction of such rules works.

#### 9.5.2.2   *Transformation of the Neural Cost Function*

The control policy is *implicitly* given by the cost function $Q(x, u)$ that is represented by the neural network. In state $x$ the costs $Q(x, u_i)$ are compared for all $u_i \in U(x)$. The controller chooses the action $u_{best}^x$ that minimizes the future costs:

$$Q(x, u_{best}^x) = \min_{u_i \in U(x)} Q(x, u_i) . \tag{9.6}$$

That means that $Q$ offers information about the future costs that an action is expected to produce. The idea is to transform $Q$ into a measure *qual* of quality or applicability of an action $u$ given a state $x$. We require

1. $qual(x, u) = 1$ for a very good action

2. $qual(x, u) = 0$ for a very bad action

A quality value of medium actions should be scaled relatively to the best and worst actions. $Q(x, \cdot)$ defines an ordering of actions: the lower $Q(x, u)$ the better is the choice of $u$ in state $x$. The problem is that this ordering is local—it is restricted to the chosen $x$. In order to guarantee a global (with respect to the states $x$) comparability of qualities, a global *scale* and a *shift* parameter that depends on $x$

are needed for the transformation of $Q$ into *qual*. These considerations lead to

$$qual(x, u) = 1 - \min\{1, scale^{-1} \cdot (Q(x, u) - Q(x, u_{best}^x))\} - shift(x) \qquad (9.7)$$

with

$$shift(x) \in [0, 1 - scale^{-1} \cdot (Q(x, u_{worst}^x) - Q(x, u_{best}^x))]$$

and

$$scale \leq \sup_{x \in X}\{Q(x, u_{worst}^x) - Q(x, u_{best}^x)\} =: \text{scale}_{max} .$$

The choice of *shift* answers questions like: *Is the best action* $u_{best}^x$ *in a state* $x$ *always a very good action* (qual$(x, u_{best}^x) = 1$)*? Is the worst action* $u_{worst}^x$ *in a state* $x$ *always a very bad action* (qual$(x, u_{worst}^x) = 0$)*? scale* on the other hand has great influence on the shape of *qual*: The smaller *scale* is, the greater is the differentiation between, for example, two qualities *qual*$(x, u_1)$ and *qual*$(x, u_2)$.

Figure 9.8 shows *qual* as the transformation of the neural controller of the chemical plant that is described in Section 9.6. We set *shift* $\equiv 0$, i.e. *qual*$(x, u_{best}^x) = 1$: The best action $u_{best}^x$ in a state $x$ is assigned the quality "one," all other actions are scaled relatively to it. If we chose a smaller *scale* than we did, the plateau on the right hand side of *qual* would have become an inclined plane like the one on the left side. This would have falsified the impression of the controller's uncertainty.

Now the question arises how to obtain a crisp control strategy from the fuzzy control relation *qual* and especially, if the strategy obtained from the $Q$-function through Equation 9.5 can be reconstructed from *qual*. The answer to the second question is positive: on the assumption that the strategy is unambiguous, the *mean of maxima* defuzzification fulfills the requirement.

### 9.5.2.3  *Adaptation of the Fuzzy Control Relation*

Transforming the implicit control knowledge of the neural cost function one by one into the fuzzy control relation results in the destruction of the existing control strategy of the fuzzy relation. The danger of this fact is easily understandable when the fuzzy relation is equipped with *a priori* knowledge and the neural network stochastically initialized at the beginning of learning: The existing control knowledge is held completely in the fuzzy relation and the first transformation of the ignorant network would destroy the prior knowledge. When we take into account that the neural network may run into local minima in training (cf. Figure 9.4) this problem can obviously be generalized to all stages of learning. The solution to this problem is the interpretation of the value *qual*$(x, u)$ as a criticism of action $u$ in state $x$. Instead of defining the control relation, written as $\tilde{R}$, by $\tilde{R}(x, u) := qual(x, u)$ for all $(x, u)$—this is done by the static transformation—we *adapt* $\tilde{R}(x, u)$ locally according to *qual*$(x, u)$. The basic algorithm can informally be described as follows:

*In state* $x$ *the fuzzy control relation applies action* $u$:

1. Calculate the evaluation $qual(x, u)$.
2. If $qual(x, u)$ is high, then raise $\tilde{R}(x, u)$.
3. If $qual(x, u)$ is low, then lower $\tilde{R}(x, u)$.

Formally the basic adaption rule reads

$$\tilde{R}(x, u) := (1 - \alpha)\tilde{R}(x, u) + \alpha \cdot qual(x, u)$$

with a learning parameter $\alpha \in (0, 1]$. More complicated forms also adapt the neighborhood of $(x, u)$ or use relaxation terms.

The adaptation rule can simply be applied to the case of two fuzzy control relations: support distributions for positive knowledge and possibility distributions for negative knowledge.

- If the quality $qual(x, u)$ is high, then raise the support of $(x, u)$ (positive knowledge)

- If the quality $qual(x, u)$ is low, then lower the possibility of $(x, u)$ (negative knowledge)

Arguments for the choice of action $u$ in state $x$ (high quality $qual(x, u)$) are "collected" in the support distribution, arguments against (low quality $qual(x, u)$) are summarized in the possibility distribution.

The learning phase can be stopped if the two relations meet. Then support and possibility of all $(x, u)$ have become identical. The greater the difference between support and possibility is, the less we know. If the support overshoots the possibility then we have detected inconsistent knowledge that will be transformed into ignorance. In order to achieve this, support and possibility are changed in a way such that the support will be smaller than the possibility. The size of the gap between support and possiblity is a measure of the level of ignorance. These adaptation algorithms including the treatment of ignorance and inconsistent knowledge, are explained in detail in (Spott and Weisbrod, 1996).

### 9.5.2.4  *Interpretation of the Fuzzy Control Relation*

In this chapter interpretation of the fuzzy control relation $qual$ means an approximation of $qual$ by the aggregation of a set of fuzzy rules. That means that the input space $X$ and the space of actions $U$ of the controller will be divided into fuzzy regions (fuzzy sets) $\tilde{X}_i$ and $\tilde{U}_i$. We can assign linguistic terms, like *negative small* or *positive small*, to the fuzzy regions and relate them by rules of the form "If $x$ is negative small then $u$ is positive small." A rule is represented by a fuzzy relation that is calculated from its *premise* $\tilde{X}$ and its *conclusion* $\tilde{U}$. The formula for this calculation is determined by the semantics and type of rule we want to use (see Section 9.4.2.4). We concentrate on the logical interpretation with Mamdani-type (logical conjunction) and Goedel-type (logical implication) rules, since they play an important role in the theory of possibility (negative knowledge) and evidence (positive knowledge) (Weisbrod, 1995).

As already mentioned in Section 9.4.2.4, the degrees of freedom in the process of interpretation are the number of rules and the shape and location of the premises and conclusions. In our opinion the interpretation must fit the user's subjective idea of it. For example, he may require a certain number of rules or define the location of the premises. On the other hand, the task of restricting the degrees of freedom (e.g. to give the premises) may be too difficult for the user, because he does not know enough about the plant or the controller. In that case, the system should be able to determine or, at least to suggest, these variables. To achieve this the fuzzy relation *qual* will be analyzed.

### *Analysis of Fuzzy Relations*

Since a rule holds local information about the control policy, it is responsible for a part of the space $X \times U$. The aggregation of all rules must then cover the complete space $X \times U$. The fuzzy relation will be analyzed in order to reduce $X \times U$ to regions that are assigned to rules. The general idea is the following:

- We need only a few rules in areas where the fuzzy relation does not change much.

- We need many rules in areas where the fuzzy relation changes substantially.

The solution is a measure for the changes in the fuzzy relation. For the sake of simplicity we assume discrete universes $X = \{x_1, x_2, \ldots, x_n\}$, $U = \{u_1, u_2, \ldots, u_m\}$. In this chapter we focus on the choice of the premises.

With varying $x$ the changes in $qual(x, \cdot)$ must be quantified. The following measure[3] appears to be quite meaningful:

$$density_k(x_i) := \|\vec{u}_{x_{i+1}} - \vec{u}_{x_i}\|_k \qquad (9.8)$$

with vector $\vec{u}_{x_i} = (qual(x_i, u_j))_j$ and standard k-th vector norm $\|\cdot\|_k$.

Now the task is the inference of the distribution of the premises from the measure *density*, e.g. "If *density* is nearly constant in a region of $X$ then uniformly distribute $\alpha \cdot density$ premises in this region" with a parameter $\alpha$. The finding of such heuristics is a current research topic. In the example in Section 9.1 the premises were distributed by hand. We used the image of the fuzzy control relation and the measure *density* as deciding factors.

Figure 9.10 shows the function $\frac{1}{n} \cdot density_2$ and the premises for the fuzzy relation *qual* in Figure 9.8.

---

3. Indeed, this is only a basic example of a class of measures.

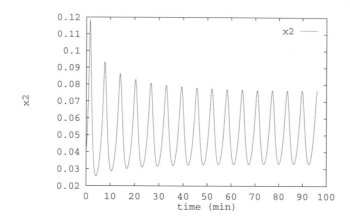

**Figure 9.2**   $x_2$ vs. time—behavior of the uncontrolled chemical reactor

### Calculation of the Rules

When the premises are distributed the conclusions must be determined with respect to the following requirement: The aggregation[4] of all rule relations must be a good approximation of the fuzzy relation *qual*. Solving it is an optimization problem. A measure *approx* of the quality of approximation, such as the quadratic difference between *qual* and its approximation, must be minimized. More complex measures also take care of the comprehensibility of conclusions. For example, they punish big overlaps that make it difficult to distinguish different rules. For each conclusion $\tilde{U}_j$ the degree of membership of each $u_i \in U$ has to be optimized with respect to *approx*. The method is explained in detail in (Bolten and Spott, 1997).

## 9.6   Control of a Chemical Plant

### 9.6.1   Task Description

The control of a chemical plant represents a challenging benchmark for nonlinear controller design. The task can be shortly described as follows (for a detailed description see (Föllinger, 1993)): In a reactor there is a chemical substance with concentration $x_1$. The substance chemically reacts with the fluid in the reactor in an energy-emitting decay process. This leads to a rise of the temperature $x_2$ in the reactor. On the other hand, the temperature $x_2$ influences the rate of decay of the

---

4. In general, a fuzzy relation cannot be modeled exactly by a finite number of rules. Besides, this is not the aim of interpretation. We only expect a simple explanation of the controller's behavior that is qualitatively correct.

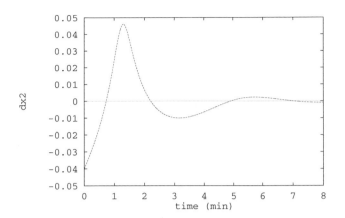

**Figure 9.3**   $dx_2$ vs. time—behavior of a nonlinear analytical controller

substance. Thus we observe two highly interacting processes of concentration and temperature (see Figure 9.2) coupled via a nonlinear function $\gamma(x_1, x_2)$:

$$\dot{x}_1 = -a_1\,x_1 + \gamma(x_1, x_2)$$
$$\dot{x}_2 = -a_{21}\,x_2 + a_{22}\,\gamma(x_1, x_2) + b\,u$$
$$\gamma(x_1, x_2) = (1 - x_1)\,k_0\,e^{-\frac{\epsilon}{1+x_2}} \tag{9.9}$$

The task is to control the reactor from an initial working point $(x_1(0), x_2(0)) = (0.42, 0.01)$ to a new working point $(x_1, x_2)^{target} = (0.75, 0.05)$. The behavior of the process can be influenced by applying external heating or cooling. Only the temperature inside the reactor, the state variable $x_2$, can be measured. Thus the input to the controller consists of the difference between the current temperature $x_2(t)$ and the target temperature $x_2^{target}$:

$$dx_2(t) := x_2(t) - x_2^{target}$$

In the following the performance of a nonlinear analytical control approach is compared to the performance of the self-learning FYNESSE controller.

### 9.6.2   A Nonlinear Controller

One of the goals of the FYNESSE approach is to show a good final control quality that is comparable to the quality of conventional controller design. The following nonlinear control law is taken from (Föllinger, 1993). It is derived using the complete knowledge of the nonlinear plant behavior. This is also expressed in the structure of the nonlinear control law:

$$u = -k(y)\,y$$
$$= -[C_0\,y + C_1\,y\,e^{-\frac{-\epsilon}{1+y}}$$
$$+ C_2\,y\,\frac{e^{-\frac{-\epsilon}{1+y}} - e^{-\frac{-\epsilon}{1+y_R}}}{y - y_R}]$$

The derivation of this control law is beyond the scope of this chapter. The intention is to present the behavior of a carefully designed analytical controller as a standard of comparison for the self-learning FYNESSE approach. The temporal behavior of the difference between reactor temperature and its target value, $dx_2(t)$ is shown in Figure 9.3.

### 9.6.3   Learning with FYNESSE

The rest of the section is dedicated to the application of the FYNESSE architecture to control the chemical reactor. Three main points will be addressed:

- Learning an optimal policy without *a priori* knowledge.
- Integration of *a priori* control. knowledge.
- Extraction of the acquired control knowledge in terms of fuzzy rules.

The degrees of freedom in this application are restricted as follows:

- Crisp linear controller as *a priori* knowledge.
- One fuzzy control relation.
- Mean of maxima defuzzification.
- Static transformation of the neural cost function into the fuzzy control relation.
- Interpretation of the fuzzy control relation with the distribution of premises by hand and optimization of the conclusions.

### 9.6.4   Self-Learning from Scratch

In contrast to conventional controller design, the self-learning approach used here assumes no initial knowledge of the plant's dynamic behavior. The only 'information' is the specification of the control target. In the self-learning approach (Section 9.5.1.3) this target is used to determine the choice of the direct cost function $r(x, u)$. The control task is to bring the temperature $x_2$ of the plant as fast as possible to its target value $x_2^{target} = 0.05$. This means that

$$r(x, u) := \begin{cases} 0 & , \quad \text{if } |x_2(t) - x_2^{target}| < \delta \\ c & , \quad \text{otherwise} \end{cases}$$

where $\delta = 0.01$ defines the range of maximum tolerance between output and target value. Here, $c$ denotes a constant value. This means that every control signal applied

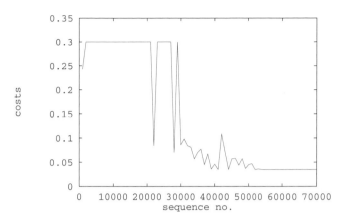

**Figure 9.4**   Average costs over number of training sequences.

when the plant is outside its target region implies the same immediate costs. Thus, when the *accumulated* costs are minimized, the number of control steps outside the target region is minimized. This means that by this special choice of $r(x, u)$ we express our wish to learn a *time optimal* control law. Note that by the definition of $r(x, u)$ we just express how the final behavior should look like. No idea of how to realize this behavior is introduced. No information of the nonlinear control behavior is available. The self-learning controller has to learn an appropriate control law all by itself. To do this, the controller repeatedly controls the plant. Each control sequence begins with a different initial state of the plant. After a certain amount of time, the trial is stopped and a new trial begins. During each control trial, the neural value function, which represents the current approximation of the cost function, is updated according to the *value iteration* rule. By improving the approximation, the control strategy, which is determined by the neural value function (Equation 9.3) also improves. This, vice versa, leads to an improvement of the neural approximation of the optimal costs.

The learning process is shown in Figure 9.4 in terms of the average accumulated costs per control trial. At the beginning, the control law is determined by the randomly initialized neural net and is accordingly very poor (average costs $\approx 0.3$). After about 30,000 trials one can see a very rapid improvement of the control strategy (average costs between 0.1 and 0.04). At this time, the controller is able to control the plant, but not perfectly optimal. An optimal control law is learned after about 52,000 control trials. The average costs per trial have reached a minimum of 0.035. The controller has learned to control the plant quickly to its target value. The target value is reached even faster than with the carefully derived nonlinear control law (Figure 9.5).

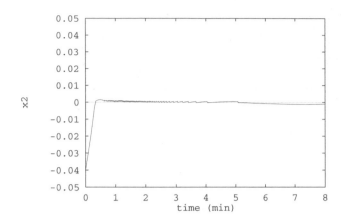

**Figure 9.5**   $dx_2$ over time—behavior of the FYNESSE controller

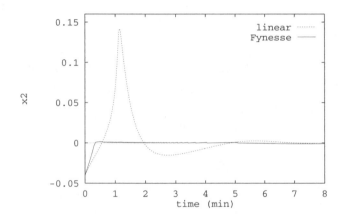

**Figure 9.6**   $dx_2$ over time—behavior of linear controller.

### 9.6.5   Use of *a priori* Knowledge

The benefit of the proposed method that learns an optimal control strategy only by clever evaluation of previous experiences is paid for by a rather large amount of training sequences. This may be no problem if there exists a computer model of the plant and learning may be performed in simulation. But if we try to learn control of a real plant directly, we may not have the opportunity of performing some ten thousands of trials. One solution is not to learn completely from scratch, but to incorporate *a priori* knowledge as far as available. The fuzzy module in the FYNESSE architecture allows the integration of crisp control laws (as below) or formulation of our *a priori* control knowledge as rules of a fuzzy controller. Then this initial policy is used to pretrain the neural value function.

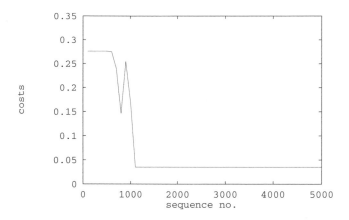

**Figure 9.7**  Average costs over number of training sequences.

To demonstrate the benefits of incorporating *a priori* knowledge, we start from a crisp linear control law  described in (Föllinger, 1993). The very simple linear control law is given by

$$u(t) = -0.8 \left( x_2(t) - x_2^{target} \right).$$

The control behavior using this simple linear controller is rather poor. This is shown by the output trajectory (dotted line in Figure 9.6). This initial idea of a linear control law was now used to pretrain the neural value function. Therefore, the control policy was fixed and the value function was adapted along the control trajectories as before. Although the linear control law used as *a priori* control knowledge is far from being optimal, pretraining has a tremendous effect on the learning process. Figure 9.7 shows the decrease of the average costs per control trial as the training proceeds. After only 1,100 trials an optimal control performance was achieved. Note that without the use of *a priori* knowledge, previously over 50,000 sequences were used to get to the same level of performance. The control behavior itself was significantly changed by the learning process. To see this, the resulting control behavior (thick line) is plotted against the control behavior of the linear controller (dotted line) (Figure 9.6).

### 9.6.6   Interpretation of the Controller

At each learning step the neural cost function can be transformed into the fuzzy control relation *qual*. Figure 9.8 shows the transformed neural network cost function at the end of learning. As explained in section 9.5.2.2 the defuzzification of *qual* with the method *mean of maxima* is equivalent to action selection using Equation 9.5. This crisp control strategy can be illustrated easily in Figure 9.8: In state $x$ choose the action $u$ with the highest quality $qual(x, u)$. For the interpretation in terms of linguistic fuzzy rules the analysis of *qual* leads to the reduction of the state space

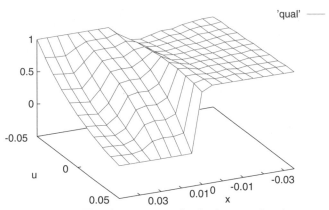

**Figure 9.8**   The fuzzy control relation $qual(x, u)$

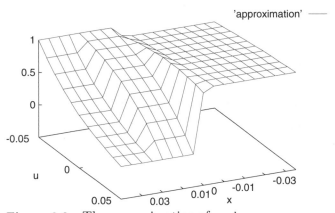

**Figure 9.9**   The approximation of *qual*

$X$ into four fuzzy premises (cf. Figures 9.10, 9.8). The quality of approximation is indeed very high, which is illustrated in Figures 9.8 (the original control relation) and 9.9 (the approximation by four rules).

This means that the policy of the neural controller can be described by four rules (Figures 9.11-9.14):

1. If $x$ is negative then $u$ is slightly positive.

2. If $x$ is zero then $u$ is around zero.

3. If $x$ is positive small then $u$ is negative small.

4. If $x$ is positive big then $u$ is negative medium.

The premises reduce $X$ to nearly sharp regions, whereas the conclusions are quite *fuzzy*. If $x$ is negative then the quality of all actions is similar—cf. the conclusion of

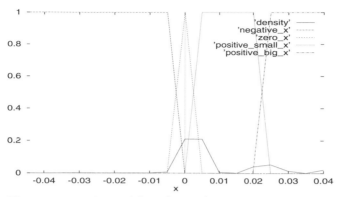

**Figure 9.10**   $density(x)$ and premises

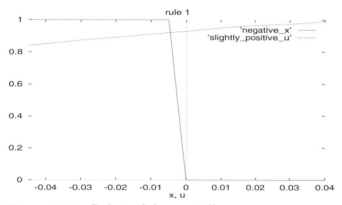

**Figure 9.11**   Rule 1 of the controller.

rule 1 in Figures 9.11-9.14. Positive actions receive a higher reward than negative actions, but the difference is not really big. On the other hand if $x$ is positive then the quality of positive and negative actions is clearly separated—cf. the conclusions of rules 3, 4 in Figures 9.11-9.14. The fuzziness of the neural controller's policy does not affect its quality: The controller always chooses the best action, i.e. it does not matter if the other actions are much or only a little bit worse. There are two main explanations for a high degree of fuzziness:

1. The controller did not learn long enough; a clear distinction of good and bad actions cannot be expected.

2. All actions in fact are of similar quality, even the worst action is good with respect to the target of control.

The degree of fuzziness of a conclusion can be used to control the process of learning: The higher the fuzziness in a region the greater is the need for learning. If the degree of fuzziness does not decrease then the second point occurs and learning can be stopped.

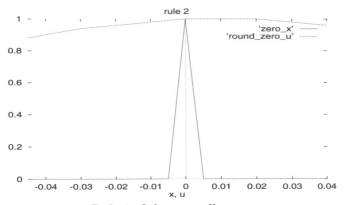

**Figure 9.12**   Rule 2 of the controller.

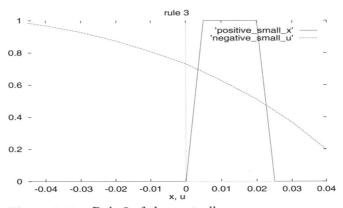

**Figure 9.13**   Rule 3 of the controller.

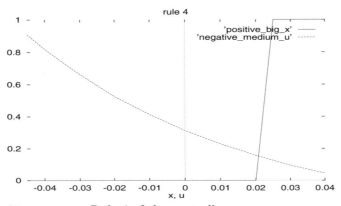

**Figure 9.14**   Rule 4 of the controller.

### 9.6.7 Summary

In this section we showed the exemplary application of the FYNESSE controller to an analytically hard-to-solve nonlinear chemical process. Aspects of all five requirements as established in section 9.2 were addressed. The plant shows nonlinear dynamic behavior and the only training information was given in terms of the target value for the new temperature inside the reactor. Nevertheless, by learning from scratch, FYNESSE acquired a very high control quality, based on minimizing the time to reach the target value. It has further been shown how the use of *a priori* knowledge can dramatically improve the learning process even if the a priori knowledge used did not itself establish a very good solution to the problem. Finally, the interpretation of the acquired critic knowledge allowed further insight into the policy of the controller.

## 9.7 Conclusions

Derived from five essential requirements for a self-learning controllerr, this chapter introduces the main concepts of the novel FYNESSE control architecture. The demand for learning capabilities on the one hand and the ability to integrate and extract explicit control knowledge on the other hand led to a hybrid approach using fuzzy and neural information processing techniques. In contrast to many other approaches, the fuzzy and neural computation modules are strictly separated, and rely on a coprocessing mode of cooperation.

Three main issues characterize the functional properties of the FYNESSE architecture: *Self-learning* is based on a neural dynamic programming approach that allows the acquisition of optimal control strategies for dynamical systems by requiring only a minimum of training information. In fact, only the control target must be specified in advance. The second point is the *possible use of a priori control knowledge* formulated either as a crisp control law or as fuzzy control rules. The *interpretation* of the learned control strategy is the third important feature of the FYNESSE approach. For example, this allows checking of the control strategy for plausibility.

The generality of FYNESSE offers some degrees of freedom which the user can adjust according to the application. A priori knowledge about the control strategy may be given as crisp analytical mappings, rule-based fuzzy systems or statistical information, etc. Many forms of interpretation of the fuzzy control relation are also possible. In this chapter we proposed a method to extract fuzzy control rules that facilitates a linguistic interpretation of the controller. One of our main research topics is the investigation of different types of interaction between the fuzzy control relation and the neural network. While in the application to the chemical reactor, learning takes place mainly in the neural network module (the fuzzy control relation is obtained by a static transformation), we currently work on real interactive learning procedures. Both modules are adapted; they learn and profit from one another, thus the result will be a shorter and more robust learning phase.

The principles of learning and interpretation are demonstrated on a highly nonlinear benchmark problem, namely the control of a chemical reactor. The acquired control behavior shows a very high quality. The controller has learned to deal perfectly with the nonlinear dynamics of the plant. The integration of *a priori* knowledge dramatically reduced the number of training sequences needed. The posterior interpretation of the acquired strategy in terms of fuzzy rules gives insight in the strategy that FYNESSE uses to control the chemical reactor.

# References

Barto, A. G., Bradtke, S. J., and Singh, S. P. 1993. Learning to act using real-time dynamic programming. Tech. rep.

Barto, A. G., Bradtke, S. J., and Singh, S. P. 1995. Learning to act using real-time dynamic programming. *Artificial Intelligence*, 72(1-2):81–138.

Barto, A. G., Sutton, R. S., and Anderson, C. W. 1983. Neuron-like adaptive elements that can solve difficult learning control problems. *IEEE Transactions on Systems, Man, and Cybernetics*, 13:834–846.

Bellman, R. E. 1957. *Dynamic Programming*. Princeton, NJ: Princeton University Press.

Berenji, H. R. and Khedkar, P. 1992. Learning and tuning fuzzy logic controllers through reinforcements. In *IEEE Trans. Neural Networks*, vol. 3, pp. 724–740.

Bersini, H., Nordvick, P. J., and Bonarini, A. 1993. A simple direct adaptive fuzzy controller derived from its neural equivalent. In *3rd IEEE Int. Conf. on Fuzzy Systems*, pp. 345–350.

Bertsekas, D. P. and Tsitsiklis, J. N. 1996. *Neuro Dynamic Programming*. Belmont, Massachusetts: Athena Scientific.

Bolten, E. and Spott, M. 1997. Fuzzy rule extraction from fuzzy relations. In *Proc. of EUFIT'97*, pp. 1019–1023, Aachen, Germany.

Eppler, W. 1993. *Prestructuring of Neural Networks with Fuzzy Logic (in German)*. Ph.D. thesis, University of Karlsruhe, Germany.

Föllinger, O. 1993. *Nichtlineare Regelungen*. Oldenbourg, 7th edn.

Geva, S. and Sitte, J. 1993. A cartpole experiment benchmark for trainable controllers. *IEEE Control Systems*, pp. 40–51.

Glorennec, P. Y. 1993. A neuro fuzzy inference system designed for implementation on a neural chip. In *Proc. of the 2nd Int. Conf. on Fuzzy Logic and Neural Networks*, pp. 209–212, Iizuka, Japan.

Jang, R. 1992. *Adaptive Network Fuzzy Inference System*. Ph.D. thesis, University of California, Berkeley.

Nauck, D., Klawonn, F., and Kruse, R. 1993. Combining neural networks and fuzzy controllers. In *Fuzzy Logic in Artificial Intelligence (FLAI93)*, eds. E. P. Klement and W. Slany, pp. 35–46. Berlin: Springer-Verlag.

Riedmiller, M. 1996a. Application of sequential reinforcement learning to control dynamic systems. In *IEEE International Conference on Neural Networks (ICNN '96)*, Washington.

Riedmiller, M. 1996b. *Autonomously learning neural controllers.* VDI-Verlag. Dissertation University of Karlsruhe (in German).

Riedmiller, M. 1996c. Learning to control dynamic systems. In *Proceedings of the 13th. European Meeting on Cybernetics and Systems Research—1996 (EMCSR '96)*, ed. R. Trappl, Vienna.

Spott, M. and Weisbrod, J. 1996. A new approach to the adaptation of fuzzy relations. In *Proc. of EUFIT'96*, vol. 2, pp. 782–786, Aachen, Germany.

Sulzberger, S. M., Tschichold-Gürman, N. N., and Vestli, S. J. 1993. Fun: Optimization of fuzzy rule based systems using neural networks. In *Proc. IEEE Int. Conf. on Neural Networks*, pp. 312–316, San Francisco.

Sutton, R. S. 1988. Learning to predict by the methods of temporal differences. *Machine Learning*, 3:9–44.

Sutton, R. S. 1990. First results with Dyna, an integrated architecture for learning, planning and reaction. In *Neural Networks for Control*, eds. W. T. Miller, R. S. Sutton, and P. J. Werbos. MIT Press.

Wang, L. 1994. *Adaptive Fuzzy Systems and Control.* Prentice-Hall.

Watkins, C. J. 1989. *Learning from Delayed Rewards.* Phd thesis, Cambridge University.

Weisbrod, J. 1995. Fuzzy control revisited—why is it working? In *Advances in Fuzzy Theory and Technology, Vol. III*, ed. P. P. Wang, pp. 219–244. Durham (NC): Bookwrights.

Weisbrod, J. 1996. A combined approach to fuzzy reasoning. In *Proc. of EUFIT'96*, vol. 1, pp. 554–557, Aachen, Germany.

Werbos, P. J. 1990. Overview of designs and capabilities. In *Neural networks for control*, eds. T. Miller, R. S. Sutton, and P. J. Werbos, pp. 59–66. Massachusetts: MIT Press.

# 10     Data Mining Techniques for Designing Neural Network Time Series Predictors

Radu Drossu and Zoran Obradović

*A real-life time series prediction system is usually subject to two constraints— accuracy and time, meaning that a sufficiently accurate prediction has to be provided in an imposed time frame. The objective of this chapter is to demonstrate that the knowledge obtained through relatively simple data mining can be embedded into a neural network time series predictor in order to both reduce its design time and improve its accuracy. Direct knowledge embedding methods, based on information theoretical modeling, dynamical system analysis, and stochastic modeling are discussed. It is illustrated that direct methods can produce a wealth of prior information regarding the choice of an appropriate neural network architecture, data sampling rates, as well as starting values for the model parameters, which otherwise have to be found as a result of costly trial-and-error procedures. In addition to direct knowledge embedding, the chapter also discusses indirect embedding methods which exploit known properties of the target function and non-stationarity detection techniques. The use of known properties of the target function can enlarge scarce data sets or enforce more accurate learning through constrained optimization. Non-stationarity analysis can considerably improve the computational efficiency of time series forecasting by avoiding the neural network model redesign more often than needed.*

## 10.1   Introduction

The outcomes of a phenomenon over time form a *time series*. Time series are encountered in sciences as well as in real life. The voltage measured every second across a resistor in an electrical circuit, the number of cars passing a marker on a highway every minute, the yearly power consumption of the United States, the hourly exchange rate of German mark versus U.S. dollar, the daily car production of Chrysler corporation are just a few examples of time series. Although sometimes outcomes of processes described through mathematical closed forms (known deterministic functions) are also viewed as time series, most commonly time series are the result of unknown or not completely understood processes. Therefore, more formally, a time series $\{x_t\}$ can be defined as a function $x$ of an independent variable $t$, stemming from an unknown process. Its main characteristic is that its evolution can not be described exactly as in the case of a known deterministic function of $t$.

It is human nature to have the desire to know in advance what is likely to happen in the future. The observation of past outcomes of a phenomenon in order to anticipate its future behavior represents the essence of *forecasting* (prediction). If a mathematical model describing a studied phenomenon is known, forecasting becomes a trivial and degenerate task. However, if a model of the phenomenon is either unknown or incomplete, different attempts can be made for predicting its future evolution. A typical approach is to try to predict by constructing a model which takes into account solely previous outcomes of the phenomenon while ignoring any other additional exterior influence. Alternatively, a prediction model can be constructed which incorporates all the factors which presumably influence the process under consideration. For example, the simplest attempt to predict the United States power consumption would be by using a prediction model based just on previous values of power consumption which neglects any other information that might also be available. On the other hand, we could construct a model which incorporates additional variables that presumably influence the power consumption, like temperature, time of day, season, etc. The choice of one or the other of the two approaches is problem dependent and care must be taken when developing a prediction model in order not to include variables that do not bear any influence on the phenomenon under study, since these would merely act as input noise.

Real-life time series are often the result of complex and insufficiently understood interdependencies. Hence, prediction models make use of incomplete information, while other factors not included in the models act as noise. In addition, real-life time series are often non-stationary, meaning that the data distribution is changing over time. Therefore, for non-stationary domains, a single model built on a certain data segment and used for all subsequent predictions is generally inadequate. A straightforward attempt is to stationarize the data by performing a de-trending preprocessing, e.g. a first or a second order discrete differentiation. More sophisticated methods provide solutions for certain types of non-stationarity, e.g. a reversible power transformation is successfully used to stabilize the variance of a series affected by a strong trend that cannot be removed by differentiation (Abecasis and Lapenta, 1996). However, not all non-stationary processes can be stationarized through data preprocessing. Forecasting such processes requires *on-line learning*, where a given model is used for a limited time and a new model is constructed whenever a change of the underlying data distribution is detected.

The two issues which have to be addressed by any time series prediction system are *accuracy* and *time*, meaning that a sufficiently accurate prediction has to be provided in an imposed time frame. Quite often these two constraints are contradictory, signifying that usually, given more time for designing a prediction model a better accuracy could be achieved. If time is not an issue, like when predicting the yearly power consumption of the United States, accuracy would be the only constraint that the design process has to deal with. In these cases multilayer perceptron neural networks are often used in practice. Their popularity is due to their universal approximation capabilities, meaning that they can represent non-linear complex functions to any desired accuracy (Cybenko, 1989), and to their significantly better scaling with the dimensionality of the input space as compared to traditional approximation techniques (Barron, 1993).

However, the design of an appropriate neural network for time series prediction problems with high data arrival rates (e.g. Internet traffic predictions or financial intra-day predictions) can be a challenging task, due to time consuming trial-and-error architecture selection, non-linear parameter optimization and the need to devise new prediction models whenever the underlying data distribution changes. For these reasons, any prior knowledge that could be extracted from a time series under study can dramatically decrease the design time of a predictor and also improve its prediction accuracy significantly.

This chapter discusses two categories of prior knowledge extraction techniques, which are embeddable into neural network prediction models. The first category, discussed in Section 10.2 and denoted as *direct knowledge embedding* encompasses information theory, non-linear dynamics, and stochastic analysis. These techniques of exploratory data analysis can provide prior knowledge regarding appropriate neural network architecture, initial network parameters and adequate data sampling rate. A real-life time series (compressed video traffic data), as well as an artificial, non-linear, chaotic time series (Mackey-Glass data) are used to illustrate the embedding of prior knowledge extracted from stochastic analysis into the neural network design process. The second category, *indirect knowledge embedding*, addressed in Section 10.3, includes the use of known properties of target functions and non-stationarity detection. The use of known properties of the target function can enlarge scarce data sets by creating additional artificial training examples, or enforce more accurate learning through constrained optimization. Non-stationarity analysis can considerably improve the computational efficiency of time series forecasting by avoiding the neural network model re-design more often than needed. Therefore, different distribution-change signaling techniques for deciding whether to reuse "trusted" models or retrain new ones are discussed and compared on low-noise and high-noise, artificially generated, non-stationary time series.

## 10.2  Direct Information Extraction Procedures

### 10.2.1  Information Theory

It has been hypothesized (Barlow, 1989) that the redundancy between different input signals allows the brain to discover their statistical relationships, and to use them for object recognition and associative learning. A representation has further been proposed in which the individual signals are statistically independent, as being the most appropriate for storing statistical information. In order to acquire the statistical independence (*factorial code*) of the input signals, a multiple-stage learning process can be employed in which every stage reduces the redundancy between its input signals generating more decorrelated output signals. This redundancy reduction strategy is applied in an unsupervised fashion to the problem of eliminating redundancies from English text (Redlich, 1993a).

In order to make redundancy reduction effective for pattern recognition or time series prediction problems, supervision has to be incorporated into the learning process. The goal of the redundancy reduction process, denoted as *factorial learning* (Redlich, 1993b), is to approximate the joint probability $P(x_1, x_2, \dots, x_d) = P(\bar{x})$, where $d$ represents the number of input signals, as a product of the individual probabilities, $P(x_1), P(x_2), \dots, P(x_d)$. The individual learning stages represent better and better approximations to the joint probability. In order to evaluate the quality of the factorial approximation at different learning stages, we can make use of the entropy function. Considering that each learning stage represents an $\mathcal{R}^d$ to $\mathcal{R}^d$ mapping, we can use as a cost function the sum of output entropies (Redlich, 1993b), expressed as

$$E = \sum_{i=1}^{d} H_i, \tag{10.1}$$

where the individual entropies are computed as

$$H_i = -\sum_{x_i} P(x_i) \log_2 \left[ P(x_i) \right], \tag{10.2}$$

with the sum running over all the discretized values of the output variable $x_i$. This cost function is minimal when the code is factorial (Redlich, 1993b), so that reducing $E$ in stages improves the factorial representation of the joint probability. In order to be able to obtain an approximation to the global joint probability after a number of stages, which is solely a function of probabilities at the output level of the last stage, we need to impose that information is preserved from one learning stage to the next. Denoting by $\bar{x}$ the input vector to a certain learning stage and by $\bar{y}$ the corresponding output vector, the information preservation condition can be written as

$$H\left[P(\bar{x})\right] = H\left[P(\bar{y})\right], \tag{10.3}$$

with $H[\cdot]$ denoting the total entropy at input or output level. With this additional constraint, minimizing $E$ will produce a factorial approximation to the input joint probability, due to the independence bound on the entropy, according to which

$$H \leq \sum_{i} H_i, \tag{10.4}$$

with equality only when the code is factorial. A network named *almost reversible cellular automata* (ARCA) has been proposed by Redlich (Redlich, 1993b), which can be used, both in an unsupervised and in a supervised fashion, for factorial learning. The ARCA network proposed for supervised learning, a viable alternative to multi-layer perceptron networks, constructs additional computational layers as needed, in a fashion similar to cascade correlation networks (Fahlman and Lebiere, 1990). However, its applicability appears to be restricted to classification problems. Therefore, we will illustrate an approach proposed by Deco and collaborators (Deco and Schurmann, 1995; Deco and Brauer, 1995), similar to the unsupervised ARCA networks, which could be incorporated as a preprocessing module in a time series prediction system.

The goal is to construct a one stage neural network which attempts to statistically decorrelate the components of its output vector (Deco and Schurmann, 1995; Deco and Brauer, 1995). In order to impose the constraint of no information loss from input to output, we can use the mutual information between input and output as a measure of information transmission, defined as (Deco and Obradovic, 1996)

$$I(\bar{y}; \bar{x}) = H(\bar{x}) - H(\bar{x}|\bar{y}), \tag{10.5}$$

with $H(\bar{x})$ denoting the input entropy and $H(\bar{x}|\bar{y})$ denoting the conditional entropy of $\bar{x}$ given $\bar{y}$. The output entropy satisfies the inequality (Deco and Schurmann, 1995)

$$H(\bar{y}) \leq H(\bar{x}) + \int P(\bar{x}) \ln\left[\det\left[\frac{\partial \bar{T}}{\partial \bar{x}}\right]\right] d\bar{x}, \tag{10.6}$$

with equality holding only when the transformation $\bar{T}$ is bijective, thus reversible. Bijectivity is therefore satisfied if the Jacobian of the transformation has a unit determinant,

$$\det\left[\frac{\partial \bar{T}}{\partial \bar{x}}\right] = 1. \tag{10.7}$$

The architecture proposed in (Deco and Schurmann, 1995; Deco and Brauer, 1995), which fulfills the previous requirement and has the same structure as the ARCA network, is presented in Figure 10.1.

The transformation computed by this network can be expressed analytically as

$$y_i = x_i + f_i(x_1, \ldots, x_j, \bar{w}_i), \quad j < i, \tag{10.8}$$

with $\bar{w}_i$ denoting some parameter vector which intervenes in the computation of function $f_i$. It is obvious that the Jacobian of the network transformation is an upper triangular matrix, with all the diagonal elements equal to 1, which yields a determinant equal to unity and thus represents a transformation without information loss. The specific form assumed for the functions $f_i$ in (Deco and Schurmann, 1995; Deco and Brauer, 1995) is polynomial, resulting in network outputs computed according to

$$y_i = x_i + \sum_{j=1}^{i-1} w_{ij} x_j + \sum_{j,k=1}^{i-1} w_{ijk} x_k x_j + \ldots \tag{10.9}$$

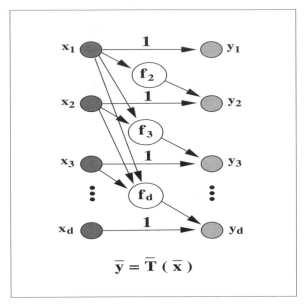

**Figure 10.1**   Information preserving transformation.

Viewed as a preprocessing module for a time series prediction problem, $x_1, \ldots, x_d$ would represent $d$ previous samples from a univariate time series  and $y_1, \ldots, y_d$ the outputs that tend to be decorrelated as a result of the learning process.

In order to obtain the decorrelation of the output signals, the following alternatives are proposed (Deco and Schurmann, 1995):

1. The minimization of an upper bound on the mutual information between the components of the output vector;

2. Cumulant expansion of the output distribution followed by imposing the independence condition.

Thus, the decorrelation can be achieved by gradient descent error minimization using either the cost function (see Appendix A),

$$E = \sum_{i=1}^{d} \ln(\sigma_i^2), \tag{10.10}$$

with $\sigma_i^2$ being the variance of component $i$ of the output vector, or (see Appendix B),

$$
\begin{aligned}
E = {}&\alpha \sum_{i<j} <y_i y_j>^2 + \beta \sum_{i<j\leq k} <y_i y_j y_k>^2 \\
&+\gamma \sum_{i<j\leq k\leq l} <y_i y_j y_k y_l>^2 \\
&+\delta \sum_{i<j} \left(<y_i^2 y_j^2> -3 <y_i^2><y_j^2>\right)^2,
\end{aligned}
\tag{10.11}
$$

with

$$< x_1 x_2 \ldots x_n > = \int x_1 x_2 \ldots x_n p\left(\bar{x}\right) d\bar{x}, \tag{10.12}$$

and $\alpha$, $\beta$, $\gamma$, and $\delta$, representing the inverses of the number of elements in their corresponding summations.

The decorrelation transformation implemented using the previously introduced neural network and either of the two cost functions presented leads also to an implicit determination of an appropriate embedding dimension (number of neural network inputs), by discarding the outputs with a variance which is below an imposed threshold. Set in the unsupervised learning framework, the information preserving transformation is not directly applicable to prediction problems. Nevertheless, it could be used as a building block inside a prediction system, whose general structure could be as follows:

■ Decorrelation module (performs previously described decorrelation transformation);

■ Predictor module (feedforward or recurrent neural network performing a "spatial" prediction in the transformed space obtained after decorrelation);

■ inverse transformation module (computes the inverse of the transformation computed by the decorrelation module, in order to provide an informative prediction in the original data space).

### 10.2.2  Dynamical System Analysis

Dynamical system analysis provides a potential means of obtaining information regarding an appropriate neural network architecture (more precisely, regarding the number of neural network inputs), as well as regarding an appropriate data sampling rate in prediction problems with prediction horizon larger than one (Lapedes and Farber, 1987).

A dynamical system is described in terms of a set of *state variables*, whose values at any given time $t$ are assumed to contain sufficient information to describe the future evolution of the system (Haykin, 1994). The *state vector* for a univariate time series can be constructed from delayed samples of the series $\bar{x}(t) = [x\left(t\right), x\left(t - \tau\right), \ldots, x\left(t - (M - 1)\tau\right)]$. Assuming that the system can be represented in terms of $M$ state variables which can be grouped together to form a state vector, $\bar{x}(t) = [x_1(t), \ldots, x_M(t)]$, the evolution of a dynamical system can be observed as a *trajectory* in the $M$-dimensional state space, also known as the *phase space* of the system. The phase space can be a Euclidean space or a subset thereof. It can also be a non-Euclidean space such as a sphere or a torus, or some other differentiable manifold (Haykin, 1994). Many dynamical systems can be described by a set of differential equations

$$\frac{d}{dt}\bar{x}(t) = V\left(\bar{x}(t)\right), \tag{10.13}$$

where $V(\cdot)$ is a non-linear (vector) function of the state vector. The family of trajectories which result when starting from different initial conditions, form the *phase portrait* of the system. The phase portrait includes all the points in the phase space where $V(\bar{x})$ is defined.

In general, a *dissipative system* (a system which "looses" energy), is characterized by the convergence of its trajectories in phase space onto manifolds of lower dimensionality, $m < M$, which form the dynamical system's *attractor* (Haykin, 1994). Attractors represent equilibrium states of a dynamical system which can be observed on experimental data. Different methods are employed in practice for determining the dimensionality of a system's attractor, the most representative ones, probably, being based on estimating either the (generalized) *Renyi dimensions*, or the *Lyapunov exponents*.

The Renyi dimensions represent a spectrum of dimensions, $D_0 \geq D_1 \geq D_2 \geq \ldots$, defined as (Pineda and Sommerer, 1993),

$$D_q = \frac{1}{q-1} \limsup_{\epsilon \to 0} \frac{\log(\sum_i p_i^q)}{\log(\epsilon)}. \tag{10.14}$$

Their computation assumes that the attractor is covered by $M$–dimensional boxes of side length $\epsilon$, and $p_i$ represents a measure of the attractor in box $i$, with the sum taken only over occupied boxes (boxes containing at least one data point). For finite data sets, the $p_i$'s can be approximated as $n_i/n$, with $n_i$ being the number of data points in the $i$–th box and $n$ representing the total number of data points. The first three generalized dimensions, also known as *capacity dimension*, *information dimension* and *correlation dimension*, respectively, can further be expressed as

$$D_0 = \limsup_{\epsilon \to 0} \frac{\log N(\epsilon)}{\log(1/\epsilon)}, \tag{10.15}$$

with $N(\epsilon)$ representing the number of non-empty boxes,

$$D_1 = \limsup_{\epsilon \to 0} \frac{-\sum_i p_i \log p_i}{\log(1/\epsilon)}, \tag{10.16}$$

and

$$D_2 = \limsup_{\epsilon \to 0} \frac{-\log\left(\sum_i p_i^2\right)}{\log(1/\epsilon)}. \tag{10.17}$$

The technique proposed in (Pineda and Sommerer, 1993) for computing $D_0$, $D_1$ and $D_2$ starts by plotting the numerators in the formulas for $D_0$, $D_1$, and $D_2$ versus $1/\epsilon$ for different space dimensions $M$, yielding three families of curves for $D_0$, $D_1$, and $D_2$, respectively, represented on separate plots. For each curve (corresponding to an individual value for $M$), the slope of its linear region before saturation is determined. These slopes are then plotted versus space dimension and the value at which the resulting curve saturates, provides the value for the generalized dimension under consideration. To check whether the data support the dimension computations, a final graph should be provided which contains the slope versus space dimension curves for all of $D_0$, $D_1$, and $D_2$. The fulfillment of the condition $D_0 \geq D_1 \geq D_2$ at any space dimension supports the hypothesis that enough data were provided in order to compute the generalized dimensions. A lack of saturation of the previously mentioned curves can be an indication of either a stochastic (non-deterministic) process, or of insufficient data. Different alternate measures exist, which allow the distinction between deterministic chaos and random noise (Grassberger and Procaccia, 1983). Any of $D_0$, $D_1$ or $D_2$ could in principle be used to estimate $m$, since they are usually very close, but in practice $D_1$ is the most commonly used. Based on Takens' theorem (Takens, 1981), an estimate of the dimension $m$ of the time series' attractor can be used to construct a multi-layer perceptron neural network of $2m + 1$ external units (Lapedes and Farber, 1987).

Instead of computing the generalized dimensions, we can alternatively compute the Lyapunov exponents using the available experimental data (Wolf et al., 1985). Loosely speaking, the Lyapunov exponents represent measures of change for geometric bodies of increasing dimensionality, as produced by the trajectories of the dynamical system. Thus, the first Lyapunov exponent, $\lambda_1$, measures the average logarithmic growth of the relative error per iteration between two initial conditions on neighboring trajectories of a dynamical system (Jurgens and Saupe, 1992). In other words, $e^{\lambda_1}$ represents the maximal average factor by which an error between neighboring trajectories is amplified. Expressed mathematically, the first Lyapunov exponent is given by (Jurgens and Saupe, 1992)

$$\lambda_1 = \lim_{n \to \infty} \lim_{E_0 \to 0} \frac{1}{n} \sum_{k=1}^{n} \log \left| \frac{E_k}{E_{k-1}} \right|, \tag{10.18}$$

with $E_0$ representing the initial error and $E_k/E_{k-1}$ denoting the error amplification from one step to the next. The second Lyapunov exponent, $\lambda_2$, represents a measure of how an area is changed along the "flow" of the dynamical system. Expressed differently, $e^{\lambda_1 + \lambda_2}$ represents the maximal average factor by which an area changes. Similarly $e^{\lambda_1 + \lambda_2 + \lambda_3}$, where $\lambda_3$ represents the third Lyapunov exponent, expresses the maximal average factor by which a volume changes. The process of determining Lyapunov exponents can continue with exponents of higher order, all of them being subject to the ordering

$$\lambda_1 \geq \lambda_2 \geq \lambda_3 \geq \ldots \tag{10.19}$$

with positive exponents standing for expansion along a certain direction and negative exponents denoting contraction along a direction.

Finally, the *Lyapunov dimension* can be computed as

$$D_L = \begin{cases} i + \frac{1}{|\lambda_{i+1}|} \sum_{k=1}^{i} \lambda_k, & \text{if } \lambda_1 \geq 0 \\ 0, & \text{otherwise,} \end{cases} \tag{10.20}$$

with $i$ being the maximum integer with $\lambda_1 + \ldots + \lambda_i \geq 0$. In theory, the Lyapunov exponents and the Lyapunov dimension are computed in a relatively straightforward manner for a continuous time series (generated from a set of differential equations). However, in practice, when dealing with a discrete time series, the effect of lacunarity (finite amount of data) has a negative impact on the accuracy of the results for both generalized dimensions and Lyapunov exponents. The Lyapunov dimension can be related to the information dimension in accordance to the *Kaplan-Yorke conjecture*, which claims their equality. Hence, denoting by $m$ the dimension (information dimension or Lyapunov dimension) of a given time series, a potentially adequate multi-layer perceptron for predicting the time series should have a number of input units which is equal to $2m + 1$.

Dynamical system analysis can further provide an indication of an appropriate data sampling rate (time delay), to be used in prediction problems with larger prediction horizon (predicting further into the future) (Liebert and Schuster, 1989; Pineda and Sommerer, 1993). Pineda and Sommerer consider the original time series, $\{x_t\}$, as well as its time-delayed counterpart $\{x_{t-\tau}\}$ with time origin shifted by $\tau$ (Pineda and Sommerer, 1993), which are discretized in units of $\epsilon$ (e.g. bits). Consequently, denoting by $X$ the random variable associated with the process values for $\{x_t\}$ and by $Y$ the random variable corresponding to the process values for $\{x_{t-\tau}\}$, we can define the discrete probabilities

$$P_X(x) = \text{Prob}\{X = x\}, \tag{10.21}$$

$$P_Y(y) = \text{Prob}\{Y = y\}. \tag{10.22}$$

and

$$P_{XY}(x, y) = \text{Prob}\{X = x \text{ and } Y = y\}. \tag{10.23}$$

Taking into consideration the quantized process values, we can define the scale-dependent entropies (Deco and Obradovic, 1996)

$$H_X(\epsilon) = -\sum_i P_X(x_i) \log_2 P_X(x_i), \tag{10.24}$$

$$H_Y(\epsilon) = -\sum_i P_Y(y_i) \log_2 P_Y(y_i), \tag{10.25}$$

as well as the scale-dependent cross-entropy,

$$H_{XY}(\epsilon) = -\sum_i P_{XY}(x_i, y_i) \log_2 P_{XY}(x_i, y_i), \tag{10.26}$$

with the sums taken over all the occupied one-dimensional and two-dimensional boxes, respectively. Additionally, we can also define the mutual information between the random variables $X$ and $Y$ as

$$M_{XY}(\epsilon) = H_X(\epsilon) + H_Y(\epsilon) - H_{XY}(\epsilon). \tag{10.27}$$

Making explicit the dependence on the delay $\tau$, we can rewrite the mutual information in the approximate form,

$$M_{XY}(\epsilon, \tau) = [2D_X - D_{XY}(\tau)] \log_2 \epsilon, \tag{10.28}$$

with $D_X$ being the information dimension $D_2$ computed for a space dimension $M = 1$ and $D_{XY}$ being the information dimension computed for $M = 2$. This expression allows the definition of a box size independent mutual information as,

$$D_\mu(\tau) = 2D_X - D_{XY}(\tau). \tag{10.29}$$

Finally, the optimal value of $\tau$ is chosen to be the one corresponding to the first minimum of the mutual information between the actual time series and the delayed one.

Although prone to lacunarity effects and not effective for stochastic processes, dynamical system analysis is still useful in providing an indication of whether the underlying time series stems from a deterministic or from a stochastic process. This information is especially useful, since domain-specific analysis techniques are likely to provide more accurate results than general ones.

### 10.2.3  Stochastic Analysis

Time series prediction is traditionally approached using stochastic methods (Box et al., 1994). A popular and theoretically well founded stochastic model for a stationary time series is the autoregressive moving average model of orders $p$ and $q$, denoted as ARMA(p,q), which describes the process value as a weighted sum of $p$ previous process values and the current one as well as $q$ previous values stemming from a random process. Formally, the stationary ARMA(p,q) process with zero mean $\{x_t\}$ is represented as

$$x_t = \varphi_1 x_{t-1} + \ldots + \varphi_p x_{t-p} + a_t + \psi_1 a_{t-1} + \ldots + \psi_q a_{t-q}, \tag{10.30}$$

where $x_{t-1}, x_{t-2}, \ldots, x_{t-p}$ represent the process values at $p$ previous time steps, $a_t, a_{t-1}, \ldots, a_{t-q}$ are the current and the $q$ previous values of a random process, usually emanating from a normal (Gaussian) distribution with zero mean, and $\varphi_1 \ldots \varphi_p, \psi_1 \ldots \psi_q$ are the model parameters.

The ARMA(p,q)–based predictor approximates the real process value $x_t$ by a predicted value $\hat{x}_t$, computed as

$$\hat{x}_t = \psi_1 x_{t-1} + \ldots + \varphi_p x_{t-p} + \psi_1 a_{t-1} + \ldots + \psi_q a_{t-q}, \tag{10.31}$$

The residual $a_{t-i}$ represents the error between the real process value $x_{t-i}$ and the predicted value $\hat{x}_{t-i}$.

The mean AR(p) and MA(q) models are special cases of the ARMA(p,q) model, where AR(p) is described as

$$x_t = \varphi_1 x_{t-1} + \varphi_2 x_{t-2} + \ldots + \varphi_p x_{t-p} + a_t, \qquad (10.32)$$

and MA(q) is described as

$$x_t = a_t + \psi_1 a_{t-1} + \psi_2 a_{t-2} + \ldots + \psi_q a_{t-q}. \qquad (10.33)$$

ARMA modeling is very fast, but of limited applicability due to strong modeling assumptions, e.g. stationary process, linear interdependencies and Gaussian noise.

A natural, less restrictive, generalization of the linear ARMA and AR models to the nonlinear cases leads to the NARMA model

$$x_t = h(x_{t-1}, x_{t-2}, \ldots, x_{t-p}, a_{t-1}, \ldots, a_{t-q}) + a_t, \qquad (10.34)$$

and the NAR model

$$x_t = h(x_{t-1}, x_{t-2}, \ldots, x_{t-p}) + a_t, \qquad (10.35)$$

where $h$ is an unknown smooth function.

The AR–, MA–, NARMA– and NAR-based predictors are obtained from their corresponding models analogous to obtaining the ARMA-based predictor (Equation 10.31) from the ARMA model (Equation 10.30). However, the NARMA and NAR models are very complex, thus difficult to use in real life applications. Fortunately, they are closely related to more practical nonlinear models, the neural networks. Recurrent and feedforward neural networks have been proposed in (Connor et al., 1994; Werbos, 1992) for simulating NARMA and NAR models respectively. An invertible (Box et al., 1994) NARMA-based predictor can be approximated as

$$\hat{x}_t = h(x_{t-1}, \ldots, x_{t-p}, a_{t-1}, \ldots, a_{t-q})$$
$$\approx \sum_{i=1}^{m} W_i f(\sum_{j=1}^{p} w_{ij} x_{t-j} + \sum_{j=1}^{q} w'_{ij}(x_{t-j} - \hat{x}_{t-j}) + \theta_i) + \Gamma, \qquad (10.36)$$

where $f$ represents a nonlinear, smooth and bounded function and $a_k = x_k - \hat{x}_k$, for all $k \in \{t - q, \ldots, t - 1\}$. This approximation of the NARMA-based model corresponds to the recurrent neural network from Figure 10.2, in which $w_{ij}$ are the weights between external inputs and hidden neurons, $w'_{ij}$ are the weights between context inputs and hidden neurons, $W_i$ are the weights between hidden and output neurons, $\theta_i$ are the hidden neuron biases, $\Gamma$ is the output neuron bias and $f$ is the activation function of the hidden neurons. Similarly, a NAR-based predictor can be approximated as

$$\hat{x}_t = h(x_{t-1}, \ldots, x_{t-p}) \approx \sum_{i=1}^{m} W_i f(\sum_{j=1}^{p} w_{ij} x_{t-j} + \theta_i) + \Gamma, \qquad (10.37)$$

obtained by disconnecting the context inputs $a_{t-1} \ldots a_{t-q}$ in Figure 10.2. The parameters $w_{ij}$, $w'_{ij}$, $W_i$, $\theta_i$ and $\Gamma$ can be estimated from examples by gradient

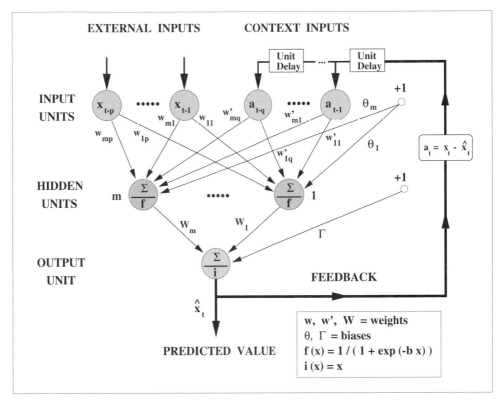

**Figure 10.2**   Stochastic model approximation.

descent optimization (Werbos, 1994).

A special case of a particular interest in this study is the approximation of a linear AR model by a feedforward neural network. Although the neural network from Figure 10.2 in which the hidden layer and the feedback connections are removed is computationally equivalent to the linear AR model, such a trivial network is of no interest since it is not able to perform better than the equivalent AR model. More interesting (see Appendix C) is the approximation of an AR(p) model with parameters $\varphi_1, \ldots, \varphi_p$ by a neural network with $p$ inputs, $p$ hidden units and interconnection parameters

$$
\begin{aligned}
w_{ij} &= \delta_{ij} \\
\theta_i &= 0 \\
W_i &= \frac{4}{\beta}\varphi_i \\
\Gamma &= -\frac{2}{\beta}\sum_{i=1}^{p}\varphi_i,
\end{aligned}
\tag{10.38}
$$

for all $i, j \in \{1, \ldots, p\}$.

In (Drossu and Obradovic, 1996a) it was shown that the neural network weight initialization based on AR model parameters could significantly shorten the neural network training process by providing an initial position on the error surface which is closer to the minimum as compared to a randomly chosen position. In addition, stochastic analysis could provide some initial knowledge regarding appropriate neural network architecture and data sampling rate. The attempt to use linear stochastic analysis prior knowledge is supported by the fact that "many non-linear systems can be described fairly well by linear models and for such systems it is a good idea to use insights from the best linear model to select the regressors for the neural network model" (Sjöberg et al., 1994, 1995). The objective of the approach proposed in (Drossu and Obradovic, 1996a) is not to obtain "the optimal" neural network architecture for a given problem, but to rapidly provide an architecture with close to optimal performance. Since information is obtained from a linear model, for more complex problems the neural network might be over-dimensioned (similar performance could be obtained using a smaller model and less learning examples). However, the exhaustive trial and error procedure involved for determining such an optimal model could be costlier than the stochastic analysis based alternative.

### 10.2.4    An Illustrative Example

Our experiments performed in (Drossu and Obradovic, 1996a) tested whether the most appropriate linear stochastic model can provide an indication of the appropriate number of neural network inputs. Additionally, they explored whether initial neural network weights obtained from the stochastic model as described by Equations 10.38 are appropriate. In the case of larger prediction horizons, the experiments also analyzed whether an adequate data sampling rate could be obtained from stochastic modeling.

All experiments encompassed preprocessing, consisting of both a logarithmic smoothing and a first order differentiation for stationarization purposes, and the neural network weight optimization was performed using gradient descent. The validity of the stochastic modeling prior knowledge for selecting an adequate neural network architecture, initial weights and sampling rate was tested in the context of two very different data sets:

- Mackey-Glass data.

The first data set is a deterministic time series, also known as the Mackey-Glass series, obtained by integrating the delay differential equation,

$$\frac{dx(t)}{dt} = \frac{Ax(t-\tau)}{1 + x^{10}(t-\tau)} - Bx(t)$$

Experiments were performed for $A = 0.2$, $B = 0.1$, $\tau = 17$, case in which the system exhibits chaotic behavior. The difficulty associated with this data set is the high *nonlinearity*. The data set consisted of 12000 samples, the first 2000 shown in Figure 10.3. The time series appears to be quasi-periodic with fairly long smooth segments. This suggests that the prediction of most of the series (except for the turning points, possibly) should be fairly easy for an adequate predictor. In accordance to previously published results (Lapedes and Farber, 1987), a sampling

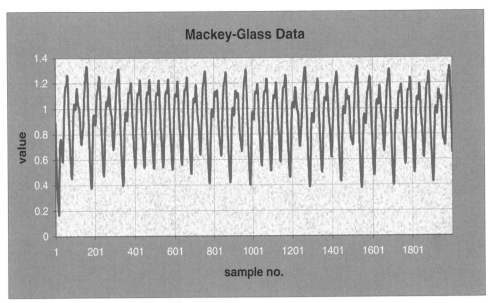

**Figure 10.3**   Mackey-Glass data.

rate of six was used for predicting 6 or 6*k steps ahead. Hence, the original data set was sampled at a rate of 6 to generate a new 2000 samples data set which was used for experimentation on prediction horizons 1 and $k$. The first 1000 samples of this "filtered" data were used for training, whereas the last 1000 samples were used for testing.

- Entertainment video traffic data.

The second data set used in the experiments consisted of a real life, compressed, entertainment video traffic data used in an ATM (Asynchronous Transfer Mode) network, in which each sample represents the size of a corresponding compressed video frame (Drossu et al., 1995). The characteristics of this data set are *non-stationarity* (data distribution changes over time) and the existence of "outliers" (values very different from neighboring ones). The problem is especially difficult since the outliers contain useful information that cannot be discarded through filtering. Hence, it is not sufficient to be able to accurately predict the (easily predictable) smooth sections of the time series, but the outliers also need to be predicted. The data set considered in our experiments consisted of 2000 samples (shown in Figure 10.4).

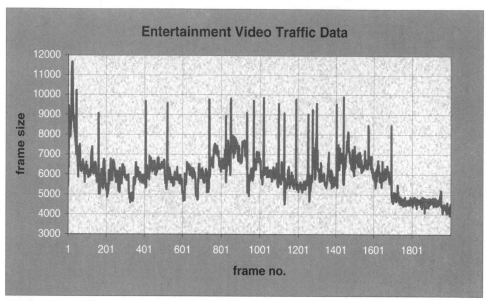

**Figure 10.4**    Entertainment video traffic data.

### 10.2.4.1   Predicting the Near Future

In these experiments, the neural network predictors attempted to predict one step ahead of time using the Mackey-Glass time series. The neural network weights were initialized either with small random values, or from the corresponding AR parameters as in Equations 10.38. The results presented for the neural networks initialized with random weights were averaged over 10 runs.

The results were compared versus an earlier reported "optimal" neural network topology with 4 inputs and two hidden layers of 10 units each (Lapedes and Farber, 1987), in which the number of inputs was determined based on dynamical system analysis and applying Takens' theorem, as discussed in Section 10.2.2, while the number of hidden layers and hidden units was determined through extensive experimentation on a supercomputer. The predictors' accuracy was evaluated according to the coefficient of determination (Anderson-Sprecher, 1994), computed as

$$r^2 = 1 - \frac{\sum_{t=1}^{N}(x_t - \hat{x}_t)^2}{\sum_{t=1}^{N}(x_t - \bar{x})^2}, \qquad (10.39)$$

where $N$ represents the number of samples, $x_t$ and $\hat{x}_t$ denote the actual and the predicted process values, respectively, while $\bar{x}$ denotes the mean of the actual data. For a perfect predictor, the coefficient of determination should be 1, whereas for a trivial mean predictor (one whose every prediction equals the mean of the actual data), the coefficient of determination is 0.

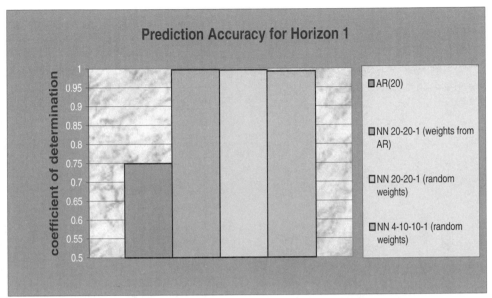

**Figure 10.5**   Prediction accuracy for horizon 1 on Mackey-Glass data.

The $r^2$ values, summarized in Figure 10.5, indicated an AR(20) model as the most appropriate linear model, thus suggesting the use of a feedforward neural network with 20 inputs. Varying the hidden layer size suggested that a number of hidden units equal to the number of inputs was an appropriate choice, thus allowing the neural network weight initialization using AR model parameters as well. Whether starting from random weights or initializing the weights from the AR parameters, the neural networks yielded a very similar prediction accuracy. Starting the neural network learning process with weights initialized from the AR parameters could, nevertheless, offer the benefit of being close to a minimum of the error surface, hence shortening the learning process. It would also eliminate the necessity of running a number of experiments in which the weights are initialized with different random values in order to obtain an averaged performance. On the other hand, to avoid the "freezing" of the learning process in a local minimum a small additive noise to the initial weight values could be desirable.

The conclusions drawn from this experiment are (Drossu and Obradovic, 1996a):

• The performance of the neural networks was much better compared to the most appropriate stochastic model, this being consistent with the nonlinearity of the time series.

• The neural network based on stochastic prior knowledge (both regarding the number of inputs and appropriate initial weight values) performed similar to the "optimal" neural network architecture, supporting the stochastic information

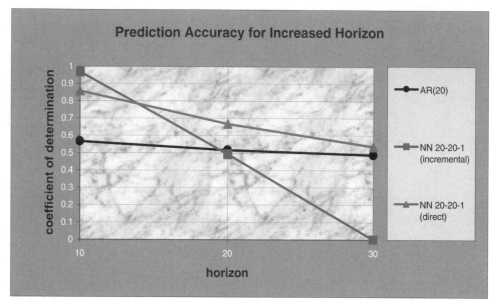

**Figure 10.6** Coefficient of determination for increased prediction horizon on Mackey-Glass data.

based design approach. This is a very useful finding, since it confirms that useful information can be extracted from a linear model even in the case where the underlying time series is highly nonlinear.

### 10.2.4.2 *Predicting further into the Future*

For horizon $h$ larger than one, the prediction can be done either in a *direct* or in an *incremental* fashion. In the direct approach, the neural network is trained to predict directly the $h$-th step ahead without predicting any of the intermediate $1, \ldots, h-1$ steps. In the incremental approach, the neural network predicts all the intermediate values up to $h$ steps ahead by using the previously predicted values as inputs when predicting the next value. The experiments, also performed on the Mackey-Glass series, were concerned with the decrease in prediction accuracy when significantly increasing the prediction horizon (Drossu and Obradovic, 1996a). For this purpose the AR(20) and the NN 20–20–1, trained as in the experiment for prediction horizon 1, were used to incrementally predict the process values up to 30 steps ahead (this corresponds to 180 steps ahead in the "unfiltered" series presented in Figure 10.3). In the case of the neural network, the weights were initialized from the AR parameters. The values for the coefficient of determination resulting from these experiments are presented in Figure 10.6.

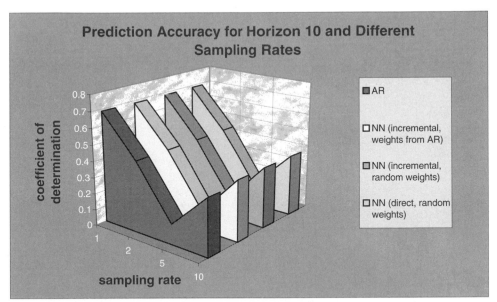

**Figure 10.7**  Prediction accuracy for horizon 10 and different sampling rates on entertainment video traffic data

The results indicated that the performance of the neural network was much better when predicting the near future, but it decreased dramatically and after about 30 steps ahead the predictor became completely unusable. This was an indication of the instability of the trained neural network (an undesirable error accumulation when using the incremental approach). For this reason, three 20–20–1 neural networks were trained in the direct fashion for predicting 10, 20 and 30 steps ahead, respectively. The values for their coefficients of determination, obtained as averages over 10 runs with different initial random weights, are also included in Figure 10.6 and they are significantly better than the corresponding ones for the AR(20) model. However, for prediction horizon 10 the coefficient of determination for the direct approach was worse than for the incremental approach.

The conclusion drawn from this experiment is (Drossu and Obradovic, 1996a):

• Although an incremental approach for neural network training in the case of an increased prediction horizon has the advantage of training a single neural network and using it afterwards for predicting as many steps ahead as desired, the system can be unstable, resulting in a dramatic error accumulation when increasing the prediction horizon. For this reason for larger prediction horizons it is desirable to analyze both the incremental and the direct training approach and to select the more appropriate one for each particular prediction horizon.

### 10.2.4.3   Selecting the Sampling Rate

For a larger prediction horizon different sampling rates can be employed, making the trial and error neural network architecture selection even more impractical. Consequently, in this experiment the choice of an appropriate sampling rate based on the stochastic modeling prior knowledge was explored. In addition, it was also tested whether an appropriate AR(p) model indicated the use of a feedforward neural network with $p$ external inputs whose initial weights could be set according to the AR parameters.

The entertainment video traffic data was used for experimentation for a prediction horizon 10 (the 10th step ahead process value is predicted) (Drossu and Obradovic, 1996a). To predict the process at time step $t + 10$ using $k$ process values up to time $t$, the following uniform sampling rates (divisors of the prediction horizon) were considered:

- sampling rate 1, where the $k$ previous process values are
  $$x(t), x(t-1), x(t-2), \ldots, x(t-k+1);$$
- sampling rate 2, where the $k$ previous process values are
  $$x(t), x(t-2), x(t-4), \ldots, x(t-2*(k-1));$$
- sampling rate 5, where the $k$ previous process values are
  $$x(t), x(t-5), x(t-10), \ldots, x(t-5*(k-1));$$
- sampling rate 10, where the $k$ previous process values are
  $$x(t), x(t-10), x(t-20), \ldots, x(t-10*(k-1)).$$

All neural network results were obtained either by initializing the weights from the AR parameters, or averaged over 10 runs with different initial random weights.

The coefficient of determination for the most appropriate AR models obtained for different sampling rates, as well as for the corresponding neural network models are presented in Figure 10.7. The stochastic models indicated a sampling rate of 1 as the most appropriate, confirmed also by their neural network counterparts. It could also be observed that the performance of the neural networks with weights initialized according to the AR parameters was very similar to that of the neural networks averaged over 10 runs with different initial random weights.

The results obtained for the most appropriate stochastic model, as well as for different representative neural networks when using a sampling rate of 1 indicated that the neural network having a number of inputs equal to the order of the most appropriate AR model yielded the best prediction.

The conclusions that could be drawn from these experiments are (Drossu and Obradovic, 1996a):

• The data sampling rate indicated by the stochastic models seems to be appropriate also for the neural network models.

• The prior knowledge provided by the stochastic analysis regarding the number of external inputs, and appropriate initial weight values is effective also for larger horizons.

- The performance of the AR models and the corresponding neural networks is comparable, this indicating the linearity of the problem under consideration.

---

## 10.3  Indirect Information Extraction Procedures

### 10.3.1  Knowledge of Properties of the Target Function

Whenever a prediction model, whether neural network or other, is trained on a data set, the only information that the model can extract is from the data itself. In many real-life applications, however, some properties of the function to be approximated are known ahead of time. The use of these properties, called *hints* (Abu-Mostafa, 1995a,b), is of major importance especially in problems with scarce, costly to obtain, or noisy data, like financial forecasting problems in which hints can improve the model's accuracy dramatically. Nevertheless, a non-valid hint can deteriorate the performance of the model considerably (Abu-Mostafa, 1995b), so care must be taken in order to analyze the validity of hints. Hints play an important role in improving the generalization ability (predictive accuracy) of the model by imposing constraints on the target function which has to be learned. This would correspond to restricting the search space for valid target functions by eliminating those which could potentially fit the noise instead of focusing on the relevant information contained in the data.

Two modalities for incorporating hints in the neural network learning process are proposed in (Abu-Mostafa, 1995a,b):

- creating additional "virtual" training examples;
- imposing constraints on the learning process by modifying the cost function.

The two modalities of embedding hints into the learning process will be illustrated in the context of two examples presented in (Abu-Mostafa, 1995a). The first one deals with the case in which the target function to be approximated is known to be odd. In this case, if $(x, y)$ is known to be a valid training example, a virtual example $(-x, -y)$ can be created which could provide an additional ready-to-use training example (if not already present in the training set). On the other hand, learning the oddness property of the target function can be enforced during the learning process, e.g. using gradient descent optimization. Similar to learning a function by minimizing the squared error between desired and real neural network output, $(y(x) - \hat{y}(x))^2$, the oddness property can be enforced by minimizing $(\hat{y}(x) + \hat{y}(-x))^2$. This requires the input of both $x$ and $-x$ to the network and minimizing the difference between the two outputs. A second example of incorporating hints assumes the target function to be invariant to certain transformations, e.g. scaling, translation and rotation in pattern recognition problems. Virtual examples can be produced by considering an available training example $(x, y)$ and creating the virtual example $(x', y)$, in which $x'$ represents the value obtained from $x$ by applying the invariance transformation. The invariance property can also be imposed during learning by minimizing, in addition to the squared error sum, a sum of terms of the form $(\hat{y}(x) - \hat{y}(x'))^2$. Many other additional hints like symmetry, monotonicity, etc., can also be easily incorporated into neural network learning.

Although not an actual way of accelerating the neural network design process, the use of known properties of the target function is an easy and cost-effective way of improving a time series predictor's accuracy, which can be used in conjunction with any other direct method presented earlier.

### 10.3.2   Non-Stationarity Detection

A *non-stationary* time series can be described as a time series whose "characteristic parameters" change over time. Different measures of stationarity can be employed to decide whether a process is stationary or not (Papoulis, 1984). In practice, confirming that a given time series is stationary is a very difficult task unless a closed-form expression of the underlying time series is known, which is rarely the case. On the other hand, non-stationarity detection can be reduced to identifying two sufficiently long, distinct data segments that have significantly different statistics (distributions). In practice, common tests for comparing whether two distributions are different are (Press et al., 1992):

- Student's t-test;
- F-test;
- Chi-square test;
- Kolmogorov-Smirnov test.

The *Student's t-test* is applied to identify the statistical significance of a difference in means of two distributions assumed to have the same variance, whereas the *F-test* evaluates the statistical significance of a difference in variances. More commonly, if there aren't any assumptions regarding the means or variances of the distributions, a chi-square or a Kolmogorov-Smirnov test, summarized in Appendix D, are performed.

If time is not an issue, non-stationary time series prediction can be accomplished by performing on-line learning using a *sliding window* technique (Chenoweth and Obradovic, 1996), in which a new prediction model is built whenever a new data sample becomes available. However, in many real-life problems the data arrival rate is high, which makes this approach completely infeasible due to the computational complexity involved in repeatedly building neural network prediction models. An alternative encountered in practice is the *uniform retraining* technique, in which an existing neural network prediction model is used for a pre-specified number of prediction steps (which we call a *reliable prediction interval*), followed by the replacement of the existing model by one constructed using more recent data. A major disadvantage of uniform retraining is that it is often hard to determine an appropriate reliable prediction interval, as it might be changing over time.

Although theoretically possible, in practice it might be very difficult to efficiently learn a single global neural network model for a non-stationary time series prediction. An obvious difficulty of such a global approach is the selection of neural network modeling parameters that are appropriate for all data segments. Additional serious problems include different noise levels in various data segments resulting in local overfitting and underfitting conflicts (it would be desired to stop training to prevent overfitting some data segments, while other data segments would still require additional training).

An interesting multi-model attempt to predict *piecewise stationary* time series , where the process switches between different regimes, is by using a *gating network*, in which a number of neural network experts having an identical structure are trained in parallel, and their responses are integrated by another neural network trained simultaneously with the expert networks (Weigend et al., 1995). Briefly, due to an adequate combination of activation and error functions that encourages localization, in a gating network each expert network tends to learn only a subset of the training data, thus devoting itself solely to a sub-region of the input space. This competitive integration method showed quite promising results when predicting a non-stationary time series having two regimes, but is not likely to extend well to more complex non-stationary processes due to overfitting problems of training a gating network system consisting of too many expert networks. In addition, the time required to train a complex gating network is likely to be prohibitively long for many real-life time series prediction problems.

In (Drossu and Obradovic, 1996b) we proposed three different time series prediction scenarios which depend on the amount of prior knowledge regarding a potential data distribution:

1. Switching among the historically successful neural network models (SWITCH);

2. Reusing one of historically successful available neural network models, or designing a new one (REUSE);

3. Retraining a neural network model when signaled, without relying on any historically successful model (RETRAIN).

The SWITCH scenario assumes a piecewise stationary, multi-regime time series and a library containing models for all regimes. To simplify the presentation we will assume two regimes and their associated historically successful models. The objective is to detect in real-time which of the two models to use for prediction at any given time step. The REUSE scenario assumes the potential existence of a repetitive regime along with an associated library model. The objective is to decide in real-time whether to use the existing previously successful historical model for prediction, or to retrain a new neural network on current data. Finally, the RETRAIN scenario does not assume any prior knowledge regarding the non-stationarity type. The objective is to decide in real-time when to discard a neural network predictor and retrain a new one on current data. The SWITCH and the REUSE scenarios are proposed in order to efficiently forecast piecewise stationary

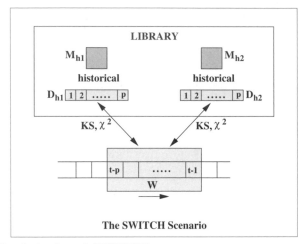

**Figure 10.8**   Statistics-based SWITCH.

processes with full or partial understanding of the number of different regimes, while the RETRAIN scenario is proposed for forecasting completely unknown higher order non-stationary processes.

The three scenarios can be used in the context of statistics– and accuracy-based distribution-change signaling techniques, discussed below.

### *10.3.2.1   Statistics-Based Signaling*

This signaling technique attempts to identify changes in the data distribution by comparing the similarity of different data segments using either the chi-square or the Kolmogorov-Smirnov statistics.

For the SWITCH scenario (see Figure 10.8), two historical data segments, $D_{h1}$ and $D_{h2}$, both of length $p$, along with their neural network models, $M_{h1}$ and $M_{h2}$, trained on these segments are kept in a library. A current window, $W$, containing the $p$ latest available data is compared in distribution (using either the chi-square or the Kolmogorov-Smirnov tests) to $D_{h1}$ and $D_{h2}$, in order to decide which of the two historical data segments is more similar to it. The library model corresponding to the more appropriate historical data segment is then used for predicting the next time series value.

For the REUSE scenario (see Figure 10.9), a single historical  data segment, $D_h$, used to build a previously successful neural network model, $M_h$, as well as a temporary data segment, $D_t$, used to build a temporary neural network model, $M_t$, both of length $p$, are kept in a library. The models $M_h$ and $M_t$ are also stored in the library. A current window, $W$, containing the $p$ latest available data is compared in distribution to $D_h$ and $D_t$, in order to decide whether to continue using one of the library models or to train a new model. For this purpose, a threshold has to be imposed on the confidence value obtained from the chi-square or Kolmogorov-Smirnov tests. If the test indicates more confidence in $M_h$, provided

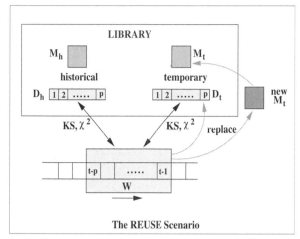

**Figure 10.9** Statistics-based REUSE.

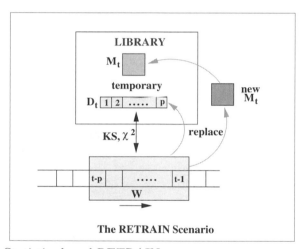

**Figure 10.10** Statistics-based RETRAIN.

that the confidence value for $M_h$ is larger than the specified threshold, then $M_h$ is used for the current prediction. Similarly, if we are more confident in $M_t$ and the confidence value is larger than the threshold, then $M_t$ is used for the current prediction. Otherwise (none of the confidence values is larger than the imposed threshold), a new temporary neural network model is trained on $W$ and it replaces $M_t$, whereas $W$ replaces $D_t$ in the library. The new model is then used for the current prediction.

In the case of the RETRAIN scenario (see Figure 10.10), a data segment, $D_t$, of length $p$ used to build a temporary neural network model, $M_t$, is stored in a library. A current window, $W$, containing the $p$ latest available data is compared in distribution to $D_t$, in order to decide whether to continue using $M_t$, or discard it and train a new neural network model. Once again, a threshold has to be imposed on

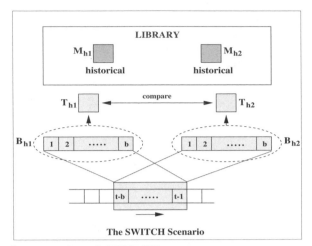

**Figure 10.11**   Accuracy-based SWITCH.

the confidence value obtained from the chi-square or Kolmogorov-Smirnov tests in order to decide when the current model becomes inappropriate. If $M_t$ is considered to be inadequate, $W$ replaces $D_t$ and a new neural network model trained on $W$ replaces $M_t$ in the library, which is used for the current prediction.

### 10.3.2.2   Accuracy-Based Signaling

The objective of this signaling technique, also proposed in (Drossu and Obradovic, 1996b) is to identify data distribution changes by measuring recent prediction accuracies of previously successful models.

For the SWITCH scenario (see Figure 10.11), two historically successful neural network models, $M_{h1}$ and $M_{h2}$, are kept in a library. At each time step, the two models are compared based on their accuracy measured on a buffer containing the $b$ most recent process values, and the more accurate model is used for the current prediction.

For the REUSE scenario (see Figure 10.12), a historically successful neural network model, $M_h$, as well as a temporary neural network model, $M_t$, are kept in a library. Similar to the SWITCH scenario, the accuracy of the two models is compared on the $b$ most recent process values. The model having a better accuracy is used for predicting the current step, unless none of the models is a sufficiently good predictor on the $b$ most recent process values. A model is considered to be sufficiently good if its accuracy on the $b$ most recent process values is above $\alpha \min\{A_h, A_t\}$, where $\alpha$ is a pre-specified threshold in the (0,1) range, while $A_h$ and $A_t$ are the training accuracies for the historical and the temporary model, respectively, computed on the process values used to build them. If none of the two existing models is satisfactory, a new neural network model is trained that replaces $M_t$ in the library and is also used for the current prediction.

In the case of the RETRAIN scenario (see Figure 10.13), a temporary neural

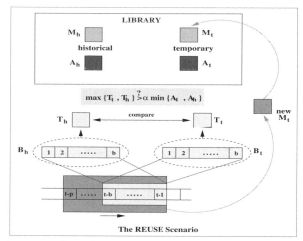

**Figure 10.12**   Accuracy-based REUSE.

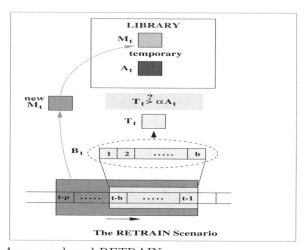

**Figure 10.13**   Accuracy-based RETRAIN.

network model, $M_t$, is stored in a library. Additionally, a corresponding training accuracy, $A_t$, is measured as for the REUSE scenario. If the accuracy $M_t$, measured on the $b$ most recent process values is $\alpha A_t$, model $M_t$ is used for the current prediction. Otherwise, a new neural network model is trained which replaces $M_t$ in the library and is also used for the current prediction.

### 10.3.3   An Illustrative Example

In (Drossu and Obradovic, 1996b), non-stationary time series prediction experiments were performed on generic data which allow a rigorous control of regime switching between distributions, as well as the possibility of computing the performance of an optimal predictor.

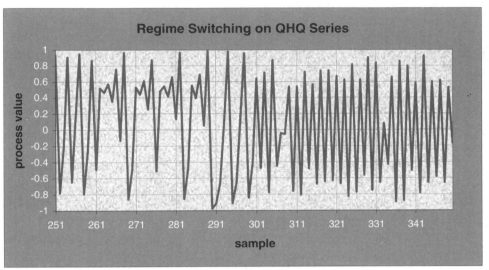

**Figure 10.14**   Regime switching on the QHQ series.

The time series used there were constructed by mixing data stemming from a deterministic chaotic process (Q) and a noisy, non-chaotic process (H) used earlier in (Weigend et al., 1995). The processes Q and H were generated according to the following rules:

$$x_{t+1} = 2(1 - x_t^2) - 1 \quad (Q)$$

$$x_{t+1} = \tanh(-1.2x_t + \epsilon_{t+1}) \quad (H),$$

where $\{\epsilon_t\}$ is a white noise process with mean 0 and standard deviation 0.32.

A first time series, denoted by QHQ, was created by concatenating three data sections of lengths 300, 400, and 500 samples, respectively, in which the first and the last data segments stemmed from the Q process, whereas the second data segment stemmed from the H process.

A segment of the QHQ time series comprising the first regime switch from process Q to process H (time series data samples 251–350) is presented in Figure 10.14. Although the Q and H processes have basically the same means and variances, as well as data ranges, Figure 10.14 illustrates the different time behavior of the two processes. Indeed, the autocorrelation plots for lags up to 50 on the first 300 and the next 300 time series data samples, shown in Figures 10.15 and 10.16, indicate a dependence of autocorrelation on time origin, meaning that the underlying mixed time series is not wide-sense stationary (Papoulis, 1984).

Two feedforward neural networks having 2 input units, two hidden layers of 4 units each and 1 output unit were trained (using the gradient descent algorithm)

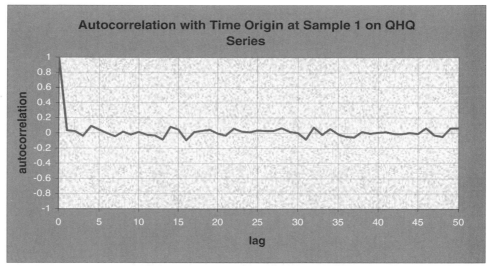

**Figure 10.15**  Autocorrelation with time origin at sample 1 on the QHQ series.

on two data segments stemming from the Q and the H processes, respectively.

### 10.3.3.1  The SWITCH Scenario

The experiments compared statistics-based signaling and accuracy-based signaling to a single-model predictor as well as to an optimal predictor (see Figure 10.17). The single-model predictor is a library model used for predicting the entire time series, whereas the optimal predictor is obtained by using both library models and assuming that the switching points between distributions are detected without any delay (this is infeasible in practice unless the regime switching rules are entirely understood).

Although the statistics-based signaling technique yields a significantly better prediction accuracy as compared to the single-model predictor, the results show the drastic superiority of accuracy-based signaling, which provides excellent results for buffer sizes over a fairly wide range of 2–30. It could also observed that these buffer sizes lead to performance which is comparable to that achieved when the regime switching points are completely known (optimal predictor curve).

### 10.3.3.2  The REUSE Scenario

The results obtained in (Drossu and Obradovic, 1996b) using the accuracy-based signaling technique for buffer sizes 50 and 100, averaged over ten runs, are shown as the first two bars in Figure 10.18. The bars represent the 99% confidence regions for the $r^2$ means, based on the *Student's t* distribution with 9 degrees of freedom. In all

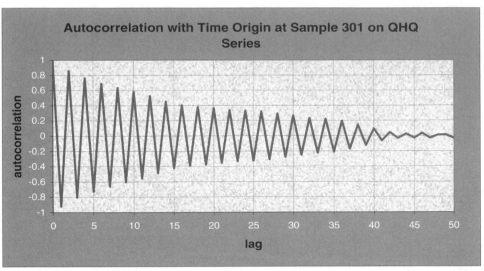

**Figure 10.16**    Autocorrelation with time origin at sample 301 on the QHQ series.

experiments the mean values for the coefficient of determination were significantly better than those obtained by the SWITCH scenario with statistics-based signaling, with small deviations given by the 99% confidence regions. Consequently, results obtained using the statistics-based signaling were not reported for the REUSE scenario. On the other hand, although the averaged value of the coefficient of determination was larger for all experiments using a shorter buffer, a statistically significant difference could not be claimed (the 99% confidence regions overlap). The number of neural network retrainings in the experiments with buffer length 100 varied between 3 and 7, whereas it varied between 5 and 14 in the case of buffer length 50. These figures indicate that the experiments on longer buffers are computationally more efficient. However, even for the shorter buffer, the number of retrainings is very small compared to the total number of predictions.

### 10.3.3.3    *The RETRAIN Scenario*

The 99% confidence regions for the averaged coefficient of determination obtained in (Drossu and Obradovic, 1996b) using the RETRAIN scenario are shown as the last two bars in Figure 10.18. Once again, the statistics-based signaling was not considered since the accuracy-based signaling results were better (with small deviations) than those obtained by the statistics-based signaling in the SWITCH scenario. The difference in performance for buffer sizes 50 and 100 was not statistically significant, while the experiments on longer buffers needed less computational resources (3 to 8 retrainings for buffer length 100, compared to 6 to 16 retrainings for buffer length 50).

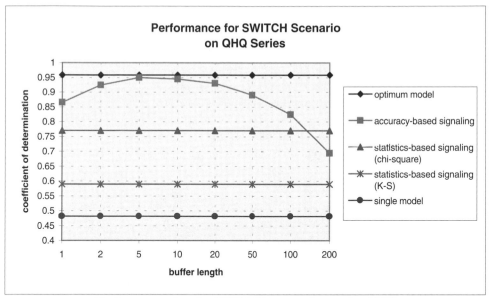

**Figure 10.17**   Performance for the SWITCH scenario on the QHQ series
(© Finance & Technology Publishing, used with permission, see Copyright Acknowledgment)

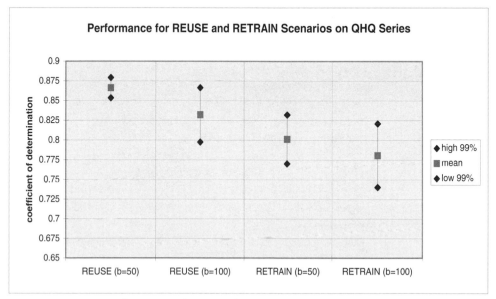

**Figure 10.18**   Performance for REUSE and RETRAIN scenarios on the QHQ series.

In (Drossu and Obradovic, 1996b), additional experimentation was performed on an HQH series (in which the mixing order of the Q and H processes was reversed). To get insight into the robustness of our proposed methodology with respect to the data noise level, two high-noise time series were constructed by corrupting the QHQ and the HQH time series with Gaussian additive noise of zero mean and standard deviation equal to half of the standard deviation of the uncorrupted data. In spite of an extremely high noise level, the accuracy-based signaling technique led once again to performance that was close to optimal. However, the statistics-based signaling technique was not only significantly less accurate, but not even consistently better than the single-model predictor that used a library model trained entirely on one distribution. As expected, due to a much larger amount of noise, the "optimal" buffer sizes for the accuracy-based signaling were larger compared to the corresponding ones from the low-noise experiments. The number of neural network retrainings in the high-noise experiments was consistently larger compared to the low-noise ones, but still reasonably small compared to the length of the time series.

## 10.4  Conclusions

Neural networks are powerful computational models which have been used in a multitude of time series prediction problems ranging from power consumption (Mangeas et al., 1995) and compressed video traffic (Drossu et al., 1995) to currency exchange (Abu-Mostafa, 1995a). However, because of their inherent complexity, the design of an appropriate neural network predictor for a real-life problem is often a time consuming trial-and-error procedure. In order to shorten the design process, as well as to improve the overall prediction accuracy, different sources of prior knowledge are *directly* embeddable into the neural network models, including, among others, information theory, dynamical system analysis, and stochastic analysis. Each of them has specific advantages but is also prone to various shortcomings. Nevertheless, the combination of different sources of prior knowledge is likely to provide a more robust predictor, likely to exploit the strengths of each individual knowledge source and to circumvent its weaknesses (Fletcher and Obradovic, 1993). This was illustrated by embedding stochastic analysis in the neural network design process in the context of an artificially generated, nonlinear, deterministic time series (Mackey-Glass data) and a real-life, non-stationary, stochastic time series (entertainment video traffic data).

In addition to the direct sources of prior knowledge, different *indirectly* embeddable sources are also worth considering. The chapter briefly illustrates the usefulness of known properties of the target function to be learned and describes in more detail different non-stationarity detection methods which incorporate various amounts of prior knowledge, and which significantly improve the efficiency of the neural network predictors. A novel accuracy-based distribution change detection method has been shown to provide significantly more accurate results than traditional statistics-based techniques (Drossu and Obradovic, 1996b).

## APPENDIX

*A. Minimization of a Mutual Information Upper Bound*

Applying Equation 10.5 to the components of the output vector leads to

$$
\begin{aligned}
I(y_1; y_2; \ldots ; y_d) \quad &= H(y_1) - H(y_1|y_2, y_3, \ldots y_d) \\
&= H(y_2) - H(y_2|y_1, y_3, \ldots y_d) \\
&\;\;\vdots \\
&= H(y_d) - H(y_d|y_1, y_2, \ldots y_{d-1}).
\end{aligned}
\tag{10.40}
$$

Adding up the left and the right hand sides of the previous $d$ expressions for the mutual information, we obtain

$$
\begin{aligned}
M = d \cdot I(y_1; y_2; \ldots ; y_d) = \\
= \textstyle\sum_{i=1}^d H(y_i) - \sum_{i=1}^d H(y_i|y_1, \ldots, y_{i-1}, y_{i+1}, \ldots, y_d).
\end{aligned}
\tag{10.41}
$$

Applying the chain rule for entropies (Deco and Obradovic, 1996), we obtain

$$
M = \sum_{i=1}^d H(y_i) - H(\bar{y}).
\tag{10.42}
$$

It can be shown that the mutual information is always greater or equal to zero, with equality holding only when its variables are independent, thus uncorrelated (Deco and Obradovic, 1996). Therefore, we can express the statistical independence of the components of the output vector as

$$
\sum_{i=1}^d H(y_i) - H(\bar{y}) = 0.
\tag{10.43}
$$

Due to the imposed condition of no information loss between input and output in the decorrelation transformation, minimizing the mutual information between the components of the output vector can be reduced to minimizing $\sum_{i=1}^d H(y_i)$. According to Gibbs' second theorem (Deco and Obradovic, 1996), the entropy of a distribution is upper bounded by the entropy of a normal distribution with the same variance. Therefore, instead of attempting to minimize $\sum_{i=1}^d H(y_i)$, we can attempt to minimize the sum of $d$ Gaussian distributions with individual variances equal to the variances of their corresponding non-Gaussian distributions. Since the entropy of a univariate Gaussian distribution is given by

$$
H(X) = \frac{1}{2}\ln(2\pi e \sigma^2),
\tag{10.44}
$$

with $\sigma^2$ being the variance of the Gaussian distribution, the minimization process reduces to minimizing the cost function

$$E = \sum_{i=1}^{d} \ln(\sigma_i^2). \tag{10.45}$$

which can be easily implemented using the gradient descent non-linear optimization technique.

### B. Cumulant Expansion of the Output Distribution

A more general approach for decorrelating the components of the output vector is provided by the cumulant expansion of the output distribution. The *moment generating function* or *characteristic function* of a univariate distribution is given as the Fourier transform of its probability density function (Gardiner, 1983),

$$\phi(\omega) = \int p(x)e^{j\omega x}dx, \tag{10.46}$$

where $j = \sqrt{-1}$. We can observe that the derivatives of the moment generating function evaluated at the origin can be expressed in terms of moments (this explains also the function's name), since

$$\phi^{(n)}(\omega) = \frac{\partial^n \phi}{\partial \omega^n} = \int (jx)^n p(x)e^{j\omega x}dx, \tag{10.47}$$

and hence,

$$\phi^{(n)}(0) = j^n m^{(n)}, \tag{10.48}$$

where $m^{(n)}$ represents the moment of order $n$ defined as

$$m^{(n)} = \int x^n p(x)dx. \tag{10.49}$$

Therefore, assuming that all the moments exist and are finite, the moment generating function can be expanded in a power series around the origin, expressed as

$$\phi(\omega) = \sum_{n=0}^{\infty} \frac{j^n \omega^n}{n!} m^{(n)}. \tag{10.50}$$

Similarly, the moment generating function of a multivariate distribution can be expressed as

$$\phi(\bar{\omega}) = \int p(\bar{x})e^{j\bar{\omega}\cdot\bar{x}}d\bar{x}. \tag{10.51}$$

The inverse Fourier transform of the moment generating function will therefore provide the probability density function,

$$p(\bar{x}) = (2\pi)^{-d} \int \phi(\bar{\omega})e^{-j\bar{\omega}\cdot\bar{x}}d\bar{\omega}, \tag{10.52}$$

with $d$ representing the dimension of the vector of random variables. In accordance with this inversion formula, the moment generating function determines the probability density function with probability 1. Therefore, the independence condition expressed as

$$p(x_1, x_2, \ldots, x_d) = p_1(x_1)p_2(x_2)\ldots p_d(x_d), \tag{10.53}$$

can also be expressed as

$$\phi(\omega_1, \omega_2, \ldots, \omega_d) = \phi_1(\omega_1)\phi_2(\omega_2)\ldots\phi_d(\omega_d). \tag{10.54}$$

The natural logarithm of the characteristic function is named the *cumulant generating function*,

$$\psi(\bar{\omega}) = \ln\phi(\bar{\omega}). \tag{10.55}$$

Assuming that all the higher order moments exist and are finite, we can expand the cumulant generating function in a power series around the origin, expressed as (Gardiner, 1983)

$$\psi(\bar{\omega}) = \sum_{n=1}^{\infty} \frac{j^n}{n!} \sum_{(i)} \ll x_1^{i_1} x_2^{i_2}\ldots x_d^{i_d} \gg \cdot \\ \omega_1^{i_1}\omega_2^{i_2}\ldots\omega_d^{i_d}\delta\left(n, \sum_{k=1}^{d} i_k\right), \tag{10.56}$$

where the quantities $\ll x_1^{i_1} x_2^{i_2}\ldots x_d^{i_d} \gg$ represent the multi-dimensional cumulants of the variables $x_1, x_2, \ldots x_d$, and $\delta\left(n, \sum_{k=1}^{d} i_k\right)$ represents Kronecker's delta function, which is 1 if $\sum_{k=1}^{d} i_k$ equals $n$ and 0 otherwise. In a similar fashion, we can also expand a univariate cumulant generating function in a power series in terms of uni-dimensional cumulants,

$$\psi_i(\omega_i) = \sum_{n=1}^{\infty} \frac{j^n}{n!} \ll x_i^n \gg \omega_i^n, \tag{10.57}$$

with $\ll x_i^n \gg$ representing the uni-dimensional cumulants. Condition 10.54 can also be expressed in terms of cumulant generating functions as,

$$\ln\left(\phi(\bar{\omega})\right) = \sum_{i=1}^{d} \ln\phi_i(\omega_i), \tag{10.58}$$

which is equivalent to

$$\psi(\bar{\omega}) = \sum_{i=1}^{d} \psi_i(\omega_i). \tag{10.59}$$

The last condition can be made explicit by using Equations 10.56 and 10.57 and hence rewritten as,

$$\sum_{n=1}^{\infty} \frac{j^n}{n!} \sum_{(i)} \ll x_1^{i_1} \ldots x_d^{i_d} \gg \omega_1^{i_1} \ldots \omega_d^{i_d} \delta \left( n, \sum_{k=1}^{d} i_k \right)$$
$$= \sum_{i=1}^{d} \sum_{n=1}^{\infty} \frac{j^n}{n!} \ll x_i^n \gg \omega_i^n \tag{10.60}$$

The method of computing the multi-dimensional cumulants $\ll x_1 x_2 \ldots x_n \gg$ of any desired order $n$ can be presented in an algorithmic fashion as (Gardiner, 1983):

■ Write a sequence of $n$ dots, .......

■ Divide this sequence into $p + 1$ subsequences, each enclosed in angular brackets, with $p$ varying from 0 to $n - 1$,

$$< .. >< ... >< \ldots\ldots > \ldots < . > . \tag{10.61}$$

■ Replace the dots by the symbols $x_1, \ldots, x_n$, in such a fashion that all the *different* expressions occur, thus

$$< x_1 >< x_2 x_3 >= \ \ < x_1 >< x_3 x_2 >$$
$$\neq \ \ < x_3 >< x_1 x_2 >, \tag{10.62}$$

where

$$< x_1 x_2 \ldots x_n >= \int x_1 x_2 \ldots x_n p\left(\bar{x}\right) d\bar{x} \tag{10.63}$$

$$< x_i^n >= \int x_i^n p(x_i) dx_i, \tag{10.64}$$

with $\bar{x} = (x_1, x_2, \ldots, x_n)$.

■ For every $p$, take the sum of all the terms containing $p + 1$ subsequences and call this sum $C_p(x_1, x_2, \ldots, x_n)$.

■ Compute the multi-dimensional cumulant as

$$\ll x_1 x_2 \ldots x_n \gg \ = \ \sum_{p=0}^{n-1} (-1)^p \, p! C_p(x_1, x_2, \ldots, x_n). \tag{10.65}$$

■ In cases in which a cumulant contains a repeated term, like $\ll x_1^2 x_2 x_3 \gg$, compute $\ll x_1 x_2 x_3 x_4 \gg$ and in the resulting expression set $x_4 = x_1$.

Although cumulants of whichever desired order can be computed theoretically, in practice cumulants of order four will rarely be exceeded. The first four multi-dimensional cumulants can be expressed as,

$$
\begin{aligned}
\ll x_i \gg \;&=\; <x_i> \\
\ll x_i x_j \gg \;&=\; <x_i x_j> - <x_i><x_j> \\
\ll x_i x_j x_k \gg \;&=\; <x_i x_j x_k> - <x_i x_j><x_k> - \\
&\quad <x_j x_k><x_i> - <x_k x_i><x_j> + \\
&\quad 2<x_i><x_j><x_k> \\
\ll x_i x_j x_k x_l \gg \;&=\; <x_i x_j x_k x_l> - <x_i x_j x_k><x_l> - \\
&\quad <x_j x_k x_l><x_i> - <x_k x_l x_i><x_j> - \\
&\quad <x_l x_i x_j><x_k> - <x_i x_j><x_k x_l> - \\
&\quad <x_i x_k><x_j x_l> - <x_i x_l><x_j x_k> + \\
&\quad 2<x_i x_j><x_k><x_l> + 2<x_i x_k><x_j><x_l> + \\
&\quad 2<x_i x_l><x_j><x_k> + 2<x_j x_k><x_i><x_l> + \\
&\quad 2<x_j x_l><x_i><x_k> + 2<x_k x_l><x_i><x_j> - \\
&\quad 6<x_i><x_j><x_k><x_l>,
\end{aligned}
\tag{10.66}
$$

whereas the uni-dimensional cumulants up to fourth order are

$$
\begin{aligned}
\ll x_i^1 \gg \;&=\; <x_i> \\
\ll x_i^2 \gg \;&=\; <x_i^2> - <x_i>^2 \\
\ll x_i^3 \gg \;&=\; <x_i^3> - 3<x_i^2><x_i> + 2<x_i>^3 \\
\ll x_i^4 \gg \;&=\; <x_i^4> - 4<x_i^3><x_i> - \\
&\quad 3<x_i^2>^2 + 12<x_i^2><x_i>^2 - 6<x_i>^4 \, .
\end{aligned}
\tag{10.67}
$$

Replacing the $x_i$'s by $y_i$'s, to indicate the components of the output vector, the independence condition Equation 10.60 can be rewritten by replacing the expressions for the multi-dimensional and the uni-dimensional cumulants, resulting in

$$
\begin{aligned}
&-\tfrac{1}{2} \sum_{i,j} \omega_i \omega_j \left\{ \ll y_i y_j \gg - \ll y_i^2 \gg \delta_{ij} \right\} - \\
&\tfrac{j}{6} \sum_{i,j,k} \omega_i \omega_j \omega_k \left\{ \ll y_i y_j y_k \gg - \ll y_i^3 \gg \delta_{ijk} \right\} + \\
&\tfrac{1}{24} \sum_{i,j,k,l} \omega_i \omega_j \omega_k \omega_l \left\{ \ll y_i y_j y_k y_l \gg - \ll y_i^4 \gg \delta_{ijkl} \right\} \\
&= 0.
\end{aligned}
\tag{10.68}
$$

Considering additionally that the mean of the output vector has been removed, the previous condition can be further expressed as (Deco and Schurmann, 1995)

$$
\begin{aligned}
&-\tfrac{1}{2} \sum_{i,j} \omega_i \omega_j \left\{ <y_i y_j> - <y_i^2> \delta_{ij} \right\} \\
&-\tfrac{j}{6} \sum_{i,j,k} \omega_i \omega_j \omega_k \left\{ <y_i y_j y_k> - <y_i^3> \delta_{ijk} \right\} \\
&+\tfrac{1}{24} \sum_{i,j,k,l} \omega_i \omega_j \omega_k \omega_l \left\{ <y_i y_j y_k y_l> \right. \\
&\left. -3<y_i y_j><y_k y_l> - \left( <y_i^4> - 3<y_i^2>^2 \right) \delta_{ijkl} \right\} = 0.
\end{aligned}
\tag{10.69}
$$

The $\delta_{i...j}$ denote Kronecker's delta, which equals 1 only when all the subscripts are equal to each other and equals 0 otherwise. Since the previous relation has to be satisfied for all $\bar{\omega}$, the terms inside each summation must be equal to zero. Hence, for all $i, j, k, l$

$$
\begin{aligned}
&< y_i y_j > - < y_i^2 > \delta_{ij} = 0, \\
&< y_i y_j y_k > - < y_i^3 > \delta_{ijk} = 0, \\
&< y_i y_j y_k y_l > -3 < y_i y_j >< y_k y_l > \\
&\quad - \left(< y_i^4 > -3 < y_i^2 >^2\right) \delta_{ijkl} = 0.
\end{aligned}
\tag{10.70}
$$

According to (Deco and Schurmann, 1995), the previous conditions can be expressed in the equivalent form

$$
\begin{aligned}
&< y_i y_j >= 0, \quad \text{if } (i \neq j), \\
&< y_i y_j y_k >= 0, \quad \text{if } (i \neq j \vee i \neq k), \\
&< y_i y_j y_k y_l >= 0, \quad \text{if } (\{i \neq j \vee i \neq k \vee i \neq l\} \wedge \neg L), \\
&< y_i^2 y_j^2 > -3 < y_i^2 >< y_j^2 >= 0, \quad \text{if } (i \neq j),
\end{aligned}
\tag{10.71}
$$

with $L$ being the logical expression

$$
\begin{aligned}
L = \{ \quad &(i = j \wedge k = l \wedge j \neq k) \vee \\
&(i = k \wedge j = l \wedge i \neq j) \vee \\
&(i = l \wedge j = k \wedge i \neq j) \ \}.
\end{aligned}
\tag{10.72}
$$

These conditions can be imposed by using gradient descent non-linear optimization applied to the cost function

$$
\begin{aligned}
E =\ &\alpha \sum_{i<j} < y_i y_j >^2 + \beta \sum_{i<j\leq k} < y_i y_j y_k >^2 + \\
&\gamma \sum_{i<j\leq k\leq l} < y_i y_j y_k y_l >^2 + \\
&\delta \sum_{i<j} \left(< y_i^2 y_j^2 > -3 < y_i^2 >< y_j^2 >\right)^2,
\end{aligned}
\tag{10.73}
$$

with $\alpha$, $\beta$, $\gamma$, and $\delta$, representing the inverses of the number of elements in their corresponding summations.

### C. AR(p) Approximation by a Neural Network

Consider the approximation of an AR model of order $p$ by a feedforward neural network with $p$ input units, $p$ hidden units and a single output unit. It is assumed that each hidden unit uses an activation function of the form $f(x) = 1/(1 + e^{-\beta x})$, whereas the output unit uses the identity function $i(x) = x$ as its activation function. In this neural network, for all $i, j \in \{1, \ldots, p\}$, let us set the hidden unit biases to

$$
\theta_i = 0,
\tag{10.74}
$$

and the input-to-hidden layer weights to

$$w_{ij} = \delta_{ij}, \tag{10.75}$$

where $\delta_{ij}$ is Kronecker's delta function. Using the notation from Figure 10.2, on input $(x_{t-1}, \ldots, x_{t-p})$, the neural network output can be written as

$$\hat{x}_t = \sum_{i=1}^{p} \left( \frac{W_i}{1+e^{-\beta x_{t-i}}} + \gamma_i \right) = \sum_{i=1}^{p} g(x_{t-i}), \tag{10.76}$$

where $\sum_{i=1}^{p} \gamma_i = \Gamma$. On the same input, the AR(p)–based predictor outputs

$$\hat{x}_t = \sum_{i=1}^{p} \varphi_i x_{t-i} = \sum_{i=1}^{p} h(x_{t-i}). \tag{10.77}$$

Equation 10.76 approximates Equation 10.77 for any combination of inputs that are small enough if each $g(x_{t-i})$ approximates the corresponding $h(x_{t-i})$. Expanding $g(x_{t-i})$ in a Taylor series around the origin and keeping just the terms up to order 1, we obtain

$$g(x_{t-i}) \simeq g(0) + g'(0)x_{t-i} = \frac{W_i}{2} + \gamma_i + \frac{\beta W_i}{4} x_{t-i} \tag{10.78}$$

Hence, setting $g(x_{t-i}) = h(x_{l-i})$ leads to

$$W_i = \frac{4\varphi_i}{\beta} \tag{10.79}$$

$$\gamma_i = -\frac{W_i}{2}, \tag{10.80}$$

So, the neural network with $p$ inputs, $p$ hidden units and interconnection parameters

$$\begin{aligned}
w_{ij} &= \delta_{ij} \\
\theta_i &= 0 \\
W_i &= \frac{4}{\beta} \varphi_i \\
\Gamma &= -\frac{2}{\beta} \sum_{i=1}^{p} \varphi_i,
\end{aligned} \tag{10.81}$$

where $i, j \in \{1, \ldots, p\}$, approximates an AR model of order $p$ with parameters $\varphi_1, \ldots, \varphi_p$.

For the Approximation 10.78 to be reasonably accurate, $x_{t-i}$ has to be close to zero. For $x_{t-i} \in [-1, 1]$, the maximum relative error when approximating $h(x_{t-i})$ (given in Equation 10.77) by $g(x_{t-i})$ (given in Equation 10.76), with $W_i$ and $\gamma_i$ computed according to Equations 10.79 and 10.80, respectively, is 8% for $\beta = 1$, 2% for $\beta = 0.5$ and 0.08% for $\beta = 0.1$.

*D. Chi-square and Kolmogorov-Smirnov Tests*

In the *Chi-square test*, the data range of the two data sets to be compared is divided into a number of intervals (bins). Assuming that $R_i$ and $S_i$ represent the number of data samples in bin $i$ for the first and the second data set, respectively, the Chi-square statistic computes

$$\chi^2 = \sum_i \frac{(R_i - S_i)^2}{R_i + S_i},$$

with the sum taken over all bins. The complement of the incomplete gamma function,

$$Q(\nu, \chi^2) = \frac{1}{\Gamma(\nu)} \int_{\chi^2}^{\infty} e^{-t} t^{a-1} dt,$$

where

$$\Gamma(x) = \int_0^{\infty} t^{x-1} e^{-t} dt,$$

is then evaluated and a small value of $Q$ (close to 0) indicates that it is unlikely that the two distributions are the same. Here, $\nu$ represents the number of degrees of freedom which in the case when the two sets have the same number of data samples ($\sum R_i = \sum S_i$), equals the number of bins minus one. If the previous restriction is not imposed, than $\nu$ equals the number of bins.

The *Kolmogorov-Smirnov (K-S) test* measures the absolute difference between two cumulative distribution functions $S_{N_1}$ and $S_{N_2}$ with $N_1$ and $N_2$ data points, respectively. The K-S statistic computes

$$D = \max_{-\infty < x < \infty} |S_{N_1}(x) - S_{N_2}(x)|.$$

The function $Q_{KS}$ defined as

$$Q_{KS}(\lambda) = 2 \sum_{j=1}^{\infty} (-1)^{j-1} e^{-2j^2 \lambda^2}$$

is computed for

$$\lambda = D(\sqrt{N_e} + 0.12 + 0.11/\sqrt{N_e}),$$

where $N_e$ is the effective number of data points,

$$N_e = \frac{N_1 N_2}{N_1 + N_2}.$$

A small value of $Q_{KS}$ (close to 0) indicates that it is unlikely that the two distributions are the same.

## Copyright Acknowledgment

Figure 10.17 was reprinted with permission from J. of Computational Intelligence in Finance, © Finance & Technology Publishing, PO Box 764, Haymarket, VA 20168, from (Drossu and Obradovic, 1996b).

## References

Abecasis, S. M. and Lapenta, E. S. 1996. Nonstationary time-series forecasting within a neural network framework. *NeuroVe$t Journal*, 4(4):9–16.

Abu-Mostafa, Y. 1995a. Financial applications of learning from hints. In *Advances in Neural Information Processing Systems*, eds. J. D. Cowan, G. Tesauro, and J. Alspector, vol. 7, pp. 411–418.

Abu-Mostafa, Y. 1995b. Hints. *Neural Computation*, 7:639–671.

Anderson-Sprecher, R. 1994. Model comparisons and $R^2$. *The American Statistician*, 48(2):113–117.

Barlow, H. B. 1989. Unsupervised learning. *Neural Computation*, 1:295–311.

Barron, A. R. 1993. Universal approximation bounds for superposition of a sigmoidal function. *IEEE Transactions on Information Theory*, 39(3):930–945.

Box, G. E. P., Jenkins, G. M., and Reinsel, G. C. 1994. *Time Series Analysis. Forecasting and Control. Third Edition.* Prentice Hall.

Chenoweth, T. and Obradovic, Z. 1996. A multi-component nonlinear prediction system for the S&P 500 index. *Neurocomputing*, 10(3):275–290.

Connor, J. T., Martin, R. D., and Atlas, L. E. 1994. Recurrent neural networks and robust time series prediction. *IEEE Transactions on Neural Networks*, 5(2):240–254.

Cybenko, G. 1989. Approximation by superpositions of a sigmoidal function. *Mathematics of Control, Signal, and Systems*, 2:303–314.

Deco, G. and Brauer, W. 1995. Nonlinear higher-order statistical decorrelation by volume-conserving neural architectures. *Neural Networks*, 8(4):525–535.

Deco, G. and Obradovic, D. 1996. *An Information-Theoretic Approach to Neural Computing.* Springer.

Deco, G. and Schurmann, B. 1995. Learning time series evolution by unsupervised extraction of correlations. *Physical Review E*, 51(3):1780–1790.

Drossu, R., Lakshman, T. V., Obradovic, Z., and Raghavendra, C. 1995. Single and multiple frame video traffic prediction using neural network models. In *Computer Networks, Architecture and Applications*, eds. S. V. Raghavan and B. N. Jain, pp. 146–158. Chapman and Hall.

Drossu, R. and Obradovic, Z. 1996a. Efficient design of neural networks for time series prediction. *IEEE Computational Science and Engineering*, 3(2):78–89.

Drossu, R. and Obradovic, Z. 1996b. Regime signaling techniques for non-stationary time-series forecasting. *NeuroVe$t Journal*, 4(5):7–15.

Fahlman, S. and Lebiere, C. 1990. The cascade-correlation learning architecture. In *Advances in Neural Information Processing Systems*, ed. D. S. Touretzky, vol. 2, pp. 524–532.

Fletcher, J. and Obradovic, Z. 1993. Combining prior symbolic knowledge and constructive neural networks. *Connection Science: Journal of Neural Computing, Artificial Intelligence and Cognitive Research*, 5(3-4):365–375.

Gardiner, C. W. 1983. *Handbook of Stochastic Methods.* Springer.

Grassberger, P. and Procaccia, I. 1983. Measuring the strangeness of strange attractors. *Physica D*, 9:189–208.

Haykin, S. 1994. *Neural Networks. A Comprehensive Foundation.* MacMillan.

Jurgens, H. O. P. H. and Saupe, D. 1992. *Chaos and Fractals: New Frontiers of Science.* Springer.

Lapedes, A. and Farber, R. 1987. Nonlinear signal processing using neural networks: Prediction and system modeling. *Technical Report, LA-UR87-2662, Los Alamos National Laboratory.*

Liebert, W. and Schuster, H. G. 1989. Proper choice of time delay for the analysis of chaotic time series. *Physics Letters A*, 142:107–111.

Mangeas, M., Muller, C., and Weigend, A. S. 1995. Forecasting electricity demand using nonlinear mixture of experts. In *World Congress on Neural Networks*, vol. 2, pp. 48–53.

Papoulis, A. 1984. *Probability, Random Variables, and Stochastic Processes. Second Edition.* McGraw-Hill.

Pineda, F. and Sommerer, J. C. 1993. Estimating generalized dimensions and choosing time delays: A fast algorithm. In *Time Series Prediction: Forecasting the Future and Understanding the Past*, eds. A. S. Weigend and N. A. Gershenfeld, pp. 367–385. Addison-Wesley.

Press, W. H., Teukolsky, S. A., Vetterling, W. T., and Flannery, B. P. 1992. *Numerical Recipes in C. Second Edition.* Cambridge University Press.

Redlich, A. N. 1993a. Redundancy reduction as a strategy for unsupervised learning. *Neural Computation*, 5:289–304.

Redlich, A. N. 1993b. Supervised factorial learning. *Neural Computation*, 5:750–766.

Sjöberg, J., Hjalmarsson, H., and Ljung, L. 1994. Neural networks in system identification. In *Proc. 10th IFAC Symposium on System Identification (SYSID) '94*, vol. 2, pp. 49–72, Copenhagen, Denmark.

Sjöberg, J., Zhang, Q., Ljung, L., Benveniste, A., Deylon, B., Glorennec, P., Hjalmarsson, H., and Juditsky, A. 1995. Nonlinear black-box modeling in system identification: A unified overview. *Automatica*, 31(12):1691–1724.

Takens, F. 1981. Detecting strange attractors in turbulence. In *Lecture Notes in Mathematics*, eds. D. Rand and L. Young, pp. 366–381. Springer.

Weigend, A. S., Mangeas, M., and Srivastava, A. N. 1995. Nonlinear gated experts for time series: Discovering regimes and avoiding overfitting. *International Journal of Neural Systems*, 6:373–399.

Werbos, P. 1992. Neural networks, system identification and control in the chemical process industries. In *Handbook of Intelligent Control. Neural, Fuzzy, and Adaptive Approaches*, eds. D. A. White and D. A. Sofge, pp. 283–356. Van Nostrand Reinhold.

Werbos, P. 1994. *The Roots of Backpropagation: From Ordered Derivatives to Neural Networks and Political Forecasting*. John Wiley and Sons.

Wolf, A., Swift, J. B., Swinney, H. L., and Vastano, J. A. 1985. Determining Lyapunov exponents from a time series. *Physica D*, 16:285–317.

# 11     Extraction of Decision Trees from Artificial Neural Networks

Gregor Schmitz, Chris Aldrich and Francois Gouws

*Despite the fact that neural networks can represent complex systems with a high degree of accuracy, they are usually difficult to interpret. This can constitute a severe limitation in practice, where reliability and comprehensibility of the model may be of critical importance. In this chapter, a novel knowledge-based neurocomputing algorithm (ANN-DT) is therefore proposed, which is designed to extract binary decision trees from trained neural networks. In contrast to existing techniques, ANN-DT can extract rules from feed-forward neural networks with continuous inputs as well as continuous outputs, while not making any assumptions regarding the neural network or the features of the data. The selection of attributes based on an analysis of the significance of attributes with regard to the output of the neural network is also proposed and compared to the standard methods using information entropy criteria for discrete outputs or variance minimisation for continuous outputs. The ANN-DT algorithm compared favorably with ID3, C4.5 and a regression tree evolved with CART's splitting procedure.*

## 11.1   Introduction

The development and application of artificial neural networks has grown significantly in recent years, owing to their ability to represent non-linear relationships that are difficult to model by means of other computational methods. In addition, neural networks do not require a priori knowledge with regard to the distributions of data, are easy to implement, are robust under the influence of noise, and can be parallelized where rapid computation is critical.

Despite their attractive qualities, neural network models are notoriously difficult to interpret. As a consequence, erroneous assumptions during model development can remain undetected during development and even application. Moreover, neural networks have large degrees of freedom in the assignment of weights, so that two completely different sets of weights can yield nearly identical outputs. This drastically complicates the analysis and comparison of similar processes that are modeled or controlled by different neural networks. The lack of transparency of neural networks is a major barrier to their implementation in a number of fields, such as medicine and engineering where mission critical applications demand a high degree of confidence in the behavior of relevant models.

In order to overcome this limitation, various attempts have previously been made to develop explanatory facilities for neural networks, an area which concerns the use of explicit knowledge within the neurocomputing paradigm. The majority of these approaches have been based on the generation of explicit rules explaining the behavior of the neural network. Unfortunately, most rule extraction techniques require special training methods and architectures for neural networks, or are based on assumptions that tend to restrict the ability of the neural network to generalize the underlying relationships in the data.

A more general algorithm not subject to these limitations is therefore proposed in this chapter. Like other knowledge-based neurocomputing algorithms, it enables the characterization of the behavior of the neural network by means of a set of heuristic rules. Unlike other algorithms however, this algorithm does not depend on any assumptions with regard to the structure of the neural network or the input-output data. Since neural networks are generally better able to approximate complex relationships between continuous variables, the rules extracted from the network also tend to be more accurate in some cases than those derived direct from the data by other machine learning methods, such as ID3 (Davis et al., 1977; Quinlan, 1986), C4.5 (Quinlan, 1993) or CART (Breiman et al., 1984).

## 11.2  Extraction of Rules from Neural Networks

The extraction of rules from neural networks can be classified as decompositional, pedagogical  and eclectic (Andrews et al., 1995; Craven and Shavlik, 1994), based on the approach used to characterize the internal model of the network in terms of a set of explicit rules. Decompositional techniques such as those used by (Towell and Shavlik, 1993; Fu, 1991; Gallant, 1993) focus on extracting rules separately for each unit of the neural network. With these techniques the activation of the individual neurons is approximated in terms of threshold functions, by assuming that the units are either maximally active or inactive. Each non-input unit in the neural net can therefore be interpreted as a step function or a Boolean rule, so that the rule extraction problem is reduced to finding conditions under which certain rules are valid. The drawback of this approach is that the architecture of the neural network and training procedures may have to be simplified to realize this approximation. This may lead to inadequate models. In addition, hard-thresholding of the units can make them sensitive to noise in the data. Although this problem can be alleviated by making use of soft thresholding (Sethi, 1995), these and other similar methods constrain the distributed non-discrete internal states of a neural network and prevent the use of many advanced network implementations.

In the approach taken by pedagogical techniques, the rules that map inputs to outputs are extracted directly, even for multilayered neural networks. The neural network is thus essentially treated as a black box. An example of this is Thrun's method (Thrun, 1994, 1995) called validity interval analysis (VIA), which uses linear programming to determine if a set of constraints placed on a network's activation values is consistent. The technique does not approximate the activation levels of the hidden units as threshold functions, but it is assumed that these activations are independent of one another. This assumption is not always appropriate and hence the algorithm does not always find maximally general rules. Other techniques such as those developed by Pop et al., as well as by Craven and Shavlik are in their current state limited to discrete inputs /(Pop et al., 1994; Craven and Shavlik, 1994). Furthermore, Craven and Shavlik's technique is implemented using either the VI analysis (Thrun, 1995) or the KT method described by Fu (Fu, 1991), whereby it is implicitly assumed that the activations of the hidden layers are independent, or that they can be treated as threshold functions.

Saito and Nakano (Saito and Nakano, 1988) have likewise pursued a pedagogical concept by searching for combinations of input values which activate a given output unit. This resulted in a search space that grew exponentially with the number of input variables, which limited the number of rules that could be explored. A similar approach was recently followed by Narazaki et al., where regions were defined, the boundaries of which were based on the signs of the partial derivatives of the neural network function, as well as on the class predicted by the neural network (Narazaki et al., 1996).

Eclectic techniques combine elements of the two basic approaches discussed above. These methods, such as exemplified by the DEDEC (Tickle et al., 1994) and BRAINNE systems (Sestito and Dillon, 1992), draw inferences from the magnitudes of the weights in a neural network. This has to be done carefully, as certain weights in a neural network can be large, but nevertheless insignificant to the final outcome, owing to cancellations of their contributions in higher layers of the network. Interdependent inputs tend to complicate this problem even further (Masters, 1993).

Based on the above descriptions, the ANN Decision Tree (ANN-DT) algorithm proposed in this chapter can be seen as pedagogical, although it does not suffer from the drawbacks of the above strategies. Two variants of the algorithm are investigated, which differ only with regard to the way in which variables, features or attributes and associated split points are selected. Instead of attempting to extract rules from the original data or interpreting the internal structure of neural networks, as mentioned above, the proposed techniques are based on sampling of a (neural network) model of the original data, which is subsequently used as a basis for the extraction of rules. The idea of sampling the neural network was introduced recently by Craven and Shavlik (Craven and Shavlik, 1994), for discrete inputs and outputs and was extended by Craven and Shavlik's TREPAN algorithm (Craven and Shavlik, 1996). The TREPAN algorithm grows nodes in a best first order (Craven and Shavlik, 1996) and uses the greedy gain ratio criterion (Quinlan, 1993) to evaluate M-of-N splits. It is therefore limited to discrete outputs. The method that will be discussed in this chapter can be applied to data sets where both the inputs and outputs can assume discrete or continuous values. A variant of the ANN-DT algorithm, applicable to discrete output data only has been applied previously to characterize froth structures in a flotation plant (Schmitz et al., 1996). As will be shown below, the significance analysis proposed in this chapter has a distinct advantage over greedy attribute selection criteria as far as problems requiring look-ahead criteria are concerned.

## 11.3  ANN-DT Algorithm for Extraction of Rules from Artificial Neural Networks

The ANN-DT algorithm generates a univariate decision tree from a trained neural network, as indicated in Figure 11.1. A given decision node in the tree returns 'true' if the node's single specified variable has a higher value than a certain threshold and 'false' otherwise. For each node the algorithm decides on which variable to partition the set of data, after which the threshold of that variable has to be determined. This is accomplished by examining the responses of the neural network in the feature space and conducting a sensitivity or significance analysis of the different attributes or explanatory variables pertaining to these responses in order to construct the decision tree.

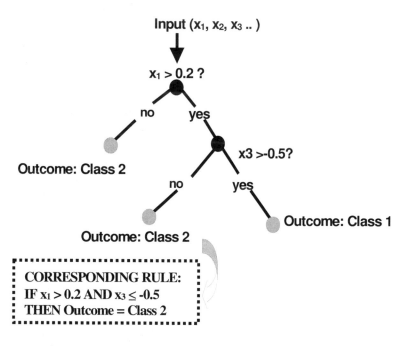

**Figure 11.1**  A simple univariate binary decision tree.

### 11.3.1 Training of the Artificial Neural Networks

Figure 11.2 gives a schematic representation of the ANN-DT algorithm. The first stage of the algorithm consists of training a suitable neural network on a set of training data. The ability of the neural network to generalize the underlying trends in the data is typically assessed via cross-validation on a separate set of test data. In this particular investigation both multilayer-perceptron and radial basis function neural networks were used, each of which is briefly described below.

#### 11.3.1.1 Multilayer Perceptrons

In general a multilayer perceptron consists of a layer of input nodes, one or more hidden layers of inner product nodes and an output layer. Each layer is completely connected to the previous layer by a set of weights. Input signals propagate through the network from the input layer onwards to the output layer in a feed-forward manner (Haykin, 1994).

The multilayer perceptron is usually trained by gradient descent methods (Werbos, 1974), in which the error is propagated backwards through the network (Rumelhart and McClelland, 1986). The frequently used error is the root-mean square error, however, especially for classification problems, cross-entropy and other error functions (Humpert, 1994) seem to be able to improve backpropagation learning.

#### 11.3.1.2 Radial Basis Function Networks

It can be shown that classification of non-linearly separable patterns can be improved if the input space is mapped into a new space of higher dimension. This

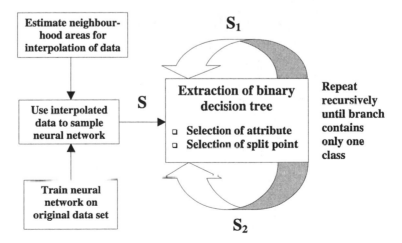

**Figure 11.2** A diagrammatic representation of the algorithm to extract rules from an artificial neural network.

non-linear mapping effectively transforms a non-linearly separable problem into a linearly separable one. This is the basic idea behind a radial basis function network (Powel, 1985; Broomhead and Lowe, 1988). The general structure of the radial basis function (RBF) network is $y(\mathbf{x}) = w_0 + \sum_i w_i \Phi_i(\mathbf{x}, \mathbf{c_i})$ where $\mathbf{c_i} \in \Re^d$ is the centre of the hidden layer or basis node $i$ and $\Phi_i$ is the activation of the node. This activation is usually a Gaussian function of the form $\exp\left(\frac{-|x-c|}{2d}\right)$, where $|.|$ is the Euclidean norm defined in $\Re^d$ and $d$ is the width of the basis node. If there are more hidden layer nodes than input features, the hidden layer of the radial basis function network performs a non-linear mapping of the inputs to the higher-dimensional feature space.

Training the radial basis function network entails finding a suitable set of basis nodes such that the problem becomes linearly separable or can be well approximated by a linear combination of the basis functions' activations. Owing to the fact that the training of the connection weights ($\mathbf{w}$) of the output layer can be done by iterative or direct numerical solutions to the least squares problem, the most difficult task is finding a good set of basis functions. The centre co-ordinates are usually determined by an unsupervised clustering phase such as k-means clustering of the input data (Moody and Darken, 1989), while the distance to the nearest cluster centre are then used as the widths of the basis functions.

### 11.3.2   Induction of Rules from Sampled Points in the Feature Space

If the rules are generated by a systematic search through the input or feature space, as can be done by the methods of Thrun, Fu, Gallant, and Saito and Nakano, their number can be overwhelming for many real-world problems (Thrun, 1994, 1995; Fu, 1991; Gallant, 1993; Saito and Nakano, 1988). Even when the feature space is properly bounded, decision boundaries generated by the neural network which are not parallel to the boundaries of the feature space can lead to an intractably large number of rules required to represent the behavior of the network to some arbitrary degree of accuracy. For example, Thrun (Thrun, 1994) reported that over 8000 rules were needed to describe the movements of a robot arm. Consequently restrictions to the depths of these kinds of searches have to be imposed. Even with these constraints the number of rules can remain large. For example, Saito and Nakano found that more than 400 rules were extracted for just one output unit in a neural network with 23 possible outputs (Saito and Nakano, 1988).

It may therefore be necessary to increase the granularity of the rules in order to improve their intelligibility. This can be done by limiting the depth to which the rules can be induced or by pruning the rules afterwards as will be discussed later.

ANN-DT uses a form of sampling, which can similarly lead to numerous rules depending on the number of sample points that are generated. However, it is necessary to ensure that the sampled points are restricted to those regions of the (often high-dimensional) search space on which the neural network model is based. This is accomplished by taking the distribution densities of points in the feature space into account, not only during sampling of the network, but also when the resulting branches of the trees require pruning.

### 11.3.3   Interpolation of Correlated Data

An artificial data set is generated by randomly sampling the input or feature space, and computing target or class labels for these sampled points by means of a neural network assumed to model the underlying trends or decision boundaries in the data satisfactorily.

To ensure that the newly generated data have the same distribution as the original training data and do not only reflect the behavior of the particular neural network model, it is essential that sampling is only allowed in the neighborhood of points or clusters present in the training data set. This can be accomplished by using a nearest-neighbor method, in which the distance of a sampled point to the nearest point in the training data set is calculated. If this distance is larger than a predetermined critical value, the sampled point is deemed unlikely to be typical to the data in the training set and is discarded.

For continuous variables the normal Euclidean distance is used as a distance measure. For discrete data a measure of similarity is defined and inverted. Various measures of similarity can be defined (Krzanowski and Marriott, 1995). For mixed data the Euclidean distance or a metric defined by Gower can be used (Gower, 1971). In cases where there are few discrete variables, the data sets belonging to the various possible combinations of the discrete variables can be treated separately. The reader is referred to (Krzanowski and Marriott, 1995) for a discussion on this topic.

In this investigation the critical distance was based on the distances between points in the training data set. In relatively small data sets with $N$ data points, all $\frac{N(N-1)}{2}$ distances can be calculated. In larger data sets this becomes computationally expensive, in which case a random sample of a number of interpoint distances can be used. The critical distance was subsequently set equal to the average distance between the points and their respective $k\,(=10)$ nearest neighbors in the training data set. Each artificially generated exemplar is subsequently presented to the neural network, from which a corresponding output value is computed.

### 11.3.4   Selection of Attribute and Threshold for Splitting

#### *11.3.4.1   Gain Ratio Criterion*

Consider a set $S$ of $n$ exemplars with $m$ corresponding discrete output classes $\{C_1, C_2, \cdots C_m\}$. Let $P(C_i, S)$ be the proportion of exemplars in $S$ which are in class $C_i$ . The class entropy of any subset $S_k$ of $S$ is defined as (Quinlan, 1986):

$$I(S_k) = -\sum_{i=1}^{m} P(C_i, S) \times \log_2\left(P(C_i, S)\right) \tag{11.1}$$

Assume that a value $T$ of a particular attribute $X$ has been chosen which splits $S$ into two subsets $S_1$ and $S_2$ . The average class entropy after such a partitioning is:

$$E\left(X, T, S\right) = -\sum_{k=1}^{2} \frac{|S_k|}{|S|} \times I\left(S_k\right) \tag{11.2}$$

The information gain generated by the split can now be defined as:

$$G\left(X, T, S\right) = I\left(S\right) - E\left(X, T, S\right) \tag{11.3}$$

It was found that when Equation 11.3 is maximized by the selection of the attribute and the threshold it is biased towards features with a large number of values (Quinlan, 1988; White and Liu, 1994). A normalized measure of information gain performed more satisfactory (Quinlan, 1988; White and Liu, 1994). The normalization factor for an attribute $X$ was defined by Quinlan as:

$$I\left(X, S\right) = -\sum_{k=1}^{n} \frac{|S_k|}{|S|} \log_2 \left(\frac{|S_k|}{|S|}\right) \tag{11.4}$$

where $n$ is the number of possible outcomes of the attribute. The normalized information gain, or gain ratio, is now given by

$$G_R = \frac{G\left(X, T, S\right)}{I\left(X, S\right)} \tag{11.5}$$

The attribute, together with the numeric threshold $T$, which will result in the maximum information gain ratio is selected for the Boolean splitting test.

For continuous outputs and a least absolute deviation measure, the attribute and threshold are selected in order to minimize the normalized standard deviation ($NSD$) averaged over the different branches in the same way as the entropy.

$$NSD = \sum_{k=1}^{2} \frac{|S_k|}{S} Stdev\left(O_k\right) \tag{11.6}$$

where $O_k$ are the outputs of the data set $S_k$.

For continuous output and a least squares error measure the attribute and threshold are selected which cause the maximum decrease in the normalized variance ($NS^2$) over the two branches.

$$NS^2 = \sum_{k=1}^{2} \frac{|S_k|}{S} Stdev^2\left(O_k\right) \tag{11.7}$$

By minimizing the normalized variance or standard deviation the resulting branches effectively reduced the RMS error or the sum of absolute errors (Breiman et al., 1984). For discrete outputs Equation 11.5 maximizes a normalized measure of information entropy gain. If one of these error or entropy criteria is used to select the attribute as well as the threshold, the algorithm will be referred to asANN-DT(e).

### 11.3.4.2  Analysis of Attribute Significance

An alternative method to those discussed above can be used for the selection of attributes. This method examines the significance of the various inputs on the behavior of the neural network. Consider a neural network model or functional relationship $f$ between attributes (inputs) and classes (outputs) that is evaluated at a set of points $S$ lying inside a domain $D$. If the magnitudes of the partial derivatives of the function with respect to the inputs are to be a measure of the significance, it is implicitly assumed that the variables can change freely and independently from one another. For the analysis of experiments where the influencing factors can be varied independently, this assumption is valid. However, if the measured attributes are correlated this is not appropriate as far as the system represented by the neural network is concerned, as the change in one input feature may be accompanied by a change in another covariant feature.

These interrelationships need to be taken into account by focusing on the variations of $f$ that actually occur inside the domain $D$. This can be done by looking at the variation of $f$ when moving between the points of $S$. Define the absolute variation $\nu(f)$ of the function $f(\mathbf{x})$ between the points $i$ and $j$ as the absolute value of the directional derivative of $f(\mathbf{x})$ integrated along a straight line between the two points. Thus

$$\nu_{ij}(f) = \int_{\mathbf{x}_i}^{\mathbf{x}_j} |\nabla f(\mathbf{x}) \bullet \mathbf{u}| \, d\mathbf{x} \tag{11.8}$$

where $\mathbf{u}$ is the unity vector in direction $\mathbf{x}_i - \mathbf{x}_j$.

This variation can be computed between all pairs of points in $S$. When an attribute is insignificant to the function for the domain $D$, the variation in the function will be unrelated to the variation in the attribute. Note that for a function where the effect of one attribute is cancelled out by another covariant attribute, e.g. $f(\mathbf{x}) = x_1 - x_2 + sin\{x_3\}$ and a domain in which $x_1 \approx x_2$, only variations in the other attributes, in this case $x_3$, will cause notable variations in $f(\mathbf{x})$. Therefore variations in the attributes with more influence, i.e. $x_3$, will correlate with the absolute variations in $f(\mathbf{x})$, while the variation in the attributes such as $x_1$ and $x_2$ will be uncorrelated with $\nu(f)$. Thus a measure of the *significance* $\sigma(f)_a$ of an attribute $a$ for a function $f$ over a data set $S$ would be the correlation between the absolute variation of the function and the *absolute variation* of that attribute taken between all possible pairs of points in $S$:

$$\sigma(f)_a = \text{correlation}\left(\{\nu_{ij}(f)\}, \{\nu_{ij}(a)\}\right) \text{ for all pairs } i,j$$

$$= \frac{\sum_i^N \sum_{j>i}^N \{\nu_{ij}(f) - \overline{\nu}(f)\}\{\nu_{ij}(a) - \overline{\nu}(a)\}}{\sqrt{\sum_i^N \sum_{j>i}^N \{\nu_{ij}(f) - \overline{\nu}(f)\}}\sqrt{\sum_i^N \sum_{j>i}^N \{\nu_{ij}(a) - \overline{\nu}(a)\}}} \tag{11.9}$$

At a given node the attribute with the maximum significance for the neural network function over the data set of the particular node was selected. In cases where Equation 11.9 led to excessive computations, the result was approximated using a randomly selected subset of data pairs. This attribute selection approach is henceforth referred to as the ANN-DT(s) variant of the algorithm.

The threshold at which the selected attribute is split is chosen by minimizing the gain ratio, the normalized standard deviation or the normalized variation depending on the type of error that is to be minimized.

## 11.3.5   Stopping Criteria and Pruning

A two-way split is generated, dividing the current set of data into two subsets. This splitting process continues recursively, successively splitting the data into smaller subsets. For discrete output data recursion halts when a node contains data with only one output class. Where data with continuous outputs are being used, recursion is terminated when the standard deviation or the variance is zero.

Recursion can also be prematurely terminated when a certain stopping criterion is met. Such stopping criteria prevent tree branches from being created where the outcome of one of the sub-branches would not be significantly different from the outcome of the other. These so called pre-pruning methods are usually implemented for two reasons. The first is to prevent the tree from modeling noise in the data and the second is to improve tree intelligibility. Many neural network architectures and training algorithms are available which can adequately compensate for noise in the training data. Therefore in the context of rule extraction from neural networks pre-pruning techniques are primarily used to improve the intelligibility of rules.

Statistical tests are applied to the outcomes of the data contained in the two new branches. For discrete outcomes the Pearson's $\chi^2$ (chi-square) test (Hays, 1988) can be used to find out whether the outcome class of a record is not independent from the branch into which the record is to be put. Where continuous outputs are concerned, an F-test (Hays, 1988) can be used to ascertain whether the mean output of the records of each of the two sub-branches are significantly different from each other. Both these tests show whether continued recursion would be meaningful or not. If the selected termination criterion fails at some confidence level $\alpha$, the current node is converted into a terminal node. Note that the $\chi^2$-test becomes less accurate as the number of data points per subset decreases (Hays, 1988). For the ANN-DT algorithm the outcomes stem from a neural network, which usually has continuous outcomes even when trained on data with discrete outputs. Therefore both the $\chi^2$-test and the F-test may be applied simultaneously as stopping criteria. In the ANN-DT algorithm both tests had to fail before a terminal node was formed. These stopping criteria can fail at a certain tree depth, even though future splits further down the tree could become statistically significant again. To prevent premature cessation of tree growth as a result of the above tests failing, these tests were only applied to nodes occurring below a certain minimum depth in the tree.

Three other criteria were applied to prevent unnecessarily large, and therefore incomprehensible trees from being formed. The first was that the tree could only grow to a user-defined maximum depth. The second was a so-called lower branching limit. This criterion prevents a node containing less than $s_{min}$ exemplars from splitting, or nodes containing less than $n_{min}$ exemplars from being formed. The third criterion, applicable to data having continuous outputs, prevents nodes from splitting if the variance of the output of the node falls below some threshold ($\nu_{th}$).

## 11.4   Splitting Procedures of ID3, C4.5, and CART

The ID3 and C4.5 algorithms generate classification trees from data by recursively splitting the data until a stopping criterion is reached in all the terminal nodes. ID3 and C4.5 use the gain ratio to determine the attribute on which to split the data set. The C4.5 algorithm by default prunes the trees using the resubstitution error rate (Quinlan, 1993) with a confidence limit of 25%. Furthermore C4.5 has the ability to group discrete attribute values together (Quinlan, 1993) and various other advanced options. However apart from the pruning mechanism, C4.5 with default settings does not differ appreciably from the ID3 algorithm. As a further comparison to the ANN-DT algorithm the trees generated by the ID3 algorithm were also pruned statistically.

The CART algorithm follows a different splitting procedure based on the minimization of a given error measure. The least-squares regression version of the CART algorithm, used in this chapter, forms a regression tree by iteratively splitting nodes on an attribute and threshold value in order to minimize the weighted variance (Breiman et al., 1984) over the branches. This is the same as minimizing the normalized variance of Equation 11.7.

The variant of CART used in this chapter did not make use of the minimal error complexity pruning (Mingers, 1989) and cross-validation estimates (Breiman et al., 1984), but pruned trees statistically instead. It should be noted that all pruning techniques, including those using cross-validation (CART or C4.5), can also be applied to the trees developed by the ANN-DT algorithm.

## 11.5   Illustrative Examples

The performance of both the ANN-DT(e) algorithm and the ANN-DT(s) variant was compared to that of the ID3 and C4.5 algorithm on a number of classification problems and to an algorithm using CART's splitting criteria on continuous output data. Three-fold cross-validation was used where the data sets contained few exemplars

The neural networks used for the problems considered in this chapter were multilayer perceptrons with hyperbolic tangent transfer functions and weights trained with the generalized delta learning rule with momentum, as well as radial basis function neural networks. The hidden layers of the radial basis function neural networks were trained with the k-means clustering algorithm and their output layers with the generalized delta learning rule.

Except for the problems pertaining to artificial data (Examples 1 and 4) the ANN-DT algorithm sampled the trained neural network 20 times for every training point. In other words, for every original training point, 20 sample points were synthesized for querying the trained neural network. It should be noted that during the integration steps, the ANN-DT(s) algorithm made additional queries to the neural network in order to determine the most significant inputs.

Two trees were built by the ANN-DT algorithm for each classification problem. The growth of the first tree was not constrained by any stopping criterion, whereas specific stopping criteria and pruning methods were applied during the formation of the second tree. In particular the maximum depth to which the second tree could grow was limited to 6. Statistical pre-pruning commenced at a depth of 3 with a confidence level $\alpha$ of 95%. The lower branching limit criterion was also implemented. The minimum number of exemplars required for a split, $s_{min}$, was set at 10 and the minimum number of exemplars that a particular node had to contain, $n_{min}$, was set at 2.

The same stopping criteria were used for those examples consisting of data with continuous outputs. A further stopping criterion, i.e. the minimum output variance required to continue splitting, $\nu_{th}$, was also implemented. The threshold value was 0.0025. The experiments with ID3 and the CART variant used the same settings as ANN-DT, except that $s_{min}$ was set to 4. This is in fact implicitly enforced because $n_{min}$ was set to 2. For all examples other than example 4 (discussed below) the results of the various algorithms on the validation sets were found to be fairly insensitive to changes in the above-mentioned settings.

### 11.5.1    Example 1: Binary Classification of Points in a Circular Domain.

In the first example a simple artificial data set was analysed. It consisted of points in two dimensions homogeneously distributed on a square with sides of unit length and bottom left corner at the origin, as shown in Figure 11.3. A decision boundary was defined by a quarter circle with centre at the origin and radius 0.8, which separated the points in the square into two classes. The class was designated as positive if the points were located outside the perimeter of the circle, and negative otherwise. The training set consisted of 100 exemplars of the form $[x, y, |\text{CLASS}]$, where $x$ and $y$ denoted the co-ordinates of the points, and CLASS the group membership of the points (designated by 0 or 1). A radial basis function neural network with 20 hidden nodes was trained on the 100 points. For the extraction of rules from the neural network with ANN-DT(s) and ANN-DT(e), 1000 points lying randomly inside the square space were used to sample the trained neural network for its corresponding outputs. A decision tree was also extracted from the training data by means of the ID3 algorithm.

This case study was extended to study the influence of noise on the performance of the decision tree algorithms. A set of data consisting of 300 exemplars was corrupted

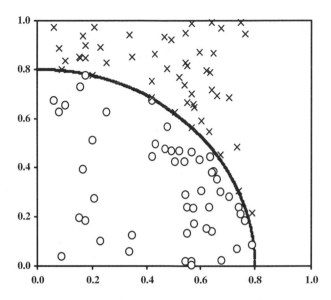

**Figure 11.3** The training patterns of case study 1.1. A decision boundary is defined by the quarter circle with centre at the origin and radius 0.8, which separates the points in the square into two classes, as indicated by ($+$) and ($\circ$) markers.

through inversion of the outcome class of randomly selected exemplars in the data set. The percentage of noisy sample points in the training data sets were 0, 5, 10, 15, 20, 25, 30 and 35. The data set used for testing the neural networks and decision tree algorithms trained on the noisy data, consisted of a set of 2000 exemplars which did not contain any noise. For comparative purposes, a hyperbolic tangent backpropagation neural network with 14 hidden nodes, as well as a radial basis function neural network with 40 hidden nodes were also evaluated.

### 11.5.2   Example 2: Characterization of Gas-Liquid Flow Patterns

Transitions between various fluid flow patterns are of substantial importance for many technical applications that rely on pressure, as well as heat and mass transfer. Reiman et al. have conducted experiments with multiphase fluid flow systems (air and water) in horizontal pipes yielding 175 experimental observations. Depending on the flow pressure ($P$), diameter of the pipe ($D$), superficial liquid velocity ($v_L$) and superficial gas velocity ($v_G$), flow regimes characterized by slug flow or non-slug flow could develop, including transitional phases such as slug-annular and slug-wave flow) (Reimann et al., 1992). A backpropagation neural network with 4 input nodes, 3 hidden nodes and a single sigmoidal output node was trained with the generalized delta rule to distinguish slug flow from non-slug flow, given exemplars of the form $[P, D, v_L, v_G, |\text{FLOW}]$, where FLOW denoted either slug or non-slug flow.

### 11.5.3   Example 3: Solidification of $ZnCl_2$

This data set consisted of 108 exemplars obtained from an experiment where zinc chloride is hydrolysed in watery ammoniacal-ammonium chloride solution (Limpo et al., 1995). Three phases of zinc chloride can occur, viz. $Zn(NH_3)_2Cl_2$, $Zn(OH)_2$ and $Zn(OH)_{1.6}Cl_{0.4}$. Usually only one phase is present, but under certain conditions more than one phase can occur. The objective of this example is to predict the expected formation of the three phases from the temperature of the solution ($^\circ$C), the concentration of chloride anions ($Cl^-$), the concentration of zinc cations ($Zn^{2+}$) and the ammonia concentration ($NH_3$).

The outputs are non-exclusive and therefore for each of the three phases a multilayer perceptron with 4 input nodes, 5 hidden nodes with hyperbolic tangent transfer functions and a hyperbolic tangent output node was trained on the data. Separate decision trees were likewise induced on each of the three outcomes to indicate whether a specific phase was present or not.

### 11.5.4   Example 4: Sine and Cosine Curves

This is a synthetic problem with four inputs, three continuous ($\theta$, $x$, $s$) and one ($\phi$) discrete. The single continuous output ($y$) is given by Equation 11.10.

$$y = \sin\left(4\pi\theta - \phi\right) + \mathrm{a}x + \mathrm{b}s + \mathrm{c}\varepsilon \qquad (11.10)$$

with $0 \leq (\theta, x, s) \leq 1$ and the discrete variable $\phi$ assuming either the value 0, or $\frac{\pi}{2}$, while $\varepsilon$ was a random variable with a normal distribution with zero mean and a standard deviation of unity.

A training set of 300 uniformly distributed random data points were generated with equation parameters a = 0.3, b = 0.0 and c = 0.2. Note that although the parameter b is zero, and the influence of variable $s$ therefore non-existent, the various algorithms will still have to deal with what will essentially be a nuisance variable. The test set consisted of 1200 points for which the outputs were computed without the error term, i.e. c = 0.

This is a difficult problem to solve for algorithms such as CART that use a greedy heuristic to induce the decision tree, because the data points need to be split on attribute $\phi$ and several times on $\theta$ (not necessarily in that order). Initially nothing is gained in terms of reducing the error from a split on $\theta$ and only after several splits on $\phi$ is the error reduced significantly. Algorithms employing greedy heuristics have difficulty finding good solutions under these circumstances. Other than possibly reducing the variance resulting from the error term, a split on $x$ will reduce the variance only marginally. Moreover, the noise factor, $c\varepsilon$, causes methods that produce rules that are supported by insufficient numbers of exemplars to overtrain. Since the initial splits do not reduce the error, premature pruning would give undesirable results. Therefore the F-tests were only applied at the second last possible level. For example, for a maximum depth of 6 the F-test was only applied at a depth of 5. The minimum number of data exemplars required for a continued splitting ($s_{min}$) was set at 4 for the ANN-DT algorithms (and for the variant of CART by default). Even so, different settings of $s_{min}$ did not change the results of any of the techniques appreciably.

A multilayer perceptron with 20 hyperbolic tangent hidden nodes was trained on the data generated by Equation 11.10. The ANN-DT(e) and ANN-DT(s) algorithms were used to extract rules from the trained neural network. For 5 different experiments the effect of the number of sample exemplars on the quality of the extracted rules was examined. Different numbers of sample points were used to query the trained neural networks, viz. 0, 250, 500, 1000 and 1500 exemplars.

In another experiment the effect of noise on the performance of the algorithms was examined. The noise factor c was therefore set at different levels, specifically 0.0, 0.1, 0.2 and 0.3. In this experiment the number of sample exemplars used to query the trained neural networks was held constant at 500 exemplars.

### 11.5.5   Example 5: Abalone Data

This data set was obtained from a study aimed at predicting the age of abalone based on the physical characteristics of the specimens examined (Reimann et al., 1992). The data have 8 inputs, namely the sex of the specimen (male, female or infant), the length, the diameter, the height, the total weight, the shucked weight, the weight of the viscera and finally the shell weight of the specimen. The current method to determine the age of a specimen is to cut the specimen's shell through the cone, stain the shell and then count the number of shell rings using a microscope. This is a time-consuming task and therefore it would be useful to obtain a specimen's age from the more easily obtainable physical characteristics. The data were obtained from the UCI Repository of Machine Learning Databases at Irvine. Records with missing data were removed. The data consisted of 3133 training records and 1044 records for evaluation of the trained models. In our experiment the sex input feature was encoded as $\{1; 0\}$ for type male, $\{0; 1\}$ for type female and $\{0; 0\}$ for the infant type. Although the output is actually discrete (the age is an integer ranging from 1 to 30) it was decided to treat the output as continuous and the root-mean-square error was minimized. After performing some experiments on the training data, it was decided to use a multilayer perceptron with 6 nodes in the hidden layer, and trained for a total of 5000 epochs.

### 11.5.6   Example 6: Sap Flow Data in Pine Trees

This data set consisted of 9 continuous inputs, namely temperature, relative humidity, differential vapor pressure, photoactive radiation, leaf mass, height of the

**Table 11.1** The percentage of examples classified correctly on the test data set by the various algorithms. The standard deviations of this percentage over the 3 cross-validation sets (where applicable) are indicated in brackets. Where indicated statistical pruning was done with an $\alpha$ value of 0.05. C4.5 used error reduction pruning with a 75% confidence limit.

| Case Study | ANN | ANN-DT(e) | ANN-DT(e) Pruned | ANN-DT(s) | ANN-DT(s) Pruned | ID3 | ID3 Pruned | C4.5 |
|---|---|---|---|---|---|---|---|---|
| (1) Circle | 97.8 | 98.2 | 97.2 | 97.9 | 97.0 | 94.6 | 91.2 | 91.2 |
| (2) Slug-Flow | 73.2 (3.4) | 72.8 (4.2) | 68.3 (5.5) | 72.4 (2.55) | 69.9 (3.1) | 69.8 (2.2) | 63.9 (4.5) | 72.1 (4.1) |
| (3) Solidi-fica-tion of $ZnCl_2$ | 92.0 (1.9) | 92.9 (2.3) | 91.4 (2.0) | 91.4 (2.2) | 80.6 (3.7) | 87.7 (3.5) | 88.0 (2.8) | 89.2 (2.4) |

**Table 11.2** The percentage of variance explained ($100 \times R^2$) by the various techniques on the continuous case studies. On all the decision trees statistical pruning was used with an $\alpha$ value of 0.05.

| Case Study | ANN | ANN-DT(e) | ANN-DT(s) | CART (statistically pruned) |
|---|---|---|---|---|
| Sin-Cos | 86.1 | 79.9 | 83.2 | 36.6 |
| Abalone | 57.0 | 48.4 | 46.5 | 45.5 |
| Pine | 90.4 | 83.7 | 79.7 | 83.4 |

tree, diameter at breast height, xylem pressure potential, the season, as well as the sap flow rate, which is a continuous output. An ellipsoidal basis function network with 20 axis-parallel ellipsoidal basis function networks was trained with an evolutionary algorithm. The decision trees were extracted from this neural network with the ANN-DT algorithm. The data consisted of 6612 records of which two-thirds were used for training and the remainder for testing the various algorithms. The decision trees were all grown to a maximum depth of 7.

## 11.6 Results

The results obtained with the various algorithms as specified previously are summarized in Tables 11.1–11.6.

For classification problems (examples 1, 2 and 3) Table 11.1 contains the classification score out of a 100, and for the continuous outcomes (examples 4, 5 and 6) the score is given in Table 11.2 in terms of the coefficient of determination (Hays,

**Table 11.3**  The fidelity of the various algorithms of Table 11.1. The fidelity is given as the percentage of examples classified the same as the neural network.

| Case Study | ANN DT(e) | ANN-DT(e) Pruned | ANN-DT(s) | ANN-DT(s) Pruned | ID3 | ID3 Pruned | C4.5 |
|---|---|---|---|---|---|---|---|
| Circle | 98.0 | 97.6 | 98.0 | 97.4 | 94.5 | 93.7 | 93.7 |
| Slug-Flow | 91.4 | 89.0 | 91.8 | 91.4 | 63.7 | 79.8 | 72.7 |
| Solidification of $ZnCl_2$ | 95.4 | 91.2 | 92.8 | 86.1 | 91.7 | 90.3 | 91.0 |

**Table 11.4**  The fidelity of the continuous case studies in terms of $100 \times R^2$ with respect to the neural network output.

| Case Study | ANN-DT(e) | ANN-DT(s) | CART $^\star$ |
|---|---|---|---|
| Sin-Cos for c = 0.3 | 84.0 | 87.2 | 28.5 |
| Abalone | 84.4 | 79.7 | 81.0 |
| Pine | 92.2 | 87.0 | 86.3 |

$^\star$ An algorithm based on CART's splitting procedure and statistical pruning

**Table 11.5**  The average number of leaves of the decision trees for the case studies with discrete outcomes of each decision tree algorithm.

| Case Study | ANN DT(e) | ANN-DT(e) Pruned | ANN-DT(s) | ANN-DT(s) Pruned | ID3 | ID3 Pruned | C4.5 |
|---|---|---|---|---|---|---|---|
| Circle | 25 | 15 | 27 | 15 | 8 | 5 | 5 |
| Slug-Flow | 65 | 33 | 179 | 33 | 33 | 8 | 8 |
| Solidification of $ZnCl_2$ | 38 | 20 | 41 | 15 | 6 | 4 | 4 |

1988). The formula used is: $R^2 = 1 - \frac{\sum (y_p - y_t)^2}{\sum (y_t - y_{avg})^2}$ , where $y_p$ is the predicted value of the outcome, $y_t$ is the target value of the outcome, and $y_{avg}$ is the average target value of the outcomes. The corresponding fidelity to the neural network is given in Table 11.3 and 11.4, while Tables 11.5 and 11.6 contain the number of leaves in the decision trees, which is an indication of the complexity of the trees. For these binary trees the number of internal nodes is equal to one less than the number of leaves. For the case studies using cross-validation, the standard deviation of the accuracies over the three cross-validation runs are indicated in parenthesis in Table 11.1. For Example 1 the results reported in Table 11.1 are those pertaining to the data without noise. The results pertaining to Example 4 in Table 11.2 are associated with a noise factor of 0.3 and 1000 sample points in addition to the original training points. Note that these sample points of ANN-DT have been synthesized from the original training data and therefore no unfair advantage was given to any of the algorithms for any of the experiments.

**Table 11.6** The number of leaves for continuous case studies of the decision trees induced by the algorithms.

| Case Study | ANN-DT(e) | ANN-DT(s) | CART * |
|:---:|:---:|:---:|:---:|
| Sin-Cos | 54 | 37 | 29 |
| Abalone | 37 | 35.5 | 31 |
| Pine | 196 | 146 | 200 |

* An algorithm using CART's splitting procedure and statistical pruning.

### 11.6.1   Example 1: Binary Classification of Points in a Circle

From Table 11.1 it can be seen that on the 2000 test points the two methods ANN-DT(e) and ANN-DT(s) achieved a classification accuracy which is similar to that obtained by the neural network. The fidelity of the two algorithms with respect to the radial basis function network is also very high and stays high after rule pruning. Notably more exemplars are classified incorrectly by the ID3 and C4.5 algorithm (resulting in a statistically significant difference between the ANN-DT and ID3, C4.5 algorithm). However, the techniques making use of the neural network also derived more rules. To illustrate this, Figures 11.4 and 11.5 show, as overlapping blocks, the respective decision regions obtained for these data by the ID3 algorithm and ANN-DT(e).

It can be seen that the regions identified by means of the ANN-DT(e) algorithm follow the contour of the circle more closely than those obtained with the ID3 algorithm. Closer inspection of the training points (indicated in the figures) shows that the ANN-DT(e) algorithm interpolates better than the ID3 algorithm. However, this comes at a cost because the contour of the circle is not easily described by axis-parallel decision rules. The ratio of rules obtained after statistical pruning (C4.5 has its own default form of pruning) by ANN- DT(e) and ID3 remained roughly the same. However, pruning tended to erode the classification accuracy of the ID3 algorithm more than that of the ANN-DT(e) method.

Figure 11.6, Figure 11.7 and Figure 11.8 show the classification results of the algorithms both with and without statistical pruning for the different noise settings.

The corresponding numbers of rules obtained by the different algorithms employed are given in Figure 11.9, Figure 11.10 and Figure 11.11.

The results confirm that the ANN-DT(e) and ANN-DT(s) algorithms are as robust to noise as the neural networks from which they extracted rules. In contrast, the ID3 algorithm relies on pruning to handle the effects of noise. Even when pruning is employed the ID3 and C4.5 algorithm still performed significantly worse than the ANN-DT algorithms on virtually all noise levels, as indicated in Figure 11.7. The performance of the rules derived and pruned by ID3 and C4.5 is initially worse than that of the other algorithms but does not decrease as fast as the performance of the rules derived with the other algorithms.

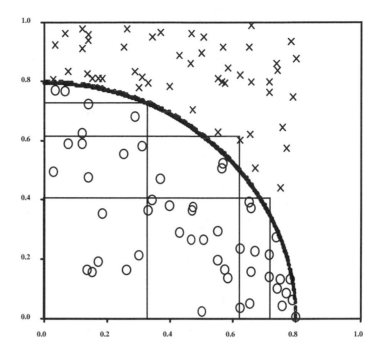

**Figure 11.4**   The decision boundaries for the case study in example 1, derived by ID3 and compared to the actual decision boundary of the problem indicated by the arc. The rectangular regions are those that were identified by the algorithm as members of class 1, while the light regions indicate the areas ID3 identified as class 0. The training points of class 1 are marked by a 'o' and those of class 0 by an '$X$'.

### 11.6.2   Real World Classification Tasks: Examples 2 and 3

The fidelity of the rules derived by the ANN-DT algorithms is for all these case studies notably higher than that of the rules obtained using either ID3 or C4.5.

Note that for Examples 2 and 3 the rules evolved by the ANN-DT(e) and the ANN-DT(s) algorithms are more accurate than those induced by ID3 and C4.5 algorithm but by a smaller margin than in the previous examples. Note too that the ANN-DT(e) algorithm performed slightly better than the ANN-DT(s) variant. A paired t-test was performed containing each of the three cross-validation results of the real-world classification problems (9 in total). This was to see whether the higher accuracy of the unpruned decision trees evolved by the ANN-DT(e) method is significantly different from the accuracy of the trees evolved by the ANN-DT(s), ID3 or C4.5 algorithm. With the double-sided t-test (Hays, 1988) it was found to be true with a 94% confidence level for ID3, with 91% confidence for ANN-

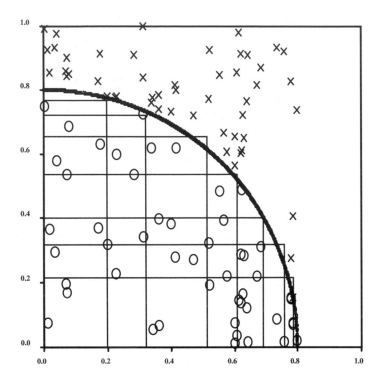

**Figure 11.5**  The corresponding decision regions of the case study in example 1, as derived by the ANN-DT(e) algorithm.


DT(s) but with less than 90% confidence for the C4.5 algorithm. Furthermore, the improvement of the results obtained by ANN-DT(s) over those of the ID3 algorithm was not significant at a 90% confidence level.

The number of rules derived by the ANN-DT algorithm is much greater than the number of rules generated by ID3 and C4.5 respectively. Although this number could be reduced by statistical pruning it was found in Example 3 that after pruning the trees evolved by the ANN-DT algorithm are no longer more accurate than the C4.5 decision trees or the unpruned ID3 decision tree. It seems that for this case study the extra information that is contained in the neural network and not in the ID3 or C4.5 decision trees cannot be represented by both intelligible and accurate axis-parallel rules.

In contrast, the ANN-DT(e) algorithm achieves a higher classification score on Example 3, both with and without statistical pruning. As three independent decision trees and neural networks were induced for each of the three non-exclusive outcomes, the three outcomes will be assumed independent. Under this assumption a paired t-test can be performed on the nine results obtained (three outcomes for every cross-validation run) to see whether the ANN-DT(e) algorithm performs significantly differenty from the ID3 or C4.5 algorithms. The classification scores of

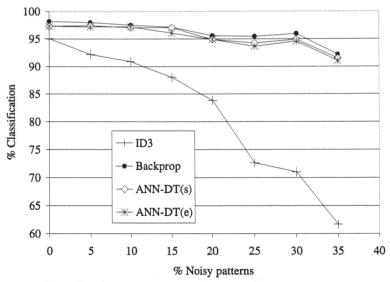

**Figure 11.6** Classification accuracy on the test data versus percentage of noisy patterns for the data in example 1. The ANN-DT(s) and ANN-DT(e) techniques were used to extract the rules from the backpropagation network, while the ID3 algorithm extracted the rules directly from the data. No pruning was applied to any of the evolved decision trees.

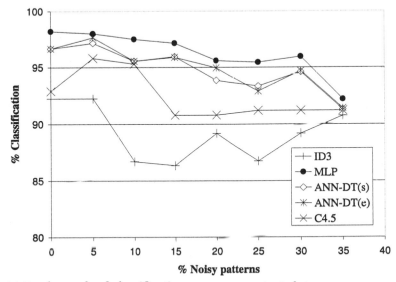

**Figure 11.7** A graph of classification accuracy on test data versus percentage of noisy patterns in case study 1 (after pruning).

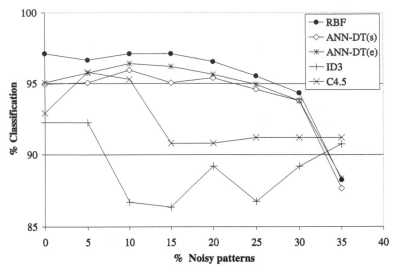

**Figure 11.8**   The classification of the decision trees induced by the algorithms in case study 1, based on the use of a radial basis function neural network, and plotted against the percentage of noisy patterns.

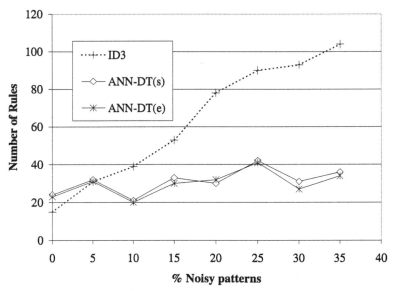

**Figure 11.9**   The corresponding number of leaves for the decision tree methods versus the percentage of noisy patterns in case study 1.

the pruned ANN-DT rules were significantly higher (at over 95% confidence level for a two-sided t-test) than both those of the unpruned and pruned sets of rules derived by ID3 or C4.5. The same result was also true for the ANN-DT(e) algorithm

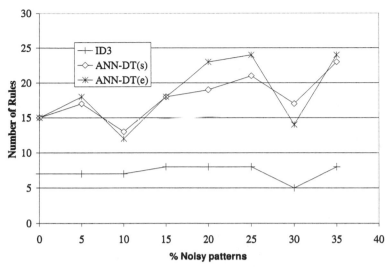

**Figure 11.10**   The numbers of leaves of the decision trees induced by the algorithms in case study 1, based on the use of a multilayer perceptron, and plotted against the percentage of noisy patterns.

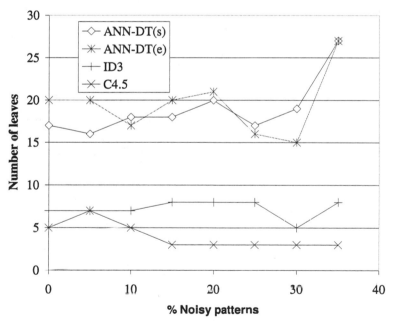

**Figure 11.11**   The numbers of leaves induced by the algorithms for case study 1, based on the use of a radial basis function neural network.

**RULE 1**

*If* Zn < 0.54
*and* NH$_3$ < 0.24
*then* 0 Prob.= 0.89, Size = 18.7%

**RULE 2**

*if* Cl$^-$ < 3.11
*and* Zn < 0.54
*and* NH$_3$ ≥ 0.24
*then* 1 Prob.= 0.94, Size = 30.9%

**RULE 3**

*if* Cl$^-$ ≥ 3.11
*and* Cl$^-$ < 3.61
*and* Zn < 0.54
*and* NH$_3$ ≥ 0.24
*and* NH$_3$ < 0.57
*then* 0 Prob.= 1.00, Size = 1.0%

**RULE 4**

*if* Temp. < 35
*and* Cl$^-$ ≥ 3.11
*and* Cl$^-$ < 3.61
*and* Zn < 0.32
*and* NH$_3$ ≥ 0.57
*then* 1 Prob.= 1.00, Size = 0.2%

**RULE 5**

*if* Temp. < 35
*and* Cl$^-$ ≥ 3.11
*and* Cl$^-$ < 3.61
*and* Zn ≥ 0.32
*and* Zn < 0.54
*and* NH$_3$ ≥ 0.57
*then* 0 Prob.= 0.95, Size = 1.0%

**RULE 6**

*if* Temp. ≥ 35
*and* Cl$^-$ ≥ 3.11
*and* Cl$^-$ < 3.61
*and* Zn < 0.54
*and* NH$_3$ ≥ 0.57
*then* 1 Prob.= 0.82, Size = 3.4%

**RULE 7**

*if* Cl$^-$ ≥ 3.61
*and* Zn < 0.54
*and* NH$_3$ ≥ 0.24
*then* 0 Prob.= 1.00, Size = 1.8%

**RULE 8**

*if* Zn ≥ 0.54
*then* 0 Prob.= 0.98, Size = 43.1%

**Figure 11.12**  The rules evolved by the ANN-DT(e) algorithm for example 3 for the presence (1) or absence (0) of the Zn(OH)$_2$ phase in the solidification of ZnCl$_2$. The 'Size' given below each rule indicates the percentage of the exemplars covered by the rule. The probability is the ratio of the number of exemplars in the dominant class to the total number of exemplars.

without pruning. A typical set of statistically pruned rules derived by the ANN-DT(e) algorithm indicating the formation of Zn(OH)$_2$ is given in Figure 11.12.

### 11.6.3  Example 4: Sine and Cosine Curves

The fidelity and accuracy (of ANN-DT(s) and ANN-DT(e)), given in terms of the coefficient of determination ($R^2$), for different numbers of neural network sample points, are plotted in Figure 11.13.

The number of rules obtained by the respective algorithms for the test runs is given in Figure 11.14.

The figures show that the ANN-DT(s) algorithm obtained satisfactory results, even if only a few sample points are available for training. In contrast, in such a situation the ANN-DT(e) algorithm almost completely fails to capture the overall trends in the data. Furthermore, even with no extra sample points beyond the training points (in which case the neural networks only performs noise filtering) the ANN-DT(s) algorithm yields satisfactory results, as well as performing much better than the ANN-DT(e) algorithm. This implies that the significance analysis enables the ANN-DT(s) method to place the attributes $\phi$ and $\theta$ high up in the

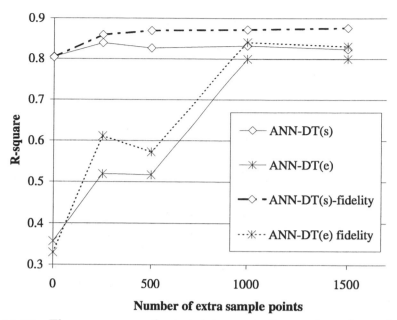

**Figure 11.13**   The accuracy on the test data versus the number of sample points beyond the training points used by the ANN-DT(s) and ANN-DT(e) algorithms to sample the trained multilayer perceptron of case study 4. The dashed line indicates the fidelity with respect to the multilayer perceptron from which the rules were extracted. The noise factor was held constant at 0.3.

decision tree. If one considers this example 4 as a whole, these attributes clearly have the greatest influence on the outcome of the neural network. For c = 0.3 and with 1000 sample points, ANN-DT(s) calculates $\sigma\left(f\right)_{\theta}$ as 0.45 and $\sigma\left(f\right)_{\phi}$ as 0.30 at the first split. The other two attributes each had a level of significance less than 0.02. It can be seen from the decision tree in Figure 11.15 that $\phi$ is selected once at tree depth of 1 and twice at a tree depth of 2.

The greedy attribute selection measure of ANN-DT(e) and CART splits only relatively late on the attribute $\phi$, because a split on this attribute causes very little immediate gain. Not shown in the figure is that CART splits the data on this attribute once at a depth of 2, 3 and 4 and ANN-DT(e) even lower at a depth of 3, 4 and 5. After too many splits on insignificant attributes the data are too sparse to pick up any underlying trends. This shortcoming of the greedy attribute selection measure that is used by CART cannot be compensated for at a later stage by pruning. Pruning will attempt to replace a sub-branch by leaves, but will not recalculate existing splits. Noise will make this task even harder. That is why CART's performance decreases further with added noise, as can be observed from a plot of the algorithm's performance against the noise as indicated in Figure 11.16.

Figure 11.14 and Figure 11.17, which give the respective number of rules obtained by each of the algorithms, reveal that the simpler trees generated by the ANN-DT(s)

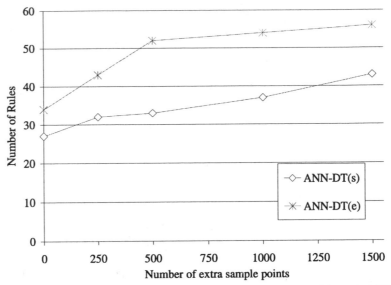

**Figure 11.14**    The number of rules induced by the ANN-DT(s) and ANN-DT(e) algorithms against the number of additional sample points in case study 4.

algorithm are also associated with better performance.

### 11.6.4   Example 5 and 6: Abalone and Pine Data

For the Abalone problem the ANN-DT algorithms perform notably worse than the neural network, although still slightly better than the variant of the CART algorithm. A paired t-test on the square errors of the 1044 test points showed that this improvement is significant with a 98% confidence level for the ANN-DT(e) method. A further run with different initial states confirmed the result. For the Pine data set both ANN-DT(e) and CART performed similarly, and both significantly better than the ANN-DT(s) algorithm. For both case studies the complexity of the trees as indicated by the number of leaves generated by the various algorithms in Table 11.6 is very similar.

## 11.7   Discussion

ANN-DT successfully extracted a faithful rule representation from the trained neural network on all the case studies. In particular the ANN-DT(e) variant seemed to be more capable with regard to classification problems, while the ANN-DT(s) method was shown to be more robust for continuous output data.

An interesting result is that the rules induced by the ANN-DT algorithm are more accurate than those induced by the ID3 algorithm or variant of the CART algorithm

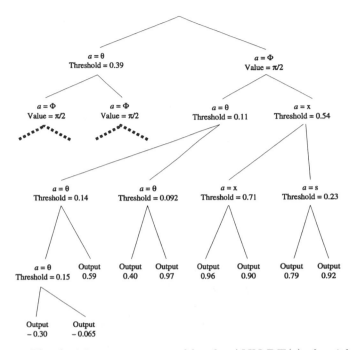

**Figure 11.15** The decision tree extracted by the ANN-DT(s) algorithm from the trained neural network for case study 4 with c = 0.3 using 1000 points to sample the neural network. If attribute a < Threshold the right sub-tree applies, else the left sub-tree is valid.

using the same pruning techniques. A similar result was also found by Craven and Shavlik, who compared the TREPAN (Craven and Shavlik, 1996) algorithm to classification trees induced by C4.5 (Quinlan, 1993) and ID2–3 (Limpo et al., 1995). The results indicate that for many problems the inductive techniques like C4.5 and CART do not use all the information that is contained in the original data. A possible source of this loss of information is that the technique splits the data recursively into branches in such a way that the data to be processed in the underlying branches are isolated from one another. This means that any trend that might exist between the inputs and the output of the data which are distributed over points belonging to different branches will not be discovered by the algorithms. It also means that points not complying with this trend as a result of noise cannot be identified and a rule can arise out of these exceptions that does not generalize very well.

If it is assumed that the neural network detects these trends and does not overtrain on outliers in the data, the ANN-DT(e) and ANN-DT(s) algorithms are evolved on data where these exceptions are already removed. Moreover, the more densely sampled points help in identifying the exact threshold value at which the data should be split. The C4.5 and CART algorithm can only estimate this value

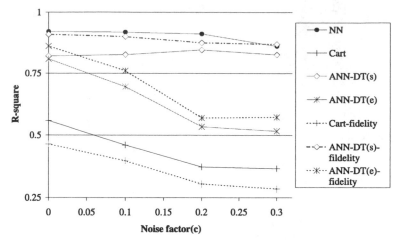

**Figure 11.16** A plot of the accuracy of the algorithms for different noise factors in the test data of case study 4. The dashed line indicates the fidelity with respect to the neural network, a multilayer perceptron from which the rules were extracted. The size of the data set with which the ANN-DT(s) and ANN-DT(e) algorithms sampled the neural network beyond the 300 training points, was held constant at 500. All the decision trees were pruned statistically with an $\alpha$ value of 0.05.

to lie somewhere between two points of that subset of the original data points that belongs to the branch in which the next split is to be made. This subset is much denser in the case of the ANN-DT(e) and ANN-DT(s) algorithms.

Moreover contours, such as class boundaries that extend over different branches of the tree, can be continued over the regions where there is very little training data or no data to support them. This is because the neural network does not split the data and can extend such a decision boundary between the training points via interpolation. The ANN-DT algorithm can sample in these regions and produce additional rules to cover these regions. Such behaviour is illustrated in Figure 11.4 and Figure 11.5. Unfortunately the higher accuracy in such cases is also associated with more rules. For the same reasons the ANN-DT algorithms also tend to maintain a significant higher fidelity with respect to the neural network.

From the classification results (Case Studies 1–3) it can be seen that the unpruned ANN-DT(s) algorithm produced significantly larger trees than the ANN-DT(e) algorithm, while also yielding a slightly lower classification. This can possibly be attributed to the fact that the significance analysis for classification problems could find high correlations between the output and one of the variables, even when the variations in the output that correlate with the variations in the attribute do not cause a change in the class. Consider the case in which all outputs of the sampled neural network with a value of higher than 0.5 will belong to class 1 and those with a lower output value than 0.5 to class 0. Then a change from 0.1 to 0.4 in the output is weighted by the significance analysis as much as a change from 0.4 to 0.7,

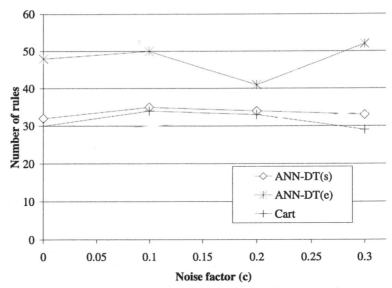

**Figure 11.17**   The numbers of rules induced by the algorithms in case study 4.

despite the fact that in the latter case a shift in class occurred and in the former not. This causes splits in the data that are non-optimal in terms of separating points of different classes from one another. The gain ratio criterion on the other hand is computed only from the class values (either 0 or 1).

## 11.8   Qualitative Analysis

Both ANN-DT(s) and ANN-DT(e) can be applied to any non-parametric model, other than feed-forward neural networks, without making any assumptions about the model's internal states or the nature of the data.

The computational time of the ANN-DT algorithm scales linearly with the neural network size and is only dependent on the time it takes the neural network to assign a label to a data point. However, the algorithm's computational time does suffer from the curse of dimensionality. In order to achieve a higher density of points than that of the training points, progressively more sample points are required as the dimensionality of the data increases. This problem can be reduced somewhat by initially using fewer sample points and growing the tree from a node in a *best-first* manner. This is performed in the TREPAN algorithm (Craven and Shavlik, 1996) by presenting the node that is most likely to increase fidelity with sufficient samples. Naturally the number of these sample points also needs to grow exponentially with the dimensionality of the data in order to achieve the same accuracy, as once a split is made in the tree it cannot be adjusted later.

In case study 4 it was seen that using the significance analysis in attribute selection can hold significant advantages over the greedy variance criterion. For this particular problem specification we know that although single splits on attributes $\phi$ and $\theta$ do not cause a significant decrease in the normalized variation of the data, changes in these attributes are nevertheless correlated with changes in the output of the neural network and will therefore have a high $\sigma_f$ value. This is again based on the assumption that the neural network has learnt the unknown function represented by the data. The significance analysis therefore learns from the trained neural network function which attributes have the most influence over the data set covered by a particular node. The greedy splitting criteria of CART and ANN-DT(e) on the other hand, do not compensate for the periodicity of the function with respect to the attribute $\theta$. The ANN-DT(e) algorithm could use additional sample points to obtain a respectable performance, whereas the CART algorithm no longer has sufficient data points to identify the periodic functional behavior, after performing the initial greedy splits. Although case study 4 concerned a synthetic data set, such periodic response of the output to one of the attributes with relatively sparse noisy data can also occur in real world data sets. The fact that both ANN-DT(e) and especially ANN-DT(s) could overcome such a pitfall is at least in theory a significant benefit of the ANN-DT algorithm compared to the CART algorithm.

## 11.9   Conclusions

- A new method has been developed to extract explicit IF-THEN rules from a trained feed forward neural network, regardless of the structure of the network. It was found that these rules are significantly more representative of the behavior of the neural network than rules extracted from the training data alone.

- Alternatively, the algorithm can be used as a method to extract rules from data sets. These rules appear to be of comparable accuracy as those obtained with C4.5 and an algorithm using procedures similar to CART's splitting and pruning algorithm. However in some cases a significant improvement could be obtained with the ANN-DT algorithm. Pruning can in some cases simplify the trees, while retaining relatively high accuracy.

- In order to focus the extracted rules on the relevant domain, it is important to sample the neural network on data similar to the original training data set.

- The ANN-DT algorithm tended to produce somewhat more complex trees for classification problems than ID3 and C4.5.

- For classification problems the ANN-DT(e) algorithm, which selects attributes and split points using a gain ratio criterion, appeared to perform better than the ANN-DT(s) algorithm, especially in terms of the number of rules extracted. The latter algorithm bases the selection of attributes and split points on a significance analysis of the input attributes. Unlike a sensitivity analysis that only considers the partial derivatives, the significance analysis takes the correlational structure of the data into account.

- For a problem with continuous outputs it was demonstrated that the significance analysis of ANN-DT(s) could correctly identify the most important attributes, whereas a greedy error driven procedure, such as used in ANN-DT(e) and standard decision tree techniques (e.g. CART), failed to identify the attributes. The significance analysis would therefore seem to be a suitable splitting criterion near the root of the decision tree, whereas a greedy splitting criterion would better split the lower branches of the tree.

# References

Andrews, R., Diederich, J., and Tickle, A. B. 1995. Survey and critique of techniques for extracting rules from trained artificial neural networks. *Knowledge-Based Systems*, 8(6):373–383.

Breiman, L., Friedman, J. H., Olshen, R. A., and Stone, C. J. 1984. *Classification and Regression Trees*. New York: Chapman & Hall.

Broomhead, D. S. and Lowe, D. 1988. Multivariable functional interpolation and adaptive networks. *Complex Systems*, 2:321–355.

Craven, M. W. and Shavlik, J. W. 1994. Using sampling and queries to extract rules from trained neural networks. In *Proceedings of the 11th International Conference on Machine Learning*, San Francisco.

Craven, M. W. and Shavlik, J. W. 1996. Extracting tree-structured representations of trained networks. *Advances in Neural Information Processing Systems 8*.

Davis, R., Buchanan, B. G., and Shortliffe, E. 1977. Production rules as a representation for a knowledge-based consultation program. *Artificial Intelligence*, 8(1):15–45.

Fu, L. M. 1991. Rule learning by searching on adapted nets. In *Proceedings of the Ninth National Conference on Artificial Intelligence*, pp. 590– 595, Anaheim.

Gallant, S. I. 1993. *Neural Network Learning and Expert Systems*. MIT Press Cambridge MA: MIT Press.

Gower, J. C. 1971. A general coefficient of similarity and some of it's properties. *Biometrics*, 27:857–872.

Haykin, S. 1994. *Neural Networks: A comprehensive foundation*. 866 3rd Avenue NY 10022: Macmillan College Publishing Company.

Hays, W. L. 1988. *Statistics*. Orlando Florida 32887: Holt, Rinehart and Winston Inc.

Humpert, B. K. 1994. Improving backpropagation with a new error function. *Neural Networks*, 7(8):1191–1192.

Krzanowski, W. J. and Marriott, F. H. C. 1995. *Kendall's Library of Statistics 2 Multivariate Analysis*, vol. 2. London: Arnold Publishers.

Limpo, J. L., Luis, A., and Cristina, M. C. 1995. Hydrolysis of zinc chloride in aqueous ammoniacal ammonium chloride solutions. *Hydrometallurgy*, 38:235–243.

Masters, T. 1993. *Practical Neural Network Recipes in C++*. Boston Mass.: Academic Press.

Mingers, J. 1989. An empirical comparison of pruning methods for decision tree induction. *Machine Learning*, 4:227–243.

Moody, J. and Darken, C. J. 1989. Fast learning in networks of locally-tuned processing units. *Neural Computation*, 1(4):281–294.

Narazaki, H., Watanabe, T., and Yamamoto, M. 1996. Reorganising knowledge in neural networks: An explanatory mechanism for neural networks in data classification problems. *IEEE Transactions on Systems, Man and Cybernetics*, 26(1B):107–117.

Pop, E., Hayward, R., and Diederich, J. 1994. RULENG: extracting rules from a trained artificial neural network by stepwise negation. QUT NRC.

Powel, M. J. D. 1985. Radial basis functions for multivariable interpolation: A review. In *IMA Conference on Algorithms for the approximation of functions and Data*, eds. J. C. Mason and M. G. Cox, pp. 143–167, Oxford. U.K. University Press.

Quinlan, J. R. 1986. Induction of decision trees. *Machine Learning*, 1:81–106.

Quinlan, J. R. 1988. Decision trees and multi-valued attributes. *Machine Intelligence*, 11:305–318.

Quinlan, J. R. 1993. *C4.5: Programs for Machine Learning*. San Mateo CA: Morgan Kaufmann.

Reimann, J., John, H., and Seeger, W. 1992. Transition from slug to annular flow in horizontal pipes. *Multiphase Science and Technology*, 6.

Rumelhart, D. E. and McClelland, J. L., eds. 1986. *Parallel Distribution Processing: Exploration in the Microstructure of Cognition 1*. Cambridge: MIT Press.

Saito, K. and Nakano, R. 1988. Medical diagnostic expert systems based on PDP model. In *Proceedings of IEEE International Conference on Neural Networks*, pp. 255–262, San Diego. vol. 1.

Schmitz, G. P. J., Aldrich, C., and Gouws, F. S. 1996. Extracting decision trees from artificial neural networks. *Proceedings of Minerals & Materials '96*, 1:250–257. Somerset West, South Africa.

Sestito, S. and Dillon, T. 1992. Automated knowledge acquisition of rules with continuously valued attributes. In *Proceedings of the 12th International Conference on Expert Systems and their Applications*, pp. 645–656, Avignon France.

Sethi, I. K. 1995. Neural implementation of tree classifiers. *IEEE Transactions on Systems, Man, and Cybernetics*, 25(8):1243–1249.

Thrun, S. 1994. Extracting provable correct rules from artificial neural networks. Tech. rep., Institut für Informatik III Universität Bonn, Bonn, Germany.

Thrun, S. 1995. Extracting rules from artificial neural networks with distributed representation. *Advances in Neural Information Processing Systems*, 7.

Tickle, A. B., Orlowski, M., and Diederich, J. 1994. DEDEC: Decision detection by rule extraction from neural networks. QUT NRC.

Towell, G. and Shavlik, J. W. 1993. Extracting refined rules from knowledge based neural networks. *Machine Learning*, 13:71–101.

Werbos, P. J. 1974. *Beyond regression: New Tools for prediction and analysis in the behavioural science.* Ph.D. thesis, Harvard University, Harvard University Cambridge MA.

White, A. P. and Liu, W. Z. 1994. Bias in information-based measures in decision tree induction. *Machine Learning*, 15:321–329.

# 12     Extraction of Linguistic Rules from Data via Neural Networks and Fuzzy Approximation

Andrzej Lozowski and Jacek M. Zurada

*Rule extraction is an important issue within Knowledge-Based Neurocomputing. Large sets of data, usually produced by experiment, can be interpolated easily with neural networks, providing a means for generalization. Based on generalized knowledge, many useful conclusions concerning the analyzed experiment can be drawn. This, however, indicates a great need for representing the knowledge in a readable and intuitive form. Soft quantization of factors taking part in the analysis allows representation of the generalizations by a set of linguistic rules. The rules determine a reasoning algorithm for a fuzzy system approximating the network function and inasmuch, they provide expert knowledge created automatically.*

## 12.1   Introduction

Soft computing techniques extensively use numerical data which characterize input/output relationships of various systems that support decision-making, advising, and diagnostics. These techniques have been successfully applied in engineering, medicine, chemical analysis, control, agriculture, financial and insurance management, and many other areas. Unlike formal and mathematically rigorous types of analysis and design, soft computing techniques possess features allowing the description of cause-effect relationships in terms of verbal statements and common sense rules. Informal notation is especially suitable for acquiring information from experts in a given field, who are not always used to giving a precise explanation of facts and algorithmic routines for solving given tasks. Yet, they often have years of experience and intuitive knowledge that is extremely difficult to grasp within restrictive formalisms. This kind of knowledge emerges as a result of learning from examples.

Neural networks play a significant role in modeling systems for which no analytical formulas are known. Effective tools for system identification are usually crucial for successful control. Although neural networks require quantitative examples for learning in the form of numerical data describing the desired input/output

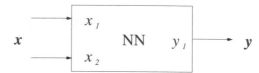

**Figure 12.1** Neural network classifier for the XOR problem. The network is assumed to perform a smooth mapping $y_1 = -x_1 x_2$. Hence, this simple decision system gives an answer *yes* if $y_1 > 0$ or an answer *no* if $y_1 < 0$.

mapping, the significance of neural networks in soft computing is rooted in their unique ability to interpolate nonlinear relations even in a multidimensional space. Moreover, neural networks are fairly tolerant to noise in the data, which becomes an issue when modeling involves a process of measurement. In such cases efficient model identification may require a careful validation of the model under construction, especially when the data is limited or incomplete. Nevertheless, an effort in this direction is usually beneficial in that a smooth interpolation outperforms a simple data-driven look-up table.

With models developed through learning from abundant data, the user can input facts and compute the system's outputs. This, however, provides no interpretation, justification or explanation of responses. The rules embedded in models are not directly accessible. Another domain of soft computing, namely fuzzy approximation, is much more reasoning-oriented and allows one to uncover the rules in a very suitable linguistic form. A closed-form algorithm for rule extraction from data can be derived within the framework of the fuzzy reasoning system.

Earlier fuzzy inference methods have been based on learning directly from examples (Takagi and Sugeno, 1985). Later approaches have focused on generating rules by adaptive-network-based fuzzy models (Sun, 1994). Genetic algorithms have also been employed for generating compact linguistic if-then rules (Ishibuchi, 1995). In our approach, we facilitate the modeling of relationships in data via multilayer perceptron networks followed by a rule generation algorithm applied to the smoothed neural network model.

## 12.2    Fuzzy Rule Extraction Algorithm

Learning results in an approximation of the input/output relationships of a given system. The approximation allows for imitating actions of the observed system based on the acquired data. The learning process is considered to be completed once the imitated actions of the system are within expected tolerances. To describe the system actions requires an informative representation of the learning results. It should reveal the entire process of reasoning used by the approximating model. Assuming that the system is a classifier, its actions can be described by a set of rules of the form $\pi \Rightarrow \varrho$ (Viktor and Cloete, 1995). Each rule is an implication that relates an input instance $\pi$ to an output instance $\varrho$. In general, both the input instance

**Table 12.1**  The data set used for developing an XOR classifier. There are 16 input pairs $(x_1, x_2)$, which sample the input space. The neural network responses are denoted by $y_1$ and classified as crisp values $\varrho_1 \in \{no, yes\}$.

| $x_1$ | $x_2$ | $y_1$ | $\varrho_1$ |
|-------|-------|-------|-------------|
| -0.4 | -0.3 | -0.12 | *no* |
| -0.4 | 0.2 | 0.08 | *yes* |
| -0.3 | -0.4 | -0.12 | *no* |
| -0.3 | 0.3 | 0.09 | *yes* |
| -0.2 | -0.2 | -0.04 | *no* |
| -0.2 | 0.1 | 0.02 | *yes* |
| -0.1 | -0.1 | -0.01 | *no* |
| -0.1 | 0.4 | 0.04 | *yes* |
| 0.1 | -0.3 | 0.03 | *yes* |
| 0.1 | 0.3 | -0.03 | *no* |
| 0.2 | -0.1 | 0.02 | *yes* |
| 0.2 | 0.4 | -0.08 | *no* |
| 0.3 | -0.4 | 0.12 | *yes* |
| 0.3 | 0.2 | -0.06 | *no* |
| 0.4 | -0.2 | 0.08 | *yes* |
| 0.4 | 0.1 | -0.04 | *no* |

$\boldsymbol{\pi} = (\pi_1, \pi_2, \dots)$ and the output instance $\boldsymbol{\varrho} = (\varrho_1, \varrho_2, \dots)$ are multidimensional. Hereafter, Greek letters are used for describing the instances in a linguistic form.

In order to introduce the rule extraction algorithm, a simple XOR decision system will be used as an example. XOR is a logical function and the extracted rules are expected to agree with its truth table. The decision system is shown in Figure 12.1. It uses two inputs $\boldsymbol{x} = (x_1, x_2)$ and provides one output $y_1$. Roman letters denote numerical values. Although the nature of the rules is logical, they are extracted from systems that use numerical data. Therefore, the exemplary problem of XOR is introduced in terms of real-valued numbers (Zurada, 1992). Its function can be performed by a neural network. For simplicity, the neural network in Figure 12.1 is already assumed to perform function $y_1 = -x_1 x_2$. Note that this function precisely evaluates the logical XOR considering numbers $-1$ and $1$ as *no* and *yes*, respectively. Other values of the output are classified as *no* or *yes* depending on the sign of $y_1$, that is *no* for the negative sign and *yes* for positive.

Typically, real-life systems need to be identified by inspecting their actions for various inputs. In the XOR example, the input space can be sampled using several input data points. These data are shown in Table 12.1. The output value $y_1$ is evaluated for each input instance $(x_1, x_2)$ and then classified as *no* or *yes*. The result of this classification is denoted by $\varrho_1$, which is the linguistic output instance.

For the sake of rule creation, the system input should be expressed in terms of linguistic variables. In other words, the correspondence between numerical values

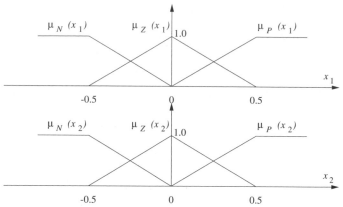

**Figure 12.2** Fuzzification of the XOR decision system inputs. Inputs $x_1$ and $x_2$ are characterized by fuzzy numbers $\pi_1 \in \{N, Z, P\}$ and $\pi_2 \in \{N, Z, P\}$, respectively. The graphs represent membership functions $\mu_{\pi_1}(x_1)$ and $\mu_{\pi_2}(x_2)$. For example, $\mu_N(x_1) = 0.5$ at $x_1 = -0.25$.

$(x_1, x_2)$ and crisp input instances $(\pi_1, \pi_2)$ should be established. A very suitable approach to soft quantization of the input leads through changing the input domain from real-valued into fuzzy (Zadeh, 1965; Sun, 1994). Fuzzy numbers provide an excellent link between linguistic input/output rules and numerical mappings that handle only continuous variables. Approximating the object of interest with a fuzzy system offers an opportunity to create fuzzy rules that can be used for describing the actions in the linguistic form.

Depending on the complexity of the input space, a fuzzification scheme for the inputs can be more or less complex. In the XOR example a set of three fuzzy numbers is constructed arbitrarily. Input instances $\pi_1$ and $\pi_2$ take values from the set $\{N, Z, P\}$. These letters stand for *negative*, *zero*, and *positive*. The correspondence between the numerical values $x_i$ and the fuzzy numbers $\pi_i$ is defined by selecting membership functions $\mu_{\pi_i}(x_i)$. As shown in Figure 12.2 triangular membership functions are chosen. Linguistic variable $\tilde{x}_i = (\mu_N(x_i), \mu_Z(x_i), \mu_P(x_i))$ describes input $x_i$ by three numbers indicating the degree of membership of that input to classes $N$, $Z$, and $P$. Membership functions can have values between 0 and 1. Their centers are selected such that every point in the data set, shown in Table 12.1, can be unambiguously represented by linguistic variables $\tilde{x}_1$ and $\tilde{x}_2$.

Assume now that the input domain of the XOR classifier is sampled at various points as shown in Figure 12.3. Numerical coordinates $x_1$ and $x_2$ of the points are indicated on the bottom and on the right side of the array. The corresponding linguistic variables $\tilde{x}_1$ and $\tilde{x}_2$ label the top and the left side of the array. All the points from Table 12.1 can be found at appropriate locations in this array, where the output instances *no* or *yes* are placed. The topology of the classifier's decision regions can be clearly seen. Decision region $D_{\varrho_1}$ is a set of all the input instances $(x_1, x_2)$, for which the output instance equals $\varrho_1$. Hence, the decision region $D_{no}$ is the region of the input space where $x_1 < 0$ and $x_2 < 0$, or $x_1 > 0$ and $x_2 > 0$. All

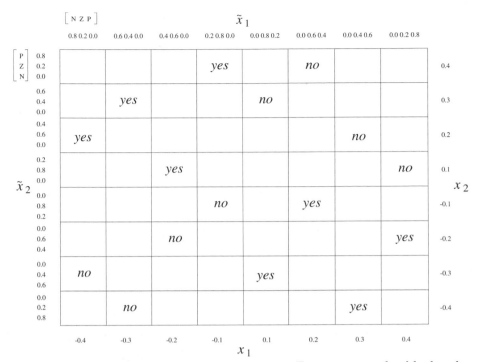

**Figure 12.3**  Decision regions in the input space. Every rectangular block, where the output class $\varrho_1$ is marked as *yes* or *no*, represents an input instance as shown in Table 12.1. For example, instance $x_1 = -0.4$ and $x_2 = -0.3$ is marked by *no* since $y_1 = -0.12 < 0$. In terms of linguistic variables this instance is represented by membership values $\tilde{x}_1 = [0.8, 0.2, 0.0]^T$ and $\tilde{x}_2 = [0.6, 0.4, 0.0]^T$.

the points outside this area constitute the decision region $D_{yes}$.

In order to create rules describing actions imitating the XOR decision system, input instances need to be expressed in terms of fuzzy numbers $\pi_i \in \{N, Z, P\}$ rather than linguistic variables $\tilde{x}_i$ involving membership values. Note that each rectangular block of the array in Figure 12.3 allows nine $(3^2)$ combinations of the fuzzy numbers $(\pi_1, \pi_2)$. Every combination determines a pair of membership values $(\mu_{\pi_1}(x_1), \mu_{\pi_2}(x_2))$. Consider, for example, point $(-0.4, -0.3)$. Its linguistic coordinates are $\tilde{x}_1 = (0.8, 0.2, 0.0)$ and $\tilde{x}_2 = (0.6, 0.4, 0.0)$. The membership function values assigned to this point equal $\mu_N(-0.4) = 0.8$, $\mu_Z(-0.4) = 0.2$, $\mu_P(-0.4) = 0.0$, and $\mu_N(-0.3) = 0.6$, $\mu_Z(-0.3) = 0.4$, $\mu_P(-0.3) = 0.0$. Therefore, instance $(N, N)$ would be validated by a membership pair $(0.8, 0.6)$, instance $(N, Z)$ would be validated by $(0.8, 0.4)$, and so on.

In fuzzy reasoning, the instances are assigned t-norms of the membership pairs (Zurada and Lozowski, 1996). For simplicity, a min function is selected as a t-norm operator. Thus an instance $(\pi_1, \pi_2)$ gets validated by a single number $\min(\mu_{\pi_1}(x_1), \mu_{\pi_2}(x_2))$. In this manner, t-norms for the exemplary instances $(N, N)$ and $(N, Z)$ of the point $(x_1, x_2) = (-0.4, -0.3)$ are equal to 0.6 and 0.4, respectively. These two t-norm val-

**$\varrho_1 = no$** (left table), $\pi_2$

| | N | | Z | | P | |
|---|---|---|---|---|---|---|
| **P** | 0.0 | 0.0 | 0.0 | 0.6 | 0.0 | 0.2 |
| | 0.0 | 0.0 | 0.0 | 0.6 | 0.0 | 0.4 |
| | 0.0 | 0.0 | 0.0 | 0.4 | 0.0 | 0.4 |
| | 0.0 | 0.0 | 0.0 | 0.2 | 0.0 | 0.2 |
| **Z** | 0.4 | 0.0 | 0.2 | 0.4 | 0.0 | 0.2 |
| | 0.2 | 0.0 | 0.2 | 0.2 | 0.0 | 0.2 |
| | 0.4 | 0.0 | 0.6 | 0.4 | 0.0 | 0.6 |
| | 0.2 | 0.0 | 0.8 | 0.2 | 0.0 | 0.8 |
| **N** | 0.6 | 0.0 | 0.2 | 0.0 | 0.0 | 0.0 |
| | 0.6 | 0.0 | 0.4 | 0.0 | 0.0 | 0.0 |
| | 0.4 | 0.0 | 0.4 | 0.0 | 0.0 | 0.0 |
| | 0.2 | 0.0 | 0.2 | 0.0 | 0.0 | 0.0 |

$\varrho_1 = no$    $\pi_1$

**$\varrho_1 = yes$** (right table), $\pi_2$

| | N | | Z | | P | |
|---|---|---|---|---|---|---|
| **P** | 0.4 | 0.0 | 0.2 | 0.0 | 0.0 | 0.0 |
| | 0.6 | 0.0 | 0.4 | 0.0 | 0.0 | 0.0 |
| | 0.2 | 0.0 | 0.2 | 0.0 | 0.0 | 0.0 |
| | 0.2 | 0.0 | 0.8 | 0.0 | 0.0 | 0.0 |
| **Z** | 0.6 | 0.0 | 0.2 | 0.4 | 0.0 | 0.2 |
| | 0.4 | 0.0 | 0.4 | 0.6 | 0.0 | 0.4 |
| | 0.4 | 0.0 | 0.6 | 0.2 | 0.0 | 0.2 |
| | 0.2 | 0.0 | 0.2 | 0.2 | 0.0 | 0.6 |
| **N** | 0.0 | 0.0 | 0.0 | 0.6 | 0.0 | 0.2 |
| | 0.0 | 0.0 | 0.0 | 0.2 | 0.0 | 0.2 |
| | 0.0 | 0.0 | 0.0 | 0.4 | 0.0 | 0.6 |
| | 0.0 | 0.0 | 0.0 | 0.2 | 0.0 | 0.4 |

$\pi_1$    $\varrho_1 = yes$

**Figure 12.4** Lists of t-norms (here, minima of membership values) for output classes $\varrho_1 = no$ and $\varrho_1 = yes$. In terms of fuzzy numbers input instances can be represented by pairs $(\pi_1, \pi_2) \in \{N, Z, P\} \times \{N, Z, P\}$. This results in 9 combinations. Consider, for example, instance $\pi_1 = N$ and $\pi_2 = N$, and the output class $\varrho_1 = no$ (bottom-left block of the table on the left.) Eight figures in this block are the minima $\min(\mu_N(x_1), \mu_N(x_2))$. The membership values $\mu_N(x_1)$ and $\mu_N(x_2)$ can be found in Figure 12.3 as assigned to the blocks marked by *no*.

ues can be found in the left table in Figure 12.4 (in the blocks whose coordinates are $\pi_1 = N$, and $\pi_2 = N$ or $\pi_2 = Z$). Each block in Figure 12.4 contains eight t-norms because there are eight points in Figure 12.3 classified as *no* (as well as eight points classified as *yes*).

Verbal description of the introduced number rearrangement in tables is somewhat complicated, but in certain programming languages such a multi-level matrix transposition can be done with a single command. Tables shown in Figure 12.4 group the t-norms separately for output classes *no* and *yes*. The consecutive step in fuzzy reasoning is evaluation of s-norms for every input instance $(\pi_1, \pi_2)$ (Wang and Mendel, 1992). The simple s-norm operator for a given instance is a maximum of all its t-norms. The s-norms evaluated based on values from Figure 12.4 are presented in Figure 12.5. Every input instance provides a value for the output membership function $\mu_{no}(\varrho_1)$ and $\mu_{yes}(\varrho_1)$. These values can be compared in order to create rules.

For example, instance $(N, N)$ generates two rules: $(N, N) \Rightarrow no$ and $(N, N) \Rightarrow yes$, validated by the output membership value of 0.6 and 0.0, respectively. Since the first rule is represented by a significantly larger membership function value, it should be included in the generated rule set. If some instances generate rules with less distinct difference in the output membership, like the case $(Z, P)$, the rule creation should be considered from the point of view of required accuracy of the rules being created. To address this problem, an arbitrary uncertainty margin $\varepsilon$ is introduced. If a given instance $(\pi_1, \pi_2)$ generates rules for which the difference of the respective s-norms $|\mu_{yes}(\varrho_1) - \mu_{no}(\varrho_1)|$ is less than $\varepsilon$, than none of the rules is included in

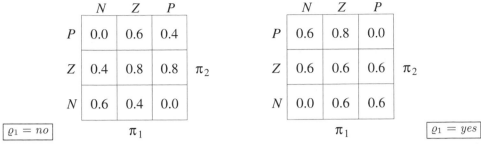

|   | N | Z | P |     |   | N | Z | P |     |
|---|---|---|---|-----|---|---|---|---|-----|
| P | 0.0 | 0.6 | 0.4 |     | P | 0.6 | 0.8 | 0.0 |     |
| Z | 0.4 | 0.8 | 0.8 | $\pi_2$ | Z | 0.6 | 0.6 | 0.6 | $\pi_2$ |
| N | 0.6 | 0.4 | 0.0 |     | N | 0.0 | 0.6 | 0.6 |     |

$\varrho_1 = no$      $\pi_1$      $\pi_1$      $\varrho_1 = yes$

**Figure 12.5** Lists of s-norms (here, maxima of the minima of membership values) for output classes $\varrho_1 = no$ and $\varrho_1 = yes$. Each input instance $(\pi_1, \pi_2)$ is represented by the value of the membership function $\mu_{no}(\varrho_1)$ and $\mu_{yes}(\varrho_1)$. These values are the maxima of the figures included in the corresponding blocks in Figure 12.4.

| $0.0 < \varepsilon < 0.2$: | | | $0.2 < \varepsilon < 0.4$: | | | $0.4 < \varepsilon < 0.6$: | | |
|---|---|---|---|---|---|---|---|---|
| $\pi_1$ | $\pi_2$ | $\varrho_1$ | $\pi_1$ | $\pi_2$ | $\varrho_1$ | $\pi_1$ | $\pi_2$ | $\varrho_1$ |
| N | N | no | N | N | no | N | N | no |
| N | Z | yes | N | P | yes | N | P | yes |
| N | P | yes | P | N | yes | P | N | yes |
| Z | N | yes | P | P | no | | | |
| Z | Z | no | | | | | | |
| Z | P | no | | | | | | |
| P | N | yes | | | | | | |
| P | Z | yes | | | | | | |
| P | P | no | | | | | | |

**Figure 12.6** XOR rule creation for selected uncertainty margins $\varepsilon$. Comparing output membership function values for classes $yes$ and $no$ (in Figure 12.5), a rule $(\pi_1, \pi_2) \Rightarrow \varrho_1$ is created provided that the difference between the output membership function values for classes $yes$ and $no$ is significant, namely $|\mu_{yes}(\varrho_1) - \mu_{no}(\varrho_1)| > \varepsilon$. Rule $(\pi_1, \pi_2) \Rightarrow no$ is created if $\mu_{no}(\varrho_1) > \mu_{yes}(\varrho_1)$. Rule $(\pi_1, \pi_2) \Rightarrow yes$ is created otherwise. Rules created with three different uncertainty margins are shown.

the rule set. If the difference is larger than $\varepsilon$, then either rule $(\pi_1, \pi_2) \Rightarrow no$ or $(\pi_1, \pi_2) \Rightarrow yes$ is included in the rule set, depending on which one determines a greater s-norm.

It can be seen that the uncertainty margin $\varepsilon$ controls the number of rules extracted from the XOR decision system example. The maximum number of rules is created when $\varepsilon = 0$. Increasing $\varepsilon$ lowers the number of rules by eliminating the less decisive ones. Finally, with $\varepsilon = 1$ no rule can be created, since the membership functions are bounded between 0 and 1. Rule sets extracted from the XOR classifier with various uncertainty margins are shown in Figure 12.6. Note that for $\varepsilon \in [0.2, 0.4]$ the rules recover the XOR truth table.

## 12.3  Gentamycin Dosage Problem

The rule extraction algorithm introduced in the previous section has been used in the problem of predicting an appropriate dose of gentamycin (a medicine used to treat kidney disease) (Lozowski et al., 1996b). The required amount of drug can be estimated by a trained physician based on a few parameters known by inspection or by measurement, such us: a person's weight, height, body surface area, sex, and age. The history of treatment is also important as are factors like the dosage time interval, recent gentamycin dose levels, gentamycin peak and trough concentration levels, serum creatinine, and creatinine clearance.

Given so many input factors, estimating the accurate dosage of gentamycin is not a simple task. Still, the appropriate dosage of gentamycin is of great importance in achieving the desired peak and trough levels of the gentamycin concentration in a patient's body. Simplifying, given an instance of relevant parameters (Karayiannis and Venetsanopoulos, 1994), the problem is to predict the amount of gentamycin needed to produce the desired peak and trough concentration levels.

By inspection of correlation coefficients between the inputs and outputs, three parameters were found the most significant in the observation of treatment: the body weight, serum creatinine, and peak concentration. These parameters will be referred to as the system inputs $x_1$, $x_2$, and $x_3$. The system output, $y_1$, is the prediction of the necessary gentamycin dose at a time.

A data set of measurements, each consisting of the three patient characteristics and routine dosage levels, was used as a training set for a neural network classifier with three inputs and one output. A fragment of these data is shown in Figure 12.7(a). For the sake of fuzzy rule extraction the input fuzzifiers have been formed using the standard triangular membership function shapes (see Figure 12.7(b)). Each input has been quantized into three classes with centers of gravity located in the middle and at both ends of the range of changes of the input (Setiono and Liu, 1996).

Rules for the gentamycin dosage have then been created with the uncertainty margin $\varepsilon = 0.01$. Totally undecidable rules were subsequently pruned from the rule sets. The resulting rule set reduced to a disjunctive normal form (Shavlik, 1994; Towell and Shavlik, 1993; Craven and Shavlik, 1994) is shown in Table 12.2. The rules can be represented graphically on a cube whose corners and sides correspond to input instances while the output classification is indicated in three grey-levels (see Figure 12.8). In the figure, variables $x_1$, $x_2$, and $x_3$ are the vertical, horizontal and axial dimensions, respectively. Roughly, this diagram shows a monotonic relationship between the dose and a linear combination of the inputs. Even though increasing the number of fuzzy classes at the inputs and the output would improve the approximation of the neural network mapping, the small set of rules provides an indication of the solution to the dosage problem.

| Weight | Serum creatinine | Peak | Dose |
|--------|------------------|------|------|
| 57.6   | 0.5 | 4.0  | 80  |
| 81.2   | 0.6 | 4.8  | 130 |
| 66.0   | 2.2 | 11.4 | 100 |
| 110.0  | 1.2 | 3.1  | 100 |
| 38.2   | 0.6 | 8.0  | 80  |
| 59.9   | 0.7 | 4.5  | 80  |
| 55.3   | 0.9 | 5.7  | 80  |
| 75.7   | 0.7 | 4.4  | 80  |
| 61.2   | 0.8 | 5.0  | 90  |
| 42.2   | 1.5 | 7.6  | 80  |
| 72.6   | 0.6 | 1.8  | 80  |
| 63.0   | 0.7 | 6.5  | 100 |
| 68.0   | 0.7 | 3.5  | 80  |
| 63.5   | 0.6 | 3.8  | 120 |
| 52.8   | 1.4 | 3.4  | 60  |
| 85.5   | 1.4 | 5.7  | 80  |
| 92.5   | 0.6 | 3.0  | 80  |
| 83.0   | 0.8 | 2.4  | 80  |
| 60.0   | 2.0 | 7.6  | 70  |
| 63.7   | 0.6 | 3.6  | 60  |

(a)                                                    (b)

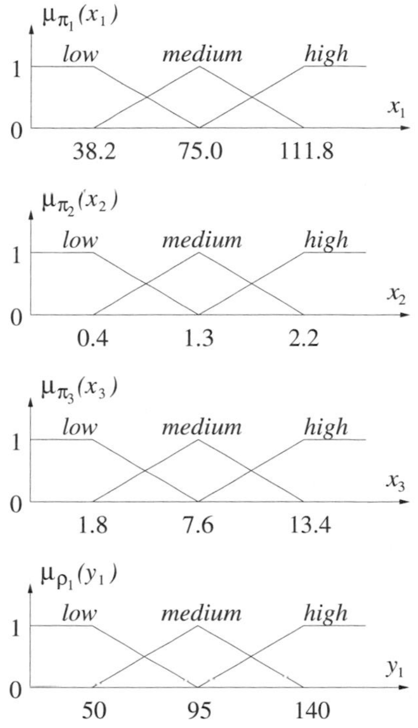

**Figure 12.7**   Gentamycin dosage problem. (a) Fragment of the measurement data set. The recommended drug dose $y_1$ depends on parameters $x_1$, $x_2$, and $x_3$ which remain under systematic observation. (b) Fuzzification scheme of variables $x_1$, $x_2$, $x_3$, and $y_1$ for the rule extraction.

**Table 12.2**   Linguistic rules for gentamycin dosage in disjunctive normal form.

| Weight | Serum creatinine | Peak | Dose |
|--------|------------------|------|------|
| ¬high  | high   | medium | low    |
| low    | ¬low   | low    | low    |
| –      | low    | low    | medium |
| –      | medium | medium | medium |
| low    | –      | high   | medium |
| ¬high  | low    | medium | medium |
| ¬low   | medium | low    | medium |
| medium | ¬low   | high   | medium |
| high   | high   | ¬high  | medium |
| high   | low    | medium | high   |
| high   | medium | high   | high   |
| ¬low   | low    | high   | high   |

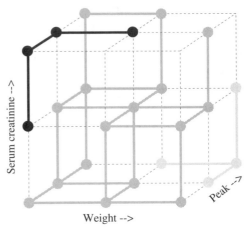

**Figure 12.8**  Graphic representation of the rules. The cube represents the three-dimensional parameter space for weight, serum creatinine, and peak value in terms of fuzzy numbers $\{low, medium, high\}^3$. Black, grey, and light-grey nodes indicate low, medium, and high drug dosage required.

## 12.4   Iris Flower Classification Problem

Iris is a well known benchmark problem concerning classification of flowers (Duch et al., 1997; Lozowski et al., 1996a). Three Iris flower classes are known: Setosa, Versicolor, and Virginica. The classification is based on four leaf attributes, namely, sepal length, sepal width, petal length, and petal width. These attributes, denoted by $x_1$, $x_2$, $x_3$, and $x_4$ were measured in millimeters and collected in the Iris database shown in Figure 12.9(a). Proper classifications, encoded by variables $y_1$, $y_2$, and $y_3$, form the output for a decision system. A neural network classifier has been trained first using the data. Given an unseen input instance, the trained network is able to classify the instance as having features of one of the flower types. The network output response is considered as a valid classification provided that only one output is positive, whereas the other two remain negative. The positive output indicates the flower type.

Figure 12.9(b) shows the fuzzification scheme used for rule extraction from the network. Following the algorithm described in the previous section, the classifier input is encoded in terms of fuzzy numbers. Using the uncertainty margin $\varepsilon = 0.01$ rules of two different kinds can be obtained. A fully decidable rule provides an output instance which has one *yes* and two *no*'s, such as $(\pi_1, \pi_2, \pi_3, \pi_4) \Rightarrow$ $(yes, no, no)$ indicating Setosa. Another kind of a rule can have one *no* and two "no information" entries, denoted by symbol "$-$", in the output instance. An example of such a rule is $(\pi_1, \pi_2, \pi_3, \pi_4) \Rightarrow (no, -, -)$, which excludes Setosa from consideration at a given input instance.

Rules extracted from the Iris classifier are presented in Figure 12.10 in disjunctive normal form. The number of rules have been reduced by grouping together input

| $x_1$ | $x_2$ | $x_3$ | $x_4$ | $y_1$ | $y_2$ | $y_3$ |
|---|---|---|---|---|---|---|
| 50 | 33 | 14 | 02 | 1 | −1 | −1 |
| 64 | 28 | 56 | 22 | −1 | −1 | 1 |
| 65 | 28 | 46 | 15 | −1 | 1 | −1 |
| 67 | 31 | 56 | 24 | −1 | −1 | 1 |
| 63 | 28 | 51 | 15 | −1 | −1 | 1 |
| 46 | 34 | 14 | 03 | 1 | −1 | −1 |
| 69 | 31 | 51 | 23 | −1 | −1 | 1 |
| 62 | 22 | 45 | 15 | −1 | 1 | −1 |
| 59 | 32 | 48 | 18 | −1 | 1 | −1 |
| 46 | 36 | 10 | 02 | 1 | −1 | −1 |
| 61 | 30 | 46 | 14 | −1 | 1 | −1 |
| 47 | 32 | 13 | 02 | 1 | −1 | −1 |
| 65 | 30 | 52 | 20 | −1 | −1 | 1 |
| 56 | 25 | 39 | 11 | −1 | 1 | −1 |
| 65 | 30 | 55 | 18 | −1 | −1 | 1 |
| 58 | 27 | 51 | 19 | −1 | −1 | 1 |
| 68 | 32 | 59 | 23 | −1 | −1 | 1 |
| ⋮ | ⋮ | ⋮ | ⋮ | ⋮ | ⋮ | ⋮ |

(a)

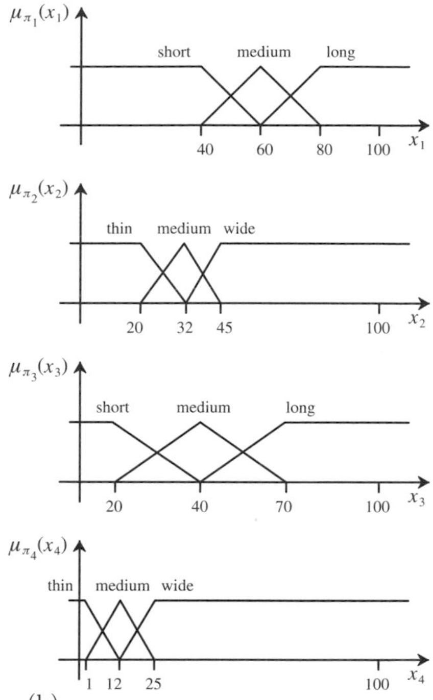

(b)

**Figure 12.9** Iris problem: **(a)** The data set used for neural network training. Variables $x_1$, $x_2$, $x_3$, and $x_4$ are the measurements of the leaf attributes: sepal length, sepal width, petal length, and petal width, given in millimeters. The classifier has three outputs $y_1$, $y_2$, and $y_3$ assigned to three Iris species: Setosa, Versicolor, and Virginica; **(b)** Fuzzification scheme of the Iris classifier inputs.

| $\pi_1$ | $\pi_2$ | $\pi_3$ | $\pi_4$ | $\varrho_1$ | $\varrho_2$ | $\varrho_3$ |
|---|---|---|---|---|---|---|
| long | wide | medium | medium | no | – | – |
| long | thin | short | medium | no | yes | – |
| ¬long | thin | medium | thin | no | yes | – |
| ¬short | wide | long | medium | no | – | – |
| ¬long | ¬wide | short | wide | no | yes | no |
| ¬long | ¬wide | long | thin | no | yes | no |
| ¬short | wide | ¬short | wide | no | no | yes |
| – | ¬wide | ¬short | ¬thin | no | – | – |
| ¬long | wide | medium | medium | yes | – | – |
| ¬long | – | short | thin | yes | no | – |
| ¬long | ¬thin | short | medium | yes | no | – |
| ¬long | ¬thin | medium | thin | yes | no | – |
| long | thin | medium | medium | – | no | – |
| long | wide | long | medium | – | no | yes |
| – | wide | medium | medium | – | no | – |
| – | ¬wide | long | medium | – | no | yes |
| – | ¬wide | ¬short | wide | – | no | yes |
| medium | thin | medium | medium | – | yes | – |
| ¬short | medium | medium | medium | – | yes | – |
| short | wide | medium | medium | – | – | no |
| long | medium | medium | medium | – | – | no |
| medium | – | medium | medium | – | – | no |
| ¬long | – | short | medium | – | – | no |
| ¬long | – | ¬long | thin | – | – | no |
| long | ¬medium | medium | medium | – | – | yes |

**Figure 12.10** Linguistic rules for the Iris classification problem. Input instances $\pi_1$, $\pi_2$, $\pi_3$, and $\pi_4$ refer to the Iris attributes: sepal length, sepal width, petal length, and petal width, respectively. Output instances $\varrho_1$, $\varrho_2$, and $\varrho_3$ determine the plant species: Setosa, Versicolor, and Virginica.

| $\pi_3\backslash\pi_4$ | thin | med. | wide |
|---|---|---|---|
| short | $\pi_1\backslash\pi_2$ \| th md wd<br>sht \| St. St. St.<br>md \| St. St. St.<br>lng \| — — — | $\pi_1\backslash\pi_2$ \| th md wd<br>sht \| Ve. St. St.<br>md \| Ve. St. St.<br>lng \| — — — | $\pi_1\backslash\pi_2$ \| th md wd<br>sht \| Ve. Ve. —<br>md \| Ve. Ve. —<br>lng \| — — — |
| med. | $\pi_1\backslash\pi_2$ \| th md wd<br>sht \| Ve. St. St.<br>md \| Ve. St. St.<br>lng \| — — — | $\pi_1\backslash\pi_2$ \| th md wd<br>sht \| — — St.<br>md \| Ve. Ve. St.<br>lng \| Vi. Ve. Vi. | $\pi_1\backslash\pi_2$ \| th md wd<br>sht \| Vi. Vi. —<br>md \| Vi. Vi. Vi.<br>lng \| Vi. Vi. Vi. |
| long | $\pi_1\backslash\pi_2$ \| th md wd<br>sht \| Ve. Ve. —<br>md \| Ve. Ve. —<br>lng \| — — — | $\pi_1\backslash\pi_2$ \| th md wd<br>sht \| Vi. Vi. —<br>md \| Vi. Vi. —<br>lng \| Vi. Vi. Vi. | $\pi_1\backslash\pi_2$ \| th md wd<br>sht \| Vi. Vi. —<br>md \| Vi. Vi. Vi.<br>lng \| Vi. Vi. Vi. |

**Figure 12.11** Iris rule diagram for a quick reference.

instances for which a class negation, denoted by "¬", or a "don't care" entry, denoted by "−", were possible to use. Large sets of rules may be inconvenient to read in a tabular form. A more readable quick reference diagram for the Iris rules is shown in Figure 12.11. It is a four-coordinate array organized as embedded matrices. The inner matrices label the flower sepal measurements $\pi_1$ and $\pi_2$, while the outer matrix describes the petal measurements $\pi_3$ and $\pi_4$.

## 12.5 Concluding Remarks

The method of extracting crisp rules from data or a trained neural network discussed above is one of many approaches in the area of soft computing. The rules have the form of those used in fuzzy reasoning. The neural network may become a necessary element if the training data is noisy, since the neural network provides filtration of the training data and thus the number of conclusive rules becomes reasonable. Even one noisy data point would cause an enormous increase in the number of created rules if the rules were obtained based on the training data instead of the network outputs. Here we assume that the network is trained with a sufficiently large final MSE to allow smooth filtration of data (Zurada and Malinowski, 1993; Zurada et al., 1994).

Moreover, by choosing the parameter $\varepsilon$, the number of rules (after pruning the totally undecidable ones) can be adjusted; the number of rules is related to the accuracy of a fuzzy classifier using the created rules. The aim is to extract knowledge from the a classifier (Ishikawa, 1996; Yasui et al., 1995), not to build its replica, since it is more important for the rules to be as compact as possible even if classification with such rules is less than optimum. The numeric complexity of the rule extraction algorithm increases with the number of fuzzy classes used for each input and with the number of inputs with a factor larger than 1. However, the algorithm presented is relatively insensitive to the size of the training data, and even large data sets can be handled efficiently.

# References

Craven, M. W. and Shavlik, J. W. 1994. Learning symbolic rules using artificial neural networks. In *Proceedings of the 10th International Conference on Machine Learning*, pp. 73–80, Amherst, Mass.

Duch, W., Adamczyk, R., and Grabczewski, K. 1997. Extraction of crisp logical rules using constructive constrained backpropagation networks. In *Proceedings of the 1997 International Conference on Neural Networks (ICNN'97)*, vol. 4, pp. 2384–2389, Houston, Texas.

Ishibuchi, H. 1995. Selecting fuzzy if-then rules for classification problems using genetic algorithms. *IEEE Transactions on Fuzzy Systems*, 3(3):260–270.

Ishikawa, M. 1996. Structural learning with forgetting. *Neural Networks*, 9(3):509–521.

Karayiannis, N. B. and Venetsanopoulos, A. N. 1994. Decision making using neural networks. *Neurocomputing*, 6:363–374.

Lozowski, A., Cholewo, T. J., and Zurada, J. M. 1996a. Crisp rule extraction from perceptron network classifiers. In *Proceedings of the 1996 IEEE International Conference on Neural Networks (ICNN'96). Plenary, Panel and Special Sessions*, pp. 94–99, Washington DC.

Lozowski, A., Cholewo, T. J., and Zurada, J. M. 1996b. Symbolic rule representation in neural network models. In *Proceedings of the Second Conference on Neural Networks and Their Applications*, vol. 2, pp. 300–305, Szczyrk, Poland.

Setiono, R. and Liu, H. 1996. Symbolic representation of neural networks. *IEEE Computer*, 29(3):71–77.

Shavlik, J. W. 1994. Combining symbolic and neural learning. *Machine Learning*, 14:321–331.

Sun, C. T. 1994. Rule-base structure identification in an adaptive-network-based fuzzy inference system. *IEEE Transactions on Fuzzy Systems*, 2(1):64–73.

Takagi, T. and Sugeno, M. 1985. Fuzzy identification of systems and its application to modeling and control. *IEEE Transactions on Systems, Man and Cybernetics*, 15(1):116–132.

Towell, G. G. and Shavlik, J. W. 1993. Extracting refined rules from knowledge-based neural networks. *Machine Learning*, 13:71–101.

Viktor, H. L. and Cloete, I. 1995. Extracting DNF rules from artificial neural networks. In *From Natural to Artificial Neural Computation*, eds. J. Mira and F. Sandoval, Lecture Notes in Computer Science, pp. 374–381. Berlin, Germany: Springer-Verlag.

Wang, L. and Mendel, J. M. 1992. Generating fuzzy rules by learning from examples. *IEEE Transactions on Systems, Man, and Cybernetics*, 22(6).

Yasui, S., Malinowski, A., and Zurada, J. M. 1995. Convergence suppression and divergence facilitation: New approach to prune hidden layer and weights in feedforward neural networks. In *Proceedings of the IEEE International Symposium on Circuits and Systems*, vol. 1, pp. 121–124, Seattle, WA.

Zadeh, L. A. 1965. Fuzzy sets. *Information and Control*, 8:338–353.

Zurada, J. M. 1992. *Introduction to Artificial Neural Systems*. Boston: PWS.

Zurada, J. M. and Lozowski, A. 1996. Generating linguistic rules from data using neuro-fuzzy framework. In *Proceedings of the Fourth International Conference on Soft Computing (IIZUKA'96)*, pp. 618–621, Iizuka, Fukuoka, Japan.

Zurada, J. M. and Malinowski, A. 1993. Sensitivity analysis for pruning of training data in feedforward neural networks. In *Proceedings of Australian-New Zealand Conference on Intelligent Information Systems*, pp. 288–292, Perth, Australia.

Zurada, J. M., Malinowski, A., and Cloete, I. 1994. Sensitivity analysis for minimization of input data dimension for feedforward neural network. In *Proceedings of the IEEE International Symposium an Circuits and Systems*, pp. 447–450, London, England.

# 13 Neural Knowledge Processing in Expert Systems

Jiří Šíma[1] and Jiří Červenka

*In this chapter knowledge-based neurocomputing is applied to expert systems. Two main approaches to represent the knowledge base, namely explicit and implicit representations are first introduced and compared in rule-based and neural expert systems, respectively. Then, several possible integration strategies that make an effort to eliminate the drawbacks of both approaches in hybrid systems, are surveyed. To illustrate the full power of knowledge-based neurocomputing, the main ideas of the prototypical, strictly neural expert system MACIE will be sketched. Here, a neural network is enriched by other functionalities to achieve all required features of expert systems. Neural knowledge processing will further be demonstrated on the system EXPSYS which exploits the powerful backpropagation learning to automatically create the knowledge base. In addition, EXPSYS introduces interval neuron states to cope with incomplete information and provides a simple explanation of the results. The chapter concludes with an EXPSYS application to a toy economic problem which is compared to a parallel conventional rule-based solution.*

## 13.1 Knowledge Representation in Expert Systems

In this section we discuss the difference between explicit and implicit representation of knowledge in expert systems. We focus mainly on two typical representatives of these different approaches. Namely, we compare rule-based systems and neural networks. To make our exposition self-contained we will first recall some basic notions from expert systems (Biondo, 1990; Giarratano and Riley, 1993; Ignizio, 1991, Jackson, 1990) to motivate representation issues.

---

1. This research was supported by GA ČR Grant No. 201/98/0717 and partially by grants MŠMT ČR OK–304 and INCO-COOP 96–0195.

### 13.1.1   Expert Systems

#### *13.1.1.1   Definition and Requirements*

The representation of large amounts of knowledge which would ensure their integrity, consistency, and effective exploitation is one of the main issues of artificial intelligence. For this purpose expert systems have been proposed to manage knowledge processing. An *expert system* is a computer program that performs a complex decision-making task within a particular narrow *problem domain* that is normally done by a human expert. It is based on the idea of taking on the knowledge from a specialist and expressing it in an appropriate representation to exploit the knowledge in the same way as the human expert does and above all with the same result. The expert system can replace an expert who can be too expensive and sometimes even not available to advise, analyze, consult, diagnose, explain, forecast, justify, monitor, plan, etc.

A typical example of the type of program introduced above is a diagnostic medical expert system. Its domain is usually confined to a particular area of medical expertise handled by a physician—a specialist, e.g. an internist. The system can help to diagnose a subclass of diseases and possibly advise the manner of their treatment. In the sequel we will use medical examples to illustrate some key concepts of expert system design. However, it must be stated here that for the sake of clarity of exposition all these examples will be oversimplified from a medical point of view. Furthermore, in Section 13.3.5, we will present an expert system application for a real-world economic problem.

Generally, the expert system is required to possess the following functional features:

- A user of the expert system usually presents his particular problem in interactive mode. The system builds an internal model of this case and asks questions to acquire new information which is most relevant for solving the task. In our example of the diagnostic medical expert system, the user first presents basic information about a patient's condition to the program, e.g. the apparent symptoms of a patient's complaints. Then the system asks additional questions or recommends relevant medical examinations to improve its internal model of the patient's condition which is finally used to infer a diagnosis. The system should ask its questions in the order of their relevance for the case being examined, e.g. it should not require all patients to be X-rayed first.

- The expert system should infer a solution for the problem even from incomplete or imprecise information, e.g. when the user replies "I don't know" to some of the questions or when some numerical values are only determined within intervals, etc. The conclusions of the program are usually evaluated by confidences given as a percentage which measure the credibility of a solution. For the medical expert system, some information on the patient's anamnesis, symptoms or results of laboratory analyses may not be available, e.g. because of the patient's inability to describe his symptoms, lack of time to carry out a particular test, insufficient laboratory equipment, contra-indications that disable required examination, etc. In spite of this, the system should always infer some diagnosis and compute its confidence, which obviously also depends on the input completeness and accuracy. For example, the medical system infers the diagnosis of hepatitis with a 58% confidence having been told that the patient has yellow skin and the results of urine and blood tests (for bilirubin) recommended by the system are unknown. After providing the program with these results the diagnosis confidence can either increase, e.g. up to 95%, or hepatitis is excluded.

- The expert system should also provide the user with some explanation of its conclusions to justify the inference and to give the user insights into the problem or to avoid fatal errors caused by the computer solution. The system usually exhibits how the conclusions have been reached by a sequence of internal logical steps which lead to its results. For example, the user of the medical system can ask why the program recommends, with high confidence, to take out the appendix by an operation. The system explains this conclusion by the acute appendicitis which has been inferred by a typical stabbing abdomen pain.

### 13.1.1.2  Modular Architecture

In Section 13.1.1.1, the definition of the expert system as well as the requirements for its functional features have been presented from an external perspective. We now turn to the description of the internal modular structure of expert systems. Of course, the expert system is a computer program and therefore its architecture can differ as the case may be. However, the following major parts of the expert system are usually distinguishable:

- The **knowledge base** is a typically large static data structure which contains all the important information about the problem domain, i.e. knowledge from the area of program expertise, and thus, it is problem-oriented. This base models an expert's knowledge which may not only be exact but it can also be intuitive, imprecise, incomplete, and even questionable or contradictory. The representation of such a knowledge base in a computational framework is the main concern of this chapter. For example, the knowledge base of the medical expert system consists of a specialist physician's knowledge. This includes, for example, sets of symptoms and characteristics indicating particular diseases, together with procedures for differentiating between them and therapeutical schemes for their treatment. This knowledge, of course, comprises not only known facts about diseases but also subtle techniques for their diagnosis gained by long practical experience. Therefore, it is difficult to express in a computer-acceptable representation.

- The facts or **fact base** is typically a small dynamic data structure which contains information about a particular problem which is currently being solved by the system. It includes the input facts provided by the user as well as the solutions of subproblems or partial solutions, i.e. the corresponding inferred conclusions with confidence concerning the considered task. Thus, the fact base serves as an internal model of the case at hand which is built by the system to solve this problem. The manner of representing facts in this base is usually the same, or at least consistent with the knowledge base representation. In our medical system example, the fact base contains information about a patient's condition and his diagnosis with the confidence being inferred so far.

- The **inference engine** is the controlling procedural part of the expert system. It consists of cooperating programs which establish the general mechanism of reasoning and inference. The inference engine exploits knowledge from the field of expertise which is stored in the knowledge base to build an internal model of the currently solved problem in the fact base. Besides making the proper inferences to develop the model internally, it collects relevant input facts into the fact base interactively from the user. This means that the inference engine determines the appropriate questions which the user is asked to obtain relevant information about the case at hand. This information should attempt to complete the model and consequently, increase confidence of the conclusions. Furthermore, the inference engine is problem-independent, i.e. it implements a general inference algorithm which should still work for other knowledge bases from different problem domains providing that their representation format is preserved. The empty expert system which does not contain a particular knowledge base, is called an *expert system shell*. Such a shell consisting only of the inference engine of the diagnostic medical expert system can be exploited for doing other diagnostics, e.g. the diagnostics of a nuclear power plant operation after a relevant knowledge base is created.

- The **explanation mechanism** traces the operation of the inference engine and exploits it to explain a particular conclusion when it is asked.

- The **user interface** of the expert system links the inference engine to the external environment, i.e. it collects and preprocesses information about the problem at hand and outputs the results.

### 13.1.2  Explicit Knowledge Representation and Rule-Based Systems

The most difficult part of building the expert system is the construction of its knowledge base. This task is usually done by *knowledge engineers* who cooperate with specialists in the problem domain to acquire relevant knowledge. In a conventional approach the representation of this information is based on a symbolic expression of the human expert's knowledge, skills, and experience. This is called the *explicit knowledge representation* because the expert knowledge is formulated in a comprehensible way. Typically, the knowledge representation is specified by a data format in which the information is expressed to be stored in the knowledge base. This format should accomodate the naturally imprecise and incomplete character of the expert knowledge. The knowledge base representation also determines how information is processed by the inference engine. The knowledge engineer normally spends a lot of effort and time by consulting the expert to debug the knowledge base, since, the specialist is usually unable to transform his knowledge immediately to a prescribed formalism, and the explicit representation formalism of the knowledge base may not be entirely adequate for all types of expert knowledge.

There are many ways of representing the expert knowledge explicitly. Traditional expert systems generally employ so-called *IF-THEN rules* to represent this information and hence, these programs are called *rule-based systems*. For example, the most famous expert system MYCIN (Buchanan and Shortliffe, 1984), which diagnoses microbial diseases of blood, is also based on rules. The rules usually have the following form:

```
IF <condition> THEN <conclusion> (<confidence>)
```

The condition is typically a logical expression which contains relevant variables whose values can be inferred from the fact base or are acquired from the user. The conclusion determines the new value of some variable providing that the corresponding condition is satisfied. The probabilistic nature of the rule is expressed by its percentual confidence. For example, the knowledge base of our hypothetical medical system can include the following rule:

```
IF (skin-color=yellow) and (bilirubin-blood-tests=true)
   THEN hepatitis=true (0.9)
```

which means that the diagnosis hepatitis is concluded with 90% confidence if the patient's skin is yellow and his blood tests are positive.

The inference engine usually examines several rules to satisfy their conditions starting with those rules whose conclusions are of main interest to the user. If a condition of some rule is fulfilled, i.e. the values of relevant variables in the fact base meet the condition with sufficiently high confidences, then this rule is applied so that a new value of the variable from the conclusion can be inferred and its confidence computed. This information is stored in the fact base. The conclusion confidence depends on the confidences of facts which are tested in the condition and on the confidence of the rule itself. The confidence manipulations are based on fuzzy logic. In the above-mentioned example of the IF-THEN rule, suppose that the confidence of the fact that a patient has yellow skin is 0.8 and that his bilirubin blood tests are positive with confidence 0.95. Then the conjunction of the condition is satisfied with the confidence which is determined as the minimum of these confidences, i.e. $\min(0.8, 0.95) = 0.8$. The resulting confidence of the diagnosis of hepatitis is computed as the product of this value and the confidence of the rule, i.e. $0.8 \times 0.9 = 0.72$.

In order to determine whether the conditions are satisfied, the inference engine recursively examines those rules whose conclusions affect the conditions of the current rules being checked. If such rules are not found, the user is asked about relevant facts. Note that the order in which the rules are examined is given by the recursive calls. This inference engine strategy is called *backward chaining* which is, for example, employed in MYCIN. An alternative approach is *forward chaining* in which the values of initially known variables are being completed by applying those rules whose conditions have already been satisfied or by questioning the user if there are no such rules. This approach is employed in the commercially successful expert system R1/XCON (McDermott, 1981) which configures computers. Generally, it is obvious that rule-based systems can be directly implemented in programming languages like Prolog, LISP, etc.

Besides IF-THEN rules, it is possible to represent the expert knowledge in so-called inference networks which are, for example, used in the system Prospector (Duda and Reboh, 1983) for geological exploration, or in the expert system shell FEL-EXPERT (Mařík et al., 1990, 1992, 1993). Furthermore, the well-known Internist-I (Miller et al., 1982), which is one of the largest medical expert systems, makes use of tables with probability-related information. The probability calculations in these systems were motivated by Bayesian theory.

### 13.1.3   Implicit Knowledge Representation and Neural Networks

In Section 13.1.2, we discussed explicit knowledge representation. However, the knowledge is often difficult to express in some computer formalism. This is the case when the specialist is unable to formulate his knowledge and experience using rules because, in fact, human experts do not usually apply formal logic to each situation, but rather they associate the new case with some old pattern to derive a solution. Moreover, some problem domains naturally include numerical data instead of rules, e.g. visual images, signals, etc. These data require additional processing to be understood properly and thus, they represent implicit knowledge. Within this context, when one tries to represent a knowledge base explicitly, e.g. by rules, a new rather inadequate representation results which may preserve the original knowledge or can even violate it in such a way that the inference engine fails to infer correct conclusions from the knowledge base.

A more natural approach is suggested by the way we envisage that the expert's brain does it. The knowledge is represented directly without further knowledge transformation into an inadequate explicit format which deforms the original information. On the other hand, one can argue that the human brain is so complex that no one really understands how information is stored there. However, the simulations of even very simplified mathematical models of neural networks exhibit surprisingly "intelligent" behavior similar to human intelligence, e.g. the ability to learn new knowledge and to generalize previous experience. *Neural expert systems*, (*connectionist expert systems* or briefly, *expert networks* (Gallant, 1993; Mitra and Pal, 1995; Šíma, 1995) ) in which the knowledge base is implemented by a neural network present a promising alternative to rule-based systems. In what follows we will recall basic notions from neural network theory (Fausett, 1994; Haykin, 1994; Hecht-Nielsen, 1990; Hertz et al., 1991; Lippmann, 1987; Rojas, 1996; Simpson, 1990) which will be used later in technical parts of this chapter.

*Neural networks* are computational models which were inspired by neurophysiology. They consist of a multitude of simple units—the so-called *neurons* which are densely interconnected. Every inter-neuron connection in the network is associated with a numerical *weight*. First, we will describe the function of a single neuron. A neuron $j$ collects its real *inputs* from the *outputs* $y_i$ of incident neurons $i \in j_\leftarrow$ where $j_\leftarrow$ denotes the set of all neurons which are connected to neuron $j$. Let these connections be labeled with the real weights $w_{ji}$ for $i \in j_\leftarrow$. Moreover, denote by $w_{j0}$ the so-called *bias* of neuron $j$ which can be viewed as the weight of a formal input $y_0 = 1$ whose value is constantly 1. Then, the so-called *excitation level* $\xi_j$ of neuron $j$ is computed as the weighted sum of its inputs:

$$\xi_j = w_{j0} + \sum_{i \in j_\leftarrow} w_{ji} y_i \,. \tag{13.1}$$

The *state*, i.e. the output, $y_j$ of the neuron $j$ is determined from its excitation level $\xi_j$ by applying an *activation function* $\sigma$ as follows:

$$y_j = \sigma(\xi_j) \tag{13.2}$$

where

$$\sigma(\xi) = \begin{cases} -1 & \text{for } \xi < 0 \\ 1 & \text{for } \xi \geq 0 \end{cases} \tag{13.3}$$

is the *hard limiter*.

Furthermore, we will restrict ourselves to the most widely used neural network architecture—the *feedforward neural network* which we outline briefly. In this network, neurons can be grouped into a sequence of layers so that neurons in one layer are connected only to neurons in subsequent layers. The first so-called *input layer* which consists of $n$ *input neurons* serves as the input for the network while the last so-called *output layer* composed of $m$ *output* neurons is used for the output. The intermediate layers are called *hidden layers* and they include *hidden neurons*. The computation proceeds from the input layer via hidden layers up to the output layer. At the beginning the states of the input neurons are set to the input of the network. In a general step, suppose that all neuron outputs are determined up to a certain layer, then the states of neurons in the next layer are computed according to Equations (13.1) and (13.2). At the end the states of output neurons represent the output of the network.

It is clear that the function $\mathbf{y}(\mathbf{w}) : \Re^n \longrightarrow \Re^m$ computed by a neural network (briefly, the *network function*) is parametrized by the vector $\mathbf{w}$ of all its weights which is called the *configuration* of the network. Neural networks learn this function, i.e. are "programmed," from example data—the so-called *training patterns*. A training pattern is a pair $(\mathbf{x}, \mathbf{d})$ of a sample input $\mathbf{x} \in \Re^n$ with the corresponding desired output $\mathbf{d} \in \Re^m$. The patterns create the so-called *training set*

$$T = \{(\mathbf{x}_k, \mathbf{d}_k) \,;\, \mathbf{x}_k \in \Re^n, \, \mathbf{d}_k \in \Re^m, \, k = 1, \ldots, p\} \tag{13.4}$$

which is used during the learning phase to adapt the configuration automatically so that the new network function is consistent with $T$, i.e. $\mathbf{y}(\mathbf{w}, \mathbf{x}_k) = \mathbf{d}_k$ for $k = 1, \ldots, p$. In addition, the network function should generalize the implicit rules from the training set and respond reasonably to previously unseen inputs.

There are many learning rules and heuristics used in neural networks. They usually minimize an error between the actual network function and the desired behavior which is specified by a training set. Given a training set (13.4), the error $E(\mathbf{w})$ of the network function $\mathbf{y}$ with respect to $T$ is defined as a function of $\mathbf{w}$ in the following way:

$$E(\mathbf{w}) = \frac{1}{2} \sum_{k=1}^{p} \sum_{j=1}^{m} \left( y_j(\mathbf{w}, \mathbf{x}_k) - d_{kj} \right)^2 \tag{13.5}$$

where $y_j(\mathbf{w}, \mathbf{x}_k)$ is the actual state of the output neuron $j$ for the input $\mathbf{x}_k$ (and the configuration $\mathbf{w}$) while $d_{kj}$ is the corresponding desired value. The task of the learning algorithm is to minimize the error (13.5) in the configuration space, i.e. to find $\mathbf{w}$ which minimizes $E(\mathbf{w})$. This represents a non-trivial optimization task because the error includes the complex non-linear network function. Gradient methods can be applied here provided that the gradient of the error function $E(\mathbf{w})$ can be computed. For this purpose, the hard limiter (13.3) is approximated with a differentiable activation function , e.g. hyperbolic tangent:

$$\sigma(\xi) = \frac{1 - e^{-\xi}}{1 + e^{-\xi}} \, . \tag{13.6}$$

The gradient computation can be achieved by the well-known *backpropagation* algorithm (Rumelhart et al., 1986). However, the whole learning procedure is a very complex time-consuming optimization process in which the implicit knowledge contained in the training set is automatically learnt and represented by weight parameters.

As we have mentioned above, to perform the desired task the network function should not only memorize the training set but it should generalize the rules from the training set in order to be able to derive solutions for similar inputs. It is known that the generalization ability of the network depends on the *architecture (topology)*, i.e. on the number of neurons and their pattern of network connections, which also determines the dimension of configuration. If the architecture is rich enough, then the network can memorize the training set without problems, however, it may respond incorrectly to previously unseen inputs. This is called *overfitting*. On the other hand, poor architectures are probably too weak to solve complex tasks. It has been experimentally confirmed that, for a particular task, there exists an "optimal" architecture which is strong enough to solve the problem and, at the same time, it generalizes well. This architecture is usually searched in such a way that different network architectures are adapted to the training set. Then, these networks are evaluated, using the so-called *test set* which is a part of the training set that is not used for learning. The architecture whose function is the most consistent with the test set is chosen to perform the task.

In neural expert systems, the user interface encodes the inputs and outputs of the system by the states of the input and output neurons and the knowledge base is implemented by a neural network configuration. This means that instead of elaborating artificial rules with the aid of an expert, the neural network automatically adapts to example inferences during a learning phase and the network function generalizes implicit rules from the training set. The set of example inferences which is encoded into a training set can be generated by observing solutions of domain experts to the problem. In our medical example the clinical records of patients can be exploited for this purpose where symptoms and test results in each case present a sample input and the corresponding diagnosis and treatment recommended by a physician is the desired output. For example, we can define the following inputs and outputs of the medical system:

```
INPUTS:  TEMPERATURE,ANOREXIA,CHOLESTEROL,SKIN-COLOR,SCLERAE-COLOR,
         ...,LIVER-TENDERNESS,BLOOD-TEST,URINE-TEST
OUTPUTS: DIAGNOSIS,HOSPITALIZE,...
```

Then, an example of such inference pattern can look like:

```
[(38.2,YES,NORMAL,YELLOW,YELLOW,...
   ...,HIGH,unknown,{BILIRUBIN,UROBILINOGEN}),
  (HEPATITIS,YES,...)]
```

Thus, after the network is trained, the expert knowledge is distributed in numerical weights throughout the network without identifying the purpose of any weight or neuron within this representation. This is called the *implicit knowledge representation* because the expert knowledge cannot be extracted easily from the knowledge base without additional processing.

Furthermore, the inference engine in neural expert systems collects all inputs for the neural network. Then it evaluates the network function using (13.1), (13.2) for these inputs and obtains the corresponding outputs from which the conclusions are decoded. It is clear that, during the network computation, the neuron states implement the fact base.

### 13.1.4 Comparison of Rule-Based and Neural Expert Systems

In Sections 13.1.2, 13.1.3, two different approaches to representing the knowledge base in expert systems have been introduced, namely rule-based and neural expert systems. Now, we compare these systems from various perspectives.

#### 13.1.4.1 Task Size

The size of a knowledge base (and even fact base) and its complexity are not limited in rule-based systems. It can include plenty of rules which serve as a way to solve very large and complex problems. The system can generate many questions including irrelevant ones which can upset the user. An example of a medical system is known which always started its consultation with the question "Is the patient alive?' Furthermore, a large rule-based system can create a lot of various auxiliary statements and can reach many different output hypotheses.

On the other hand, it has been proven (Šíma, 1996) even for a very simple fixed feedforward architecture that backpropagation learning is an NP-hard problem. Therefore, learning larger tasks can be intractable in neural expert systems. Practical experiments prove that the learning process is very time-consuming (even weeks of PC computation) and it is possible to manage tasks only up to hundreds of neurons and training patterns. Therefore, the size of a neural knowledge base is limited and neural expert systems are suitable for partial subproblems with a very restricted problem domain. They can be linked in a hierarchy to handle larger tasks.

### 13.1.4.2   *Knowledge Acquisition and Editing*

The main difference between the rule-based and neural approach to expert system design is found in their knowledge acquisition. In rule-based systems, a knowledge engineer together with an expert from a problem domain formulates the particular rules, evaluates confidences for them and debugs the resulting knowledge base to achieve a reasonable performance of the inference engine. For example, the appropriate order of rules is found and confidences are refined. This is a very time-consuming process (even years) and a satisfactory result is not guaranteed. Moreover, further editing can cause undesired side-effects. The explicit knowledge representation in these systems confines their applicability to the problems that are sufficiently understood and where the rules are available and adequate to solve the task.

In neural expert systems, the expert knowledge is included implicitly in the training set, which consists of example inferences, and an expert is generally not necessary to create the neural knowledge base. The training set should include a reasonable number (due to learning time) of representative patterns which sufficiently cover the problem domain. Their combinations and generalization is left for the learning phase. Therefore, the neural approach is more suitable for problems in which a data set is available and where there is a lack of rules. It is also possible to select the representative patterns automatically from a large database by using cluster analysis. On the other hand, it is better to apply the rule-based system than try to translate a complete set of rules into a training set because one rule can cover an unmanageable amount of data. The main advantage of the neural approach is that the knowledge base, which is implemented by a neural network, is created automatically by a learning algorithm after the training set is prepared. Therefore, building a neural expert system takes only a few weeks or months. Moreover, the editing of a neural knowledge base can easily be achieved by additional learning.

### 13.1.4.3   *Partial Matching*

The problem of *partial matching* appears in rule-based systems when no condition of all rules in the knowledge base is entirely satisfied in the fact base, although the conditions match the facts partially. The inference engine is sometimes able to exploit the partially satisfied rules to infer reasonable conclusions, e.g. by using fuzzy logic. In neural expert systems, this problem corresponds to the situation where the presented input for the network has not occurred in the training set. Supposing this input is from the problem domain which was covered sufficiently by the training set and the neural network generalizes well, then the conclusion provided by the network is a good solution for the problem at hand. We contend that neural networks are especially suitable for partial matching.

### 13.1.4.4   *Incomplete Information*

Incomplete or even imprecise input information is handled in rule-based systems by using confidence calculations and fuzzy logic. The system gradually builds the internal model of the case currently being solved on the basis of a possibly incomplete set of input information which is being acquired from the user step-by-step while it provides partial hypotheses and conclusions.

On the other hand, in neural expert systems, all network inputs (including unknown and irrelevant inputs) have to be specified to compute the network function, i.e. to perform the inference and to get the relevant solution of the case at hand. This makes operating with incomplete information difficult or even impossible (Drucker, 1990). Sometimes, the input and output neuron state can be interpreted as confidence in the corresponding facts to cope with imprecise information in neural networks. However, this should be taken into account in the training set to let the network generalize the confidence calculations during learning.

### 13.1.4.5   *Explanation Capabilities*

Due to explicit knowledge representation the rule-based systems have perfect explanation capabilities. It is sufficient to display the process by which the inference engine has reached the conclusions, which are transparent and comprehensible due to the explicitness of its logical steps. On the other hand, the implicit knowledge base representation in neural expert systems makes such an explanation difficult or even impossible. The expert knowledge is distributed in the network configuration and the neural network is used only as a "black box" to compute its outputs for given inputs without justifying these conclusions.

As it can be seen from the preceding comparison of rule-based and neural expert systems, their advantages and disadvantages are complementary. If knowledge is explicitly represented, its acquisition and the creation of the knowledge base for an expert system must be done manually. The debugging of rule-based systems is difficult and time-consuming. On the other hand, for the same reason these systems work well with incomplete information and provide excellent justification of inference. The opposite is true for a neural expert system whose knowledge base, despite its limited size, is created automatically by learning from example inferences in a relatively short time. However, these systems do not allow inference from incomplete information easily and have little or no explanation capability.

## 13.2   Neural Networks in Expert Systems

In this section we will briefly survey several possible integration strategies of explicit and neural knowledge representations in hybrid systems. Then we will focus on a strictly neural approach to illustrate information processing within the framework of the knowledge-based neurocomputing paradigm. Some applications of neural expert systems will be mentioned.

### 13.2.1   Hybrid Systems

The advantages and disadvantages of explicit and implicit knowledge base representations which have been demonstrated by rule-based and neural expert systems in Section 13.1 are complementary. Therefore, there is a natural tendency to integrate the advantages of both representation approaches in hybrid systems. *Hybrid systems* attempt to integrate the explicit knowledge with neural networks to cope simultaneously with different types of information. In the following various integration strategies (Caudill, 1991) will be discussed and illustrated by examples of existing systems.

#### *13.2.1.1   Divide and Conquer*

One of the simplest ways of combining neural networks and rule-based systems is a *divide-and-conquer* strategy. A large problem is broken into pieces which are solved separately by using the most appropriate methods. A subtask in which rules are known and justification of inference is required, is suitable for a rule-based solution. The other part of the problem, where only data are available, can be processed by neural network technology. Sometimes, a neural solution does not even need any explanation because the solution itself gives reasons for the conclusions, e.g. the optimization process is justified by its result. Thus, in the modular expert system architecture, the problem is first partitioned, i.e. the inputs are distributed to respective rule-based and neural network modules. Then these modules work in parallel to solve relevant subtasks. Finally, their solutions are collected to provide the user with resulting conclusions.

For example, in the daily scheduling of large numbers of delivery trucks it must be determined what packages should be combined on each truck and what the most efficient route is for that truck to follow for all its stops. This complex problem can be naturally divided into two subtasks: grouping the packages into trucks which can be solved by rules and route scheduling where an optimizing neural network is employed to find an efficient path for each truck. The final system which has been proposed by researchers Bigus and Goolsbey (Caudill, 1991) works very well indeed.

### 13.2.1.2   *Embedded Neural Network*

Another method of implicit and explicit knowledge integration is to make the neural network a part of the rule-based system. For example, the network can evaluate conditions of some rules. This approach is especially suitable for pattern matching, e.g. for visual or signal inputs, etc. where logical expressions cannot be applied. Thus, the neural network is employed for a rule matching process to decide whether a rule is applicable for the case at hand. Similarly, the applications of some rules can be executed by neural networks. The network can develop the internal model of the currently solved problem by inferring new facts and re-computing the confidences in the fact base or simply by performing the particular desired action (as in an application such as robot-arm control). Besides the network function computation, this can even include the neural learning and adaptation to the particular problem. In this way, the neural networks are embedded into a rule-based system to implement some rules or their parts while the remaining ones represent classical explicit knowledge. Such a hybrid system is controlled by a procedural inference engine.

Furthermore, even some parts of the conventional inference engine can be implemented by neural networks. For example, the selection of the most effective rule from a particular set of applicable rules is usually done by some heuristics. Several neural network architectures, e.g. Kohonen networks, respond with a single-best-response category and thus, they can be exploited for the best rule selection task. In this case, the neural network is embedded into the inference engine of a rule-based system to perform some of its heuristics. In addition, since in the embedded approach the application of rules still follows a logical sequence, the explanation capability is preserved.

An example of the embedded approach is a hybrid system *COLE* (COnnectionist Logic programming Environment) (Kasabov and Petkov, 1992a,b) which is an empty experimental rule-based system. It is implemented in Prolog and, in addition, includes neural network simulators as objects for which three predicates are defined: *create_net, train_net, recall_net.* It is clear that a hybrid rule-based system which exploits neural networks to solve partial subtasks can be built using COLE. A similar example is a hybrid production system *COPE* (COnnectionist Production systems Environment) (Kasabov, 1993) which employs forward chaining. The application of a production rule in COPE can again involve commands to cope with neural networks. This integration method can also be applied in the above-mentioned expert system FEL-EXPERT (Mařík et al., 1992) whose knowledge base representation is based on inference networks. In a medical application of FEL-EXPERT, neural networks are substituted for parts of the inference network (Družecký, 1992). Yet another interesting example of the embedded approach is a rule-based system for robotic control (Handelman et al., 1989) which initially finds acceptable first-cut solutions and simultaneously supervises the training of neural network by examples provided by rule-based task execution. The resulting integrated system is controlled by the rule-based part and enables a natural division of labor.

### 13.2.1.3   *Neural Implementation of Explicit Knowledge*

Another strategy is to transform explicit knowledge, e.g. rules, into a neural network in order to make use of neural network advantages like parallelism, competition, cyclic (recurrent) architecture, gradient minimization, partial matching, additional learning, etc. The neurons in the created network represent microconcepts, propositions, etc. and the connections among them express causal relationships, logical dependencies, and so on. Since the architecture is built from explicit knowledge each neuron and connection have their own purposes in the network and thus, the explicit knowledge representation is preserved although a neural network is utilized. The inference in this network is achieved by neural network computational dynamics which can be interpreted in logical terms due to the explicitness of the knowledge. Hence, justification of conclusions is guaranteed in such systems.

For example, the system *RUBICON* (Samad, 1988) implements rule-based architectures using feedforward neural networks in which individual layers represent parts of rules. Kasabov and Shishkov describe similar approaches (Kasabov and Shishkov, 1993; Kasabov, 1994). Or the so-called *fuzzy cognitive maps* (Kosko, 1987; Styblinski and Meyer, 1988; Taber and Siegel, 1987) are generally cyclic networks where neurons represent phenomena and connections are labeled with signs to express positive or negative causal relationships. The computational network dynamics model the actual development of a studied case. An application of the fuzzy cognitive map to modelling the political situation in South Africa has been described (Kosko, 1987). Another example of neural implementation of explicit knowledge employs again a cyclic network architecture (Narazaki and Ralescu, 1992) which is created analytically from rules by means of mathematical programming. Thus, the neurons represent propositions and constraint equations and the violation of constraints is formulated as an energy function. The inference is realized as a minimization process of the energy function to search for a truth value distribution that achieves optimum consistency with the knowledge. In contrast to the conventional microscopic inference technique based on local and piecewise evaluations of the knowledge, this method is macroscopic in that the whole set of knowledge is taken into consideration simultaneously.

### 13.2.1.4   *Incorporating Rules into Neural Networks*

The opposite approach to the preceding two strategies (see Sections 13.2.1.2, 13.2.1.3) is to incorporate explicit knowledge into a neural network after it has been trained from example data to improve its generalization capability. This strategy is suitable in the case when a training set is available, as well as when several isolated rules are known. Of course, the neural network should generalize these rules during learning from training patterns, however, it can fail to respond correctly in a few cases with respect to these rules. It is because the number of all the instances covered by these rules can be unmanageably large and thus it is impossible to include all of them into the training set to ensure perfect network function consistency with these rules. In addition, some of these rules may be essential for expert system applicability because breaking them is inadmissible or even dangerous. For example, in a medical system application a wrong diagnosis can endanger a patient's life. Therefore, it is important to have a method for incorporating rules into an already trained neural network while preserving the implicit knowledge which has been acquired from data. However, the knowledge representation in such an improved system is still implicit and hence the explanation of inference is problematic.

For example, Kasabov presents a method in which the weights of a two-layered neural network are adjusted to incorporate rules after the network has been trained (Kasabov, 1991). Namely, the weights associated with the connections leading from those input neurons which represent related facts within the condition of the rule, to those output neurons corresponding to relevant conclusions in this rule, are strengthened. This method improves the network generalization of the corresponding rule. Significantly better generalization of the explicit rules which can be expressed as differentiable functions can even be achieved during backpropagation learning using training pattern derivatives (Šíma, 1994). Thus, the error function (13.5) includes an additional term which penalizes the discrepancies between the actual and desired derivatives of the network function. In another example (Mazný, 1995) of this approach, rules are implemented as a separate so-called *rule neural network* using techniques from Section 13.2.1.3. Then the trained neural network is integrated with this rule network so that the rule network has a higher priority. This guarantees perfect network responses if a condition of some rule is satisfied and, at the same time, the computation of the original trained network is performed if this is not the case.

### 13.2.1.5  *Rule Extraction from Neural Networks*

It is also possible to use neural networks for rule extraction to replace human specialists for knowledge acquisition in rule-based systems. In this case, a neural network is trained from data to solve the problem acceptably well and then it is analyzed to extract a set of rules from the trained network with the aid of a training set. The rule-extraction process is tedious and the results may not be quite what one expects, but it is feasible. The resulting rules form the knowledge base of a rule-based system, perhaps after being refined or extended by a human expert. This approach can significantly shorten the rule-based system development time. Another exploitation of rule extraction is the explanation of inference in neural expert systems or even neural knowledge debugging. The rules which are extracted from the trained neural network are presented to a human specialist who can identify the rules which are incorrect. These rules are then used to generate the appropriate training patterns which, after being additionally learnt, correct the network function and improves its generalization capability.

The relation between inputs and outputs is usually analyzed in a trained neural network to extract rules. For example, the so-called *relation factor* (Saito and Nakano, 1988; Krysiak, 1991) has been introduced in medical diagnostic systems based on feedforward networks. Namely, denote by $C(S, D, P)$ the change in an output value of disease $D$ where a symptom $S$ of a patient $P$ (i.e. a training pattern) is switched from *on* to *off*, $Sum(S, D)$ is a summation of $C(S, D, P)$ for all patients (i.e. over the training set) and $N(S)$ denotes the number of switches of a symptom $S$. Then the relation factor is proportional to the fraction $Sum(S, D)/N(S)$. Similar statistical techniques in the network function analysis have been used to generate rules which are reasonable in physicians' opinions. Or the so-called *causal index* (Enbutsu et al., 1991) is defined to be the partial derivative of a particular network output by inputs. This index should measure the degree of the causal relationship between the input and output neurons. The causal index is evaluated for average training patterns to generate the relevant rules. Another technique of rule extraction exploits the so-called *structural learning with forgetting*, see Chapter 5 and (Ishikawa, 1996). In this method, additional penalty criteria are included in the error function (13.5) to delete connections and neurons with little contribution and to force the hidden neurons to have bipolar states in the continuous model (see (13.6)). Thus, a rough skeletal network architecture is obtained and the distributed representation in hidden neurons is dissipated during learning from example data. This enables extraction of explicit rules from the sparse architecture and clearer neural representation. Moreover, the rule extraction can be performed even for trained cyclic neural networks. These networks are computationally equivalent with finite automata whose transition functions are discovered by applying clustering algorithms in the network output space, see Chapter 3 (Omlin and Giles, 1996).

### 13.2.1.6   *Fuzzy-Rule Completion in Neural Networks*

The neural implementation of explicit knowledge described in Section 13.2.1.3 can be combined with rule-extraction methods (see Section 13.2.1.5) to complete fuzzy rules and to automate the computation and debugging of their confidences during neural learning. In this combined strategy the network with various types of constraints is first initialized from explicit fuzzy rules which are available as a first-cut problem solution. This means that the functions of respective neurons explicitly evaluate these rules and their parts, or combine them, e.g. the neurons compute prescribed fuzzy logic operations. Hence, these neuron functions may completely differ from Equations 13.1 and 13.2. Furthermore, the connections among neurons are now labeled with confidences, certainty factors or possibility measures, etc. which are partially estimated from the given rules, or they are chosen randomly. These confidence parameters represent the network configuration and may be restricted (or even fixed) within specific intervals to preserve their fuzzy-quantity interpretation. Thus, the architecture and the computational dynamics of the created network explicitly implement the set of rules and their fuzzy combinations.

The knowledge representation in such networks is fully explicit because, in fact, the original fuzzy rules are wired into the network and the role of individual neurons and connections is identifiable. In addition, the architecture of the network may be enriched (or even entirely constructed) with "empty" rules, i.e. with additional neurons and connections whose parameters will be specified during learning.

Then, the network which has been initialized from fuzzy rules is trained from example data to complete, revise    and refine the original explicit knowledge. Besides the regular training set, even the original rules may be exploited to generate training patterns in order to strengthen the prior   explicit knowledge. During the learning process, only the parameters of rules (e.g. confidences) are adapted within specific bounds while the rules themselves are preserved due to the shape of neuron functions and the fixed network architecture. For this purpose, the learning algorithm (e.g. backpropagation) is tailored to the specific network function. After the network has been trained, the adapted or even new rules can be extracted easily because the knowledge representation is explicit in this network. In this way, the confidences of fuzzy rules can be determined or refined using neural learning heuristics. This combined strategy can be modified if the extraction of rules is not needed. In this case the initial network implementation of rules does not require an explicit knowledge representation and the classical neural network function without constraints, e.g. Equations 13.1 and 13.2, can be employed. Then the explicit representation is lost during the network adaptation and rules can be restored only by applying the techniques from Section 13.2.1.5.

For example, this combined strategy can be applied to tune certainty factors in MYCIN-like expert systems  using backpropagation learning algorithm (Lacher et al., 1992). Similarly, the belief measures are accommodated in probabilistic logic and Bayesian networks  which may be implemented as neural networks (Chen, 1987). The combined method is also widely employed to refine or derive fuzzy rules and fuzzy controllers (Berenji and Khedkar, 1992; Jang, 1992; Lin and Lee, 1991; Yager, 1994). Furthermore, rules for string-to-string mapping can be extracted from a trained neural network with representation restrictions (McMillan et al., 1991). Implicit neural network implementation of rules (without the necessity of rule extraction) to refine expert system performance using neural learning has also been used by (Yang and Bhargava, 1990).

### 13.2.2  Neural Expert Systems

As we have seen in Section 13.2.1, various integration strategies of explicit and neural knowledge representations are possible. We now focus on a strictly neural approach to exploit the full power of knowledge-based neurocomputing and to illustrate neural knowledge processing. Neural expert systems attempt to weaken the disadvantages of implicit representation by introducing heuristics which analyze neural networks to cope with incomplete information, to explain conclusions and to generate questions for unknown inputs. This means that neural networks are enriched by other functionalities so that they have all required features of expert systems. Furthermore, they can still be linked into hybrid systems to manage larger tasks. We will sketch the main ideas of the prototypical neural expert system MACIE to introduce this approach.

### 13.2.2.1　*MACIE*

We briefly outline the architecture of the historically first real neural expert system shell MACIE (MAtrix Controlled Inference Engine) proposed by (Gallant, 1988). This system is based on the discrete feedforward neural network in which neurons compute the function described by Equations 13.1–13.3. Moreover, hidden neurons are, in fact, output neurons and hence their purposes are given by the application. The inputs of the system represent user's answers to questions and they may have only two values, either "yes" or "no" which are encoded by 1 or $-1$, respectively, by using the states of input neurons (similarly for outputs). In addition, an unknown state is encoded by 0.

The network configuration, i.e. the neural knowledge base is created from training patterns using the so-called *pocket algorithm* (e.g., see the paper (Gallant, 1988) for details) which computes relevant integer weights. This algorithm works only for a single layer of neurons and that is why all states of neurons in the feedforward network should be prescribed by training patterns, including hidden neurons. The simpler learning task may avoid the efficiency problems and simultaneously the visible hidden neurons serve as a better interpretation of implicit neural knowledge representation. However, sometimes auxiliary hidden neurons with random weights must be added to handle more complicated tasks.

In the case where all inputs are known, the inference engine of MACIE simply computes the network function, i.e. all outputs. This can be viewed as a forward-chaining strategy. However, as usual in expert systems, a user presents input facts about the currently solved case gradually and thus some of the inputs are temporarily unknown or may remain unknown. For an incomplete network input a modified inference heuristic is performed. The state $y_j$ of neuron $j$ is computed as follows supposing that the outputs $y_i$ of all neurons $i \in j_{\leftarrow}$ has been determined. First, two auxiliary values $KNOWN_j$ and $MAX\_UNKNOWN_j$ are computed:

$$KNOWN_j = w_{j0} + \sum_{i \in j_{\leftarrow}} w_{ji} y_i \tag{13.7}$$

$$MAX\_UNKNOWN_j = \sum_{i \in j_{\leftarrow};\, y_i = 0} |w_{ji}| . \tag{13.8}$$

Further, if $|KNOWN_j| > MAX\_UNKNOWN_j$, then the possible contributions of incident neurons $i \in j_{\leftarrow}$ with currently unknown states (i.e. $y_i = 0$) to the excitation level $\xi_j$ (see (13.1)) cannot influence the state $y_j$ which is given by known outputs

$(y_i \in \{-1, 1\})$ of incident neurons:

$$y_j = \begin{cases} -1 & \text{if } KNOWN_j < 0 \\ 1 & \text{if } KNOWN_j > 0 \,. \end{cases} \tag{13.9}$$

In the opposite case, if $|KNOWN_j| \leq MAX\_UNKNOWN_j$, then the possible contributions of incident neurons with currently unknown states to the weighted sum may change the state $y_j$ and thus, $y_j = 0$ is set to be unknown. This inference method allows MACIE to reach conclusions although only a fraction of the input values is known.

In MACIE, the confidence of the neuron state $y_j$ is also defined to be a real number $Conf(y_j)$ within the interval $[-1, 1]$ which expresses the inclination of the state $y_j$ to $-1$ or $1$, respectively. For input neurons or neurons with known states the confidence equals the state, i.e. $Conf(y_j) = y_j$. For the remaining non-input neurons $j$ with unknown states $y_j = 0$, the confidence $Conf(y_j)$ is determined as follows:

$$Conf(y_j) = \frac{w_{j0} + \sum_{i \in j_\leftarrow} w_{ji} Conf(y_i)}{MAX\_UNKNOWN_j} \,. \tag{13.10}$$

Thus, the unknown outputs can be partially evaluated and preliminary conclusions with confidences can be inferred.

The confidence is also used in the heuristics of generating questions for the most relevant unknown inputs. Here, the backward-chaining strategy proceeding from the output layer to the input layer is employed. At the beginning, the output neuron $j$ with unknown state, $y_j = 0$ and with the maximum absolute confidence $|Conf(y_j)|$ is found, i.e.

$$j = \arg \max_{k \, output, \, y_k = 0} |Conf(y_k)| \,. \tag{13.11}$$

In a general step when neuron $j$ is inspected, the incident preceding-layer neuron $i \in j_\leftarrow$ with unknown state $y_i = 0$ and with the maximum absolute influence $|w_{ji}|$ on the underlying neuron $j$ is determined, i.e.

$$i = \arg \max_{k \in j_\leftarrow, \, y_k = 0} |w_{jk}| \,. \tag{13.12}$$

If $i$ is an input neuron, then the user is asked for its unknown value, otherwise the general step, now with the inspected neuron $j$ replaced by the above-selected neuron $i$, is repeated.

Finally, the MACIE system provides a simple justification of inference by generating the IF-THEN rules. During a consultation, the user may ask for an explanation why a particular value of output neuron state is $-1$ or $1$, respectively. For example, assume that the system is asked to explain the state $y_j = 1$ (analogously for $y_j = -1$) of the output neuron $j$. Then the minimal subset of its incident neurons $i \in j_\leftarrow$ whose states ensure the state $y_j = 1$, regardless of the remaining ones, is determined in the following way. Let $I = \{i \in j_\leftarrow ; \, w_{ji} y_i > 0\}$ be a set of incident neurons which contribute positively to the excitation level $\xi_j$ of the underlying neuron $j$, so that in the result, its state is $y_j = 1$. Further, enumerate $I = \{i_1, i_2, \ldots, i_r\}$ so that $|w_{j,i_1}| \geq |w_{j,i_2}| \geq \cdots |w_{j,i_r}|$ is a non-increasing sequence of absolute values of corresponding weights. Now, the minimal $s$ such that

$$w_{j0} + \sum_{k=1}^{s} |w_{j,i_k}| > \sum_{k=s+1}^{r} |w_{j,i_k}| + \sum_{i \in j_\leftarrow \setminus I} |w_{ji}| \tag{13.13}$$

is determined. Because the meanings of hidden neurons in MACIE are known, the following IF-THEN rule can be extracted to justify the inference of $y_j = 1$:

$$\text{IF } (y_{i_1} = a_1) \& (y_{i_2} = a_2) \& \cdots \& (y_{i_s} = a_s) \text{ THEN } y_j = 1$$

where $a_1, \ldots, a_s$ represent the current actual values of the neuron states $y_{i_1}, \ldots, y_{i_s}$, respectively.

Obviously, the neural expert system MACIE can compete with rule-based systems in all functional features. However, the explicit interpretation of hidden neurons is still assumed and the full power of neural learning (e.g. backpropagation) is not exploited. This may be the restriction for knowledge representation of complex problems which require actual hidden neurons for successful generalization. Therefore, we will illustrate in Section 13.3 how the MACIE architecture can be tailored to backpropagation networks in the empty neural expert system EXPSYS (Šíma, 1995).

### 13.2.2.2   *Applications*

From the preceding exposition and discussions it follows that neural expert systems are conveniently applied to middle complex problems (or subproblems) from areas where neural networks govern analytical solutions and where example data instead of rules are available. Namely, the typical neural network domains are pattern recognition, control, prediction, forecasting, signal processing, diagnostics, fault detection, etc. To illustrate the potential of neural expert systems we discuss several successful applications to real-world problems.

A connectionist expert system *RAMBOT* that learns to play a simple computer game, called *robots*, by observing a human player has been constructed by (Mozer, 1987). RAMBOT is able to learn behavior that is dependent on a large number of variables, i.e. the robot playing board contains 400 cells, despite the inconsistent demonstrator's play. The system is able to suggest multiple hypotheses with varying degrees of certainty. The results achieved by the system were surprisingly better than those by its teacher.

A neural network trained by backpropagation was applied to the diagnosis of acute myocardial infarction (coronary occlusion) in patients presenting to the emergency department with acute anterior chest pain (Baxt, 1990). The network was trained on a randomly chosen set of about 180 retrospectively studied patients including those who had not sustained acute myocardial infarction. Then the network was tested on previously unseen patterns and it correctly identified 92% of the patients with infarction and 96% of the patients without infarction. This is substantially better than the performance reported for either physicians or any other analytical approach.

The first version of the empty neural expert system EXPSYS (see Section 13.3) has been applied to diagnostics of protection warnings for the cooling system in nuclear power plants (Šíma, 1992a). After training on 112 patterns the generalization of the system was approved on a test set of about 300 patterns where more than 90% of conclusions were accepted by an expert who had been disappointed by previous experience with rule-based systems.

A neural-network classifier for detecting vascular structures in angiograms was developed by (Nekovei and Sun, 1995). The classifier consists of a feedforward network window in which the center pixel is classified using gray-scale information within the window. The network was trained by using the backpropagation algorithm on 75 selected points from a $256 \times 256$ digitized cineangiogram. The three-layer network shows good generalization to the entire cineangiogram and other images, including direct video angiograms. In a comparative study, the network demonstrates its superiority in classification performance. Its classification accuracy is 92%, as compared to 68% accuracy derived by the application of a maximum-likelihood estimation method.

A medical neural expert system for automated brain signal diagnosis has been presented by (Moreno et al., 1995). A training set, as well as the test set, consisted of data extracted from EEG signal and diagnoses carried out by expert neurologists. The neural approach has been shown to have better performance over traditional statistical classifiers. In addition, the integration of neural networks in a higher-level knowledge-based system for brain signal interpretation has been discussed.

A collection of neural networks called *PROMNET* which are interfaced to a computerized medical record, has been built by (Bassøe, 1995). Clinical narratives were subjected to automated natural language processing, and relations were established between 14323 diagnoses and 31381 patient findings which were grouped into clinical entities to train PROMNET using the Widrow rule. The dictionary contains about 20000 words and the neural network recognizes more than 2800 disorders. PROMNET makes a clinical decision in a few seconds with a sensitivity of 96.6% and specificity of 95.7%. Thus, PROMNET is a powerful inference engine that learns from clinical narratives and interacts with medical personnel or patients in natural language. This system is comparable with the current standard, viz. Internist.

## 13.3 EXPSYS—An Example of a Neural Expert System

In this section we will demonstrate the neural knowledge processing on the empty neural expert system *EXPSYS* (Šíma, 1995) in more detail. The architecture of EXPSYS has been inspired by the system MACIE (see Section 13.2.2.1) whose ideas are adapted for feedforward neural networks trained with the backpropagation algorithm. Thus, the neural network used in EXPSYS differs from that of MACIE in two ways: learning hidden neurons is feasible although their values are not prescribed by training patterns and further, the activation function (13.6) is differentiable. According to Equation 13.6 arbitrary real numbers between −1 and 1 may represent the hidden neuron states which are further used as inputs for neurons in the following layer. Hence, it would be ambiguous and inconsistent for the incomplete information processing within EXPSYS to determine the discrete states (either −1 or 1) of hidden neurons as in MACIE according to Equation 13.9. Therefore, interval states of neurons covering all their potential values are introduced in EXPSYS and propagated throughout the network to cope with imprecise and incomplete   information. The backpropagation algorithm, on one hand, eliminates the weak learning of MACIE and improves the generalization capability of the neural network, and on the other hand, it makes the explicit interpretation of hidden neurons difficult. Moreover, the usage of a continuous activation function complicates the inference engine and explanation heuristics. Thus the tension between the implicit and explicit representations also appears in neural expert systems.

### 13.3.1   Interface

#### 13.3.1.1   *Data Types*

After one has decided to use neural network technology for building an expert system by applying the neural expert system shell EXPSYS (Šíma and Neruda, 1993), the important issue is to choose the most suitable input and output variables which should best describe the problem. The inputs of the system should cover all important information which is sufficient to solve the problem. On the other hand, the input variables should not be duplicated or irrelevant because increasing the number of inputs decreases the efficiency of the system. One can even exploit some statistical methods to discover the input irrelevancies and duplicates from data. The output variables represent the problem solutions and system conclusions.

Furthermore, the types of these inputs and outputs should appropriately be defined by a user. The system EXPSYS supports three basic data types: the numerical type (i.e. real numbers or integers), the scalar type with user-defined values and the set. The domain of the numerical type is specified by a real (integer) interval. The domain of the scalar type is defined by a vector of possible values which are chosen by a user. Similarly, for the set type the universe of possible elements is given by a vector of these elements. The difference between the scalar and set types is that the scalar value is exactly one item from the domain while any subset (including the empty set) of elements from the universe may appear in the set type.

For example, in a simplified medical problem the inputs and outputs and their types are chosen as follows:

```
INPUTS:    TEMPERATURE: real of [36,42]
```

```
                    SKIN-COLOR: scalar of (NORMAL,YELLOW)
                    SCLERAE-COLOR: scalar of (NORMAL,YELLOW)
                    LIVER-TENDERNESS: scalar of (NORMAL,HIGH)
                    CHOLESTEROL: scalar of (LOW,NORMAL,HIGH)
                    URINE-TEST: set of (BILIRUBIN, UROBILINOGEN)
          OUTPUTS:  DIAGNOSIS: scalar of (HEALTHY,PSEUDO-JAUNDICE,
                                         OBSTRUCTIVE-JAUNDICE,HEPATITIS)
```

### *13.3.1.2   Encoding*

The interface of EXPSYS encodes the input and output values into the states of input and output neurons, respectively. The states of neurons with the activation function (13.6) are within the interval $[-1, 1]$ and hence only the values from this range are used for this purpose. Three possible ways of coding are supported: floating point, unary and binary codes. Almost any combination of a variable type and coding is allowed (excluding unary-coded numerical type) where a binary-coded real value is, in fact, integer. We will describe only the natural combinations of type and coding, which are floating-point for reals, unary-coded scalar type and binary-coded set, while the remaining ones are similar and their descriptions can be found in (Šíma, 1995).

A numerical value may be encoded directly using the real state of one neuron, i.e. floating point representation. However, the values of variables should somehow be normalized because remarkably different scales of two variables would require different scales of the corresponding weights in the network configuration and consequently complicate the learning process. Therefore, the domain of the numerical type, say $[a, b]$, is linearly mapped to the neuron state $[-1, 1]$. Hence, a real value $x \in [a, b]$ is encoded by the state

$$y = 2\frac{x - a}{b - a} - 1 \in [-1, 1].  \tag{13.14}$$

The scalar type with the domain of $k$ possible values is encoded in unary code using $k$ neurons where each neuron is reserved for one value. Thus, a particular value is encoded in such a way that all states of $k$ neurons are set to $-1$ except the only one which corresponds to this value and has state 1. Similarly, each element from the universe of the set type corresponds in the binary code to one neuron whose state is 1 if this element is in the set, otherwise it is $-1$. Hence, the number of neurons needed to encode the set with possibly up to $k$ elements is $k$. For example, the empty set is encoded by all $k$ states being $-1$.

The method of encoding the inputs and outputs is crucial for learning and it may even influence its tractability (Blum and Rivest, 1992). The training task is easier when more significant features of the problem can be extracted, preprocessed and presented to the network in the simplest form. Besides normalizing numerical values, the expert knowledge about the problem can be useful for deciding which code is suitable to use for individual inputs and outputs to create appropriate knowledge representations. Compressed representation saves the number of input and output neurons (i.e. the network size) but, on the other hand, it employs hidden neurons for its decoding. Therefore, the sparse unary code is always recommended provided that the number of input and output neurons is manageable. For example, even the numerical variable can be represented with the scalar type including items such as low, medium, high, etc.

### 13.3.1.3  *Incomplete information*

The system EXPSYS handles incomplete information by introducing interval states of neurons (Šíma, 1992a). The interval state is any non-empty (even one-point) subinterval of $[-1, 1]$. Then a crisp value is represented by one-point intervals, e.g. $[1, 1]$ stands for 1. Further, an unknown value is encoded by complete intervals $[-1, 1]$. Even the imprecise value can be expressed by using interval neuron states. For example, this is straightforward for the numerical type, or for the binary-coded set an unknown membership of particular elements can be encoded by corresponding complete intervals; see EXPSYS—Students' Software Project (EXPSYS, 1994) for details. In our medical example the values are encoded as follows:

```
[ ( [-0.2,-0.2],                            38.4
    [-1,-1],[1,1],                          YELLOW
    [-1,-1],[1,1],                          YELLOW
    [-1,-1],[1,1],                          HIGH
    [-1,1],[-1,1],[-1,1],                   unknown
    [1,1],[1,1] ),                          {BILIRUBIN,UROBILINOGEN}
  ( [-1,-1],[-1,-1],[-1,-1],[1,1] ) ]       HEPATITIS
```

### 13.3.2  Neural Knowledge Base

### 13.3.2.1  *Interval Neuron Function*

As we have already mentioned the knowledge base of EXPSYS is a feedforward neural network trained with the backpropagation algorithm. Hence, the functions (13.1), (13.2), and (13.6) of neurons are differentiable. In addition, this function is generalized to intervals to cope with incomplete information (see Section 13.3.1.3). The interval neuron state is the minimal interval which covers all its possible values with respect to incomplete interval inputs. This property should be preserved throughout the network computation. Therefore, the interval function of neurons should preserve monotonicity with respect to interval inclusion. Namely, if an input value is made more accurate, i.e. the corresponding interval is narrowed down to a subinterval (e.g. down to a one-point interval), then the output intervals may only contract and the new intervals are subsets of the preceding ones. Thus, the output intervals cover all possible results for all possible specifications of incomplete inputs. In what follows the corresponding interval function of neurons is derived.

Let $[a_i, b_i]$ be the interval states of neurons $i \in j_{\leftarrow}$ which are connected to the neuron $j$. The interval excitation level $[\alpha_j, \beta_j]$ and the interval output $[a_j, b_j]$ of the neuron $j$ are determined so that they meet the following requirement. For any single inputs $y_i \in [a_i, b_i]$, for $i \in j_{\leftarrow}$, from the given interval states, the corresponding unique output $y_j$ of the neuron $j$ computed by (13.1), (13.2), and (13.6) must fall in the output interval, i.e. $y_j \in [a_j, b_j]$. Hence, the lower bound $\alpha_j$ of the excitation level (13.1) is determined as its minimum for $y_i \in [a_i, b_i]$. The corresponding contribution of the $i$-th neuron ($i \in j_{\leftarrow}$) to this minimum is $w_{ji}a_i$ if the weight $w_{ji} > 0$ is positive and it is $w_{ji}b_i$ for negative weights $w_{ji} < 0$. Similarly, the upper bound $\beta_j$ is computed:

$$\alpha_j = w_{j0} + \sum_{w_{ji}>0; i\in j_{\leftarrow}} w_{ji}a_i + \sum_{w_{ji}<0; i\in j_{\leftarrow}} w_{ji}b_i \qquad (13.15)$$

$$\beta_j = w_{j0} + \sum_{w_{ji}>0; i\in j_{\leftarrow}} w_{ji}b_i + \sum_{w_{ji}<0; i\in j_{\leftarrow}} w_{ji}a_i \,. \qquad (13.16)$$

Further, formula (13.2) for the output $y_j$ can be rewritten easily for the interval output $[a_j, b_j]$ because the activation function (13.6) is increasing:

$$a_j = \sigma(\alpha_j) \qquad b_j = \sigma(\beta_j)\,. \qquad (13.17)$$

It is obvious that the interval function (13.15)–(13.17) coincides exactly with the original single-state function (13.1), (13.2), and (13.6) for one-point intervals and, simultaneously, it satisfies the monotonicity with respect to interval inclusion. However, this interval neuron function is not smooth as required for gradient-based learning, namely the bounds (13.15), (13.16) of the excitation level are not differentiable with respect to weights at the points with a zero weight. In spite of that it is possible either to compute one-sided derivatives when a discontinuity of derivatives appears, and thus the gradient method can still be tailored to this case (Bělohlávek, 1997) or the interval function (13.15)–(13.17) can also be made differentiable by a continuous approximation of the monotonicity property (Šíma, 1992b). Although the strict monotonicity property is partially lost in the latter case the system EXPSYS employs this approximate approach as follows.

To make the interval bounds (13.15), (13.16) of the excitation level differentiable, the auxiliary continuous sigmoid functions

$$s(x) = \frac{1}{1+e^{-x}} \qquad \bar{s}(x) = \frac{1}{1+e^{x}} \qquad (13.18)$$

are introduced to approximate the weight signs:

$$s(w_{ji}) \doteq \begin{cases} 1 & \text{for } w_{ji} \gg 0 \\ 0 & \text{for } w_{ji} \ll 0 \end{cases} \qquad \bar{s}(w_{ji}) \doteq \begin{cases} 0 & \text{for } w_{ji} \gg 0 \\ 1 & \text{for } w_{ji} \ll 0. \end{cases} \qquad (13.19)$$

Note that $s(x) = \bar{s}(-x)$ and $s(x) + \bar{s}(x) = 1$ for every real $x$. Thus, the Equations 13.15 and 13.16 for the interval excitation level can be rewritten:

$$\alpha_j = w_{j0} + \sum_{i \in j_\leftarrow} w_{ji} \left( s(w_{ji})a_i + \bar{s}(w_{ji})b_i \right) \tag{13.20}$$

$$\beta_j = w_{j0} + \sum_{i \in j_\leftarrow} w_{ji} \left( \bar{s}(w_{ji})a_i + s(w_{ji})b_i \right) . \tag{13.21}$$

This means that the weight $w_{ji}$ is proportionally divided into contributions with $a_i$ and $b_i$ according to the positiveness and negativeness of $w_{ji}$ because

$$s(w_{ji}) + \bar{s}(w_{ji}) = 1$$

. Furthermore, the so-called *gain parameter* $\lambda_j$ is supplied to the activation function (13.6) of neuron $j$:

$$\sigma_j(\xi) = \frac{1 - e^{-\lambda_j \xi}}{1 + e^{-\lambda_j \xi}} . \tag{13.22}$$

The gain parameter $\lambda_j$ determines the steepness of the activation function $\sigma_j$ around zero, e.g. for $\lambda_j \to \infty$ this function coincides with its discrete version (13.3). This parameter belongs to the network configuration and thus it is subject to adaptation which gives the gradient method more freedom to converge (Hořejš and Kufudaki, 1993). However, $\lambda_j$ can become negative during the adaptation for which the activation function $\sigma_j$ is decreasing according to (13.22), and hence the correctness of (13.17) is violated because this would imply $a_j \geq b_j$. This problem can be solved by introducing the same gain parameter $\lambda_j$ into the auxiliary sigmoid functions (13.18) of neuron $j$:

$$s_j(x) = \frac{1}{1 + e^{-\lambda_j x}} \qquad \bar{s}_j(x) = \frac{1}{1 + e^{\lambda_j x}} . \tag{13.23}$$

Now, for the negative gain parameter $\lambda_j < 0$ the values of $s_j(w_{ji})$ and $\bar{s}_j(w_{ji})$ are exchanged due to $s(w_{ji}) = \bar{s}(-w_{ji})$ and thus $\alpha_j$ and $\beta_j$ are switched as well, i.e. $\alpha_j \geq \beta_j$. This exchange is then corrected by the activation function $\sigma_j$ which is decreasing for $\lambda_j < 0$ and hence, $a_j \leq b_j$. In addition, it is noteworthy that for $\lambda_j \to \infty$ the monotonicity property is satisfied.

Finally, the above-derived interval function of neuron $j$ is summarized as follows:

$$a_j = \sigma_j(\alpha_j) \qquad b_j = \sigma_j(\beta_j) \tag{13.24}$$

$$\alpha_j = w_{j0} + \sum_{i \in j_\leftarrow} w_{ji} \left( s_j(w_{ji})a_i + \bar{s}_j(w_{ji})b_i \right) \tag{13.25}$$

$$\beta_j = w_{j0} + \sum_{i \in j_\leftarrow} w_{ji} \left( \bar{s}_j(w_{ji})a_i + s_j(w_{ji})b_i \right) \tag{13.26}$$

$$\sigma_j(\xi) = \frac{1 - e^{-\lambda_j \xi}}{1 + e^{-\lambda_j \xi}} \tag{13.27}$$

$$s_j(x) = \frac{1}{1 + e^{-\lambda_j x}} \qquad \bar{s}_j(x) = \frac{1}{1 + e^{\lambda_j x}}. \tag{13.28}$$

This function is employed by hidden and output neurons during the computation of the interval network function except by those output neurons which encode the expert outputs using a floating point (see Section 13.3.1.2). For these output neurons the activation function $\sigma_j$ is not applied, instead the output intervals equal the interval excitation levels, i.e. $a_j = \alpha_j$, $b_j = \beta_j$ and, for example, $\lambda_j = 1$ for the auxiliary sigmoid functions $s$, $\bar{s}$. It is because the activation function $\sigma_j$ tends to saturate the output $y_j$ towards its limits of $-1$ or $1$, and hence the medium state values which represent current numerical outputs in floating point would be discriminated against. Thus, the underlying interval network function depends on the network configuration $(\mathbf{w}, \boldsymbol{\lambda})$ which consists of all weights and gain parameters within the network.

### 13.3.2.2 Learning Algorithm

Before the learning process starts the user of EXPSYS must specify the architecture of the feedforward neural network. It suffices to determine the number of hidden layers and the number of hidden neurons in each layer since the number of input and output neurons is given by the number of expert inputs and outputs by their types and the way they are encoded (see Sections 13.3.1.1 and 13.3.1.2). In addition, it is implicitly assumed that every neuron in one layer is connected to all neurons in the next layer. Thus, by specifying the hidden layers the network size is established (see also Section 13.1.4.1) which should correspond to the complexity of the problem to achieve the best generalization capability as it has been described in Section 13.1.3. Typically, one or two hidden layers are used in which the number of neurons is of the same order as the number of input and output neurons.

Furthermore, the file of example inferences must be provided to the learning algorithm. The interface of EXPSYS can be used either to create or to load this file. The example inferences are immediately transformed to the training set by encoding the input and output values using the input and output neuron states (see Section 13.3.1.2). These example inferences may even include incomplete information which is encoded using interval training patterns as described in Section 13.3.1.3. The principles of selecting appropriate training patterns to cover the problem domain were introduced in Sections 13.1.3 and 13.1.4.2. The third version of EXPSYS even has a preprocessing procedure for automatic selection of representative patterns from larger files based on Kohonen networks; see EXPSYS—Students' Software Project (EXPSYS, 1994) for details. One should also not forget to reserve a subset of example inferences for the test set which is used in EXPSYS to evaluate the network outputs with generalization confidences (see Section 13.3.2.3).

Thus, the training set of interval patterns has the following form:

$$T = \{(\mathbf{X}_k; \mathbf{D}_k) \; ; \; k = 1, \ldots, p\} \tag{13.29}$$

where for the $k$-th training pattern $\mathbf{X}_k$ is the vector of intervals of input-neuron states and

$$\mathbf{D}_k = ([A_{k1}, B_{k1}], \ldots, [A_{km}, B_{km}]) \tag{13.30}$$

is the corresponding desired vector of intervals $[A_{kj}, B_{kj}]$ of the network outputs in which $j$ denotes the relevant output neuron. The error $E(\mathbf{w}, \boldsymbol{\lambda})$ of the network function, depending on the configuration $(\mathbf{w}, \boldsymbol{\lambda})$ with respect to the training set (13.29), can be generalized for intervals. Because the interval network function introduced in Section 13.3.2.1 approximately preserves the monotonicity of the interval inclusion, this error depends only on the bounds of relevant intervals:

$$E(\mathbf{w}, \boldsymbol{\lambda}) = \sum_{k=1}^{p} E_k(\mathbf{w}, \boldsymbol{\lambda}) \tag{13.31}$$

where $E_k(\mathbf{w}, \boldsymbol{\lambda})$ is a partial error with respect to the $k$-th training pattern:

$$E_k(\mathbf{w}, \boldsymbol{\lambda}) = \frac{1}{2} \sum_{j \; output} \left( (a_j(\mathbf{w}, \boldsymbol{\lambda}, \mathbf{X}_k) - A_{kj})^2 + (b_j(\mathbf{w}, \boldsymbol{\lambda}, \mathbf{X}_k) - B_{kj})^2 \right) \tag{13.32}$$

where $[a_j(\mathbf{w}, \boldsymbol{\lambda}, \mathbf{X}_k), b_j(\mathbf{w}, \boldsymbol{\lambda}, \mathbf{X}_k)]$ is the actual interval state of the output neuron $j$ computed for the interval input $\mathbf{X}_k$, while the network configuration is $(\mathbf{w}, \boldsymbol{\lambda})$.

The learning algorithm of EXPSYS minimizes the error function (13.31) in the configuration space using the following gradient method. At the beginning the weights $\mathbf{w}^{(0)}$ are chosen randomly close to zero and the gain parameters $\boldsymbol{\lambda}^{(0)}$ around 1, for instance. Then, at the discrete adaptation time $t = 1, 2, \ldots$ the new configuration $(\mathbf{w}^{(t)}, \boldsymbol{\lambda}^{(t)})$ is computed as follows:

$$w_{ji}^{(t)} = w_{ji}^{(t-1)} + \Delta w_{ji}^{(t)} \qquad \lambda_j^{(t)} = \lambda_j^{(t-1)} + \Delta \lambda_j^{(t)} \tag{13.33}$$

where the increments $\Delta w_{ji}^{(t)}$, $\Delta \lambda_j^{(t)}$ of the configuration at the adaptation time $t$ are determined in the following way:

$$\Delta w_{ji}^{(t)} = -\varepsilon \frac{\partial E}{\partial w_{ji}} \left( \mathbf{w}^{(t-1)} \right) + \mu \Delta w_{ji}^{(t-1)} \tag{13.34}$$

$$\Delta \lambda_j^{(t)} = -\varepsilon' \frac{\partial E}{\partial \lambda_j} \left( \boldsymbol{\lambda}^{(t-1)} \right) + \mu' \Delta \lambda_j^{(t-1)} \tag{13.35}$$

where $\frac{\partial E}{\partial w_{ji}}(\mathbf{w}^{(t-1)})$ (similarly $\frac{\partial E}{\partial \lambda_j}(\boldsymbol{\lambda}^{(t-1)})$) is the partial derivative of the error function $E$ by $w_{ji}$ at the point $\mathbf{w}^{(t-1)}$. The so-called *learning rate* $0 < \varepsilon, \varepsilon' < 1$ and the *momentum parameter* $0 < \mu, \mu' < 1$ are the adjustable parameters of the gradient method ($\varepsilon, \varepsilon'$ should be sufficiently small to converge and a reasonable value of $\mu, \mu'$ is 0.9).

To implement the gradient method (13.33) the partial derivatives $\frac{\partial E}{\partial w_{ji}}$ from (13.34) and $\frac{\partial E}{\partial \lambda_j}$ from (13.35) must be determined. For this purpose, the backpropagation strategy is generalized for the interval network function (Šíma, 1992b). For notational simplicity we will describe the formulas only for the network without output neurons which encode floating point. The generalization for the opposite case is straightforward and can be found in (Šíma, 1995) . First, the rule for the derivative of the sum is used for (13.31):

$$\frac{\partial E}{\partial w_{ji}} = \sum_{k=1}^{p} \frac{\partial E_k}{\partial w_{ji}} \qquad \frac{\partial E}{\partial \lambda_j} = \sum_{k=1}^{p} \frac{\partial E_k}{\partial \lambda_j} . \tag{13.36}$$

To compute $\frac{\partial E_k}{\partial w_{ji}}$, $\frac{\partial E_k}{\partial \lambda_j}$ the chain-rule for composite function derivatives is applied:

$$\frac{\partial E_k}{\partial w_{ji}} = \frac{\partial E_k}{\partial a_j}\frac{\partial a_j}{\partial \alpha_j}\frac{\partial \alpha_j}{\partial w_{ji}} + \frac{\partial E_k}{\partial b_j}\frac{\partial b_j}{\partial \beta_j}\frac{\partial \beta_j}{\partial w_{ji}} \tag{13.37}$$

$$\frac{\partial E_k}{\partial \lambda_j} = \frac{\partial E_k}{\partial a_j}\frac{\partial a_j}{\partial \lambda_j} + \frac{\partial E_k}{\partial b_j}\frac{\partial b_j}{\partial \lambda_j} . \tag{13.38}$$

Thus, the following derivatives from (13.37), (13.38) can be calculated directly using the explicit form (13.24)–(13.28) of the interval neuron functions:

$$\frac{\partial a_j}{\partial \alpha_j} = \frac{1}{2}\lambda_j \left(1 - a_j^2\right) \qquad \frac{\partial b_j}{\partial \beta_j} = \frac{1}{2}\lambda_j \left(1 - b_j^2\right) \tag{13.39}$$

$$\frac{\partial \alpha_j}{\partial w_{ji}} = a_j s_j(w_{ji})\left(1 + \lambda_j w_{ji}\bar{s}_j(w_{ji})\right) + b_j \bar{s}_j(w_{ji})\left(1 - \lambda_j w_{ji} s_j(w_{ji})\right) \tag{13.40}$$

$$\frac{\partial \beta_j}{\partial w_{ji}} = a_j \bar{s}_j(w_{ji})\left(1 - \lambda_j w_{ji} s_j(w_{ji})\right) + b_j s_j(w_{ji})\left(1 + \lambda_j w_{ji}\bar{s}_j(w_{ji})\right) \tag{13.41}$$

for common weights $w_{ji}$ with $i \neq 0$ and $\frac{\partial \alpha_j}{\partial w_{j0}} = \frac{\partial \beta_j}{\partial w_{j0}} = 1$ for the biases. Further,

$$\frac{\partial a_j}{\partial \lambda_j} = \frac{\partial \sigma_j}{\partial \lambda_j} + \frac{\partial a_j}{\partial \alpha_j}\frac{\partial \alpha_j}{\partial \lambda_j} =$$

$$= \frac{1}{2}\left(1 - a_j^2\right)\left(\alpha_j - \lambda_j \sum_{i \in j_\leftarrow} w_{ji}^2 s_j(w_{ji})\bar{s}_j(w_{ji})(b_j - a_j)\right) \tag{13.42}$$

$$\frac{\partial b_j}{\partial \lambda_j} = \frac{\partial \sigma_j}{\partial \lambda_j} + \frac{\partial b_j}{\partial \beta_j}\frac{\partial \beta_j}{\partial \lambda_j} =$$

$$= \frac{1}{2}\left(1 - b_j^2\right)\left(\beta_j + \lambda_j \sum_{i \in j_\leftarrow} w_{ji}^2 s_j(w_{ji})\bar{s}_j(w_{ji})(b_j - a_j)\right) . \tag{13.43}$$

The computation of the remaining derivatives $\frac{\partial E_k}{\partial a_j}$, $\frac{\partial E_k}{\partial b_j}$ in (13.37), (13.38) starts in the output layer and it is propagated back to the input layer as the name "backpropagation" suggests. So, first assume that $j$ is an output neuron. Then, the relevant derivatives can be directly calculated from (13.32) as follows:

$$\frac{\partial E_k}{\partial a_j} = a_j(\mathbf{w}, \boldsymbol{\lambda}, \mathbf{X}_k) - A_{kj} \qquad \frac{\partial E_k}{\partial b_j} = b_j(\mathbf{w}, \boldsymbol{\lambda}, \mathbf{X}_k) - B_{kj} . \tag{13.44}$$

Further, let $j$ be a hidden neuron and denote by $j^{\rightarrow}$ the set of neurons to which the connections from the neuron $j$ lead. Moreover, assume that the values of the partial derivatives $\frac{\partial E_k}{\partial a_r}$, $\frac{\partial E_k}{\partial b_r}$ have been computed for all neurons $r \in j^{\rightarrow}$. Then the chain-rule for the derivative of a composite function can be applied again:

$$\frac{\partial E_k}{\partial a_j} = \sum_{r \in j^{\rightarrow}} \left( \frac{\partial E_k}{\partial a_r} \frac{\partial a_r}{\partial \alpha_r} \frac{\partial \alpha_r}{\partial a_j} + \frac{\partial E_k}{\partial b_r} \frac{\partial b_r}{\partial \beta_r} \frac{\partial \beta_r}{\partial a_j} \right) =$$

$$= \frac{1}{2} \sum_{r \in j^{\rightarrow}} \lambda_r w_{rj} \left( \frac{\partial E_k}{\partial a_r} \left( 1 - a_r^2 \right) s_r(w_{rj}) + \frac{\partial E_k}{\partial b_r} \left( 1 - b_r^2 \right) \bar{s}_r(w_{rj}) \right) \qquad (13.45)$$

$$\frac{\partial E_k}{\partial b_j} = \sum_{r \in j^{\rightarrow}} \left( \frac{\partial E_k}{\partial a_r} \frac{\partial a_r}{\partial \alpha_r} \frac{\partial \alpha_r}{\partial b_j} + \frac{\partial E_k}{\partial b_r} \frac{\partial b_r}{\partial \beta_r} \frac{\partial \beta_r}{\partial b_j} \right) =$$

$$= \frac{1}{2} \sum_{r \in j^{\rightarrow}} \lambda_r w_{rj} \left( \frac{\partial E_k}{\partial a_r} \left( 1 - a_r^2 \right) \bar{s}_r(w_{rj}) + \frac{\partial E_k}{\partial b_r} \left( 1 - b_r^2 \right) s_r(w_{rj}) \right) . \qquad (13.46)$$

This completes the gradient computation as well as the description of the learning algorithm.

### 13.3.2.3  *Expert Checking*

After the feedforward neural network has learnt the training set of interval patterns, it is necessary to check whether the created neural knowledge base can be exploited to infer usable conclusions from it. This can be done by a human expert who can evaluate the quality of the system answers in typical situations, or by the test set which is used for computing generalization confidences of individual expert outputs. A *generalization confidence* of a particular expert output is a fraction of the number of patterns from the test set, whose desired values for the respective output coincide with its actual values computed by the inference engine (see Section 13.3.3) for the corresponding inputs, over the size of the test set. Typically, the neural knowledge base is not perfect after the first learning and it is further debugged. This can even include a change of the network architecture (see Section 13.1.3) and new learning from the beginning. Usually, additional training of the network suffices to improve its generalization capability. In this case, the mistaken network responses serve for creating the appropriate training patterns which are learnt additionally to correct the network function. It is useful to iterate the cycle of learning and testing until the neural network inference is sufficiently accurate. At the end of neural knowledge base checking the generalization confidences of all expert outputs are computed by using the test set.

### 13.3.3  Inference Engine

After the neural knowledge base is created it is used for the inference from generally incomplete inputs. During a consultation, the user of EXPSYS presents some (typically not all) values of inputs to the system that provides him with the partial conclusions and their confidences. These partial conclusions are gradually made precise, refined and the confidences increase when the user completes the inputs. The inference engine always re-computes the outputs and their confidences after every input value is presented. An example of the inference in the medical expert system follows:

```
TEMPERATURE = unknown
SKIN-COLOR = YELLOW
SCLERAE-COLOR = NORMAL
LIVER-TENDERNESS = NORMAL
CHOLESTEROL = unknown
URINE-TEST = unknown


----> DIAGNOSIS = PSEUDO-JAUNDICE          conf.: 0.86
```

We now describe how the inference engine of EXPSYS works. The expert inputs including unknown ones, are encoded using the interval states of input neurons by the system interface (see Sections 13.3.1.2 and 13.3.1.3). Then the interval network function is computed according to (13.24)–(13.28) to find out the corresponding interval excitation levels and the interval states for all output neurons which are used to determine the expert outputs and their confidences. Further, we again restrict ourselves to unary and binary coded outputs while the description of the floating point case can be found in (Šíma, 1995). Hence, the states of output neurons should represent only two values, either 1 or $-1$. However, the actual state $y_j$ of the output neuron $j$ computed by (13.24) is a number within the interval $[-1, 1]$ (even $-1 < y_j < 1$), due to the continuity of the activation function (13.27). Therefore, the actual output should be rounded off. For this purpose, the optional so-called *separation parameter* $0 < \gamma < 1$ is introduced so that the state $y_j \in [\gamma, 1]$ of output neuron $j$ is considered as 1 and similarly, the output $y_j \in [-1, -\gamma]$ is interpreted as $-1$ while the state $y_j \in [-\gamma, \gamma]$ means an unknown value. It is clear that the separation parameter controls the precision of the network output.

For the output neuron $j$ the separation parameter $\delta_j$ for its excitation level is computed by applying the inverse of the activation function (13.27):

$$\delta_j = \sigma_j^{-1}(\gamma) = \frac{1}{\lambda_j} \ln \left( \frac{1 + \gamma}{1 - \gamma} \right) . \tag{13.47}$$

In the sequel, assume that $\lambda_j > 0$ and hence $\delta_j > 0$ while the opposite case is similar. Now, comparing this parameter $\delta_j$ with the bounds $\alpha_j \leq \beta_j$ $(\lambda_j > 0)$ of the interval excitation level (13.25), (13.26) for the output neuron $j$, the positive confidence $0 \leq c_j^+ \leq 1$ of the *rounded output* $v_j = 1$ as well as the negative confidence $0 \le c_j^- \le 1$ of the rounded output $v_j = -1$ are computed as follows:

$$
c_j^+ = \begin{cases} 1 & \text{for } \delta_j \le \alpha_j \\ \frac{\beta_j - \delta_j}{\beta_j - \alpha_j} & \text{for } \alpha_j < \delta_j < \beta_j \\ 0 & \text{otherwise} \end{cases} \tag{13.48}
$$

$$
c_j^- = \begin{cases} 1 & \text{for } \beta_j \le -\delta_j \\ \frac{-\delta_j - \alpha_j}{\beta_j - \alpha_j} & \text{for } \alpha_j < -\delta_j < \beta_j \\ 0 & \text{otherwise}. \end{cases} \tag{13.49}
$$

Finally, the rounded state $v_j$ of the output neuron $j$ together with its so-called *inference confidence* $c_j$ is determined from the dominant confidence:

$$
v_j = \begin{cases} 1 & \text{for } c_j^+ > c_j^- \\ -1 & \text{for } c_j^+ < c_j^- \\ unknown & \text{otherwise} \end{cases} \tag{13.50}
$$

$$
c_j = \max\left(c_j^+, c_j^-\right). \tag{13.51}
$$

Then, every (known) output of the expert system is decoded from the corresponding known rounded states of output neurons and it is associated with the confidence. This confidence is computed as a product of the inference confidences of relevant coding states multiplied by the corresponding generalization confidence (see Section 13.3.2.3). It can happen that the rounded states of relevant output neurons do not represent any code of an expert output value (see Section 13.3.1.2), e.g. there are more states equal to 1 in unary code or some of the neuron states are unknown (see (13.50)). In these cases the corresponding expert output is considered as unknown or even imprecise; see EXPSYS—Students' Software Project (EXPSYS, 1994) for details.

### 13.3.4   Explanation of Conclusions

The neural expert system EXPSYS provides a simple explanation of the conclusions which are inferred by the inference engine. During a consultation the user can ask why a particular output value has been concluded. EXPSYS determines a list of selected input values with their relative percentual influence measures which have mostly influenced the inference of the underlying output. Thus, the corresponding total (100%) influence is distributed only to the influence measures of these selected inputs while the influence of remaining inputs is neglected. In our medical example we can obtain:

```
   DIAGNOSIS = OBSTRUCTIVE-JAUNDICE ?
----> URINE-TEST = {BILIRUBIN}     51%
      CHOLESTEROL = HIGH           27%
      TEMPERATURE = unknown        22%
```

The results of the explanation can be exploited not only for the justification of the inference, but it is also possible to debug the neural knowledge base by means of them (see Section 13.3.2.3). For example, using the explanation of incorrect answers the appropriate example inferences can be proposed which, after being additionally learnt, correct the expert system behavior. In addition, the explanation of the conclusions is used in EXPSYS for generating questions for unknown inputs (see Section 13.3.4.2).

### 13.3.4.1   Explanation Heuristics

The explanation heuristics for the output which is encoded by using floating point representation is based on the causal index (Šíma, 1995) and will again be omitted here. The explanation heuristics for the unary and binary coded expert output employs a backward-chaining strategy and discovers the dominant influences of neurons on the underlying output. For its description an auxiliary data structure, namely a *LIST* of records $Z$ is used. The record $Z$ consists of the following three items:

**Z.N** ... neuron identification number
**Z.S**  ... influence sign ($-1$ or $1$)
**Z.M** ... influence measure

The list of records is ordered according to $Z.N$ in such a way that neurons in one layer always precede neurons in the preceding layers, e.g. the output neurons are at the top of *LIST*. Moreover, the records with the same $Z.N$ follow each other in this list. Furthermore, the following operations are implemented for *LIST*:

**insert(Z)** ... insert $Z$ into *LIST* with respect to the ordering
**get(Z)**    ... get the first (top) record $Z$ from *LIST*
**LIST↑**     ... access (buffer) variable to the first (top) record in *LIST*

Denote by $Y$ the set of output neurons encoding the given (known) expert output value for which an explanation was asked. At the beginning of the explanation procedure the records for these output neurons $j \in Y$ are created and inserted into *LIST*. Their rounded states (13.50) represent influence signs and their inference confidences (13.51) determine influence measures. In addition, the variable $F_q$ for an influence of the expert system input $q$ $(q = 1, \ldots, z)$ on the underlying output is introduced and initialized by zero. For the detailed description of the explanation heuristics a Pascal-like pseudocode will be used:

{ initialization }
$LIST \leftarrow$ empty list;
**forevery** $j \in Y$ **do**
   $Z.N \leftarrow j$;
   $Z.S \leftarrow v_j$;
   $Z.M \leftarrow c_j$;

$insert(Z)$
**enddo**;

**forevery** $q = 1, \ldots, z$ **do** $F_q \leftarrow 0$ **enddo**;

In a general step the total influence, sign and measure of the neuron, whose records are at top of the $LIST$, are determined from its multiple occurrences. Namely, in the course of the explanation procedure it may even happen that one of these records considers the current neuron to have a positive influence sign which should explain the underlying expert output, while the other one prefers the same neuron to have a negative sign for the same reason. This is caused by the dense network architecture in which a hidden neuron may influence two different neurons in the following layer oppositely. Thus, the sign associated with the dominant influence measures is assigned to this neuron and its resulting influence measure is evaluated with respect to this sign. Furthermore, if the current neuron is from the input layer (i.e. $LIST$ contains only input neurons), then its contribution to $F_q$ is added:

**repeat** { general step }

    { multiple occurrences of one neuron in $LIST$ }
    $M1 \leftarrow 0; M2 \leftarrow 0;$
    **repeat**
      $get(Z);$
      **if** $Z.S = 1$ **then** $M1 \leftarrow M1 + Z.M$
                 **else** $M2 \leftarrow M2 + Z.M$
      **endif**
    **until** $LIST \uparrow .N \neq Z.N;$
    **if** $M1 > M2$ **then** $Z.S \leftarrow 1$ **else** $Z.S \leftarrow -1$ **endif**;
    $Z.M \leftarrow |M1 - M2|;$

    **if** $Z.N$ is input neuron
      **then**
          $q \leftarrow$ expert input coded by neuron $Z.N$;
          $F_q \leftarrow F_q + Z.M$

If the current neuron $j$ is not from the input layer, then the contributions $R_i$ of incident neurons $i \in j_\leftarrow$ to its excitation level (13.25), (13.26), namely either to $\alpha_j$ or to $\beta_j$ depending on the associated influence sign, are determined. Further, only those neurons $i \in j_\leftarrow$ whose contributions $R_i$ have consistent signs are selected. In particular, assume the gain parameter $\lambda_j > 0$ is positive (similarly for $\lambda_j < 0$), i.e. the activation function $\sigma_j$ is increasing and $\alpha_j \leq \beta_j$. Now, if the influence sign $Z.S = 1$ is positive then all neurons with positive contributions $R_i > 0$ are selected otherwise all neurons with negative contributions $R_i < 0$ are chosen:

    **else** { $Z.N$ is non-input neuron }

{ contributions to excitation level of $Z.N$ }
$j \leftarrow Z.N$;
**forevery** $i \in j_\leftarrow$ **do**
   **if** $Z.S = 1$ **then** $R_i \leftarrow w_{ji}(\bar{s}_j(w_{ji})a_i + s_j(w_{ji})b_i)$
           **else** $R_i \leftarrow w_{ji}(s_j(w_{ji})a_i + \bar{s}_j(w_{ji})b_i)$
   **endif**
**enddo**;

{ selection of contributions with consistent signs }
$I \leftarrow \{i \in j_\leftarrow ; Z.S \times \lambda_j R_i > 0\}$;

Furthermore, only the neurons $i \in I$ with dominant contributions $R_i$ are included into $LIST$. For this purpose the neurons in $I$ are sorted with respect to the associated absolute contributions $|R_i|$ into a non-increasing sequence. Then sufficient neurons from the beginning of this sequence are selected such that the sum of their absolute contributions is enough to equal or exceed the sum of the remaining ones. The influence signs of these selected neurons $i$ are determined from the corresponding weights $w_{ji}$ to strengthen the original sign associated with neuron $j$. Namely, providing that the gain parameter $\lambda_j$ is positive (similarly for $\lambda_j < 0$) then if the weight $w_{ji}$ is positive then the influence sign assigned to neuron $i$ is positive otherwise it is negative. Similarly, the influence measures of the selected neurons correspond to their absolute contributions $|R_i|$ multiplied by the original influence measure associated with neuron $j$. This completes the general step:

{ selection of dominant contributions }
sort $I = \{i_1, \dots, i_r\}$ so that $|R_{i_1}| \geq |R_{i_2}| \geq \cdots |R_{i_r}|$;
$r' \leftarrow \min\left\{u ; \sum_{k=1}^{u} |R_{i_k}| \geq \sum_{k=u+1}^{r} |R_{i_k}|\right\}$;
$I' \leftarrow \{i_1, \dots, i_{r'}\}$;

{ insertion of influential neurons into $LIST$ }
**forevery** $i \in I'$ **do**
  $Z1.N \leftarrow i$;
  **if** $Z.S \times \lambda_j w_{ji} > 0$ **then** $Z1.S \leftarrow 1$ **else** $Z1.S \leftarrow -1$ **endif**;
  $Z1.M \leftarrow Z.M \times |R_i|$;
  *insert*$(Z1)$
**enddo**

**endif** { end of non-input neuron processing }

**until** $LIST = empty$ { end of general step }

By using the preceding procedure, the influences $F_q \geq 0$ of expert inputs $q = 1, \dots, z$ on the given output value which is being explained are determined. Again, only the dominant influences are considered. For this purpose, they are sorted so that $F_{q_1} \geq F_{q_2} \geq \cdots \geq F_{q_z}$ and the minimal $z'$ is determined in such a way that

$$\sum_{k=1}^{z'} F_{q_k} \geq \sum_{k=z'+1}^{z} F_{q_k} \,. \tag{13.52}$$

In order not to overload the user the number of influential inputs is further restricted to $L = \min(z', 10)$. Thus, the desired list of inputs which have mostly influenced the underlying expert output value is $q_1, \ldots, q_L$ with the corresponding percentual influence measures:

$$M_{q_k} = 100 \frac{F_{q_k}}{\sum_{i=1}^{L} F_{q_i}} \qquad k = 1, \ldots, L \,. \tag{13.53}$$

The limitation of the above-described explanation heuristics is that it is impossible to give reasons for an unknown expert output value because the influence signs of the respective neurons cannot be determined.

### 13.3.4.2   *Question Generating*

In EXPSYS the explanation heuristics described in Section 13.3.4.1 is used for generating questions for relevant unknown expert system inputs. The strategy is to ask for such an unknown input that, given its value, the completeness and confidences of expert system outputs would mostly increase after the next inference. This is not only a matter of one question but of a sequence of questions because the user can respond that the answer to the first question is unknown. Thus, all known expert output values are gradually explained and the corresponding percentual influence measures (13.53) are added separately for each unknown input. Then the sequence of questions for unknown input values is given by a decreasing order of these sums. If no unknown input has influenced the known output values according to the explanation heuristics, then a random sequence of questions for all unknown inputs is generated.

### 13.3.5   Example of Application

The three versions of the neural expert system shell EXPSYS have been successfully applied to solve several real-world problems: the diagnostics of protection warnings for the cooling system in nuclear power plants (Šíma, 1992a); the diagnostics and progress prediction of hereditary muscular diseases, namely Duchenne's and Becker's dystrophy (Šíma and Neruda, 1994); the diagnostics of ear diseases on the basis of brainstem auditory evoked potentials (Mechlová, 1994); and others. In this paragraph the application of EXPSYS to a toy economic problem is compared with the rule-based system solution to demonstrate the differences in the processing of implicit and explicit knowledge representations.

### 13.3.5.1   Problem Description

Consider the problem of developing a banking expert system that would decide, after screening some personal data of an applicant, whether he is to be granted credit or not. Our example will be based on Japanese credit screening data (JCS Data, 1992). This data set contains examples of people that were or were not granted credit from a Japanese banking company.

As the first natural step towards this goal we need to choose which items of personal data are relevant for our decision making. However, as we employ an existing data set, this choice was made for us beforehand. Thus, our expert system will examine the following information: whether the applicant has a job and if so, how long he is with the current company, the item that the loan is for, sex, age, marital status, region he lives in, bank deposit, monthly loan payment and, finally, number of months to pay off the loan.

The data set has 125 example inferences: 85 positive (people that were granted credit) and 40 negative (people that were rejected). All examples are complete.

### 13.3.5.2   Applying EXPSYS

Our task of applying EXPSYS to this problem has to start with definition of data types. We used the following definition:

```
INPUTS:  JOBLESS: scalar of (NO,YES)
         ITEM: scalar of (PC,CAR,STEREO,JEWEL,MEDINSTRUMENTS,
                          BIKE,FURNITURE)
         SEX: scalar of (FEMALE,MALE)
         UNMARRIED: scalar of (NO,YES)
         PROBLEM-REGION: scalar of (NO,YES)
         AGE: real of [0,150]
         MONEY-IN-BANK: real of [0,999]
         MONTHLY-PAYMENT: real of [0,100]
         MONTHS-TO-PAYOFF: real of [0,60]
         YEARS-AT-COMPANY: real of [0,99]
OUTPUT:  CREDIT: scalar of (NO,YES)
```

Then one of our example inferences appears as follows

```
[(NO,CAR,MALE,YES,NO,25,150,10,20,2),YES].
```

Since we chose unary encoding for the attribute ITEM, binary encoding for all the other scalars and natural floating-point encoding for reals, we obtain altogether 16 neurons in the input layer and 1 neuron in the output layer.

The crucial moment in the learning process of a neural network is making a decision about a particular network architecture and finding some good representative subset of the set of patterns.

As a first attempt, we put 10 neurons in the one and only hidden layer. Then we split the patterns into two parts: one containing patterns used in the process of learning, the other patterns used for testing network performance. In our case the learning set has 62 patterns (42 of them positive) and the testing set 63 (43 of them positive).

Thus, we started the learning procedure with a 16–10–1 architecture. After approximately 7 hours of learning on a 133 MHz Pentium PC the learning algorithm got stuck with an error of roughly 5 and three unlearned patterns. By examining these patterns we found that two of them are almost contradictory and that the third pattern is the only positive example of a person without a job in the whole learning set. As a next step, we omitted two patterns from the learning set: one of the contradictory patterns and the positive jobless example, and relearned the whole set. After 2 hours the net learned all the examples and ended with an error of 0.2. This network classified roughly 70% patterns of the test set correctly. We obtained very similar results for architectures with two (16–8–4–1) and three (16–6–4–4–1) hidden layers. The network with architecture 16–8–4–1 showed the best generalization on the test set: 71%.

Yet 71% generalization confidence is quite unsatisfactory. As several variations of the network architecture did not influence the quality of generalization very much, the learning set was probably ill-chosen—it did not capture the knowledge well.

As a second attempt, we chose the 16–8–4–1 architecture and divided the patterns into learning, auxiliary and test sets with 42, 42 and 41 patterns, respectively. The purpose of the auxiliary set was to serve as a resource of new example inferences from which it would be possible to draw appropriate patterns and enrich the learning set. The net then learned during an iterative process comprising three steps, namely (re)learning the current learning set, checking the performance of the net on the test set and successive modification of the learning set. The learning set was modified by removing contingent unlearned patterns and adding some patterns from the auxiliary set that were "similar" to those misclassified in the test set.

We iterated the whole process three times (see Section 13.3.2.3). After the first run, the net generalized on 68% of cases from the test set. Finally, after the third run, we obtained 93% generalization confidence on the test set (of 41 patterns). In the last run we used 72 patterns in the learning set. Learning in each run took approximately 6–8 hours.

Here we can give some examples of EXPSYS inferences. For instance, when we present the system with the following incomplete information:

```
ITEM = BIKE
SEX = FEMALE
PROBLEM-REGION = YES
MONEY-IN-BANK = 9.5
YEARS-AT-COMPANY = 7.5
```

it infers

```
----> CREDIT = NO                 conf.: 0.77
```

Now we can ask for an explanation of the inference and we obtain the following:

```
    CREDIT = NO ?
----> YEARS-AT-COMPANY = 7.5        54%
      MONTHLY-PAYMENT = unknown     20%
      ITEM = BIKE                   15%
      MONEY-IN-BANK = 9.5           11%
```

Not having a human expert at hand, we can judge the quality of inference only by confronting it with the data. However, this is rather a vague strategy and may require application of various types of methods for retrieving information from data. In our simple example, we easily inspected the data and noted some obvious facts. For example, the average length of present occupation of people who were granted credit is 9.2 years, whereas for those not granted it is only 2.4 years. Moreover, 70% of people applying for a loan for a bike were rejected and the average amount of bank deposits for the accepted applications was 81.6 units. Thus we can conclude at least that the above inference is not in contradiction with the data.

Now we can present an example of a positive inference:

```
    JOBLESS = NO
    ITEM = MEDINSTRUMENTS
    AGE = 58
    MONEY-IN-BANK = 70
    MONTHLY-PAYMENT = 1.5
    YEARS-AT-COMPANY = 36.5
----> CREDIT = YES               conf.: 0.75
```

and its explanation:

```
    CREDIT = YES ?
----> ITEM = MEDINSTRUMENTS         35%
      MONTHLY-PAYMENT = 1.5         27%
      JOBLESS = NO                  21%
      SEX = unknown                 10%
      PROBLEM-REGION = unknown       7%
```

We can also specify a value of an up-to-now unknown attribute so as to obtain a higher confidence rate of the inference, e.g. we can add a value of attribute PROBLEM-REGION and we obtain:

```
    PROBLEM-REGION = NO
----> CREDIT = YES               conf.: 0.93
```

Again, by inspecting the data, we find that 80% of people applying for a loan for a PC were granted credit, 75% of applicants that have a job also obtained credit, as well     % of people that live in a non-problem region. For other attributes,

**Table 13.1**  Network interval states for the positive inference example.

| Expert System Input | Input Layer | Hidden Layers | Output |
|---|---|---|---|
| JOBLESS = NO | $[-1, -1]$ | | $[-0.992, 1]$ |
| ITEM = MEDINSTRUMENTS | $[-1, -1]$ | First Layer | |
| | $[-1, -1]$ | $[-0.683, -0.398]$ | |
| | $[-1, -1]$ | $[0.583, 0.919]$ | $\alpha = -0.915$ |
| | $[-1, -1]$ | $[-0.993, 0.986]$ | $\beta = 4.548$ |
| | $[1, 1]$ | $[-0.059, 0.921]$ | $v = 1$ |
| | $[-1, -1]$ | $[-1, 0.848]$ | $c = 0.807$ |
| | $[-1, -1]$ | $[-1, -0.916]$ | conf.$= c \times 0.93$ |
| SEX = unknown | $[-1, 1]$ | $[-0.527, 0.216]$ | conf.$= 0.75$ |
| UNMARRIED = unknown | $[-1, 1]$ | $[0.424, 0.522]$ | |
| PROBLEM-REGION = unknown | $[-1, 1]$ | | |
| AGE = 58 | $[-0.227, -0.227]$ | Second Layer | |
| MONEY-IN-BANK = 70 | $[-0.86, -0.86]$ | $[-1, 0.666]$ | |
| MONTHLY-PAYMENT = 1.5 | $[-0.97, -0.97]$ | $[0.319, 0.506]$ | |
| MONTHS-TO-PAYOFF = unknown | $[-1, 1]$ | $[-0.523, -0.039]$ | |
| YEARS-AT-COMPANY = 36.5 | $[-0.263, -0.263]$ | $[-0.063, 1]$ | |

however, the dependencies are not so clear. At least we come to the conclusion that the inference performed by the expert system does not contradict the data.

At this point, it is instructive to use the above example of positive inference to demonstrate the performance of the EXPSYS interval neuron function (see Section 13.3.2.1). We illustrate this with values of network interval states for the positive example in Table 13.1 and, for comparison, values of interval states for the same example after specification of one more attribute (namely, PROBLEM-REGION = NO) in Table 13.2.

The first column of both tables contains the expert system input (i.e. values of attributes), the second column contains their corresponding encodings as interval states of input neurons (for details on input encodings see Section 13.3.1.2). The third column contains values of interval states of neurons in both hidden layers—eight neurons in the first hidden layer and four neurons in the second hidden layer. The last column contains the interval state and excitation level of the output neuron together with final results of inference.

We describe here briefly the steps of the inference procedure for the example in Table 13.1; the case for Table 13.2 is similar (for details on the inference engine see Section 13.3.3). Since we chose the value of the separation parameter $\gamma$ to be 0.4 and the gain parameter of the output neuron is $\lambda = 6.094$, we obtain the value of the separation parameter of the output neuron $\delta = 0.139$ by Equation 13.47. Then, for the interval excitation level of the output neuron $[\alpha, \beta] = [-0.915, 4.548]$, we get the positive confidence $c^+ = 0.807$ and the negative confidence $c^- = 0.142$ from Equations 13.48 and 13.49, respectively. Now we can determine the rounded output of the output neuron $v = 1$ by (13.50) and the inference confidence $c = 0.807$

**Table 13.2** Interval states for the positive example with one more attribute specified.

| Expert System Input | Input Layer | Hidden Layers | Output |
|---|---|---|---|
| JOBLESS = NO | $[-1, -1]$ | | $[0.889, 1]$ |
| ITEM = MEDINSTRUMENTS | $[-1, -1]$ | First Layer | |
| | $[-1, -1]$ | $[-0.686, -0.403]$ | |
| | $[-1, -1]$ | $[0.706, 0.939]$ | $\alpha = 0.465$ |
| | $[-1, -1]$ | $[-0.947, 0.992]$ | $\beta = 4.559$ |
| | $[1, 1]$ | $[0.045, 0.933]$ | $v = 1$ |
| | $[-1, -1]$ | $[-1, 0.886]$ | $c = 1$ |
| | $[-1, -1]$ | $[-1, -0.997]$ | conf.$= c \times 0.93$ |
| SEX = unknown | $[-1, 1]$ | $[-0.372, 0.344]$ | conf.$= 0.93$ |
| UNMARRIED = unknown | $[-1, 1]$ | $[0.357, 0.45]$ | |
| PROBLEM-REGION = NO | $[-1, -1]$ | | |
| AGE = 58 | $[-0.227, -0.227]$ | Second Layer | |
| MONEY-IN-BANK = 70 | $[-0.86, -0.86]$ | $[-1, 0.279]$ | |
| MONTHLY-PAYMENT = 1.5 | $[-0.97, -0.97]$ | $[0.347, 0.525]$ | |
| MONTHS-TO-PAYOFF = unknown | $[-1, 1]$ | $[-0.528, -0.051]$ | |
| YEARS-AT-COMPANY = 36.5 | $[-0.263, -0.263]$ | $[0.281, 1]$ | |

according to (13.51). Finally, by multiplying the inference confidence $c$ by the above-mentioned generalization confidence 0.93 we obtain the resulting confidence 0.75 (see Section 13.3.2.3).

By comparing values in Table 13.1 and Table 13.2 we can see how specifying a previously unknown input influences network interval states. Particularly, Table 13.2 shows the network states after setting the value NO to the attribute PROBLEM-REGION, which was left unknown in Table 13.1. Thus the states of the neurons in the input layer differ only for the neuron which encodes the value of the PROBLEM-REGION attribute and which becomes $[-1, -1]$ in Table 13.2. When comparing states of the neurons in hidden layers we can observe that several intervals have contracted. Namely, the intervals of the second and the fourth neurons in the first hidden layer and the intervals of the first and the fourth neurons in the second hidden layer show substantial contraction. Indeed, we can also observe that some neurons shifted their interval states slightly and thus do not preserve the strict monotonicity property (see Section 13.3.2.1). The interval state of the output neuron shows the biggest contraction. However, it is the value of the interval excitation level of the output neuron which is relevant for the expert system output. Here, the lower bound of the excitation level $\alpha$ increases from $-0.915$ in Table 13.1 to 0.465 in Table 13.2, and thus becomes greater than the separation parameter $\delta = 0.139$. This forces the rounded output $v = 1$ with inference confidence $c = 1$ and resulting confidence 0.93.

We conclude this paragraph by listing the questions that are generated by the system together with the measures of their influence on a particular output. Since there is only one output in the system, the order in which the questions are generated coincides with decreasing significance of individual unknown inputs (see Section 13.3.4.2). This is demonstrated for the case when all input attributes are left unknown:

```
CREDIT = YES ?                      (conf.: 0.48)
----> YEARS-AT-COMPANY = unknown    56%
      MONTHS-TO-PAYOFF = unknown    20%
      ITEM = unknown                13%
      MONEY-IN-BANK = unknown       11%
```

### 13.3.5.3   *Comparison with a Rule-Based Solution*

The Japanese credit screening data (JCS Data, 1992) also contains a domain theory—i.e. information obtained by interviewing banking experts who make decisions about granting credits. This information, transformed to several rules, represents the knowledge base of a rule-based banking expert system which examines the trustworthiness of people applying for a loan. The list of rules follows:

```
#1: IF jobless=yes & sex=male
    THEN credit=no
#2: IF jobless=yes & sex=female & unmarried=yes
    THEN credit=no
#3: IF jobless=yes & item=bike & sex=female & unmarried=yes
    THEN credit=no
#4: IF jobless=yes & sex=female & unmarried=no &
        & (money-in-bank < monthly-payment * months-to-payoff)
    THEN credit=no
#5: IF problem-region=yes & (years-at-company <= 10)
    THEN credit=no
#6: IF (age > 59) & (years-at-company < 3)
    THEN credit=no
#7: IF credit<>no
    THEN credit=yes
```

Two aspects can be observed here. First, no confidences for individual rules are used in this simple example. This means that all rules have absolute validity. Second, the rules form a chain of exclusions—i.e. each rule rejects a class of applicants for a loan.

Since we are not in contact with the banking expert, the only way to verify validity of the above rules is to test their performance on the data set. For this purpose we have incorporated the rules into an empty expert system toolkit—we employed the Prolog-based system MIKE (Eisenstadt and Brayshaw, 1990; MIKE, 1990). Tests have shown that the rules err on 25 examples out of 125. However, it is important to distinguish between positive and negative misclassifications. There are

22 examples wrongly classified by the system as yes, whereas only 3 were wrongly classified as no. With respect to the exclusive form of the rules this means that the rules are incomplete rather than incorrect. Thus, through the consultation of a banking expert we could devise additional exclusive rules that would set aside the remaining wrongly classified positive cases.

When comparing neural and rule-based approaches to building an expert system for granting credits, we must confine ourselves only to comparison of performance with respect to the data set. Having done so, we can conclude that the neural solution is not worse than the rule-based one. Particularly for the rules contained in the Japanese credit screening data (JCS Data, 1992), we observe that the neural solution shows much better performance.

Nevertheless, the main purpose of this application example is to demonstrate some key differences between neural and rule-based approaches in the process of developing an expert system. From this point of view it appears that the main difference consists of creating and debugging the knowledge base. While the rule-based solution has been proposed by banking experts who made an effort to express their credit granting strategy analytically, the neural approach issues from particular examples of their credit granting decisions in practice. On the basis of these examples the representative training patterns have been selected and an adequate neural network architecture was determined. It has been confirmed that these two optional parameters are crucial for neural network learning and generalization, and their debugging represents the important part of the neural knowledge base development. Thus, instead of improving the analytical solution the neural knowledge engineer trains different network architectures using various training sets to achieve the best performance of the neural inference engine on the test set. It follows that knowledge-based neurocomputing exploits a different methodology when applying statistical techniques rather than the formal logic which is used in conventional rule-based systems.

In addition, the application has also demonstrated that the expert system functionalities of EXPSYS which analyze implicit neural knowledge can compete with a rule-based solution. Particularly, the neural expert system decides about credit granting when only incomplete personal data of applicants is available. Furthermore, the system asks additional questions to complete the information about an applicant which is most relevant for the resulting decision. Finally, the system simply explains why the loan is provided or rejected. Thus, we can conclude that the neural expert system EXPSYS represents a respectable alternative to rule-based systems.

## References

Bassøe, C.-F. 1995. Automated diagnoses from clinical narratives: A medical system based on computerized medical records, natural language processing, and neural network technology. *Neural Networks*, 8(2):313–319.

Baxt, W. G. 1990. Use of an artificial neural network for data analysis in clinical decision-making: The diagnosis of acute coronary occlusion. *Neural Computation*, 2(4):480–489.

Bělohlávek, R. 1997. Backpropagation for interval patterns. *Neural Network World*, 7(3):335–346.

Berenji, H. R. and Khedkar, P. 1992. Learning and tuning fuzzy logic controllers through reinforcements. *IEEE Transactions on Neural Networks*, 3(5):724–740.

Biondo, S. J. 1990. *Fundamentals of Expert Systems Technology: Principles and Concepts.* Norwood, NJ: Ablex Publishing Co.

Blum, A. L. and Rivest, R. L. 1992. Training a 3-node neural network is NP-complete. *Neural Networks*, 5(1):117–127.

Buchanan, B. and Shortliffe, E. 1984. *Rule-Based Expert Systems.* Reading, MA: Addison-Wesley.

Caudill, M. 1991. Expert networks. *Byte*, 16(10):108–116.

Chen, S. 1987. Automated reasoning on neural networks: A probabilistic approach. In *Proceedings of the IEEE International Conference on Neural Networks, San Diego*, vol. II, pp. 373–378.

Drucker, H. 1990. Implementation of minimum error expert system. In *Proceedings of the International Joint Conference on Neural Networks IJCNN'90, San Diego*, vol. I, pp. 291–296.

Družecký, P. 1992. *Expert System for Medical Diagnostics.* Master thesis, Department of Control Engineering, Faculty of Electrical Engineering, Czech Technical University, Prague.

Duda, R. O. and Reboh, R. 1983. AI and decision making: The PROSPECTOR experience. In *Artificial Intelligence Applications for Business*, ed. W. Reitman. Norwood, NJ: Ablex Publishing Co.

Eisenstadt, M. and Brayshaw, M. 1990. A knowledge engineering toolkit. *Byte*, 15(10):268–282, (12):364–370.

Enbutsu, I., Baba, K., and Hara, N. 1991. Fuzzy rule extraction from a multilayered neural network. In *Proceedings of the International Joint Conference on Neural Networks IJCNN'91, Seattle*, vol. II, pp. 461–465.

EXPSYS 1994. *EXPSYS—Students' Software Project.* Department of Software Engineering, Faculty of Mathematics and Physics, Charles University, Prague.

Fausett, L. V. 1994. *Fundamentals of Neural Networks: Architectures, Algorithms, and Applications.* Englewood Cliffs, NJ: Prentice-Hall.

Gallant, S. I. 1988. Connectionist expert systems. *Communications of the ACM*, 31(2):152–169.

Gallant, S. I. 1993. *Neural Network Learning and Expert Systems.* Cambridge, MA: MIT Press.

Giarratano, J. and Riley, G. 1993. *Expert Systems: Principles and Practice.* Boston,

MA: PWS Publishing.

Handelman, D. A., Lane, S. H., and Gelfand, J. J. 1989. Integration of knowledge-based system and neural network techniques for autonomous learning machines. In *Proceedings of the International Joint Conference on Neural Networks IJCNN'89, Washington*, vol. I, pp. 683–688.

Haykin, S. 1994. *Neural Networks*. New York: Macmillan College Publishing Company.

Hecht-Nielsen, R. 1990. *Neurocomputing*. California: Addison-Wesley.

Hertz, J., Krogh, A., and Palmer, R. G. 1991. *Introduction to the Theory of Neural Computation*, vol. I of *Lecture Notes, Santa Fe Institute Studies in the Sciences of Complexity*. California: Addison-Wesley.

Hořejš, J. and Kufudaki, O. 1993. Neural networks with local distributed parameters. *Neurocomputing*, 5(4-5):211–219.

Ignizio, J. P. 1991. *Introduction to Expert Systems: The Development and Implementation of Rule-Based Expert Systems*. New York: McGraw-Hill.

Ishikawa, M. 1996. Structural learning with forgetting. *Neural Networks*, 9(3):509–521.

Jackson, P. 1990. *Introduction to Expert Systems*. California: Addison-Wesley.

Jang, J. S. 1992. Self-learning fuzzy controllers based on temporal back propagation. *IEEE Transactions on Neural Networks*, 3(5):714–723.

JCS Data 1992. Japanese credit screening data. Machine Learning Repository, University of California, Irvine, ftp://ftp.ics.uci.edu/pub/machine-learning-databases/credit-screening/.

Kasabov, N. K. 1991. Expert systems based on incorporating rules into neural networks. Technical University in Sofia, Bulgaria.

Kasabov, N. K. 1993. Hybrid connectionist production systems: An approach to realising fuzzy expert systems. *Journal of Systems Engineering*, 1:15–21.

Kasabov, N. K. 1994. Connectionist fuzzy production systems. In *Proceedings of the Fuzzy Logic in Artificial Intelligence: IJCAI'93 Workshop, Chambery, France*, vol. 847 of *LNAI*, pp. 114–127, Berlin. Springer-Verlag.

Kasabov, N. K. and Petkov, S. H. 1992a. Approximate reasoning with hybrid connectionist logic programming systems. In *Proceedings of the International Conference on Artificial Neural Networks ICANN'92*, eds. I. Aleksander and J. Taylor, pp. 749–752. Elsevier Science Publisher B. V.

Kasabov, N. K. and Petkov, S. H. 1992b. Neural networks and logic programming—a hybrid model and its applicability to building expert systems. In *Proceedings of the $10^{th}$ European Conference on Artificial Intelligence ECAI'92*, ed. B. Neumann, pp. 287–288. John Wiley & Sons.

Kasabov, N. K. and Shishkov, S. I. 1993. A connectionist production system with partial match and its use for approximate reasoning. *Connection Science*,

5(3&4):275–305.

Kosko, B. 1987. Adaptive inference in fuzzy knowledge networks. In *Proceedings of the IEEE International Conference on Neural Networks, San Diego*, vol. II, pp. 261–268.

Krysiak, A. 1991. Application of parallel connectionist model in medical expert system. Institute of Computer Science, Polish Academy of Sciences.

Lacher, R. C., Hruska, S. I., and Kuncicky, D. C. 1992. Back-propagation learning in expert networks. *IEEE Transactions on Neural Networks*, 3(1):62–72.

Lin, C. T. and Lee, C. S. G. 1991. Neural-network-based fuzzy logic control and decision system. *IEEE Transactions on Computers*, 40(12):1320–1336.

Lippmann, R. P. 1987. An introduction to computing with neural nets. *IEEE ASSP Magazine*, 4(2):4–22.

Mařík, V., Vlček, T., Kouba, Z., Lažanský, J., and Lhotská, L. 1992. Expert system FEL-EXPERT version 3.5: Description and user's manual. Technical Report TR-PRG-IEDS-06/92, FAW Linz-Hagenberg-Prague-Vienna.

Mařík, V., Vlček, T., Šedivá, I., Maříková, T., Hyanek, J., Campr, V., Tjoa, A. M., and Gierlinger, C. 1993. FEL-EXPERT applications—some pilot case studies. Technical Report TR-PRG-IEDS-13/93, FAW Linz-Hagenberg-Prague-Vienna.

Mařík, V., Zdráhal, Z., Kouba, Z., and Lhotská, L. 1990. The FEL-EXPERT project: Applications in education. In *Proceedings of the CEPES-UNESCO International Symposium: Artificial Intelligence in Higher Education*, Berlin. Springer-Verlag.

Mazný, M. 1995. *Integrating Rule-Based and Neural Approaches to Expert System Design*. Master thesis, Department of Software Engineering, Faculty of Mathematics and Physics, Charles University, Prague.

McDermott, J. 1981. R1: The formative years. *AI Magazine*, 2(2):21–29.

McMillan, C., Mozer, M. C., and Smolensky, M. 1991. Learning explicit rules in a neural network. In *Proceedings of the International Joint Conference on Neural Networks IJCNN'91, Seattle*, vol. II, pp. 83–88.

Mechlová, S. 1994. *Applications of Neural Networks*. Master thesis, Department of Control Engineering, Faculty of Electrical Engineering, Czech Technical University, Prague.

MIKE 1990. Mike: Micro interpreter for knowledge engineering. ftp://hcrl.open.ac.uk/pub/software/src/MIKEv2.03/.

Miller, R. A., Pople, H. E., and Myers, J. D. 1982. INTERNIST-I, an experimental computer-based diagnostic consultant for general internal medicine. *New England Journal of Medicine*, 307:468–476.

Mitra, S. and Pal, S. K. 1995. Fuzzy multi-layer perceptron, inferencing and rule generation. *IEEE Transactions on Neural Networks*, 6(1):51–63.

Moreno, L., Piñeiro, J. D., Sanchez, J. L., Mañas, S., Merino, J. J., Acosta, L., and

Hamilton, A. 1995. Using neural networks to improve classification: Application to brain maturation. *Neural Networks*, 8(5):815–820.

Mozer, M. C. 1987. Rambot: A connectionist expert system that learns by example. In *Proceedings of the IEEE International Conference on Neural Networks, San Diego*, vol. II, pp. 693–701.

Narazaki, H. and Ralescu, A. L. 1992. A connectionist approach for rule-based inference using improved relaxation method. *IEEE Transactions on Neural Networks*, 3(5):741–751.

Nekovei, R. and Sun, Y. 1995. Back-propagation network and its configuration for blood vessel detection in angiograms. *IEEE Transactions on Neural Networks*, 6(1):64–72.

Omlin, C. W. and Giles, C. L. 1996. Extraction of rules from discrete-time recurrent neural networks. *Neural Networks*, 9(1):41–52.

Rojas, R. R. 1996. *Neural Networks: A Systematic Introduction*. Berlin: Springer-Verlag.

Rumelhart, D. E., Hinton, G. E., and Williams, R. J. 1986. Learning internal representations by error propagation. In *Parallel Distributed Processing: Explorations in the Microstructure of Cognition*, eds. D. E. Rumelhart and J. L. McClelland, vol. I, pp. 318–362. Cambridge, MA: MIT Press.

Saito, K. and Nakano, R. 1988. Medical diagnostic expert system based on the PDP model. In *Proceedings of the IEEE International Conference on Neural Networks, San Diego*, vol. I, pp. 255–262.

Samad, T. 1988. Towards connectionist rule-based systems. In *Proceedings of the IEEE International Conference on Neural Networks, San Diego*, vol. II, pp. 525–532.

Šíma, J. 1992a. The multi-layered neural network as an adaptive expert system with the ability to work with incomplete information and to provide justification of inference. *Neural Network World*, 2(1):47–58.

Šíma, J. 1992b. Generalized back propagation for interval training patterns. *Neural Network World*, 2(2):167–173.

Šíma, J. 1994. Generalized back propagation for training pattern derivatives. *Neural Network World*, 4(1):91–98.

Šíma, J. 1995. Neural expert systems. *Neural Networks*, 8(2):261–271.

Šíma, J. 1996. Back-propagation is not efficient. *Neural Networks*, 9(6):1017–1023.

Šíma, J. and Neruda, R. 1993. Designing neural expert systems with EXPSYS. Technical Report V-563, Institute of Computer Science, Academy of Sciences of the Czech Republic, Prague.

Šíma, J. and Neruda, R. 1994. The empty neural expert system and its application in medicine. In *Proceedings of the 12th European Meeting on Cybernetics and Systems Research, Vienna*, ed. R. Trappl, vol. II, pp. 1825–1832, Singapore.

World Scientific.

Simpson, P. K. 1990. *Artificial Neural Systems: Foundations, Paradigms, Applications, and Implementations.* New York: Pergamon Press.

Styblinski, M. A. and Meyer, B. D. 1988. Fuzzy cognitive maps, signal flow graphs, and qualitative circuit analysis. In *Proceedings of the IEEE International Conference on Neural Networks, San Diego*, vol. II, pp. 549–556.

Taber, W. R. and Siegel, M. A. 1987. Estimation of expert weights using fuzzy cognitive maps. In *Proceedings of the IEEE International Conference on Neural Networks, San Diego*, vol. II, pp. 319–326.

Yager, R. R. 1994. Modelling and formulating fuzzy knowledge bases using neural networks. *Neural Networks*, 7(8):1273–1283.

Yang, Q. and Bhargava, V. K. 1990. Building expert systems by a modified perceptron network with rule-transfer algorithms. In *Proceedings of the International Joint Conference on Neural Networks IJCNN'90, San Diego*, vol. II, pp. 77–82.

# Index